Up from Communism

Also by *John P. Diggins*

Mussolini and Fascism: The View from America
The American Left in the Twentieth Century

CONSERVATIVE ODYSSEYS IN

Up from Communism

AMERICAN INTELLECTUAL HISTORY

John P. Diggins

HARPER TORCHBOOKS
HARPER & ROW, PUBLISHERS
NEW YORK, HAGERSTOWN, SAN FRANCISCO, LONDON

To the memory of Baila Feldman (1935–1972)

*the text of this book is printed
on 100% recycled paper*

Grateful acknowledgment is made for permission to reprint lines from "East Coker" in *Four Quartets* by T. S. Eliot. Copyright 1943 by T. S. Eliot; copyright renewed 1971 by Esmé Valerie Eliot. Reprinted by permission of Harcourt Brace Jovanovich, Inc.

Designed by Sidney Feinberg

A hardcover edition of this book is published by Harper & Row, Publishers, Inc.

First HARPER TORCHBOOK edition published 1977

ISBN: 0–06–131899–X

77 78 79 10 9 8 7 6 5 4 3 2 1

Contents

Illustrations

Preface

The final struggle will be between the communist and the ex-communist.

IGNAZIO SILONE, 1949

This book is an intellectual history of the "final struggle" in America. It is a critical examination of conservative minds haunted by radical memories. The study arose out of a conviction that the moral and philosophical roots of the cold war must be sought much further back in time than political or diplomatic scholars seem to realize. In America as well as in Europe the experience of Stalinism pressed like a tumor on the brain of a whole generation of writers who came of political age between 1917 and 1939, and that experience has done much to shape American attitudes toward communism for the past fifty years. In order to understand anti-communism as a genuine intellectual proposition, and not merely as a politics of ambition, we must first understand ex-communism.

One aim of this work is to explain how the radical experience of a generation of writers influenced the cultural and political climate of post–World War II America, providing much of the conservative rationale for America's hard-line stance in the early years of the cold war. My larger goal is to deal with broader theoretical issues relating to the course of American intellectual history and social philosophy. I am primarily concerned with the impact of European totalitarianism upon American intellectual life in a variety of disciplines: philosophy, political theory, literature, sociology, economics, ethics, and theology. This book explores ideas undergoing philosophical reconsideration by a nucleus of thinkers who are in the process of political transformation. Basically it is a biogtaphical approach to the history of ideas moving from Left to Right. It could be called a study of progress—up to a point.

Wherever ideology is involved the historian has a special obligation to be honest with his readers and, perhaps more important, with himself. A man in the middle writing about the Left and the Right should make no effort to exclude or, above all, pretend to exclude value judgments. To establish the context within which my judgments may have been formed, perhaps a brief political memoir may help.

This book was conceived around 1969, during the height of the New Left confrontations. At the time I was teaching at San Francisco State College, a riot-torn campus that remained under a state of siege for nearly three years. I had reached the "age of reason"— that age when, as Catholic educators put it, one is responsible for one's choices—during the "silent generation" of the fifties, a period in which there seemed to be no choices to make other than to consent and conform. Too young to have experienced personally the traumas of the Old Left (the Depression, fascism, the Popular Front, the Spanish Civil War, the Nazi-Soviet pact), I was too old—thirty in 1965—and too "adjusted" to embark upon the fresh causes of the New Left (Selma, the Free Speech Movement, SDS, Vietnam, Castro). Caught between the tired negations of the fathers and the arrogant affirmations of the sons and daughters, I felt like a man without a generation. Still, I respected the intellectual achievements of the radicals of the thirties, and tried unsuccessfully to convey a sense of those achievements to my students—whenever classes could be held before the picket lines formed and the "tactical squad" moved in. I also admired the political commitments and morally inspired madness of some factions of the New Left. Yet, having been brought up on Camus, Melville, and Niebuhr, having read too much about the degeneration of one left-wing revolution after another, having watched the Haight-Ashbury neighborhood deteriorate from a garden of flower children into a ghetto of violence, freak-out, and crime ("hippie capitalism"), and having turned thirty (that age when one knows he will always be what he is), I found it was no longer possible for me to re-enact the ceremony of innocence and go whoring after the young. It was no longer possible, that is, to become a teacher who need not think.

To be young is to aspire, to be a historian is to remember, and herein lies the rub. Between the dream and the memory lies understanding. Historical experience alone can be as misleading as the imagination trying to do the work of the intellect: one can be imprisoned by historical memories as well as enraptured by ideological fantasies. The generation of the thirties remembered Munich, and many of its members therefore condoned Vietnam; the generation of the sixties ignored Russia's purges, and many of its activists therefore applauded China's "Hundred Flowers" episode. Santayana's aphorism needs a corollary: If those who ignore the past are condemned to repeat it, those who remember it too well are determined to universalize it.

This book is written in an effort to illuminate some continuity among generations. One need not accept the political legacy of the Old Left in order to re-examine its rich intellectual heritage. A decade ago such a task would have been as futile as asking students to read Edmund Burke. Today the signs are more encouraging. Even "old" New Left historians are beginning to see that many ex-radical "consensus" scholars were describing a condition, not celebrating a solution. There is much that can be learned from a study of the problems that the Old Left had to face. Almost all the theoretical issues that emerged in the sixties and that remain in the forefront of debate today had been discussed and analyzed in the thirties: the dream of class conflict and the reality of liberal hegemony; the validity of Marxism and its relation to Hegelian philosophy; the crisis of bourgeois capitalism and the emergence of corporate capitalism, bureaucracy, elitism, and the managerial state; power and morality; means and ends; and, above all, the problem of "American exceptionalism." In their conservative stance the writers discussed in this book also analyzed a number of issues that have urgent relevance today: the riddle of power and the legitimacy of authority, the question of religious truth versus scientific knowledge, the historical conditions of freedom, the failure of socialism and the threat of collectivism, the heritage of the American Enlightenment, the philosophies of humanism and existentialism, and the Christian paradox of spiritual alienation. These are some of the issues that will be explored as they arose at critical moments in modern American intellectual history.

The paths to conservatism I have chosen to study all end with William F. Buckley, Jr., and the *National Review*, which may seem to some the road to Damascus, to others a descent into purgatory. My purpose is not to deliver the reader to the Right or to save him from the Left; nor do I wish to leave the reader stranded in the liberal center with the author, who may be a skeptic but is not a sadist. Nothing, surely, would be more pretentious than to try to write a political road map to guide us out of the dilemmas of our time. After surviving the sixties, we find that it seems truer now than ever that the central task before us is to return to first principles, to abandon outworn formulas, and to raise again basic questions that will help clarify theoretical problems. If this study makes a contribution to that modest aim, the author will be satisfied that his purpose has been achieved.

Acknowledgments

In the course of my research a number of obligations have been incurred. I wish to thank the following institutions for their assistance and hospitality: the Alderman Library, University of Virginia; the Butler Library, Columbia University; the Hoover Library, Stanford University; the Houghton Library, Harvard University; the Lilly Library, Indiana University; the Newberry Library, Chicago; the New York Public Library; the Oral History Research Office, Columbia University; the Rutgers University Library; the Tamiment Library, New York University. I am also grateful to Irene Wechselberg and Yvonne Wilson, librarians at the University of California, Irvine.

Several persons facilitated my research by granting me interviews or by responding to my queries. For their generous cooperation I thank James Burnham, Theodore Draper, Will Herberg, Sidney Hook, Herbert Marcuse, Henry Pachter, David Reisman, Arthur Schlesinger, Jr., the late Max Shachtman, and Bertrand D. Wolfe. I am especially indebted to Daniel Aaron, who made available his materials on the Old Left and who has sustained my efforts by his encouragement and by the inspiration of his own scholarship.

A number of scholars were kind enough to read sections of the manuscript. I am pleased to acknowledge my gratitude for the helpful comments of David Caute, Peter Clecak, Allen Guttmann, David Hollinger, Irving Howe, Allen Lawson, Henry F. May,

Gerald Meaker, and Hayden White. I also wish to convey my thanks to Robert Huberty, a graduate student who has taught me a great deal about the nuances on conservative philosophy, and to Lauren Gibbs, who patiently helped a disorganized author prepare a text. And a very special note of obligation is due to Jeannette Hopkins, whose perceptive editorial suggestions have been of considerable value.

In addition, the author is indebted to Elizabeth H. Dos Passos, Yvette Eastman, and Elena Wilson, for permission to quote from the respective letters of John Dos Passos, Max Eastman, and Edmund Wilson; to Daniel Bell, James Burnham, Irving Kristol, Peter Viereck, and Sol Stein, for permission to quote from their letters in the files of the American Committee for Cultural Freedom; to William Buckley, Jr., for permission to quote from his correspondence in the Eastman papers; to John Howard Lawson, for permission to quote from his correspondence in the Dos Passos papers; to Mrs. M. Lincoln Schuster and Mrs. Daphne Mebane, for permission to quote from their respective husbands' correspondences in the Eastman papers; to Dr. Louis M. Starr, Director of the Oral History Research Office, Columbia University, for permission to quote from the Max Shachtman transcripts; to Dr. Jo Ann Boydston, Director of the Center for Dewey Studies, Southern Illinois University, for permission to quote from a letter by John Dewey; Peter Dzwonkoski, Assistant to the Curator, Collection of American Literature, The Beinecke Rare Book and Manuscript Library, Yale University, for permission to use letters of Mabel Dodge; Diana Haskell, Curator of Modern Manuscripts, The Newberry Library, for permission to quote from the letters of Floyd Dell; and Dr. Neda Westlake, Director of Manuscripts, University of Pennsylvania Library, for permission to quote from a letter of Theodore Dreiser; and to Richard Rovere, for permission to quote from his letters to Arthur Schlesinger, Jr.

The author is deeply grateful to the University of California for a Humanities Institute Fellowship, and to the National Endowment for the Humanities for a Younger Humanist Fellowship, which made possible the research on this book.

Earlier versions of sections of the book appeared in various scholarly journals. They are used here, in revised form, with the kind permission of the editors of the following journals: *American Historical Review*, *American Literature*, *Antioch Review*, and *Dissent*.

The book is dedicated to the memory of a close friend who defied her tragic fate through her work, exquisitely vivid canvases painted with an intense fascination and a joyous affirmation of life that was heroically sustained right up to the known end. She conquered the king of terror.

JPD
Laguna Beach, 1975

In order to arrive at what you are not
You must go through the way in which you are not.
T. S. Eliot, "East Coker," 1940

Up from Communism

Introduction

This book focuses specifically on the ideological careers of four important American writers: Max Eastman, John Dos Passos, Will Herberg, and James Burnham. These figures have been chosen because they underwent the complete shift from the Old Left of the 1930s to the New Right of the 1950s. Unlike so many other writers who repudiated communism (e.g., Sidney Hook, Dwight Macdonald, Edmund Wilson), Eastman, Dos Passos, Herberg, and Burnham were among the few notable ex-radicals who found their way to the editorial board of William F. Buckley's *National Review*, and who proudly, though sometimes awkwardly, identified themselves as converts to the "New American Conservatism."

There are risks in selecting any group of intellectuals who may have little in common save their own individuality. But there are compensating advantages in concentrating upon these four particular writers. For one thing, their case histories offer the opportunity of spanning a half century of American intellectual history. While none may be regarded as a representative thinker, their political careers reveal a remarkable range of talents: Eastman, the poet-philosopher of lyrical rebellion and scientific experiment; Dos Passos, the novelist-historian of anarcho-individualist sensibilities; Herberg, the anguished theologian of moral man in immoral society; Burnham, the intensely logical philosopher of power in a universe of protracted conflict. As conservatives as well as radicals, all of these writers experienced the critical sting of emotions as

1

they re-examined their convictions, and if their reactions to any particular historical event were rarely identical, each attempted to justify a change in political behavior by offering a new social theory or historical vision. As we reach the end of their odyssey, it is the validity and consistency of their respective theories, historical arguments, and ethical philosophies that the author attempts to examine critically, quite apart from, though not entirely unrelated to, their politics. So far no historian has undertaken such a task, presumably convinced that the errors of the ex-radical who becomes a conservative are not corrected but compounded. This attitude puts the answer before the question, resolves issues by ignoring them, and discredits the adversary instead of answering him. I remain curious.

Were Eastman, Dos Passos, Herberg, and Burnham only half-baked radicals? Were they "Marxists of the heart" who passed through a revolutionary adolescence and "grew up" to become the respectable brain men of Buckley's *National Review*? It is necessary to raise this question, for the charge has often been made that the Left in America is politically feeble because it is intellectually sterile. The allegation is generally made by European Marxists,[1] but interestingly enough, it also derives support from America's own "consensus" historians (in some cases ex-radicals themselves) who are determined to deny the role of ideas, theory, and ideology in American life. The reason I take the time to examine, in Part I of the book, the radical writings of the four American neo-conservatives is to correct this false impression about the intellectual shallowness of American radicalism and also the canard of the alleged "opportunism" of Old Left renegades in the United States. The American Left may live a short life, but it dies from head wounds and heart failures, not stomach politics.

Did Eastman, Dos Passos, Herberg, and Burnham become genuine conservatives in their later years? Aside from defining what we mean by "conservative,"* this question brings us to the

---

* For a useful taxonomy of the various meanings, see Clinton Rossiter, *Conservatism in America* (New York: Vintage edn., 1962), pp. 2–10. My study

title that was finally decided on for the present book. When William Buckley wrote his political manifesto in the late fifties, he titled it *Up from Liberalism*. The sarcastic reference to Booker T. Washington's *Up from Slavery* was clear to everyone. Given the writers I am dealing with, this book is appropriately titled *Up from Communism*. About half of the *National Review*'s editorial board was, after all, Stalin's gift to the American Right. But Buckley wrought better than he knew when he chose his title. If Eastman, Dos Passos, Herberg, and Burnham had one thing in common, it was contempt for liberalism. There is, in fact, a continuity of disdain for liberalism that runs through their careers like a red thread. Eastman criticized the polite liberal reformer who could not see the "beauty" of the revolutionary deed; Dos Passos looked upon liberal intellectuals as a "milky lot" armed only with "tea-table convictions"; Herberg dismissed liberal pragmatism as the ideology of the bourgeoisie; and Burnham saw liberalism as a philosophy of hope without a philosophy of power. When the four writers became conservatives, an ironic twist emerged in their indictment. Once they accused liberals of being intolerant of communism, now they attacked them for being "soft on communism." Formerly they scorned the impotence of liberalism, now they complained about its power and influence. But whether weak or strong, liberalism was still held responsible for all that had gone wrong in the modern world. If in the thirties the very fragility of liberal ideology made fascism possible in Germany and Italy, in the postwar period presumably it was only the timidity of a power-

---

deals with two kinds of conservatism, anti-communist and philosophical. Allen Guttmann has defined perceptively the role of the latter in America: "Pushed in disarray from the battlefield of political activity, Conservatism has taken refuge in the citadel of ideas. The democratization of American society has made Conservatism increasingly feeble as an institutionalized force, but the Conservative's dream of a hierarchically structured society of prescribed values and restrained liberty has continued on as an important and usually unrecognized aspect of American literature." Guttmann, *The Conservative Tradition in America* (New York, 1967), p. 11. In the concluding chapter I discuss the difficulties of reconciling anti-communist conservatism and philosophical conservatism.

ful Western liberalism that made Stalinism possible in Eastern Europe. Previously liberalism was rejected for its inability to make a revolution, now it was repudiated for its inability to prevent one.

In domestic matters modern liberalism was also seen as a curse that had crept over the nation and produced the welfare state, the eclipse of moral authority, the decline of educational standards, and the corruption of the young. In economics, liberalism meant the death of free enterprise (Eastman); in social life, the disease of bureaucracy (Dos Passos); in philosophy and theology, the ethical relativism that poisoned authentic religion (Herberg); in diplomacy, "the ideology of western suicide" (Burnham). At one time anti-liberal radicals, the four writers became anti-liberal conservatives, equally frustrated by the liberal consensus of American life.

It is a measure of their intellectual honesty, however, that these writers on the Right remained discontented with American conservatism as well—or as Herberg would put it, "with what passes for conservatism in America." This critical attitude deserves admiration, for when one thinks of the status of genuine intellectual conservatism in America it seems necessary to reverse William Faulkner's adage: Conservative man will not prevail, he will endure. The hegemony of liberalism in America points up the weakness of conservatism as a political force, but the follies of liberalism itself also suggest the wisdom of conservatism as a philosophical persuasion.

The rise of the New American Right out of the ashes of the Old American Left was one of the great political surprises of our time. How Eastman, Dos Passos, Herberg, and Burnham got from one side of the political spectrum to the other is an intriguing chapter in modern American intellectual history. Their odyssey warrants some preliminary observations and questions.

Max Eastman was the founding father of the twentieth-century American Left. A flamboyant poet-philosopher, Eastman embodied the adventurous innocence of flesh and spirit that has characterized various generations of American rebels. To Eastman existence was a celebration of life as it is experienced in all its variety, a joyous affirmation of freedom and possibility. This lyrical impulse inspired the Greenwich Village Left of 1912 to 1917, the generation that invoked the dionysian spirit of youth, love, poetry, and heroism. Together with the romantic revolutionary John Reed and the sexual freedom advocate Floyd Dell, Eastman published the lively and open-hearted The Masses, a satiric journal that outraged the sensibilities of post-Victorian America. The Masses' editors were animated by eight passions: "fun, truth, beauty, realism, freedom, peace, feminism, revolution."[2] Eastman and his comrades were the "movers and shakers" of the first counterculture in modern American history. A half century before the hippies and the New Left of the 1960s, the Greenwich Village rebels spoke of imagination as liberation and denounced repression as a tedious hang-up. Eastman, a glamorous libertine who was, as one admirer later put it, "fatal to women," declared the new morality of his generation in three words: "Lust is sacred." Revolution would also be sublime.

When the Bolsheviks seized power in Russia in October 1917, shocking the liberals and even the moderate socialists, Eastman supported them to the hilt in his new journal, The Liberator. He also helped raise money to send Reed to the new Soviet Republic, a voyage of adventure that resulted in the epic Ten Days That Shook the World. Though the country was in the grip of wartime fever and hysteria, Eastman was one of the few "reds" who somehow managed to stay out of jail, and his magazine functioned as the voice of Bolshevism in Wilsonian America. At peak circulation The Liberator reached sixty thousand readers. When Lenin's pamphlet The Soviets at Work was published—the document that won Whittaker Chambers to communism—Eastman instantly became "enraptured" by Lenin's "factualness" and "experimental" mind. He visited Russia in 1922, and he returned home twenty-one months later to defend without reservation Lenin's program of action and his new regime. After Lenin's death in 1924

Eastman sided with Leon Trotsky, the hero of the Red Army; and for more than a decade he would serve as Trotsky's best literary translator and staunchest defender. The golden boy of the American Left, Eastman was as proud of his communism as he was of his erotic conquests. "I supported every step," he boasted to Trotsky in 1933, "taken by the Bolshevik party and by you and Lenin from the seizure of power and the dissolution of the Constituent Assembly (horrible to all other American editors) to the condemnation of the Social Revolutionaries. I was for six years alone in America in supporting the Left Opposition. I was the Left Opposition."[3]

He who did more than any writer of his generation to celebrate and popularize communism to the American public would be, some twenty years later, the very person William F. Buckley turned to for advice in starting a national magazine to champion the cause of conservatism. What did Eastman have to offer Buckley, and why would the old Greenwich Village rebel be willing to collaborate with the pompous young author of God and Man at Yale? Could Buckley's National Review accommodate both a devout Catholic and a lusty atheist? Aside from ecumenical problems, what of Eastman's passionate political convictions? The writer who had once protested eloquently the injustices of capitalism and spoken rhapsodically of a cooperative socialist society would now, two decades later, address an annual convention of the American Federation of Labor and offer the American worker four words of wisdom: "Don't Kill the Goose."[4] And the activist who had valiantly resisted the Red Scare of 1919 would later defend the House Un-American Activities Committee and describe the campaign against Senator Joseph McCarthy as "vicious and unprincipled." Was Eastman an opportunist? Hardly. Both stands were unpopular; both took courage; and Eastman was no more afraid of making new enemies than of losing old friends. But who were Eastman's new allies and admirers? In his revolutionary days Eastman satirized the respectable wealthy class and sympathized with the cultural underworld of immigrants, bohemians, anarchists, and feminists. Now he emerged as the political sage of both the American Establishment and of Middle America, praised by Congresswoman Clare Booth Luce and by movie star Barbara Stanwyck. Once admired by the followers of John Reed, he came to be lauded by the fans of John Wayne. Is Eastman's career a case of *la trahison des clercs*, or can a man who moved from Left to Right still be fighting the same fight?

Similar questions can be asked of John Dos Passos. After World War I Dos Passos emerged upon the literary scene a bitter young novelist who wanted to bring down the entire social order. He found war horrifying, the state a monstrous fraud, and society the spectacle of oppressed humanity. Everywhere he saw power beating down upon the individual; nowhere could he find freedom. These unfocused convictions crystallized during the Sacco-Vanzetti trial in 1927. To Dos Passos the arrest and trial of the two Italian anarchists represented a blatant betrayal of the ideals of the Republic and the clearest indication of the power of the forces of order. Politically radicalized, Dos Passos agreed to serve as a reporter for the *Daily Worker*, and he was arrested in a police roundup of picketers marching in front of the Boston statehouse. The execution of the two accused left Dos Passos filled with shock and indignation. He later recorded his bitterness in *U.S.A.*:

they have clubbed us off the streets they are stronger they are rich they hire and fire the politicians the newspapereditors the old judges the small men with reputations the collegepresidents the wardheelers (listen businessmen collegepresidents judges America will not forget her betrayers) they hire the men with guns the uniforms the policecars the patrolwagons . . .

we stand defeated America

Although Dos Passos never joined the Communist Party, he lent his name to its causes and participated in communist-led industrial strikes. He was also hailed as a proletarian ally by Marxist intellectuals. His sense of rage and conflict, his bitter outbursts of class hatred, and his artful use of the collective novel to capture the totality of society seemed proof that he was America's first genuine literary practitioner of "socialist realism." Communist writers saw in him the American Maxim Gorky. "Comrade" Dos Passos appeared to be fulfilling this role in 1932, when he gave his signature to *Culture and Crisis*, an intellectual manifesto endorsed by fifty-two leading American writers and artists in support of the Communist Party presidential candidate, William Z. Foster. "However much we may cavil at the Communists," wrote Dos Passos that same year, "they mean it when they say they are fighting for socialism, i.e., the cooperative commonwealth." And Roosevelt's New Deal? "The upshot of it," he told Edmund Wilson the following year, "is that you and me and the Forgotten Man are going to get fucked plenty."[5]

Thirty years later, on March 7, 1962, eighteen thousand excited Young Americans for Freedom gathered in Madison Square Garden to rejoice in the revival of conservatism, the "cause of the Christian West," as one speaker put it. Amid the bright drapings of red, white, and blue, the fluttering of American flags and anti–United Nations banners, the strains of "Battle Hymn of the Republic," and the boos and hisses heaped upon the name of President John F. Kennedy and the tumultuous applause at the mention of African leader Moise Tshombe, Dos Passos walked humbly to the stage to accept his "Freedom Award" along with Senator Strom Thurmond, economist Ludwig von Mises, actor John Wayne, and other messiahs of the new American Right. Almost thirty years earlier the same novelist stood in this same arena together with communists and socialists protesting the reactionary terror in Austria. What is one to make of a writer whose ideological travels have taken him from William Z. Foster to Barry Goldwater, from the *New Masses* to the *National Review*, without so much as an apologia? How can a man who once denounced Woodrow Wilson for taking America into war maintain, a half century later, that President Nixon "deserves acclaim" for "having had the courage" to order the invasion of Cambodia? In *U.S.A.* the brilliant young essayist Randolph Bourne is depicted as a martyr for his heroic resistance to America's involvement in World War I. In 1970, just before his death, Dos Passos said of student anti-war protesters, "The rank criminal idiocy of the younger generation in this country is more than I can swallow."[6]

Dos Passos's politics are also hard to swallow. A former communist sympathizer justifies America's intervention in Vietnam, then supports a president who desires more than anything else a détente with Red China. A Jeffersonian individualist spends his whole literary life protesting the bureaucratic state, then turns against a younger generation who opposed the same technological society that he had attacked in every novel from One Man's Initiation (1920) to Midcentury (1960). No one was more puzzled by Dos Passos's conservative positions than the great literary critic Edmund Wilson. In the forties Dos Passos had joined his close friend in denouncing Stalinism; two decades later he openly attacked Wilson for failing to support the cold war. Dos Passos's political career has remained a riddle to literary scholars and intellectual historians. Wilson tried to sum up its meaning in a simple couplet:

> On account of Soviet Knavery
> He favors restoring slavery.[7]

Fair or foul?

The ideological career of Will Herberg is equally puzzling. It may even be unique in the annals of American radicalism. Herberg became a Marxist revolutionary, youth organizer, and Daily Worker contributor in the early twenties when the Communist Party was being hounded by the forces of law and order. In some respects Herberg was the young Rabbi of the Revolution, the Talmudic scholar of the militant Left, the intellectual wanderer who could not find a home even in the Communist Party itself (which had banished his faction in 1928). An intense, learned young philosophy student, Herberg devoted his entire being to the world of ideas, rising to every intellectual challenge at a time when theoretical matters were usually settled by a cablegram from Moscow. He attempted to reconcile Marxism and Einstein's relativity physics, correct Edmund Wilson's views on proletarian literature, and argue with Sidney Hook over the textual validity of Marx's ambivalent position on revolution. In the thirties Herberg became a familiar ideologue and polemicist in the *Modern Quarterly*, one of the chief theoretical journals of the Old Left generation. Elevating political discourse to the highest level of sophistication, he conceived his mission as that of the philosopher who would expedite the revolution by explicating the meaning of dialectical materialism and the theory and practice of Leninism.

Less than a decade later this same writer would be explicating fervently the meaning of sin, despair, *Angst*, and dread, the existential anxiety of "finitude" and the tragedy of the "human condition." As a Marxist, Herberg had dismissed religion as the illusion of the oppressed. When he now spoke as a conservative, God came alive in almost every utterance. The revolutionary who once believed that class conflict and working class struggle would redeem the world discovered some terrible secret about man, and with that discovery he also assumed a new mission. "At its deepest level, the conflict between Soviet Communism and the free world is a religious conflict," Herberg told a conference of ministers, priests, and rabbis in 1952. "Quite literally, it is a struggle for the soul of modern man." In Herberg the theologian the cold war took on spiritual dimension, the forces of light against the forces of darkness. And in the drama of salvation there could be no "coexistence."[8]

Why did Herberg become a communist and why did he then repudiate communism as though he were fleeing the dark night of his soul? Was Herberg another Whittaker Chambers, a pilgrim who abandoned revolution for revelation? Is such behavior evidence of a failure of nerve or, in Herberg's case, of an authentic mind probing the depths of existential understanding? The theological problems are as difficult as the psychological and political. If communism ultimately brought Herberg to religion and to

William Buckley, should Buckley thank Stalin for doing God's work?

The odyssey of James Burnham is another strange chapter in modern American intellectual history. In the early thirties he endorsed, after some hesitation, the whole program of revolutionary communism: the "contradictions" of capitalism, the party as the agency of history (*partiinost*), the power "morality" of the Bolshevik tradition, the historical necessity of violence, class warfare, and the dictatorship of the proletariat. In the mid-thirties he became perhaps the leading intellectual exponent of Leon Trotsky, absorbing completely the entire outlook of Trotskyism: the doctrine of permanent revolution, reformism as "petty-bourgeois impotence," and the fantasy of the Fourth International as the true embodiment of the October Revolution. Burnham articulated these ideas in *The New International*, a sophisticated theoretical journal that influenced a number of important left-wing writers and nurtured the minds of young radicals like Irving Howe and Michael Harrington. Burnham was also a highly respected member of the *Partisan Review's* editorial board, which included such learned intellectuals as F. W. Dupee, Dwight Macdonald, William Phillips, and Philip Rahv. In addition, he helped organize the Trotskyist Workers Party, and as the leading theoretician of its "political bureau" and "secretariat," he was consulted on political decisions and often directed the party's tactical moves against rival factions and devised various strategies of New York–styled backdoor Bolshevism—absorption by infiltration. During the late thirties, when many leading radical intellectuals began to sense a "crisis in Marxism" due to the unexpected triumphs of fascist dictatorships, Burnham remained the faithful voice of Lenin, admonishing other writers for their faltering belief in the socialist revolution. In a twenty-page essay, "Intellectuals in Retreat," Burnham and Trotskyist Max Shachtman scrupulously analyzed the presuppositions of every important writer who had turned away from revolutionary Marxism. The politics of Max Eastman, John Chamberlain, Sidney Hook, Edmund Wilson, John Dewey,

Eugene Lyons, James T. Farrell, and Philip Rahv were, declared Burnham and Shachtman in 1939, "negative, irresponsible and unprincipled."[9]

A year later Burnham himself broke with Trotsky, repudiated Marxism, and pronounced the socialist revolution a foolish day-dream. This was only the first of a series of surprising turns in Burnham's political career that left his admirers and critics dumb-founded. His writings in the forties are an ideological mystery. First, he calmly predicts the collapse of the Soviet Union and the victory of fascist Germany and Japan (*The Managerial Revolution*, 1941); he next sets out to prove that democracy and freedom are "myths" (*The Machiavellians*, 1943); and he then proceeds to explain to readers of *Partisan Review* why Stalin must be recognized as a "genius" who, instead of betraying the revolution as Trotsky had maintained, had actually "fulfilled" it ("Lenin's Heir"). After the war a new James Burnham appeared. He now advocates full use of military force to resist the Stalinism he had just recently seemed to credit with inexorable power, and he now calls upon Americans and Europeans to fight for democratic ideals that he had earlier dismissed as theoretically unrealizable (*The Struggle for the World*, 1947). With the advent of the cold war, Burn-ham's positions became clear, if not consistent. He emerged as the leading diplomatic theoretician of the Right, a nuclear confronta-tionist whose articles were read by the hundred thousand sub-scribers to the *National Review*. At the time of the Korean war, his writings had considerable influence in the State Department, the Pentagon, and the Central Intelligence Agency, especially among those officials who wanted to oppose the policy of contain-ment with a new strategy of "liberation-rollback." As a conserva-tive, Burnham also retained his obsession for prophecy and conspiracy. He again predicted the end of the democratic world in *The Suicide of the West* (1964), and he had earlier warned Americans about the threat of internal communism in *The Web of Subversion* (1954), an espionage report that the John Birch Society would later publish as part of its "Americanist Library."

Burnham surprised many writers by becoming America's leading intellectual cold warrior. Even the astute George Orwell failed to anticipate the ex-Trotskyist's sudden turn to the Right. Attempts have been made to explain Burnham's politics, but it is instructive to note that even his closest comrade during the Old Left era confesses his shock and bewilderment at Burnham's behavior. Listen to Max Shachtman's "oral history" recollections:

The only time after the break with the Workers party that I saw him again was—I must admit to my utter surprise, absolutely unexpectedly—at the hearing that we finally, finally, finally got from the Department of Justice on our being on the so-called subversive list, a listing that we had contested for years before we could even get a hearing on it. When we got the hearing we had testifying for our side such people as Dwight Macdonald, Daniel Bell, Norman Thomas. They scoured the country—these Department of Justice people, especially among ex-members of ours—looking for somebody who could reveal our big secret subversive activities and our true secret doctrine to overthrow the government by violence. They couldn't find one single solitary soul, not one. They dug up a professor from Columbia, an expert on the Russian Revolution, who had never even heard of the Independent Socialist League. That was their first expert. And our attorney—this wonderful Joe Rauh—absolutely made a monkey of him. So the first witness for the government was a disaster, especially after we had gotten Norman Thomas to testify for us. This was long before we had joined the Socialist party. They promised that they were going to get somebody who in his field is as prominent and as expert as Mr. Thomas is in his field, and we were breaking our heads trying to figure out, "Whom have they got?" There just cannot be anybody! We had learned through the grapevine of the literally dozens of people they had tried to induce to testify against us, and no one had consented. Whom could they possibly have found!?

Well, one morning the session opened when this big surprise witness was to turn up and it turned out to be none other than James Burnham. I must say it was a shock. It wasn't because we expected him to be a fine, outstanding liberal or an old friend of ours who for old time's sake wouldn't do anything dirty to us. We just didn't expect a man of his type, this suave, above-the-battle, academic, political man to descend to this sewage of the government's attempt in effect to gag and outlaw a tiny little left-wing propagandist society. And there he was, urbane as usual, greeting me with a polite smile, which I tried my best to return with an angry and contemptuous look, because that's exactly how I felt. And he did his little stint. It wasn't very effective, because we were removed from the subversive list after all. . . .

You know, it's far from the first time that someone far more prominent and far more active and far more devoted and far more integrated into the radical movement had turned into the opposite of what he had been. But to read about such things is one thing, and to experience it personally and directly is another thing. And it shocked all of us, and we all felt that our hands were dirty. Even now, even now I like to feel that Burnham was not very happy and not very proud about this . . . disgraceful job that he felt called upon to perform for the police.[10]

Is it necessary to have dirty hands to clear one's conscience? Is the ex-communist intellectual compelled to collaborate with the anti-communist politician? McCarthyism was also part of the bitter conflict in America that drove Burnham, Eastman, Dos Passos, and Herberg into the arms of William Buckley.

Here we have, then, four gifted but diverse men who made the peculiar odyssey from the revolutionary Left to the militant Right, without so much as pausing in the "Vital Center." The burden of the present work is to probe each of these political migrations and to try to illuminate the dynamics that governed them and, above all, to suggest what common impulses or reactions might underlie the flight from one extreme to the other. If, indeed, "the extremes touch," what is it that forms the bridge between them?

PART ONE

Arrival and Departure

1912–1940

CHAPTER 1

Exorcising Hegel: Max Eastman

Hegel's concept of reason . . . denies the hegemony of every prevailing form of existence by demonstrating the antagonisms that dissolve it into other forms. . . . Hegel's dialectic is permeated with the profound conviction that all immediate forms of existence—in nature and history—are "bad" because they do not permit things to be what they can.

HERBERT MARCUSE, *Reason and Revolution*, 1941

Once catch well the knack of this scheme of thought and you are lucky if you ever get away from it. It is all you can see.

WILLIAM JAMES, "Hegel and His Method," 1909

Hegelism is like a mental disease—you cannot know what it is until you get it, and then you can't know because you've got it.

MAX EASTMAN, *Marx and Lenin*, 1927

The Joyous Life and Lenin's Triumph

The story of the central figure of the generation of 1912 begins where it ought to begin—in bed with Mabel Dodge.

I remember sitting up in bed one dark, stormy morning and I could hear the rain beat against the house. Looking through my bedroom door, across the sitting room, I saw panes of the front window streaked with rain. How good the cool water felt to the earth. An immense satisfaction flooded me as I realized in myself the fast flow of nature and its excellent enjoyments. At that moment the figure of Max Eastman passed the window. Head down, contracted against the wind and wet, he pressed up the road, the picture of misery and unrest. He seemed an outcast of the earth—one of those who are fair-weather lovers, whose spirits depend upon sunshine and slump into dismay when the storm comes. I felt superior, somehow, and glad I knew what I knew.[1]

Mabel Dodge, the notorious hostess of the Greenwich Village Left, knew many of the pre–World War I rebels, and at her famous salon at 23 Fifth Avenue she "collected" a number of prominent literary intellectuals and journalists. But whatever else she may have known, Mabel Dodge never really understood Max Eastman, any more than she understood why her lover, John Reed, abandoned her smothering affection in order to save his "spirit." Her "intimate memoirs" were published in 1936, when she and Eastman were engaged in a bitter quarrel over the political reputation of her former lover Reed. Eastman could share Reed's passion for political freedom and personal independence, and ironically he described Reed's departure in 1915 much as Dodge had described seeing Eastman outside her window: "Mabel was just lifting herself out of a tumultuous love affair with John Reed. I remember his stamping out of her bedroom in the small hours of the night, slamming the door and plunging away in a heavy rainstorm, none of us knew where." In Dodge's eyes, Eastman and Reed alike were "outcasts of the earth"; both were men who, as Reed wrote in a poem dedicated to Eastman, "loving quiet beauty best/Yet could not rest," men who chose instead to fan up "the noble flames that smoulder in the breast/Of the oppressed."[2]

In 1936, the year Dodge published her memoirs, Joseph Freeman published his autobiography, *An American Testament*. Freeman had been a teen-age camp follower of the earlier Lyrical Left of Eastman and Reed, and his autobiography offers perhaps the best portrait of Eastman by one who had actually experienced the power of his presence. Freeman, at the time he wrote his memoirs, was an ardent communist literary intellectual who had broken with his old comrade and idol. Nevertheless, he described Eastman as an ideological mentor who "looked Beauty and spoke Justice." For Freeman could understand, as Dodge could not, that the true radical must always be a lonely "outcast" and "perpetual renegade," a rebel who can change causes without betraying ideals.

Freeman could discern in Eastman the paradoxes as well as the promises of American radicalism. A complex, controversial figure, with a mind and temper of contradictory impulses, Eastman combined the revolutionary earnestness of a Trotsky, the sexual adventurousness of a Casanova, and the honest self-introspection of a Stendhal. His life was a voyage of discovery through a revolutionary epoch, an episodic political romance that left many friends stranded when he pressed forward with Lenin's legacy, or bewildered when he later turned away from Trotsky. But for those who had once caught the flame of Eastman his memory never faded. Two decades later, in 1958, when Eastman was an outspoken conservative defender of capitalism, Freeman still expressed the fascination of Eastman's "broad humanity" and "miraculous personality": "What a man! I ought to say what a god—because it seems to me that he is very much like Apollo must have been both in appearance and in temper. In him you have wisdom without timidity, strength without insolence, and beauty without vanity."[3]

The life of Max Eastman offers one of the most remarkable careers in twentieth-century American intellectual history. During his rich and active literary years, he wrote more than twenty books on art, science, poetry, philosophy, humor, journalism, aesthetics, anthropology, religion, capitalism, socialism, Soviet culture, German politics, Freudian psychology, and Marxism. He composed five volumes of verse, a novel, two volumes of memoirs, a pioneering analysis of the young Trotsky's personality, and two collections of brilliant biographical portraits of an unlikely gallery of close friends and acquaintances: Eugene Debs and Albert Einstein, Carlo Tresca and Edna St. Vincent Millay, Ernest Hemingway and George Santayana, John Dewey and Sigmund Freud, Bertrand Russell and Charles Chaplin, E. W. Scripps and Pablo Casals. He published the radical journals *The Masses* and *The Liberator* and later became, ironically, a "roving editor" for *Reader's Digest* and one of the first editorial advisers to William Buckley's conservative *National Review*. After having mastered Russian in a little more than a year, he skillfully translated Pushkin as well as Trotsky's monumental three-volume *History of the Russian Revolution*, edited and abridged *Das Kapital* for the Modern Library, smuggled out of the Soviet Union a copy of Lenin's "Testament," and produced a historic documentary film on the Russian Revolution.[4]

Eastman's reputation was as magnetic as his writings were prolific. Tall, lean, tanned, strikingly handsome with blond wavy hair and dashing, gay eyes, he was one of the best-known literary radicals of the Greenwich Village generation and one of the dominant figures in American cultural life between 1912 and 1923. His career before World War I was a sustained round of intellectual and political activism. While writing poetry, lecturing in philosophy at Columbia University, and editing the lively, sardonic *The Masses*, he championed the cause of the anarcho-syndicalist Wobblies, became a leading spokesman for the radical feminist movement, and, with his sister, Crystal, organized the American Union against Militarism. During these joyous years Eastman emerged as the orphic bard of the Left, the eloquent lyricist of liberation. "When I was up at Columbia University," wrote publisher M. Lincoln Schuster two decades later,

one of the most unforgettable and most glamorous experiences I recall in my student life was the first lecture I heard by Max Eastman before the Socialist Study Club. He came before us then as the fair-haired apostle of the new poetry, the knight errant of a new and rebellious generation, the man who was making his dreams come true—as poet, as thinker, as editor, as teacher, as psychologist, as philosopher, as a yea-sayer of the joy and adventure of living in the fullest and richest sense of the word. Even then Max was already a glamorous, exciting figure in the world of letters and in the world of adventure. Life was bursting in all its radiance all around him. For him existence was a fight, a song, a revolution, a poem, an affirmation.

Max is a dazzlingly many-sided person, but his lust after the real, the intense, the beautiful enriches and colors his whole life, and his revolutionary ideology gives it direction and discipline. Thus an exuberant vitality courses through all his personal history—an uncompromising courage and passion for justice control it at every critical point. Whether life is a pageant or a predicament, a crisis or a contemplation, Max is always feeling and celebrating the qualities of things. The high spiritedness of youth and the deep thinking and clear seeing of radical teaching enabled him to integrate the qualities of the poet, the scientist, and man of action, and above all, the man who never betrays his sense of beauty or sense of humor.[5]

Max Eastman's radicalism sprouted from native soil. Before he had become a convert to Marxian socialism in 1912, he had already taken his stand on the Left as a staunch agnostic, a severe critic of nationalism and militarism, and a witty castigator of class distinctions. His early intellectual heroes included Mark Twain, whom he had known as a youth in Elmira, New York; Walt Whitman, the democratic poet of "communion" and "amativeness"; and Thorstein Veblen, whose Theory of the Leisure Class offered him both a critique of orthodox economics and a justification for his assault upon respectability. Eastman drew his inspiration from America's liberal intellectual tradition and from his parents' moral idealism, yet he vigorously opposed the contemporary idea of gradual reform. He disdained liberal rhetoric and had contempt for electoral politics. Liberals were "soft-headed idealists" who clung to outworn moral platitudes, and reformers missionaries who wanted to do for the oppressed what only the oppressed could do, and must do, for themselves. The philosophy of Marxism, which Eastman had picked up casually from his girl friend and later wife, Ida Rauh, seemed to offer a better grasp than liberal reform of the nature of economic power and the necessity of struggle and conflict. Marxism appeared to Eastman to be an "experimental" approach to society and history, a "hypothesis" that could be tested and revised like the theories of physical science. This image appealed to Eastman's empirical temperament, and in the theory and practice of revolutionary Marxism he believed he had at last found a system of ideas that enabled man to transform the real into the ideal and a program of action that furnished the means of overcoming the brutalities of class society.

So inspired, Eastman went on to become one of America's most eloquent spokesmen for the Bolshevik Revolution. Other Village radicals like John Reed and Emma Goldman were troubled by Lenin's reversal of trade union policy, by the Comintern's twenty-one "demands," and by the ill-fated Kronstadt uprising. But not Eastman. The sharp twists and turns in Bolshevik policy merely demonstrated to him the superiority of Lenin's intellect—"that of astute, flexible, undoctrinaire, unbigoted, supremely purposive, and I judged experimental, intelligence."[6] Lenin emerged as the "free-minded engineer of revolution," the man of action as well as ideas, the revolutionary who alone had the nerve to impose will upon reality and to seize history with both hands. In 1918, when the Bolshevik leader lay stricken by an assassin's bullet, Eastman published a poem in praise of Lenin's steadiness of will and fluidity of mind:

> Men that have stood like mountains in the flood
> Of change that runs like ruin through the earth,
> When murder takes the sanctity of birth,
> When food is fire and harvest-treasure blood,
> Men that like fixed eternal stars have stood,
> Their faith clear-shining sadly, and their mind
> Unmaddened by the madness of their kind—
> They were the godlike, they the great and good.
> With light, and mountain steadiness, and power,
> And faith like theirs in this all-fluid hour,
> You to the dreadful depth of change descend,
> And with its motions moving it, you blend
> Your conquering purpose as blue rivers roll
> Through all the ocean's waters toward the pole.[7]

The following year Eastman devoted all his energies to opposing the Allied intervention in the young Soviet republic and to struggling against the Red Scare in the United States. The year 1919 was, as Dos Passos observed, "the springtime of revolution," a year that saw labor strikes spread from the longshoreman halls of San Francisco to the great steel mills of the Midwest and even to the police stations of Boston. The radicalized American intelligentsia regarded Eastman's new journal, The Liberator, as something of an English Iskra, Lenin's theoretical "spark" of revolution. Because other left-wing publications had been suppressed by the government, *The Liberator* became the only source of news on the bloody civil war in Russia. Even European radicals turned to *The Liberator* for information. So tight was the blockade around the Bolsheviks that Antonio Gramsci and other communist leaders in Italy were forced to rely on Eastman's editorial reports. In *The Liberator* Eastman also answered Morris Hillquit and other socialist critics of the Bolsheviks, and published Lenin's "Letter to American Workingmen," which the poet Carl Sandburg had brought back from Stockholm. *The Liberator* became a beacon of hope to many literary intellectuals. It was, as Theodore Draper called it, "a kind of Who's Who of artistic and literary Americans for the next two or more decades." It published contributions from such important writers as Edna St. Vincent Millay, William Carlos Williams, Elinor Wylie, E. E. Cummings, John Dos Passos, Ernest Hemingway, Louise Bogan, Robert Hillyer, Elmer Rice, S. N. Behrman, Sherwood Anderson, Claude McKay, James Weldon Johnson, Vachel Lindsay, Amy Lowell, Heywood Broun, Edmund Wilson, and Bertrand Russell.[8]

In 1922 Eastman left *The Liberator* to visit Russia "to find out whether what I have been saying is true." He was impressed by the triumphs of the Red Army and by the energy and health of the Russian people. Bolshevik leaders received him gracefully, and Trotsky befriended him as an intellectual comrade. But while Eastman toured the countryside and studied Russian in the Marx-Engels Institute Library, Stalin's campaign against Trotsky began. Eastman attended the 1923 Party Congress unaware of the struggle for power behind the scenes. Then the *danse macabre* unfolded with Lenin's death in January 1924. As the party *apparatchiks* began to move against the anti-Stalinist opposition, Trotsky advised Eastman to leave the country with documents that would expose Russia's internal struggle for power. Those documents included important extracts from what later came to be known as Lenin's last "Testament," in which the premier, dictating to his wife from his deathbed, called for Stalin's removal from the post of general secretary. Eastman gave them to the New York *Times* shortly after he arrived in London late in 1924. He started his long and lonely campaign to promote Trotsky, "the most universally gifted man in the world today," as the Bolshevik whose "superior moral and intellectual revolutionary greatness" made him Lenin's legitimate successor. He put forth this argument in *Since Lenin Died* (1925), a book which contained a complete account of the methods by which the Stalinist faction had dethroned Trotsky and discredited his authority. The anti-Stalinist opposition in Russia, however, failed to act decisively upon the revelations of Lenin's last will and testament, and even Trotsky himself felt compelled to renounce Eastman. When Eastman saw the following headline of the London communist paper, *Sunday Worker*, he collapsed into a chair, "so sick to my heart" that his wife thought he was about to faint:

> TROTSKY TROUNCES EASTMAN
> Lenin's "Will" a Myth—
> Eastman No Warrant for His Assertions
> By Leon Trotsky[9]

Eastman was also attacked in the *Workers Monthly*, an American communist publication that had absorbed the independent *Liberator*. A few months later he moved to Paris and began working in the Bibliothèque Nationale on a book which, as a defense of Bolshevism and at the same time a theoretical critique of Marxism, would bewilder the communist world.*

Throughout the twenties, when many American literary intellectuals expatriated to Paris and bade farewell to radical politics, Eastman continued to defend communism as the "science of revolution." With the rise of fascism in Italy, he was certain that the bankruptcy of liberalism left radical intellectuals with "this inexorable alternative—Lenin or Mussolini."[10] Eastman still believed that only Trotsky, the hero of the Red Army, could restore the legacy of Lenin and save Russia from creeping bureaucratic despot-

---

* Eastman's important philosophical treatise is discussed on pp. 44–51 passim.

ism. Hence Eastman was one of the first intellectuals to support, financially as well as politically, the organization of a Trotskyist party in the United States. Young Trotskyists like Max Shachtman and James P. Cannon were grateful to Eastman, but even they could not understand his position. Eastman had assumed the difficult role of expounding what appeared to be three incompatible viewpoints: protesting the corruption of Bolshevism under Stalin, questioning Marxism as a philosophical system, and defending a communist revolution that supposedly had been "made" in the name of Karl Marx.

Although Eastman's ambiguous position infuriated communists, to the Old Left intellectuals, the radicals of the thirties, the relationship between literature and politics was far more important than one's attitude toward the fine points of dialectical materialism and the philosophical riddle of freedom and determinism. Yet Eastman's position on literature also made him a maverick. Indeed on aesthetic issues Eastman became to the Left what Trotsky was politically to Stalin: he knew too much.

Radicalism and the Literary Mind

Eastman had taught aesthetics at Columbia University before World War I. He devoted one whole term to the exposition of twenty-three definitions of beauty, only to annihilate each and send his students away with the conclusion that beauty must be experienced, not explained. Skeptical of any claim to absolute truth, Eastman remained critical of the Greenwich Village artists' and writers' attempt to break down all classical dualisms in order to synthesize, in Joseph Freeman's words, "politics, poetry, and science; justice, beauty, and knowledge."[11] Eastman believed with Yeats that poetry and politics, imagination and truth, private vision and public life were conflicting, irreconcilable values. In an introduction to a collection of his poems, *Colors of Life*, he denied an absolute value under which all branches of knowledge could be assimilated and toward which man may guide his thoughts and actions. Only life itself, as the highest value, higher than even liberty or revolution, could encompass all that is valuable.

After World War I, when Eastman was caught up in the glorious triumphs of Bolshevism, he had momentarily succumbed to the temptation to subordinate creative life to political organization. In his debates with Romain Rolland, and later with Henri Barbusse and the *Clarté* circle of French intellectuals, Eastman maintained that writers, as conveyers of experience and hence free agents of "inspiration," needed the guidance of a political party because they themselves did not constitute a revolutionary vanguard.[12] This was as far as Eastman ever would go in trying to reconcile the conflicting demands of cultural autonomy and political dedication. A few years later Eastman's acute perception of the dual nature of cognition—first expressed in 1913 in the *Enjoyment of Poetry*—returned in full force as he warned radicals to resist all efforts to instrumentalize art as a class weapon and to reject a communist manifesto summoning the intellectual to establish an "International Proletarian Literature":

In other words art and poetry, having with difficulty escaped from their bondage to religion, must now enter into bondage in politics. They must be subordinated to a single practical enterprise. No great or consecrated poet or artist in the world could sincerely subscribe to such a manifesto. Poetry and art may contribute vitally to purposive effort, but they are in their essence and definition distinct from it and independent of it. Their interest is in experience and not purpose, in being and not becoming. The only ultimate distinction which can be made between poetic and practical language is that poetic language pauses to realize the existing nature of things mentioned, practical language merely indicates them for the purpose of action and adjustment.[13]

Poetry and art are concerned with "being" because they deal with the pure contemplation of things as the writer and painter attempt to communicate the quality of an experience. Eastman elaborated this thesis in *The Literary Mind: Its Place in an Age of Science*. Published in 1932, the book was directed primarily at New Criticism aestheticians like I. A. Richards and New Humanism scholars like Irving Babbitt. Here Eastman declared that general truth is not the province of poetry, which is the enhancement in consciousness of a particular experience in terms that can be felt, touched, and seen but not logically defined or rationally comprehended. Science is not the province of ultimate knowledge either, since science does not tell us what reality is but merely how to operate on and experiment with the practical potentialities of nature.[14] Although Eastman was addressing the aesthetic theoreticians of the conservative Right, The Literary Mind had severe implications for the Left as well. Dialectics enables us to conceive history as mediated through the mind of Hegel and Marx but not to perceive the real meaning and direction of history itself. Neither the philosophy of literature nor the philosophy of history must pretend to offer knowledge of a superior kind, for human knowledge is as incomplete as reality is indefinite. "A skepticism about the power of the human mind to solve any ultimate problem honestly confronted is all the philosophy I have," Eastman later remarked in his conversations with Albert Einstein.[15]

Eastman's sensibility to the disorder of experience would be compatible with the vision of history around which Dos Passos organized his masterpiece, U.S.A. But The Literary Mind offended many intellectuals on all sides of the political spectrum: conservatives who saw poetry as the last domain of value in a world of science; liberals who were uneasy with Eastman's attack on modernist writers like Joyce and Eliot; and, above all, Marxists who could not tolerate Eastman's sharp distinction between art and politics.[16] The book was published just when the Old Left was in the thick of an intense literary war over the issues of proletarian realism and the relationship of art to propaganda. For the most part Eastman stayed out of these debates which engaged the minds of important writers like Edmund Wilson, Joseph Wood Krutch, Archibald MacLeish, and Granville Hicks—as well as many lesser minds who had contempt for the political impotence of the literary intellectual. While the debates were raging and communist intellectuals were publishing Voices in October in an effort to rhapsodize the joyful rebirth of cultural freedom in the Soviet Union, Eastman was at work on another book, *Artists in Uniform*. Here he brought to public light Stalin's literary inquisition against independent authors, which had been carried out in the Soviet Union through the Russian Association of Proletarian Writers and in the United States through the John Reed Clubs. Chapters of the book had been published in *Modern Monthly* while Eastman was battling with Sidney Hook over Marxism. Responding to these articles in the *Partisan Review*, the Russian novelist Boris Pilnyak denied, and challenged Eastman to prove, that the Soviet government had forced him to repudiate his writings. Eastman easily did so in an article entitled "Artists in Strait Jackets," but before its appearance Hook remarked to Calverton that Eastman "may have invented a few details to fill out the picture" of the Pilnyak case even though he was right about the Soviet Union. Editor Calverton's willingness to quote Hook's casual remark caused Eastman to resign from *Modern Monthly's* editorial board.[17]

Eastman sought Trotsky's support in exposing the fate of artistic freedom under Stalin. Trotsky could not recommend Eastman's book to his American followers because of their disagreements over dialectical materialism. In a private letter he admitted to Eastman, "It is needless to say that you write with full knowledge of your subject." From the American Trotskyist Max Shachtman came more encouraging words: "Your stuff on arts and letters under Stalin . . . is gorgeous. One of my spies tells me that Mike Gold was seen, surrounded by copies of your articles, uttering low groans and running around on his belly eating grass in Washington Park while a compassionate mob looked on."[18]

The "groans" of Gold and other communist writers reached a crescendo of invective when *Artists in Uniform* appeared in June 1934. Joseph Freeman, once an intellectual protégé of the old *The Masses*, devoted six double columns in the *Daily Worker* to describing Eastman as a "liar," a "literary jesuit," a "forger," and a writer of "scurrilous diatribes." Gold, editor of the *New Masses*, added predictable epithets: "Shameful! Disgusting! Horrible!

Nauseating! Criminal!" "I have never turned away from a friend who lost his path through drink, disease, or personal weakness. But Max Eastman, former friend, you have sunk beneath all tolerance. You are a filthy and deliberate liar! . . . Nay, you are worse, since you yourself were once the Bolshevik leader of a generation of young intellectuals. The world has always loathed Judases more than Pontius Pilates."[19]

Eastman wrote a thirteen-page reply, a "quixotic performance" intended more for his own personal files than for the *Modern Monthly*, which, he felt, would have no room for a detailed, factual refutation of Freeman's and Gold's febrile polemics. The following year, when the Popular Front in America remade Russia's image into a respectable ally among the common enemies of fascism, Eastman found himself more politically alone than ever. His once towering reputation now became a matter for ridicule as amateur psychologists on the Left subjected his personality to scrutiny. Haakon Chevalier, a specialist in French literature, a translator of Malraux, and, years later, a key witness in the J. Robert Oppenheimer affair, described Eastman as a rebel without a cause, a half-baked American Leninist who could not sublimate his personal life into the higher imperative or organized political life.

Look at the two men: Lenin—compact as a bullet, single-minded, undramatic to the point of self-effacement; uncompromising and relentlessly steering a straight course through the mad chaos of the world in upheaval; the whole wealth of his genius harnessed to a single purpose; a man without a personal life, the living incarnation of the *will* of a whole people. Max Eastman—genial, easy-going, wayward, passionately individualistic, with a colorful life full of personal emotions and adventures, his gifts flowing out in many directions; a dramatic figure, a Bohemian, a free soul whose center of gravity is always with himself.[20]

American Trotskyists, though grateful for Eastman's revelations of "the ghastly depredations of Stalinism on the body of art," also dismissed his views on literature and philosophy as "childish prattle." The pseudonymous Chester Ernest exploded his scorn upon the bohemian playboy from upstate New York:

The present fire-cracker boyishly placed by Max Eastman under the great chair of Papa Marx is but the latest of a whole series of similar adolescent pranks that have won some public notice. It is hard to take seriously these utterances, which together constitute the Defiance of the Lone Rebel of Croton, the Last Survivor of the Old Masses gang, to the invading hordes of Marxism. . . . No Marxist-Leninist can rest content while the best available attack on pseudo-Marxist regimentation of the artist (squeezing art into army-cap and high-boot uniform) remains one written from the viewpoint of a Left Wing nudist.[21]

The Greenwich Village radical, claimed the Trotskyists, devoted his literary talents to exposing the cultural crimes of Soviet Russia because he had sold his mind and pen to the capitalist press, a charge that infuriated Eastman. His first critical work on communist ideology, *Marx and Lenin: The Science of Revolution*, had been so specialized and unpopular a topic that Eastman was forced to contribute to the cost of its publication. *Artists in Uniform* and *Art and the Life of Action*, another work which challenged the Marxist approach to literature, each sold fewer than five hundred copies. Eastman suspected that potential sales on the latter books were sabotaged by pro-communist bookstore agents. By 1936 he could no longer dip into his own pockets to help out Calverton and the *Modern Monthly*. With his bank account down to forty-three dollars, he decided to write a sequel to his early popular treatise *The Sense of Humor* (1922). The second volume, *Enjoyment of Laughter* (1936), was a brief best seller, and the royalties freed him from continuing his lecture tours for the next several years. In contrast, Eastman's prolific writings on Marxism and Soviet culture were no profitable venture and, one might add, no laughing matter.[22]

John Reed Redivivus: Greenwich Village and Stalin's Russia

In 1936 Granville Hicks, for a brief time the literary spokesman for the Communist Party, published a biography of Eastman's old comrade and fellow *The Masses* editor, John Reed. The patron saint of the CP, a former Greenwich Village rebel who was buried near the Kremlin, Reed had become a legend who, if properly exploited, could help establish continuity between the communist Old Left and the anarcho-libertarian Left of the pre–World War I years. To do so, Hicks had to explain away Reed's disillusionment with communism just before his death in 1920. In Hicks's account, Reed did not resign from and permanently break with the Comintern's executive committee when it ordered American communists to accept its organizational policies, but he withdrew his resignation from the Comintern and offered his "apologies" to the executive committee when fellow delegates persuaded him that such an action was not "a thing a disciplined revolutionary would have done." This version of Reed's political repentance incensed Eastman, who had refused to assist Hicks with his biography because, he said, Hicks's association with the New Masses and his defense of Stalinism "betrayed every essential value for which John Reed fought and which he loved."[23] To set the story straight and demolish the legend, Eastman interviewed Louise Bryant, Reed's wife, and Angelica Balabanoff, the first secretary of the Comintern. Eastman's own account appeared in the Modern Monthly, and as the controversy developed Hook advised Calverton to "play up the Eastman on Reed feature."[24]

Eastman's interpretation, which has Reed struggling to the end against the Comintern and giving up communism before his death, was based largely on the dim recollections of Louise Bryant. Mabel Dodge challenged Eastman in a private letter: "I cannot help feeling that you use the roly-holy Reed just as much as the others, as a tool to carve your own prejudices into a satisfactory form. Just as much as the insignificant Hicks, you use the innocent Reed as proof of this and that." You are also "using," Mabel Dodge continued, "hoar Louise as a support of your theory about Reed's motivation and conduct." She was certain that she knew the "lovable" and "amorphous" Reed better than Louise Bryant did, and that her own "physiological" explanations of his rebellious "enthusiasms," spelled out in her published memoirs, remained the basis for a true biography of Reed. A mistress could well claim she knew her lover better than a wife knew her husband, but Eastman told Mabel Dodge she did not know enough about Reed's life after the affair; nor did she know anything about the Russian Revolution and the Comintern, about Reed's unwavering syndicalist beliefs, and, above all, "the political passion—a primitive and animal trait which does not conflict at all with the other things you think about Jack. (You don't know about it because, as you say, you don't possess it.)"[25]

Mabel Dodge's expressed "lack of interest in progress" made her, Eastman felt, incapable of understanding why Reed and *The Masses* rebels would become disciples of Lenin and why they would be able, in different circumstances, to change their minds without changing their convictions. Eastman believed that he was remaining within the spirit of Reed's legacy when he applied the same moral and political criticisms to Stalin's Russia that the Greenwich Village Left had once applied to Woodrow Wilson's America. In this assertion Eastman was correct. The earlier rebels wanted to bring down a corrupt old order, not impose a new one. Out of an impulse born of repression, the generation of Eastman and Reed chose moral and aesthetic freedom; out of a necessity born of desperation, the generation of the Depression era chose economic order and rationalization. The Old Left was fascinated by centralized planning and industrial growth, the earlier Lyrical Left, by the joys of unorganized struggle. But in the thirties the ritual of innocence seemed to be repeating itself in the false hopes of the fellow travelers. The radicals of the thirties saw emerging in Stalin's Russia what Eastman had thought he had earlier seen in Lenin's Russia: a "scientific" experiment in socialism that signified the reaffirmation of the sane and rational values of the historic Enlightenment. For Eastman, however, the romance with history had ended. Freedom had nothing to do with the future. The values of the past were the only guide, even the unrealized ideals of Greenwich Village—Reed's libertarianism against Stalin's totalitarianism, the rebel against the commissar.

Eastman's first serious effort at evaluating Soviet Russia was undertaken in summer 1934. After having been "pounced on" from many quarters for his writings on dialectical materialism and proletarian literature, he felt it necessary to "launch a statement of my true position into the mainstream." The result was an article that represented, he told Calverton, "the crystallization of my opinions."[26] Apparently he had no luck in getting it published in Harper's or the New Republic and had to settle for the Modern Monthly, an important theoretical journal but hardly the "mainstream" magazine whose readers he was trying to reach. The article bore the title "Discrimination about Russia."

To Eastman Soviet Russia was an "experiment" which would either confirm or disprove the "hypothesis" of socialist revolution. Since there was no "historical necessity" or "dialectical inevitability" inherent in communism, one must compare emerging realities with ideals. "Therefore," Eastman prefaced his analysis, "if the soviet culture as it developed did not bear out in essential ways the hopes predicated upon it, I should be ready to abandon the idea of improving human society by guiding a revolution toward socialism. This will, I hope, add force to my assertion that the soviet culture does bear out those hopes." The Soviet Union demonstrated, Eastman proceeded to explain, the two psychological fallacies of the bourgeois mind: the old wail that "initiative" would die out in a non-competitive society, and the old whimper that interests and profits as "rewards for saving" are essential to capitalist accumulation. The great economic strides being achieved under the five-year plans, Eastman maintained, were sufficient proof that there was more than one road to modernization. Eastman recognized that the agricultural problem was, and always had been, "the skeleton in the closet of all Marxians"; he regarded Stalin's policy of forced collectivization as avoidable and therefore "savage, licentious, and stupid." Once sufficient farm machinery was introduced in the countryside, Russia would at last be brought into the twentieth century and the agricultural crisis would subside. Even more encouraging were the glowing reports brought back from "the suburbs of paradise" to America by fellow travelers who hailed Soviet reforms in education, birth control, crime and prostitution and drug addiction, race relations, mental health, and other aspects of urban life.

Eastman perceived the blemishes and the beauties of socialist reconstruction, as did Lenin just before his death. Particularly galling to him were the bigotry and bureaucracy, the growing Stalinist cult of personality, the emergence of Russian nationalism, and the abandonment of all hope for world revolution—as evidenced in Foreign Minister Litvinov's new policy of disarmament and rapprochement with the capitalist powers of the West. Such developments represented to Eastman, as they did to Trotsky, a "betrayal" of the October Revolution. Eastman became much more pessimistic as he contemplated the unthinkable—a continuous degeneration of Marxist Leninism and even a permanent state of terror. The only course left to a "thoughtful revolutionist" was to "support and defend the soviets and yet at the same time criticize the Stalin bureaucracy and reject its international leadership." Such a position, Eastman added, "required a certain emotional equilibrium."[27]

Six months later Eastman took another hard look at the Soviet Union and declared that the experiment in socialism had ended. The Kremlin's decree ordering Russian people to multiply the population was "the last straw," he told Calverton, "the ultimate end of a dream."[28]

Two years afterward Eastman spelled out the reasons for his disillusionment in a two-part essay in *Harper's*. The Moscow purge trials, which occupied the dazed minds of so many radicals of the thirties, appeared to Eastman merely the bloody climax of a trend toward counterrevolutionary repression. But in his *Harper's* article Eastman chose to concentrate rather on those social problems that had inspired the moral impulse of the older Greenwich Village Left: "education, prison reform, public health, women's freedom, sex and family relations, birth control, prostitution, yellow journalism, drug addiction, alcoholism, rights of national minorities, elimination of anti-Semitism, mental hygiene, administration of justice, peace, war and patriotism, economic planning." Eastman cited a battery of statistics to show that income differentials between workers and management were as great in the USSR as in the United States, and the social and cultural privileges of the party bureaucrats even greater than the inequities of capitalist society. Still, the problems of class were not as important to Eastman as world peace and cultural freedom—ideals for which he had been willing to go to jail in 1917.

He returned again and again to three basic issues: Russia's position on peace and war, education and youth, sex and family relations. All three Soviet promises had been violated. Instead of the working class solidarity that had been the hallmark of the Second International, Stalin had embarked upon a program of nationalism and military alliances with the capitalist West under the "fascist" slogan, expressed in *Pravda* (June 9, 1934), "Defense of the fatherland is the supreme law of life." Instead of the bold experimental schools that John Dewey thought he saw emerging in 1928, Stalin's "Decree of Academic Reform" of 1935 imposed upon educational life a uniformity that strangled the mind's natural curiosity. His decree applying the death penalty for theft to minors over twelve years of age made Stalin more brutal than the industrial capitalists or the Social Darwinists of the nineteenth century. Finally, Stalin did not liberate women from the drudgery of domesticity and the compulsion of motherhood, but emerged as more tyrannical than the worst male chauvinist of the Victorian age, proceeding to raise the cost of divorce and alimony, denying the right of birth control, and redefining into a crime the right of abortion—"one of woman's few real guarantees of liberty." "Every girl," Eastman quoted *Pravda* as stating (June 7, 1935), "must be treasured not only as a textile worker, a bold parachute jumper or an engineer, but as a future mother. The mother of one child must be treasured as the future mother of eight." This attitude toward women, closer to Mussolini than to Marx, brought from Eastman a remark closer to Emma Goldman than to Joseph Stalin: "Just how far the mother of eight children will go as an engineer or a parachute jumper, is well known to those who use their brains when they think."[29]

In Eastman the libertarian "heart" struggled privately with the Leninist "head," bohemian anarchism with party centralism. Not until the last years of his life would he acknowledge that the bureaucratic apparatus Stalin used to carry out his counterrevolution derived, directly or indirectly, from Lenin's theory of party dictatorship. Eastman indicted Stalinism not as a liberal or democratic socialist but as a cultural critic from the old Lyrical Left, a position entirely consistent with his ideological career, and one that might well be read as John Reed redivivus.

In *Harper's* Eastman had finally reached the "mainstream," and his articles drew praise from people in all walks of life: a Seattle banker; a New Deal economic planner; J. B. Matthews, the ex-communist journalist; and John Dewey, who complimented Eastman's "powerful statement." Little, Brown & Company contacted Eastman to reprint in book form the first of the *Harper's* essays, "The End of Socialism in Russia," with promise of extensive publicity and a plug from the columnist Dorothy Thompson. Eastman rushed the revised manuscript to the publishers. But for some reason—Eastman attributed it, in *Love and Revolution*, to a new president of the house who brought to "that staid old New England firm . . . a seizure of pro-Soviet enthusiasm"—the book was published quietly, received no comment in Miss Thompson's column, and sold fewer than two hundred copies. E. F. Tompkins of the *New York American* wrote to Little, Brown for permission to serialize the book in the Hearst papers. Eastman refused. (A year earlier, when asked to write on Russia for that vast conservative newspaper chain, Eastman replied to the offer, "I feel that in working for any Hearst publications at present time I would be strike-breaking.") A short while later when he tried to publish, with Scribners, another manuscript on the state of socialism in Russia, Maxwell Perkins informed him there were no sales prospects for such a book. Save the manuscript, Perkins advised in a letter, much of it "is essential material for your spiritual biography."[30]

Turned down by important liberal publishing houses he sought, approached by a right-wing press he deplored, Eastman was also attacked by the left-wing press to which he had once devoted his life. Trotsky, at one time a comrade-in-opposition, asked James Burnham to respond to Eastman's articles in the New International.* Trotsky himself announced his dissociation from Eastman publically, spurred on when Eastman, interviewed in the New York Times, told reporters that Trotsky's new book, The Revolution Betrayed, identified the Soviet and fascist regimes as almost politically synonymous. Trotsky vehemently denied the identification. In a letter to the Times, he wrote, "I hope the readers will understand my ideas better than my translator." Unruffled, Eastman went on to elaborate his argument in the conservative magazine Liberty in an article, "Stalinism Becomes Fascism," that brought an angry reply from Burnham and from Eastman's old friend Max Shachtman. In a personal letter to them both Eastman admitted it was a mistake to send the article to Liberty. Its editors had "mercilessly slashed" key paragraphs and introduced Eastman with the sobriquet "onetime radical." His "experiment with a characterless capitalist magazine," Eastman assured Burnham and Shachtman, "will be my last experiment in that direction."[31]

Eastman's attempt to equate Stalinism and fascism was an expedient historical analogy that enabled him to avoid what he inevitably would have to confront: the relationship between Leninism and Stalinism. He was reluctant to reconsider his earlier apologia for Lenin. Yet Lenin's seizure of power and his method of party organization were the crux of the problem. Eastman's early boast that Lenin had broken the spell of Marxism had serious implications. For if the transition to socialism was inevitable, then the revolution made by Lenin was superfluous. On the other hand, if the transition was not inevitable, then Eastman's defense of Lenin as a socialist was spurious. To be sure, Eastman

---

* For Burnham's critique of Eastman's writings, see pp. 173–79.

was correct about the un-Marxist nature of the Bolshevik Revolution, but his glorification of the role of "will" in history, his hero worship of Lenin, and his indifference to doctrinal issues deprived the Revolution of the intellectual legitimacy of the Marxist heritage. And without an intellectual and moral criterion, it is difficult if not impossible to tell where Leninism ends and Stalinism begins.

By 1940 Eastman was willing at least to mention Lenin's name when making general criticisms of Soviet communism. Lenin, along with Trotsky, Eastman observed, placed the party above "moral judgment" in the struggle for power. Eastman was not invoking "any Kantian imperatives or supernatural admonitions of conscience," he was asking that communists practice the "truth-telling" that is the essence of empirical knowledge instead of claiming, as did Trotsky, that " 'Lies and worse' are an inseparable part of the class struggle." Eastman now conceded that Lenin as well as Trotsky failed to behave properly when he arrogated to himself the standards of revolutionary conduct. Yet Eastman's argument carried more sentiment than substance. He cited Goethe's injunction that a "harmful truth" is better than a "useful error," but both Stalinism and fascism seemed to prove that "lies and worse" are useful truths. There was something old-fashioned and paradoxical in Eastman's demand for scientific behavior as a guarantee of moral conduct.[32]

Even more seriously, Eastman never, until the very last years of his life, faced squarely the monster that Lenin had wrought, the party apparatus that made "truth-telling" the victim of power politics. Whether or not Leninism begat Stalinism, Lenin divorced the democratic means and ends of Marxism from the authoritarian methods of the Bolshevik Party, thereby severing the "unity of theory and practice" and making power and success the standard for political action. In bringing to light the Hegelian content in Marxism, Eastman ignored completely the democratic foundations of Karl Marx's thought and the totalitarian consequences of

Lenin's system of party dictatorship.* His faith in Lenin's personal character, and his willingness to elevate revolution to the status of a "science," made him incapable of seeing what another disillusioned radical, Herberg, would come to recognize as the ethical bankruptcy of empirical politics. Eastman also failed to discern what fellow radicals Dos Passos and Burnham would come to perceive: Marx plus Lenin equals Weber, that is, bureaucracy and managerialism. And Eastman's effort to divorce Leninism from Marxism—our next subject—could lead to an equally perilous equation: Lenin minus Marx equals Mussolini, that is, revolution for revolution's sake, or mere *putschismo*.

Marxism and Metaphysics

In March 1938, during the height of the Moscow show trials, the *Daily Worker* came out with a front-page headline: "MAX EASTMAN IS A BRITISH AGENT." In Stalinist circles Eastman was now identified as part of the Trotsky "conspiracy," despite Trotsky's public repudiation of him the year before. Stalin classified Eastman as a "notorious crook" and a "gangster of the pen," perhaps the only American writer, as Daniel Aaron has wryly noted, to be so honored.[33]

Stalin had good reason to be upset about Max Eastman. But that Kremlin authorities should have attributed Eastman's writings to a Trotskyist plot was a desperate joke. The irony is that Stalinists had more to fear from Eastman than from Trotsky, though neither posed a serious political threat to the Soviet Union.

* The discussion of Hegelianism follows. Sidney Hook, to his credit, undertook before a hostile American public during the McCarthy era the important, and perhaps thankless, task of drawing the distinction between the democratic traditions of Marxism and the authoritarian consequences of Leninism. See Hook, *Marx and the Marxists: The Ambiguous Legacy* (Princeton, 1955). For an important criticism of Eastman, see B. Herman, "Is Marxism Totalitarian?" *Workers Age*, IX (March 30, 1940), 4; id., "Marx-Engels on Democracy," ibid. (April 6, 1940), 4; id., "Why It Happened in Russia," ibid. (April 13, 1940), 3.

Trotsky claimed that Stalin had violated Marxism by betraying the dream of Bolshevism; Eastman had maintained all along that Marxism itself had violated the canons of science, thereby betraying the heritage of the Enlightenment. Trotsky challenged the political consequences of Stalinism; Eastman questioned the philosophical foundations of the Soviet state itself. In the realm of ideas Trotsky was a nuisance to Soviet communists; Eastman was a problem for communists who took Marxism seriously, as well as for Trotsky himself. Indeed, Eastman had written the earliest and most penetrating critique of Marxist philosophy in the English language, with the possible exception of Bertrand Russell's. He had gone beyond Russell in subjecting Marxism to a psychological analysis based on Freudian insights. Moreover, Eastman was perhaps the first writer in the Western world to draw a critical distinction between the ideas of Marx and the actions of Lenin that would make a case for the October Revolution to infuriate both Bolsheviks and Mensheviks. Many of the philosophical issues he raised remain worthy of attention after a half century of debate and revisionism. While most contemporary Marxists concede the terrors of the Stalin regime, few concede the limitations of Marxism as a philosophy of history. Thanks to the revival of Hegel and the recent attention devoted to the writings of the Frankfurt school, philosophic Marxism is more alive today than it has been since the 1930s.

Before we know why Eastman rejected Marxism it is necessary to know why he first embraced it. The philosophical proposition of Marxism answers needs that are rooted in psychological conditions. Eastman's mind and character had been shaped in his early childhood environment. Although Eastman committed his life to the cool rationalism and scientific methodology of Veblen and Dewey, he was imbued with a religious idealism inherited from his "heroic" mother and "saintly" father, both ordained Congregational ministers. Their "Christian ideal," he later reflected, "demands that life itself, as we live it, be transcended and superseded and changed. It is a utopian ideal and ethically, at least, revolutionary." The generational transfusion of idealism came particularly from his mother, whom Eastman always looked back upon as his "first great companion." As a freshman at Oberlin College, Annis Ford Eastman had written a theme which proposed "the theory that God himself *is* joy—a vast stream of joy surrounding all of us." His mother impressed upon him the idea that life should be lived intensely as a continuous adventure in self-realization and social responsibility. "She believed that the essential secret of the joyous life, no matter where you start from, is to be ever in a state of growth."[34]

Eastman's early intellectual development held a basic tension he believed Marxism would resolve. His idealistic thirst for a "vast stream of joy" found an outlet in poetry, in the subjective realm of emotion, mystery, imagination, love, beauty, moral vision, and freedom. His agnostic revolt against religion found an outlet in science, in the objective world of fact and experience, in the verifiable processes of natural causation, and in logical analysis and empirical explanation. Eastman was aware of the dichotomy. Poetic man, he pointed out in 1913, is interested in describing the immediate qualities of things and receiving and realizing experience for the sake of experience, not as a means to an end, but as a "lust after the intense," not to learn about the world, but "to taste the flavor of its being." Scientific man, on the other hand, substitutes appreciation for achievement; his desire is to alter, manipulate, and control the environment with little comprehension of what is being transformed and even less capacity for enjoying what has been made. Eastman originally hoped—as would Dewey—that the poetic and practical impulses within man could be reconciled, that creative vision and social action could be made compatible. For poetry is also "instrumental" knowledge, since it "affects that significant imagery" in our mind and thereby renders abstract ideas concrete. And in life, if not in art, "the realization of ideas is part of the adventure of being."[35]

Eastman's two contradictory impulses—his yearning for the imaginative world of the possible beyond the actual, and his dispassionate respect for the actual world of fact and experience—found resolution in a Marxism that was more sensed than understood. "It was this clash of impetuosities, the thirst of extreme ideals and argumentative clinging to facts, which led me to seize so joyfully upon Marx's idea of progress through working class struggle." Marxism also appeared to him to have answered one of the greatest problems in social philosophy: how to build a perfect society out of imperfect human beings. Eastman recalled Mark Twain's answer when the novelist was asked what he thought about socialism: "I can't even hope for it. I know too much about human nature." Marxism offered an answer to Twain's and Eastman's dilemma. While acknowledging the limitations of historic man, it fulfilled contemporary man's "need to line up fiercely with the ideal against the real." Instead of trying to change human nature, Marx took humankind "as it is" and used the class struggle as a "driving force" to abolish the conditions that made human nature "work badly." Psychologically, Marxism gave Eastman what poetry gave Yeats: the ability to hold together justice and truth within a single thought. "Here was a method," Eastman exclaimed, "of attaining the ideal based upon the very facts that made it seem unattainable. I need no longer extinguish my dreams with my knowledge. I need never again cry out: 'I wish I believed in the Son of God and his second coming.'" Eastman did not exult in his new-found creed but accepted Marx's philosophy simply as a "matter of fact interpretation of history."[36]

Torn between his skeptical knowledge of human limitations and his will to believe in the possibility of transcendence, Eastman saw Marxism as a rational answer to an emotional predicament. After the Bolshevik Revolution, however, he became disturbed at seeing Russian officials applying Marxism not as a "working hypothesis" but as a body of "sacred scripture." His doubts grew stronger when he was in Russia, and by 1925, after he had published *Since Lenin Died*, he realized that it was necessary to plunge into a full exploration of the philosophical foundations of Marxism.

The historical context in which Eastman was investigating the intellectual origins of Marxism was a critical period for the future of Marxist philosophy. In the early 1920s the Comintern embarked upon the task of "bolshevizing" national communist parties, an effort that led Soviet officials to lay claim to the whole corpus of Marxism as interpreted by the Russians Plekhanov and Lenin. By and large the Soviet school of thought consisted in the scientific codification of Marx's ideas worked out by Engels after his mentor's death. This version, which also pervaded much of Western socialist thought before World War I, had been prevalent among many Bolshevik Party members before the Revolution. After 1921, when older professors of philosophy had been removed from Russian universities, official Soviet Marxism amounted to what Gustav Wetter has aptly called a "crude" and "vulgar materialism."[37]

Three important European communist philosophers reacted to the petrification of Marxism: the Italian Antonio Gramsci, the Hungarian Georg Lukacs, and the German Karl Korsch. All three desired to rehumanize Marxism by returning to its classical heritage. Lukacs and Korsch especially sought to recapture the Hegelian dimension of Marx's thought. The "dialectical conception of totality," Lukacs announced in 1923, would end the debate over materialism and idealism by reunifying subject and object and synthesizing theory and practice in the transforming power of the proletariat, whose universal class consciousness manifested the character of an idea realized as material force. Invoking a similar imperative, Korsch called upon philosophers to grasp the "essential and necessary relation between German philosophy and Marxism." Only when the true function of the dialectic is properly conceived will Marxism remain a permanent revolutionary approach to history and reality. For a Marxism without Hegel can easily lose its power of negation, just as a Hegelianism without Marx lost its power of realization. To reunite the two systems of thought was the role of the revolutionary philosopher. "If we do this," Korsch advised, "we can see at once not only the interrelations between German idealist philosophy and Marxism, but also their internal necessity."[38]

Eastman was unaware of the writings of Lukacs and Korsch. But it is a revealing irony in comparative intellectual history that the first American to grasp the connection between Hegel and Marx went on not to reaffirm it but to repudiate it. Eastman's *Marx and Lenin: The Science of Revolution* (1926) is an unusual specimen in the vast historiography of Marxism. Eastman did not plunge into traditional issues that made Marxism so controversial in the disciplines of economics, sociology, and political science—the labor theory of value, the principle of class struggle, and the Marxist theory of the state. Neither did he indict Marxism for offering a false science of "prophecy," as would the anti-historicist scholars during World War II. Nor did he maintain, as would many American liberals in the late 1930s, that the failure of the Soviet Union to realize the ideals of Karl Marx disproved the ideas of Marxism. Although he would come to regard Stalinism as further proof of the fallacies of Marxism, Eastman's original critique was philosophical rather than political. Essentially it revolved around two simple but embarrassing epistemological questions: How did Marx come to know what he knew? and How do we know that it is true?

Appropriately, the book opens with a chapter on the function of thought. Drawing upon Darwin and Freud, Eastman explained how discoveries in biology and psychology naturalized man's conception both of the world and of himself. By illuminating the foundations of human behavior, these genetic sciences demonstrated that mind functioned as an instrument governing either the conscious interests or the unconscious desires of man. The "instrumental interpretation of consciousness" denied that mind could free itself from the natural drives that motivate it in order to comprehend an immaterial "spirit" that allegedly inspires it. "Not only the prior thing in the world is matter and not mind," observed Eastman, "but the prior thing in mind is impulse and not reason."[39]

Eastman recognized that Marx, in the "Theses on Feuerbach," had developed a functional view of intelligence that resembled the modern pragmatic mode of knowledge. But the "internal necessity" between Marxism and German idealism hailed by Korsch and Lukacs seemed to Eastman an internal fallacy. What separated Marx from Hegel were two different ontologies about the role of mind. Whereas Marx located consciousness in "practical-critical action," Hegel believed that the nature of consciousness was to be "discovered by examining the relation between categories of pure logic." For Marx, that is, truth was made in action and praxis; for Hegel "absolute knowledge" was non-instrumental, something found in thinking about thinking, knowledge knowing itself. According to Eastman, Marx passed over this crucial distinction when he found himself at an impasse with Feuerbach's materialism, a doctrine that could show Marx and Engels that matter is more fundamental than spirit but could not tell them where matter "is going." Driven by the need to find purpose in the material universe, Marx and Engels thus returned to Hegel and found in the principle of the dialectic the meaning and direction of history.

Eastman illuminated the way in which Marx had retained the central Hegelian principles of historical understanding: that history is a "process" unfolding without regard to the interests of the historian; that the process has "some one cause" which explains "all" and which does not necessarily derive from the conscious purposes of men; and that "this cause has the property of being logical in development, and of advancing by contradiction, and by the negation of negation." These Hegelian principles played havoc with Marx's language of historical description, and Eastman proceeded to subject that language to the test of causal analysis. He found, for example, the alleged "logical contradiction" between "productive forces" and "production relations" to be a species of "speculative logic" which allowed Marx to confuse the terms "contradiction," "conflict," and "rebellion." He criticized Marx for interchanging the verbs "condition" and "cause," for mixing the two distinct ideas of "reflection" and "result" when discussing culture and the superstructure, and for absorbing contingency into necessity by insisting that historical accidents are "compensated by other accidents." Marx, Engels, and Trotsky had expressed qualifications about unilateral determinism, but no Marxist, not even Plekhanov, had developed precise canons of inquiry that would help analyze the degrees of determinism in order to do justice to the complexity of historical events.

To Eastman, Hegel's quest for totality—to "penetrate the unity" of all phenomena—not only violated the rich diversity and particularity of human experience but identified the historian with history itself. There was an essential dualism between the historian as subject and history as object. With Hegelian Marxism this distinction collapses. Hegel's "subject-object identity" led to the doctrine of historical necessity with causal explanations shrouded under the bloodless abstraction of an "inner logic." The practical upshot was that Hegel's disembodied philosophy of history precluded bold action as well as precise explanation. To Eastman it was man, not "logic," that made events happen; it was human intelligence, not "Absolute Mind," that must interpret experience; and it was Karl Marx, not "history," who was determined to produce a social revolution. There was only one way to salvage Marxism from the errors of Menshevism and to "escape the bonds of German idealism" as well: "That is to take the revolutionary motive out of 'history,' where Marx and Engels surreptitiously projected it, and locate it in the human breast where it belongs."

Eastman simply could not accept the dialectic as a "universal law of motion" either in human thought or in the material universe. He rejected, as a procedure of knowing, "the whole myth about negating negations, and seeking in everything for its opposite, and never resting in an affirmative statement, and studying everything in its logical self-movement, its inner-hostility against itself, and remembering that things can be both themselves and their opposites, and that cause and effect merge into each other, and that quantity becomes quality, and that nature makes jumps— this whole mixture of scientific commonplace with Hegelian higher-logical buncombe." All this represented to Eastman a form of "animistic thinking," an exercise in which Marx projected his own "desires" onto external reality, read into the unconscious material world the unfolding "spirit" of German idealism, and thus found in Hegel a philosophy of the universe in which he already believed. Eastman realized that Engels was more guilty than Marx in attributing human qualities to the properties of matter. Thus Engels's attempt to take Hegel's definition of free-dom as "necessity become conscious" and apply it to the "laws of nature" showed "either a naïve innocence of the problem he is talking about, or that Hegelian sophistication which is a mockery of innocence." Still, Marx, as well as Engels, accepted Hegelianism in much the same way as man accepts "religion" as a means of reconciling himself to an alien universe. Hegelianism answered a psychological need. It enabled Marx and Engels to "rationalize their aspirations" by "cooperating" with a world view in which both consciousness ("self-change") and conditions ("changes of circumstances") are moving dialectically in a "congenial direc-tion," ascending "from the lower to the higher" (Engels's words); a world view in which "true thought and the material world are doing the same thing, and doing it together."[40]

This was a most audacious indictment.* At the turn of the century Benedetto Croce had criticized the metaphysical deifica-tion of historical materialism, but Eastman was broaching an attack articulated at the same time in Germany by the Hungarian sociologist Karl Mannheim—Marxism itself may be regarded as an

* The charge of "animism," of reading into matter the attributes of human values, is similar to the "pathetic fallacy" of some nineteenth-century romantic writers, who carried over to inanimate objects the emotions of human beings and thereby made nature sympathize with their own feelings. Eastman would allow the poet such license (and he tolerated it in George Santayana), but not the Marxist who calls his philosophy "science" in the British and Latin sense of the concept, as opposed to the German *Wissenschaft*. For Eastman's discus-sions of poetry and science, see *Marx and Lenin*, pp. 182–85.

"ideology" subject to a socio-psychological analysis of the derivation of its meaning.† Eastman boldly argued that Marx's mind,
too, was influenced by a cultural matrix that prevented him from
seeing the genesis of his own ideas. He could scorn the human
ideals that motivated him—"morality and justice"—only because
he confined their realization to the material forces of history in the
unconscious process of rendering the external world obedient to
his moral wish. Marx's "immanent laws" of capitalist production,
which supposedly brought centralization and class conflict, seemed
to Eastman like a reification of the "iron laws" of classical economics, which supposedly brought social harmony and competition. To Marx's declaration that capitalism "creates with the
necessity of a natural process the negation of itself," Eastman
simply asked, "Is it not quite obvious that it is not Marx's knowledge, but his purposes, that is being expressed?"[41] To read purpose into history, to perceive a dialectic of negation whose essence
is disclosed not by empirical perception but by philosophical
reflection, was to Eastman the very "false consciousness" of ideology that must be challenged by the true knowledge of science.*
He believed the new psychology of Freud would aid in this effort,
and he attempted to relate Freud's analysis of personality to

† Two years after Eastman's book appeared, Mannheim observed, "It is no
longer the exclusive privilege of socialist thinkers to trace bourgeois thought
to ideological foundations and thereby discredit it. Nowadays groups of every
standpoint use this weapon against all the rest. As a result we are entering
upon a new epoch in social and intellectual development." Noting that Max
Weber, Werner Sombart, and Ernst Troeltsch had begun to move in this
direction, Mannheim added, "The analysis of thought and ideas in terms of
ideologies is much too important a weapon to become the permanent monopoly of any one party. Nothing was to prevent the opponents of Marxism
from availing themselves of the weapon and applying it to Marxism itself."
Ideology and Utopia: An Introduction to the Sociology of Knowledge (Harvest edn., New York, n.d.), p. 75.
* "It is impossible, once you have defined ideology as thinking which is
unconscious of its motives, to let Marxism continue to hide its motives in an
animistic philosophy of the universe. Marxism as a system of dialectical metaphysics is ideological, just as all metaphysics is, but it is certainly the tendency
and true end of Marxism to become a science." Marx and Lenin, p. 88.

Marx's analysis of society.† Marx himself had begun this effort at developing a "science of human behavior," Eastman pointed out, and the "essence of Marx's historical wisdom," and "one of the deepest and wisest intuitions in the history of genius," was Marx's own critique of ideology as the distortion and falsification of conscious thought by society and culture. "The abolition of religion, the illusory happiness of people, is a demand for their real happiness. The demand that one reject illusions about one's situation, is a demand that one reject a situation which has need of illusions." In effect, the American agnostic asked Marxists to abolish their own religion, to discard Hegel and reject the opium of a "theology" that will overcome alienation, and thus to accept a world without myths, a history without redemption, and a philosophy that has no need of illusions:

That rejection of illusions—religious, moralistic, legal, political, aesthetic—is the immortal essence of Marx's contribution to the science of history, and to history itself. And if he did not succeed in rejecting also the illusions of philosophy, those who really esteem his life and his genius ought to carry out that process. Marx himself declared that philosophy, like law and politics and religion and art, is subject to an economic interpretation at the hands of science. But he also declared —and within a year of the same date—that Hegel wrote the true history of philosophy. Since Hegel's history of philosophy is a history of "the self-developing reason," a "history of thought finding itself," these two statements are directly contradictory, and we have to choose between them. We have to choose between Marxism as a Hegelian philosophy, and Marxism as a science which is capable of explaining such a philosophy.[42]

The one true revolutionary who chose "scientific" Marxism was Lenin. It was that great Bolshevik leader, Eastman argued in the

† Eastman feared that unless Marxists assimilated Freudianism, reactionaries would use it for their own purposes. When the French communist Charles Rappoport critically reviewed his book, Eastman responded, "Have you really got nothing to say about the problem of the relation between Marxism and modern psychology? Have you read Hendrik De Man's counter-revolutionary revision of Marxism on the basis of modern psychology? Do you really know what is going on in the intellectual world?" Eastman to "Dear Comrade Holy Father," Dec. 1926, Eastman Papers.

second part of his book, who rescued history from the false consolations of Hegel. Lenin's call for a "vanguard" of professional revolutionaries indicated that he did not regard revolution as the inevitable outcome of the laws of history and the spontaneous struggle of the working class. Lenin displayed great insight in defining the Bolshevik Party in psychological rather than in class terms, choosing for his cadre those who possessed "purposive ideas" and an appropriate revolutionary "state of mind." Lenin's *What to Do?** denied the "assertion that the material elements of the world are automatically evolving toward socialism, and [the] assertion that the thoughts of socialists are a mere reflection of the process." The year 1917 dramatized both these truths, for Lenin demonstrated that the nature of political organization, and not the stage of economic or social development, was the decisive factor in revolution. Hence Lenin's grasp of the autonomy of politics, his "policy of sharp turns," showed that the October Revolution was a "violation of Hegelian-Marxism." Moreover, Lenin's effort to build socialism through the very political superstructure he created indicated that Bolshevism did not evolve from the "ripening" of the "contradictions" of capitalism. "No person," stated Eastman as though he were replying to Lukacs, ". . . could possibly declare that the political forms existing in Russia, and the ideas propagated by the Communist party, are a reflection of existing economic conditions. Never did a reflection put forth such gigantic efforts to produce its likeness in the object reflected."[43]

Eastman was fully aware that Lenin had "recommended—but never began—'a systematic study of the Hegelian dialectic from the materialist point of view.'" He learned from Hegel that "truth is always concrete" and from Marx that praxis is the criterion of knowledge that the "maximum of flexibility" is called for in "revolutionary moments." In his philosophical writings Lenin could believe that mind "reflects" the "ordered movement of matter," while in his political actions he behaved in a way that gave mind a

* Eastman insisted that this title—and not *What Is to Be Done?*—was the true English equivalent to the heading of Lenin's 1902 organizational manifesto.

"dynamic function," enabling him to interact with and act upon the movement of history. Lenin's awareness that the "revolutionary will" resided in the revolutionist did not result in the arrogance of power; it led to "an unusual moral responsibility." Here Eastman was not resorting to the precepts of religious or Kantian morality; nor was he proposing a return to the revisionist belief of ethical socialism, a proposition of Eduard Bernstein's that Eastman dismissed as "absurd." He was suggesting that the revolutionist must be existentially aware that one cannot escape from political morality by invoking the laws of history. "Whenever the word 'ought' has meaning, it will be affirmed that such a man ought to know his own motives, and be honest with those whom he leads." Lenin possessed this critical self-awareness when he demanded that the professional revolutionist be (in Lenin's words) "devoted," "heroic," "self-sacrificing," and "honest." Hegel relegated ultimate ethical issues to absolute "reason" and Marx to the end of "pre-history." Eastman saw in Leninism the possibility of restoring political responsibility to the mind and will of man. "There is no element in the Bolshevik tactics of Lenin more vitally important than the transparent purity of his motives, and his perfect intellectual honesty before the proletariat."[44] With Leninism, then, the imperative of revolutionary praxis is liberated from the deceptions of metaphysics; the true humanization of Marxism has begun.

Eastman versus Hook

When Eastman's book *Marx and Lenin: The Science of Revolution* appeared in the United States in 1927, its author had already been ostracized by the Communist Party. Party leader William Z. Foster had remarked two years earlier that Eastman had "killed himself in the Movement by his treatment of the Trotsky question"; and Mike Gold, soon to become editor of the *New Masses*, advised V. F. Calverton that Eastman, despite his "fine mind," was "a thorough bourgeoisies [sic] in esthetics" who preferred the "Platonic" way of life. Eastman was dismissed as an amateur philosopher whose effort to assimilate Freud and Marx and expunge Hegel could not be taken seriously.[45]

Liberal intellectuals were impressed by the book's lively style and anti-Hegelian witticisms but expressed serious reservations about its content. The *Nation's* reviewer, Henry Raymond Mussey, noted that the exaltation of "will" was characteristic of right-wing movements. T. V. Smith shrewdly pointed out that Eastman had inadvertently denied Lenin the right to make a revolution, since the only Marxist justification for revolution was the presumption of its inevitability. The philosopher Horace Kallen warned Eastman that Leninism itself could become a "religion" of empirical power worship. In your "eagerness to escape the hypostasis of Hegelian dialectics," Kallen told Eastman, you are in "danger of hypostasizing organizing leadership as 'scientific.' "[46]

Eastman had copies of *Marx and Lenin* sent to leading European intellectuals, and he received warm praise from George Bernard Shaw, H. G. Wells, and Sigmund Freud.[47] Continental Marxists who read the book (it was translated into French and Spanish) tended to respond according to their views of Freudian psychology on the one hand and Hegelian philosophy on the other. A Swedish writer hailed the work as the start of a "Copernican revolution" in making Marxism a science and in "laying the psychological basis of Marxian sociology."[48] A young student in the Frankfurt am Main Institut für Sozialforschung welcomed the book as a relief from the tedious, abstract "fetishism" of a metaphysical Marxism.* The more seasoned communist thinkers,

---

* Professor Martin Jay, author of *The Dialectical Imagination: A History of the Frankfurt School of the Institute for Social Research, 1923–1950* (Boston, 1973), informs me that the following letter "captures perfectly" the mood of the Institute for Social Research in its early years. "All this is the more gratifying to one," the student told Eastman, "who has spent hours of exasperating argument in a Marxist Institute with a younger generation setting down to an orthodox religion and the worship of an iconographical literature, not to mention blackboards full of mathematical juggling with blocks of 1000 k I 400 w of Marx's divisions of capital's functions, and the like. God! the hours I've spent listening to the debate of seminaries and student circles on the Hegelian

however, saw concealed in the bud of Eastman's argument the worm of revisionism. Charles Rappoport, a founder of the French Communist Party, attacked the American "sophist" for failing to see that a Hegelian philosophy that replaced the "immobilismo" of "Being for the eternal youth of Becoming, is eminently revolutionary."[49] Georg Lukacs, the Hungarian philosopher who would later renounce Hegelian idealism under the pressures of Stalinism, claimed Eastman was attempting to provide a theoretical platform for the "international Trotskyist" movement based upon "Anglo-American empiricist nonsense." Lukacs sarcastically termed Eastman's description of the "primitive animism" of dialectics a "grand and indubitably original conclusion," and he felt it necessary to "renounce categorically" Eastman's psychological "additions" to Marxism as completely as the "contributions" of Max Adler. Lukacs, the most learned Hegelian Marxist of the period, never came to grips with Eastman's argument. Lukacs described Eastman's critique of dialectical materialism as a reflection of the "skepticism" which inflicts the "socially rootless, déclassé" intellectual with corrosive doubt, while he himself remained skeptical of any attempt to "round out" orthodox Marxism with the ideas of Freud.[50]

Lukacs's criticisms would not have disturbed Eastman even had he been aware of them. The "illusions of philosophy" were, after all, the curse of a European mind supposedly "expiring" before the advance of science and psychology. In America, the land of scien-

---

dialektik, with not a single voice to point out that the problems can no longer be solved (if they ever were) by means of straw-splitting philosophical conceptions. Even the leader, faced with an audience of enthusiastic youth convinced that Relativity is a further installment of bourgeois ideology substituting fluctuating ideas for Newton's absolute materialism, that Freudianism and Bergsonism are insidious attacks from the rear, and that the war can be waged with the sword in one hand and the 'Geschichte der Historikomaterialismus' in the other . . . is constantly being brought up against the inherent contradictions in a Marxist M.I.H. and being forced to devise defenses against the logical conclusion that we may sit with our arms folded and wait the millennium to blossom from the dung of capitalist decay." The student told Eastman he had mentioned his book to a colleague at the Institute, who replied, "Ah, yes. Just a journalist!" Oscar Swede to Eastman, Oct. 1, 1927, Eastman Papers.

tific intelligence, Eastman was proud enough to believe that only he understood the limitations of philosophical Marxism, vain enough to claim that he alone was "the Left opposition." Yet the champion of Lenin and Trotsky would soon meet his match—a young American philosophy student who in 1928 was in Germany on a Guggenheim fellowship absorbing Marx and attending lectures on contemporary philosophical Marxism. Ironically, Eastman's antagonist was not a European metaphysician but a home-grown pragmatist—Sidney Hook.

Eastman "bungled a great theme," Hook announced in the *Modern Quarterly* that year. Eastman interpreted Marx's views as "the confused, personal expression of a queer German—at once hard-headed (scientific) and quasi-religious—trying to liberate himself from the metaphysical superstitions of a still queerer German—Hegel." The shafts of the scrappy young philosopher sparked a sardonic debate that dragged on for five years, when editor V. F. Calverton wearily stepped in and put an end to the affair so that two Marxists would no longer "vent their spleen in public to the obscene enjoyment of the bourgeois world."[51]

Three issues divided Eastman and Hook in the first phase of the debate (1928–1930). As a thorough rationalist and a student of John Dewey, Hook questioned whether Freudianism would, as Eastman assumed, advance Marxian analysis. Freud not only made psychic reality prior to social reality, he formulated theories of human behavior that represented the "grossest violation" of scientific method. The extent of determinism in Marx's philosophy was also at issue. Hook agreed with Eastman that the theory of historical materialism suffered because of the failure to distinguish necessary and sufficient causes and because of the "oscillating between the anthropomorphic and functional" conceptions of causation. Eastman erred, however, in failing to see that Marxism poses no "inevitable ends" but only "effects" and "objective *tendencies*." Eastman also failed to acknowledge that Marx, in *The Holy Family*, had declared that "History does nothing, it 'possesses no colossal riches,' it 'fights no fight'! It is rather man—real, living man—who acts, possesses, and fights in everything." But the most troubling issue was the philosophy of Hegel. No one "swallows Hegel whole," Hook maintained, least of all Marx. Marx used dialectical reasoning not to establish a universal law but to illuminate social "contradictions." Eastman was "poking fun" at Hegel and "ridiculing" his "cumbrous language" instead of trying to penetrate the great insights within his Teutonic prose. Eastman, Hook advised, ought to read Hegel's *Phänomenologie des Geistes* "as punishment."[52]

Hook could not so easily dismiss Eastman's *Marx and Lenin*, and when he began to work out his own interpretation of Marxism he emphasized the "systematic contrasts" between Hegel and Marx in order to "close the door tight to attempts at 'Ergänzung' Marx by Hegelianizing him."[53] Yet Hook, perceiving the important elements of continuity as well as change between Hegel and Marx, set himself two basic tasks: first, to demonstrate how Hegel and Marx shared a common belief in the centrality of process, movement, and development on the one hand, and a common opposition to Kantian ethical idealism, sensationist empiricism, and bourgeois social atomism on the other; and second, to explain how Hegel and Marx were "utterly opposed in substance and spirit" on the role of philosophy, the function of mind, and the meaning of the dialectic. Thus, against Hegel's philosophy of speculation and reflection (which arrives "too late"), Hook contrasted Marx's philosophy of praxis and transformation; and against Hegel's theory of mind as the vessel of logically necessary truths, he contrasted Marx's view of mind as the instrument of social action. As for the dialectic, Hook was certain that once Marx's version was stripped of its Hegelian terminology one could grasp its meaning in its application. The dialectic enabled Marx to appreciate the structural interrelationships of society and to perceive the causal factors of social change in the processes of contradiction and resolution. Hook pointed out similarities between dialectical thinking and "instrumentalist logic" in which knowledge expresses itself in practical activity arising from the conflict between human needs and social conditions. Moreover, Marxism and pragmatism shared a common criterion of verification. As a "method" of thinking, Marxism must be considered "a huge judgment of practice, in Dewey's sense of the phrase, and its truth or falsity (instrumental adequacy) is an experimental matter. Believing in it and acting upon it helps to make it true or false."[54]

As epistemology, Marxism and American pragmatism did have something in common,[55] and had Hook confined himself to treating the dialectic as a "method" that sensitizes the mind to social antinomies he would have avoided what Eastman called the "metaphysical pretensions" of philosophy. But never quite able to separate form from content, Hook was tempted to see meaning as well as method in the dialectic. Hook clearly went beyond the limitations of instrumentalist knowledge when he maintained that the "dialectical principle explains how human beings, although conditioned by society, are enabled through activity to change both themselves and society"; when he asserted that "in Marx as well as in Hegel the dialectic is, so to speak, the philosophical rhythms of conscious life"; when he argued that Marxism is "a 'partial' or 'partisan' theory without ceasing to be an objective expression of the interests of the proletariat"; and when he declared that Marx offered the clear choice between "communism" and "barbarism."[56] His language was Deweyite, his stance that of a Jamesian radical, a "Marxist of the heart" who was not reluctant to invoke the will to believe and to act in order to "make" communism come true. Marx's philosophy of history, Hook declared in a moment of Roycean lyricism, "fuses the logic of analysis with the poetry of passion."[57]

It was this fusion, this systematic effort to synthesize objective description with subjective desire, that had earlier seduced Eastman the poet into declaring himself a Marxist. Now the whole effort seemed psychologically understandable and, therefore, philosophically unacceptable. In numerous articles and letters to the Modern Quarterly, and in a forty-seven-page pamphlet entitled The Last Stand of Dialectical Materialism, he answered Hook in customary lucid language unencumbered by philosophical jargon. Why must Hook, Eastman complained, characterize Marx's philosophy "as 'naturalistic activism,' 'social behaviorism,' 'revolutionary voluntarism,' 'voluntaristic humanism,' 'voluntaristic realism,' 'activistic atheism,' 'critical historicism,' 'realistic evolutionary naturalism,' 'Aristotelianism saturated with temporalism,' and other long-tailed horny epithets very disheartening to a man who is not accustomed to take his vacations in the library." The crux of the issue was not, as Hook implied, whether Marxism could be made compatible with the principles of American pragmatism. Eastman never had much regard for the pragmatic definition of truth, which he sensed had more to do with power and control than with knowledge or wisdom. And while John Dewey may have carried over from Hegel the ideal of identifying theoretical and practical consciousness, Dewey never studied Marx and did not deduce the idea of class struggle from the concept of the dialectic.* Nor was historical inevitability the issue, for Hook eschewed the deterministic elements of Marxism: socialism was a probability, not a necessity. The crux, which had been buried in

* Both Hook and Eastman had studied under Dewey at Columbia University. "But I studied under Dewey," Eastman insisted, "not as a disciple of his pragmatist or instrumentalist philosophy, but always with a feeling that I stood 'to the left' of him—not only politically, but in the direction of scientific skepticism." Eastman had begun a thesis under Dewey criticizing pragmatism from this viewpoint, "and I never receded from that thesis. Its bright point, I remember, was the rather impertinent remark that, 'if "the meaning of an idea is its results in action," then the meaning of pragmatism is to resign your chairs in philosophy.' " Eastman, "A Master Magician," Modern Monthly, VII (June 1933), 290–93. See also Eastman's affectionate portrait of Dewey, "The Hero as Teacher," in Heroes I Have Known (New York, 1942), pp. 274–321.
Eastman had urged Dewey to preside over a debate between himself and Hook. Although Dewey declined, stating he did not "know enough Marx," he was willing to write the following statement for the possible reissue of Eastman's book: "Mr. Eastman has not only disentangled Hegelian metaphysics in a masterly fashion from Marx's fundamental contribution to thought; he has done much more by exhibiting the corroding animism which afflicts much philosophic, economic, and psychological writing even today." Dewey to Eastman, Feb. 7, 1933, Eastman Papers. See also Dewey's "Why I Am Not a Communist," in The Meaning of Marxism: A Symposium (New York, 1934), pp. 86–90.

the earlier debates, was the relation of mind to the external world. How is reality to be perceived? Can the scientific mind, as opposed to the philosophic or poetic mind which relies upon reflection and intuition, identify the perception of reality with reality itself? Eastman returned to the "Theses on Feuerbach" for the answer and seized upon the kernel of Marx's advice:

The chief fault of all materialism heretofore (including Feuerbach's) is that object, reality, sensibility (*Sinnlichkeit*), is conceived only under the form of object or of contemplation; not as human-sensible activity, Praxis, not subjectively. Hence the active side developed in opposition to materialism abstractly from idealism—abstractly, because idealism naturally did not recognize sensible activity as such. Feuerbach wants objects of sense reality distinguished from objects of thought, but he does not conceive of human activity itself as objective activity.

As Eastman interpreted the passage, Marx was asserting that subject and object are identical, that the activity of the human mind and the motion of the material world are "*the same thing,* and that the thing is to be conceived *subjectively as practical human sensible activity.*" To see man as an objective being who conceives subjectively, to regard human activity itself as objective activity, comes close to asserting that what is perceived is identical to *how* it is conceived. This advice seemed to Eastman to be a reversion to the idealist fallacy of attributing reality to the knowing subject. Marx assumed he had saved the "rational kernel" and eliminated the "mystical shell" in Hegel's philosophy. When Marx made material activity the agency of spiritual realization, he inverted Hegel's ontology only to absorb his teleology. However it might be clothed in the language of materialism, philosophic Marxism would remain for Eastman a form of "animism," an attempt to read "subjectively" the ideal into the real in order to identify human purposes and desires with historical processes and developments.[58]

Hook had tried to resolve the metaphysical problems of Marxism in somewhat the same way that Dewey had tried to resolve the metaphysical problems of pragmatism,[59] but Eastman could accept neither effort. Marxism and pragmatism demonstrated that knowledge was action and power, but neither could prove to Eastman that the ultimate nature of reality would be anything more than an alienated man's need to find meaning in a meaningless universe. Eastman believed in "progress," and he believed that Lenin's great achievement showed that the world could be improved by acting upon it and transforming it. Hegelian Marxism could not overcome the acute tensions at the heart of Eastman's aesthetic sensibility: the dualisms between moral vision and factual description, between mind and object, purpose and process, desire and reality. To Eastman, history would remain a problem for which philosophy offered no solution.

This "doctrinal crisis" in Marxism made Eastman the first major infidel of the Old Left, the first radical philosopher to question the philosophical assumptions of radicalism.[60] Yet, his skepticism was itself based on the illusion that radical man can live without radical illusions. He demanded that Marxism divorce itself from Hegelianism in order to acquire a self-critical understanding of its own myths. Such a demand is a psychological if not a theoretical impossibility. A Marxist need not believe in man, but he must believe in the meaning of history illuminated by philosophy. Eastman could believe in Lenin and revolution, love and sexual liberation, the joy of living, and nothing more.

The Dialectic Repudiated

The Eastman-Hook dialogue fascinated some American radicals and frustrated others. Eastman's refutation of Hegelian Marxism seemed to identify him with Eduard Bernstein and revisionism, yet his continued espousal of Leninism made him a staunch Bolshevik. Hook's defense of Marxism identified him as an authentic revolutionary, but his increasing doubts about the principle of the "dictatorship of the proletariat" made him appear, to Will Herberg and others, less a Leninist than a Kautskyist reformer.[61] To find out who was left of whom, several independent radicals, especially those connected with the newly formed American Workers Party, tried unsuccessfully to bring Eastman and Hook together for what Max Shachtman called "The Debate of the Colossi."[62]

From Prinkipo, Turkey, Leon Trotsky had been following the divisive affair. He was critical of Hook's effort to strip Marxism of its doctrinal significance and reduce it to a "method," but more upset by Eastman's assault on Hegel and the dialectic. In *The Militant* he warned his American followers that Eastman was "carrying out a systematic fight against materialist dialectics, the philosophical foundation of Marxism"; and he advised Calverton and the *Modern Quarterly* against his "retrograde adventure." Trotsky's attack stung Eastman. During these years he had been helping Trotsky publish his books and articles in the United States, always making sure the near-destitute exile received good terms from American publishers. He also had tried to help him get a visa to enter the United States, and he tried to gather support for him among writers like Theodore Dreiser (who refused on the grounds that Trotskyism endangered the Soviet Union). What distressed Eastman most, however, was not Trotsky's ingratitude but his willingness to condemn *Marx and Lenin* before he had studied it. (Trotsky admitted he had "only turned over the pages.") In 1940 Trotsky would write a defense of dialectical logic; in the early thirties he asked James Burnham to answer Eastman for him.[63] At times Trotsky's own argument on the primacy of revolutionary "will" seemed to echo the case Eastman had been trying to make in divorcing Lenin the revolutionist from Marx the Hegelian.*

A philosophical enemy of Trotsky, a political enemy of Stalin, and a literary enemy of the Old Left, Eastman was a solitary figure

---

* "It is necessary to remember that Marxism both interprets the world and teaches how to change it. The will is the moving element in the domain of knowledge, too. If Marxism loses its will to transform political reality, it loses the ability to understand it." Trotsky, "Perspectives on American Marxism," Ms. to Calverton, Nov. 4, 1932, Trotsky Archives.

in the late thirties. He was also a worried man. He could not take lightly the Stalinist accusation that he was a Trotskyist conspirator and a "British spy." His brother-in-law had already fallen victim to the purges. He knew that anyone casually mentioned in the trials had met with foul play or disappeared from public life. "This means it's open season on you, Max," Carlo Tresca said when he called him as soon as he saw the *Daily Worker* headline. Tresca, an old anarchist friend, had been branded an "enemy" for publicizing the GPU's alleged involvement in the disappearance of Juliet Poyntz and the Stalinist responsibility for the murder of Andrés Nin during the Spanish Civil War. Tresca advised Eastman to sue the *Daily Worker* for libel. Eastman did so, not to seek a retraction but, as Tresca instructed, to use the publicity to protect himself against the fate of other anti-Stalinists at the hands of the GPU.[64]

Eastman had always regarded companionship and fraternal happiness as one of the great pleasures in life. The insults of former comrades and the loss of old friends, especially the "massacre of honesty and political clear thinking by our famous 'liberals,' "[65] left him distraught. His isolation was, however, a prelude to his vindication. Although the Popular Front made him a pariah, intellectual countercurrents began to surface. John Dewey addressed himself critically to Marxism in a manner that resembled Eastman's own earlier analysis. Doubting that methods of political action could be "deduced" from a "*fixed law*" of social development, Dewey questioned whether means and ends could be "read out of" the presumed laws of society or nature. "Orthodox Marxism," Dewey observed, "shares with orthodox religionism and with traditional idealism the belief that human ends are interwoven into the very texture of existence—a conception inherited presumably from its Hegelian origins."[66]

As the decade drew to a close, American Trotskyists like James Burnham and Max Shachtman also challenged the validity of Hegelian Marxism. "Comrade Trotsky," wrote Burnham just before resigning from the Socialist Workers Party, "you have absorbed too much of Hegel, of his monolithic, his totalitarian, vision of a block universe, in which every part is related to every other part, in which everything is relevant to everything else, where the destruction of a single grain of dust means the annihilation of the Whole."[67] More telling were Sidney Hook's second thoughts on the dialectic in particular and on Marxism in general. Having investigated the writings of the nineteenth-century Left Hegelians, Hook reported disparities and distortions between the historical materialism of Marx and the dialectical materialism of Engels. In a brilliant philosophical analysis of Engels, "Dialectic and Nature," Hook acknowledged that the concept of the dialectic had been appropriated uncritically from Hegel's speculative ontology and erroneously accorded universal status in mathematics, physics, chemistry, biology, geology, as well as in history and philosophy. As a constitutive principle inherent in every conceivable aspect of the universe, the dialectic functioned more as "mythology" than methodology.[68] Several years later Hook went on to juxtapose Lenin, the "event-making man," to the principle of historical determinism in order to demonstrate some of the same weaknesses in Marx's philosophy of history that Eastman had disclosed fifteen years earlier.[69]

Even more encouraging was the support Eastman received from the greatest literary mind of his generation—Edmund Wilson. In 1937 Wilson dug up a copy of Eastman's out-of-print Marx and Lenin. It was, he said, "the best critical thing I've read on this philosophical aspect of Marxism." Even though the book, Wilson informed Eastman, "suffers a little" from an abstract and negative tone and lack of dramatic style, "it would have been a good thing if people had read it a few years ago when everybody was going crazy about Marxism." Wilson had studied Eastman's book in preparing for his own work on the intellectual history of European socialism. "What I have written," he told John Dos Passos in 1938, "will fill the Marxists with horror." That fall he published a section of his manuscript, "The Myth of the Dialectic," in the Partisan Review. The editors wanted to have Hook, Burnham,

Bertram D. Wolfe, and Meyer Shapiro reply, but, as editor William Phillips observed, these writers were no longer committed to the issue and thus there was little chance of getting "a real 100% dialectical materialist." Two years later, during the period of the non-aggression pact between Hitler and Stalin, Wilson's magisterial *To the Finland Station* appeared. In it he described Eastman's book as a "remarkable study" to which he owed "a special debt." Wilson's analysis was far more comprehensive in treating the complex development of Marxism; still, it essentially followed Eastman's critique of the dialectic as a "religious myth" and his celebration of Lenin as the revolutionary who turned ideas into flesh and made intellectual history the study of action as well as thought.[70]

In 1940 three important American books rejected the dialectic as either a disguised theology—Eastman's *Marxism: Is It Science?* —as a pseudo logic of organic totality—Hook's *Reason, Social Myths and Democracy*—or as a Pythagorean illusion suggesting the insurgent power of a phallic symbol—Wilson's *To the Finland Station*. The following year in an erudite treatise that scarcely raised an eyebrow among America's disenchanted Marxists—*Reason and Revolution: Hegel and the Rise of Social Theory*—a German exile scholar, Herbert Marcuse, attempted to explain Hegel to the Anglo-Saxon world, to rescue German idealism from its perversions in the writings of Italian and German fascists, to present the dialectic as a revolutionary concept that retains the tension between the "is" and the "ought," between what is immediately given and what is ultimately real, and thus to offer a radical "critical theory" of existing society. But to most Old Left intellectuals in America, Hegel's philosophy was too ambiguous, too full of unresolved contradictions. At once a philosophy of negation and reconciliation, Hegelianism seemed to comprehend everything metaphysical and explain nothing political.[71]

The German exile scholars at the Institute for Social Research in New York did not bother to respond to the American critiques of Hegel and dialectical reasoning. The Frankfurt philosophers and sociologists dismissed the affair as an extension of the "positivist emasculation of Marxism" that had begun in Europe, a subject to which Max Horkheimer had fully addressed himself a decade earlier.[72] Is it true, as the German émigrés charged, that the philosophical empiricist acquiesces to political conservatism? This attitude raises a difficult question in intellectual history: What is the relationship of philosophical ideas to political positions?[73]

Sidney Hook believed there was a clear relationship. Hook was no positivist, but he did tend to associate the empirical, pragmatic habits of thought with progressive and radical tendencies, and the Hegelian, idealist modes of knowledge with conservative and authoritarian movements.[74] This distinction may collapse before the vagaries of European intellectual history, but in twentieth-century America it did make sense in view of Dewey's and James's reaction to the idealism of Josiah Royce and the resistance to scientific thought by conservative intellectual defenders of Southern Agrarianism, classical humanism, or Roman Catholicism. Max Eastman, however, was an intellectual who came to radicalism by way of poetry, perfectly aware of the Kantian and Hegelian idealism that had influenced Whitman and the American Transcendentalists. Yet poetic idealism could only inspire an indictment of society; it could not offer the basis for analyzing and changing society. Poetry, like philosophy, afforded only the "emotional realization" of ideas. "Why not say," Eastman remarked in reference to Marx's dictum, " 'Poets have sung the world . . . painters have painted the world; the thing is to change it.' "[75] Only science enabled man to transform the world so that the transcendent ideas born of poetry or philosophy could be realized.

What science could realize, however, it could also destroy. Science spelled the end of philosophical idealism. With Veblen, Eastman believed that science would make man less "anthropomorphic," free him of the "animism" and "superstition" with which nineteenth-century thinkers had reified metaphysical ideas like natural law, thereby rendering those man-made conventions beyond the control of man.[76] This radical change in American social thought meant that history would now be studied in naturalistic terms in which there would be no place for the operation of disembodied forces, immaterial laws, or teleological systems. The American revolt against German idealism—most pronounced in the works of Dewey and Veblen—appears to be quite different from European positivism, which was also hostile to idealism.[77] For Eastman, as well as for Veblen and Freud, the naturalization of knowledge did not deny the reality of subjective factors like will, imagination, and instinct as it did for the positivists; it simply meant that metaphysical thought could no longer assert the right to reach historical truths independent of the findings of natural science. The Frankfurt scholars' case against positivism was that its methodology isolated and compartmentalized phenomena, treated all forms of social existence as ontologically permanent, focused on factual data at the cost of ignoring normative ideals, and hence succumbed to "uncritical objectivism."[78] This description hardly applied to Eastman, who originally wanted to make Marxism "scientific" in order to assert its power of transformation:

> Mind's task is not to blur the real
> With mimic tints from an ideal,
> But to change one into the other by an act.[79]

Eastman believed that Lenin, not Marx, carried out this task, and his admiration of Lenin is perhaps best understood in light of Veblen's respect for the "matter of fact" engineer as the revolutionist of the future.

Whatever "scientific" Marxism implied, the Old Left's repudiation of the dialectic does reveal a great deal about the bias against formal metaphysics in American social thought. Long before most other writers, Eastman perceived that any debate over the meaning of Marxism would ultimately be a debate over the meaning and validity of Hegelianism. His contribution to the critique of dialectical materialism would gain considerable recognition in British scholarship, particularly in the work of Sir Isaiah Berlin,

R. N. Carew-Hunt, and Raymond Postgate.[80] In America only those of Eastman's generation who had followed his entire career could sufficiently appreciate his role as the critical conscience of the Stalinist era. This appreciation was perhaps best expressed in 1941 by Edmund Wilson. Reviewing Eastman's *Marxism: Is It Science?* and *Stalin's Russia and the Crisis of Socialism* in the *New Republic*, he praised the "natural genius" and "toughness" of a thinker who, like Trotsky, had been a hero to one generation of radical intellectuals only to become a heretic to another generation. Characteristically, Wilson found much to criticize in Eastman because he found much more to admire:

Max Eastman's comprehension of the modern world is limited in certain respects, and this is probably another reason for the recent neglect of his work. As his novel [*Venture*, 1926] is quite non-naturalistic, so his discussion of the Soviet Union and of the general situation of the West does not include an adequate picture of economic and social conditions. It is strange that this student of Marxism should never have learned from Marx what is certainly most valid in his system: the class analysis of historical happenings. Max Eastman, as Philip Rahv has pointed out, tends to talk as if the fallacies of Marxism had by themselves wrecked the Leninist revolution, and is not interested in finding out how the development of social forces has affected the application of ideas. But though it is true that he thinks mainly in terms of psychological motivations, of philosophical and moral positions, his criticism along these lines has, nevertheless, proved extremely salutary at a time when people were trusting to arrangements of statistical figures to demonstrate the rights and wrongs of History without being able to smell the corpses in the Lubyanka or to take stock of what was healthy at home. Max Eastman has continued to perform for us the same function that he did in the first World War: that of the winter log that floats in the swimming-pool and prevents the concrete from cracking by itself taking the pressure of the ice.[81]

Philosophy Negated by History: Eastman versus Trotsky

It would be wrong to conclude, as did Wilson and Rahv, that Eastman's writings on Marxism amounted "only" to a study of ideas, a discourse on a disembodied metaphysical theory, and hence an abstract philosophical critique of no real significance because it gave no attention to "economic and social conditions." On the contrary, Eastman's writings became even more important to the study and interpretation of contemporary history. The debate over dialectical reasoning in the thirties reached its political climax in the historical issue of Stalinism, an unparalleled political phenomenon that has continued to this day to intrigue and baffle scholars of all ideological persuasions. To the Old Left, in general, and to Eastman, Hook, and Burnham in particular, the problem of understanding Stalinism became almost the problem of understanding history itself. In the writings of their former hero, Leon Trotsky, the concept of the dialectic descended, as it were, from the metaphysical heights of pure philosophical discussion into history as a real, vital idea whose validity was manifested in the "contradictions" of the Soviet bureaucracy. Many of the intellectual origins of what came to be called, misleadingly I believe, "anticommunism," lie in this philosophical debate over the nature of Stalinism.

For the generation of the 1930s the most significant analysis of Stalinism from the perspective of economic and social conditions was Trotsky's The Revolution Betrayed, which Eastman translated and praised as a "prodigious feat of intellect." To the readers of Harper's Eastman showed just how sensitive he was to "social forces" when he described Trotsky's brilliant mode of explanation:

The amount of free and fluid judgment he achieves within the framework of a rationalistic metaphysics is amazing—a tribute to his dexterity and the ingenuity of old Hegel. His sustained sense of human society as a process rather than a thing—the real wisdom concealed under the cant about "dialectic"—is also admirable. I find much truth too in his concrete demonstrations of the results of Russia's backwardness, and much empirical good sense in his insistence upon the interdependence of the nations in any basic economic change they make. The idea of capitalist encirclement and the war danger—used by Stalinists to "blackmail the intellectuals and keep down the workers," as James T. Farrell truly says—is used by Trotsky with honesty and a just sense of its significance.[82]

Nevertheless, Eastman remained unconvinced by Trotsky's essential thesis—that Russia's isolation as a proletarian power and her "backward technic of production" accounted for the degeneration of the Revolution and the emergence of Stalinism. Such an explanation ignored fundamental problems of human behavior that could hardly be dismissed as mere "survivals in a backward country of a 'petty-bourgeois psychology.'" Above all, confronted with the mutation of Marxist sociology by the unexpected growth of Soviet bureaucracy, Trotsky refused to reconsider his Marxist philosophy of history. Eastman questioned what Wilson felt he should have learned most from Marx: "The class analysis of historical happenings." It was precisely this obsolete analysis that could not fully explain Stalinism, a phenomenon that developed out of novel historical conditions in which the property relations Marx had emphasized as the root of power no longer determined class behavior.

To a certain extent, it is true, Eastman did tend to engage in the genetic fallacy of tracing a political consequence to its philosophical origins (Hegelianism) in order to claim, as Wilson and Rahv expressed it, that "the fallacies of Marxism had by themselves wrecked the Leninist Revolution." The immediate issue between Eastman and Trotsky, however, was not what had destroyed the Revolution but what would save it, not the social conditions of backwardness that plagued Russia but the philosophical ideas that were still being invoked to restore Russia to her original revolutionary course. Insofar as Trotsky claimed to embody the heritage of Leninism, Eastman could argue that in an ultimate sense it was indeed the "fallacies of Marxism" that prevented Trotsky from both understanding the historical significance of Stalinism and offering a political answer to it.

Trotsky's theory of Stalinism contains a historical explanation with a philosophical solution. Drastically simplified, Trotsky's interpretation held that Stalinism must be seen as a temporary "Bonapartist" political phenomenon, an "episodic relapse" which, like the Thermidorian phase of the French Revolution, would be undermined by its own "social contradictions" and ultimately destroyed by the proletariat as it rises again to resume the second act of the unfinished October Revolution. Although he would modify aspects of his theory and revise his timetable in response to events, Trotsky never doubted that Stalin's Russia stood suspended at a momentous historical turning point, a "bureaucratic interval" that could lead backward to "capitalist restoration" or forward to socialist revolution. Everything depended upon the proletariat and, equally important, upon the intellectuals' commitment to the creation of a Fourth International and their willingness to defend the Soviet Union as a "workers' state," which, however "deformed" and "betrayed," had succeeded in preserving the collectivization of property and the means of production, the historic victory of the Russian Revolution.[83]

Many Old Left intellectuals in America could readily sympathize with Trotsky's opposition to Soviet totalitarianism, a stance that characterized all that was best and noble in a world that was asked to choose the bad against the worst, Stalin against Hitler. They could not agree that Stalinism, any more than fascism, would be brought down by a revolutionary proletariat whose historical mission was determined not by a sociological analysis of its character but solely by what Eastman called its "metaphysical position" in the Marxist scheme of philosophy.[84] As the controversy developed, Trotsky realized that the sum and substance of the entire issue turned on the dialectical logic he employed both to affirm that the proletariat would break the "shell" of Stalinism and to deny that Russia's bureaucracy was an autonomous social stratum. He tried to draw Burnham into a debate over "The ABC of Materialist Dialectics." Burnham, the last of the "literary Trotskisants," declined, stating, "I stopped arguing about religion long ago." Trotsky could only reply glumly, "I once heard Max Eastman voice this same sentiment."[85]

On that note it could be said that for some American writers the intellectual cold war had begun. For Trotsky had called upon his followers to continue to resist Stalinism as "reactionary" and at the same time to support Stalin's foreign policy in Eastern Europe as "progressive."[86] This paradoxical proposition was offered not solely on the basis of Russia's national security, the rationale used a year earlier by Stalinists to excuse the non-aggression pact and used two decades later by some New Left historians to excuse Yalta;[87] it derived from a fantastic philosophy of history that could justify supporting Stalinism in Poland as revolutionary while continuing to oppose it in Russia as counterrevolutionary. At this critical point the issue of dialectical reasoning became almost a matter of life and death to Trotsky, for never did so much depend upon how the human mind perceived the unfolding nature of historical reality. Trotsky now plunged into intellectual history with all the passion, if not the sense of irony, of Perry Miller or Arthur O. Lovejoy as he tried to find in Aristotle and classical philosophy arguments to use against Eastman.* He wrote letter

* Trotsky's compelling argument and Eastman's equally compelling rebuttal suggest how important intellectual history can become even to historical materialists.
    Formal logic, Trotsky argued, prevailed in the ancient classical world before man had knowledge of evolution. It was then believed that a thing cannot both be and not be, cannot be itself and that which it is not. But Aristotle's logic of identity (A=A) underwent a revolution when man became aware that reality is changing and not static. Once the universe was perceived as dynamic and evolutionary, Hegelian-Marxist thought was the only way man could understand the laws of development. Now the logic of contradiction replaced the logic of identity, for a thing was seen to be in the process of becoming that which it is not, of growing, changing, and transforming itself into something else. Indeed, Trotsky insisted with dialectical flourish, any other perception of reality would deny the existence of reality. For the antiquated axiom that "A is equal to A signified that a thing is equal to itself if it does not change, that is, if it does not exist." (Trotsky, "A Petty-Bourgeois Opposition in the Socialist Workers Party," New International, VI [March 1940], 35–42.)
    In response to Trotsky's exposition, Eastman pointed out that the idea of evolution was quite familiar to Aristotle in the writings of Thales, Anaximander, Xenophanes, and Anaxagoras, who were discussed in his chapters on metaphysics, and it was also familiar to the classical world of Heraclitus and Solon. Eastman then maintained—and here he may have pushed his argument too far—that formal logic had no ontological status. When the Greek philosopher declared that A=A he was not writing a "science of being" but an approach to reasoning, "not talking about existent things but consistent thinking. . . . The

after letter from Coyoacán, Mexico, to the New York office of the Socialist Workers Party in a desperate attempt to persuade his dwindling band of followers. Seemingly fighting a one-man war with the ideas of Hegel against the power of Stalin, confronted by the "retreat of the intellectuals" in America, Trotsky remained convinced that the "dual nature" of Stalinism could be understood only if one maintained a dialectical interpretation of history:

It is not surprising that the theoreticians of the opposition who reject dialectical thought capitulate lamentably before the contradictory nature of the USSR. However the contradiction between the social basis laid down by the revolution, and the character of the caste which arose out of the degeneration of the revolution is not only an irrefutable historical fact but also a motor force. In our struggle for the overthrow of the bureaucracy we base ourselves on this contradiction.[88]

Trotsky remained equally convinced that it was "Eastman and his ilk" who had so corrupted the mind of a whole generation of American Marxist intellectuals that it lost the capacity to see "all things and phenomena in their continuous change" (but not the workers, who are "naturally inclined to dialectical thinking.") Since he held the epistemological key that would unlock the riddle of Stalinism, and since he saw himself as the last remaining revolutionary with the Hegelian vision of history that would illuminate the meaning of events, Trotsky proceeded to instruct Americans on how to think and how not to think. "Dialectical training of mind, as necessary to a revolutionary as finger exercises to a pianist," is superior to "pragmatism" and the "banalities of 'common sense,'" wrote Trotsky,[89] as he endeavored to show how the "housewife," the "illiterate peasant woman," and the "fox" in the

---

principle, A equals A, means that if you are going to be rational, or in other words talk sense, the meaning of your terms must not shift while you are talking. You cannot even argue . . . that all existence is a process, unless by existence you mean existence and by process process. You could not even state that a pound of sugar is always unequal to itself, unless the term pound of sugar remained identical in meaning with the term itself. That is what Aristotle perceived; that is what formal logic is about." (Eastman, Marxism: Is It Science? pp. 286–87.)

woods all demonstrated in their everyday behavior unconscious "Hegelian tendencies."*

Trotsky, believing World War II would be the ultimate test of his theory of Stalinism as a transitionary episode about to explode, was prepared to concede that if the proletariat demonstrated its "congenital incapacity . . . of accomplishing the task placed upon it by the course of development, nothing would remain except openly to recognize that the socialist program, based on the internal contradictions of capitalist society, ended as Utopia."[90] Trotsky did not live to see the death of the dream to which he dedicated his whole political life; his former followers were left to face Stalinism alone, without the historical certainties that Marxism had once guaranteed them. Stalinism, then, not "commu-

---

* After delving into Aristotle to refute Eastman, Trotsky embraced the entire universe in his "Open Letter to Comrade Burnham":

> Every individual is a dialectician to some extent or other, in most cases, unconsciously. A housewife knows that a certain amount of salt flavors soup agreeably, but that added salt makes the soup unpalatable. Consequently, an illiterate peasant woman guides herself in cooking soup by the Hegelian law of the transformation of quantity into quality. Similar examples from daily life could be cited without end. Even animals arrive at their practical conclusions not only on the basis of the Aristotelian syllogism but also on the basis of the Hegelian dialectic. Thus a fox is aware that quadrupeds and birds are nutritious and tasty. On sighting a hare, a rabbit, or a hen, a fox concludes: this particular creature belongs to the tasty and nutritive type, and—chases after the prey. We have here a complete syllogism, although the fox, we may suppose, never read Aristotle. When the same fox, however, encounters a wolf, it quickly concludes that quantity passes into quality, and turns to flee. Clearly, the legs of a fox are equipped with Hegelian tendencies, even if not fully conscious ones. All this demonstrates, in passing, that our methods of thought, both formal logic and the dialectic, are not arbitrary constructions of our reason but rather expressions of the actual inter-relationships in nature itself. In this sense, the universe throughout is permeated with "unconscious" dialectics. But nature did not stop there. No little development occurred before nature's inner relationships were converted into the language of the consciousness of foxes and men, and man was then enabled to generalize these forms of consciousness and transform them into logical (dialectical) categories, thus creating the possibility for probing more deeply into the world about us. [Trotsky, *In Defense of Marxism*, p. 84.]

This fantastic discussion, which suggests a structure of mind in nature mediated through forms of language and behavior, could make Trotsky something of a precursor of French Structuralism. As Carl Becker might have said, Not being a fox, I'm in no position to judge.

nism," was the terror and the mystery of the anti-Stalinist Old Left. And in a curious way, writers like Eastman, Hook, and Burnham would continue to carry on their old struggle against Stalinism unencumbered by the intellectual legacy of Trotskyism —the myth of the dialectic and its philosophical counterpart, the proletariat.[91] The process by which anti-Stalinism may have grown into a morally indiscriminate crusade to defend a democratically illegitimate "free world" is questionable, yet the dissolution of these twin-myths was necessary. Stripped of its mystical "motor force" and mysterious power of self-negation, history could now be studied on its own terms, without the consolations of philosophy, and Soviet totalitarianism could be faced squarely as a permanent reality that had defied the author of "permanent revolution."

Eastman's original philosophical quarrel with Marx ended with Trotsky. Once championed as Lenin's rightful heir, Trotsky was now regarded as the last heroic antagonist to Stalin, tragically continuing his struggle with nothing left save a philosophy of history "saturated with optimism."[92] Ironically, the "metaphysical illusions" Eastman believed Lenin had purged from Marxism re-emerged in the mind of Trotsky, whose entire edifice of belief in the meaning of events in Europe lay ultimately in the dialectic, and whose valiant but desperate hopes for the Fourth International would lie ultimately in ruins on the battlefields and in the concentration camps of World War II—history's answer to Hegel.

"Organization Is Death": John Dos Passos

We must organize everything.

LENIN, 1918

Who says organization, says oligarchy.

ROBERT MICHELS, 1908

A Man without a Country

John Dos Passos was one of the most respected novelists of the twentieth century. This is not an aesthetic judgment of his work. As a human being Dos Passos was respected—one is almost tempted to say "loved"—because of his exceptional honesty and humility, qualities that remained incorruptible despite his continuous political involvements. Even Mike Gold could not bring himself to denounce Dos Passos as he had Max Eastman. One gathers, from reading various memoirs from the thirties, that to have known Dos Passos was to know the meaning of old-fashioned ideas like integrity, kindness, and decency. The novelist had a few political enemies, to be sure, but against him they stood morally powerless like Milton's Satan: "Abash'd the devil stood/And felt how awful goodness is."

Dos Passos and Eastman would arrive at a similar political destination, but no two temperaments and personalities were more dissimilar. The affable Eastman found Dos Passos "so shy that he seems cold as an empty cellar with the door locked when you meet him." The novelist did appear a monkish ascetic. Balding, nearsighted, slightly stooped-shouldered, he was painfully modest, afraid of publicity, uneasy at social gatherings, and inclined to shudder when women spoke openly of sex. In the twenties Dos Passos, Malcolm Cowley recalls, wore a pair of spectacles with "gollywog lenses," dressed usually in a rumpled nondescript gray suit, talked in a low voice with an occasional stutter, his "mouth curving upward at the corners into apologetic grins," peering at people with his head thrust forward as though he were an "inquisitive, easily frightened bird."[1]

Although Dos Passos was not of the "lost generation," he knew the meaning of the phrase even before Gertrude Stein uttered it. Other American literary intellectuals expatriated to Paris in the twenties in order to find a new spiritual home, but Dos Passos had experienced homelessness from the beginning of his conscious life. In his early years he was a rootless wanderer, a man without a "chosen country," a "bastard" of history. Dos Passos was alienated as Eastman was not.

Whereas Eastman enjoyed a secure and happy childhood with loving and understanding parents, Dos Passos's childhood could have been material for a Dreiser novel. He had been born in a Chicago hotel room on January 14, 1896, the illegitimate son of a fifty-two-year-old attorney and a forty-eight-year-old genteel Southern woman. The father, John Randolph Dos Passos, son of the Portuguese shoemaker Manuel Dos Passos, rose to prominence in the 1880s as a specialist in corporation law and later wrote books on legal history. He was married at the time of his son's birth and reluctant to divorce his invalid wife, thus suffering loss of social and professional standing. Not until John was fourteen did his father openly acknowledge him as his son. Young Dos Passos spent much of his time traveling abroad with his mother, Lucy Addison Sprigg, the only source of emotional warmth during his adolescence. This nomadic, fatherless existence clearly affected the young novelist. Just before his own death in 1970, Dos Passos would describe affectionately his father, "The Commodore," author of *The Anglo-Saxon Century*, as having written out of a conviction that, in the son's words, the English "tradition of law and representative government was the only possible basis for the development of a worldwide Christian civilization."[2] This nostalgic portrait, drawn by an elder conservative coming to terms with his past, belies the anger that once characterized his attitude toward the upper classes to which he himself belonged, the nouveaux riches lawyers and manufacturers whom he bitterly ridiculed in his early novels. Much of the source of that anger was filial before it was political. The hideous caricatures he drew of the business world expressed his resentment toward a capitalist class whose idea of paternal love was a lecture on "getting ahead." In Dos Passos's thinly disguised autobiographical novel, Chosen Country, the encounter between father and son reads like a dialogue of the deaf. Worshiping his distant father and yet denied his immediate love and companionship, Jay Pignatelli exclaims,

What a horrible childhood, he said to himself so nearly out loud that his lips moved. A hotel childhood. . . . A Man Without a Country. Lord I cried over that story and Ishmael the wanderer in deserts and Cain, that birthmark on the forehead the mark of the accursed like Cain, like all history's bastards.[3]

The instability and emotional deprivation of Dos Passos's youth offer a clue to his political behavior. More than any other figure we shall encounter on the road to conservatism, Dos Passos was truly seeking social identity as well as political liberty. His odyssey would end where it began.

No one could have predicted this pattern of rebellion and reconciliation. Dos Passos, who was born illegitimate, grew up to become an angry young castigator of all that was legitimate and respectable. After enduring the ordeal of prep school at fashionable Choate, he entered Harvard reluctantly in 1912, prodded by his father. Here the awkward, self-conscious student first felt the fascination of Froude, Gibbon, and Pater. He associated with a group of young literary intellectuals later known as the "Harvard Aesthetes." Writing in the Harvard Monthly in company with

E. E. Cummings and other poets, he denounced industrialism, mass culture, and the frantic rush of modernity which made him wonder whether "civilization had outlived life."[4] When war broke out in Europe his *Kulturpessimismus* turned to political rage. He attended pacifist meetings, sang "The International," and watched "the cossack tactics of the New York police force." Who would stop the orgy of violence? Certainly not the "milky lot" of Harvard graduates. Only the East Side Jews and a few "isolated 'foreigners'" were resisting. The activities of Eastman, Reed, and *The Masses* group did not encourage Dos Passos. The intelligentsia were too polite, products of an effete education. Harvard was an "ether cone" that turned out "nice men." "These stupid colleges," he complained in a letter to a friend, were "instillers of stodginess—every form of bastard culture, middle-class snobbism."

And what are we fit for when they turn us out of Harvard? We're too intelligent to be successful businessmen and we haven't the sand or the energy to be anything else.

Until Widener is blown up and A. Lawrence Lowell assassinated and the Business School destroyed and its site sowed with salt . . . no good will come out of Cambridge.

His bloody thoughts exploded in a Bakuninite fantasy as though he were an early Weatherman-of-the-pen.

My only hope is in revolution—in wholesale assassination of all statesmen, capitalists, war-mongers, jingoists, inventors, scientists—in the destruction of all the machinery of the industrial world, equally barren in destruction and construction.

My only refuge from the deepest depression is in dreams of vengeful guillotines.[5]

In his senior year Dos Passos left school to study painting and architecture in Spain. Upon his father's death in 1917, he returned to the United States for a few months, then enlisted in the Norton-Harjes medical unit and served in the war as an ambulance driver in France and Italy. He was sent home in 1918 for violating censorship regulations and returned to Europe as an enlisted private in the U.S. Army. The war was Dos Passos's chance to witness behavior under stress, to test his own capacity for courage, and to find the companionship his childhood had denied him. Both fascinated and horrified by what he saw, he recorded vividly his impressions in letters from the front: the mutilated bodies, the grime and fleas of the trenches, the rum-sotted soldiers, the "ghoulish dust-powdered faces," the horses choking to death in poison gas. Politically the war was a "ridiculous farce." Only the liberals took it seriously, the tender souls who mourn for the dead while enshrining the holocaust with the "halo" of a noble cause. "Like the Jews at their wailing place, the Liberals cover their heads with their robes of integrity and wail, wail, wail—God, I'm tired of wailing. I want to assassinate."[6]

Out of the war experience came Dos Passos's first two novels, *One Man's Initiation* (1920) and *Three Soldiers* (1921), dramatizing in the barracks and on the battlefield the aesthetic tensions he felt as a student. The primary characters are not political radicals but artists, sensitive musicians or novelists who cry out, "First we must burst our bonds, open our eyes, clear our ears. No, we know nothing but what we are told by the rulers. Oh, the lies, the lies, the lies, the lies that life is smothered in! We must strike once more for freedom, for the sake of the dignity of man. Hopelessly, cynically, ruthlessly we must rise and show at least that we are not taken in; that we are slaves but not willing slaves. Oh, they have deceived us so many times."[7]

Who were "they"? It was characteristic of Dos Passos that he would never be able to identify the enemy in ideological terms. Nor did he place much hope in the anarchists and socialists whose dialogues provided the only political reflections in his early novels. They would not be taken in, but neither would they take power. Everyone, revolutionary activists and artists alike, struggles vainly against the "machine," the novel's central metaphor. The war to Dos Passos was not so much an encounter with death, as it was to Hemingway, but a way of life. War was an institution, and the army a microcosm of modern civilization, with the soldier an instrument to be "moulded" into the social organism. The militarization of life at the front was merely the extension of the regimentation of life at home. "Over organization," Dos Passos declared, "is death."[8] The threatening mechanization of social existence would become one of Dos Passos's enduring themes.

The Anatomy of Industrial Society

Several contemporaries believed that Dos Passos's anti-war novels flowed from the same romantic emotions as Hemingway's *A Farewell to Arms*: the politics of generational disillusionment, the sensibility of wounded innocence, the existentialist philosophy of *nada*. But Dos Passos would never completely follow the lost generation's retreat into the private world of the self, the interior psyche of the tragic "I" that haunted Hemingway and Fitzgerald. Unlike many postwar writers, Dos Passos would be unable to find personal meaning in social withdrawal. Even in Spain while writing his seemingly escapist travel book, *Rosinante to the Road Again* (1922), he pondered the political truths found in a country resisting modernization. During the same period he gathered together a collection of his earlier poems, *Pushcart at the Curb*, the last lyrical statement of a former undergraduate aesthete. Two years later, in the *Streets of Night* (1924), he probed the psychological sources of repression that plagued youths who rebelled against their parents, only to discover that their internalized Puritan inhibitions had paralyzed their will to be free. Thereafter Dos Passos's focus moved steadily outward. The poet of lyrical negation now became the anatomist of social malaise. Long before other writers abandoned their various poses of cultural alienation in response to the Depression, Dos Passos immersed himself in social reality in an effort to capture America's collective consciousness. As his quest for personal identity broadened into a deeper search for historical meaning, he concentrated all his powers of perception upon the social and political structure of modern industrial civilization. This subject, which had preoccupied sociologists like Thorstein Veblen and Max Weber, was to become Dos Passos's lifelong obsession.

Dos Passos chose the city as the topic for his first explicit social novel, *Manhattan Transfer* (1925). He lived in New York from 1923 to 1925, and sometime during this period he read "at one gulp" Joyce's *Ulysses*. "Parts I found boring," he later recalled, "and parts I found magnificent."[9] No doubt it was Joyce's surrealistic style that impressed him: the artful succession of sense impressions, the interior monologues run together in liquefied word sequences expressing arbitrary patterns of thought, the disjointed narrative broken by a seemingly arbitrary panorama of fleeting scenes. Dos Passos used the Joycean technique to capture the turbulent power and chaos of the city and to convey the frantic lives of those caught in its swirl. New York became symptomatic of all the social evils that had troubled Dos Passos, and the dozen or so aimless characters and the series of unrelated episodes in the novel seemed to have no point other than to dramatize the fragmented tone of modern city life. The dehumanized, listless quality of his characters—even the anarchists and communists are ineffectual or corruptible—led Paul Elmer More to describe *Manhattan Transfer* as an "explosion in a cesspool"; Edmund Wilson protested that Dos Passos condemned the "sufferers" along with the "disease."[10]

The nature of the "disease"? Dos Passos followed the naturalist tradition of viewing personal failure as a consequence of impersonal forces, but his curiosity about American life yielded no simple economic explanation. "God I wish I could blame it all on capitalism the way Martin does," states one sensitive character in *Manhattan Transfer*. Like Eastman, Dos Passos would not allow wish to dominate intellect in order to render history responsive to his own desires. But Eastman's reservations about Marxism arose from a skeptical mind informed by philosophical reflection; those of Dos Passos came from the sensibility of a poet at war with a world that was too big, too powerful, and too chaotic to be reduced to political formulas. "I don't think it's time for any group of spell-binders to lay down the law on any subject whatsoever," Dos Passos told the communist Mike Gold in 1926. "Particularly I don't think there should be any more phrases, badges, opinions, banners, imported from Russia or anywhere else. . . . I'd like to see a magazine," he stated in reference to the founding of the *New Masses*, "full of introspection and doubt that would be like a piece of litmus paper to test things by."[11]

While Dos Passos was planning his greatest work, the trilogy *U.S.A.*, he came as close as he ever would to formulating what appeared to be a Marxist conception of society. That was in the summer of 1927, when he threw all his energies into the Sacco-Vanzetti defense campaign. Dos Passos was willing to write articles on the case for the *Daily Worker*, maintain a vigil outside the Charlestown prison, and undergo arrest and stand trial for picketing. The execution of the two Italian anarchists shook him with horror. He started writing *U.S.A.* shortly after the event, and the traumatic experience provides the éclaircissement for the last novel in the trilogy. It is a hymn of hatred, a prose-poem of class warfare:

all right you have won   you will kill the brave men our friends tonight . . .
America our nation has been beaten by strangers who have turned our language inside out who have taken the clean words our fathers spoke and made them slimy and foul
their hired men sit on the judge's bench they sit back with their feet on the tables under the dome of the State House they are ignorant of our beliefs they have the dollars the guns the armed forces the power-plants.
they have built the electricchair and hired the executioner to throw the switch
all right we are two nations

Communists hailed *U.S.A.* as a masterpiece of political art, and many radical intellectuals assumed that America's greatest social novelist would go on to hail communism as the wave of the future. Clearly there was no turning back, particularly for a writer without a country. Or was it the Marxists who were the "bastards" of history?

The Reluctant Communist

Dos Passos expressed admiration for the communist editor Mike Gold, "a worker and not an unclassed bourgeois," who accepted the "discipline of the Worker's Party."[12] Suspicious of discipline himself, Dos Passos nevertheless desired, even before Wall Street crashed, to sink his roots into the laboring classes and write about the worker and his tools. Thus during the early years of the Depression he saw nothing wrong in associating with communist-infiltrated organizations. He helped establish the Emergency Committee for Southern Prisoners and he was willing to become chairman of the National Committee to Aid Striking Miners Fighting Starvation. In fall 1931, Dos Passos and Theodore Dreiser went to Harlan County, Kentucky, in an effort to bring to public attention the violation of civil rights of the communist-led striking coal miners. The following year Dos Passos added his name to the pamphlet *Culture and Crisis*, a manifesto signed by fifty-two of America's most important writers and artists endorsing the communist presidential candidate, William Z. Foster. For Dos Passos the endorsement was a protest gesture against all other political alternatives, including the democratic Socialist Party of Norman Thomas. "Becoming a socialist right now," he wrote in 1932, "would have just about the same effect on anybody as drinking a bottle of near-beer." Should a writer join the Communist Party? "It's his own goddam business," Dos Passos replied to a *Modern Quarterly* questionnaire. "Some people are naturally party men and others are natural scavengers and campfollowers. Matter of temperament. I personally belong to the scavenger and campfollower section."[13]

Dos Passos would never be comfortable with the Communist Party even as a curious camp follower. On two important issues the novelist found himself at odds with communist orthodoxy: the function of the literary artist, and the interpretation of American history and society.

Like Eastman, Dos Passos opposed the view, prominent among the "vulgar" Marxists, that literature should be reduced to ideological formulas in order to be more effective as a class weapon. Both believed that America's naturalistic novelists offered better examples of social realism than the writers in the communist camp did, and Eastman shared Dos Passos's conviction that "Walt Whitman's a hell of a lot more revolutionary than any Russian poet I've ever heard of." Whatever the relationship of aesthetics to politics, "good writing was good writing under Moses and the Pharaohs and will be good writing under a soviet republic or a money oligarchy." The novelist would be committed but not collected. "Intellectual workers of the world unite," he once shouted in a cafe to a table of radicals, "you have nothing to lose but your brains."[14]

On the second issue, Dos Passos departed from Eastman as well as from the communists. Eastman had criticized Marxism as a philosophical system, but he did not bother to question its sociological principles. Dos Passos doubted that the doctrine of class struggle applied to conditions in the United States—the debate over "American exceptionalism" that would occupy Will Herberg and other communist theoreticians. To Dos Passos America was not only exceptional but exemplary. The novelist sensed that his country was too vast and complex to be confined to the logic of a systematic social philosophy, particularly one that mistook a contradiction for an explanation. "Do you believe that American capitalism is doomed to inevitable failure and collapse?" he was asked in 1932. "We've got the failure. . . . What I don't see is the collapse." It was more probable, Dos Passos added, that the capitalism would "ripen" into a "centralized plutocracy" rather than a social revolution. The key to the future lay in the middle classes, not in the amorphous working class and the elusive proletariat. Convinced that the various elements in the bourgeois strata must be neutralized, he warned both the communist *New Masses* and the liberal *New Republic* that the struggle against capitalism must be conducted "under the most humane conditions possible."[15]

His advice seemed confirmed when Hitler came to power in 1933. Now more than ever it became clear that a savage warfare of class hatred must be avoided in America. Victory over capitalism might still be won, for one class of workers who had the "least stake" in the system were the "engineers, scientists, independent manual craftsmen, writers, actors, and technicians of one sort or another." These elements could combine with "young men of the left" and with "farmers, mechanics, railroad men, miners, garment workers" and other alienated artists and productive citizens who must be won over if democratic processes were to be preserved. The very identification of these diverse occupations suggests Dos Passos's Whitmanesque respect for the healthy complexity of American society; it also reveals his Veblenesque skepticism of class consciousness and his sensitivity to the uniqueness of America's social structure. The American working class represented neither the negation of capitalism nor the fulfillment of Marx's historical mission. The lesson for the Left? "Somebody's got to have the size to Marxianize the American tradition before you can sell the American workers on the social revolution. Or else Americanize Marx."[16]

Americanize Marx. That proposition blew the mind of a whole generation of radicals. Sidney Hook attempted to reinterpret Marx in light of Dewey's thought; but Dos Passos, on the other hand, believed that America's dominant school of philosophy offered merely an unfocused methodology, a plea for intelligence without the power of social analysis or critical theory. "Theories are extremely rare in our country," he told a French interviewer in 1936. "The habit of not entertaining ideas—Pragmatism—is so strong in the United States it is a kind of veritable malady."[17] Dewey was a meliorist and a democratic socialist, too insipid a brew for Dos Passos's thirst. Far more potent and less polite was Veblen's mordant intellect. Dos Passos found Veblen's masquerade of solemnity and satire congenial, and Veblen's ability to question everything and promise nothing fascinated the novelist who aesthetically preferred to abandon U.S.A. than to bring it to a political conclusion.

Dos Passos chose to Americanize Marx by reorienting the last volume of U.S.A. around the philosophy of Veblen. While he was writing The Big Money, however, the first of a series of events occurred that would lead Dos Passos to reject communism as well as Marxism. In February 1934 the Socialist Party sponsored a rally at Madison Square Garden to honor the socialist workers of Vienna who had been shot down by Chancellor Dollfuss's troops. Attempting to take over the rally, communists stormed the meeting and provoked a riot. Outraged by their "unintelligent fanaticism," Dos Passos signed, together with twenty-four others, an "Open Letter to the Communist Party" protesting the disruption. The New Masses was saddened to find Dos Passos's name on the letter. What is this truly radical "literary guide and inspiration" doing in the "queer company" of democratic socialists who are no more than "revolutionary butterflies"? When Dos Passos replied, condemning the violent sectarianism of the communists, the Communist Party concluded that the misguided novelist confused Bolshevik firmness with "fanaticism." The New Masses continued to try to win him back to the movement as America's foremost "revolutionary writer" and political "comrade."[18] The communist literary intelligentsia could not afford to lose Dos Passos, as playwright John Howard Lawson explained to him in a thirteen-page personal letter:

> You, who have been the nearest thing this country has to a Proletarian writer, are desperately needed right now—the Communists know how badly you're needed and feel bitterly that you're turning away from them. And I certainly hope you analyze the situation a lot more before you take any steps that are definitely unsympathetic.

After admonishing Dos Passos for reacting emotionally to the Madison Square Garden incident, and informing him that he was being attacked at John Reed Club meetings for writing for *Common Sense*, Lawson offered a final word of advice:

The Communists are beginning to accuse you for consorting with their enemies—that's likely to make you angry, and to make you feel that they are narrow-minded and didactic and unreasonable (which is true)—but there's a basis for the charge, just as there's a basis for Mike Gold calling me "a bourgeois Hamlet," however stupidly he put it. My own plan is to work very closely with the communists in the future, to get into some strike activity, and to accept a good deal of discipline in doing so. It seems to me the only course open to people like ourselves.[19]

Dos Passos chose a different course, and during the mid-thirties, when he was working on *The Big Money*, his political views shifted considerably. By the time he finished the novel, communist characters like Mary French and Ben Compton appeared as pathetic if not neurotic. The "Camera Eye" conveys what is on the author's mind: "and all the time in my pocket that letter from that collegeboy asking me to explain why being right which he admits   the radicals are in their private lives such shits". Dos Passos now warned eminent intellectuals like John Dewey against associating his name with communist causes (even Trotsky's countertrial in Mexico). Other independent radicals, like Margaret De Silver, wife of the colorful anarchist Carlo Tresca, appealed to him to resist the presumed communist takeover of the American Writers Congress.[20] During this period Dos Passos also expressed a renewed respect for the American traditions of civil liberty and representative government. Recoiling from European totalitarianism, he began to explore the American past not as a naturalistic novelist of impersonal social forces but as a citizen and political moralist. He had turned to the past in desperation. "I'm trying to take a course in American history," he wrote F. Scott Fitzgerald in 1936, "and most of the time the course of world events seems so frightful that I feel absolutely paralysed—and the feeling that I've got to hurry to get the stuff out before the big boys close down on us."[21]

Dos Passos's suddenly developed historical sense enabled him to reject the communist myth of the false alternative: that America must either move forward to socialism or "revert" to fascism. "Frankly I don't see all this fatalism about fascism on the part of the communists," Dos Passos told Robert Cantwell. "If you mean repressive violence, sure, we've always had that tougher than anywhere; if you mean Hearstian demagoguery, sure—Hearst is handsome Adolph's schoolteacher—but fascism organized into the state I can't see—I don't think its in the breed—I think you've got to have the feudal pattern in the social heritage to make it stick—and that's one thing we haven't got." A novelist sensed early what it would take "consensus" historians long to discover: America is "unique," a country that lacks the feudal heritage that made both communism and fascism possible in Europe. America has no proletariat to forge a social revolution against an *ancien régime*, and no feudal class that would destroy its liberal traditions. It is the American Marxists, Dos Passos told Edmund Wilson, who are men without a country.

The Marxians have gotten into one of those hopeless situations like the French Huguenots in the years before St. Bartholomew, where everything they do helps the reaction— The Huguenots were right and so are the Marxists right—but I think we're fast getting into a situation where there'll be nothing left to do but go to the stake with as much dignity as we can muster— The only alternative is passionate unmarxian revival of Anglo Saxon democracy or an industrial crisis helped by a collapse in the director's office— That would be different from nazi socialism only in this way: that it would be a reaction towards old time Fourth of July democracy instead of towards feudalism—as we haven't any feudalism in our blood I dont see very well how we can react towards feudal habits the way the heinies do.[22]

Dos Passos's doubts about communism remained a private matter until 1937. The ideological differences between him and the Marxist Left were real and irreconcilable, but unlike Eastman, he responded more to deeds than to doctrine. His final break with communism was less a matter of theoretical reflection than an immediate, personal crisis of conscience. For Dos Passos the "wound in the heart" came during the Spanish Civil War.

Spain, 1937

The war in Spain had personal as well as political repercussions for Dos Passos. For one thing, it meant the breakup of an old, close friendship with Ernest Hemingway. Dos Passos first met Hemingway in 1918 when they were driving ambulances on the Italian front. Their paths crossed frequently after the war, and in the twenties they prowled the cafes of Paris together, went fishing in Montana and Key West, and spent their Christmas holidays with the Gerald Murphys in the Swiss Alps, Murphy being a patron of the Lost Generation. Dos Passos met his wife, Katharine Smith, while on a fishing trip on Hemingway's boat, and Hemingway met his second wife, Pauline Pfeiffer, through Katy Dos Passos.[23] The two novelists were drawn together by common intellectual concerns as well. Hemingway shared the same reverence for the dignity of work, the moral duty of a technical task brought to fruition that was so heroically expressed in Robert Jordan of *For Whom the Bell Tolls*. He also shared Dos Passos's scorn for the "slimy words" that pass for political ideals, phrases like "honor" and "glory" that nauseated Frederick Henry of *A Farewell to Arms*. The mystification of ideological abstractions violated both novelists' respect for concrete truth and immediate experience. In 1932, when Hemingway was being attacked by the Left for not writing about the social injustice of the "system," he wrote Dos Passos a series of letters. He warned his friend to resist communist appeals and pressures to subordinate his writing to the service of the Party. He wanted Dos Passos to keep the Joycean "Camera Eye" section in the last volume of *U.S.A.* and not allow himself to be upset by Malcolm Cowley's criticisms. Above all, Dos Passos must continue to write about people as people and not as symbols of institutions or social forces. The novelist, Hemingway advised, is interested in the human race, not in ideologies or political causes. Describing himself as an anarchist, Hemingway protested that it was Christianity that killed Christ, and the institutionalization of Marxism will do in Karl Marx as well. Justice, he concluded, could only be found in character.[24]

If character transcends conditions—an anti-naturalist argument Dos Passos must have found difficult to accept—Spain was the country where human character could be found in its purest form. Both novelists deeply admired the Iberian world. It proved to Hemingway that justice could not function in any social unit larger than a pueblo; and Dos Passos, who earlier had tried to justify the ways of Spain to Americans in Rosinante to the Road Again, became convinced that the villages were the heart and soul of Spain.[25] In the isolated communities of Andalusia and Catalonia both novelists could find a clearer understanding of their own values and a clearer perspective on America. Impressed by Spanish culture as well, the two American writers drew up a commentary for the New York exhibition of the Spanish painter Luis Quintanilla. Hemingway visited Spain about a dozen times and Dos Passos went there in 1916, 1920, and 1933. In 1937 Dos Passos journeyed there again to write about the war and to collaborate with Hemingway in the filming of the pro-Loyalist documentary The Spanish Earth.

Dos Passos and Hemingway began to clash almost as soon as they met in Madrid. They differed over the proper focus of the film: Dos Passos wanted to concentrate the camera on the human sufferings of the Spanish people, Hemingway on the military aspects of the war.[26] Far more serious were their conflicting interpretations of the war itself. Dos Passos was deeply moved by the Spanish working class, which had been defending itself with a "magnificent heroism that will remain one of the bloodstirring episodes of European history." Yet he also observed developing behind the lines "a struggle as violent as the war . . . between the Marxist concept of the totalitarian state, and the Anarchist concept of individual liberty." The anarchists and socialists, with their ideals of local freedom and self-government, would be unable to resist the organized leadership and discipline of the Communist Party that was so necessary for victory. Dos Passos saw tragedy on every side. For even if the Loyalists win, a militarized Spain will undergo centralization at the hands of the Stalinists, and the forces of the Left will give way before "this tremendously efficient and ruthless machine for power."[27]

Hemingway regarded Dos Passos's fears as unfounded. In a personal letter he told his friend that he was doing a disservice to the anti-fascist cause by exaggerating the extent of Soviet influence among the Loyalist forces. Had you been on the front lines, Hemingway lectured Dos Passos, you would have seen that there were no Russian generals but only Polish, Bulgarian, and Yugoslavian military advisers, all welcomed as liberators by the Spanish populace. An even graver matter was the fate of Andrés Nin and José Robles Pazos. The former was a leader of the Trotskyist POUM organization; the latter a Spaniard who had taught literature at Johns Hopkins University, a close friend of Dos Passos, and a colonel in the Loyalist army. Both had been mysteriously arrested by Stalinist agents and subsequently executed in secret. Hemingway believed Dos Passos had no business writing about the death of Nin in the American press, since neither he nor anyone else could confirm the fact. The swaggering Hemingway, boasting of the "good" Russians he had met in Spain, accepted the Stalinist version of Robles's guilt and attributed Dos Passos's belief in his innocence to the naïveté of "a typical American liberal attitude."[28] When he learned of the death of Robles, Hemingway broke the news to Dos Passos, who immediately left Madrid, reeling from the shock that his friend had followed Nin's fate.

After the Spanish experience Dos Passos could see little moral distinction between communism and fascism. Like George Orwell, he came home from abroad convinced that the butchery of language and the abuse of power were characteristic of the Left as well as the Right. With the fate of Robles searing his conscience, Dos Passos wrote *Adventures of a Young Man*, his final testament to the perils of radical innocence. The hero, Glenn Spottswood, becomes disillusioned with communism in America after discovering the Party exploiting the Harlan County miners' strike for its own ends. He goes to Spain hoping that the final struggle against oppression and fascism could be fought in the open battlefield. He is arrested by the GPU, charged with Trotskyism, released from jail, and sent to his death on a suicidal mission. The novel, published in 1939, produced an uproar in Marxist literary circles. The *New Masses* described it as "a crude piece of Trotskyist agit-prop." Malcolm Cowley, who had earlier published a letter from Dos Passos in the *New Republic*, thereby inadvertently jeopardizing the attempt to free Spanish prisoners like the artist Luis Quintanilla,[29] pronounced the novel artistically unconvincing and politically unreliable in a review in which he also took Hemingway's side on the Robles affair. John Howard Lawson, an old friend from the New Playwrights Theatre experiment of the twenties, complained to Dos Passos that his analysis of what was happening in the world was bereft of "any coherent theoretical basis." Declared a renegade by the last remnants of the Popular Front, Dos Passos nevertheless still had the support of an important minority on the literary Left: the Trotskyist James T. Farrell, the anarcho-"cynicalist" Dwight Macdonald, the essayists Edmund Wilson and Lionel Trilling, a few anti-Stalinist intellectuals of the *Partisan Review*, and the loneliest rebel of all, Max Eastman.[30]

After his experience with the atrocities of the Spanish Civil War, Dos Passos announced his "farewell to Europe." Although he desired to see Roosevelt revise the Neutrality Laws and lift the embargo that prevented America from aiding the Spanish Republic, Dos Passos continued to oppose the Popular Front's call for intervention and to attack the "war spirit" of the Communist Party. The purges and the non-aggression pact confirmed his deepening mood of isolationism from the "total bankruptcy of

Europe." Dos Passos's sense of isolationism was moral more than political. When the Germans invaded the Soviet Union in June 1941, he realized that the United States could not remain indifferent to the forces of totalitarianism.

In September 1941 Dos Passos published an article, "To a Liberal in Office," admitting he had been wrong in his earlier criticism of the New Deal, an experiment which had been, despite many false starts, "productive of real living good in the national life." Three months later, with the attack upon Pearl Harbor, Dos Passos did not, like other isolationists, publicly criticize Roosevelt's precipitous foreign policy that had, perhaps, led to the attack. Nor did he oppose Congress's declaration of war. Dos Passos's curious silence would later puzzle his friends when the novelist subsequently turned against Roosevelt.[31]

When World War II broke out, Dos Passos was steeped in the study of the American past. He now began to feel that the fate of Western democracy was somehow bound up with the health of American society and history. The threat of European totalitarianism compelled him to embrace the very heritage he had all but disowned twenty years earlier, and his ruminations in the American past gave him a new sense of political belonging. His first investigation resulted in two essays in 1939 on Tom Paine— another fellow traveler whose revolutionary idealism had drowned in the Jacobin terrors of the eighteenth century—and then his first historical work in 1941, The Ground We Stand On. The libertarian novelist could readily identify with the great figures of colonial American history—Roger Williams, Joel Barlow, Franklin, Jefferson. A recurring allegory in the book is the dialectic of American innocence and European experience, the bright dawn of a new life of virtue and happiness juxtaposed to the dark historical record of defeated hopes and betrayed ideals. His chapter on "Citizen Barlow of the Republic of the World" ends with a quatrain by the poet that might have been written by Dos Passos upon his return from Madrid in 1937:

Yet other Spains in victim smoke shall rise
And other Moskows suffocate the skies,
Till Men resume their souls & dare to shed
Earth's total vengence on opression's head.

The Riddle of Dos Passos

Dos Passos's career differs from those of the other three thinkers studied here. His intellectual history cannot be readily divided into periods, for the ideas and values that concerned him remained constant throughout his life, and the causes he later championed as a conservative were implicit in his early radical protests. One may discern important changes of attitude about the nature of historical reality and human character when Dos Passos shifts from fiction and explores the American past as a historian. His historical studies, to be considered in the second part of the book, are peculiarly an outcome of America's confrontation with European totalitarianism and the cold war. Here we shall discuss some psychological and ideological themes in Dos Passos's prose fiction, themes and perspectives that suggest an underlying unity in his politics, and then examine both Dos Passos's philosophy of history and the unexplored implications of his fictional works for social and political theory, the relationship between the literary imagination and historical reality.

The psychosocial functions of Dos Passos's art can profitably be extended to the novelist's politics.[32] Indeed, if the child is father to the man, the implications of Dos Passos's childhood—the Oedipal tensions toward his father and his traumatic experience of homelessness—offer clues both to his early radicalism and his postwar conservatism. In most of Dos Passos's novels the narrator either has no clear memory of his father or is driven to shame and anger whenever the shadowy image of the father appears. Through several of his characters, especially those in *Streets of Night*, the author could express obliquely a deeply rooted filial aversion that had its origins in his own unstable domestic life as a child. This unconscious frustration manifested itself in Dos Passos's desire to make a complete break with the past, his family, and with all the values symbolized in his father's profession as a business lawyer.

Can Dos Passos's anti-capitalism be reduced to a simple "Freudian quarrel" with his father? Only by ignoring sources of radical sentiment that were intellectual and historical as well as psychological. Still, if one cannot fully explain Dos Passos's radicalization in terms of hidden psychic compulsions, neither can one adequately explain his later deradicalization solely as a conscious act of intellect. Even while rebelling against his family Dos Passos had so implicated himself in his father's personality that he could never make an ultimate repudiation. He managed to overcome these ambivalent tensions in U.S.A., but two decades later, in his autobiographical Chosen Country, the hero makes himself over in his father's image. As Blanch Gelfant observes: "Thus the search for identity leads ultimately, by a circuitous path, to the acceptance of the total identity of the father as the reality of one's self."[33]

Applying Gelfant's psychological analysis to Dos Passos's shifting political positions, a similar contour of consciousness emerges. In both cases self-awareness leads to social adjustment, for the psychological reconciliation to the father parallels Dos Passos's own political reconciliation to the economic way of life he would like to believe his father represented—a theme openly and joyously expressed in one of his last writings, his memoir The Best Times. Perhaps this is one reason why Dos Passos's attack upon capitalism evoked a strange mixture of hatred and sentimentality. He assailed the abuses of industrial capitalism but seldom questioned the individualistic, competitive values that made the historic culture of American capitalism possible. He rebelled against the authority of his father, but he could never bring himself to question the internalized values of work and opportunity that his father had instilled into his conscience as a youth. The novel Midcentury (1961), one of the first important American books to treat the businessman as the hero of civilization, enabled Dos Passos to re-embrace his father as part of his true self that he had tried so long to suppress.

The psychological analysis also helps explain Dos Passos's chronic rebelliousness, his stubborn individualism, and his belated discovery of a libertarian tradition in America that contains countercurrents of both radicalism and conservatism. The suppressed respect and conscious fear in which he held his father contributed to his distrust of all forms of authority and social forces that deny individual autonomy: the regimentation of military life (*Three Soldiers*), the atomization of city life (*Manhattan Transfer*), the alienation of historical life (*U.S.A.*), the domination of party life (*Adventures of a Young Man*), the bureaucratization of political life (*The Grand Design*), and the managerialization of business life (*Midcentury*). The rebellion against the father as an authority symbol became a rebellion against power in general—not only its abuses, but the exercise of power itself. At first his struggle was with the lone individuals whose freedom was subject to the will of others, with the powerless people who get pushed around. "My sympathies," he wrote in 1939, "lie with the private in the front line against the brass hat; with the hod-carrier against the straw-boss, or the walking delegate for that matter; with the laboratory worker against the stuffed shirt in a mortarboard; with the criminal against the cop."[34] As Dos Passos moved further to the right in the fifties and sixties he discovered new sources of authority and new victims of power: the economic state standing over the self-employed entrepreneur. As he began to probe the American past, moreover, he discovered a new definition of freedom in Jeffersonian individualism. In the Founding Fathers he also assumed he had discovered what he had earlier longed for in his own father: legitimate moral authority that could be entrusted with power. The discovery evolved logically—or psychologically—from *U.S.A.*, where Dos Passos's protest against the capitalist world of his father was made in the ironic name of "our fathers" of American colonial history.

Yet long before Dos Passos discovered the republican virtue of colonial America he had been attracted by an idea that had caused the Founding Fathers' blood to curdle—the idea of anarchism, the political dream of total statelessness and classlessness.[35] This quest for pastoral innocence and pure freedom brought him to Spain in the early twenties. Seeking the tradition denied him in America, this grandson of a Portuguese immigrant traveled through the Iberian peninsula in search of spiritual ancestry. "Telemachus had wandered so far in search for his father he had quite forgotten what he was looking for," announces the opening sentence in *Rosinante to the Road Again.* Dos Passos may have forgotten the psychological need that drove him abroad, but he found much else in the essential "gesture" of Spain that nourished his political development: the village spirit of communalism; that skepticism and defiant individualism of the writer Pio Bajora; and the Spanish instinct for "lo flamenco," a principle of life that resembled Thoreau's distinction between "getting a living" as a means and the joys of simple, spontaneous "living" as an end in itself. In the twenties Dos Passos could look to Spain as a land of freedom and agrarian anarchism. But as Spain itself succumbed to social conflict in the thirties, he was forced to turn to American colonial history as the seemingly last incorruptible idyl of decentralized, pre-industrial life. As a historian he found in the American past what he once thought he had found in the Spanish present: a healthy tradition of dissent (Thomas Paine), a legacy of libertarian tolerance (Roger Williams), and an agrarian philosophy of local self-government (Thomas Jefferson).

Dos Passos's rebellion against the authority of his father and his attraction to the idea of anarchism help explain the ironies of his political career. But these themes scarcely illuminate the nature of American society against which the novelist defined his political self. The psychological analysis tells us more about Dos Passos's relationship with his family than why he arrived at his peculiar social philosophy. The same is true of the anarchist strain in his thought, which is something of a natural moral position that tells us more about his personal character than about his political convictions. We must be wary of an explanation by childhood determinants which leaves no room for the intellectual development of Dos Passos's political mind and thought. His anarchism can easily be reduced to an adolescent instinct, his conservatism to infantile regression. We may grant the dialectical tension between authority and rebellion, but to do justice to Dos Passos's social thought we need to go beyond psychology and examine both his early theory of history and the problems of modern society that he perceived but could not resolve. Such an exercise may help us understand Dos Passos not as a radical activist who became a conservative apologist but as a conservative who became what he always was.

Visions of Chaos: Dos Passos's Philosophy of History

When communist intellectuals praised *U.S.A.* as the highest expression of socialist realism they were either politically desperate or philosophically dumb. Given the crude examples of what passed for "proletarian" literature in the thirties, we cannot blame communists for seeking a first-rate novelist. Yet it is significant that no American Marxist literary critic discerned the un-Marxist premises upon which Dos Passos structured his approach to reality and history in *U.S.A.*[36] Critics did complain about the absence of a sustained class conflict élan, but much else was missing. Above all, there was no coherent philosophy of history, no vision of the meaning of events, and thus no drama of promise. An examination of the implicit philosophical and aesthetic assumptions underlying *U.S.A.* should reveal why Dos Passos's mind and temperament remained alien to Marxism.

In 1928, about the time he began work on the first volume of *U.S.A.*, Dos Passos was formulating his credo of literary art as a mode of historical understanding. The true function of the writer was that of a "sort of second-class historian of the age he lives in," an artist who is "able to build reality more nearly out of his factual experience than a plain biographer can." There were several reasons why Dos Passos believed that it was possible for him, as a novelist, to write history. First of all, the reality of the past could be reconstructed not by scavenging through historical archives but by recapturing its language. "The mind of a generation is its speech," Dos Passos wrote in the 1932 introduction to *Three Soldiers*. In the preface to *U.S.A.* the meaning of America is identified with American speech, and the trilogy itself proceeds to expose the use and abuse of words, the corruption of language that results in a nation's self-deception. The dual task of the novelist-historian is to penetrate the social reality obfuscated by banal rhetoric, thereby overcoming the lies and illusions of an age by employing fresh, inspiring language that represents reality as it really is. With this mimetic function, a novelist not only perceives history but makes it. "A writer who writes straight is the architect of history." Furthermore, the best history is usually produced by an author who has participated in the events about which he writes. When Trotsky's *History of the Russian Revolution* was published in 1932, Dos Passos suggested that one would have to go back to Thucydides "to find anything like the sort of narrative whose facts, explanations and political convictions are welded into granite by the hot and clear intelligence of a man who's accustomed to being an actor as well as an observer of events. That's what history ought to be. Classical in the best sense."

Could Dos Passos do for 1919 what Trotsky had done for 1917? Clearly he shared Trotsky's literary attitude toward history and society. From Dos Passos's naturalistic perspective, social forces predominate but society itself has no essence, no meaning beyond experience. Having no nature, it has only its past. And since history is the totality of human events and society the totality of human activities, we can comprehend the social organism only by telling its history. "The writer's business," Dos Passos declared in response to a 1932 *Modern Quarterly* questionnaire, "is to justify God's way to man as Milton said. For God read society, or history."[37]

He said this after he had completed *1919* and was starting the third volume of *U.S.A.*, *The Big Money*. Yet Dos Passos himself could neither justify nor explain the ways of history to his fellow man. The historical dimension, to be sure, emerges in U.S.A. both as a structural device and as a mode of comprehension. In the trilogy that covers the years between the turn of the century and the economic crash of 1929, Dos Passos develops from youth to adulthood the lives of a number of characters, each swept along by the stream of events headlined in the "Newsreel" sections. History like society becomes the protagonist. In the biographical sketches it is often the ironic chorus of conscience, the voices of Debs, La Follette, Veblen, and John Reed. In the biographies, however, history is all memory, studies of moral heroes who are actually noble losers, "masterless" men who, though not deceived by society, have been defeated by the crushing might of historical events. Their lives suggest that the locus of historical force and energy does not lie in men—men have only "words against power / SUPER POWER." Dos Passos renders the human mind and will subordinate to external forces so that good men and bad, Joe Williams and J. Ward Moorehouse, cannot ultimately be regarded as authors of their actions.

This deterministic philosophy of history pervading U.S.A. differs from Marxism in several respects. For one thing, U.S.A. denies both freedom and progress. Man cannot liberate himself; instead his destiny has been foreordained by a betrayed past and a chaotic present. In U.S.A. humanity is condemned rather than invested with a redemptive purpose. In Marxism, on the other hand, man is determined by history but he is also the maker of history, the homo faber who overcomes alienation through the self-actualizing activity of human labor. Marx, of course, was hopelessly ambiguous on the question of determinism and freedom; but whether he chose to stress the inexorability of history or the activities of man, he clearly believed that fate and will both meant progress and ultimate freedom. Dos Passos, in contrast, could not see truth, rationality, and freedom developing out of the sequence of temporal events. Marx advised radical man to draw his "poetry" from the future, but Dos Passos's moral orientation is clearly retrospective.

The novelist confounded liberals as well as radicals by drawing an ideological connection between the immigrant anarchists Sacco and Vanzetti and the immigrant "founders of the Massachusetts" who landed at Plymouth Rock. To locate freedom in the American past, to suggest that at one time Americans were truly free, made no sense to those who accepted either the progressive or the Marxist interpretation of history. Underlying the eloquent rage of *U.S.A.* is a conservative desire to restore what contemporary radicals wanted to transcend. "We stand on quicksand," the "Camera Eye" speculates, until modern man is able to "ponder the course of history and what leverage might pry the owners loose from power and bring back (I too Walt Whitman) our storybook democracy." Unable to see the fulfillment of a historical mission in the working class, Dos Passos could only see history as a modern Cato. The country has been conquered by "strangers" who have infiltrated the American Garden and "cut down the woods for pulp and turned our pleasant cities into slums and sweated the wealth out of our people." History itself has been captured by alien elements. It is an insidious power without justification or even vengeance, an inscrutable force unleashed by a mysterious "they" against an unidentified "we." Dos Passos's vague but passionate conspiratorial view of history denied human events a moral teleology. The epistemological dread lies in his honest inability to locate the real source of evil or oppression. Hence the almost "paranoiac"[38] response to the Sacco and Vanzetti execution: "they have clubbed us off the streets / we are beaten / all right we are two nations."

The polar imagery of the "two nations" implies conflict, yet *U.S.A.* is more naturalistic than Marxist, more disposed to record the social history of alienation than to conceive the drama of history as following an upward movement of consciousness. The denial of a redemptive *telos*, of an unfolding unity behind the diversity of events, Dos Passos achieved through his brilliant stylistic innovations. The novelist had been influenced by the montage experiments of film directors like David W. Griffith and Sergei

Eisenstein, and by the Italian Futurists and French poets who adopted from Cubist painters the idea of "simultaneity"—the effort to "produce something that stood off the page."[39] Borrowing the techniques of the filmmaker and painter, Dos Passos strove to represent his vision of reality and, further, to enable the reader to encounter it as an immediate personal experience.

Four interrelated devices were used to produce this effect: "Newsreel" sections that chronicled the irrationalities of world events; biographies of contemporary historical figures, mostly studies in political defeat or economic and technical success at the cost of moral failure or the loss of independence; personal lyrical impressions of the "Camera Eye," the broken consciousness of the author himself; and segmented narratives of twelve representative characters from almost all social levels whose lives overlap and tie together a collective portrait of American society that spanned three decades of American social history. The biographies are commentaries upon the impersonal forces of social organization that have rendered all Dos Passos's heroes victims of history; the fleeting, disjointed impressions of the "Newsreels" convey the discontinuity of historical experience; the narratives treat individual characters as fragments of a collective consciousness so alienated it cannot experience its own alienation; and the "Camera Eye," the one vehicle through which consciousness rises to social knowledge, expresses a growing realization of the incoherence and estrangement of the self, the loss of identity that renders man faceless—"an unidentified stranger / destination unknown / hat pulled down over the   has he any   face?"

With these stylistic devices Dos Passos found a framework to hold together a subject too vast for the traditional forms of the novel. The creation of a new genre that held the artistic possibility of representing both the reality of society and the power of history presented Dos Passos with a problem of definition. After completing the final volume of the trilogy he attempted to discover a category that would best describe the potent literary object he had wrought. He came up with the definition of "chronicle." A literary scheme that can begin and end anywhere, a chronicle is not so much a narrative as an impression. It is, in Dos Passos's hands, the method of measured disarray, a device that enabled him to capture the disjointed, fragmented nature of society and the random, indeterminate nature of history:

A chronicler has to use the stories people tell him about themselves, all the little dramas in other people's lives he gets glimpses of without knowing just what went before or just what will come after, the fragments of talk he overhears in the subway or on a streetcar, the letter he picks up on the street addressed by one unknown character to another, the words on a scrap of paper found in a trashbasket, the occasional vistas of reality he can pick out of the mechanical diction of a newspaper report.[40]

The essential disconnectedness of Dos Passos's subject suggests the possibilities of *U.S.A.* as a work of art and its limitations as a radical work of historical literature. Benedetto Croce's familiar distinction between history and chronicle may be useful here: The historian attempts to penetrate the core of events by entering into history and reliving in his own mind the experiences of the past; the chronicler treats his materials as inert, empty of determinate content and thus devoid of self-actualizing interpretive potential, like Dos Passos's "scrap of paper found in a trashbasket." History, observed Croce, "is principally an act of thought, chronicle an act of will." *U.S.A.* may be regarded as more willed than understood, for Dos Passos was determined to arrange a panorama of utterances and gestures the total meaning of which he did not pretend to comprehend. In this audacious literary experiment the choice of chronicle was proper and perhaps inevitable. No other method could have so deadened the human dimension of history while animating its naturalistic forces. The anti-naturalist Croce believed that two different "spiritual attitudes" distinguished the historian and the chronicler: the former regards characters and events as alive because their meanings "vibrate in the historian's mind"; the latter regards characters and events as relics because he makes no attempt to understand their ultimate significance. Hence, "History is living chronicle, chronicle is dead history."[41]

History becomes chronicle in *U.S.A.* because Dos Passos dissociates himself from the very characters he has created. He cannot enter their lives and experience their thoughts in the Crocean sense, because they themselves are hardly conscious of the meaning of historical events. Writing about a society that was spiritually dying, Dos Passos was thus forced, as Croce might have expected, to record and describe rather than analyze and explain. Thus *U.S.A.* violates the two canons of Marxist theory. It is neither guided by a principle of historical explanation nor inspired by a vision of historical meaning. The pattern of causality is never revealed in the random sequence of the story. Instead history unfolds as a kind of indeterminate determinism, a series of happenings that can be told without explicit interpretation, told only through the disconnected flashes of newspaper headlines. There is no causal order of understanding behind the disorder of events. What happens, happens.

It was Jean-Paul Sartre, I believe, who first discerned the epistemological implications of Dos Passos's work. Reviewing *1919* in the *Nouvelle Revue Française* in 1938, the French philospher concluded his metaphysical essay with the highest compliment: "I regard Dos Passos as the greatest writer of our time." Sartre regarded Dos Passos as superior to even Faulkner or Kafka because the author of *1919* was bold enough to relate the problem of historical time to the problem of collective consciousness. Dos Passos's idea of "narrating means adding," Sartre observed, the complication of each irreducible, isolated event, "a gleaming solitary thing that does not flow from anything else, but suddenly arises to join other things." Our bewildering impression of an inchoate present, where everything develops and nothing relates, also affects our memory of the past. By imposing upon the reader an unsettling impression of the "indeterminacy of detail," Dos Passos succeeds in expressing what he himself cannot explain—the lawless nature of historical events. And since the present is the continuation of an "irremedial" past, history is not hope but fate. Sartre found Dos Passos's vision aesthetically exciting but psychologically almost unbearable. "Close your eyes and try to remember it *that way*," he stated in reference to the inanimate, petrified lives of Dos Passos's characters. "You will stifle. It is this unrelieved stifling that Dos Passos wanted to express. In capitalist society, men do not have lives, they have only destinies."[42]

In *U.S.A.* Dos Passos's historical perspective is the totality of chaos, a vision that enabled him to "comment on" history but not necessarily to write it.[43] As a novelist Dos Passos avoided narrating historically and allowed his great work to unfold without any ordering principle based upon the assumption of causality. The juxtaposition of the Joycean "Camera Eye" amid the "Newsreels," biographies, and narratives suggests that the inner eye of the author cannot perceive the meaning of history because it sees only the effects of causeless events ("if not why not? walking the streets rolling on your bed eyes sting from peeling the speculative onion of doubt"). The surrealistic quality in *U.S.A.* as well as in Kafka's novels serves to reinforce the impression that nothing that happens in history has any discernible cause. Without some feeling that events have an explanation we have no capacity to comprehend experience. The historical implications of *U.S.A.* negate the idea of history itself. For if the problem of history is the problem of consciousness, the problem of consciousness is the problem of causal understanding. Dos Passos was too honest a writer to resort to an act of faith to overcome either of these problems. The Joycean nightmare quality in Dos Passos's sense of history also lies in his unwillingness to accept completely either one of two "awakening" resolutions: the Marxist view of causality without consciousness, or the existentialist view of consciousness without causality.* One violated freedom, the other denied meaning. In

---

* Marxists regarded Joyce's cry—"History is a nightmare from which I am trying to awake"—with much the same scorn they expressed toward Eliot's "Prufrock": the whimper of bourgeois decadence. But Dos Passos had been

U.S.A. Dos Passos does allow the denial of both these values to prevail, and by artfully avoiding the necessity of causality, he offers us a history that can be experienced but not comprehended. This vision of chaos, however, reveals a deeper, personal quest for order and meaning. Dos Passos desired, above all, to believe and affirm, to do what Veblen was incapable of—get his "mouth around the essential yes."

The Prism of Sociology: Durkheim, Veblen, Weber

"A satirist," stated Dos Passos in reference to the artist George Grosz, "is a man whose flesh creeps so at the ugly and the savage and the incongruous aspects of society that he has to express them as brutally and nakedly as possible to get relief."[44] In responding to the incongruities of modern society in his novels, Dos Passos was also refracting some of the major theoretical problems that had occupied many profound social thinkers in Europe and America. The novelist's deep concern for the relationship of personality to institutions, the fate of autonomy and individuality in the mass society of the modern city, and the institutionalization of life and labor in the social structure of industrial civilization made him an unrecognized intellectual comrade of sociologists like Thorstein Veblen, Charles Cooley, Émile Durkheim, Max Weber, Georg Simmel, and Werner Sombart. With the exception of Veblen's writings, Dos Passos was unfamiliar with contemporary sociology. Yet his novels seem to bear out Ezra Pound's dictum that the writer is an "antenna" who senses the problems of modern society even before he fully understands them. Dos Passos's writings also reflect the same concern of many contemporary sociologists for the emotional warmth of the older pre-industrial

---

deeply impressed by Joyce's sense of historical consciousness as the brutality of existence that is at once futile and unintelligible. *Ulysses* is a "classic," he wrote in 1932, ". . . a profound study of the human animal and its environment at the height of capitalist culture. It deserves the respect that a scientific work on a similar theme would get." (Dos Passos to Bennett Cerf, June 1, 1932, Cerf Papers, Butler Library, Columbia University.)

values. The novelist never read Cooley, but *Manhattan Transfer* dramatizes aesthetically the pathos or urban *Angst* as Cooley had once depicted the pattern of "discontinuous lives" in metropolitan America.[45] The themes that emerge in Dos Passos's works have an amazing sociological prescience—alienation, estrangement, separation, privatization, anonymity, disaffection, isolation, and withdrawal. All these ideas have long since passed into the standard vocabulary of social criticism, but it is significant that a half century ago Dos Passos occupied himself with themes similar to those that troubled the social philosopher. Appropriately, *U.S.A.* begins and ends as a commentary upon the homelessness of the human spirit in modern society. The lonely, solitary "young man," given the name "Vag" at the conclusion of the trilogy, walks the "night streets" of America as a deracinated exile: "No job, no woman, no house, no city."

It is in the sociological ramifications of Dos Passos's work that one most readily discerns the conservative sensibility underlying it. At the basis of his social philosophy is the desire to preserve or restore the old values of his idealized America, the country of "our fathers." Even his anarchistic rebellion against authority and the structure of power reveals a deeper quest for the need of authority and moral order. We may appreciate this essentially conservative quest if we examine briefly in light of sociological theory Dos Passos's two city novels, *Manhattan Transfer* and especially *Streets of Night*, perhaps the most overlooked and least discussed of all Dos Passos's works of fiction.

The better-known *Manhattan Transfer* opens with a description of people pouring off a ferryboat down the sluiceway into a strange city and immediately asking directions ("men and women press through the manuresmelling wooden tunnel of the ferryhouse, crushed and jostled like apples fed down a chute into a press"). What Dos Passos senses is a condition that develops when large numbers of people are thrown with relative suddenness into an environment where there are no group ties resting upon traditional customs and standards. As a symbol, the city is an independent power set over and apart from individuals, an external force which Dos Passos depicts, in some of his chapter titles, as a kind of mechanical rhythm that imposes itself upon the inhabitants. Ironically, the new urban environment appears to be free and open and full of promises, but it is also destabilizing, since there are no fixed ethical principles or cultural goals. In the mass pictorial ugliness of *Manhattan Transfer* we find the condition of anomie that Durkheim had introduced to sociological thought. Technically anomie means the absence of norms, an ethical dizziness that victimizes the central character, Jimmy Herf, who is trying to find in motion what has been lost in space:

And he walks round blocks and blocks looking for the door of the humming tinsel windowed skyscraper, round blocks and blocks and still no door. Everytime he closes his eyes the dream has hold of him, everytime he stops arguing audibly with himself in pompous reasonable phrases the dream has hold of him. Young man to save your sanity you've got to do one of two things. . . . Please mister where's the door to the building? Round the block? Just round the block . . . one of two unalienable alternatives: go away in a dirty soft shirt or stay in a clean Arrow collar. But what's the use of spending your whole life fleeing the City of Destruction? What about your unalienable right, Thirteen Provinces? His mind unreeling phrases, he walks on doggedly. There's nowhere in particular he wants to go. If only I still had faith in words.

The novel's final two lines express succinctly the total loss of orientation, that feeling people have when they sense that they are no longer "getting anywhere" (Durkheim). Herf hitches a ride from a driver, who asks, "How fur ye going?"

"I dunno . . . Pretty far."

Dos Passos's early characters are victimized by external social pressures, as the novelist's critics have stressed; they also suffer from internal malaise, an unfocused longing for some lost ideal or faith that will restore wholeness and purpose. In Durkheim's analysis of the tensions between values and structural integration, the sense of confusion and frustration that results from the loss of moral direction reaches its most desperate expression in the act of

suicide. The phenomenon of suicide is a consequence of the oppression of a static society, as radicals maintain, but even more a
result of the very absence of discipline and restraint that results
from change itself, a state of normlessness caused by the lack of
internalized values that in turn derive from external sources of
moral power and authority. Without discipline, Durkheim observed, human desires and passions become unlimited, and man
sets out in a desperate search for the impossible.[46]

The disease of anomie afflicts several of Dos Passos's characters;
it drives David Wendall, the precocious, Prufrock-like student in
Streets of Night, to the ultimate act of self-annihilation. Having
rebelled against his father's authority, Wenny finds himself in a
vacuum of non-resistance, free to do anything he wants but not
knowing what it is he wants to do. "Before I came to college I
spent my time dreaming, and now I spend it gabbing about my
dreams that have died and begun to stink. Why the only genuine
thing I ever did in my life was get drunk, and I haven't done that
often."

A creature of desire, he has no knowledge of the desirable. The
result is, as Durkheim could have predicted, moral nausea: "To
be free of this sickness of desire. I must break down my fear. Of
what, of what?"

Just before his suicide he thinks of the urge for oblivion swelling
within him as bringing the end of social disequilibrium and the
cessation of personal desire. Death is a release, a quiescence found
in the return to the primordial unity of the pre-anomic spiritual
womb:

I have nerve enough for this suicide, why not for the rest, for walking
with Nan down streets unaccountable and dark between blind walls
that tremble with the roar of engines, for her seagray eyes in my eyes,
her lips, the sweetish fatty smell of Ellen's lips. Maybe death's all that,
sinking into the body of a dark woman, with proud cold thighs, hair
black, black.

The conservative sociological themes of *Manhattan Transfer*
and *Streets of Night* yield in *U.S.A.* to what appears to be a radical

vision of hope and possibility. The ideological inspiration of the greatest of Dos Passos's works came from the economist and sociologist Thorstein Veblen. In the twenties Dos Passos was "very much interested in the 'Technocrats' . . . and was certainly very much influenced by my reading of Veblen";[47] and while working on U.S.A. he also compiled a folder of "Vebleniana" and wrote to several scholars and government officials who once had been students of the eccentric professor.[48] Of all the biographical sketches in U.S.A., Veblen received the most extended and sympathetic treatment. Clearly Dos Passos could identify with the estranged Norwegian immigrant's son, the intellectual who asked "too many questions" and "couldn't get his mouth around the essential yes." The great American social scientist, Dos Passos wrote in U.S.A.,

> established a new diagram of a society dominated
> by monopoly capital,
>   etched in irony
>   the sabotage of production by business,
>   the sabotage of life by blind need for money
> profits,
>   pointed out the alternatives: a warlike society
> strangled by the bureaucracies of the monopolies forced
> by the law of diminishing returns to grind down more
> and more the common man for profits,
>   or a new matter-of-fact commonsense society dominated
> by the needs of the men and women who did the work and
> the incredibly vast possibilities for peace and plenty
> offered by the progress of technology.

If there is a scheme of social conflict in U.S.A. it is not labor against capital but the Veblenian cleavage of industry against business. Beginning with the trilogy, all of Dos Passos's novels reveal an admiration for the technician and workman, for the craftsman and mechanic, for those who are close to the real productive operations of society. Part of Dos Passos's literary mission was to explore the precarious status of the independent artisan in industrial society. "To tell truly," he wrote in 1934, "about the relation between men and machines and to describe the machine worker are among the most important tasks before the novelist today."[49] Dos Passos's attitude toward various forms of human labor derived from a moral rather than a class distinction. Whether proletariat or professional, his fictional heroes were more interested in productivity than profit, guided by what Veblen called the "instinct of workmanship." Opposed to the worthy doers and makers stood the businessman, the antagonist who haunts the pages of Veblen's sociological treatises. With pecuniary gain as his sole objective, the businessman manipulates the economic levers of power and conspires against the productive instruments of the industrial system.

The novel's central character, J. Ward Moorehouse, sustains this theme from beginning to end. He is, as befits a Veblenesque satire, "etched in irony." We are repelled not so much by what he does but by the nature of the character that performs the deed, the banality of thought behind the act. Moorehouse's rise to wealth makes a mockery out of the Protestant ethic. "By gum, I can do it!" thinks Moorehouse, who wants to keep himself "clean for the girl he was going to marry" only to wed a rich, promiscuous older woman to further his career. Born in the late nineteenth century, Moorehouse represents Veblen's "new captain of industry," the salesman who is concerned neither with the "technical conduct" nor the "tangible performance" of the industrial system. He finds no satisfaction working at the Bessemer steel plant. What he aspires to is a public relations program which will create a favorable image of the business community and stimulate more demand for consumer goods. The pleasures of craftsmanship, the joys of laboring upon the materials of nature, do not interest him. Completely removed from the humanizing sources of work, he becomes obsessed with "ideas, plans, stockquotations unrolling in endless tickertape in his head." When his public relations outfit begins to lag in 1916, the advice of his partner does not go unheeded: "Whoever wins, Europe will be economically ruined. This war is America's great opportunity." With a display of patriotic bravado he goes off to Europe as a publicity director for the Red Cross. Peace as well as war brings out in Moorehouse what

Veblen called the "pecuniary calculus." As Paris was celebrating the announcement of the Armistice, "J.W. was preoccupied and wanted to get to a telephone. . . . He must get in touch with his broker."

Through a combination of charm and cupidity Moorehouse achieves success and becomes, in Veblen's words, the "prince and priest" of the business world. He also becomes an institution ("After all J. W. Moorehouse isn't a man, it's a name"). In his skillful characterization of Moorehouse Dos Passos seemed to understand, as did Veblen, the mechanisms and psychology through which the ruling class legitimates itself, dominates the political order, perpetuates its values, and sustains its cultural hegemony. Moorehouse's life was patterned, Dos Passos revealed fifty years later in an interview, after the career of Ivy Lee, the famous publicity agent of the Rockefeller interests.[50] Moorehouse, like Lee, believed he could sell the capitalist system to working class America. "It was the business of the industry to educate the public by carefully planned publicity extending over a term of years," Moorehouse advised. To cement ties between capital and labor he helped establish a labor relations board. Aside from serving as the pacifier of class conflict, Moorehouse is also Veblen's "prehensile" tribal leader who sees himself as the élan vital of the economic system. Dick Savage, Moorehouse's protégé, who, as the name implies, represents the predatory instincts of capitalism, defends the role of his alter ego in the name of progress and civilization. "Whether you like it or not the molding of the public mind is one of the most important things that goes on in this country. If it wasn't for that American business would be in a pretty pickle. . . . It's only through public relations work that business is protected from the wildeyed cranks and demagogues who are always ready to throw a monkeywrench into the industrial machine."

The irony in Savage's speech is as clear as the satire in Dos Passos's portrait. Although Moorehouse and Savage conceive of themselves as the driving force behind the industrial machine, and rationalize their own material interests in the name of higher ideals—the hegemonic phenomenon of ideology—Dos Passos demonstrates, by the third volume, that their propensity to manipulate and "mold" is essentially destructive. They compose the "monkeywrench," or what Veblen called the "saboteurs" of the economy.

If Moorehouse is the villain who conspires against technological rationality, Charley Anderson is the victim who betrays his better self. As a skilled mechanic and aviator, Anderson found satisfaction in his work and tried to remain loyal to his calling. "Hell, I ain't no boss. . . . I belong with the mechanics . . . don't I Bill? You and me, Bill, the mechanics against the world." Yet the lure of lucre was too strong. "I don't know what it is, but I got a kind of feel for the Big Money." Driven by an unanalyzable obsession for the wealth and kitsch of the leisure class, he realizes he is caught and cannot return to his craft. "Aw Christ, I wish I was still tinkering with that damn motor and didn't have to worry about money all the time." The passion for "pecuniary emulation" overcame the instinct of workmanship. Anderson forsook his métier, and in doing so his salvation as well. His drunken smashup at the conclusion of the novel points up what Dos Passos called, in his sketch of Veblen, "the sabotage of life by the blind need for money."

A lesser character, Bill Cermak, Anderson's mechanic, presents an interesting contrast. He is one of the few healthy characters in all of Dos Passos's fiction. A rare specimen in U.S.A., Cermak is happy to remain a worker. He is the hope of Veblen's technocratic dream, the independent craftsman who takes pride in his trade. It is Cermak who, speaking for Dos Passos, perceives that new production methods are divorcing the worker from the use of his skills. The massive industrial machine was causing his men to lead lives of automated desperation. Yet when Cermak complains to Anderson he is told that the "oldtime shop" is obsolete and that from now on every unit must "click like a machine." Protests are futile, for Anderson no longer has the engineer's conscience. He has subordinated the life-enhancing joys of human artifice to the calculus of profits and dividends. The "Big Money" wins.

The conservative restoration leitmotif in *U.S.A.* emerges in minor figures like Cermak, honest, independent workmen who achieve some sense of worth and identity in the production of useful goods. But the modern industrial system displacing Cermak was undermining the moral foundations of society. Dos Passos's transformation from a radical to a conservative becomes more apparent than real when we penetrate to the core of his convictions and discover a rather homely gospel of work ethic. Certainly he had every right, a quarter century later in his introduction to William F. Buckley's *Up from Liberalism*, to assert that the radical ideologies that had earlier influenced him grew out of a basically conservative impulse. "The aim of all the diverse radical movements of that politically fertile period was somehow to restore the dignity of the man who did the work."[51]

Dos Passos's conviction that labor is a source of virtue and salvation is a politically ambiguous proposition that contains radical as well as conservative implications. Marx also desired to restore dignity and value to the life of labor. Indeed the theme of the alienation of the worker under industrial capitalism was shared alike by Marx, Veblen, and Dos Passos. The separation of the worker from the products and the processes of labor, the division of labor and isolation of man from fellow man, the reification of the commodity fetish, and the "thingification" of life were phenomena that Dos Passos saw developing everywhere in industrial society. "Millions of men," he wrote in 1916, "perform labor narrow and stultifying even under the best conditions, bound in the traces of mechanical industry, without ever a chance of self-expression, except in the hectic pleasures of suffocating life in the cities." The realization of the "fullness of man," he protested, was being thwarted by "the filthy darkness of meaningless labor," and man himself was being deceived by the fetish of conspicuous consumption, ensnared by "a silly claptrap of unnecessary luxuries, a clutter of inessentials which has been the great force to smother the arts of life and the arts of creation."[52] A decade later, in *U.S.A.*, he used the Joycean device of fusing words together to express in tonal reverberation the alienating nature of work on the assembly line:

(fifteen minutes for lunch, three minutes to go to the toilet, the Taylorized speedup everywhere, reach under, adjust washer, screw down bolt, shove in cotterpin, reachunder, adjustwasher, screwdownbolt, reachunderadjustscrewdownreachunderadjust until every ounce of life was sucked off into production and at night the workmen went home grey shaking husks)

Marx, Veblen, and Dos Passos all grappled with the problem of labor alienation in modern society. Yet their respective solutions are profoundly incompatible. Marx accepted industrialism as historically necessary and progressive, and Veblen saw in the "discipline of the machine" the salutary development of the empirical habit of mind. For Marx, industrialism created the material for revolution in the proletariat; for Veblen, it nurtured the mentality for revolution in the scientist and engineer. Although Veblen remained skeptical of Marx's Hegelian philosophy and his doctrine of class consciousness, he agreed that man can transform society by acting upon nature through "industry," which Marx called, in a fit of technological rapture, "the open book of man's essential powers."[53] It is here, where Marx and Veblen come together to embrace technology, that Dos Passos departs to uphold humanity. The novelist could never accept the redemptive claims of science and engineering. The Industrial Revolution was the "bastard of science," he protested in 1916. A machine culture enables man to control nature, but it is dumb to all other human needs. Science defines knowledge as power while leaving the more important question of wisdom and happiness unanswered. As a method or instrument science was a limited tool with which to realize human ideals. In *U.S.A.* Luther Burbank, "The Plant Wizard" who experimented with new hybrids, "died / puzzled" when he saw an ungrateful society "cash in on Natural Selection" while rejecting Darwin. And Frederick Winslow Taylor, the efficiency genius who died "with his watch in his hand," is less the master of his scientific American plan than its victim.[54] Not only was science powerless to oppose the superstitions of society and challenge the hegemony of the ruling class, it dehumanized the spirit by objectifying value. As a positivistic mode of analysis that breaks everything down into component parts, science destroys feeling and imagination. Truth to Dos Passos could never be simply a matter of experimentation, nor could it be a Marxist exercise in praxis. As a humanist he believed with Kant that knowledge of the objective world depended upon the moral health of the knowing subject:

It is possible that, from over-preoccupation with what is at the other end of our telescopes and microscopes, we have lost our true sense of proportion. In learning the habits of the cells of man's epidermis, it is easy to forget his body as a unit. In the last analysis, the universe is but as we see it, all relative to the sense perceptions of the body. In this consuming interest in science, in knowledge of the exterior, in the tabulation of fact, haven't we forgotten the *Know thyself* of the Greeks?[55]

Dos Passos's rejection of scientific knowledge and his resistance to industrialism are further evidence of the basic conservatism that underlies his early writings.[56] The critical sting of Veblen's sociology served the radical purpose of enabling Dos Passos to "put the acid test to existing institutions, and to strip the veils off them"— the role he so admired in the anarchist novelist Pio Bajora.[57] Without a coherent and optimistic analysis of society and history, however, *U.S.A.* confesses a radical agony while concealing a conservative sensibility. Indeed his fear of large-scale organizations suggests that his quarrel was not so much with entrepreneurial capitalism as with the advent of industrial corporatism. The late stages of capitalist development, which Marxists could welcome because they were supposedly "contradictory," and which Veblen could even smile upon because of his belief that science would ultimately triumph over superstition, seemed to Dos Passos a permanent condition without a radical solution.

It is this foreboding sense of historical pessimism that makes

Dos Passos closer to Weber than to Marx or Veblen. Later the novelist would attack government despotism and trade union tyranny as he became more aware of the problem that had been the central focus of Weber's sociology—the problem of bureaucracy. From Weber's perspective, however, even Dos Passos's respect for the entrepreneurial capitalism of an earlier age represented a false nostalgia. For once the acquisitive activities of enterprise are loosed from the bonds of tradition, capitalism has no inherent limits and leads inevitably to larger and larger units of organization. Dos Passos would later acknowledge that "man in society can, I think, be most aptly described as an institutionbuilding animal. He builds institutions the way the ants build hills."[58] In U.S.A. he glimpsed but did not fully grasp the implications of what Weber called "rationalization"—the tendency of capitalism to overcome its own irrational stresses and submit to hierarchical structures of authority, indeed the tendency of all aspects of modern life, government and labor as well as business, to become systematized as they grow into vast, petrifying institutions. There is in U.S.A., in the portraits of Henry Ford, Luther Burbank, Thomas Edison, and particularly the scientist Charles Steinmetz (who "was the most valuable piece of apparatus General Electric had / until he wore out and died"), the feeling that even Veblen's technological heroes would be unable to cope with the incipient institutions their inventions had wrought. Henry Ford built an automotive empire only to long for "the way it used to be / in the days of horses and buggies." No career ends in happiness and fulfillment. The men of genius or simple craftsmen were either broken by the system or sucked into it. Thus Dos Passos describes, with acute Weberian prescience, the victory of organization over spontaneity, institutions over individuality, and ultimately the domination of life by the administration of life.

Unlike Weber, however, Dos Passos stubbornly refused to accept large-scale institutions as necessary and inevitable. (Nor would he be able to accept Burnham's managerialism as an answer to Marxism.) The novelist who had once declared that "overorganization is death" wanted to strip all institutions of their veils. But of the veil that had changed capitalism from a religious impulse to a secular institution, Weber could only say, "Destiny has transformed this veil into a cast-iron shell."[59] For the rest of his life Dos Passos would struggle to break out of that very feature of modern society that Marx and Veblen had failed to anticipate and that Weber had reconciled himself to in order to live without illusions—the "iron cage" of bureaucracy.

CHAPTER 3

The Quest for Transcendence: Will Herberg

The intellectually gifted Jew is in a peculiarly fortunate position in respect of this requisite immunity from the inhibitions of intellectual quietism. But he can come in for such immunity only at the cost of losing his secure place in the scheme of conventions into which he has been born, and at the cost, also, of finding no similarly secure place in that scheme of gentile conventions into which he is thrown. For him as for other men in the like case, the skepticism that goes to make him an effectual factor in the increase and diffusion of knowledge among men involves a loss of that peace of mind that is the birthright of the safe and sane quietist. He becomes a disturber of the intellectual peace, but only at the cost of becoming an intellectual wayfaring man, a wanderer in the intellectual no-man's land, seeking another place to rest, farther along the road, somewhere over the horizon. They are neither a complaisant nor a contented lot, these aliens of the uneasy feet.

THORSTEIN VEBLEN, 1919

The Seeker as Radical

"The terrible danger to explorers," Dos Passos had advised the *New Masses*, "is that they always find what they are looking for. . . . I want an expedition that will find out what it's not looking for."[1] To the young Will Herberg such advice would have been incomprehensible. Communism may have been a political adventure and a social "experiment" to Old Left intellectuals like Eastman and Dos Passos. To Herberg it was, above all else, an *idée maîtresse*.

Herberg's early radicalism and his later conversion to conservatism derived from an inner need so intense that it can only be described as religious in nature. In Herberg's odyssey the tendencies of self-surrender and self-transcendence, the need to believe in order to know, remain characteristic. Eastman also embraced Marxism to overcome the pains of religious doubt and thereby ease the Blakean anguish of the modern skeptic—"The Tree of Knowledge has killed the Tree of Life." Yet Eastman could believe in no systematic philosophy save the "method" of science, and when he abandoned communism his behavior was like that of an empiricist dropping a hypothesis into the wastebasket. Eastman was also content to live the rest of his life a gay agnostic, as William Buckley was to discover. Not so Herberg. The epitaph "The God That Failed" takes on literal meaning in Herberg's career. Of the four thinkers examined in this study, Herberg alone seemed to be born to live for belief, to commit himself completely to a search for transcendent truth. Because his commitment to communism was far more intense than that of Eastman and Dos Passos, his final break and disillusionment were more painful and reflective, and his ultimate critique more searching and illuminating.

Will Herberg was born in New York City in 1909, the son of Hyman Lewis Herberg and Sarah Wolkov, Russian immigrants who came to America near the turn of the century, bringing with them the cultural passions of the Russian intelligentsia class—critical thinkers in a barbarous society. His father had been trained in science and engineering at the University of St. Petersburg and his mother had been a gymnastics instructor in a lyceum. His father died when Herberg was ten, a crucial age for any youth, and Herberg was raised by a remarkable mother who believed deeply in self-education. Sarah Herberg shared her husband's "passionate atheism," and, like him, had "contempt" for the American public school system. Herberg's real education took place at the kitchen table of an apartment in a lower middle class Jewish neighborhood in Brooklyn. By the time he was a teen-ager Herberg knew Latin, Greek, French, German, and Russian. To make ends meet at home he tutored fellow high school students. He was graduated from high school at sixteen, attended Columbia University, where he studied history and philosophy for an AB degree in 1928, stayed on at Columbia for an MA in 1928 and a PhD in 1932. His doctoral dissertation in philosophy was on "Philosophy of Science and Scientific Philosophy."[2]

Precocious, learned, versatile, Herberg brought to radical politics a theoretical sophistication that helped elevate American Marxism as an intellectual proposition. He also brought a combative intellect that other partisans had to reckon with, often at their peril. Sidney Hook, who affectionately referred to Herberg as "the Rabbi," once introduced him to an audience as an ideologue who had been born with "a political spoon in his mouth." "I remember him," Hook stated, "when he was perhaps the most articulate and the most dialectic representative of a political point of view, to the point where even those who disagreed with him acknowledged that if he wanted to find an argument for a position Will Herberg would find the argument." Bertram D. Wolfe, another former communist who had been a close friend and political associate of Herberg's in the thirties, recalls his old comrade as an "omnivorous reader" who approached communism as an encyclopedist approached ideas. To learn about everything there is to know, and to bring the totality of knowledge under a rational scheme of order, this was Herberg's daily mission. Years later, when Herberg began to develop the foundations of his own theological conservatism, his critics found him a hopeless moralist whose cosmic meditations could not be refuted by historical knowledge. "To polemicize against Herberg," Irving Howe quipped, "is somewhat like depreciating a man who has just delivered a solemn lecture against sin; the innocent and malicious alike may conclude that one is for sin."[3]

Central to an understanding of the political and spiritual odyssey of Herberg is the condition of the Jewish intellectual in America. Religion defines the possibilities of being a person in America, Herberg would later observe in *Protestant, Catholic, Jew* (1955). There the problem of Jewish identity would be seen as a clash of opposing forces: first in the tripartite encounter of Sephardic, German, and East European cultures, then in the American conflict of generations that separated the ghetto-spawned working classes of the twenties and thirties from the middle class professionals of the forties and fifties. Herberg became deeply impressed with the immigrant historian Marcus Hansen's "law" of generations: The second generation immigrants reject their religious and ethnic past for the sake of Americanization, but the third generation grandsons, now thoroughly assimilated, try to "remember" what their fathers tried to "forget" because of the new need for religious identity and social definition. To a certain extent this pattern of rejection and re-embracement characterizes Herberg's own intellectual career, which culminates in his conversion to Judaism. Yet the pressures that account for this pattern are immediate political experience and painful theoretical reflection. When he was a communist in the twenties and thirties, Herberg never deigned to regard religion as anything but an illusion born of the sigh of resignation.[4] As a conservative in the fifties, religion and theology became an inspiration which sprung from *le crise du coeur*.

Marxism and the Challenge of Einstein's Relativity Theory

If Eastman and Dos Passos were more prolific writers, Herberg was more catholic. He came later to admire Jonathan Edwards, the brilliant eighteenth-century theologian; and he made effective use of the most advanced philosophical ideas of the age to support the most ancient religious beliefs. He played a similar role in his early radical years, when he stood in the forefront of modern scientific thought to support unscientific political ideas. Herberg's career, in both its radical and conservative phases, resembles Veblen's description of the Jewish thinker who "becomes a disturber of the intellectual peace," the restless philosophical "wanderer" whose critical skepticism places him in "the vanguard of modern inquiry." Even the work of Freud, which many Marxists dared not assimilate, appeared to Herberg as the acid test of illusions and thus the liberation of modern consciousness. As a radical Jew, Herberg hailed Freud, as he did Marx and Einstein, as a modern prophet. "The world of socialism—to which nothing human is alien and which cherishes every genuine manifestation of the human spirit—lays a wreath of homage on the grave of Sigmund Freud," wrote Herberg in 1939.[5]

Herberg entered the communist movement as a teen-ager. The "passionate atheism" of his parents served him well as a budding exponent of science and scientific philosophy. His academic training helped him make one of the boldest contributions to radical thought—he tried to reconcile Marxism to the new Einsteinian cosmology, the "second scientific revolution" that had gone virtually unnoticed among other left-wing writers in America. In the intellectual history of modern American radicalism, the complex relationship of Einstein and Marx is a missing chapter which every historian seems to have overlooked. The story needs to be told.

Herberg saw natural science as the highest attainment of human culture. Eastman had turned to science as an answer to religious dogma and as a generational weapon. To Eastman, as to Hook and other students of pragmatism, science was a tool of analysis; to Herberg it was more the vessel of truth. For Herberg Charles Darwin had provided the underlying foundation, if not the ultimate philosophy. He saw in the idea of evolution no savage chaos of competition as trumpeted by the Social Darwinists, no simple confirmation of historical materialism as lauded by the "vulgar" Marxists. To Herberg evolution was the metaphysics of naturalism. Darwin's world view had replaced the classical, static, and mechanistic concept of the universe and made man aware of the organic stream of change, process, and development (a perspective foreshadowed, Herberg noted, in the writings of Lyell, LaPlace, and even Kant). After Darwin's great discoveries, no philosophical justification for the existing forms of society could claim permanent ontological status. Social Darwinists could scarcely assert that the ultimate aims of man and nature had been realized in the capitalist stage of history. Yet Darwinism itself, Herberg noted, is incomplete. Although the doctrine of evolution illustrates the inevitability of change and transformation, the principle of natural selection is unilateral, gradualistic, and "hopelessly" undialectical. Darwinism prepared the way for the ultimate triumph of Marxism. Between evolution and revolution lies an essential philosophical concept that escaped British natural science —the critical, self-transforming power of the dialectic.[6]

It was more than a decade before Herberg came to see the quasi-religious dimension embedded in the dialectic that Eastman had exposed in the twenties. He then dismissed Marxism, in a discerning article written in 1943, as a mere secular expression of "Christian mythology." But before he came to this critical juncture, Herberg was one of the most fertile and creative defenders of Marxism as a philosophical proposition and a scientific paradigm, a synthesis that offered mankind the essence of human rationality. He performed this role in 1931, when Nikolai Bukharin, speaking before a thousand delegates at a Moscow conference on Planning Scientific Research, delivered a report on the relationship between science and socialist construction. The address provoked indignation among some liberal scientific intellectuals from the West. They criticized the "crass utilitarianism" of any approach to science that sacrificed the search for truth to the cause of socialism. Herberg in response drew upon Veblen's *Theory of the Leisure Class* and Bukharin's *Historical Materialism* to defend communism against the charge that it was "enchaining" science to a non-empirical enterprise. The quest for truth is the demand of ruling class intellectuals who insist on perpetuating the distinction between "those who think" and "those who do" in order to preserve their own "priestly" function. The demand is a false cultural fetish, not a methodological imperative. Indeed, with the ·abolition of classes, the distinction between manual and mental labor will disappear, theory and practice will be reunited, and the "pretentious academicism" that divorces thought from life will at last be overcome. "With this reconciliation," Herberg said, "science loses its esoteric character and assumes a social-practical aspect."[7]

Herberg could draw upon Marx and Veblen—and even Dewey—to answer the liberal attack upon the communist version of science as applied social reconstruction. Yet the real challenge to Marxist science came from the new philosophies of nature that derived from the collapse of classical mechanics. By the end of the twenties, their primary reference points were Einstein's physics of relativity, Werner Heisenberg's "uncertainty relation," Niels Bohr's "complementarity principle," and Max Planck's "quantum mechanics." The exciting new developments denoted by these terms placed Herberg in a difficult position. Einstein, like Marx and Freud, represented the vanguard of modern consciousness, and his bold contributions to theoretical physics, which revolutionized man's conception of the universe, could hardly be alien to the human spirit. Communist officials, on the other hand, repudiated relativity theory as a threat to the philosophical foundations of Marxism. Thus Herberg found himself almost alone among left-wing intellectuals in America, one of the few Marxist thinkers willing to defy orthodoxy and to attempt to assimilate the latest discoveries in physics with the principle of dialectical materialism.

Herberg expressed bemusement and concern about the publicity accorded the work of James Jeans, Arthur Eddington, and Einstein in the popular press. He took note of this curious development in the first installment of a four-part article published in 1930–1931 in the short-lived communist journal *Revolutionary Age*. Why the sudden "human interest" in the scientific ideas propounded by an esoteric genius like Einstein? The German physicist is "almost a recluse," and his "theories on the nature of time and space and the structure of the universe are as unintelligible to the overwhelming majority of newspaper readers as the lost language of the Etruscans." Herberg could only suspect that the new physics was exploited by the popular press as an answer to Marxism, with the public misled by scientists who experienced a failure of nerve when they were compelled to confront the politically revolutionary implications of scientific materialism and determinism. Herberg was certain that relativity theory, even if it focused on contingencies instead of certainties, could not undermine Marx's "scientific" efforts to revolutionize society.[8] The sovereignty of science as the basic means of comprehending reality remained unscathed. How then account for the "retreat from reason to mysticism" indulged in by contemporary scientists? What indeed was the threat of Einstein and Heisenberg to Marx?

The challenge was—or appeared to be—twofold, epistemological and metaphysical, the problem of knowledge and the nature of reality. Regarding the former, classical Newtonian science held that all physical things are subject to law, that all phenomena are interrelated, and that the universe is fundamentally an intelligible and meaningful unity. New discoveries in microphysics, which demonstrated the impossibility of measuring or predicting traditional concepts of position and momentum, challenged these Newtonian certitudes. Henceforth, electrons and atoms, particles and waves, and the traditional categories of time and space could no longer in any ultimate sense be knowable, because they were ultimately unmeasurable in relation to one another. Scientists could describe either velocity or position accurately, but not both, for the behavior of one affected and distorted the measurement of the other. Without an absolute reference point of observation, the scientific world lost its innocence and awoke to find itself in a bedlam of subjectivity and relativism. This discovery, disturbing enough to liberal humanists, was shattering to Marxists. At least one implication of relativity theory led modern philosophy "back" to idealism, as Herberg was aware.[9] For what one could know about physical objects depended upon what one chose to isolate and observe; and thus the meaning and explanation attributed to objects may not be inherent in physical properties themselves but derived from the mind of the observer. The physical laws of nature had lost their solid character, knowledge had become blurred and ambiguous, and the possibility of scientific certainty seemed to have vanished from the modern mind. By confessing their own limitations, scientists were setting the stage for the revival of idealism and even of "mysticism."

In the second realm, metaphysics, quantum theory also brought about the "crisis of causality." The essence of empirical causality is predictability, implying a predetermined, law-bound behavior in physical matter. Yet causal determinism was overturned when modern scientists rediscovered in the laboratory the shocking claim of the philosopher David Hume—that there may be no real, objective relationship between cause and effect. Infected by this virus of doubt, empirical theorists now chose to speak in terms of "statistical probability." Scientists like Jeans, moreover, discovered that radioactive atoms and subatomic particles had what appeared to be a self-determining life of their own that rendered their behavior unpredictable and hence unexplainable. "The individual atom," observed Arthur Koestler, "seemed to experience freedom at least in the sense that no explanation of its behavior was possible in the language of physics."[10] The denial of causality had serious implications for Marxism, for when a scientist admits that he finds he can assign no discernible cause to the behavior of things, the concept of causality is undermined in other fields of knowledge that touch upon Marxism—economics, sociology, and, above all, history. As we saw in discussing Dos Passos's U.S.A., the ability to understand the world, not to mention "predicting" its future development, is linked to the idea of cause and effect, the assurance that events have an intelligible explanation and that experience is comprehensible. Small wonder that unlearned communists recoiled from Einstein's blackboard like seventeenth-century Jesuits before Galileo's telescope. The appeal of scientific Marxism to the Old Left lay in its predictive utility. Marxism supposedly enabled one to anticipate as well as analyze, foretell as well as explain.[11] Thus the principle of indeterminate causality posed a direct threat to the Marxist principle of historical inevitability. Science, it seemed, had overtaken history.

With the new physics, space, time, causality, and the notion of fixed material substances suffered a loss of philosophical dignity and scientific status. Herberg accepted the challenge of the new cosmology ushered in by the "second revolution" in physical science. Such discoveries did not mean that the older hope of achieving perfect objectivity and total knowledge had come to an end. On the contrary, the quest for the unity of objective reality and human knowledge had taken another departure. The real question was whether the new universe of Einstein had rendered obsolete the old world view of Marx. In attempting to reconcile Einstein and Marx, Herberg had less difficulty with the problem of causality than with the problem of material reality. In the first instance he could cite the authority of Einstein himself and demonstrate that relativity theory did not have the same implications as the quantum theory elaborated by Heisenberg and Bohr. Notwithstanding new discoveries in intra-atomic behavior, Einstein still believed in the possibility of a universal causal law inherent in the nature of matter, even though the human mind had yet to penetrate its mystery. Herberg could demonstrate that even the genius who had done so much to make man aware of the limitations of scientific knowledge was himself unsatisfied with the incomplete and tentative quality of his investigations. To reduce cause-effect relations to statistical approximations is to mistake expectations for explanations. The true aim of science, Herberg quoted Einstein as saying, "is describing the things themselves, not merely the probability of their happenings."[12] The most prestigious exponent of the physics of relativity had rejected the popular impression that he himself was a "relativist." In the end Einstein, like Marx, believed in a nature of universal causality.*

More serious was the epistemological challenge to the doctrine of materialism brought on by the upheaval in theoretical physics. Einstein had demonstrated that space and time were interchange-

* Einstein's insistence on searching for a uniform basis for the lawful behavior of physical properties led Eastman to engage him in a debate of freedom versus determinism. See Eastman, "Three Visits with Einstein," in *Great Companions: Critical Memoirs of Some Famous Friends* (New York, 1959), pp. 21–39.

able, depending on the motion-bound position of the observer; and he suggested that events should replace particles as the constituent elements of the universe, which would make "matter" merely a semantical catchword for describing subatomic events having physical properties. Herberg was fully aware that Einstein's relativity theory reintroduced subjectivity into scientific investigation and thus gave, however inadvertently, support to metaphysical idealism. He was also aware that the principle of indeterminism strongly suggested that there may be a force at work in the universe other than matter. Thus he drew upon Marx's "Theses on Feuerbach" and Lenin's *Materialism and Empirico-Criticism* to demonstrate that relativity theory, rather than contradicting dialectical materialism, actually confirms it. First of all, Herberg pointed out, Einstein's criterion of existence—"What cannot essentially be observed, cannot be said to exist"—need not lead to the idealist conclusion that all reality exists only in the act of observation, that is, in the mind of the knowing subject. On the contrary, Einstein also insisted that the "definition of a thing is given through its measurement." Herberg seized on this dictum to argue that Einstein, like Marx, was merely declaring that we know things by encountering them and acting upon them, by allowing them to enter into our experience. True cognition is not a passive contemplation of an eternal and immutable reality. To "measure" something is not to know the thing in itself. What we want to know is not its nature but its behavior, and this procedure of knowing is arrived at through the activist mode of praxis.[13]

So far Herberg could assume that he had reconciled Marx's epistemology with Einstein's methodology. Yet a central problem remained. There is an important difference between the ulterior nature of knowledge and how we acquire knowledge, between what truth is and how we find it out, as Arthur O. Lovejoy observed in his brilliant critique of pragmatism. And this distinction becomes something of an intellectual embarrassment in the cruder epistemology of Lenin. For if, as Lenin insisted, human thought is the "reflection" in mind of the independently existing natural world, how can we know that thought corresponds with the external object it reflects when Einstein has demonstrated that the basic categories of perception, such as space and time, are relative to the position of the perceiver? Herberg honestly acknowledged that Einstein's theories had demolished the principle of "invariance," the assumption that there are absolute natural laws for all space-time transformations regardless of the observer. But he did his best to prove the existence of objective, material reality independent of and prior to human thought:

A more serious problem is the question of the apparent subjectivity of relativity. We say: "A length (space-interval) on System A (moving at constant velocity in reference to System B) is shorter to an observer on System A than to one on System B." Does this not make the length of an object depend upon the existence (or condition) of an observer so that if there were no observer there would be no length and therefore no object? A real understanding of Einstein's ideas will show that this idealistic conclusion is thoroughly illegitimate. A length is shorter as measured from one system than another not because of the subjective condition of the observer but because of an *objective relation* between the systems of reference—their state of relative motion. The observer could well disappear, yet the objective relation would remain just the same and so would the effects on length-intervals and time-intervals. A simple illustration will make this clearer. We say Chicago is "to the East" if the observer is in San Francisco but "to the West" if the observer is in New York. But, of course, this does not mean that if there were no observer Chicago would lose its directional location! Here, in the theory of relativity, we use "observer" not as an essential thinking mind upon whom reality depends but as the designation for the objective basis of reference *relative to which* the direction of a city, or the length of an object, is determined.

Pushing further, Herberg maintained that the Einsteinian conception, which makes place and time depend solely upon the relation between objects and events, reaffirms the meaning of dialectical materialism. Time, space, matter, and energy are not exclusive concepts, as the "old physics" insisted; nor are they useless metaphysical fictions, as the logical positivists insisted. Instead these very scientific concepts prove the existence of an organic structure in the universe because they reveal themselves only in relation to one another. Thus the atomicity and discontinuity of nature become more apparent than real when we appreciate the dialectical connection of opposite concepts:

But the bottom falls out of this hitherto insuperable obstacle [Newtonianism] once we approach nature from the point of view of relativity physics. The "fixed lines of demarcation" disappear, the "irreconcilable contradictions" (space vs. time, matter vs. energy) are synthesized in the relativity physics into a higher organic unity, the space-time world, the equivalence of matter and energy. Out of disparate categories—dialectical unity![14]

Herberg's articles, written in an obscure journal in 1930, when relativity was a forbidden subject to many communist intellectuals, presage much of the reasoning used two decades later by Russian scholars and scientists in the last years of the Stalin era—when Einstein's equation of mass and energy could hardly be denied by anyone working on nuclear reactors.[15] But Herberg's arguments, as well as those of Soviet intellectuals, failed to confirm the relationship between relativity theory and dialectical materialism. The most that such arguments could prove was the existence of an objective reality given independently of the thinking subject. This exercise merely demonstrated that the world is "real," not that it is "materialistic." Whether matter is the only and ultimate reality, and, above all, whether matter is endowed with self-movement, were questions that could not be resolved in terms of physics and the knowledge of science. These were philosophical questions whose affirmative answers required a belief in the dialectic, a concept that mystified Einstein as much as it had infuriated Max Eastman. With the help of Hegel, Herberg managed to reconcile Einstein and Marx, but the entire synthesis rested on a structure of logic alien to the empirical, skeptical temperament of modern science. Under the all-embracing metaphysical schema of Hegelianism, relativity theory may no longer be a problem to Marxists. But one might reply, to paraphrase Wittgenstein, that with the philosophy of Hegel philosophy itself experiences "a loss of problems."

In Dubious Battle: Literature and History

Among the great majority of Old Left writers literature generated far more controversy than physics did. Herberg could not remain above the battle that was being waged over proletarian literature, socialist realism, and agit-prop culture. The controversy had been simmering for several years until it exploded like a pistol shot in a salon with Mike Gold's attacks on the novelist-playwright Thornton Wilder. The attacks first appeared in the *New Masses* and then in the *New Republic* in 1930, in an article entitled "Thornton Wilder: Prophet of the Genteel Christ." A first-rate polemicist and a third-rate Marxist, Gold accused Wilder of writing "little lavender tragedies" of decadent, effete people, "of homosexual figures in graceful gowns moving archaically among the lilies." Wilder's Anglo-Catholic religion, Gold protested, was "pastel, pastiche, dilettante . . . without the true neurotic blood and fire"; and his rhetoric had the "serenity" of a "corpse" which, when pricked, "will bleed violet ink and apéritif." The fierce debate that followed Gold's articles, and Edmund Wilson's response in the *New Republic*, "The Literary Class War," prompted Herberg to write his own version of Marxist literary theory in an essay addressed specifically to Wilson.[16]

Herberg entirely sympathized with Wilson's "forceful protest against the pretentious and wooden dogmatism that presumes to pass as Marxist criticism of art" in the *New Masses*. He also agreed that past and present bourgeois culture could not be discarded and that, in Wilson's words, "there are elements of the old culture which will carry over and help make the new." But Wilson drew a false parallel between the latest literary devices of modern writers and the latest technological innovations of capitalism, and he also tended to "*externalize* literary technique altogether too much."

The styles and techniques of bourgeois literature cannot be taken over the same way the working class will appropriate the industrial techniques of capitalism. Bourgeois artistic techniques are so integrally a part of the spirit of bourgeois culture that they cannot be detached from it and adapted by the Left to "express the spirit of another, and altogether alien, social order." The "devices" of Joyce, Eliot, and Cummings are eloquent expressions of the rich possibilities of form, but "form is not a self-determined empty vessel into which any content may be poured: it is a living reflection of the same forces that mould the content itself." Proletarian writers may take existing literary technique and tradition as a "point of departure" not because form can be drained of class content but because the proletariat has no culture of its own and bourgeois literary technique is all that is available. Moreover, the departure point does not imply that Marxists adopt the "latest mode" in bourgeois culture simply because in economics Marxists may appropriate the latest stage of industrial technology. If this were so, Marxism itself would have been superseded; Marxism is not the latest expression in philosophy but rather a historic synthesis of classical German philosophy and the French materialism of the Enlightenment. Thus the analogy Wilson offered between industrial and literary technique in order to clarify the Gold-Wilder controversy only clouded the issue (a point which Wilson implicitly conceded when he dropped the analogy from a later version of the article).[17] Lecturing one of America's greatest literary minds, Herberg understood perfectly, as did Trotsky and Rosa Luxemburg, that the whole issue of proletarian culture was premature and not a little pretentious.[18]

Herberg's brand of Marxism derived from the historicist tradition. Despite the creative power of dialectical reasoning, or perhaps because of it, the horizons of knowledge are limited by past experience. All human understanding depends upon an accurate grasp of objective reality discovered in the study of the past. Herberg brought this historicist philosophy to the courses he taught on Marxist political theory and American history at the New

Workers School in New York City. He never doubted, as did Wilson and several literary intellectuals, that Marxism offered the proper conceptual framework for approaching American history and culture. But the grandest approach to this vast subject had already been undertaken by Vernon L. Parrington. To Herberg, Parrington's *Main Currents in American Thought* revealed the limitations of an economic interpretation of history that stressed the dualisms between aristocracy and democracy, agrarianism and industrialism, idealism and realism. Herberg did not reject the democratic values of liberal historians; he rejected their false moral nostalgia. Their lamenting the decline of individualism merely reflected the disappearance of the frontier; neither land nor freedom could hold back the advance of industrial capitalism. Comparing the Marxist V. F. Calverton to Parrington, Herberg observed that liberal scholars could not account for the transmutation of the self-reliant spirit of the frontier when industrialism undermined the values of Emerson and Whitman and turned to ashes the once-buoyant optimism of Mark Twain. Parrington's alleged economic determinism forced him to treat ideas as fixed principles, but he could not explain the movement and transformation of ideas, the process by which Emersonian idealism gave way to laissez-faire materialism.[19]

Herberg's primary historical concerns were the American Civil War and Reconstruction, for it was these two episodes that constituted the first stages of an unfinished revolution that left America a violently racist society. He saw both episodes as aspects of a "bourgeois revolution" aimed at destroying the "pre-capitalist forms" of political economy in the South. The Civil War was basically a struggle between the industrial and commercial capitalism of the North and the "semi-feudal" slave plantation system and "pseudo-aristocracy" of the South. The two systems were inherently incompatible. The industrial economy could not sustain itself without expanding, while the plantation economy could not generate sufficient commodity production and capitalist accumulation without undermining the structure of slave society. Fearing

the opening of the West and Northwest to further settlement—
the "dire apogee" of America's future, according to Marx—the
South staged a counterrevolution of the plantation class when it
seceded from the Union. With the defeat of the southern slave-
owning class, Reconstruction offered Radical Republicans the
opportunity "to push the bourgeoisification of the South with the
greatest determination and ruthlessness, to complete the bourgeois-
democratic revolution." But Radical Republicans like Charles
Sumner and Thaddeus Stevens were thwarted by the conservative
wing of the party. The moderates, who wanted to come to terms
with the old ruling class in the South as they turned their efforts to
westward industrial expansion, realized that radical Reconstruction
disturbed the Northern bourgeoisie, who feared the contagious
radicalization of the working class and farming masses. Herberg's
interpretation, a mixture of Marx and W. E. B. Du Bois, was
challenged by the Marxist historian Louis Hacker, who doubted
that the South was so central to Northern capital, questioned the
"motives" of Radical Republicans, and chided Herberg for relying
upon the "dialectic rather than external evidence."[20]

In avoiding a strict economic determinism and a simple class
analysis, and in acknowledging some idealism on the part of
"bourgeois" politicians, Herberg's interpretation of the Civil War
as a struggle between two "social orders" escaped reductionism
and anticipated some of the ideas advanced decades later by the
"old" New Left historian Eugene Genovese and by the sociologist
Barrington Moore. Herberg's primary concern, however, was
neither the cultural hegemony of the planter class nor the problem
of modernization. His more immediate concern was the bearing of
the Civil War and Reconstruction upon the precarious status of
the Negro in contemporary American society. He examined and
criticized one by one the various explanations offered to account
for the subjugation of the black race: (a) the "natural antipathy"
thesis, curiously endorsed by white supremacists and Garveyites on
grounds of inherent racial differences, is rejected as unscientific;
(b) the "economic competition" theory is also inadequate, since it

fails to explain why white people entirely isolated from blacks are nonetheless prejudiced; (c) the "slave tradition" notion is similarly rejected, since racism had long outlived the abolition of slavery; and (d) the "conscious fostering" theory is unconvincing because, even though white capitalists use racism to sow dissension among the masses, it does not explain why they themselves manifest deep-seated racial attitudes. What accounts for the lingering of racial prejudice in America? It was the incomplete emancipation of the Negro during Reconstruction. Since the Civil War did not fully eradicate the slave condition of the Negro, the "material basis of racial subjection likewise did not disappear but continued in modified form." Herberg wrote in 1932 that the bourgeoisie had found it advantageous to use the image of the pre-capitalist slave status of the black man in order to confine him to the depressed economic strata. Prejudice, Herberg insisted, provided a clear illustration of the way the class interests of the bourgeoisie were transformed into a class ideology of racism.[21]

Herberg's historical reasoning did not succeed in surmounting the criticisms he raised against other explanations of racial prejudice. The suggestion that racism is an ideology which rationalizes class interests seems only a reversion to the "conscious fostering" theory of human prejudice. Nor could he satisfactorily explain why it was in the interests of capitalists to keep the Negro suppressed instead of allowing black workers to enter the white labor force in order to compete and thereby lower wage scales. The relationship between economics and racism was, and still is, an enormously complex problem in America. Nevertheless, Herberg had good reason to stress that racism must be viewed as the outcome of a "bourgeois revolution" (the Civil War), the consequences of which could only be resolved by a true proletarian revolution. For at the time Herberg was writing his articles a distinction was being drawn between the class question and the race question, with the clear implication that an answer to the latter must wait upon the solution to the former.

The distinction had been propounded by the American Communist Party, possibly at the suggestion of Joseph Stalin. At its Sixth World Congress in 1928, the Comintern issued a thesis that came to be known as the "Black Belt" doctrine. American Negroes, it was declared, constituted an "oppressed nation" within a nation, and the solution to their situation lay in "self-determination." The doctrine applied mainly to blacks in the South. Seventy-two per cent of all Negroes in the United States then lived in twelve Southern states, two thirds in the rural parts of those states. In 189 Southern counties the blacks constituted more than half the population. With a map in hand outlining the "Black Belt" areas where Negroes were in the majority, the Party began to wax Wilsonian in championing "self-determination" and the creation of a "Negro Republic."[22]

Herberg regarded the Party resolution as bad Marxism and poor history. The American Negroes did not constitute a nation of people. Stalin himself, in his 1913 pamphlet on *Marxism and the National Question*, had defined a nation as "an historically developed, consolidated and enduring community of languages, territory, economic life, psychic structure—which manifests itself in the community of culture." Since American Negroes lacked all these characteristics of nationhood, they could not be likened to, say, the Croats in Yugoslavia, Herberg maintained. Even more preposterous was the Comintern's assertion that the "Negro zone" was once a real political unity and had been artificially divided into a number of states "for the purpose of facilitating national oppression." All this Herberg found to be an "absurd" distortion of American history. The Comintern and the Party not only ignored the lessons of Reconstruction—when Negroes were also left to their own fate in the South—but played into the hands of the Garveyites in the North and the Jim Crow racists in the South, both of whom demanded a separate status for the Negro and even special segregated schools. The real "organic bond" uniting communists and blacks would not be found in Stalin's writings or in the Comintern's resolutions. It would be found in American history itself—in the career of Wendell Phillips, the Brahmin radical who "hailed

the heroes of the Paris Commune and who passionately defended
the revolutionary terrorists of the Czarist Russia of the 1870's,"
the one abolitionist who realized that the color question and the
class question were inseparable.[23]

Yet the real dilemma facing Herberg had also confronted Phillips: How can the working class ally with Negroes in a common
movement when the proletariat itself is so infected with racism
that black Americans distrust the rule of white labor as much as
white capitalism? Marxists had no easy answer to this question,
and the Comintern's resolutions and the Party's "Black Belt" doctrine may have been eagerly accepted by communists in order to
skirt the issue. But Herberg faced it squarely and openly. He acknowledged the violent depths of prejudice in the American working class. He found encouragement in the status of the Jews. The
"Jewish problem" in Russia offered an example of a people who
had suffered "caste" oppression and religious and ethnic persecu-
tion, and yet had been "completely emancipated" by the Bolshevik Revolution. Both the subjection of the Jews in Tsarist Russia
and of the Negroes in the old South could be traced to the "pre-
capitalist conditions" in the early nineteeth century.

Herberg's historical reasoning was clearly faulty, proceeding as it
did from a partial resemblance to an exact correspondence and
hence a similar revolutionary solution. (The penchant for historical analogies is not confined to Marxists; as a conservative historian, Dos Passos, too, would become obsessed by false parallels.)
When one thinks of the plight of the blacks in the old and the
"new" South, and that of the Jews (and Gypsies, Cossacks, and
other "non-Russian" peoples) in both Tsarist and Stalinist Russia,
one is tempted to revise Marx's dictum: History repeats itself, the
first time as tragedy, the second as catastrophe.

Even more dubious was Herberg's attempt to grapple with
racism, which, like anti-Semitism, may have had roots elsewhere
than in capitalism and hence may survive the abolition of slavery
and caste. Herberg believed that the remnants of racism in American society were due to the "backwardness" of a working class not

fully emancipated. American workers could purge themselves of prejudice only through the heightening of class consciousness in the struggle for power. Herberg's belief in the transforming and clarifying power of revolution takes on mythic overtones: "Karl Marx repeatedly emphasized that the process of revolution involves not only an 'external' change of the social structure and functioning but implies an 'inner' transformation, a revolution in the 'human nature' of the masses."

To prove his point Herberg quoted Marx himself: "A revolution is needed not only because there is no other way to overthrow a ruling class but also because the class that does the overthrowing is able only through a revolution to cleanse itself of all the filth of the old regime and thus to become capable of building a new society."[24] Herberg made much of the "cleansing" phenomenon of the revolutionary act, obviously believing, with Marx, that the emancipation of the proletariat as a "universal class" included the emancipation of humanity as a whole, black as well as white. But the reference to an "inner" transformation and a "revolution in . . . 'human nature' " is completely foreign to Marx's thought. Rejecting the imperatives of moral philosophy, Marx exempted man from the ethical responsibility of striving to change himself. With Herberg the need to believe in moral revolution and self-transcendence was paramount, and it touched his early radicalism with a religious conscience that was bound to come to terms with questions that Marx had left unanswered.

The Lonely Ordeal of a Lovestoneite: Polycentrism Presaged

Herberg entered the Communist Party shortly after high school and at the precocious age of seventeen became a leading organizer of the Young Workers League. The YWL grew to about three thousand members in the twenties. Though only an appendage of the Communist Party, YWLers saw themselves as the juvenile vanguard of the revolution. On purely doctrinal grounds, the YWL was an oddity. Marx and Engels had distrusted radical student movements; young intellectuals were like a philosophical head without a proletarian body, or, as Engels put it, "officer candidates without an army."[25] Herberg did his best to create an ideology for the YWL by quoting Lenin ad infinitum and by depicting the October Revolution as a glorious generational synthesis that saw, for the first time in history, fathers and sons on the same side of the barricades. As a director of the YWL summer camps, Herberg had to justify military training while young communists were calling for the abolition of ROTC on the campus of City College of New York. The distinction was simple: collegiate military drill served the cause of imperialism, that of the YWL the cause of revolution. Young communists should not be "shocked" at discovering militarism in their curriculum; we need to purge ourselves of "pacifist illusions."[26]

When the American communist movement split into two factions in 1929, Will Herberg, then twenty-one, followed the Lovestone group out of the Party. This small splinter group took the name of, first, "The Communist Party (Majority Group)," and then, "The Communist Party of the U.S.A. (Opposition)." The history and politics of the Lovestone opposition did much to shape Herberg's ideological education.

A small circle of young college-bred intellectuals and labor organizers, the Opposition was headed by Jay Lovestone, a Lithuanian who came to the United States at the age of nine and who studied at City College of New York and Columbia University. In the early twenties Lovestone had been one of the rising stars in the Communist Party. In 1927, upon the death of Charles Ruthenberg, the Party's general secretary, a succession struggle developed between Lovestone and William Z. Foster. Lovestone had the support of the overwhelming majority of CP members in the United States, but not the support of the CP in the Soviet Union. For the factional disputes in the American party had taken place against the background of the "Trotsky heresy," the alleged danger of "Right deviationism," and Stalin's struggle against his opponents within the Russian central committee. Slow to grasp the shifting power alignments in the Soviet Union, Lovestone made the mistake of identifying with Bukharin, the Bolshevik theoretician who had been Stalin's ally in the campaign against Trotsky. The Lovestoneites had also been articulating a doctrine that came to be known as "American exceptionalism." Lovestone and his former CCNY colleague, Bertram D. Wolfe, had maintained that there were certain unique features in the development of American economic life that set it apart from the general trend of economic history in other capitalist countries. They did not deny the inevitability of an economic crisis in America, only its imminence. This theoretical position, although at variance with Comintern views, was scarcely decisive in determining Lovestone's fate. It is more likely that he was simply the victim of the numerous splits that had shocked the communist world as a result of Russia's internal power struggle. In November 1929 Stalin began to move against Bukharin and the alleged "Right danger" in the Russian party. A few days later the Comintern's executive committee sent a letter to the American CP, denouncing its sectarianism, demanding a reorganization, and ordering the expulsion of Lovestone.[27]

Stunned but defiant, Lovestone and several associates, including Wolfe and Benjamin Gitlow, decided to take their case to Moscow and appeal the Comintern's decision. Stalin himself attended the session of the American delegation before the Comintern, and at the climactic meeting of the Presidium, the permanent governing organ of the Executive Committee of the Communist International (ECCI), he brusquely told the Lovestoneites that they did not represent the majority within the American CP and that henceforth they must subordinate themselves to Comintern policy. Gitlow directly challenged Stalin, declaring that he opposed the Presidium's decision and would fight against it upon his return to the United States, whereupon Stalin jumped to his feet and assailed the Lovestoneites as anarchists and strikebreakers. According to Wolfe, Stalin said, "Who do you think you are? Trotsky defied me. Where is he? Zinoviev defied me. Where is he?

Max Eastman, graduate student of John Dewey at Columbia University, 1908.

Eastman with his first wife, feminist Ida Rauh, in their Greenwich Village apartment, c. 1912.

John Reed, young hero of Greenwich Village Left and co-editor of Eastman's *The Masses*, in 1916 before leaving for Russia, where he died in 1920.

Eastman in Hollywood in 1919 with Charles Chaplin.

Portraits by Eastman's second wife, Eliena Krylenko, of two Leftist heroes of the 1920s, both later assassinated: Leon Trotsky, whom Eastman met in 1922 in Moscow; and Carlo Tresca, friend of Eastman and John Dos Passos.

Eastman in Moscow in 1922 with James P. Cannon, a founder of the Socialist Workers Party, an American Trotskyist faction, and "Big Bill" Haywood, leader of the anarcho-syndicalist Wobblies.

Eastman with Socialist Party leader Eugene V. Debs and Rose Pastor Stokes, labor activist, at the 1918 trial of Debs and Stokes for pacifist speech under the Espionage Act; both were convicted, and their sentences commuted after several years' imprisonment.

John Dos Passos, arrested for protesting in a picketline against the death sentences for Sacco and Vanzetti, Boston, 1927.

Edmund Wilson, literary critic
and friend of Dos Passos and
Eastman, in the 1920s.

James Burnham in 1927, the
year of his graduation from
Princeton University.

Floyd Dell, rebel, feminist, co-
editor of *The Masses*, who broke
with communist intellectuals
and later with Eastman over
anti-communism, 1922.

Bolshevik admirer Lincoln Steffens (*standing*) with New York *Herald* foreign correspondent Frederick O'Brien (*l.*), Steffens's baby, and Max and Eliena Eastman, San Pedro, Italy, 1925.

Ernest Hemingway, skiing instructor Fraulein Maria Glaser, Dos Passos and Gerald Murphy, friend of Lost Generation intellectuals, skiing in the German Alps, March 1926.

Hemingway as war correspondent for the *North American Newspaper Alliance* in the Spanish Civil War, 1936 or 1937–1938.

Eastman (r.), nudist and feminist, at swimming party with *Nation* drama critic Joseph Wood Krutch (*foreground*), his publisher Charles Boni, Rex Stout, Eliena Eastman, Norman Habicht, Ruth Arena, c. 1930.

Will Herberg, c. 1935, a time when he was questioning the Popular Front.

At a political rally on November 7, 1938, Communist Party leader Earl Browder and Granville Hicks, Harvard instructor and literary critic.

John Dewey, professor emeritus of philosophy at Columbia University, greeting Leon Trotsky before Trotsky's "counter-trial" on charges of disloyalty to the Soviet Union, Mexico City, April 13, 1937.

Bukharin defied me. Where is he? And you? When you get back to America, nobody will stay with you except your wives."

Lovestone, who later described Stalin's tirade as the "graveyard speech," recalls Stalin's warning the Americans that for strike-breakers "there is plenty of room in our cemeteries." Theodore Draper has described vividly the funeral exit of the Lovestoneites from the international communist movement:

> Stalin stepped down from the platform and strode out first. Guards and secretaries flocked after him. No one moved until he had walked down the aisle. But as he reached the Americans, he stopped and held out his hand to the Negro delegate, Edward Welsh, who stood next to Lovestone.
>
> Welsh turned to Lovestone and asked loudly, "What the hell does this guy want?" and refused to shake Stalin's hand.
>
> The American delegates, totally shunned by everyone else, walked out into the gray dawn and bought oranges from a street peddler.[28]

The Lovestoneites, isolated and dejected, having suffered the loss of ninety per cent of the CP members who had supported them at the Sixth Party Convention in March 1929, and now reduced to about two hundred adherents, started their own journal, *Revolutionary Age*. Within a year this bi-weekly would be banned from the government postal service and forced to change its name to *Workers Age*. Its subtitle was "An Organ of Marxism-Leninism in the United States," and its masthead read, "For Communist Unity in the Revolutionary Class Struggle." Those who wrote for these publications—Gitlow, Herberg, Lovestone, Wolfe, James Cork, Herbert Zam, and Charles Zimmerman were the frequent contributors—would later become bitter anti-Stalinists. Many would spend the rest of their lives denouncing communism. In the early thirties, however, their aim was to become better communists than the communists themselves, and to prove their doctrinal purity by converting members of the CP back to Leninism and the principle of "democratic centralism." Such invocations came a little late. For in the twenties Lovestone had himself denied the principle of open discussion to Trotsky and other dissidents. The Lovestone faction was born and took its shape as an "opposition," but only after spending many years campaigning against those who opposed the communist code of discipline and loyalty. The Lovestoneites had been willing to use the Comintern to destroy their rivals within the CP; now they were struggling against the Comintern to win over their former enemies. To Herberg, who loved to live and breathe the pure air of doctrinal consistency, Lovestoneism was an ordeal of ethical paradoxes to be overcome only by a deep faith in the ultimate judgment of history.

The Communist Opposition assigned Herberg to study and report on the Plenum proceedings of the Tenth ECCI, which met just after the orders had been issued to expel Lovestone. Herberg's critical analysis ran for three straight months in *Revolutionary Age*. It gradually led to an exposition of the principles of the Communist Opposition. Before long Herberg was recognized as one of the leading theoreticians of the Lovestoneites, and in 1933 Victor F. Calverton, who had asked Herberg for copies of lectures he had delivered at the New Workers School, asked him to write an article for the *Modern Quarterly* on the crisis of the Comintern from the viewpoint of the Communist Opposition.[29]

The fundamental principle of the Opposition, Herberg informed other Left intellectuals in America, was the conviction that the United States must develop its own revolutionary strategy and tactics. This was not exactly a restatement of the idea of "American exceptionalism" propounded earlier by Lovestone and Wolfe, for the economic crash rendered academic the older debate over the stability, if not the durability, of American capitalism. Now the emphasis was on the need for national self-determination, if not complete autonomy, within the world communist movement. Herberg was willing to grant the Comintern a dominant role at its inception, when it possessed "revolutionary authority" and when all Western communist parties could do no other than support the imperiled Bolshevik Revolution. After 1923, however, the development of the Soviet Union and that of Western countries diverged.

Each had to adjust to its own particular conditions and opportunities. Now more than ever Marxists must heed Lenin's advice that "the development of the revolution in different countries proceeds along varying paths with varying rapidities." Anything less, Herberg insisted, would lead to the "mechanical transference" to other countries of methods suitable to Russia, a forced "uniformity" of ideas and tactics that would ignore all that is concrete, specific, peculiar and unique.[30]

In stressing the need for each nation to find its own road to the goals of Marxism, Herberg anticipated the idea of "polycentrism" that Palmiro Togliatti advocated in 1956, when the Italian communist leader observed the great "objective differences" in the economic and political conditions confronting communist parties throughout the world. Herberg and the Lovestoneites also insisted, as did Togliatti, Tito, and other polycentrists twenty years later, that they represented not a separate party but an "organized tendency" within the international communist movement. *Revolutionary Age* used the writings of the German August Thalheimer, the Pole Karl Radek, the Indian M. N. Roy, and other independent communists who had run afoul of the Comintern. Had Herberg and the Opposition succeeded in drawing the CP into a real debate on "American exceptionalism," a re-examination of the relationship between the historical development of European and American capitalism might have occurred. A theoretical discussion of this nature may have made some communists more aware of the unique features of American society that necessitated an independent exploration of American communist strategy. The Stalinization of the CP precluded such debate, and as a result American communists proceeded upon three disastrous courses that Herberg fought vigorously.

The first was "dual unionism." Herberg and the Lovestoneites opposed splitting the labor movement in America in order to form "Red" unions like the Trade Union Unity League. Such a tactic was another example of "mechanically" universalizing a technique that had its origins in the particular Soviet experience. As a result of such practices, communist influence would never gain among organized workers. The trade unions, no matter how conservative in America, have always been more than "capitalist" agencies, and indeed they contain the potential for organizing the working class on a true mass basis. The second disastrous tactic of the CP, the "united front from below," excluded from the movement all non-Party Left elements and prevented communists from entering electoral alliances with socialists. Again this tactic derived from the Soviet experience, where the CPSU did not have to work with other organizations and stoop to politics in order to conquer power. In the United States, Herberg pointed out, this same policy led to the "fatal isolation" of the CP that was, like dualism, "well-nigh suicidal."[31]

Finally, the most tragic policy of the CP, and one that proceeded from the assumptions of the other two tactics, was the doctrine of "social fascism." The notion that the social democrats were the "moderate wing of fascism," and the notion that fascism was "a universal stage of development" through which capitalist countries must pass before the proletarian revolution turned the entire phenomenon of fascism into "an unrecognizable, all-pervading generality." Such a policy, based on the non-Leninist assumption of the "homogeneity" of the social democrats, prevented a united front in Germany and totally disoriented communists everywhere else. Indeed the debility of the German CP was further proof that American communists must reformulate their own strategy and tactics on the basis of "democratic centralism," which Herberg defined as "the right of the free expression of opinion within the party and the free discussion of all vital issues, side by side with the disciplined execution of decisions regularly arrived at." Only through such new procedures and policies could communists win over the workers from the socialists and trade unionists and begin to develop a true class consciousness among the American masses. Without this radically new strategy of "democratic centralism" the Left would remain impotent, for the Opposition realized that the economic crash was not the beginning of the end of capitalism. As events in Germany proved, capitalism could overcome every crisis it encountered, even the mythical "final crisis." After identifying the disastrous policies of the CP, Herberg issued a dire warning:

> The excesses to which the stupid bureaucracy dominating our move-ment has led are almost indescribable. The most irresponsible falsifica-tions, the most conscienceless slander and abuse, the most disgusting anti-proletarian hero-cults are all its fine flowers. The spiritual degra-dation and corruption of thousands of militant workers, especially the youth, will be a charge that the present leadership of the official Com-munist movement will find it difficult indeed to meet in the future![32]

Herberg himself, one is bound to report, would find it difficult to answer a charge that could be leveled at the Lovestoneites: While demanding that the CP return to "democratic centralism," they could not bring themselves to advocate a multi-party democ-racy within the CP broad enough to include anti-Stalinists. On the "Trotsky heresy," in short, the Opposition revealed its narrow, sectarian nature. Herberg, unlike Eastman, saw nothing heroic in the figure of Trotsky, and despite his moral outrage toward the CP he seemed to fear Trotskyism more than he hated Stalinism. He viewed the Trotskyist movement as an "inverted Stalinism," an attempt on the part of frustrated, manqué Bolsheviks to oust Stalin, establish a new International, and keep the Soviet system itself intact.

Was Herberg right? There was nothing in the history of Trot-sky's few years in power to indicate that he was wrong. But how could Herberg condemn Trotsky without condemning Bolshevism itself? Whatever his reservations about Soviet bureaucracy, Her-berg still felt powerfully the myth of the October Revolution.

Herberg also dismissed the first formulations of a theory that would become the basis of considerable debate among American Trotskyists and eventually lead to James Burnham's break with the Socialist Workers Party—the theory of the "Soviet Thermidor." According to Trotsky, Stalin's dictatorship represented a reversed "Kerensky period," a moment in history when power changes directions and flows backwards from the proletariat to the bourgeoisie. Herberg criticized Trotsky's belief that Stalinism signified the beginnings of a capitalist restoration in Russia—a criticism that might have carried more weight had Herberg made some attempt to explain what was going on in the Soviet Union.[33]

While suspecting Trotsky of "ultra Leftism" because of his argument for "permanent revolution," Herberg also accused him of Right "opportunism" because of his curious response to the German crisis. After Hitler's advent to power, Trotsky believed, the Nazi dictatorship would generate among the German people a desire to restore the democratic freedoms of the Weimar Republic, just as the despotism of Tsarist Russia had stimulated a growing sentiment for liberal reforms. Herberg denied Trotsky's analogy between bourgeois Germany and feudal Russia, and he maintained that the restoration of a "discredited system" of parliamentary government in Germany would make the proletarian revolution "more difficult and more painful." Here Herberg's historical reasoning lost all perspective. For if Trotsky's parallel between Russia and Germany did not obtain, neither did Herberg's hopeful analogy between 1917 and 1933. The Bolshevik Revolution could not be repeated in Berlin and the bourgeois state smashed by the German CP—Hitler saw to that. Herberg felt the power of Lenin's historic example; but even more than Eastman, he continued to believe in the myth of the inevitable recurrence of the October Revolution. Although he would argue for "American exceptionalism" against the CP, he assumed that Leninism was the sole authority of revolutionary theory and practice. Herberg was a "permanent revolutionist" *malgré lui*.[34]

The subject of Leninism, however, was bound to rise among the Old Left, and one of the first writers to broach it was Sidney Hook. Originally Herberg had much more respect for Hook than for Eastman, whose writings on Marxism in the *Modern Monthly* he found "characteristically thin and substanceless."[35] But while Herberg had no quarrel with Hook as a Marxist philosopher, the political implications of Hook's *Towards the Understanding of*

Karl Marx and his essay on "Workers' Democracy" were disturbing to the Lovestoneites. In these studies Hook sought to refute Lenin's thesis that the "essence of the Marxist theory [of the State] is the doctrine of the dictatorship of the proletariat." Herberg responded to Hook in a series of articles in *Workers Age*: a battle followed, with the weapons of textual criticism, quotesmanship, logic chopping, italics shifting, and occasional sound historical reasoning mixed with fine-spun casuistry that had all the polemical brilliance, if not the notoriety, of the Eastman-Hook debates.

Herberg attempted to demonstrate that the concept of proletarian dictatorship was central to Marxism and not, as Hook had maintained, a "mere phrase" and "verbal symbol" that Lenin seized upon as a principle of Party organization. Herberg's argument combined intellectual elitism with what he called "high expediency." Contrasting Lenin's brilliant achievements in 1917 with the dismal course of history a decade later, he insisted that the CP could "conceive" the ultimate interests of the working class better than the workers themselves. And making a distinction between "form" and "substance," between political institutions and their class nature, he felt no compunction in defending Lenin's actions during the Kronstadt uprising and the Bolshevik suppression of the Baku Soviet. Against these lessons of history Hook appeared a naïve Kautskyist still steeped in the "outworn superstitions of parliamentary democracy" and caught up in a "philistine worship of the abstract forms of democracy." Hook's "entire viewpoint," scoffed Herberg, "is the crudest sort of democratic fetishism disguised in a Marxist mantle."[36]

Hook immediately responded in the *Modern Quarterly* in an article entitled "Manners and Morals of Apache-Radicalism." He accused Herberg, whose "methodological thuggery" blinded him to the "full enormity of his crime against the spirit of Marxism," of expounding a "Communist-Catholic theory of party infallibility." In his rejoinder, "Professor Hook Loses His Temper," Herberg confessed astonishment at the "unbecoming spleen" and the "unphilosophical peevishness exhibited by this eminent philosopher." At issue above the dialogue of sarcasm was a theory of "soviet parliamentarianism" or "workers' democracy" that Hook had been articulating as a social democratic spokesman for the newly formed American Workers Party. Hook had cited the 1917 Bolshevik Left–Social Revolutionary alliance as an instance of the possibility of an immediate coalition based upon a plurality of revolutionary forces all representing the working classes. He also argued for the necessity of recognizing rival workers' parties in the postrevolutionary period in order to represent different factions and interests (though he agreed with Herberg that "non-proletarian influences" deserved no political voice). Herberg found the suggestion unthinkable. The continuation of different working class parties after the revolution could only mean that those parties had profound differences on "fundamental principles." No "coexistence" among parties could be possible without risking the danger of allowing a counterrevolutionary party to emerge within Hook's "soviet parliament." As would the historian E. H. Carr years later in his scholarly study of the Bolshevik Revolution, Herberg insisted that "the very hegemony that the leading party has won in the revolution is evidence enough of the effectiveness of its strategical course." The victory of the Bolsheviks over all other parties proved that only one party was necessary to embody the historical interests of the working class.[37]

The Herberg-Hook debates reveal the difficulties Marxists get themselves into when they try to solve liberal problems like representation, consent, legitimacy, and authority. Indeed the whole debate could scarcely serve to reinforce the Lovestoneite argument for readmission into the CP and the Comintern. If Herberg could cite Lenin's success over his opponents to demonstrate the correctness and historical necessity of a one-party dictatorship, the CP could also cite Stalin's victory over his rivals to demonstrate the virtues of a one-man dictatorship. The Lovestoneites were, after all, the losers in their struggle with the Fosterites. If history belonged to the winners in 1917, where did that leave the Lovestoneites in 1929? Herberg's overly subtle distinctions would return to haunt him as he and the Lovestoneites used the authority of Lenin in an attempt to regain the grace of Stalin. The difference between the mystique of a one-party dictatorship of the proletariat and the cult of a one-party dictatorship of personality was, from the Stalinist point of view, only a distinction in "form," not in "substance."

Analogy between Russia and Spain: Critique of the Popular Front

When John Dos Passos shrewdly commented, in response to a *Modern Quarterly* questionnaire in 1932, that America was witnessing the "failure" of capitalism but not necessarily its "collapse,"[38] he was expressing accurately Herberg's response to the Great Depression. But what Dos Passos seemed to understand instinctively Herberg arrived at after long excursions through the writings of Marx and Lenin—that the present economic crisis was in the system but not yet of the system. The Wall Street crash undermined the country's faith in its economic institutions, but the legitimacy of its political institutions and the hegemony of capitalist culture remained unchallenged. Citing Marx's *Class Struggles in France*, Herberg could only conclude that "there is no inevitable and necessary connection between an economic crisis (however deep!) and a maturing revolutionary situation." The key to the impasse that prevented an economic crisis from turning into a political crisis lay in the working class, which had yet to show any signs of taking what Lenin called "independent historical action."[39]

Herberg had immersed himself in the world of ideas to reconcile modern science, literature, and history to Marxism, yet he could not ignore the most noble idea of all—the idea of the proletariat. Without a proletariat Marxism remained only a theory in search of praxis, an idea whose time was yet to come. In America in the early thirties the times did seem ripe for the emergence of a genuine proletariat. Many workers had become radicalized as they participated in prolonged strikes in coal mines, steel mills, auto assembly plants, and waterfront warehouses. The Lovestoneites observed these developments carefully; to ally themselves with the struggles of the working class they would adopt the organizational title of the Independent Labor League of America. In Workers Age Herberg wrote extensively on the condition and prospects of American labor, and in 1935 he became educational director of the International Ladies Garment Workers Union. But however closely Herberg identified with the labor movement, he did not misinterpret workers' demands as proletarian consciousness. The Depression had radicalized much of the working force, yet the sporadic militancy of strikers displayed more personal desperation than historical direction, while the passive bewilderment of the unemployed indicated the depth of self-reproach more than the hostility of class warfare. The New Deal introduced a novel dimension into relations between capital and labor, making it questionable whether American society would polarize along class lines. Roosevelt's NRA, Herberg believed, would not revitalize the economy through its price-raising schemes, nor would it give labor, despite the "right" to collective bargaining, real power and equity in government decision making. Herberg was convinced that corporate wealth would ultimately win out over labor in Washington, even though businessmen, as in the febrile activities of the American Liberty League, were too shortsighted to see that Roosevelt wanted to stabilize capitalism, not abolish it. The only force capable of resisting a business-government alliance—which through "organizational rationalization" was producing a new form of "state capitalism"—was labor, and by 1936 the American labor movement was rapidly becoming absorbed, "swallowed up completely and entirely in the Roosevelt whirlpool."[40]

Herberg, less hostile to the New Deal than many other Old Left intellectuals, praised in 1937 the administration's legislation governing wages and hours, child labor, and social welfare. He had rejected the widespread belief, expressed monotonously in the left-wing press, that the New Deal would usher in a fascist state. The American labor movement, Herberg noted, was presently too weak to make a bid for power and produce a reaction from the Right, while the Roosevelt administration was too dependent upon the working class vote to move openly against organized labor. Amid this equilibrium of social forces the crucial factor was the political status and freedom of action of the trade unions in particular and the labor movement in general. Thus Herberg found some encouragement in the emergence of the American Labor Party, established in 1934 by A. J. Muste. Here was an organization, however small, that could provide the nucleus of a labor movement independent of both the CP and the Democratic Party. The dream collapsed as quickly as it arose. When the CP gave "unofficial support" to Roosevelt in 1936 and the American working class voted overwhelmingly for his re-election, Herberg concluded that labor's "first few sparks of political class independence [were] completely extinguished."[41]

Herberg thought that the inability of labor to achieve unity and political independence could be traced to the policies of the CP. Everything that went wrong in the thirties, it seemed, could be blamed upon the CP, and what was true of the CP in America was equally true of the Comintern in Europe. In 1934 Herberg's thoughts grew dark and gloomy as he wrote about events in Germany and Austria. Hitler's elimination of the inept German CP and the failure of the Austrian Left to resist suppression at the hands of the Dollfuss regime offered final proof of the fallacies of the "third period." This Comintern policy had been formulated at the Sixth World Congress in 1928. The doctrine of the "third period" assumed that the period of capitalist stability had passed and that the time had now arrived for a revolutionary upsurge in the international communist movement, its two tactical corollaries dual unionism and social fascism. The Lovestoneites criticized these tactics from the beginning; Herberg could now cite the bleak record of historical experience. Dual unionism fragmented the labor movement everywhere, and in the United States especially it isolated the CP from powerful unions like the AFL. The theory of social fascism also proved fatal. In Europe it all but disarmed the proletariat with the insane charge that social democracy was the "left wing of fascism," and in America its attacks upon the Socialist Party and conservative trade unions confused workers even more about who their real enemies were and rendered impossible any real solidarity on the Left. The answer to these debacles, Herberg and the Lovestoneites had pleaded all along, was unity and more unity, specifically a "united front."[42]

The CP eventually did adopt the radically new policy of the "Popular Front" at the Seventh Congress of the Comintern in the summer of 1935. At first Herberg and the Opposition welcomed the new turn as the end of "the ultra-left madness [that] ravaged the world communist movement like a dreadful plague for five years." But the decision to call off dual unionism, drop the slander of social fascism, and ally with liberals and socialists came not from the Lovestoneites' headquarters on West Fourteenth Street in New York, but from the premier's palatial office in the Kremlin. It soon became evident that the Popular Front did not include the unpopular Lovestoneites, who originally had assumed that they would now be readmitted into the CP and allowed to participate on the basis of open discussion and internal "self-criticism." Once this exclusion was understood, Herberg and the Opposition attacked the "Peoples' Front" with sulky arguments. Where Herberg earlier assailed the CP for being unduly hostile toward liberals, socialists, and trade unionists, he now felt it was being unduly hospitable; where he once criticized the CP for seeing fascism behind every New Deal legislation, he now criticized it for supporting Roosevelt and failing to see the threat of fascism in the expansion of executive power; and where he formerly cited Lenin's *Left-Wing Communism: An Infantile Disorder* to argue the case for American "exceptionalism" and communist participation in electoral activity and trade unionism, he now cited Marx's *Eighteenth Brumaire* and *The Civil War in France* as a universal lesson in the futility of a working class–bourgeoisie alliance. In view of these shifts, the *Daily Worker* had grounds for accusing the Communist Opposition of "sheer lack of consistency of principle." Herberg, however, would soon have grounds for also accusing the CP of shifting from "ultra-left madness" to the "ultra-right" tactic of "unbridled opportunism." For the test case of the Popular Front would be Spain.[43]

In Herberg's eyes the Popular Front was betrayed on the battlefields of Spain during the Civil War. Spanish communists, at the instigation of the Comintern, suppressed all manifestations of revolutionary action, allowed the Loyalist government to force peasants to return seized land, and denounced the "popular excesses" of the Catalonian masses. Examining the main points of the program adopted by the Spanish CP in January 1936, Herberg discovered that there would be no land confiscation, no nationalization of banks, and no workers' control of industry. Instead the Spanish CP demanded political amnesty, the re-establishment of civil rights and the Cortes, and in general the restoration of a "bankrupt" bourgeois liberalism. Herberg could only view this "minimum" program as a repudiation of the October Revolution, and to outline the true path to communist victory he wrote several articles reflecting on the relationship between Spain and Russia. He found a "striking analogy" in the economic conditions of the two countries and in the events in Spain in 1936 and the stages through which the Russian Revolution passed in August and September of 1917: a similar agrarian economy characterized by backwardness and the "land question"; a similar new republic which, like Russia's Provisional Government, did not enjoy consensual comity and thus could not cope with a monarchist Right, a liberal Center, and a radical Left; a similar social revolution within a civil war in which the authority of the republic was being undermined by workers and peasant "committees" as the Provisional Government had been undermined by the soviets—hence the repetition of "dual power"; and, lastly, a similar right-wing attempted coup by Franco, which, like the Kornilov putsch in Russia, foreshadowed the collapse of the republic and the beginning of the true communist revolution.[44]

Herberg's exercise in revolutionary analogy offered a clever critique of the Popular Front, but it was not without embarrassing lapses in historical reasoning. Eastman could have reminded him that the missing link in the analogy was a Spanish Lenin, whose absence rendered history undramatic and revolution problematic. Dos Passos could have reminded him that the Spanish rural masses, upon whom the revolution depended, were imbued with anarchist doctrines, and their leaders would fight against communist authority just as they had resisted bolshevization in the Andalusian uprisings of 1919. In Herberg's historical argument, where the October Revolution becomes a model inspired by a mystique, there seemed to be no room for Spanish "exceptionalism."[45]

The Irony of Power

Although Herberg attacked Comintern policy in Spain and the atrocities of the Spanish communists, he could not bring himself to question the Soviet Union and its internal atrocities. In 1934, writing on the seventeenth anniversary of Russian Revolution, Herberg had praised Stalin's five-year plan and the policy of forced collectivization. He did not deny that there had been "grave errors," but these "unavoidable negative consequences" were due to the undeveloped internal resources of Russia, the resistance of the Kulaks, and the "capitalist remnants" left over by Lenin's New Economic Policy. Trotsky was wrong, Herberg insisted, in attributing Russia's harsh economic policies "to the perverse caprices of that particular devil, Stalin." For the devil theory of power loses its persuasion when matched against the dialectical theory of history. A socialist economy evolving "directly from the womb of capitalism" must develop, in Bukharin's words, through progressive "contradictions reproducing themselves on an ever-contracting scale, constantly though unevenly diminishing in scope and intensity." True, Herberg admitted, Soviet economic development was causing considerable social chaos and exacting great human costs. History, however, obeys necessity, not morality. "It would be the merest philistinism," he advised, "to sigh in regret or to whine in despair over these heavy sacrifices and costs. It is something much worse, something approaching unprincipled demagogy, to attempt to convert these sacrifices and costs into political capital, as Trotsky and others did, fortunately in vain."[46]

Unfortunately for Herberg—and for Bukharin!—the "contradictions" of Soviet history did not "diminish" in either scope or intensity. Two years later the Moscow trials confronted the Lovestoneites with the most grotesque contradiction of all, a spectacle that could not so easily be resolved dialectically into a higher "synthesis" of historical meaning. When the *Daily Worker* accused the *Workers Age* of "equivocating" on the trials, Herberg responded with a lengthy defense of the Opposition's position. Of the indiscriminate array of charges and allegations made during the trials, he admitted there were a number of "discrepancies, contradictions, even sheer impossibilities." But discarding the Presidium's sloppy handling of evidence, Herberg agreed that "efforts at assassination and sabotage were indeed made by some of the followers of or former followers of Trotsky and Zinoviev." He and the Lovestoneites also denied that their organization had any political allegiance to Bukharin and Rykov, whose trials were about to begin. Like Lovestone and Wolfe, Herberg seemed indifferent to the guilt or innocence of the accused. When "objective judgment" is passed on the trials, it is simply a question of who is the "bearer" of the revolutionary message of Marixst Leninism and which tendency is advancing socialist construction and which tendency is obstructing it: Stalin or the Trotskyist opposition? The Lovestoneites are not Trotskyists, Herberg assured the *Daily Worker*. "Don't," he warned, "make a game of the political struggle against Trotskyism—don't vulgarize it—don't make it so ridiculous that it becomes self-defeating!"[47]

What seemed a vulgarity soon turned into a depravity. Herberg had insisted that the trials "represented the last and concluding phase of Stalin's protracted struggle against the Trotskyist opposition." Nine months later he admitted that he and the Lovestoneites "were seriously mistaken." Instead events in Moscow were now seen as marking the "opening phase of a new terrorist offensive" that arose from Stalin's desperate effort to preserve his "oppressive" regime. The turning point was the trial and execution of Bukharin and the communist atrocities against the Spanish Trotskyists. These events of the winter and spring of 1937–1938 shocked the Lovestoneites, and Workers Age carried Charles Rappoport's account of Bukharin's defense and George Orwell's account of the fate of the POUM leadership in Spain. Jay Lovestone would now join with American Trotskyists in public speeches protesting the "menace" of Stalin. But neither Lovestone nor Herberg—who admitted that Trotsky had defended himself "brilliantly" in the hearings conducted by John Dewey in Mexico City—could accept Trotsky's version of what was happening in Russia or endorse his call for a Fourth International. This complex subject will be taken up in the following chapter on Burnham. Here it is only necessary to mention that, although Herberg felt compelled to offer a series of lectures at the New Workers School on the "New Problems of Soviet Dictatorship," he still refrained from revising his estimate of the "undoubted soundness of the Stalinist general line of socialist construction as against the Trotskyist line." The Moscow trials, Herberg maintained, indicated the extreme measures Stalin would resort to to suppress all resistance to his bureaucratic rule within Russia. At the same time, anti-Trotskyism did not indicate the strength of Trotsky's case, nor did it signify a real purge designed to eliminate Trotsky himself. Rather it was used as an excuse to smear and terrorize the "new oppositional elements" in the Soviet Union. Herberg's reasoning was as desperate as it was delusive. Insofar as he failed to question Stalin's line of "socialist construction," he seemed to argue that a new movement was rising in Russia not so much against Stalin's economic policies as against his political dictatorship. This argument was consistent with the history and philosophy of Lovestoneism, but the distinction had no clear foundation in Marxist Leninism. Since Stalin's economic and political policies were almost inseparable, since his bureaucratic regime was in large part a product of his personal rule, and since he himself was as much the creature as the creator of a one-party dictatorship that Herberg still did not question, it appeared that Herberg and the Lovestoneites wanted Stalinism without Stalin.[48]

The events of 1939–1940 left the Lovestoneites gasping for some meaningful historical perspective. No longer could Herberg return to the October Revolution to explain the Nazi-Soviet non-aggression pact, the causes of World War II, or Russia's invasion of Finland. Faced with these developments, the Lovestoneites began to drop their narrow sectarianism and praised liberals like Archibald MacLeish and John Dewey for denouncing the Popular Front, supported declarations of the American Committee for Cultural Freedom, protested the violation of Earl Browder's civil liberties when the CP leader was arrested, and endorsed Norman Thomas for president in 1940. Thoroughly committed to keeping America out of the European conflict, Workers Age serialized the writings of Charles Beard, whose theories on American interventionism now seemed as compelling as Lenin's theories on imperialism. Still stuck on historical analogies, Herberg maintained that American intervention in 1917 demonstrated that the present war had little to do with the preservation of Western democracy, and, despite the arguments of the American Labor Party and the New Leader, American involvement would again lead to the suppression of the Left. The issue of America's participation in the war was still unresolved among the Lovestoneites when, in January 1941, the Independent Labor League dissolved itself amid pleas for working class unity and diplomatic non-involvement. As former editor of the now-defunct Workers Age, Herberg lapsed into silence after disagreeing with Bertram Wolfe about the dangers of national defense and military aid to Great Britain.[49]

In the last issues of Workers Age Herberg had begun to ponder the mystery and terror that was Stalinism. He knew it was easy to bewail the dreadful consequences of the phenomenon, but like many American Marxists he was at a loss to explain its causes. The contemporary interpretations seemed inadequate: Burnham's managerial thesis on the emergence of a "new class" and Benjamin Herman's view of Stalinism as a form of "nationalist chauvinism." Nor did Herberg feel it worthwhile, as Eastman had felt it a moral duty, to trace the origins of Stalinism to the grim joke of the Marxian dialectic. More plausible was Lewis Corey's suggestion that Stalinism resulted from the imposition of collectivization upon a backward country lacking a viable middle class. Yet in focusing solely on economic factors, Corey ignored the role of "power relations" that prevail regardless of the respective social structure. The more Herberg reflected on the problem of Stalinism, the more it seemed rooted in the ambivalent nature of power itself. In April 1940, in a symposium on "Reconsidering Marxism," Herberg elaborated his theory of power as a lesson in historical irony.

According to Herberg there was nothing in the entire body of Marxist doctrine—"aside from some few stray suggestions by Marx and some very brilliant insights of Rosa Luxemburg"—to enable one to comprehend the monstrous "catastrophe" that grew out of the Russian Revolution. The central defect of Marxism was its inability to understand the contradictory relationship between socialism as an end and the means used to achieve that end. Despite Marx's great faith in the unity of theory and practice and in the organic relationship between means and ends, he failed to see that any means, whether dictatorial or democratic, can take on an existence of its own as human effort becomes institutionalized in higher and higher levels of organizations. Though Bolshevism produced victory, it also produced bureaucracy; not because Lenin's methods were immoral but because they were ironical:

Here, then, is the dilemma. The very form that facilitated—nay, was indispensable for—the struggle against Czarism and the victory of the revolution, turned out to be the form of organization that helped turn the fruits of the revolution into ashes, that led to Stalinism and totalitarianism.[50]

Arriving at this perception of the hitherto hidden dilemma of socialism, Herberg might have concluded with Dos Passos that the unforeseen fruits of Leninism proved again that "organization is death." Or he might have concluded with Eastman that Hegelian Marxism could overcome every contradiction except its own— Stalin. Or, to anticipate the next chapter, he might have concluded with Burnham that Soviet totalitarianism merely demonstrated what radicals should have known all along—the political inevitability of an elitist ruling class. But these conclusions, while perhaps politically sound, were philosophically shallow. Like Reinhold Niebuhr, Herberg retained from Marxism a dialectical sensibility that would be alien to the neo-conservative thought of Eastman, Dos Passos, and Burnham. From his experience with the failures of the Marxist interpretation of history, Herberg emerged with a heightened appreciation for the irony and ambiguity of historical events. But it would not be in Hegel's "cunning of reason" or in Bukharin's "contradiction of contradictions" that Herberg would find the explanation for the unforeseen riddles of human experience. On the contrary, his foreboding sense of irony and tragedy led ultimately to Judaic and Christian philosophy. In the crisis theology of existentialism Herberg would find a new foundation for value, and in the Christian doctrine of paradox he would find a criterion of meaning for every moment of history.

CHAPTER **4**

The Cerebral Communist: James Burnham

Who can determine when it is that the scales in the balance of opinion begin to turn, and what was a greater probability in behalf of a belief becomes a positive doubt against it?

CARDINAL NEWMAN, 1864

From Aesthetics to Politics

Among the number of Old Left radicals who made the complete transition to neo-conservatism after World War II, James Burnham was without doubt the most controversial figure. From the time he edited *The Symposium* in the early thirties to his break with Trotsky at the end of the decade, and from the publication of *The Managerial Revolution* (1941) to *Suicide of the West* (1964), Burnham's articles and books provoked a series of debates that challenged some of the most precious assumptions of the American intellectual community. In his early years a radical without illusions, in his later a conservative without delusions, he never shirked from thinking unfashionable thoughts as he gradually turned all the basic problems of history into questions of power. Until he joined the *National Review* in 1955, he appeared to be a writer who wrote not to be saved but to be damned. Before he found a following among *National Review* readers, his political friends were few and his enemies many. No one, it seemed, could abide his cold melancholy wisdom. A list of his critics throughout his career spans almost the entire political spectrum: Lionel Abel, Raymond Aron, Daniel Bell, Benedetto Croce, Lewis Corey,

Pierre Courtade, Peter Drucker, Max Eastman, Abraham Edel, Charles Frankel, Sidney Hook, Irving Howe, Frank S. Meyer, C. Wright Mills, Dwight Macdonald, Max Nomad, George Orwell, Murray Rothbard, David Spitz, Paul Sweezy, and, of course, Leon Trotsky.

In his own oral history memoirs, Max Shachtman has given us a most perceptive and sensitive portrait of Burnham.

He was very much welcomed in the Trotskyist movement, although he was regarded as something of a curio, a personal curio, not a political curio. He was very much respected by everybody—the leadership and the ranks, not just by the intellectuals but by the proletarians, including the pseudo-proletarians in the party. It was known that he came from the bourgeois aristocracy. . . . He was an outstanding student in Princeton and I think Cambridge—very scholarly. I don't mean in demeanor but in knowledge. Very urbane. Immediately acquired a reputation for impersonality, impartiality, fairness, and logical thought.

Because of his qualities and active interest in the Party, "no one ever dreamed of questioning the appropriateness of his position as a party leader," Shachtman said. Burnham was admired as a radical of a rare breed. He was one of the few Party members who tried to encourage the Trotskyists to take an interest in American politics; and he was "perhaps the only one" who had a facility with theoretical problems and could absorb the essential ideas of Trotsky and yet avoid the "particular exotic jargon" of Trotskyism itself. "Everyone felt good about having a genuine, serious, competent intellectual who was at home in political questions as well as questions of literature or art." Burnham, however, was not really "at home" in the movement. A divided man, he was a revolutionist who dreamed too little and thought too much. As Shachtman put it:

Yet all of us—and this went for Cannon and myself in particular—felt that although he was with us and with us thoroughly, he was not, so to say, of us. I don't mean that he behaved in any snobbish way or that he was standoffish or maintained an attitude of aristocratic disdain to party workers—no, it wasn't that. But we had had a training which caused us to judge party people, and above all else, party leaders, from the standpoint of their readiness to be an integral part of the party's life up to and including working for the party—working for the party as a party official, what we used to like to call "as a professional revolutionist." And try as we would—directly, by indirection, by pressure, by suggestion, by cajolery, by every device we could think of—we could never induce him to come to work in the party office. And I won't say that he thought he was above that. It was obvious—and as I became increasingly more intimate with him, increasingly obvious—that he was torn. There were clearly times when he was on the very verge of throwing it all up—namely, his job at the University—and perhaps other personal involvements and coming to work for the party, and that he felt this urge very strongly and very sincerely. It was not an act on his part. Indeed, he was not given to acting or pretending. And there were other times—especially toward the end of the fight on the so-called Russian question in 1939, 1940—when he was obviously assailed by doubts about the movement itself. And these doubts he would express to me very freely: questions that had arisen in his mind about Marxism—not just about dialectical materialism, toward which he was always skeptical, but about Marxism in general, socialism in general, about the social capacities of the working class in general. He had not made up his mind on any of these things. But, as I say, he was assailed by doubts.[1]

Burnham was tormented with doubt when he was about to break with Trotsky, but as a young radical, and later as a conservative, he was a man of certainty and decision. Matthew Josephson recalls that when he first met Burnham in the early thirties he found "a shy young mental prodigy of the type we tend to label a 'frosty intellectual.' " Other veterans of the Old Left have also remarked on the intense, abstract quality of Burnham's mind and thought. The ex-Lovestoneite Bertram D. Wolfe has described Burnham's method of reasoning as "rectilinear," a tendency to think of politics as a parallelogram of forces and to see history unfolding so predictably that one may chart it with geometric precision.[2] These characteristics became more pronounced in later years when Burnham's writings on the cold war seemed like a calculus of power moves, provoking Orwell and others to assail the neo-Machiavellian "power worship" of the ex-Trotskyist. But even as a young radical, writing on such abstruse subjects as aesthetics and ethics, Burnham was "scientifically" lucid, precise, direct; his style reads like an eloquent syllogism composed in primer simplicity, seemingly without emotional involvement. Nowhere in his writings does one find the probing moral sensibility of Herberg, the humorous rhetorical flashes of Eastman, the sensitive political rage of Dos Passos. What one does find is analytical deference to the presumably "objective" forces of history.

Behind Burnham's controlled prose was an author who scarcely fitted the stereotyped picture of the radical intellectual as a flaming confrontationist or as a loquacious bore. Polite, courteous, gracious to his friends, and, at least until provoked, respectful of his opponents; well-bred, well-mannered, well-educated, and well-connected; a devoted husband and father who, unlike Eastman, could become a radical revolutionary without questioning the bourgeois institutions of marriage and family, Burnham might have been a character in a J. P. Marquand novel. Always neatly attired, with closely trimmed hair on top of a serious forehead, below which stared a pair of rimless glasses, usually wearing a dark suit with a white collar and thinly knotted tie, he could easily have passed for a Madison Avenue advertising executive. He grew up knowing little about the struggles of the working class and life in the Jewish ghetto, the environment of Herberg. He bore no ill feelings toward the business world of his father, the early "complex" of Dos Passos. And his life style posed no challenge to conventional morality, the butt of Eastman's banter. If "alienation" describes the condition of many radical intellectuals, it does not describe the disposition of Burnham's thought and character.

James Burnham was born in Chicago in 1905 to a wealthy family, the son of Claude George Burnham, a Catholic Briton who emigrated from Britain as a child; he was vice president of the Burlington Railroad at the time of his death in 1928. At Princeton University, Burnham was an editor of the *Princeton Tiger* and the *Nassau Literary Review* and won the Latin Salutatorian, the equivalent of the "first scholar" of his class. After graduation in 1927 he went abroad to continue study of English literature at Oxford and earned an MA at Balliol College two years later. Although he had left the Church about midway through Princeton, at Oxford he studied philosophy under the Catholic scholar Father Martin C. D'Arcy (Burnham's brother, Philip, later became an editor of the Catholic *Commonweal*). In the summer of 1930, with the economic crash taking on the dimension of a worldwide depression, he began to read Marx and Engels while living in southwestern France. That fall he accepted a position in the philosophy department in the Washington Square College of New York University, where he taught courses in medieval and Thomistic philosophy and became a close friend and colleague of Sidney Hook. With another colleague, the literary critic Philip Wheelwright, Burnham wrote *Introduction to Philosophical Analysis*, a highly imaginative textbook that used the novels of Faulkner and Joyce to interest students in the technical problems of epistemology. Susanne K. Langer described this work as close to a "pedagogical masterpiece."[3]

For four years, from 1930 to 1933, Burnham and Wheelwright published *The Symposium*, a "critical review" devoted to literature and philosophy, in some respects a precursor of the *Partisan Review*. Many of its budding authors would later be writing in *Partisan Review* and would become leading figures in the academic world of literary theory and the political world of social criticism: William Phillips, F. W. Dupee, Dwight Macdonald, Harold Rosenberg, Paul Goodman, and Lionel Trilling.

Burnham, as editor and former student of English literature, was caught up in the debates over literary criticism and the epistemological status of poetry. He was sympathetic to I. A. Richards and the "New Critics" in their attempt to use the distinction between prose and verse to demonstrate how form shapes meaning. Did poetry as a means of cognition convey truth? Did it illustrate or explain anything about the external world? The questions troubled Burnham, as they did many other literary philosophers. For two years apolitical, he wrestled with the interminable issues of plot, character, and symbol, of imitation and representation, of T. S. Eliot's "objective correlative," reviewing books on Shakespeare, Restoration tragedy, romanticism, modern poetry, and the contemporary novel. Long before Malcolm Cowley or Jean-Paul Sartre, Burnham sensed the genius of Faulkner's literary metaphysics of the absurd, the novelist's "sound and fury" that signified the existential nothingness of life, his "passionate awareness of inarticulateness" as a vehicle for conveying the inadequacy of words to describe emotional experience. For at this juncture Burnham, too, found himself mired in the "metaphysical bogs" of modern thought. Uncomfortable with the scientific equation of change and progress, he was uncomfortable with the humanist claim of culture and tradition. One led to a complacent utilitarianism, the other to an uncritical historicism. And between both the radical and conservative approaches to art there remained the problem of aesthetics and linguistics: the relationship that exists between experience prior to the act of communication and language that functions as the medium of the creative act.[4]

Burnham was deeply moved when he first laid eyes on Trotsky's *History of the Russian Revolution*. The monumental trilogy reminded Dos Passos of the classical history of Thucydides, and it demonstrated to Burnham that "the medium is an integral part of what the work of art means." Several years later, when he broke with Trotsky, Burnham would say that he had found the *History*'s "style" seductive. Reviewing the book in *The Symposium*, however, he made no distinction between style and substance. What impressed Burnham was Trotsky's ability to render historical generalizations vivid through the symbolic use of characters and events, to substitute for the older personalistic great-man interpretation of the past a class approach to historical understanding, and to synthesize the historical determinism of Marxism with the political voluntarism of Lenin. Thus, unlike Eastman, whose translation of the *History* he praised, Burnham discerned no discrepancy in Trotsky's use of dialectical reasoning as a means of reconciling determinism and freedom. With Herberg, however, he realized that Trotsky's great historical study could scarcely serve as a model for modern industrial America. The "peculiarities" of America's historical development made any prediction about the future impossible.[5]

By 1933 Burnham could no longer ignore the intense political controversies raging through the American intellectual community. In January he wrote an extended and highly thoughtful essay on "Marxism and Esthetics" for The Symposium, one of the most balanced and intelligent pieces of literary analysis of the early Old Left. Here Burnham tried to find some middle ground between the New Critics, who were devoted to the autonomy of art and the self-referential criteria of aesthetic experience, and the Marxists, who desired to subordinate art not only to life but to the demands of social transformation. Burnham protested the lofty position of the New Critics, who made a fetish of the work of art as pure object. Yet he could not accept the political crudeness of the Marxists, whose cries for social "relevance" endangered aesthetic discrimination. "Those of us who are not marxists," he concluded; "must reject the dictates of socialist realism. And because I believe that marxism is, in the last analysis, false, false in this sense—inhuman and offering an order of values not acceptable to man nor in keeping with man's nature—I do not rest my hopes for art in any esthetics it can give birth to."[6]

When readers complained that The Symposium had failed to take an "unequivocal position" toward the important issues of the day, editors Burnham and Wheelwright put together "Thirteen Propositions" to explain the rationale of the journal. They conceded that capitalism was moribund, that a "revolutionary change" was necessary in property relations, and that collectivization could only be brought about by militant mass pressure from the working class. They also conceded that literary criticsm should be brought to bear more closely upon social reality, and that the relationship between theory and practice be studied in depth. Yet the Communist Party, by equating politics and culture, made the grievous mistake of confusing man's moral reconstruction with society's economic transformation; and by universalizing its tactics and ideology, it confused modern industrial America with post-feudal Russia. The Party, Burnham and Wheelwright charged,

is, on the one hand, in its exaggerated internationalism (which is actually Slavophilism), equalitarianism, "revolutionary optimism," in its conceptions of the possibilities of social development and its visions of the future anarchic heaven on earth, ridiculously utopian; and, on the other, in the cluttering ideology with which it leads and impedes its political activities, in its conceptions and analysis of literature, art, morality, religion, and human nature, it is barbaric.[7]

The "Thirteen Propositions" served to becloud rather than clarify the political position of The Symposium, bewildering both ends of the ideological spectrum. T. S. Eliot, for example, wrote an editorial in The Criterion which likened The Symposium to the right-wing American Review because of their mutual denunciation of communism, capitalism, and liberalism. On the Left, the New Masses accused editors Burnham and Wheelwright of intellectual elitism and pro-fascism because of their failure to advocate the dictatorship of the proletariat.[8] The criticisms disturbed Burnham, and when he responded in October 1933 he and Wheelwright wrote separate statements. Burnham rejected Eliot's contention that communism and capitalism were "forms of the same thing" and that the study of ethics should take priority over the study of politics. Such a position, Burnham responded, made the proper study of mankind the study of timeless principles of "the idea of the good." Burnham respected Eliot's undoubted literary genius, but he regarded the poet's Platonic search for the essence behind the shadow as a formalistic escape from life to art. Burnham knew enough philosophy to realize that Marxism did not resolve the problem of ethics; but he knew enough about the realities of the Depression to realize that ought implies can: "We should try to put men in a position where they can live like human beings before showing them how human beings ought to live." As for the communist critics on the Left, Burnham now expressed "regret" for the language he had used in describing the Party. After outlining his basis for criticizing the Communist Party six months ago—its Slavophilic subservience to the Comintern, its "Black Belt" doctrine for the American Negro, its thoughtless description of American farmers as "Kulaks"—Burnham assured his communist critics that "I do accept the dictatorship of the proletariat as the indispensable instrument of the revolution."[9]

Burnham confessed that he was "particularly anxious" to clear up the confusion because "my own position has developed considerably since the Propositions were written." Why the apologia? What caused so cautious and reflective a thinker to change his mind about communism between the spring and fall of 1933? The answer is a combination of immediate personal experience and theoretical reflection. During the summer Burnham toured the country and saw at first hand the desperation of the poor and unemployed. In the Detroit auto factories, the Illinois coal districts and steel regions, he encountered the first stirrings of an authentic "class struggle."[10] Aside from the existential experience of the Depression, Burnham could find theoretical justification for the communist position in the work of his colleague Sidney Hook, whose *Towards the Understanding of Karl Marx* appeared in 1933. Hook's translation of Marxism into the American "pragmatic" idiom was far more satisfying to Burnham than Eastman's quarrel with the ghost of Hegel. An even more important influence, however, was Adolf A. Berle's and Gardiner C. Means's *The Modern Corporation and Private Property*, also published in 1933. In this work, now a classic in economics, Burnham not only learned about the great concentration of wealth, he also discovered that the owners of corporate stock no longer controlled the use of their own property. Berle and Means looked upon this development as a blessing in disguise, for the modern sophisticated administrators of corporate wealth, in contrast to the unenlightened owners of the past, would be more inclined to make corporations serve the interests of the community. Burnham, however, saw the heralded "neutral technocracy" as part of the class co-option strategy of the New Deal, a policy founded on the illusion that a broker or "umpire" government could both mitigate the class struggle and prevent the development of a corporate fascist state in America. Moreover, although Berle and Means demonstrated that a "revolution" had taken place in the "social relations of production," Burnham doubted that class and property relations had been fundamentally altered. Thus the separation of ownership from control—a theory Burnham would later return to in *The Managerial Revolution*—altered the functional relationships of power but did not threaten the traditional structure of power; nor did it call into question the profit motive, the sanctity of property, the inequitable distribution of wealth, or the efficacy of corporate capitalism to overcome its own inner weaknesses. *The Modern Corporation and Private Property* was merely further evidence of the failure of liberal nerve.[11]

The limitations of liberal capitalism, far more than the illuminations of theoretical Marxism, drove Burnham into the camp of revolutionary communism. His move to the extreme Left was less an act of philosophical conviction than an act of political desperation. For all along Burnham expressed doubts about the utopian content of communism. Egalitarianism, absolute social justice, total statelessness and classlessness, were ideals he questioned rather than invoked; and as for the slogan "to each according to his needs," Burnham wisely observed that "need" is an impulse limited only by "imagination." Never wholly absorbed by communism, he harbored an inner struggle between emotive belief and critical reasoning, and when he decided to become a communist it was not because Marxism was true but rather because it was "our only hope." It would be the first and last time that James Burnham would allow his political intellect to hope for the best for fear of the worst.[12]

The Permanent Revolution

In 1933 Burnham joined his colleague Sidney Hook in helping to organize the American Workers Party. Led by the Dutch-born pacifist minister, A. J. Muste, the AWP appealed to a small group of independent radical intellectuals who wanted to avoid the tactical and doctrinal mistakes of the CP. Burnham wrote for the Musteites' *Labor Action* and briefly served as secretary of the AWP.[13] A majority of AWP members, including Burnham, united with the American Trotskyists in 1934 to form the Workers Party. Hook sympathized but did not join. Like the Lovestoneites, the Trotskyists were the Pharisees of the revolutionary Left. But the Lovestoneites were more like a banished tribe of reformationists who desired to be readmitted into the CP; the Trotskyists, also expelled from the CP in the late twenties, were more like proud separatists who had given up hope of reforming the Party. The Trotskyists, claiming to be the true heirs of Lenin, longed to reconstitute a new, de-Stalinized party and a new, de-Slavified Communist International—the Fourth International. After Hitler's advent to power demonstrated further the fatal errors of the CP and Comintern, they felt it imperative to have a separate monthly publication devoted to fundamental theoretical issues to add to their weekly, *The Militant*. Burnham and Max Shachtman became the chief editors of the monthly *New International*.

In the *New International* Burnham attempted to interpret two seemingly different yet related developments: the meaning and direction of America under the leadership of President Roosevelt, and the meaning and direction of Russia under the dictatorship of Premier Stalin. Although Burnham's analysis of the Roosevelt administration partook of the Marxian idiom, there were some distinctive perceptions. He did not regard Roosevelt's program simply as the last critical phase of monopoly capitalism, nor did he regard economics as the sole determining factor in historical understanding. Instead Burnham saw Roosevelt as a consummate politician, perhaps a demagogue, but nonetheless a shrewd therapist of the anxieties of the middle class, and hence an intelligent opportunist who would try to salvage capitalism by moving the nation halfway to socialism. Burnham believed the attempt impossible, for in order to realize the quasi-socialist program of welfare, public works, financial reform, and social security, Roosevelt would have to expand the power of the executive office and consolidate the power of the federal government, steps that would help "pave the way to the transition to Fascism."[14]

Thus Burnham ridiculed the socialist New Leader for hailing Roosevelt's welfare programs as a victory for socialism, and he criticized liberals who saw in the Keynesian "multiplier effect" the key to expanding and accelerating income circulation. But his severest criticisms were directed at the Daily Worker, for the communists did not know what to make of the Wagner labor relations bill other than to claim that the bourgeois press opposed it in order better to "deceive the workers." This "childish" attitude of "maneuvers" and "deceptions," Burnham insisted, may save face for the Marxist theory of the state, but the heterogeneous nature of the bourgeois classes in America, and the disunity and conflict within the business community itself, cannot be explained away. The American government, though susceptible to capitalist pressures, was not the mere "instrument" of the capitalist class. It was an institution that had recently begun to assume a life and logic of its own. Indeed all modern democratic governments, which have increasingly grown into "gigantic bureaucracies," are run by politicians who must maintain the support and sufferance of the masses while serving the needs of the capitalist order. And during the period of capitalist decline the role of the politician increases as the power of government expands. Here, in an early analysis of the New Deal, one can discern the germ of an idea that haunted Burnham for the rest of the decade until he finally brought it to fruition in The Managerial Revolution: Both Marx and Madison may be wrong and Weber right. For the modern state is neither solely a "reflection" of the interests of the capitalist class nor a "representation" of the interests of majority and minority factions. Instead it may be a new political mutation, an increasingly autonomous structural entity without exact precedent or analogy in the past.[15]

This idea still remained only an embryonic caveat when Burnham turned his attention from the American scene to Russia. The Franco-Soviet military pact and the announcement of the Popular Front in 1935 meant, from the Trotskyist viewpoint, that war between the fascist powers and the Soviet Union and the democratic West was only a matter of time. How to respond to the next war? Burnham believed that every true Marxist must avoid the mistakes of World War I, when the Second International collapsed under the pressures of war and national security. The Popular Front slogan "Defend the Soviet Union!" was a treacherous illusion. He rejected the rationale of left-wing realists, who called upon workers and intellectuals to support the Soviet Union, despite its unfulfilled promises and its "temporary" deviations from Marxist Leninism, as the only bulwark against fascism and the only great achievement of the working class in the twentieth century. To Burnham this realpolitik attitude was not realistic enough. Every additional step Stalin took as a matter of military expediency made it all the more difficult for the Soviet Union to return to the ideals of 1917. The danger to the Soviet Union was Stalinism itself. The "present bureaucratic, nationalistic officialdom, resting primarily on the apparatus and the army," was a gross departure from Lenin's concept of proletarian dictatorship and, if allowed to continue, would transform the "working class" nature of the Soviet Union. Thus the only way to truly defend Russia was to extend the October Revolution abroad, strengthen the world proletariat, and break with both democratic socialism and Stalinism and establish the Fourth International.[16]

In 1935 Burnham still regarded Russia as a "working class" state and Stalinism as an aberration of Bolshevism rather than its logical conclusion. These matters of interpretation, plus the crucial issue of whether to support Russia in the event of war, would later lead Burnham to break with Trotsky. Meanwhile the most publicized criticism of Soviet Marxism and Stalin's Russia came not from the Trotskyist opposition on the Left but from a writer who had once been America's staunchest supporter of Lenin, Trotsky, and the Bolshevik Revolution—Max Eastman.

Burnham versus Eastman

When Trotsky had warned that Eastman's critique of dialectical materialism augured the start of a "retrograde adventure," the die was cast. Trotsky's American followers would now have to choose sides. But in the early thirties Trotsky himself was too preoccupied with other matters to answer Eastman directly. Instead he asked the editors of New International to respond, and Burnham took on the challenging task.[17]

Burnham found himself agreeing with Eastman despite himself. Much as Hook had done, Burnham denied Eastman's claim that Marx, in attempting to go beyond Hegelian idealism, had actually absorbed it into his own Weltanschauung and thereby read into history his own ideals and purposes. Yet Burnham's reply to Eastman differed from Hook's in several respects. First of all, Burnham noted that Eastman's critique took the whole issue out of the context of intellectual and social history and made Marx's mind and thought subject to psychoanalysis. The proper dimension to explore, Burnham pointed out, was not Marx's "inner psychic urge" but the historical validity of his ideas, not his motives but his conclusions. Burnham then elaborated six definitions of "inevitability" to demonstrate that the dialectical, logical, and teleological elements supposedly inherent in Marxism were merely used by vulgar Marxists as a means of guaranteeing the victory of socialism. To the extent that these crude Marxists rested their case on such foundations as dialectical materialism—which Burnham cryptically dismissed as "only a disguised form of monistic objective idealism" —he agreed with Eastman that Marxism had become a religion rather than a science. Yet this Hegelian ethos was not characteristic of true Marxism, "which insolubly combines scientific objectivity with the intransigent struggle for power." Shrewdly shifting the focus, Burnham claimed it was the Stalinists who deluded themselves into thinking that socialism was inevitably predetermined in the nature of historical development. Stalin's communist opponents, on the other hand, insisted that socialism was not guaranteed but had to be won through sustained, permanent revolutionary struggle. The clever upshot of Burnham's reply was to dissociate Eastman's critique from Marxism itself and apply it to the Stalinists, "the non-revolutionary falsifiers of living Marxism."[18]

In 1935, then, Burnham tended to agree with Eastman that Marxism could be profitably liberated from the contemplative spell of nineteenth-century idealist assumptions and revised in accordance with twentieth-century knowledge and reality. Such an attitude would be in keeping with the spirit of Lenin, who himself went beyond a literal, static interpretation of Marxist inevitability to realize the October Revolution. Burnham could tolerate Eastman's critique of dialectical materialism for the sake of better realizing socialism; still, he could not stand idly by when Eastman, writing in *Harper's* three years later, pointed to developments in Stalin's Russia as evidence that the ideals themselves of socialism must be questioned. "No mind not bold enough to reconsider the socialist hypothesis in the light of the Russian experiment can be called intelligent," wrote Eastman, who was still willing to identify himself with "we socialists."[19]

Aside from his Greenwich Village cultural indictment of Stalin's Russia, Eastman criticized the proposition of socialism itself on several theoretical grounds. First, Marx never defined the socialist ideal in terms of a specified end to be reached. Of the workers, Marx had said, "They have no ideal to realize, they have only to set free the elements of the new society which the old bourgeois society carries in its womb." With no theoretical definition of ends, Marxism was vulnerable to Eastman's ridicule as he examined its following historic promises: (a) a society of free and equals summed up in the felicitous formula "From each according to his abilities, to each according to his needs"; (b) a polity without power and authority in which the state "withers away"; (c) a community of fraternity in which the distinction between manual tasks and creative endeavor is obliterated; (d) a life of meaning and purpose in which the division of labor disappears and non-alienating work becomes the "highest desire of life." Second, not only may the above ideals be unrealizable, there were also ideals implicit in Marxism that were inherently self-contradictory. According to Eastman, Marx tried unsuccessfully to combine two opposing values: the Jeffersonian ideal of freedom and "rank individualism" and least possible government, and the socialist ideal of equality, cooperativeness, and government regulation for the good of all. Third, and perhaps most disturbing to the Trotskyists, Russia's failure to realize or even approximate the above ideals was a result of the theoretical paradoxes in the ideals themselves. Here Eastman rejected Trotsky's thesis, expressed in *The Revolution Betrayed*, that the degeneration of Bolshevism under Stalin may be explained by the pressures of political backwardness and economic scarcity in a nation menaced by world imperialism.[20]

Eastman's devastating critique, which in effect showed that Marx had never really liberated his mind from the very "utopianism" he himself criticized, could not be dismissed lightly. It was a great challenge to Burnham, who, as we have seen, never subscribed to the utopian content of Marxism and who, as one of America's leading Trotskyist intellects, prided himself on being as realistic and scientific as Eastman. Burnham's reply might be characterized as a thoughtful exercise in terminological discrimination and historical reasoning. The ends of socialism may be a "wish fulfillment," Burnham conceded, but the Jeffersonian ideal of complete individual freedom was no less willed from desire rather than intellect. The important point is that great ideals, because of their "dynamic function," are not meant to be realized. Thus Eastman's ridiculing of Marxist ideals betrays an acceptance of the "tragic sense of life" and a belief in "original sin," notions that are unscientific and doom men forever to resignation and despair. Moreover, Marx's egalitarian and fraternal ideals, although they may not be ultimately reached, may be better approached in a socialist society. Even under advanced capitalism vast technical development and minimum social progress have been achieved. Even the overcoming of workers' alienation is within the realm of historical possibility, Burnham cautiously suggested:

Marx, not knowing the monotony of mass production methods, was perhaps over-optimistic in hoping that labor will become instead of drudgery "the highest desire of life." But with manual factory labor reduced to a minimum through the application of inventive technique (compare even today a continuous rolling mill with the former existing mill for the same process), and hours of that type of labor shortened to a small fraction of the day, with adequate sanitary and aesthetic conditions of work, with general education and leisure, with city and country planned as even today they are technically capable of being handled, why should not labor become if not man's highest desire at least part of a highly desirable life?[21]

Burnham had done as well as he could to justify many of the paradoxical ideals that Marx himself never bothered to analyze.[22] But the main burden of Burnham's reply was his defense of Trotsky. In refuting Trotsky's *The Revolution Betrayed*, Eastman had argued that "if the socialist idea of a free and equal cooperative commonwealth emerging from the dictatorship of the proletariat were practical under an economy of abundance, we should find under an economy of scarcity some lame approximation to it." The logic of Eastman's statement seemed to Burnham bereft of any causal connection. An economy of abundance plus the dictatorshp of the workers may make possible a "rapid" transition to socialism, he replied, but without the prerequisite of abundance there is no reason why a proletarian dictatorship can even begin a "lame approximation" of the transition. Russia's retarded technique of production, however, was not what Eastman regarded as a sufficient explanation of what went wrong in Russia. Eastman criticized Trotsky for being oblivious to recent "psychological or biological problems" of human behavior. "Developments that to the most ordinary shrewd sense reveal a conflict between Marxian theory and the universal attributes of human nature," Eastman said of

Trotsky, "are attributed by him to survival in a backward country of a 'petty bourgeois psychology.'" Burnham seized upon Eastman's careless phrases to accuse him of retreating to medieval notions of the eternal "Substance and Essence" of man, the "dead lumber" of the Thomistic and Platonic "realm of Being." Here Burnham missed the point entirely, or perhaps deliberately avoided it. The problem of human behavior was not a real problem for Marx and Trotsky. The heretofore limited nature of man would be transcended by the victory of the proletariat, a social stratum which Marx had not so much studied in terms of its actual character and behavior, but simply gave a metaphysical position in his scheme of historical negations—the old *deus ex machina* of the dialectic that both Eastman and Burnham had rejected. Eastman, then, was not substituting a functional, environmental analysis of human behavior for a medieval notion of "eternal human nature" to explain the unhappy consequences of the socialist experiment in Russia. He was suggesting that in light of Stalinism the nineteenth-century rationalistic and optimistic assumptions about man that "saturated" Trotsky's thought must be honestly re-examined—an exercise that would later engage Herberg and Burnham himself.[23]

Burnham was satisfied that he had demonstrated Eastman's failure to prove any incompatibility between the conclusions of modern science and the ideals of socialism. Whether or not he did so, the Trotskyists had nothing to fear from Eastman, the aging rebel who had seemingly run out of Left causes. Yet by 1939 a considerable section of the American intellectual community seemed to be following Eastman's path. The anti-Stalinist intellectuals with whom the Trotskyists could once ally themselves had now begun to criticize not only the Soviet Union but the Marxist-Leninist assumptions that presumably made Stalin possible. Burnham, together with co-editor Shachtman, studied this development in a twenty-page editorial analysis in *New International*, "Intellectuals in Retreat." They drew up a list of two categories of renegades from Marxism. Group One consisted of Eastman, Hook, Charles Yale Harrison, James Rorty, Edmund Wilson, Philip Rahv, Benjamin Stolberg, James T. Farrell, Louis Hacker, and others; Group Two of John Chamberlain, Louis Adamic, Eugene Lyons, John Dewey, George S. Counts, and Ferdinand Lundberg. The two groups had recently begun to coalesce as each writer "retreated" back to liberalism. Originally they were distinct. While members of the second group had been called "radical anti-Stalinist intellectuals," those of the first had been, with the exception of Eastman and Stolberg, Communist Party sympathizers in the early thirties, and after their break with Stalinism many came to be known as "the Trotskyist intellectuals." Together writers in both groups had now taken a stand on the fundamental issues that separated them from what remained of the Marxist Left in America: they were against one-party dictatorships, against dialectical materialism, against the argument that Leninism was not the source of Stalinism, and against "the harsh tone of revolutionary polemics."[24]

Burnham and Shachtman spent a great deal of time and energy attempting to rebut these positions one by one. But their efforts, however intellectually resourceful, were politically futile. By 1939 much of the American Left had turned against communism of all varieties and had begun to question all political strategies that derived from Marxist premises. That Stalinism itself was the main cause of this reorientation was cruelly ironic to the Trotskyists. For years *New International* had been protesting with almost single-minded obsession the threat of Stalin as the betrayer of world revolutionary struggle. Now American intellectuals, themselves taken in by the false promises of Soviet Russia, became so inflicted with "Stalinphobia" that they began to liken Stalin to Hitler and communism to fascism—an ideological equation so shocking to Burnham and the Trotskyists that it reminded them of the doctrine of "social fascism" originally expounded by the Stalinists themselves.

Yet what exactly was Stalinism? For several years Burnham had accepted Trotsky's interpretation of the phenomenon and used it in his debates with Eastman, Hook, and others. After the outbreak of World War II in September 1939, Burnham began to question not only Trotsky's interpretation of Stalinism but the theoretical foundations of Marxism itself more and more rigorously than he had done, beginning with his doubting of certain of Trotsky's views.

Trotsky—"A Veritable Pharos"

In some respects Trotsky was to the anti-Stalinist Old Left of the thirties what Lenin had been to the Lyrical Left of the World War I years. Eastman, Reed, and other Greenwich Village radicals saw in Lenin the glorious identity of history and will; he was the revolutionist whose daring conquest of power in 1917 seemed to symbolize the fulfillment of both the idea and the deed of Marxism. Trotsky enjoyed a similar heroic image, but for the generation of the thirties it took on a different character—the purity of an idea whose essence had been tainted by Stalin. He emerged as the "prophet outcast" who in losing power had saved the conscience of the revolution. To Irving Howe, Trotsky was "an embodiment of past grandeur, a voice of corrosive honesty attacking the terror and corruption of Stalin, a thinker in the great Marxist tradition, a revolutionist of exemplary fearlessness." To the literary critic F. W. Dupee, Trotsky was the Thucydides of the Russian Revolution. Even to the sardonic Dwight Macdonald, a writer not given to hero worship, Trotsky's career "showed that intellectuals, too, could make history." Trotsky could scarcely satisfy the intellectuals' thirst for power—a latent impulse more likely fulfilled by identifying with Stalin and the Soviet state. If some radical intellectuals saw Stalin as the only answer to Hitler, others saw Trotsky as the only answer to Stalin, the last hope that the meaning of the October Revolution would not be lost in what Isaac Deutscher called the "hell-black night" of totalitarianism. In the gloomy political atmosphere of the thirties, when writers felt the urgent necessity of choosing the bad against the worst, Trotsky and Trotskyism held out the possibility that one could choose the best and the brightest and defy the grotesque fallacy of the false alternative.

Edmund Wilson best expressed this desperate hope of his generation:

> We who of recent years have seen the State that Trotsky helped to build in a phase of combining the butcheries of the Robespierre Terror with the corruption and reaction of the Directory, and Trotsky himself figuring dramatically in the role of Gracchus Babeuf, may be tempted to endow him with qualities which actually he does not possess and with principles which he has expressly repudiated. We have seen the successor of Lenin undertake a fabulous rewriting of the whole history of the Revolution in order to cancel out Trotsky's part; pursue Trotsky from country to country, persecuting even his children and hounding them to their deaths; and at last, in faked trials and confessions more degrading to the human spirit than the frank fiendishness of Ivan the Terrible, try to pin upon Trotsky the blame for all the mutinies, mistakes and disasters that have harassed his administration —till he has made the world conscious of Trotsky as the accuser of Stalin's own bad conscience, as if the Soviet careerists of the thirties were unable to deny the socialist ideal without trying to annihilate the moral authority of this one homeless and hunted man. It is not Trotsky alone who has created his role: his enemies have given it a reality that no mere self-dramatization could have compassed. And as the fires of the Revolution have died down in the Soviet Union at a time when the systems of thought of the West were already in an advanced state of decadence, he has shone forth like a veritable pharos, rotating a long shaft of light on the seas and the reefs all around.[25]

Within American intellectual circles, Burnham was for several years the chief spokesman for the "veritable pharos" exiled in Mexico. After Trotsky directed his followers to enter the Socialist Party in 1936, Burnham would be called upon to present the position of the Workers Party at various socialist meetings and conventions. Burnham helped organize the Joint Commission of Inquiry formed to conduct Trotsky's "countertrial" in Mexico, and it was Burnham who defended to Trotsky the choice of John Dewey to head the commission. Moreover, as a contributor to the prestigious *Partisan Review*, Burnham influenced influential authors like Dwight Macdonald and Philip Rahv, who lent their support to *New International* and the Workers Party.[26]

Burnham was not, however, a mere echo of the oracle in Mexico City. On domestic political issues he often differed with Trotsky. In 1937 he asked Trotsky to reconsider his plan for splitting the Workers Party from the Socialist Party, a precipitous action that, Burnham wisely advised, would only deepen suspicion toward the Trotskyists. Trotsky nevertheless plunged ahead with his new strategy, which was based on the assumption that the year 1937 was bringing to a climax tendencies in world politics that would prove the historical wisdom of Trotskyism over both socialism and Stalinism. As evidence of these trends, Trotsky pointed to the coming "denouement" of the Spanish Civil War; the increasing tempo of Soviet persecutions that would finally expose the terror of the Stalin regime; the eventual failure of the Léon Blum government in France, and hence the exposure of the bankruptcy of the Popular Front; and the forthcoming report of the Commission of Inquiry investigating Stalin's charges against him, the publication of which "must and will be annihilating for the Stalinist clique and for the Comintern Bureaucracy." On such matters of world politics, Burnham could hardly challenge Trotsky, a man who had been in more countries and perhaps witnessed more history than even Marx or Lenin. As for Soviet internal affairs, an American philosophy professor was in no position to question the co-creator of the Bolshevik Revolution.[27]

Trotsky elaborated his fascinating interpretation of Stalin's Russia in *The Revolution Betrayed*, his last completed book, and his final effort to face squarely the unexpected turns in contemporary history and the diminishing hopes of the revolutionary Left scattered throughout the world. We have already seen how Trotsky and Burnham used the perspective of backwardness to explain the Soviet Union's failure to make the transition to socialism. The riddle of Stalinism, however, remained, for Joseph Stalin was as much the creator as a creature of a totalitarian system no one had foreseen, least of all those Marxists who believed that the contradictions of class society had been abolished in Russia in 1917. What went wrong?

To answer this question Trotsky reverted to the metaphor of the "Soviet Thermidor" that had been bandied about by the anti-Stalinist Workers Opposition in the twenties. Trotsky's use of the term was much more discriminating, even though his historical judgments were far from impeccable. Trotsky maintained that there were certain "laws" that governed bourgeois and proletarian revolutions alike and that therefore what was happening in Russia from 1923 to 1937 could be understood on the basis of what had happened in France from 1789 to 1794. Just as the French Revolution had swung from the egalitarian excesses of the Jacobins to the bourgeois consolidation of Napoleon Bonaparte, the Russian Revolution had begun its stabilizing phase in 1923, when Stalin suppressed the Left Opposition and began to build a state machinery that resembled the Consulate under Bonaparte. Neither Stalinism nor Bonapartism represented counterrevolution, for neither phenomenon expressed a tendency to turn back the social revolution and restore feudal property relations. Yet as a reactionary stage within a continuing historical process, Stalinism signified a tendency on the part of a rising bourgeoisie to regenerate itself through the political means of the new bureaucracy, just as the new French middle class reasserted itself under the Bourbon reign after 1830. In the face of this danger of bourgeois restoration, Trotsky was nevertheless convinced that the Soviet Union must be defended when the war, which he regarded as inevitable, broke out between Russia and the Western powers. Despite its "monstrous bureaucratic degeneration, the Soviet state still remains the historical instrument of the working class, in so far as it assures the development of economy and culture on the basis of nationalized means of production, and by virtue of this prepares the conditions for a genuine emancipation of the toilers through the liquidation of the bureaucracy and of social inequality." War may be the health of the Soviet state; it may also serve as the virus that would bring down the old order in the rest of Europe and usher in a true proletarian uprising in the West. "The danger of war and defeat of the Soviet Union is a reality, but the revolution is also a reality.

If the revolution does not prevent war, then war will help the revolution. Second births are commonly easier than the first."[28]

Trotsky's interpretation of Stalin's Russia, and Burnham's distillation of it in New International, were in turn analyzed by several caustic American writers who found it difficult to understand why the Soviet Union deserved "critical support" as the imperfect realization of a perfect idea gone awry. The deficiencies of Trotsky's interpretation were acknowledged many years later by his sympathetic biographer, Isaac Deutscher; but even he failed to question the Marxist premises upon which those interpretations had been founded,[29] an exercise that would soon engage Burnham himself. Trotsky's position became even more questionable because of his own role in the Thermidor. In the winter of 1937–1938, when the subject of Trotsky's involvement in the Kronstadt affair of 1921 was first raised, his acknowledged participation in the violent suppression of the uprising of anarchist-inspired sailors at the port of Kronstadt tarnished his reputation as the symbol of revolutionary virtue. The issue was debated heatedly by the Trotskyist sympathizer Dwight Macdonald in New International.[30] Soon liberals joined the discussion, and in January 1938 Common Sense published "Violence, For and Against: A Symposium on Marx, Stalin, and Trotsky."

The symposium had been prompted by Selden Rodman, a poet and fellow Yale graduate of editor Alfred Bingham, who had raised a question that could no longer be suppressed: If Trotsky were in the Kremlin today, would he be any less ruthless than Stalin? Did not both share a "common grounding in Marxist absolutism and its dependency on violence"? British notables like H. G. Wells and Aldous Huxley agreed with Rodman. Eastman and Hook, who knew far more about Marxism and the history of Soviet Russia, and who still maintained a high respect for Trotsky's integrity and intellect, defended Trotsky against the charge that a common philosophy of history must lead to a common course of action. Yet it was increasingly difficult to avoid the conclusion that Stalinism implicated, if not Trotsky himself, a philosophy which Trotsky never showed any inclination to reconsider even in light of the terror and the purges. The "Russian question" forced veteran Marxists in Europe and America to discuss the problem of ends and means and the relationship between revolutionary violence and political conscience. Soon an intellectual search was under way to discover the fatal flaw in the history of communist theory and practice, the original sin, as it were, from which Stalinism took its malignant birth. Hook and Victor Serge identified it as the principle of proletarian dictatorship, which allowed Stalin to build a one-man bureaucracy upon a one-man party dictatorship; Rodman isolated it in the historical context of the Bolshevik seizure of power in 1917, which presumably set the tone of revolutionary violence as the norm of political conduct; Herberg and Bertram D. Wolfe returned to Rosa Luxemburg for a critique of Leninist terrorism in 1918; Macdonald implicated Trotsky himself by bringing up Kronstadt; and Eastman, of course, went beyond 1917 and beyond Marx to Hegel, "in whose 'dialectical' philosophy Stalin's morals, among other prodigies, have their theoretic root."[31]

Trotsky responded to his growing number of critics in a stimulating essay, "Their Morals and Ours," in which he demonstrated that liberals, no less than Marxists, believed in moral relativism and the "ends justifies the means" criterion of praxis; he reiterated his defense of Bolshevik methods and denied a direct continuity between Bolshevism and Stalinism. Burnham published John Dewey's reply in New International. Dewey's equally perceptive statement, as Eastman's had done, traced Trotsky's contradictory assumptions about dictatorial means (class struggle) and democratic ends (socialism) to a belief in "mystical" laws of history that "presumably" had its origin in Hegelianism.[32]

Seduced by "Style": Burnham's Break with Trotsky

During this period, when revelations of the Kronstadt affair shook the moral foundations of Trotskyism, Burnham was occupied in debating Eastman and heading the tactical maneuvers of the Workers Party. Unlike other literary "Trotskisants," he seemed scarcely disturbed by the ethical dilemmas Dewey had exposed in communism. A revolutionary realist impatient with conscience-striken liberals, he looked upon their cries for "freedom, truth and science" as a hypnotism of the mind. Such "abstractions," declared Burnham a year later, cannot be invoked as universal absolutes without social content or historical context. "Simply to claim 'we seek the truth' is not enough." The concept of truth, Burnham shrewdly pointed out, as though lifting a page from Dewey, must ultimately be related to the purpose which inquiry aims to serve. The real, scientific idea of truth is inextricably bound up with the problem to be solved—and that was socialism.[33]

But the immediate solution to the problem of socialism rested upon Trotsky's assumptions about the coming war. Trotsky would regard World War II as a continuation of World War I, an imperialist struggle for territory that would sap the strength of capitalist powers and allow the proletariat to resume the second act of the unfinished October Revolution. Before the outbreak of war came, however, Trotsky, with Burnham following his interpretation of events, looked upon Stalin's foreign policy in the light of the Spanish Civil War as decidedly counterrevolutionary. Indeed the rationale for creating the Fourth International derived from the assumption that the proletariat could only be aroused to its revolutionary mission once Stalin's strategy of capitalist preservation in the West and capitalist restoration in Russia was fully exposed. Burnham and other Trotskyists had all along regarded a Hitler-Stalin alliance as logical and probable. Thus with the announcement of the non-aggression pact, in August 1939, Burnham did not experience the sudden moral shock that convulsed much of the American Left, particularly the liberal fellow travelers. What stunned Burnham was Trotsky's response to the events immediately following Germany's declaration of war against Poland a week after the pact. When Stalin's army marched into

Poland, and several months later when Russia declared war on hapless Finland, Trotsky reversed his attitude toward the Soviet Union as a reactionary force to insist that Russia's military expansion into the eastern front, and Stalin's expropriation of Ukrainian and Polish landed estates, was "progressive." Assuming a continuity between domestic and foreign policy, Trotsky arrived at the fantastic conclusion that the pressure of the Russian masses had prevented Stalin from coming to terms with Polish capitalists and landlords. Hence Stalin's foreign policy was genuinely revolutionary, and the Soviet Union, despite political deformities, was a genuine "workers' state" that must be defended by every genuine Marxist-Leninist.[34]

Shaken by the sudden turn of strategy, Burnham resisted Trotsky's new course. He attempted to convene a full session of the national committee of the Workers Party; and for the next six months, while the WP split into embittered factions, Burnham and Trotsky debated each other with eloquent ferocity. Trotsky reiterated his conviction that Kremlin foreign policy must be interpreted as the historical expression of a "Bonapartist bureaucracy of a degenerated workers' state in imperialist encirclement,"[35] a description that seemed to Burnham an empty verbal rationalization designed to justify the seemingly impossible demand of defending the Soviet Union while opposing Stalinism. Indeed, a "workers' state" no longer had meaning in a country where propertyless workers had been denied political freedom. Nor could the rubric of "Bonapartism" explain how Stalinism could carry the seeds of bourgeois restoration in Russia and social revolution abroad. The whole issue called for a redefinition of the political nature of the Soviet Union.

This effort at redefinition had already been made in Bruno Rizzi's *La Bureaucratisation du Monde*, published just before the outbreak of the war. Rizzi, an Italian ex-Trotskyist, maintained that the Soviet Union must be considered neither a movement toward socialism nor a capitalist recrudescence but rather a product of "bureaucratic collectivism," a new state administered by a new ruling class and manifesting a new system of class domination. Burnham, Shachtman, and Macdonald accepted an analysis similar to Rizzi's—indeed Burnham would soon rely on such a theory to develop his own theory of managerialism. Trotsky himself could accept many of Rizzi's descriptive categories of bureaucratization. The question was whether this phenomenon meant a transient phase of reaction or a permanent feature in the new social order. Trotsky denied that "bureaucratic collectivism" represented a "universal trend" in all modern industrial countries. In the West collectivism was only partial and by no means overcame the irrationalities of capitalism; and in Russia bureaucracy was only "a temporary growth on a social organism,"—historically a mere "episodic relapse" that did not preclude the possibility that the working class retained the power of overthrowing it. For Trotsky neither fascism, Stalinism, nor America's corporate welfare state under the New Deal was evidence that the proletariat had failed its historical mission.[36]

On that issue Burnham departed from Trotsky and from the whole program and philosophy of Trotskyism. Trotsky responded by accusing Burnham of being "anti-dialectical" and having fallen under the influence of "Max Eastman and his ilk." Burnham admitted in New International that Eastman was right about the dialectic,[37] and he and Shachtman considered a disturbing point raised by Eastman in a personal letter—Trotsky's latent nationalism. "Trotsky, you must remember, is a Russian, and also a man of state," wrote Eastman; "for him to renounce the defense of the Soviet Union would be a prodigious personal feat. But for you, after defining Stalinism as the 'theory and practice of internationally projected anti-Soviet totalitarianism,' to call upon the workers of the world to shed their blood for Stalin's regime in the name of proletarian democracy and the soviets, suggests, in my opinion, a lack of the elementary ingredients of simple political horsesense."[38]

Burnham directed a long reply to Trotsky a few months before resigning from the Workers Party in May 1940. "Science and Style" is a remarkable document. It reveals what Trotsky had once meant to Burnham, and how utterly desolate he now felt in the conviction that he had been "seduced" by a philosophy of history built upon the rhetoric of metaphors and sustained by the imagery of inexorability, how he had been deceived by the form of literary expression as a poet is deceived by the conceit that his words comprehend as well as interpret reality:

I find the Open Letter which you have addressed nominally to me more than a little disarming. It is not easy, I confess, for me to undertake an answer.

In reading it I was reminded of a conversation I had some while ago with one of our good comrades from Central Europe. We were discussing, in that idle and profligate way we intellectuals have, the possible conflicts between the aesthetic sense, the feeling for beauty, and the demands of political action. He told me a story.

A number of years ago, the country in which he lived was going through a period of social crisis. The masses were surging forward, heading, it seemed, toward revolt. One morning, near the height of the movement, a crowd of many thousand workers gathered on one side of the wonderful great square of the capital city of that country. Our comrade was assigned as captain to direct one wing of the workers' detachments.

The sky was dark blue, with the white morning sun throwing across the square the shadows of the buildings that lined its sides. From the side of the square opposite the workers, the troops of the police filed out and took formation: in straight rows, mounted on their tense horses, equipment gleaming. At the shout of command, in a single swift gesture their sabres were drawn, and flashed in the rays of that white sun. The second command came: forward against the workers.

The instant had come for reply: for our comrade to launch his wing of the workers into a driving counter-attack. But for a long moment he found his will paralyzed and his voice stopped by the sensuous beauty of the unfolded scene. And all that day, while the bitter struggle lasted—more than fifty were killed that day, hundreds wounded, our comrade among them—he could not forget that sun, those shadows, that blue sky, those whirling horses and flashing sabres.

So, too, on this verbal battleground, pale reflex—and indispensable spark—of the battles in the streets, I, when all my will should be concentrated in launching my ranked arguments into counter-attack against your letter (so wrong, so false, so very false), find I must stop awhile in wonder: at the technical perfection of the verbal structure you have created, the dynamic sweep of your rhetoric, the burning expression of your unconquerable devotion to the socialist ideal, the sudden, witty, flashing metaphors that sparkle through your pages.

How unpleasant and thankless a duty to submit that splendid structure to the dissolving acids from those two so pedestrian, so unromantic flasks: logic and science![39]

Armed with the mundane weapons of "logic and science," Burnham would soon refute Trotsky with a book that became a minor classic in political sociology.

The Managerial Revolution

Burnham's first major book, *The Managerial Revolution*, had crystallized in his mind while he was debating Trotsky in the months immediately following the outbreak of the war in Europe.[40] Published in 1941, within a year after he had resigned from the Workers Party, the book was an answer to Trotskyism and a farewell to Marxism as a philosophy of history and as a program of hope—but not as a mode of analysis. The entire Trotskyist edifice was built on the assumption that Russia must either move forward to socialism or revert to some form of capitalism. This formulation seemed to Burnham a species of syllogistic logic born of Hegel's dialectic, and he proceeded to refute it with what might be called a "neither-nor" proposition.

The new pattern of economic organization, which Burnham claimed had been developing in advanced Western countries since 1914, demonstrated that capitalism was a moribund reality and socialism a mythical dream. The coming order would be neither the competitive society of capitalism nor the classless society of socialism, but a managerial society, a political economy run by a new ruling elite which was assuming control over the means of production and thereby seizing the very power that once belonged to the capitalist class and was destined, in the Marxist view of history, to fall to the working class. The managers would be those who guide, organize, and administer the processes of production—

"operating executives, superintendents, administrative engineers, supervisory technicians; or, in government . . . administrators, commissioners, bureau heads." These new managerial occupations would be as "exploitive" as older class systems, since their control over access to the instruments of production afforded members preferential treatment in the distribution of goods and services produced by those instruments. Neither capital nor labor would be able to challenge the power of the managers, for the increasing extension of state ownership and control over the economy was developing along with the increasing managerial operation and control of the state.[41]

Burnham regarded World War II as a "major social revolution" to which the war itself was subordinate, a phase in the long-developing managerial revolution. When the war ended the world would be divided among three superpowers: Germany, a partially developed managerial society, would have control of most of Europe; Japan, the most advanced country in Asia, would have Manchuria and eastern China; and the United States, still only a "primitive" managerial state, would penetrate the remains of the British Empire in the Western Hemisphere. As for Russia, Burnham believed her backwardness and underdeveloped technology were so great that, despite her leadership in creating a managerial ruling class, she would "split apart" under the stress of war, with the eastern half gravitating toward Asia and the western toward Europe. There was no doubt in Burnham's mind that the irresistible trend toward managerialism could be seen in the transference of sovereignty from representative institutions to various centralized bodies of power: in Germany, from the Weimar Republic to the Nazi state of Hitler; in Russia, from the workers' soviets to the Communist Party of Stalin; in the United States, though considerably less pronounced, from Congress and the Supreme Court to the myriad bureaus and agencies of the Roosevelt administration. Burnham did not visualize the wave of the future as centralized despotism. As with the bourgeois revolutions and counterrevolutions of previous centuries, totalitarianism represented a new class engaged in a struggle against entrenched social strata; against older capitalists, whose interests lay in preserving a dying order; against the masses, who posed an opposition to oppression and class rule of any kind; and against managerial elites in other countries, with whom the new class must compete for international domination. These struggles would eventually subside, and the managers, realizing they needed the support of the populace and access to accurate information on public opinion, would allow some semblance of "limited democracy" to emerge. The managers would realize what the ruling classes of the past had learned: democracy is the best instrument of pacification. "Experience shows that a certain measure of democracy is an excellent way to enable opponents and the masses to let off steam without endangering the foundations of the social fabric. Discontent and opposition under an absolute dictatorship, having no mechanism for orderly expression, tend to take terroristic and, in times of crisis, revolutionary forms."[42]

After the war, sometime in the distant future, Burnham speculated cautiously, European totalitarianism might yield to minimal opposition parties and other institutionalized expressions of dissent, provided they constituted no dangerous threat to the social rule, "the power and privileges," of the managerial class or to the foundations of the new order. Yet whatever the form of government, real power would reside with the managers, the new ruling class created by the technological imperatives of the modern industrial structure. Thus Marx was right about the past: the domination of the capitalist class, which ruled by virtue of its economic role in the course of development, made democracy historically impossible; he was wrong about the future: the domination of the new managerial class, which rules by virtue of its technological and organizational necessity, makes democracy eternally impossible.[43]

The Managerial Revolution was the kind of book Max Eastman had always wanted to write—a popular treatise that reached the general reader and absorbed the attention of the intellectual community as well. More than 100,000 copies were sold in hardcover in the United States and England during the war, many more in the paperback edition; after the war it was translated into French, German, Italian, Spanish, Chinese, Japanese, Arabic, Hebrew, Russian, Polish, Ukrainian, Greek, Swedish, and Hindi. A book that seemed to open a new perspective on the future, it anticipated in some respects Milovan Djilas's *The New Class* and Jacques Ellul's *The Technological Society*. In France it would be critically praised by socialists like Léon Blum and liberals like Raymond Aron. In America it started a controversy that continues to this day, in revised form, over the question "Who governs?" To understand the ideological significance of the book we must understand its historical context.

In May 1941, after Germany had overrun France, conquered Scandinavia and the Low Countries, invaded the Balkans and was poised to march on Russia, there was a pressing need for some coherent and comprehensive explanation of the whirl of events. Burnham's book, with its visions of irresistible forces clashing together in a portentous technological melodrama, held a morbid fascination for reviewers even as they questioned its gloomy predictions. The New York *Times* devoted three separate days to reviewing the work. Such disparate journals as *Fortune* and *Partisan Review* published full-length articles by Burnham summarizing his thesis. *Time* carried a photo of the hitherto unknown author and praised his work as "the most sensational book of political theory since *The Revolution of Nihilism*"; and Peter Drucker, writing in the *Saturday Review of Literature*, described it as "one of the best recent books on political and social trends" and probably "the Bible of the next generation of Neo-Marxists."[44]

The "Burnhamian Revolution," as Dwight Macdonald called it, provoked considerable criticism in early 1942. Many writers gleefully noted the false prophecies in the book, as democratic England and Soviet Russia resisted instead of collapsing before the onslaught of the Nazi state. Aside from Burnham's planetary speculations, various substantive arguments of *The Managerial Revolution* were analyzed and found inadequate as explanations and outrageous as conclusions. Liberals would question Burnham's impulse to turn an uncertain tendency into a mechanically determined historical trend, his ignoring the role of labor unions as a counterforce to managerialism, and his Marxist disregard for the plural nature of political power. Conservatives were upset by Burnham's indifference to moral issues and his dismissal of the problem of legitimate authority. These criticisms, however, read like polite caveats compared to the denunciation from the radical Left. Lewis Corey assailed Burnham's book as the "Olympian defeatism of a doctrinaire radical gone sour"; Paul Sweezy as a justification "to retire to the ivory tower, au-dessus de la mêlée"; and C. Wright Mills as "A Marx for the Managers."[45]

The radical critique spun out a variation on a single theme: the resiliency of traditional capitalist power in three countries. In Germany, argued the radicals, the big industrialists and Junkers were still in control of the state well after Hitler's advent to office. In Russia the abolition of private property made the relationship between ownership and control tenuous and the independence of the managers from the bureaucrats dubious. In America the structure of capitalist property relations was not threatened but preserved by the managers. Indeed, the control of industries did not pass from owners to administrators; on the contrary, large stockholders still dominated corporate decision making, and what was true of major corporations was even more true of small businesses. All this would indicate that although a managerial oligarchy may be inevitable in modern industrial society, Burnham's analysis was based on a functional misconception of its position and role. Managers may give advice on "how" things should be run; they still must take orders on "what" should be done, or else risk losing their livelihood in America and their very lives in Hitler's Germany and Stalin's Russia.[46]

Contemporary research suggests that Burnham's critics were only half right and Burnham himself only half wrong. In Germany, as Ralf Dahrendorf and David Schoenbaum have demonstrated, the hegemony of the old aristocracy and Junker class was

finally broken by Hitler's "social revolution." New controlling
elites, though not necessarily managerialists, came to power. The
situation in Stalin's Russia was more complex. There the internal
power struggles clearly had something to do with the danger of a
rising technical intelligentsia assuming control of the means of
production and constituting a "new class." Perhaps this is one
reason why the Russian managerialists, specifically the engineers,
were one of the leading professional groups to fall victim to the
first purge, the industrial party trial of 1930–1931. Yet in the post-
Stalinist era scientific training appears to have been, especially for
present-day leaders like Leonid Brezhnev and Aleksei Kosygin,
"an important criterion on their way to power," according to a
recent scholar on this subject.[47] The road to power is not the same
thing as the power to rule. It remains an open question whether
the logic of occupational ascendancy, the role of ideals or ideology,
or the personal factor in bureaucratic power struggles accounts for
Soviet behavior. Closer to home the debate continues, in modified
form, on the issue of whether America is a pluralistic society of
countervailing interest groups, or whether corporate wealth controls a centralized government whose decisions are often determined by a "power elite."

Burnham's critics maintained that The Managerial Revolution
drew upon sources which its author failed to acknowledge. The
anarchist Max Nomad claimed that Burnham plagiarized the ideas
of his political hero, Jan Waclaw Machajski, the Polish author of
The Intellectual Worker (1904), an anti-Marxist essay that
Nomad introduced and published in Victor F. Calverton's The
Making of Modern Society (1937).[48] Such criticisms are incorrect
and misleading. The nineteenth-century anarchist tradition, from
Bakunin to Kropotkin, looked upon Marx's "scientific socialism"
as an ideology devised by "centralizers" who were creating a "new
aristocracy" of brain power; Machajski, in particular, considered
the intellectuals, with their thick eyeglasses and "white hands," a
new exploiting class that would use its education to deceive manual laborers and control society after the economy had been collec-

tivized. Machajski and the anarchists perceived this development as a "conspiracy of the intellectuals"; Burnham stressed managerialism as a natural technological tendency arising from the "objective" laws of history.[49]

In America, despite a rich vein of elitist thought—Hamilton's virtuous statesmen, Veblen's enlightened engineers, the public-conscious executives envisioned in Berle and Means's *The Modern Corporation and Private Property*—Burnham could not conceive of the managers as possessing the ability to transcend selfish interests in order to rule for the well-being of the community. Burnham's sociology of power drew closer to the European tradition of conservative thought, particularly to the ideas of Pareto, Mosca, and Michels, Italian political theorists whose writings he would examine in his next book, *The Machiavellians*. Burnham's *Managerial Revolution* may also be read as an American variant of German sociology, especially Max Weber's studies on bureaucracy, which likewise demonstrated that control of the channels of administration would be the basis of political power regardless of the socialization of the means of production. However, Burnham had little respect for bourgeois values and saw no role for religious or spiritual ideals, and hence his writings lacked the ethical tension between politics and morality that was the genius of Weber's mind and thought.[50]

Burnham's book was also linked to Rizzi's *La Bureaucratisation du Monde*. The Italian ex-Trotskyist was one of the first writers to conceive the category of "bureaucratic collectivism" in order to demonstrate that socialism was not the only alternative to capitalism and the proletariat nor the historical answer to Stalinism. It is difficult to say to what extent, if any, Burnham had been influenced by Rizzi's argument, which clearly permeated the air of Trotskyist debate in America in 1939–1940. Rizzi had accused Burnham of stealing his ideas, but toward the close of the war sent him articles and manuscripts to have published in the United States. Later in Paris radical intellectuals divided over whether to side with the Italian or the American ex-Trotskyist. Perhaps the major difference between the two was that Rizzi praised the emergence of bureaucracy as a "progressive" and necessary stage in the rationalization of society. Burnham refrained from committing himself to any value judgment. He was certain that the future nature of society would emerge from the present trends of history, but he never equated the inevitable with the desirable. The final paragraph of *The Managerial Revolution* is as stoical as it is stark:

> There will be those who will find this a renewed proof of what they will call the essential tragedy of the human situation. But I do not see with what meaning the human situation as a whole can be called tragic, or comic. Tragedy and comedy occur only within the human situation. There is no background against which to judge the human situation as a whole. It is merely what it happens to be.[51]

As an exercise in futurology and as an interpretation of "What Is Happening in the World" (Burnham's subtitle), *The Managerial Revolution* is a vulnerable book. As a critique of Marxism, however, it is a significant statement. Burnham carried Marxism to its logical conclusion, only to turn it back against itself. With Marx, Burnham believed that the economic would absorb the political; and with the Trotskyists of the thirties, he assumed that Stalinism, Nazism, and the New Deal were, as ideologies, mere epiphenomena, "superstructures" behind which the real sources of power lay in the economic base of Russian, German, and American society. Retaining many of the assumptions of Marxism, Burnham thus offered what would become a familar way out for Old Left intellectuals—a Marxist analysis without a Marxist solution, a description of society with a class structure and without a class struggle.

Bureaucracy had not been a problem in orthodox Marxist political theory, and technological elites had not been envisioned even by Lenin, who elevated party control to an Archimedean principle of power only to blind himself to its ultimate authoritarian consequences. Burnham was not the first writer to discern in the emergence of bureaucracy a refutation of Marx's class analysis, nor was he the first to see that hidden oligarchical tendencies are potential in all organizations. These observations had been made by Weber, Pareto, and other conservative social philosophers. Burnham, however, drew his ideas from the Left rather than the Right. He did not claim, as the anarchists did, that the new ruling class was the creation of a "plot" on the part of a displaced intelligentsia with a secret lust for power; he was, as the liberals were not, too skeptical of moral ideals to invoke democratic principles to challenge the consequences of Bolshevism; and, unlike the Trotskyists, he was certain that Stalinism represented far more than the personal "betrayal" of the October Revolution. Managerialism, of which Stalinism was an expression, evolved logically from Marx's assumption that all power and authority derived from possession of the means of production. As sociological phenomena, managerial rule, technological authority, and bureaucratic domination could be traced back to the means of production, the ownership of which Marx had regarded as the sole source of power and freedom. As the instruments of production became diversified and the division of labor magnified in the course of industrial specialization, possession of these instruments passed to a new managerial class which now "owned" property by virtue of controlling it. Burnham may have indiscriminately equated ownership with control; he may have narrowly identified economic power with political authority and class domination; and he may have falsely stressed property rather than income as the criterion of class membership. But it was perfectly Marxian to make all three assumptions, and hence the only way to avoid Burnham's conclusions was to go beyond Marx for a new theory of class and perhaps a new philosophy of history as well.[52]

Thus it could be said that Burnham's idea of a managerial revolution had the same effect as Eastman's critique of dialectical materialism. By positing the emergence of a new social stratum, Burnham demonstrated the fallacies in Marx's theory of class as a struggle of mutually antagonistic social forces climaxed by the victory of the proletariat. The messianic role of the proletariat was a philosophical assumption rooted, as Eastman noted, in Marx's dialectical scheme of historical conflict, which envisioned the emergence of only one class—the working class—as the total antithesis and "negation" of the bourgeois order. Yet Burnham was wrong in assuming that the managers would constitute a new ruling elite and that managerialism would supersede Marxism as the sociological key to modern industrial society. Burnham substituted for Marx's historical determinism an even narrower version of technological determinism in order to explain the present and predict the future. He tried to go beyond Marx, but he never took his eyes off the mode of production, the fundamental causal agency in the Marxian analysis of social change, the foundation and the apex of power in the Burnhamian analysis of society and politics. Small wonder that history would defy James Burnham in much the same way it had eluded Karl Marx: both mistook a historical trend for a natural law.

PART TWO

The Middle of the Journey

1940–1955

Most writers who emerged from the 1930s wanted to forget as rapidly and as completely as possible the years spent in the radical movement. A few wrote novels or autobiographies in an attempt to reflect on the political past, but many began to abandon politics as they turned to the issues of modern culture and mass society. For Eastman, Dos Passos, Herberg, and Burnham, however, politics continued to make great demands on intellectual life. A decade of radicalism now lay behind them, and history had presumably rendered its verdict, but the impact of European totalitarianism urged upon them a number of new questions—from the depravity of modern man to the destiny of Western civilization. The World War II years and the subsequent cold war era would be for them an acute period of introspection and speculative anxiety. In the previous decade the doctrine of socialism had seemed to them almost a self-evident truth, an enlightened doctrine of reason, justice, and progress. But Marxism had not succeeded in forcing history to satisfy its claims, and with the failure of Marxism modern American intellectual history found itself at the crossroads. Where could Eastman, Dos Passos, Herberg, and Burnham, as the intellectual leaders of the Old Left, turn to discover fresh doctrines for the new struggles that lay ahead? If, indeed, the dream of socialism had collapsed with the "end of ideology," what values remained that could still be affirmed?

CHAPTER 5

Capitalism and Freedom: Eastman

At all times sincere friends of freedom have been rare, and its triumphs have been due to minorities, that have prevailed by associating themselves with auxiliaries whose objects differed from their own; and this association, which is often dangerous, has been sometimes disastrous, by giving to opponents just grounds of opposition.

LORD ACTON, 1922

The Vigilant Anti-Stalinist

In 1940 when Eastman published *Marxism: Is It Science?* he still thought of himself as a socialist. The following year, at a cocktail party given by Freda Utley, Miss Utley asked Eastman, " 'Aside from these Russian developments, do you still believe in the socialist idea?'

"I said, 'No.' "[1]

Eastman's response surprised even himself. He had never before uttered the thought, not even privately to his closest friends or inwardly to his political conscience. Until World War II he had regarded socialism as a living idea that had been betrayed by the Soviet Union, but he never questioned the inner validity of the idea itself. In the early forties he wrote some hurried articles expressing his doubts, but not until 1955, in *Reflections on the Failure of Socialism*, did he spell out his reasons for rejecting socialism as a theoretical proposition and a practical program. Meanwhile, the crucial problems of U.S.–Russian wartime diplomatic relations and internal Stalinist subversion commanded his attention.

Eastman had always been something of a Childe Harold of lost causes. During and after World War I he espoused Bolshevism in the name of liberty, science, and progress while the American public recoiled in horror from the terrors of social revolution. During World War II Eastman denounced Stalinism in the name of liberty, science, and progress while the American public grew increasingly enamored of the Soviet Union. The majority of Americans—as indicated in mass magazines like *Collier's* and *Life* as well as opinion poll surveys—believed that Russia now had a government which was "as good as she could have for her people" and that the Soviet economy was transforming itself into a "modified" form of capitalism.[2] These hopes sprang from the psychological need to believe in the possibility of Soviet-American collaboration in time of war. But such hopes were also illusions that could serve as answers to the previous delusions of the intellectual Left and nativist Right in America. The Trotskyist Left had claimed that the Russian masses would turn the war into a social revolution, and the isolationist Right believed that the Wehrmacht would make short shrift of the Red Army. Events proved both wrong; neither had anticipated that Stalinism would be rescued by the resurgence of Russian nationalism. Patriotism, the scourge of Eastman and the intellectual class, is something the American people understand and respond to almost instinctively; and watching the Russian armies fighting valiantly and the Russian people suffering the brunt of the German attack and invasion, they could not help but feel a sense of kinship and hence moral obligation to their allies on the eastern front.

Although Eastman believed the United States must give full support to the Soviet Union in the war against Hitler, he had no illusions that Joseph Stalin had suddenly discovered the virtues of democracy and that the Soviets could be counted upon to continue the "Grand Alliance" once the threat of Nazism was removed. Eastman's suspicions arose from theoretical reflection and personal experience. The Soviet state, he now cknowledged, had inherited the Bolshevik party apparatus and Lenin's theory of vanguard revolutionary activity, both of which, lacking Lenin's "genuine purpose of liberty and enlightenment," made Stalinism monolithic, conspiratorial, totalitarian, and counterrevolutionary. Moreover, the police terror of the NKVD and the assassinations of Trotsky and Tresca increased his apprehensions. Even more personally, the disappearance in the purges of the entire family of Eliena Krylenko, Eastman's third wife, left him shaken with suspicion of Russia's every move.[3]

The war years were a frustrating time for Eastman. Well-informed on Russian internal affairs and in close contact with several Russian émigré intellectuals and early veterans of the Comintern, he was eager to proffer advice, only to find himself an author with few sophisticated readers and no significant followers. For a brief moment he had been "enormously bucked up" by Edmund Wilson's praise for his books on Marxism and the Soviet Union in a review in the New Republic.[4] The mainstream journalistic media, however, paid little attention to his writings. Orville Prescott, influential reviewer for the New York Times, described Eastman as an embittered old Trotskyist who had been tiresomely "airing" his views in print for twenty years.[5] For the most part the intellectual community responded to his wartime writings with a déjà-vu yawn. Eastman was an embattled warrior who had nothing new to say. To the intellectual Left he had committed the unpardonable sin—he actually went to the masses by writing for Reader's Digest.

During the war years Eastman was not content to thrash out the old battles of dialectical materialism and proletarian realism. Those battles had been won; new causes, more immediate and concrete, had now to be fought—causes that raised embarrassing questions about the conduct of Soviet foreign policy. Eastman was one of the first American writers to have access to news that would later have profound repercussions for Soviet-American relations. In the early forties he had heard from Alexander Barmine and Boris I. Nicolaevsky about the Soviet deportation centers and concentration camps in Eastern Europe and Lithuania. Then in spring

1943 the German government announced the discovery of a field of mass graves, on occupied Russian territory in the Katyn Forest, containing the bodies of more than 4,000 of the missing 15,000 Polish officers who had been taken prisoner by the Russians in 1939. The Germans asked for an investigation by the International Red Cross. The Polish government in exile, after much soul searching, associated itself with the investigation. The British and American governments, fearing that the inquiry would anger the Russians and jeopardize American-Soviet relations, persuaded Polish officials to withdraw their request for an international investigation. Elmer Davis, head of the Office of War Information, cast doubt on the German accusations, calling the whole story "very fishy" and possibly a product of German propaganda.[6] Nicolaevsky, who had no doubt that "Stalin is responsible," regarded Davis's radio speech as inexcusable and "stupid," but the former Menshevik informed Eastman that the delicate diplomatic situation dictated an article on general Polish-Russian relations rather than the one he had been preparing on the Katyn episode.[7] Polish officials were also cautious. Although they turned over to Eastman a "confidential memorandum" submitted earlier to the British and American governments, and although they regarded Polish-Russian relations as a "test case" for future Allied diplomacy, they informed Eastman that their government in exile must "do all in its power to establish good neighborly relations with Russia in view of collaboration in the war."[8] Eastman, sensing the tragedy of the situation, decided not to publicize the Katyn massacre.

In summer 1943 Soviet-American relations had been improving to the point of growing respect and cordiality, for in the spring of that year, during the heroic battle of Stalingrad, American feelings toward Russia blossomed into friendship, admiration, and trust. One wonders whether Eastman could have published so sensitive an article had he chosen to do so. Two years earlier he had written an article in the *American Mercury* on "Stalin's American Power," shortly afterwards published in the *Reader's Digest*, that drew upon information gathered by the American Committee for

Cultural Freedom. Eastman told the *Reader's Digest*'s five million subscribers of the huge network of communist front organizations in the United States. The *Reader's Digest*, enthusiastically endorsing the article, offered to supply three reprints free to any individual upon request. But the protests against Eastman's article were so vociferous and the threatened libel suits so intimidating that the editors changed their minds. In a circulated form letter, the *Reader's Digest* stated that the possible "effect of the article on our war morale" led to the decision not to do "anything that might operate to disturb our essential war effort."[9]

During the war years Eastman refused to be silenced, however. He named the organizations which he believed had been hoodwinking many innocent and loyal Americans, such as notables like Eleanor Roosevelt, who represented "our American democratic humanitarianism at its best."[10] Those organizations included the American Committee to Save Refugees, the National Lawyers Guild, the Progressive Committee to Rebuild the American Labor Party, the League for Democracy and Intellectual Freedom, and the Russian War Relief. Though in his anti-subversive campaign Eastman often cited Eugene Lyons's *The Red Decade*, a rather febrile exposé of the thirties that tended indiscriminately to lump together fellow travelers, Russian sympathizers, and liberal intellectuals as "dupes" of communist propaganda, Eastman was somewhat more discriminate but no less zealous in his desire to purge Stalinists from American political and cultural life. He did not favor a government investigation; he remembered the "blundering efforts" of the Dies Un-American Activities Committee of the late thirties. But he did believe in bringing to public light what many others wanted to forget and forgive. A few years earlier, in a private letter to George Acklom of E. P. Dutton, publishers, he wrote a revealing report on the manuscript, later published, of the ex-communist Benjamin Gitlow's political confessions (*I Confess*):

I have read every word of Gitlow's manuscript with intense interest. It is a faithful and resolutely candid account from the inside (and what is more important, from the top) of a vitally important phase of recent

American history. This history is secret, and might well have remained so but for the extraordinary poise and honest-hearted courage of this man, and his ultimate recovery of clear vision and unmixed devotion to his ideals. A thousand congressional investigations could not expose the facts exposed in this book. A thousand research experts, convinced of them, could not make them convincing.[11]

Eastman's conviction that no one but ex-communists could explain the meaning of communism to Americans appeared confirmed in May 1943, when the Comintern was dissolved by orders from Moscow. To American Communist Party leaders the move promised a new experiment in national autonomy. Earl Browder, president of the CP since 1936, hailed the step as leading toward the "integration of the CPUSA into our own American democratic life and national unity." There is no evidence that Browder was insincere in his hope for what he would soon call "peaceful coexistence and collaboration" between capitalism and socialism, for he had already expressed these thoughts in *Victory and After*, published in 1942, a year before the Comintern was dissolved.[12] But the policy raised again the question whether the CP was, and would continue to be, an appendage of the Kremlin. Many Americans, caught up in the wartime fusion of American and Russian patriotism, believed the Comintern's dissolution promised a new era of mutual understanding between the United States and Russia. Certainly every new sign pointed in that direction. Roosevelt, Churchill, and Stalin were amiably arranging the Teheran conference on postwar relations, and Browder not only publicly offered to help Americans overcome their fears by laying to rest the "spectre of communism," he even directed the CP to throw its support to Mayor Frank Hague of Jersey City, one of the most violent anti-communists in the country. All this was confusing. Observing these startling shifts, the New York *Times* concluded that the CP "has never stood for anything that made sense in America" and that it "does not represent Russian policy."[13]

To Eastman the new position of the CP made perfect sense. "May I suggest," he wrote in a six-page letter to the *Times*,

" . . . on the basis of a more intimate acquaintance than yours with communist activities," that it "is a mistake to confuse the lack of principle in totalitarian parties with a lack of purpose or of plan." The CP, with a "tightly woven phalanx of 50 to 100,000 zealots," is hardly a negligible factor in American political life, he reminded the *Times*. It was not the first instance the CP had embarked on a turn to the right, and even if it went further and dissolved itself as an organization, such a move would merely be a re-enactment of many previous strategies of abandoning the "legal party" in order to "go underground," only to surface again as an integral part of the international communist movement. Balancing wartime imperatives against postwar illusions, Eastman concluded:

For my part, I favor forthright cooperation with Stalin now and after the war. I favor giving all military and economic aid to Russia, all honor to her heroic soldiers and people. And I favor coming to their aid with as many western fronts as lie within our military power and judgment. But I think we should do this without kidding ourselves about Russia's total subjection to a totalitarian single party and its Boss, the close cooperation of that party with an exactly similar one here, and a not yet broken harmony in their plans and purposes.[14]

Know Thy Enemies

"The worst thing about Communism is that it produces ex-Communists." With this opening sentence Eastman was greeted in a bitter letter from Daniel Mebane, treasurer of the *New Republic*. Eastman knew that the *New Republic*, and editor Malcolm Cowley in particular, had no use for his criticisms of Marxism and Stalinism. In 1941 Edmund Wilson informed him that his long article reviewing Eastman's latest books would soon be out in the *New Republic* "unless," Eastman told his publisher, "Cowley sabotages it."[15] Thus Eastman knew what to expect when Mebane assailed him as a "major menace in this country. . . . Men like yourself, J. B. Matthews, Lyons, Waldman, Stolberg and Thomas, by playing Judas, have acquired an immense influence for evil."[16]

Such charges reinforced Eastman's distrust of the liberal publishing houses of New York. He tried in vain to advise the New York *Times* on reviewers for books on Soviet Russia; he criticized the *Atlantic Monthly* for publishing the communist Anna Louise Strong; he broke with old editorial associates when Simon & Schuster, publisher of Trotsky's *History of the Russian Revolution*, came out with the notorious pro-Stalinist apologia *Mission to Moscow* by Ambassador Joseph Davies;* and he refused to attend a dinner in honor of the *Nation*, whose editors had, Eastman charged, "by apologizing for and upholding the totalitarian regime in the Soviet Union . . . betrayed the cause not only of liberalism, but of democracy and civilized morals."[17] As a vehicle for his own

---

* The fate of Trotsky's unpublished works in the United States is a measure of pro-Soviet sentiment not only among publishers but perhaps some academic institutions as well. In the thirties Eastman had translated a number of Trotsky's anti-Stalinist writings, including *The Young Lenin*, which mysteriously disappeared for over thirty years, only to turn up in Harvard's Houghton Library a short time before Eastman's death in 1969. It was not published until 1972. Whether the Trotsky-Eastman manuscript was deliberately suppressed is unclear. But another work by Trotsky, *Stalin: An Appraisal of the Man and His Influence*, definitely was. This manuscript, which Trotsky was working on at the time of his assassination (some pages were spattered with his blood), was turned down during the war years by publishers who decided it was not "timely" to let the people know everything about the leader of America's new ally. Then, in 1945, Albert Goldman, attorney to Trotsky's heirs, tried to obtain a copy of the manuscript from Harvard University, where Trotsky had sent his archives, apparently for safekeeping. Since Harvard did not have title to the documents, its attorney, Charles B. Rugg, called Secretary of State Dean Acheson, who referred the matter to the Department of State's legal adviser. A memo clearly records the nature of Harvard's request. "Dr. Samuel Cross, head of the Slavic Department at Harvard, has read over parts of the life of Stalin and has indicated that the publication of this book, he feels, would be detrimental to Soviet-American relations. In view of the possible effect on Soviet-American relations, Harvard does not wish to release the documents to Mr. Goldman and therefore asked Mr. Rugg to call at the Department to ask assistance in finding out some way by which Harvard could refuse to release the documents. Mr. Rugg suggested that there might be something in the wartime powers of the President which would permit us to refuse to release these documents which belong to an alien (apparently Mrs. Trotsky)." The State Department's adviser could "find no legal justification for retention of the papers by Harvard." (Elbridge Durbrow to Mr. Hackworth, Oct. 25, 1945; W. W. Bishop to Mr. Hackworth, Oct. 30, 1945, DS, 711. 61/10–2545.) I am grateful to Professor Barton Bernstein for drawing my attention to this State Department correspondence. Trotsky's book was published in 1946.

views, the only sympathetic intellectual outlet Eastman could turn to was the harassed and relatively obscure social democratic journal, the New Leader. And the only noted friends who offered encouragement were Attorney General Francis Biddle, Reader's Digest editor De Witt Wallace, and an occasional celebrity like the movie actress Barbara Stanwyck.[18]

Eastman might have been able to win some support among Left intellectuals had he shown some understanding of their honest hopes and anxieties about the postwar world. But a writer who took pride in his psychological understanding of human behavior, and who had been bold enough to reduce the thought of Karl Marx to unconscious psychic drives, had little patience with the conscious motives of those he opposed. This is curious, nonetheless, for Eastman himself had once defended Lenin and the Bolshevik terror while ridiculing the sensibilities of tender-minded liberals and democratic socialists. Reminding him of this episode in his early career, the old socialist Charles W. Erwin advised Eastman to at least have "the humility to cry 'peccavi'" when writing about present Soviet sympathizers.[19] Eastman failed to heed Erwin's sound advice, and he continued to attribute sinister motives to Left intellectuals. An example of this unfortunate misjudgment occurred toward the end of the war, when Eastman pounced on Dwight Macdonald and his journal Politics for supporting the communist-led resistance forces in Greece. Eastman maintained that Macdonald had, "in more than a figurative sense, joined their [the Stalinists'] ranks." Surely Eastman must have known that Macdonald had all along opposed Stalinism as a former Trotskyist and continued to do so as a caustic political satirist.[20]

Eastman's position had hardened long before the cold war. In May 1941, seven months before Pearl Harbor, he wrote a three-column letter to the New York Times in an attempt to convince intellectuals of the necessity of America's entry into the war against Hitler, a letter that drew praise from pro-interventionist liberals like Lewis Mumford and Clarence Streit.[21] But to former

Trotskyists like Macdonald, Shachtman, and James T. Farrell, Eastman seemed to be succumbing to a patriotic hysteria that he had once—in 1917 when President Wilson asked for a declaration of war—so courageously denounced as banal idol worship. Thus Eastman's criticisms of Marxism, his second thoughts about socialism, and his recent defense of American democracy all seemed to follow a pattern of retreat from radicalism and a "swing back to bourgeois values."[22] Eastman responded to the charge in the *Partisan Review*, where he also tried to defend a number of other American intellectuals and European émigrés who were being attacked in Trotskyist circles: Lewis Corey, Louis Hacker, Sidney Hook, John Dos Passos, James Burnham, Alexander Barmine, Boris Souvarine, and Max Nomad. Drawing upon Barmine's memoirs, Eastman maintained that the two basic assumptions upon which socialism rested had been refuted by recent history: that in a collectivized economy production would rise higher than in a capitalist economy; and that exploitation would cease as the workers enjoyed the full fruits of increased productivity. To acknowledge these failures, Eastman insisted, does not change one's values. "Nobody in his right mind, from Marx down, ever denied that bourgeois democracy has values." The point is to devise better ways of defending and expanding the values of freedom and democracy through means other than economic collectivism and one-party dictatorships. In saying this, Eastman may have attributed to Marx more regard for "bourgeois values" than Marx himself shared, but there can be no doubt that Eastman now assumed he was returning to a firm belief in the organic connection between means and ends,* the very unity of democratic theory and practice that he once praised Lenin for violating.[23]

The Good Fight Is the Same Fight

Immediately after the war, when friendly U.S.–Russian relations were ebbing, Eastman emerged as one of the most articulate de-

* The problem of means and ends would become as awkward for conservative cold warriors as it had been for Leninist revolutionaries. See p. 385.

fenders of America in the coming showdown with the Soviet Union. The millions of *Reader's Digest* lowbrows had already been familiar with the name Max Eastman, and his militant writings probably prepared them for the confrontations that developed at the Potsdam conference and in the opening meetings of the United Nations. Eastman reached an even greater number of Americans in September 1946, when he debated Harold Laski, the British labor leader and political scientist, on the *Town Hall of the Air* radio program. For weeks following the debate Eastman's mail was flooded with letters of congratulations from Americans in all walks of life: housewives, war veterans, old labor combatants, students and teachers, European refugees, a coal miner, a businessman, a former Wobbly, an ex-convict, a Bible Belt fundamentalist, a Legionnaire, a timid citizen who confessed to never before having written a political letter, a widowed invalid requesting an autograph, and a host of other middle Americans whose support Eastman could welcome but whose salutations must have made the incorrigible atheist wince—"Thank God for men like you."[24]

Eastman's public, professional, and personal lives had always run in competing directions, and in his early years he had difficulty harnessing what he called his troika of ambitions: working for mankind, thinking critically and writing creatively, and earning a living. Only in the postwar period did these drives begin to merge. On the strength of an enormously popular sketch of his mother ("A Momma's Boy Grows Up") written for the *Reader's Digest*, he was asked to become a "roving editor" and to submit further articles. Eastman accepted both offers, and with payment often as high as $1200 per article, he and his wife were at last out of debt and able to purchase land and build a permanent house at Gay Head on Martha's Vineyard.[25] He now was also in demand as a visiting lecturer at colleges in the South and Midwest. In 1948 his name again became a topic of conversation in literary circles with the publication of the first volume of his memoirs, *Enjoyment of Living*. The book, a valuable document in American cultural history, was well received, and it brought heartening letters from a number of veterans of the old The Masses era: Sally and Boardman Robinson; Upton Sinclair; Oswald Villard; Harold Lord Varney, the former Wobbly leader, who was now a U.S. government "adviser" to Chiang Kai-shek's Nationalist China; Ida Rauh, Eastman's beautiful first wife, who was grateful for the sensitive manner in which he had described their relationship in his memoirs; and Floyd Dell, who informed Eastman that his book "is being compared, in its candor, to Rousseau's Confessions."[26] Dell, who had been Eastman's close companion during The Masses period, had been corresponding with him in connection with reviewing the book for the Chicago Tribune. Strongly disagreeing with Eastman's present politics, Dell chose to avoid the ideological aspects of Eastman's early career and to stress instead the "neurotic difficulties" he had in "sublimating" his sexual drives. (The Tribune's book editor required Dell to delete this.) It is puzzling, from reading the love letters that came to Eastman after his memoirs were published, to figure out what "difficulties" Dell had in mind. One woman sent Eastman her photo in an effort to kindle an affair; another old friend told Eastman of first laying eyes on him at a party in the 1920s. "Who is that?" she asked her escort. "That," he replied, "is Max Eastman. I won't introduce you to him. He is fatal to women!"[27]

The response to Enjoyment of Living may have flattered Eastman's sensitive ego and rejuvenated his lust for life. Clearly his ideological passions were as potent as ever. In the late forties he carried on a running feud with Corliss Lamont and Soviet Russia Today, whose editor, Jessica Smith, had written a ten-page "Open Letter to Max Eastman" in the New Leader, challenging, with documentation, Eastman's allegation that Russian children were subject to adult criminal law and deportation. He also advised the Reader's Digest on materials concerning the Ukrainian underground and on accepting an article by Alexander Kerensky, leader of Russia's provisional government before the Bolsheviks came to power. (Eastman recommended rejection, suggesting that Keren-

sky's discredited image was still vivid enough to provoke the attitude, "Oh, is that guy still alive and still trying to come back?")
Active abroad as well, Eastman gave advice to the Voice of
America, and he wrote a series of articles on Greece which received warm praise from George Papandreou, leader of the Demo-
cratic-Socialist Party, who years later would be a victim of a right-
wing military coup. (Eastman's article, however, drew sharp criticism from his friend Laird Archer, an official of the Near East
Foundation, who well knew that Greece did not, as Eastman
allowed the Queen to claim, develop its modest welfare programs
"without a cent of foreign money.") In Washington Eastman was
something of a consultant to the anti-communist forces. He kept
Representative Clare Boothe Luce informed on Russian affairs,
and she used his articles in congressional debates. In 1949 he was
called to give testimony on Stalin's Russia before the House Foreign Relations Committee.[28]

In the intellectual community Eastman became somewhat less
isolated. After Stalin's determination to suppress Eastern Europe
became a reality, the influential editor Maxwell Perkins complimented Eastman's prescience on the Russian question, as did the
Nation's editor Oswald Villard, the Yale economist Irving Fischer,
and the Harvard political scientist Herman Finer. Still, many literary intellectuals believed Eastman had "sold out" to the pedestrian right wing in America. "I wish you would stop writing for the
Reader's Digest and write for Max Eastman," admonished the
poet Carl Sandburg. Other writers like Louis Untermeyer and
Glenway Wescott were troubled by Eastman's attack on various
literary associations as communist fronts. Eastman's old poetry
cohorts were also hurt when, at the time of the Bollingen Prize to
Ezra Pound, Eastman openly accused Archibald MacLeish of behaving "like a Russian Commissar" for speaking, as the Librarian
of Congress, in behalf of a "traitor." Eastman spent many hours at
the typewriter trying to explain where he stood politically to
former friends and admirers. "I am fighting exactly the same fight

I was on the old The Masses and the Liberator," he replied to Sandburg. "It was always a fight for 'liberty,' and especially liberty for the working class." One cannot "support tyranny and slave labor in the name of liberty and the triumph of the working class," he told Joseph Freeman, who had once worshiped him as a teen-ager. "We were fighting for truth and human freedom" during the Greenwich Village days, he reminded the pacifist Kate Crane Gartz, another old admirer. To Untermeyer he quoted Burnham's description of the cold war as a "political, subversive, ideological, religious, economic, resistance, guerrilla, sabotage war, as well as a war of open arms." If such descriptions may be also applied to Lenin's Third International, the difference is, Eastman patiently pointed out to his bewildered old comrades, that "Stalin is the greatest counter-revolutionary in history." Thus the true ideological heir of The Masses and the Liberator is the New Leader, the one journal that "comes nearer than any other paper to carrying on the old fight."[29]

Eastman's association with the New Leader, which started during the war years, was tenuous, strained, and brief. By spring 1948 he was asking publisher Sol Levitas to remove his name as contributing editor. He now felt it intellectually dishonest to support a paper that defined itself on its masthead as "devoted to social democracy." Such a description would be "politically expedient" in Europe, Eastman noted, where the labor movement was predominantly socialist. In America it would be more accurate to call the New Leader a "Labor Liberal Weekly," and all that needs to be said on the masthead is that the journal dedicates itself to "truth, freedom and a more equal distribution of wealth."[30] Eastman's break reflected his growing criticism of the New Leader's position that a planned economy is compatible with democracy. He had earlier debated Sidney Hook on the issue of democratic socialism versus free enterprise. In the early fifties several other issues led to Eastman's gradual divorce from the old anti-Stalinist Left and his eventual alignment with the new conservative Right.

McCarthyism and the Conscience of History

In January 1950 James T. Farrell confessed that he owed Eastman a "public apology." One can now see, Farrell admitted in a
letter to the *Partisan Review*, that in our earlier debates on totalitarianism and the outcome of the war Eastman "was more right
and had more insight than I." This must be openly acknowledged,
for "all of us who are younger than Max Eastman owe him a great
debt. At a time when it took great moral courage, Eastman wrote
with frankness and honesty concerning the nature of totalitarianism."[31]

A few years after Farrell made his public apology he became
chairman of the American Committee for Cultural Freedom,
founded in 1951 as an affiliate of the International Congress for
Cultural Freedom. Eastman had some supporters among the anti-
Stalinist intellectuals in the ACCF, including the executive committee members Farrell, Hook, Burnham, Sol Stein, and Peter
Viereck. But in 1952 the executive committee believed it necessary
to draw up a resolution explaining its anti-communist position,
because Eastman, an ACCF member, had cast "an unclear
shadow" (Hook's phrase) on the organization.[32] To the conster-
nation of the executive officers, Eastman had made a statement to
the press defending Senator Joseph McCarthy. With this breach,
distinctions became more crucial than ever. The issue of Mc-
Carthyism created considerable tension within the ACCF, and it
eventually drove both Eastman and Burnham out of the organization and further into the orbit of the cold-war Right.

Was Eastman really a McCarthyite? He believed in honesty and
civility in domestic politics and hard-headed realism in foreign
relations; and, while he was concerned about internal subversion,
he did not become obsessed by the conspiratorial notion that diplomatic setbacks abroad were the work of communists in Washington. He also knew the difference between a man of good hope

and a man of bad faith. Thus he came to the defense of George S. Counts, a Columbia University professor who was attacked as a communist propagandist by John T. Flynn in the *Reader's Digest*; and, in an attempt to help another old friend, he permitted government officials to interrogate him at his home at Martha's Vineyard, where he signed an affadavit testifying that actor Charles Chaplin had never been a member of the Communist Party. (This was true political fidelity by a man who was both a believer in free love and a hater of masculine double standards: Chaplin had been the suitor of Eastman's great love, the actress Florence Deshon!)[33] Nonetheless, Eastman's growing conservative convictions on economics and foreign policy led him to support Senator Robert Taft as the Republican presidential candidate in 1952. Eastman, like Taft, believed that the issue of domestic communism could not be swept under the liberals' couch and dismissed as a "diversion," the position of the *Partisan Review*, or as a political "red herring" and "smokescreen," the position of President Truman and, later, of Republican presidential candidate Dwight Eisenhower. (Ike was, Eastman told General Albert Wedemeyer, chairman of the Citizens for Taft Committee, "apologizing already for the mushheads and will be, I judge, a highly spiritual tool in their hands.")[34]

Eastman's anti-communism was not exactly synonymous with McCarthyism—the lessons of historical experience are one thing, the lusts of political ambition another. In 1948, two years before McCarthy went before the U.S. Senate and made his reckless charge of "twenty years of treason," Eastman wrote an enthusiastic introduction to Benjamin Gitlow's *All of Their Lives*—a phrase taken from Lenin's book on party organization: "Communists are those who give all of their lives to the movement." Eastman had given part of his life to Lenin's revolutionary movement; he would spend the rest of his life attacking those who would re-enact the ceremony of progress with Stalin's "counterrevolution."[35]

But as a politician, McCarthy was an embarrassment to Eastman. He regretted "his loose-jointed wild talk," Eastman privately told Viereck.[36] "I think McCarthy is a misbehaved and sloppy-minded person functioning in a place where the prime demand was for a well-behaved and extremely accurate and exact mind," he wrote Dell. Eastman also informed Dell that *The Freeman*, a conservative monthly to which he was now a steady contributor, had once been "undiscriminatingly McCarthyist," but after Henry Hazlitt became editor it supported Truman in his conflict with the senator. In fact, Eastman pointed out, during a meeting he told the magazine's board of directors that "I wished General Zwicker had walked down from the witness stand when McCarthy told him he was unfit to wear the uniform and socked him on the jaw." Yet Eastman's reservations about McCarthy as a man were not sufficient enough for him to regard McCarthyism itself as a "menace." Only liberals had succumbed to this "hysteria," Eastman claimed, for their minds had sunk under a bad conscience. Eastman may have been correct about liberal guilt, but he was also a little callous. Not sensitive enough to the unscrupulous methods of McCarthy—who, had he possessed full constitutional power, would have compelled witnesses to betray friends, and therefore themselves, to an even greater degree—Eastman assumed one could safely confront McCarthy armed with nothing more than a personal confession of past history. The liberals are "implicated in the selling out of the world to totalitarian Communism," he wrote Dell, "and instead of coming out and saying so and stating in what way they have changed their minds, they are trying to pretend that the attempt of congressional investigations to root Communists out of the government is an assault on all liberal opinion." To Eastman the McCarthy investigations offered an opportunity to put liberalism on trial and to lay bare before the public, once and for all, the radical illusions that led a whole generation astray:

I don't like McCarthy and I think he's something of a ham and he is both ignorant and crude—to say nothing of not being a gentleman, he is not even a good sport—but my objection to him is that he is doing badly a job that has to be done, and that distinguishes me from most of the people whom I call mush-head liberals, who seem to have even less of the understanding than McCarthy has of the danger to civilization in this totalitarian movement. If it were Nazism, instead of Communism, that was being attacked in this crude way, I doubt if the majority of them would utter a peep against it—in fact, they didn't utter a peep when Roosevelt and Francis Biddle staged the trial for conspiracy of 40 odd people who had never seen each other or communicated with each other until they came into the court room—an amalgam after the best Stalinist and Hitlerite models. That was the biggest blot so far on the history of the administration of justice in America. That was a legal issue. McCarthy after all is operating within the laws and the constitutional framework of the country. The objection to him is basically moral, just as it was to Hearst all through our life time, but nobody would have thought of erecting "Hearstism" into a political menace comparable to an avowed conspiracy to overthrow the government and destroy our free way of life. I think that Communism as it developed is both worse at home and more dangerous abroad than Hitlerism was. That perhaps is the main thing that separates me from these liberals who think that "McCarthyism is a worse danger than Communism."[37]

Eastman found McCarthy repugnant, but he succumbed to many of the characteristics of McCarthyism. For one thing, he could not resist indulging in the right-wing cant of equating fascism and communism only to claim that Stalin was a greater threat than Hitler had ever been. It is undeniable that Stalin was as monstrous and, for East Europeans, as meanacing as Hitler. But an ethical verdict which equates two distinct political phenomena can present a formidable obstruction to historical understanding, enabling the scientist-turned-moralist to enjoy the luxury of condemning that which he need not comprehend. Such a verdict returns to haunt anyone who tries to answer the next logical question: If by democratic standards fascism and communism are equally repugnant, why did Western democracies watch unperturbed the spread of fascist regimes in Eastern Europe, and then cry in horror as soon as communist regimes were established there after the war? Clearly American political leaders who demanded intervention to save Poland from Gomulka were not known to have demanded intervention to save Poland from Pilsudski.

The matter of retrospective omniscience also needs mentioning.

In 1943 Eastman defended America's support of Stalin's Russia in the common struggle against the Third Reich. After the defeat of Nazism, he maintained that communism "as it developed is both worse at home and more dangerous abroad than Hitlerism was." It takes no great historical imagination to suggest that the opposite would have been true had the Soviet Union been defeated in the war. Finally there is the matter of ethics. In the thirties Eastman had been sensitive to the problem of means and ends in regard to revolutionary politics; in the fifties he seemed willing to use almost any means for the sake of purging communist and Soviet sympathizers. "We're in a political fight, not an ethical argument," he lectured Viereck when defending McCarthy. "You go into battle like women in silk dresses, more concerned with keeping your skirts clean than defeating the enemy." But who was the "enemy"? Here Eastman fell into the McCarthyite habit of establishing guilt by association: those who held a position that coincided with the Communist Party's were either knowingly or unwittingly aiding the enemy; and those who, like Senator Millard Tydings and Joseph Davies, attempted to challenge McCarthy, were "dishonest-minded Sovieteer[s]." Tydings could only answer the charges of McCarthy and Fulton Lewis, Jr., with a "lying whine," Eastman told Viereck. The senatorial campaign against McCarthy "is far more vicious and unprincipled than any McCarthy has done."[38]

Eastman led a charmed life. History never caught up with him as it did with the Old Left. Thus the psychological terror of McCarthyism never touched him. His political record in the thirties was clean, his conscience in the fifties was clear. Consequently he could demand that intellectuals confess their errors to a candid public, seemingly unaware that the historical right to have been politically wrong guarantees no mercy. Yet the enormity of Eastman's past mistakes was certainly as great as that of those who fell victim to Stalinism and McCarthyism. If it was the sin of the Stalinist Old Left to have wanted to be anti-fascist without being anti-totalitarian, surely it was Eastman's sin to have wanted to be a

Leninist without accepting the full consequences of Leninism. Eastman accused communist sympathizers of "selling out" Eastern Europe to Stalinist totalitarianism after World War II, but the accusation easily becomes a self-accusation when we go back to the period 1918–1923. Were the democratic Mensheviks, the peasant-based Social Revolutionaries, the liberal Kadets, and the Kronstadt anarchists any less the victims of the Bolshevik terrors that Eastman had once accepted as inevitable? A short memory does wonders for a clear conscience.

It was Floyd Dell who called for that sympathetic understanding that comes only from the sixth sense—the sense of history combined with psychology. "There was nothing disgraceful in having mistaken confidence in the revolutionary wisdom of Lenin," Dell wrote to Eastman in an eleven-page letter that he, at the urging of his wife, decided not to send.[39] "Nor was there anything disgraceful in your becoming a too devoted partisan defender of Trotsky." But how, Dell wondered, did his old friend come to the scandalous position of supporting McCarthy? One theory Dell proposed was that ex-communists could easily do so because they crossed over from the authoritarian Left to the authoritarian Right while all along retaining their hatred and scorn for liberalism. It is the "mush-head" liberals who "belly-ache about civil rights" in the McCarthy era, just as they could never accept, in the days of Lenin, revolutionary violence and "ruthlessness on the theory that an omelette cannot be made without breaking eggs." This anti-liberal temperament gives the pro-McCarthyite intellectuals the illusion that McCarthyism is not a danger because they could, if necessary, stand up to him and his mere "bad manners." You boast, Dell told Eastman, that if called before the McCarthy committee you would "bust the senator in the nose" as you wanted General Zwicker to do. This is sheer "fantasy," for McCarthy would probably reduce you to helplessness as he had other witnesses. One can imagine, Dell speculated, McCarthy discovering that Eastman, one of his supporters, had criticized him, and hence summoning Eastman to appear. No doubt you would, Dell continued, proudly tell the committee about all the anti-communist books you have written. And McCarthy would simply ask, "Mr. Eastman, when you wrote those books, were you under instructions from the Communist Party to write them as a cover-up for subversive activities?"[40]

Dell saw clearly the dilemma of ex-radicals supporting McCarthy's investigations while resisting the logic (or illogic) of McCarthyism itself. He also discerned much else that might have tempered Eastman's cry of *trahison des clercs*. For one thing, he pointed out to Eastman in a seventeen-page critique of the manuscript of Eastman's forthcoming book on socialism, one generation cannot rebuke another for repeating its own mistakes. Indeed Eastman himself bore grave responsibility for the radical illusions that swayed young intellectuals and students who later became communists. The young Whittaker Chambers and Joseph Freeman, Dell noted, were persuaded by our "eloquent articles" in *The Masses* and the *Liberator*, and we misguided many others by our sarcastic rebuttal of Bertrand Russell's repudiation of Bolshevism in 1922. In effect, we provided "defenses of Stalinism in advance. The reasons we gave for loyalty to the Soviet regime were splendidly broad, Max. They gave absolution for crimes as yet uncommitted." These reasons, Dell continued, amounted to prejustifications for the positions of Romain Rolland, Henri Barbusse, and even Robert Minor, the great *The Masses* illustrator who gave up a promising career in art to become a Party functionary. With this haunting my mind, "I think it would be damned unreasonable of me," Dell confessed, "to set the date on which I stopped making excuses for the Soviet regime as the date beyond which anyone who kept on was an infamous scoundrel. In Christian morality, too, there is the idea that the sinner who repenteth late should be forgiven no less heartily than the sinner who repenteth early."[41]

Dell believed that Eastman's anti-communism, while intellectually prescient, had rendered him morally insensitive and politically arrogant. Dell himself would never "repent" the sentiments that earlier brought him into the revolutionary movement. "But," he added, "if there is a 'right time' for all good men to quit, all I can feel is that it *ought* to have been 'earlier.'" This means, Dell painfully explained, that there were others who saw the truth long before either of us. In the early twenties we were the ones who remained blind to our illusions and innocent of Bolshevik propaganda. And since we gave people "eloquent" arguments for believing in Soviet Russia, we are hardly now in a position to rebuke them for taking our advice only too well. Dell then went to the heart of the problem in the following passage, which could readily apply, as Dell and Eastman must have realized, to the Stalinist fellow travelers of the thirties and forties as well as the Leninist idol worshipers of the twenties:

You are very scornful of Rolland, Barbusse, and Joe Freeman, among others, for remaining in the Soviet fold long after you had left it. You seem to think that any generous-souled person was excusable for staying in as long as you did, but those who came in or stayed in later were utterly contemptible. You are not alone in this self-righteousness; it is a trait fairly common among ex-Communists. To you it seems quite excusable to have adored Lenin, and quite inexcusable to have tolerated Stalin. But, Max, there were those who got out of the fold earlier than you did and who had found in the Soviet regime under Lenin and Trotsky *all* the hideously objectionable things that you found existent under Stalin. They could have called you, and perhaps they did, a lackey, a high priest, etc. You mention Bertrand Russell, and you give him as little credit as you can for changing his mind so quickly. The rate at which you changed your mind was the right rate. To change earlier was giddy frivolity; to change later was obsequious servility. Cromwell said to Parliament: "I beseech you, brethren, in the bowells of Christ, to conceive it possible that you may be mistaken." And I abjure you in the same spirit.[42]

Reflections on the Failure of Socialism

final "political testament" was published in 1955. No
ed by the arguments put forth in *Reflections on the*
sm. Several chapters had already appeared in the
ader's *Digest, Saturday Evening Post,* and *The*

Freeman. Yet Eastman, with his characteristic lively and lucid prose, brought together in this slender volume intellectual convictions that still burned from the fire and ashes of personal experience; and the book opens, appropriately, with a biographical introduction, a dazzling condensation of his voluminous memoirs that enables its author, as befits a part-time poet, to portray truth by concrete example.

The publication of *Reflections* was cause for celebration among conservatives. Congratulations came to Eastman from business representatives like T. W. Phillips, president of Phillips Gas and Oil Company, and Merwin K. Hart, the right-wing president of the National Economic Council. Conservative journalists like David Lawrence of *U.S. News & World Report*, Raymond Moley of *Newsweek*, and Vermont Royster of the *Wall Street Journal* lavishly praised the book in their publications. Especially grateful were several Old Left writers who had made the transition to the New Right of the fifties along with Eastman: John Chamberlain, William Henry Chamberlin, Morrie Ryskind, and William S. Schlamm. Émigré scholars such as Milorad M. Drachkovitch and Vladimir Petrov wanted to see the book published in Europe, and the State Department had a Japanese translation issued through the United States Information Agency. Eastman or his publisher, the Devin-Adair Company, planned a huge party in celebration of the book. The guest list of nearly a hundred is a veritable social document of the conservative establishment in America.[43]

Reflections is a discursive *contra-Marx* that can be reduced to three prevalent themes or arguments. First is the indictment of socialism as a utopian belief. As a theory, socialism was the product of willful idealists who ceased believing in heaven only to conceive a future paradise on earth. Whether regarded as an ethical force, the inevitable result of moral progress, as the nineteenth-century romantic communitarians believed, or as a metaphysical certainty incorporated into a "scientific" history, as Marx believed by unconsciously allowing his will to govern his intellect, socialis[m] is the perfection of an abstract idea that has continued to d[e] those who mistake dream for reality. Marx's vision of a "society of the free and equal," Engels's promise that "Socialism will abolish architecture and barrow-pushing as professions," Lenin's stirring announcement made to the Petrograd Soviet in 1917 that "We will now proceed to the construction of Socialist Society"—all were expressions of "perfect fantasy" that could only result in perfect futility, scoffed Eastman. But Eastman did not have to belabor the history of Soviet Russia. He well knew that few intellectuals still believed a proletarian dictatorship could usher in a classless society, a notion so "preposterous," said the former champion of Lenin, that it now almost seemed like "a dangerous fairy tale."[44]

Far more dangerous were socialism and liberalism. Eastman reserved his greatest scorn for the democratic socialists of Italy and Germany who were opposing the Christian Democratic governments of Alcide De Gasperi and Konrad Adenauer; and in America he singled out Arthur Schlesinger, Jr., the liberal historian who wanted to see "creeping" socialism installed through the expansion of the welfare state. The idea that a radical intelligentsia could bend a bourgeois state to its will seemed even more "utopian" than the revolutionary theories of Lenin, who at least had enough sense to smash the state. The liberal idea was equally dangerous. A planned economy, whether totalitarian, socialist, or liberal, had as its aim the destruction of the "free market" from which all other liberties were historically derived. Eastman conceded he was not an economist, and he acknowledged that much of his argument stemmed from the writings of F. A. Hayek, Wilhelm Röpke, and Ludwig von Mises, conservative European economists who had come to admire the American ex-Trotskyist.[45]

U̶n̶l̶i̶k̶e̶ ̶t̶he classical economists, however, Eastman tolerated a ̶"̶m̶i̶x̶e̶d̶ ̶e̶c̶o̶n̶omy" as long as the mass of people, as consumers and ̶v̶o̶t̶e̶r̶s̶,̶ ̶r̶e̶t̶a̶i̶n̶ed substantial control over the market; and he ac̶c̶e̶p̶t̶e̶d̶ ̶i̶n̶t̶e̶rvention in fields like TVA and advocated con̶t̶r̶o̶l̶s̶ ̶a̶s̶ a check on big business. But Eastman was ̶c̶e̶r̶t̶a̶i̶n̶,̶ ̶a̶s̶ were the European laissez-faire theorists, that a country could not continue to expand controls in the economic sphere without restricting freedoms in the political sphere. Convinced that collectivism and democracy are incompatible, he believed with Hayek that on the "road to serfdom" there is no turning back. The idea that there can be some "halfway" experiment with planning is, Eastman warned, "a little like hoping a boa-constrictor will eat only half your cow."

Aside from its utopian illusions and collectivist solutions, the major fallacy of socialism was its naïve conception of human nature—or more accurately, its "no conception." Here Eastman rebuked Marx for not bothering to ask the basic question facing every great thinker: What is Man? To assert, as Marx did, that man is simply "a complex of social relations" hardly penetrates the infinite depths of man as a total psychobiological being. Socialists rightly rejected the Christian doctrine of original sin and then wrongly assumed that nature had endowed man with potential human qualities necessary to a free, equal, and fraternal life. This mistaken assumption about natural man was made because nineteenth-century socialist thinkers conceived their notions before the birth of modern psychology, anthropology, and post-Darwinian biology. Today we know, if not the ultimate mystery of man, something about the "drives," "impulses," and "native tendencies" that make man's instinctual nature more complex and more obscure than socialists ever realized. Thus radicals, Eastman pointed out, were totally unprepared for Stalin's cult of personality, even though Freud, with his theories of "submission" and "domination," could have told them something about the psychic mechanisms of authority that would persist in a classless society. The problem goes deeper than Marx's conflict between labor and capital or even Freud's antagonism between nature and civilization. Marxists and Freudians alike believe that society and culture have distorted original human nature, and they would agree w' Whitman, who said in his praise to the animal kingdom, "N is demented with the mania of owning things." To the we now know, Eastman maintained, by pointing t "animal sociology" by Konrad Lorenz and Robert Ardrey, that "territoriality," the aggressive determination to possess and rule over a piece of land, is native to the vertebrate animal world as well as human society. As Mark Twain knew all along, the human condition of permanent conflict and struggle is the natural condition.[46]

Eastman stated the conservative case against liberalism and socialism well. He pointed up the dangers of the centralized state, dramatized the tensions between liberty and equality, and criticized Soviet sympathizers for drawing a perilous distinction between economic democracy and political freedom. He also raised a troublesome matter that most socialists had passed over in silence for almost a century: Marx and Engels never explained the perfectibility of man, they assumed it. Indeed, even Marx's theory of alienation, which became so fashionable a decade later, is a terrible simplification without empirical or theoretical justification. That the contradictions in man's social existence, which supposedly spring from capitalism, will be transcended ("aufhebung") with the abolition of capitalism is an assumption deduced from the dialectic, not from modern social science.[47] Nevertheless, when all is said and praised, Reflections on the Failure of Socialism remains a banal polemic that lacks the penetrating depth Eastman had displayed thirty years earlier when he plunged into the philosophical currents of Hegelian Marxism.

First of all, as a critique of socialism, Eastman's book suffers from too much Marxism—always a bad sign. The philosophy of Marx was his touchstone, the Soviet Union, where presumably it ⁿpplied, his historical testing ground. Those who knew East-
ew better. Like Farrell a decade earlier, Van Wyck Brooks
stman for making "a virtual identification of Socialism
ⁿ and Russia" and for claiming that writers of their
regarded socialism as a "scientific" proposition.
ⁿd it "absurd to attribute" to the rebels of the
ⁱeft the "naïve" notion that the "Socialist
he hill.'" Nor did they rest their hopes for

the future of mankind on "the Marxian dialectical-process theory of the class struggle," the "Sunday theology of the Party" that mystified only a handful of intellectuals with "Jewish habits of thought" and an "enthusiastic young minister" like Eastman himself. What earlier radicals did believe in, Dell maintained, were specific social reforms that would bring about a "gradual establishment of workers' and other human rights." And many of these reforms, far from being "utopian" and related to the Soviet experience, had since been enacted into law. Thus socialism in the United States was not the conceit of the intellectual class but "a natural reaction to the greed, brutality, arrogance, and stand-pattism of the owning class."[48]

It is highly revealing that Eastman chose to indict socialism with Marx's own favorite word of derision—"utopian." Eastman used the term, as did Marx and Engels when criticizing Charles Fourier and Robert Owen, to mock reformist socialism as a cerebral fantasy. The alternative approach of Marx and Engels was to see socialism as "scientific," not as a romantic idea springing from the mind and heart but as a necessary economic tendency discovered in the nature of historical development, not what *ought* to be, but what *had* to be. Because of his animus against Hegel, Eastman never completely accepted this fatalistic definition; but when Lenin introduced an element of voluntarism into Marxism, Eastman believed socialism could now indeed be approached as a scientific "experiment" conducted by the "engineers of revolution." Such reasoning enabled Eastman to be in the socialist movement, but not of it. For the identity of socialism with science, while consistent with Marxism, offers an easy retreat from socialism. Once the identity is made, the sole criterion of socialism is its realization. Insofar as history disproved almost all the programmatic theories of Marxism—class struggle, dictatorship of the proletariat, nationalization of the means of production, etc.—Eastman could repudiate socialism on empirical grounds. Yet surely there were other ways of thinking about socialism even while reflecting on its failures as a "hypothesis." Dell was quite right to point out to Eastman that socialism was, among other things, a moral impulse and a social obligation. "I do not think that anybody should ever 'repent' any generous and humane sentiments, despite the follies to which they may have led," he had advised Eastman when reading his manuscript.[49] Eastman had once accused Marx of treating too lightly the moral ideals that had inspired him when he confined their realization to the operation of dialectical materialism. In repenting his radical past and celebrating his "convalescence from socialism," Eastman now seemed to be renouncing all that was courageous, humane, and noble in his own career. Scorning "utopia," both Marx and Eastman had little patience for ideals that lay beyond the actual world of science and historical experience. Thus Marx believed socialism a scientific certainty, and Eastman thought it a scientific fallacy. Eastman's conclusion may have been right only because Marx's premise was wrong. Conceived strictly as a scientific proposition, or even historically as a probability, socialism became an empirical escape from an ethical imperative.

Eastman's analysis also sinks from the weight of Marxism in its historical understanding of the conditions of freedom. Marx was one of the first to observe, according to Eastman, that Western political freedoms had developed with the rise of free enterprise. Yet he was one of the last to see the permanent historical dependency of freedom upon capitalism. "It was he who informed us that the evolution of private capitalism with its free market had been a precondition for the evolution of all our democratic freedoms. It never occurred to him that, if this was so, those other freedoms might disappear with the abolition of the free market."[50] Even though Eastman regarded bourgeois liberalism with a tenderness unknown to Marx, he shared Marx's view that the economic mode of production is of primary significance in the development of political institutions. To a certain extent Eastman shared Trotsky's conviction that an industrial economy must either advance to socialism or return to capitalism. In Reflections there is no discussion of other possible alternatives such as Burnham's managerial state, Thurman Arnold's corporate capitalism, or Oscar Lange's "free market socialism." Nor is there any suggestion of the autonomy of the political over the economic. Yet, if it is ironic to find capitalists and socialists agreeing about the primacy of productive forces, the historical record is much too complex to prove a direct, unilateral causal relationship between the economic base and the political superstructure. The historical development of specific political freedoms cannot simply be explained in terms of the mode of production. The variations of modern European liberalism alone would suggest that an economy does not in itself determine any one political system or ideology.[51]

Nor does the form of an economy necessarily determine the political destiny of a nation. Eastman was convinced, fortified by Hayek's writings, that a planned economy ushered in the dictatorship of the Right and Left in Europe, and he showed little patience for discriminating between communism and fascism as different political expressions of totalitarianism.[52] Here again Eastman's historical judgment seems more willed than wise. As Sidney Hook pointed out in an earlier debate with Eastman, a planned economy did not set the stage for the death of political democracy in Russia and Germany. The destruction of democracy was already implicit in the totalitarian character of the Bolshevik and Nazi party organizations. Collectivism was the necessary result of the political seizure of power, not the sufficient cause.[53] From a broader historical perspective there also appear to be grounds to question Eastman's simple conviction that the preservation of democracy depends upon the preservation of the "free market." The chastening historical experiences of the twentieth century would indicate that the fate of democracy may very well depend upon its historical legitimacy and value in the conscience of a nation. In Europe, fascism swept into power in those countries where parliamentary democracy was weak and fragile, as in Italy; or where it had never struck deep roots, as in Poland; or where it had been discredited by military defeat and national humiliation, as in Germany. Similarly, parliamentary socialism flourished most where the traditions of universal suffrage and the institutions of liberal democracy had been deeply implanted, as in the United Kingdom and Scandinavia; while revolutionary communism successfully rose to power in the one country where neither socialism nor democracy could find political expression—Tsarist Russia.*

Eastman's reflections on human nature also deserve comment. He was convinced that socialism was doomed to failure because socialist theoreticians had never formulated a conception of human behavior that did justice to all its biological and psychological complexity. Delving into intellectual history, he pointed out that Marx wrote his major philosophical treatise before Darwin's discoveries denied teleological significance to human history, and long before Freud's explorations of the unconscious revealed the "irreducible variety of drives in man's hereditary nature." By emphasizing the competitive and acquisitive instincts of man, Eastman could readily expose the myth of equality and faternity that supposedly lies at the heart of socialism, and he could easily refute the liberal assumption "that love of freedom is the strongest of political motives."[54] These conclusions, however, rest upon a corpus of intellectual history that is open to more than one interpretation. Darwinism was so ambiguous a legacy that it could give "scientific" support to class struggle as well as competitive individualism, while Marx's vision of socialism had little to do with "equality" and "justice," the heritage of bourgeois liberalism that he once dismissed as "obsolete verbal rubbish."[55] Nor is it clear that Freudianism can be interpreted as a refutation of socialist illusions

---

* The example of Bolshevism and Soviet Russia suggests that revolutionary communism would continue to be, especially after World War II, the characteristic "solution" to the problems of backwardness and modernization in countries where parliamentary institutions and universal suffrage were unknown. Yet it is not easy to draw clear political lessons from these historical patterns. Comparative studies in Europe may indicate that democratic socialism and partial collectivization of industry do not necessarily lead to the demise of political democracy, but Castro's Cuba and Mao's China also demonstrate that one-party dictatorships cannot be sustained without the total collectivization of all phases of economic, political, and even cultural life. In one respect, then, Eastman was right: collectivization grows out of the logic of totalitarianism, even though it may not be the historical cause of it.

and hence an affirmation of capitalist realities. Freud's theory of the cultural necessity of repression is a far cry from the capitalist notion of unlimited self-aggrandizement. Indeed when we match Freud's image of man with Adam Smith's we find two entirely different conceptions of human nature. Smith and the classical economists attributed to the masses of men a healthy and robust capacity for self-direction and rational decision making, which in turn enabled the individual to exercise conscious control over the price fluctuations of the market place. Freud, on the other hand, saw man as limited and frail, an irrational, tragic creature struggling against primal emotions and impelled by self-dividing inner anxieties; and the market place was for Freud not Adam Smith's creative dynamo of value and community but the squalid spectacle of "filthy lucre." With Marx, we are still in the rational, progressive world of David Ricardo and even of Adam Smith. With Freud, we descend into the underworld of Dostoevski. "One might say anything about the history of the world, anything that might enter into the most disordered imagination," wrote Dostoevski. "The one thing one cannot say is that it is rational."[56]

Eastman used contemporary social science to prove that socialism is historically impossible. These same sources, however, offer cold comfort to anyone who wants to believe that capitalism is historically inevitable or morally preferable. Eastman wanted to relegate socialism back to nineteenth-century utopianism, but he could not explain how the "laws" of classical economics escaped many of the same false assumptions that also influenced the "laws" of Marxian socialism, rationalist assumptions that collapsed with the psychological and sociological discoveries of the twentieth century. All this suggests that Eastman was at his best as a skeptic, one who could be counted upon in his early radical years to turn easy answers into harder questions. As a conservative, he was an eclectic dilettante, scavenging here and there for ideas that would reaffirm convictions he already believed in. He wanted to bring capitalism into the twentieth century, but he chose Hayek instead of Joseph Schumpeter or Max Weber, thereby returning to the self-regulating "free market" fetish and the natural-law mentality of the nineteenth century. He wanted to leave Marx back with Hegel, but he could never bring Adam Smith past Thorstein Veblen, the first scholar to discern in classical political economy the "animism" that Eastman would discern in Marxist philosophy. His mind and intellect in one century, his heart and will in another, Eastman used the wrong ideas to support what he regarded as the right idea.

CHAPTER **6**

Visions of Order: Dos Passos

I am against bigness and greatness in all their forms, and with the
invisible molecular moral forces that work from individual to individual, stealing in through the crannies of the world like so many
soft rootlets, or like the capillary oozing of water, yet rending the
hardest monuments of man's pride, if you give them time. The
bigger the unit you deal with, the hollower, the more brutal, the
more mendacious is the life displayed. So I am against all big
organizations as such, national ones first and foremost; against all big
successes and big results; and in favor of the eternal forces of truth
which always work in the individual and immediately unsuccessful
way, under-dogs always, till history comes, after they are long dead,
and puts them on the top.

WILLIAM JAMES, 1911

A Moment of Optimism

During World War II John Dos Passos fell in love with America.
In the thirties he had invoked American ideals as an indictment of
contemporary American society. Now he embraced American society itself, still aware of its imperfections, but convinced more
than ever of its promises and possibilities.

During the war years he discovered America anew as a traveling
reporter for *Harper's, Fortune,* and *Liberty.* Impressed by the immense productivity unleashed by the war effort, he paid tribute to
an unregimented society where he found shipyard workers bustling
with energy amid the roar of rivets, farmers busily resettling on
new lands and adjusting to price ceilings, coal miners walking off
their jobs in defiance of government orders. These were the pro-

233

ducing groups Dos Passos had always admired; and it was natural for him to defend, against some angry servicemen, the rights of labor in wartime as essential to American liberties. Dos Passos was interested in the human drama quietly unfolding behind the war, the daily lives of average people doing particular jobs in particular places. Disregarding the official publicity and slogans of government agencies, and talking instead to those actually engaged in war work, he saw a spirit of local community springing up in the projects, meetings, cooperatives, and other collective efforts that put people in touch with one another. *The State of the Nation*, as he aptly entitled his journalistic excursions, was sound in spirit, a fluid, open society where people could "still change their occupations, their ways of living, their settlements as easily as they can eat their breakfasts." The war against European totalitarianism, Dos Passos was convinced, would be won on the farms and in the factories of America.[1]

This was one of the few periods when Dos Passos felt optimistic about America's future. His hopes did not diminish while touring the Pacific as a war correspondent. America's conduct in that theater of war seemed to Dos Passos intelligent, and the role of American power beneficent. The sunny optimism that blossomed in the Pacific as Dos Passos described the liberation of the Philippines suddenly wilted as he observed the course of events in Eastern Europe. Grave doubts now arose over President Roosevelt's prosecution of the war. Once again Dos Passos sank into gloom, as though the ghost of Randolph Bourne had returned. Writing in 1945—"In the Year of Our Defeat"—he expressed dismay at America's unwillingness to resist the Soviet occupation of Eastern Europe. The failure of will did not appear to Dos Passos a matter of war weariness and public indifference, nor was America's "defeat" an inevitable result of the power realities of the incipient cold war. Someone was responsible, and to Dos Passos it was "the handful of men" who had surrounded "the man in the White House," politicians and bureaucrats who had lost touch with the people and arrogated the very power the Constitution was designed to limit.[2]

After the war Dos Passos was in Europe reporting for *Life* magazine. His journalism, a varied panorama of scenes mingled with a vivid profusion of dialogue, is a human inventory of confusion and frustration. In Vienna he experienced the suspicion and misery that clouded the once-gay cultural capital. In Germany he found a dangerous cynicism and despair arising in the industrial cities, now reduced to mounds of rubble. The American military presence created a bad odor, as John Horne Burns would recount in *The Gallery*, a novel on occupied Italy greatly admired by Dos Passos. The American soldiers came as liberators, but in the eyes of the Germans themselves they appeared little better than the Russians, interested only in looting, lust, and liquor. (The Americans carried off some things, Dos Passos noted, the Russians everything.) Dos Passos was deeply disturbed by the sudden decline of America's prestige in Europe. It seemed to him a repetition of 1919, when America won the war only to lose the peace. The irony was personal as well as political. After World War I, when Dos Passos found himself bitterly estranged from America, Europeans, he recalled, perhaps a bit too nostalgically, looked to Woodrow Wilson and American democratic ideals as the last hope for peace and freedom. After World War II, now having passionately re-embraced America, Dos Passos found the fabric of European society devastated and America helpless to offer political direction and moral inspiration. Instead of offering a "bold plan of relief and reconstruction," American statesmen were full of "evasions and apologies."[3]

How should Western Europe be reconstructed? Dos Passos answered this question in "The Failure of Marxism," published in *Life* in 1948. His answer derives from many assumptions characteristic of Old Left thinkers who knew too much Stalinism and not enough Marxism. Equating socialism with Russia, Dos Passos retold the gory history of the Stalin regime as final proof of the "failure" of both socialism and Marxism. The "angry young men" of my generation, he recalled, were "naïve" and "innocent" in their desperate belief that socialism would substitute cooperation and public service for competition and profit and provide a rational alternative to international rivalry and war. Those illusions prevented us from seeing that the Russian people, emerging from the ravages of civil war, desired above all else "any kind of order," and the "only order Russians knew was despotism." The same illusion persisted into the thirties, when it was assumed that soviet collectivization was giving birth to genuine communal democracy, while in reality Russia under Stalin more closely resembled "the slave-run military autocracy of the Ottoman Turks than it did any of the European blueprints for a socialist utopia." The "dilemma of our time" is the revenge of the counter-Enlightenment, for just at the very historical moment when technology is opening up the possibility of liberating society from the historical problem of scarcity, "the masses of mankind are being plunged back into a regime of misery and servitude such as has not existed in the West since the days of serfdom." Instead of expanding human freedoms, "socialized economies . . . have backslid with dizzy speed into aboriginal oppressions."

Ah, yes! But the Russians are "barbarians," replies the English intellectual. We are civilized. Socialism will be different in Great Britain! Dos Passos had no patience with this argument. Like Eastman, he saw democratic socialism an even greater danger than the Soviet system, for the latter was a squalid reality, the former still a shining dream. It is the conceit of the British socialists to think that their country will escape the "ultimate implications" of the Russian experience, he warned the readers of *Life*. True, England has no police terror, no "quasi-religious dogma," and as yet no "universal servitude." Nevertheless, British socialism has failed to broaden personal liberty and expand individual freedom. Everywhere in England Dos Passos saw a contraction of workers' rights under the Labor government, a diminution of energy and enterprise, a debilitation of talent and leadership. The British people, who demonstrated their heroic dignity during the war, "represent in themselves at this moment just about the highest development of Western civilized man." But now the British must face the arduous tasks of economic growth and technological development, and the British ruling class and civil service corps have no experience in stimulating industrial productivity. Even more serious, the British are under the illusion that they are "free, quite free," because they have the secret ballot and parliamentary institutions. Nonsense. The "record of history" shows that voting and electoral politics are inadequate guarantees of democratic freedoms. "This great highly trained, highly disciplined and civilized nation," Dos Passos concluded with a dire warning, "is in danger of dying of inanition because in all the elaborate structure of the state there are so few cracks left where individual initiative can take hold."[4]

Dos Passos's case against socialism contains many of the questionable historical assumptions implicit in Eastman's argument. Both believed individual liberty was the historial fount of freedom; both stressed the primacy of economic institutions and values; and both maintained that man could not determine his freedom through political institutions alone. Yet, while Eastman was at least clear, if not convincing, in arguing that Soviet totalitarianism evolved from the "utopian" illusions of Marxism, it is not at all clear from Dos Passos's writings that he had any theoretical notion of the complexities of historical explanation. Questions arise: Was the failure of socialism due to the fallacies imbedded in the doctrine of Marxism itself, or to the peculiar historical traditions and national character of Russia? Was Stalinism inherent in the idea of socialism or a reversion to the repressive heritage of Tsarist Russia? In contrast to Eastman the philosopher, Dos Passos the social historian leaned toward the latter view, and hence he wrote of the Russians' yearning for "order," their familiarity with "despotism," their retrogression to the condition of "serfdom" and the "aboriginal oppressions" that run deep in Slavic history. In this respect the "failure" of Marxism is a result of the tyranny of the past, an argument with which Marx himself would be the first to agree.* But the same argument could hardly be applied to England in order to claim that socialism would be the tyranny of the future. To suggest that the failure of Soviet communism is rooted deep in the despotic past of Russia also implies that the possibility of the success of British socialism lies in her democratic heritage. Ironically, the persistent historical traits of Russia, which Dos Passos loathed, appeared to have a greater grip on the present and the future than did the Anglo-Saxon institutions and British national character, which he passionately loved. This would not be the last time that Dos Passos's historicism defeated his didacticism.

The Grand Design

The tyranny of socialism begins in the tyranny of words. Twenty years ago, Dos Passos wrote in 1948, capitalist slogans dominated social thought while socialist slogans were suspect. "Now public ownership, planned economy, controls and socialized have become words heavy with virtue, while profits, free enterprise, investments and even dividends have taken on an evil context."[5] The language of possessive individualism had indeed become stale and pernicious, and the moral significance of capitalism had clearly lost its meaning for the generation of writers who had lived through the Depression and the war. How did one restore the respectability of

---

* This is not merely a question of Russia's backwardness. Marx had a profound, almost Burkean, respect for the past as a historical force that could not be violated by the imposition of will, as Eastman had assumed in his exhortations on Lenin. "We suffer not only from the living but from the dead. Le mort saisit le vif!" wrote Marx in the preface to Capital. "Men make their own history," he stated in The Eighteenth Brumaire of Louis Bonaparte, "but they do not make it just as they please; they do not make it under circumstances chosen by themselves, but under circumstances directly found, given and transmitted from the past." Thus while a revolutionary may look to the future, he cannot merely leap the stages of history and escape the awful burden of the past. "The tradition of all dead generations weighs like a nightmare on the brain of the living." For an excellent discussion of the tragic dimension in Marx's dramatic sense of history, see Harold Rosenberg, "The Resurrected Romans," in The Tradition of the New (New York: McGraw-Hill edn., 1965), pp. 154–77.

a discredited ideology? Eastman the essayist and philosopher tried by praising the blessings of the "free market" as an enduring idea and an eternal proposition. As a novelist, Dos Passos would try to depict the virtuous character of those who embodied the idea itself, the doers and builders whose struggles and frustrations dramatized the human story of capitalism in our time.

The Grand Design, the third volume of the trilogy District of Columbia, appeared in 1949, a year after Dos Passos wrote "The Failure of Marxism" in Life. An ideological morality tale, the novel attempted to penetrate the political cant of the day and lay bare the forces thwarting the revitalization of entrepreneurial energies during the late stages of the Depression and the early war years. It is the first significant literary attack on the New Deal, the first assault on modern liberalism by an important American novelist. The book is epigraphed with the old nursery rhyme adage "A man of words and not of deeds / is like a garden full of weeds." The liberals, of course, are the word-froth politicians and administrators. Men of principle, they speak platitudes; characters with conviction, they live by compromise. Walker Watson, who combines the rhetoric of Henry Wallace with the ambitions of Harry Hopkins, epitomizes to Dos Passos all that was sanctimonious and cynical in liberalism. But there are good liberals as well as bad, and one of Dos Passos's purposes is to trace the history of the New Deal through the career of Paul Graves, an agronomist who has just returned from the Soviet Union, attracted by the idealism and experimental promises of the early New Deal. His solution to the problems of modern industrial capitalism contained the Jeffersonian vision that always inspired Dos Passos's hope that the past would redeem the present:

This was his America. If you could get the rural economy functioning well enough to reverse the trend and suck the people back out of the obsolete and gangrenous cities . . . Americans had never learned to build decent cities because they didn't need them, maybe. As the blueprints unrolled in his mind it was as if he skimmed in an imaginary plane over a model countryside contourplowed reforested resettled. God there was so much land in this country. There was room for all of us to live spaced out, to reach a balance between largescale organization and individual human stature.[6]

Convinced that America could be "made over" through determination and hard work, Graves takes a position with the Economic Scarcities Commission of the Agricultural Department. But when he visits the farm communities he discovers that government controls, subsidies, and price supports had destroyed his agrarian dream of making man more independent at the source of his livelihood. Not only political freedom but moral stature was being threatened, for the farmer was being paid not to produce, the ultimate insult to Dos Passos's Veblenian work ethic. Thus Graves turns against the politics of planned scarcity and expresses his admiration for minor figures like John Hick and Ed Hodgins, small independent farmers who are more interested in the beauties of husbandry than in the bounties of parity.

Millard Carroll, a dedicated businessman, also gives the best years of his life to government service, only to find his hopes crushed by the stifling bureaucracy in Washington. Carroll, who opposed America's entry into the war, resigns in disgust when he senses that Roosevelt deliberately manipulated the public. The "voice" in the White House "played on the American people. We danced to his tune. Third Term, Fourth Term, Indispensable. / War is a time of Caesars." Roosevelt also played at diplomacy and "got meddling with history." Collaborating with Churchill and Stalin, the president made a mockery out of his promise of "Four Freedoms" to postwar Europe. The "triumvirate"

divided up the bloody globe and left the freedoms out,
And the American people were supposed to say thank you for the century of the Common Man turned over for relocation behind barbed wire so help him God.
We learned. There were things we learned to do
but we have not learned, in spite of the Constitution and the Declaration of Independence and the great debates at Richmond and Philadelphia
how to put power over the lives of men into the hands of one man and to make him use it wisely.[7]

Dos Passos's postwar novels are fictional statements on the theme of power and freedom. His dilemma is essentially a rediscovery of the Madisonian paradox: can a government be allowed to control the governed if it cannot control itself? Yet Dos Passos was not a deeply reflective man, and from his novels it is difficult to discover just what it is "we learned" from history. The Founding Fathers feared centralized power, but they feared popular democracy as well, and the Constitution attempted to neutralize both forces. Dos Passos, on the other hand, wanted to assure the fullest measure of popular sovereignty to the people, thereby ignoring what Madison and John Adams would certainly have perceived: Roosevelt had power democratically conferred upon him by the citizenry long before he presumably abused that power. What is lacking in Dos Passos's writings is a sense of the inner essence and dynamism of power, above all, the tendency of power to continually move away from people. With almost populistic simplicity, Dos Passos attributed Roosevelt's power (and that of Huey Long in the novel *Number One*) to sheer demagogy, and in his fictive treatment of the theme in *The Grand Design* there is always the shadow or "voice" of an unseen power more sensed than understood.

Had Dos Passos possessed a greater appreciation for the historical dynamics of power he might have grasped what most conservative thinkers have maintained: only the forms through which power is expressed change, not the reality of power itself. Surely the shift of political sovereignty from Wall Street to Washington in the thirties cannot be explained by a simple conspiratorial view of history, a habit of thought that characterizes Dos Passos's anarchistic suspicion of the movement of power from one source to another. In the concluding lines of his *Life* article he warned, "Socialism is not the answer to the great concentration of power that is the curse of capitalism." True, perhaps, but to the Depression generation the crime of unregulated capitalism meant far more than concentrated power; it also meant fear and anxiety, unemployment and breadlines. Suffering from these conditions, the masses of men and women turned to the state for protection and security. Today, now that the welfare state appears to have proved incapable of effectively solving many economic and social problems, few social critics would challenge Dos Passos's prescient attack on the bureaucracy that grew under the Roosevelt adminis- tration. Indeed *The Grand Design*, once so controversial, may now seem almost prophetic. But we are still left with a condition, not an explanation. Dos Passos offered only a moral perception of a real danger; unable to provide a convincing historical analysis of the causes of that danger, he could not offer a political solution to it. Unlike Eastman, who invoked the magic of the "free market," Dos Passos knew enough about the nature of organization to real- ize that capitalism is the calculus of growth and consolidation, but he could not follow that logic to its frightful conclusion: The curse of big business means the curse of big government. Conceived in Jeffersonian protest, *The Grand Design* ends in Weberian pathos.

Pathos aptly describes the frustrated heroes of the novel. If Graves and Carroll symbolized Dos Passos's idea of a potential capitalist Risorgimento, they hardly lived up to the role. Graves, a curiously passive man, eschews politics and is incapable of assum- ing administrative leadership, while Carroll also gives up the struggle against bureaucratic domination with hardly a gesture of resistance. Dos Passos wanted to revive the virtuous concepts of capitalism, but he could not create fictional characters who affirmed them. Thus Graves speaks of restoring "individual human stature," while he himself lacks the spirit to compete with power and withdraws from the fight almost with a whimper. In Graves and Carroll we do not see the defiant resistance to authority that was the great historical achievement of bourgeois liberalism. The same paradox remains in Dos Passos's portrait of the bourgeois citizen as in his earlier characterization of working class figures in *U.S.A.* The novelist passionately believes in individual freedom, yet he cannot create individuals with the will to be free.

In the forties critics Granville Hicks and Edmund Wilson maintained that Dos Passos's imagination was no longer involved with his material and that he seemed "dissociated from the kind of reality he has chosen to deal with."[8] That Dos Passos suffered a decline of literary power is debatable; that the weakening of his creative work derived from his separation from social reality is hardly the case. For Dos Passos was deeply immersed in his material,[9] and he remained in temperament and in talent what he had been in *U.S.A.*: America's leading writer on the subject of frustration and defeat, the literary authority on political failure. Perhaps it was not the "reality" of bureaucratic organization and power that led to the dissociation of his sensibility. The divorce of will and intellect may have derived from his failure to envision an alternative to the reality he was determined to expose in the hope of restoring capitalist values. In truth, the selfless humanistic capitalism Dos Passos longed for required a moral vision that would invoke nothing less than the regeneration of man, and as a literary exercise this vision required creating characters he believed in more firmly than his mind would allow. He set out to use prose fiction to revive the words and concepts of capitalism (or his humane version of it), but his imagination proved incapable of conceiving a new man and his will incapable of infusing new life into an old idea whose time had come and gone—an irretrievable idea whose real meaning, like that of liberty, he could find only in the past, in his study of history, or in his nostalgic reflections on his father's generous, enlightened career as a corporation lawyer. Dos Passos was too honest to ask of modern capitalism more than he could expect from modern man.

Perspective at Midcentury

In 1950 Dos Passos moved with his family and new wife, Elizabeth H. Holdridge, to Spence Point, on the Northern Neck of Virginia. (Katharine Smith, his first wife, had died in 1947 in an auto accident in which Dos Passos lost an eye. *Chosen Country*, published in 1951, is in part a fictionalized autobiography and a tribute to her memory.) Dos Passos's 1800-acre farm covered a piney strip of land between the Rappahannock and Potomac near the vicinity of the birthplaces of Washington and Monroe. Now fifty-four and still vigorous, he worked his property, callusing his hands in the garden, supervising land and timber operations, and adding a new wing to his simple square brick house built in 1806. Here, in the quiet of his father's farm, Dos Passos also worked long and hard at his desk (in his lifetime he would produce almost fifty books, a literary corpus that included poetry, plays, travel diaries, political reportage, autobiography, and historical narratives as well as novels), refreshing himself after his labors with a daily swim in the bracing waters of the Potomac.[10]

The gentry life Dos Passos took up in his later years led some cynics to conclude that the ex-radical adjusted his politics to suit his newly acquired status. Dos Passos's contemporaries knew better. "Nobody," Malcolm Cowley recently wrote in his memoirs, "thought that Dos Passos was trying to profit by his new beliefs. On the contrary, they involved a financial sacrifice, since they deprived him of his former audience and plunged him into a period of partial neglect." Dos Passos managed to make a living by writing, but it was always "nip and tuck," he once replied to a *Partisan Review* questionnaire in 1939. In the early forties he informed Eastman that he could not become a steady contributor to the *New Leader* because he needed the few dollars his articles could bring from other journals. His essays in *Life* were doubtlessly remunerative, and they commanded the respect of publisher Henry Luce. But by the end of the forties even *Life*, hardly a radical magazine, found Dos Passos's articles a bit too portentous and stopped printing his reports on the state of the world. In the fifties his reputation in literary circles continued to decline. Because of your "ideological writing," James T. Farrell wrote Dos Passos, you are getting "a snobbish, unfair deal."[11]

Like Eastman, Dos Passos did not hesitate to take on the journalism establishment in America. He chastised the "New York press" for practicing "an invisible censorship" on books dealing openly with Russian life under Stalin. "It is time we heard from the underdog," he wrote the New York *Times*, "and by underdog I don't mean political dissidents, I mean the great tortured majority of Russian people." As cold war tensions increased, Dos Passos became an important figure among the American anti-communist literary intelligentsia. He also had some influence in Europe and Hispanic America, where his writings were well known. Lewis Galantière informed him that "our voices—Polish, Czech, Slovak, Hungarian, Bulgarian, Rumanian"—had asked Radio Free Europe to have Dos Passos extend a message to the literary community in their countries; and the American Committee for Cultural Freedom asked the Spanish-speaking novelist to attend a Mexico City conference of the International Congress for Cultural Freedom along with Hook, Farrell, Lionel Trilling, John Steinbeck, W. H. Auden, and Thornton Wilder.[12]

Dos Passos was delighted to participate in such activities, but many intellectuals, while welcoming his anti-communism, were disturbed by the thickening of his conservative convictions. In 1952 he joined Eastman and John Chamberlain to form the Arts and Letters Committee in support of Senator Taft for president. That same year he wrote a revealing review of Whittaker Chambers's *Witness*. Dos Passos was convinced that Chambers's confession was testimony to the suffering spirit and hence a work of literature that combined the themes of Dostoevski's *The Possessed*, Bunyan's *Pilgrim's Progress*, and George Fox's *Journal*. Likening its moral lesson to Dante's descent into hell, Dos Passos observed, "That there is something uplifting in the prospect of the immensity of pain that the human soul can contain is one of the great paradoxes that make life supportable." Dos Passos's existential grasp of the inner turmoil of the psyche is uncharacteristic of his naturalism. But what did all this mean politically? The imperative, Dos Passos maintained, of admitting the sin of self-deception and making a decision to "go down fighting" to redeem the ideals that one had betrayed. Thus those liberals who are determined to ruin Chambers's reputation pose a greater danger than the communists themselves, for their influence in America is greater. "The questions raised in the mind by the moral lynching of Whittaker Chambers by the right-thinking people of this country are so grave and urgent that a man breaks out in cold sweat to think of them." To Dos Passos it was not so much a matter of the guilt or innocence of Alger Hiss (whom he avoids mentioning) as the larger issue of communism itself, which remained for him the politics of permanent conspiracy. No doubt he had good reason to break out into cold sweat; he too had once been raked over for trying to expose the Stalinist maneuvers of the thirties, and the scars remained an open sore on his political memory. "I've seen," he told Glenway Wescott while warning against the threat of communist infiltration into the American Writers Association, "the trick turned again and again, in unions during the strikes in this country, in liberal or radical magazines, in the theatre, and in Spain during the Civil War."[13]

Dos Passos's bitter anti-communism is understandable, and even his defense of Chambers could be seen as a philosophical discourse on human frailty—the *Partisan Review*, after all, had solicited Chambers's personal reflections just before he turned on Hiss.[14] More difficult to explain is Dos Passos's alignment with the Republican Right in the early fifties. "I don't understand your politics these days," Archibald MacLeish wrote while congratulating him on the publication of *Chosen Country*. "Taft to me is the unspeakable hypocrite and symbol of everything Jay Pignatelli hated," he stated in reference to the novel's hero (and a thinly veiled portrait of the novelist himself). "But I do understand what you say of the institutions of the Republic and bless you for it. They do indeed have to be saved from those who would save them to destroy them." To talk about such patriotic ideals, MacLeish nevertheless warned, is to risk expropriation; the words turn to mush not "only in the Commies' mouths but in McCarthy's and McCarran's even more for more men listen to them." A few years later Edmund Wilson also expressed his bewilderment. In a letter written in response to the publication of *The Great Days* (1958), Wilson told Dos Passos that the novel fails to make clear the

reasons for the protagonist's quarrel with the Roosevelt administration. True, the "New Dealers begin to show symptoms of the
disease developed by people in power. But otherwise the picture
seems blank." Nor could Wilson figure out why Dos Passos's reaction against the New Deal should have led him to succumb to
"something of a panic about Russia," even to the "point of some
tenderness toward McCarthy." "What puzzles me," Wilson concluded, "is that I seem to remember your accepting at the start the
whole New Deal case for intervention, and now you are talking
about Roosevelt as a butcher as you did about Wilson after World
War One."[15]

Dos Passos's politics are indeed disconcerting. A decade earlier,
in an interview given after *The Grand Design* had been published,
Dos Passos was quoted as having said, "It was Mr. Roosevelt's
foreign—not domestic—policy that disappointed him." He meant,
one gathers, Roosevelt's refusal to carry through the liberation of
Eastern Europe from Stalinism as well as Nazism. By the fifties,
however, Dos Passos was deeply disappointed with the legacy of
Roosevelt's domestic program as well. The New Deal now seemed
as pernicious as Yalta, for the creeds and vaunted idealism of
liberalism brought expediency and corruption as much as the greed
and cynicism of the old order. Moreover, much of the New Deal
had now been absorbed by President Eisenhower and the Republican Party, and the bureaucratic state had seeped into almost every
crevice of American life. In light of these realities, a few close
friends knew what to expect of Dos Passos's future writings: the
novelist would never allow himself to be subdued by the Leviathan. "You know, Dos," wrote Farrell in 1957, "despite the fact
that we disagree on many things politically, I have always insisted
that you have not changed as a decent human being, and that the
key to your attitude was a feeling for an attitude of libertarianism,
and, with this, opposition to bigness." But despite his admiration,
Farrell was troubled. He knew that the New Deal had done much
to overcome poverty and injustice and that business needed government controls. At the same time he also knew what Dos Passos

knew—that the liberal state begins as the servant of society and becomes its master. He thus asked Dos Passos, "How much welfare should there be in the welfare state?" The novelist answered Farrell's question and several other burning issues in Midcentury.[16]

A Chronicle of Despair

Published in 1960, Midcentury is in some respects the postwar sequel to U.S.A. As in his earlier masterpiece, Dos Passos was concerned not only with the narrow corridors of power, the focus of his recent novels; he was also concerned with the full scope and reality of American society. To capture this totality he returned again to many of the literary devices used in U.S.A.—the "Newsreels" and their pastiches of bizarre headlines, the documentaries, the satirical typographical arrangements, and the topical quotations designed to give the reader a sense of the absurdity of modern life. But Midcentury is a more pessimistic novel than any of the volumes of U.S.A., where the defiant rage kept alive at least the hope of passion and dissidence during the Depression years. In Midcentury the entire social organism is sick with corruption and the total culture diseased by the comforts of pleasure and affluence. "Man," cries Dos Passos in the novel's final passage, "drowns in his own scum. / These nights are dark."

What accounts for the night of despair that overcame Dos Passos at midcentury? The answer lies, I believe, in the demise of three historical possibilities that at one time or another had given him hope in the future: the failure of the labor movement to achieve genuine trade union democracy; the failure of capitalism to free itself of external controls on the one hand and inner cupidity on the other; and the failure of science and technology to fulfill Veblen's dream of liberating modern culture from all that was irrational, wasteful, stupid, and oppressive. These three themes culminate in Midcentury, and it is here that we can best examine the reasons for Dos Passos's disillusionment with contemporary American society.

Since World War II, Dos Passos's novels had constantly shifted their focus from one threatening concentration of power to another. As an organized institution, labor unions had thus far escaped his wrath. But in the late fifties he took a close interest in the investigations of Senator John L. McClellan and his committee on the "improper activities" of labor unions. Dos Passos was allowed access to the committee's findings, and from Robert Kennedy, McClellan's chief counsel, who was preparing a case to prosecute Teamster Union leader James Hoffa, he received scores of letters from CIO workers, many of them written anonymously for fear of reprisal. He also received from Kennedy correspondence on the People's Cab Company of Pittsburgh, material he used in the novel to dramatize a taxi war, a jurisdictional dispute so brutal and bloody that it would seem that Eastman's belief in man's "territorial imperative" was being acted out on the streets of America.[17]

Dos Passos saw two phases in the American labor movement, one a heroic memory of what might have been, the other a horrendous picture of what really happened. The former vision is represented in the character of Blackie Bowman. Part-time hobo, merchant seaman, farmhand, and working stiff, he symbolizes the old rebellious spirit of the Wobblies, the anarcho-syndicalist outcasts who remained incorruptible because they did not succumb to the disease of organization. But Bowman, who tells his story from a bed in a veterans' hospital, is a broken spirit from the past. The conscience of the future labor movement is embodied in Terry Bryant. War hero, devoted family man, dedicated mechanic who finds satisfaction in doing his job well, he is Dos Passos's idea of what the unalienated workman might be. But when Bryant attempts to make suggestions for improving working conditions and eliminating wage favoritism, he runs up against the ruthless bosses of the machinists' union. "Get wise feller, get wise." He continues to clash with the hierarchy, but his fellow workers are too intimidated to support him, and a government arbiter is too timid to press matters. In a final assertion of his individuality he takes a job as a taxi driver, only to find that his union is being terrorized by a rival organization. Bryant goes down fighting, his death at the hands of hired goons symbolizing the fate of the honest workman in modern America.

To add factual substance to his fiction, Dos Passos drew devastating biographical sketches of American labor leaders, particularly the Teamster bosses Jack Tobin, Dave Beck, and James Hoffa, and the United Auto Workers' Walter and Victor Reuther. The new leisure class ("well tailored; ate in the best restaurants; hired suites in the best hotels; drove the most expensive cars"), they were the new power elite. "Unions are for Big Business," Dos Passos quotes Beck. "Why should truckdrivers and bottlewashers be allowed to make big decisions affecting union policy? Would any corporations allow it?" The American labor movement had ceased to represent labor.

Dos Passos was also convinced that those who controlled big business no longer represented capitalism—a point often missed by liberal reviewers who regretted the forbidden subject of boss unionism. Free entrepreneurial capitalism suffers a double death in *Midcentury.* Capitalism had been killed, Dos Passos makes clear in his biography of the railroad builder Robert Young, by the "strangling hand" of government; but it had also carried within itself tendencies toward self-destruction that lie in man's insatiable urge for power and profit. The second theme emerges in the life of Jaspar Milliron, a fictional character whose story had been reconstructed from Dos Passos's own investigation of the General Mills Corporation.[18] Milliron is the technician-hero who desires to make flour production more efficient by introducing the "Swiss process." But, significantly, he soon sees that the art of milling had been destroyed by overcentralization, that relations between management and labor had become coldly depersonalized, and that contemporary business life offered meager satisfaction to those who wanted to engage in honest production. In the character of Milliron, Dos Passos reintroduces the Veblenian distinction between the industrial innovator and the financial manipulator. Milliron's daring experimental milling plan is turned down by remote figures who control the economic levers of power, the "saboteurs" of maximum production who would rather "retrench" and write off losses in tax deductions. Contemporary capitalism could never be enlightened and humane, Dos Passos implies in the repugnant figure of Judge Lewin, for the ultimate decisions of business were still made by those far removed from the real productive activities of life. "When I assume control of a corporation through the use of my skills," Lewin boasts, "I have to consider it a problem of pure finance. I can't be distracted by worrying about administration, who gets fired from what job, all the grubby little lives involved." Capitalism still sacrifices humanity for profitability; the producing classes remain victims of "pure finance."

Beyond the failure of labor and business is the larger failure of modern culture itself. Dos Passos saw the fifties as a low, vulgar decade. Ironically, the only relief came during the Korean war, which dramatized the heroism of General Douglas MacArthur and General William Dean. But it was James Dean, the young movie idol, who symbolized the culture of the future. The young Dean had been brought up in Indiana, where the "Hoosier farm boys have no cows to milk . . . no wood to chop . . . no chores. . . . Freedom what good is it? Let's have social security and welfare and tailfins on our cars." Everywhere Dos Passos saw the corruption of society by the false promises of wealth, advertisement, and consumption ("Kicks . . . buy speed, buy horsepower, buy happiness"). And everywhere he saw the delusions of modern man created by the false premises of psychology ("You never understood me. And now here I lie tracing resentment back to the womb / on the analyst's couch"). Nowhere did he find the work ethic that had once been the conscience of the nation; and nowhere in the new society could he see the will to greatness and nobility. On the contrary, American culture had become crass, indulgent, neurotic, and sick with self-deception ("BEAUTY LIFT WILL BUOY WEARY EGO"). Jefferson's "pursuit of happiness" had degenerated like Gatsby's dream.

Dos Passos's portrait of America at midcentury resembled the same "one-dimensional" pessimism that Herbert Marcuse would express a few years later. In the writings of both the conservative novelist and radical philosopher we find a society without historical rationality, a society of control and manipulation wherein human relations are organized in bureaucratic terms, a society in which man lost his freedom without knowing it because he cannot recognize his servitude to a culture of endless consumption. Dos Passos attributed this false state of "happy consciousness" to the very ideas that Marcuse assumed would liberate modern culture from oppression—Freudianism and Marxism. Marcuse believed that Marxism, despite its failure as prophecy, was still a viable ideology that would enable man to overcome capitalism, since the irrationality of competitive life derives from the repression of man's natural instincts, a Freudian cultural necessity now rendered obsolete by the disappearance of economic scarcity. Dos Passos, on the other hand, believed with Veblen that economic abundance, instead of liberating man, brought out his worst "barbaric" instincts as man forsook a life of creative production for an even more aggressive life of conspicuous consumption. Marxism and Freudianism offered no escape from this dilemma, for they both lifted the moral burden from the shoulders of mankind, one by deifying history, the other by psychologizing man.

By crying up inhibition as the ultimate ill Freud disposed of thou shalt not. God
is a father image to be talked out of the system. The Marxists at least
made transcendent their anti-God principle;
for Paraclete read Dialectic; Man worships History,
Thesis, Antithesis, Synthesis
form another new Trinity; by scrupulous adherence to the Party line a man may be assured of salvation
by dialectical materialism;
these are the brainwashers, the twin myths of Marx and Freud, opposed yet interlocking, as victory interlocks with defeat, which

soared out of the scientific ruminations of the late nineteenth century
to hover like scavenger birds
over the disintegration of the Western will.

The indictment of Marxism and Freudianism was part of a
larger attack on science itself. The threat of modern science to Dos
Passos's humanism was threefold: its tendency to reduce the variety of social life to uniform laws of prediction; its urge to control
and dominate nature; and its drive to offer technological solutions
to moral problems. *Midcentury* is sprinkled with satirical comments on the vanity of behavioral engineering, systems analysis,
digital electronics, computers, chemotherapy, and other features of
biopsychological control. The machine is taking over, Dos Passos
laments; everyone is surrendering his will to the false gods of
technology and psychology. Self-reliance has given way to mathematical infallibility, even though in the final reckoning "numbers
fail." The individual has sold out his independence to the pro-
grammed security of science. Even the engineer, the old hero of
Veblen and Dos Passos, has been sucked into the system and
allows himself to be advertised more as a product than a producer
("Send your key technical people / TOP MEN FOR SALE").
Modern science, the supreme achievement of Western thought,
the cultural force that would liberate man by teaching him to
question and doubt all existing institutions, has succeeded only in
pacifying man by its wonder-working technology. Thus alongside
the bureaucratization of government, labor, and capitalism, science
has become another threatening source of power, far more dangerous because its authority is beyond the reach of the common man,
far more insidious because its miracles have turned a servant into a
savior. The advent of the space age ultimately demonstrates what
Dos Passos feared most: At the altar of science man worships
power itself. Dos Passos is not only alienated from the drift of
modern society, he is homeless in a new scientific universe that has
rendered man puny and irrelevant. The social pessimism of *U.S.A.*
takes on cosmic dimensions in *Midcentury*. Always a stranger in

the land, Dos Passos finds himself more alone than ever under the stars:

> The man walks alone.
> Thoughts swarm; braincells, as multitudinous as the
> wan starpoints that merge into the Milky Way overhead,
> trigger notions; tonight,
> in the century's decline,
> new fantasies prevail. Photoelectric calculators
> giddy the mind with numbers mechanically multiplying
> immensities by billions of lightyears.

Midcentury was Dos Passos's next-to-last novel,* a chronicle of the nation's decline, a mournful recording of the slow disintegration of those premises of value that hold society together. To rediscover what had been lost the novelist had to recapture the mind and spirit of an earlier age. Henceforth America's hope for the future would lie in the past.

Historian of the Enlightenment

Dos Passos's respect for history as the fount of lost wisdom had been implicit in many of his writings, from the wistful essays he wrote at Harvard in 1916 to the historical documentary portraits and memory-clouded flashbacks of *U.S.A.* In the fifties, when he began to associate with the *National Review*, his search for a usable past became almost his sole intellectual passion. But the quest for historical understanding, the attempt to move beyond the presentistic negations of *U.S.A.*, began to occupy his thoughts in the thirties when he broke with the Marxist *New Masses* and began to identify more and more with the liberal *Common Sense*. His awareness of the political importance of historical knowledge also took on a sense of urgency in 1933, with Hitler's advent to power. At a time when eminent academic historians like Charles Beard and Carl Becker almost despaired of the possibility of rescu-

---

* *Century's Ebb*, a novel which Dos Passos left at his death, was to be published in late 1975 by Gambit.

ing historical study from the pitfalls of relativism and value judgment, Dos Passos was certain that historical truth could be recaptured by a simple act of will. As America's confidence in itself seemed to decline, the novelist's confidence in American history grew from a political impulse to a moral imperative:

[1933] Americans who don't want to live in a society of slaves can no longer look to Europe for moral countenance. . . . We can rely on ourselves and our past and our future. Repudiation of Europe is, after all, America's main excuse for being.[19]

[1935] A people without a memory is a people without history, past or future, a group idiot. . . . Perhaps it is worth bringing out of the attic of the nation's past a certain amount of dusty equipment long forgotten there, antique conceptions of liberty, man's dignity, courage, self-respect.[20]

[1937] An American in 1937 comes back from Europe with a feeling of happiness, the relief of coming up out into the sunlight from a stifling cellar, that some of his grandfathers must have felt coming home from Metternich's Europe after the Napoleonic wars, the feeling all the immigrants have had when they saw the long low coast and the broad bays of the new world.[21]

[1939] I think there is enough real democracy in the very mixed American tradition to enable us, with courage and luck, to weather the social transformations that are now going on without losing our liberties or the human outlook that is the medium in which civilizations grow.[22]

[1941] In times of change and danger when there is a quicksand of fear under men's reasoning, a sense of continuity with generations gone before can stretch like a lifeline across the scary present and get us past that idiot delusion of the exceptional Now that blocks good thinking.[23]

The first curiosity about Dos Passos as a historian of the American past is that he does not begin at the beginning. In contrast to Perry Miller, another wanderer who came to the realization—while unloading cargo ships in Africa—that any search for self-identity as an American must begin with the New England Puritans, Dos Passos skips over the infinitely rich intellectual and social content of the seventeenth-century Calvinists, perhaps the last real "conservatives" who called upon imperfect man to perfect society. (Dos Passos does discuss Roger Williams, but his allegorical treatment serves merely as a prelude to the Enlightenment and the development of American liberty—an erroneous prelude, as we shall see.) It is also curious that as a novelist Dos Passos showed scant interest in America's literary heritage. His re-embracement of the American past was characteristic of a number of deradicalized intellectuals of the thirties who came to believe they could no longer look to Europe for political direction or cultural salvation. But Dos Passos felt no need, as did Van Wyck Brooks, Waldo Frank, and Alfred Kazin, to restore American literature to its former glories as an awakening impulse and an enduring inspiration. He believed that what must be rescued from oblivion and passed on to future generations was the sober political tone and tough moral fiber of the American Enlightenment. To this end the novelist became a romantic historian of a heroic epic, an artist who sought to recapture the "organic extension" of the Enlightenment through the historical imagination.[24]

Literary scholars have stressed the tenacious consistency and integrity that runs through Dos Passos's ideological career, Right as well as Left. An examination of his historical writings, however, reveals several significant changes of attitudes and values. One change occurs in his perception of reality. The stylistic devices of U.S.A., which he dropped in subsequent novels and then took up again in Midcentury (1960), are completely missing from his historical works. Their absence signifies the absence of that perspective of chaos which gave U.S.A. such unfocused power and passion. The historical reality that Dos Passos discovered in the eighteenth century—or willed into vision—appeared pregnant with meaning and value, an orderly, intelligible society capable of being reconstructed through the traditional storytelling function of the narrative historian. The scope of historical reality also contracted as Dos Passos abandoned the multi-class montage of

U.S.A. and focused solely on the political culture of a ruling elite. No longer were his heroes the beautiful losers, the eighteenth-century counterparts to the Wobblies: the Shaysites, the Regulators, perhaps even the Quakers and Indians. He now became fascinated by the stately activities of men of property, status, and power. And writing history from the "top down," as it were, he found a remarkable climate of opinion completely free of the milieu of conflict that reverberated through *U.S.A.* The portrait of late eighteenth-century America is characterized by consensus, continuity, harmony. Reading Dos Passos's narratives, one is hardly aware the Founding Fathers were profoundly troubled by the problems of change, instability, factions, class aggrandizement (though not class conflict), ambition, "passion," power without virtue, democracy without deference, and what Madison spoke of as the eternal and universal "propensity of mankind to fall into mutual animosities."[25] Madison advised Americans that government was necessary because men were not angels, and he and the *Federalist* writers proceeded to build a government, not of men, but of mechanisms that would check vice with vice. Dos Passos, however, does not allow his vision of reality to partake of the sordid. He elevates it above politics and perhaps above recognition.

As a historian Dos Passos's vision of character changed along with his vision of reality. Perhaps it would be more accurate to say that he discovered the possibility of moral character in the past while continuing to despair of the present. In his novels, which all dealt with the twentieth century, humanity generally "came off badly," Edmund Wilson observed of *Manhattan Transfer*.[26] Dos Passos's attitude continued to puzzle Wilson. "I've never understood why you give so grim a picture of life," Wilson wrote to him in 1939. "You yourself seem to enjoy life more than most people and are by way of being a brilliant talker; but you tend to make your characters talk clichés, and they always get a bad egg for breakfast."[27] Dos Passos's characters could seldom rise above the banal because his moral purposes could never overcome his naturalistic vision sufficiently enough to create characters who enable us to believe in man. In his novels we see uninspired and uninspiring people, but we cannot conceive of their opposites. Even his later heroes, Terry Bryant and Jaspar Milliron of *Midcentury*, go down to defeat with little suggestion of the importance and greatness of man. At their worst, Dos Passos's characters repel us; at their best, they choke on their own clichés.

In colonial American history, however, Dos Passos could find the nobility and excellence lacking in contemporary man. He could even find those exceptional qualities of character and will in Alexander Hamilton and John Marshall, two statesmen whose respective financial and judicial policies went far toward creating the corporate economy and centralized government so inimical to his social philosophy. Hamilton possessed "a simple honesty" and Marshall "the weight of character" (John Adams's description). Although vain and ambitious, neither man succumbed to the corruptions of power. The Treasury Secretary displayed deep resources of restraint when he changed his mind about the innocent Hugh Henry Breckinridge during the Whiskey Rebellion, and the Chief Justice rose above politics when he handled the Aaron Burr affair with scrupulous fairness.[28]

Implicit in Dos Passos's new-found respect for the potential of character is a new attitude toward history. With Carlyle, Dos Passos now believed that history is the study of great men, and with Emerson he felt that historical heroes represent the splendor and nobility of their age. This attitude indicates an obvious shift from the naturalistic pessimism that pervaded *U.S.A.* and rendered characters into creatures, yet when we examine Dos Passos's history the old riddle arises: Were these great men imitators or makers? How much was inherited and how much was actually creative in their thought? Can they be both great and representative? And, in ethical terms, was their behavior governed by the instincts of habit or by the imperatives of conscience? The answer is probably both, but Dos Passos never enters into the minds of his heroes sufficiently to allow us to see the nature of their character and moral strength. In 1939, in a polite quarrel with Edmund

Wilson, Dos Passos told his close friend and critic that in his novels he was attempting to "generate the insides . . . of characters by external description."[29] Much of this naturalistic method remains in Dos Passos's historical writing. Here, too, he refrains from analyzing emotions and thoughts. Instead he presents his great figures from the outside; we know them as they are behaving and responding, acting and being acted upon. Thus we know Jefferson as the doer rather than the thinker, not Jefferson the moral philosopher and political theorist, but Jefferson the farmer, surveyor, inventor, architect, and craftsman. Although Dos Passos wants us to believe in the moral excellence of the Founding Fathers, he tries to convey their character through their deeds rather than their thoughts, as though moral man is what he does and not necessarily what he thinks.

Focusing on the mundane activities of the Founding Fathers, Dos Passos's historical universe is the world of Daniel J. Boorstin rather than the world of Perry Miller, the world of historicism rather than idealism. The late novelist would probably have gagged on the label "historicist," but the term applies to Dos Passos in two respects. First, as a literary artist he romanticizes a classical period, the American Enlightenment, through the historical imagination. Second, as a political moralist he assumes that the nation had been conceived once and for all during the age of the Founding Fathers, and that their thoughts and deeds defined the possibility of America's future development.

Dos Passos's historicist conviction that the past is as binding as it is liberating, that it is our only "ground to stand on," raises a question that has troubled many contemporary historians: What is the source of American democracy? Did democracy rise from the natural environment or from the political mind? The question poses a serious dilemma for those who would claim the superiority of America's historical experience. Those who prefer the environmental interpretation must deny the creative power of the political intellect, while those who choose the intellect must acknowledge the influence of European ideas, thereby compromising America's claim to "uniqueness." Dos Passos struggles with this problem in his discussion of Daniel Defoe and Ben Franklin. Comparing their respective careers, he concludes that Franklin went further because America's social structure was freer, so open and inviting that Franklin "could go forward with a backwoodsman's beaver cap on his wise noodle instead of the wig that etiquette required." One may question whether Franklin was able to advance his station without conforming to his beliefs. But at the basis of Dos Passos's attitude is the conviction that character is somehow related to landscape and that political liberty is a product of social mobility, simply "a question of elbow room."[30] In this prosaic explanation—which scarcely accounts for why there were not more Franklins—freedom is achieved not because it is desirable but because it was possible. "It is not a question of what we want; it is a question of what is."[31] As with other historicists, Dos Passos confuses the possibility of an idea with its validity, thereby identifying the actual with the ideal.

Dos Passos could pass over this distinction because of his romantic attitude toward the American past. For the novelist-historian, democracy had always been, even in *U.S.A.*, an ideal that is not so much realized as recaptured, an invocation made in the "clean words our fathers spoke." In this allegorical exercise history becomes an act of the imagination, a feat that one could readily grant Dos Passos only if it did not get him into so many ideological difficulties. He would have us believe, for example, that Roger Williams was the torchbearer of the idea of toleration, the Milton of American democracy, when in reality the great dissenter's ideas about authority and equality are perhaps closer to Lenin's than to Jefferson's.[32] Similarly, if Williams may be too conservative to be used as a symbol of Dos Passos's libertarian ideals, Tom Paine may be too radical. Dos Passos hails Paine as the eighteenth-century spokesman for world emancipation, but he also hints that the great American revolutionist came to discover in the Jacobin terror of Robespierre what Dos Passos's generation discovered in the Soviet "republic" of Stalin. "Republic!" Paine shouts to a friend in France:

do you call this a Republic? Why they are worse off than the slaves of Constantinople; for there they expect to be beshaws in heaven by submitting to the slaves below, but here they believe neither in heaven nor hell, and yet are slaves by choice. I know of no Republic in the world except America, which is the only country for such men as you and I.[33]

Still responding to his own break with Europe in the thirties, Dos Passos wanted to dissociate America's political heroes from Europe's revolutionary tradition. The result is less an analysis than a metamorphosis. He contrasts Williams's planting a commonwealth of liberty in America with the failure of the English commonwealth and Cromwell's march on the Rump Parliament (which he likens to the Bolshevik dissolution of the Constituent Assembly), and he treats Paine as a jaded radical who repudiated revolution and re-embraced America, a typical ex–fellow traveler who lost his faith and thereby saved his reason. One would never guess that Dos Passos was talking about the Paine who dismissed government as "the badge of lost innocence," who remained a sort of pre-Trotskyist advocate of universal "permanent revolution," who had a mind so given to abstractions that political experience could not enter it ("the Peter Pan of the Age of Reason," Cecilia Kenyon aptly called him), and who offered a model of "conscience politics" that would later be rediscovered by Dos Passos's own ideological foes—the New Left. Searching for a "usable past" in the forties and fifties, Dos Passos became a literary hero of William F. Buckley, Jr., and the new American Right. He became a conservative historian without a conservative concept of history.[34]

Dos Passos's didactic history is full of ideological difficulties, and nowhere is this more obvious than in his studies of Thomas Jefferson. The novelist's dilemma confronts every conservative writer who seeks to ground his creed in Jefferson's natural rights philosophy. How can we inspire respect for the past by holding up a philosopher who himself believed that no generation could bind another, that each new-born race of men enjoyed the "sovereignty of the present," and that the "earth belongs to the living"? Every American interprets Jefferson differently, but for a conservative to comprehend his genius he must grasp the contrary tensions within a single intellect, an effort that perhaps requires what Kenneth Burke called the method of "perspective by incongruity." Dos Passos always distrusted "double-minded" temperaments. F. Scott Fitzgerald, Dos Passos lamented at the time of his friend's death, was a "split personality" who lacked the total integration of the "whole heart and whole intelligence" essential to an "unshakeable moral attitude towards the world." Dos Passos could never accept Fitzgerald's definition of a "first-rate intelligence" as "the ability to hold two opposed ideas in the mind, at the same time, and still retain the ability to function."[35]

As a result Dos Passos could never fully appreciate the tensions and ambiguities that characterized Jefferson, a statesman who could be at once a democrat and an aristocrat, a nationalist and a cosmopolite, a speculative philosopher and a practical politician, a Lockian who denied innate ideas and a humanist who believed in "self-evident" truths, a theorist of limited government and a practitioner of national sovereignty, a champion of the Bill of Rights and a violator of civil liberties, an advocate of freedom and an apologist for slavery. Indeed, one has no sense from Dos Passos that Jefferson experienced some guilt and self-doubt as he tried to reconcile black servitude with his philosophy of nature and natural rights.[36] Had he explored this problem from within the interior of Jefferson's rich mind, he would have discovered an intellect that could hold contradictory thoughts on slavery and freedom and still maintain the ability to function rationally.[37] This subject, the phenomenological-inner and political-outer world of Jefferson, contained the potential for fusing literature, psychology, and history into a brilliant portrait in paradox. (One wonders what Styron or Faulkner might have done with it.) But the subject also suggests a "doubleness" of consciousness that was repugnant to Dos

Passos's moral sense and, in his view, inconsistent with Jefferson's character and with the culture of the Enlightenment itself.

Dos Passos's handling of the Sally Hemings affair—Jefferson's liaison with a house slave—reveals his reluctance to probe the complexities of Jefferson's mind and character. In view of Dos Passos's own illegitimate birth and his lifelong search for self-identity,[38] this affair may have had some personal meaning. He seemed to be concerned with it while working on *The Heart and Head of Thomas Jefferson*. "Is there something rather interesting that has been kept out of sight about Jefferson's relations with Negroes?" Edmund Wilson asked him in 1950. "Did he have close and unprincipled relations with those that were made of brown extract for the lack of close relations with white people? I learn from the same source—and for the first time—that he had several mulatto children."[39] Dos Passos chose not to discuss the matter in the Jefferson book, published in 1954. In the mid-sixties, when a different moral awareness of American race relations emerged, he took up the Hemings affair and admitted that the "story had a kernel of truth." Yet instead of exploring the matter in depth in order to understand a political culture aspiring to egalitarianism and restrained by racism, Dos Passos resolved it with a twist of logic that was as uncanny as it was unenlightening. After quoting from a Henry Randall letter that had recently turned up in the James Parton papers at Harvard, he added his own wry judgment:

"Walking about mouldering Monticello one day with Col. T. J. Randolph (Mr. Jefferson's eldest grandson)," Randall wrote, "he showed me a smoke-blackened and sooty room on one of the colonnades and informed me it was Sally Hemings' room. He asked me if I knew how the story of Mr. Jefferson's connexion with her originated. I told him I did not. 'There was a better excuse for it,' said he, 'than you might think; she had children that resembled Mr. Jefferson so closely that it was plain that they had his blood in their veins.' "
Indeed they did, and blood even more precious to Jefferson than his own.[40]

The tendency to turn an embarrassment into a eulogy suggests the extent to which the essential strain of skepticism is missing from Dos Passos's history. The "storybook democracy" ethos of his history also suggests why he faced several difficulties in trying to transmit the meaning of Jeffersonianism to the twentieth century. First of all, his naturalistic historicism left him without a method of analyzing ideas as autonomous moral principles, ideas that would have to transcend the eighteenth-century environment in order to convey binding ethical significance for the modern world. Even when Dos Passos discusses ideas there is no evidence of his having reflected upon their significance. Indeed, the profound political and moral problems the Framers wrestled with are turned into platitudes simply through the reification of words like "freedom," "self-government," and "happiness," concepts that the authors of the Constitution themselves found difficult to reconcile.[41] Convinced that the Founding Fathers knew what they meant and meant what they said, Dos Passos was certain that the meaning of their ideas could be comprehended not by interpreting but simply by invoking them, as though the Declaration of Independence, and not Madison's The Federalist or John Adams's Discourse on Davila, provided the last word in American political theory.

Dos Passos was also in the awkward position of assuming that the past was both exceptional and exemplary, unique as well as analogous. He was attracted to colonial America because it offered a milieu politically and morally superior to contemporary industrial America. At the same time he was forced to argue that we could learn from colonial Americans, who "in spite of the changing conditions of life . . . were not very different from ourselves . . . [and] managed to meet situations as difficult as those we have to face."[42] What, then, can be learned? In 1934 Dos Passos declared that "at this particular moment in history, when machines and institutions have so outgrown the ability of mind to dominate them, we need bold and original thought more than ever."[43] Dos Passos assumed he found this "thought" in colonial history, but he was hard pressed to demonstrate that the fundamental structure of the past was so economically and culturally the same as the present that we can learn anything at all from the Founding Fathers—least of all learn how man could "dominate" machines and institutions from those who deliberately built institutions and the "machinery of government" to check democracy and control man.

Dos Passos looked forward to ruin, backward to hope. His attempt to recapture the moral and political milieu of the American Enlightenment was his way of asking us to appreciate a world that we have lost. His history is a poignant study in old moral principles long forgotten, good ways not taken. Yet Dos Passos's vision of eighteenth-century order was more willed than true, a triumph of imagination over inquiry. He was enamored of his own majestic vision of the Jeffersonian world but unclear about the forces that brought that world into being; he was even less clear about the factors that led to its decline. In *The Shackles of Power* Dos Passos marks 1831—five years after Jefferson's death—as the year of declension, the moment when commercial capitalism, mass society, and the Leviathan state began to emerge like a visitation from nowhere. But even though he drew upon the travel accounts of Tocqueville, he could not follow the Frenchman's analysis to its unsettling conclusion—that the rise of Jacksonian democracy threatened Jeffersonian liberty, that Jefferson's own Lockian "pursuit of happiness" turned every individual into a conformist and a materialist, and that Jeffersonian liberalism itself could lead to a life of mindless action and endless acquisition, "a joyless quest for joy."[44]

Dos Passos's studies of the American past ignore the right historians and celebrate the wrong heroes. In *U.S.A.* he drew upon Veblen (and to a certain extent Marx) for a radical critique of capitalist society, but in his historical works he refrained from using Tocqueville's equally brilliant conservative critique. It is also curious that Dos Passos failed to sustain a consistent standard of historical judgment that would morally bind the present to the past. In the novels *U.S.A.* and *Midcentury,* Dos Passos held up Moorehouse and Judge Lewin to execration because they trafficked in money and public relations, investing themselves in their own investments. But Robert Morris, the colonial financier who speculated profitably on the American Revolution, is cheerfully tolerated in *The Men Who Made the Nation* as "everybody's banker."[45] Even Veblen's villains, still despised in the fifties, are domesticated as Dos Passos moves back into the eighteenth century. A history without antagonists is a past too consensualized to comprehend. "Where there is no strain," R. G. Collingwood has written, "there is no history."[46]

Dos Passos was at a loss to explain how a majestic past developed into a miserable present. Without a sensibility to the demands of causal explanation, he retained in his historical works the same characteristics of chronicle writing that infused his early novels. In *U.S.A.* Dos Passos was appalled by the contingency of history; in *The Ground We Stand On* he is amazed by its rationality. The vision of chaos is gone; the meaning of events has yet to emerge from the vision of order. As a narrative historian, as a raconteur of episodes and anecdote, Dos Passos shows us this and he shows us that, but of the world that has been forsaken he does not show us "why." He asks us to move forward to yesterday, but he offers no hint how to get there. We are as lost as the characters in *Manhattan Transfer* or *U.S.A.* Even more so, for we have come further and know less.

Perhaps the real question is whether a historian has a right to demand more of Dos Passos. The answer is, I believe, no. Too honest a writer to claim more than he could see, Dos Passos was too humble a thinker to claim a privileged understanding of the movement and process of history. Through the dialectical "Logic" of perfect contradiction, Hegel and Marx may have explained how man becomes alienated from history, how the *homo faber,* the maker of history, loses his freedom to forces beyond himself. Throughout his life Dos Passos was also painfully aware of the estrangement of history from freedom, the tendency, that is, of power to "autonomize" itself, to cut itself off from its subjects and become an independent force over them.[47] Indeed fear of power is at the heart of Dos Passos's political sensibility, just as fascination with power is at the basis of Burnham's political philosophy. But Dos Passos refrained from allowing his desires to coincide with the presumed course of history. In this deliberate restraint, Dos Passos resembled Tolstoy, who likewise would not control force by becoming its agent on the assumption that man can master his destiny by identifying with history. "There is nothing stronger in us," Nicola Chiaromonte has written of War and Peace, "nothing we know with more certainty than this force about which we know nothing."[48] These words capture perfectly Dos Passos's skeptical stance in U.S.A., where he chooses with Veblen to "peel the onion of doubt" in the face of alienated force and energy. And when he rediscovers the American Enlightenment, he also follows Veblen back to a pre-industrial world of harmony and dignity, where power had presumably been humanized by character, disciplined by a healthy balance of self-determination and self-control. Dos Passos's historical works offer, then, not a teleology of deliverance but a moral vision of redemption by restrospection. His odyssey had to end with the Founding Fathers, lest his quest for freedom became a quest for power by identifying history with prophecy. The task of the historian is not so much to change history (that is being done independently) but to ponder it, even celebrate it ("I too Walt Whitman"). The American Enlightenment must catch up with American energy.

As a political moralist Dos Passos is to our modern age of unbridled power and energy as relevant as Henry Adams. But what of Dos Passos the historical artist? His historical works have suffered a sad fate in America. Among professional historians only the late Allan Nevins seemed to have taken a keen interest in the novelist's research and writing. Other historians and literary critics have dismissed his narratives as a mountain of pious Americana. Is this judgment fair? Perhaps. I prefer to paraphrase G. P. Gooch's estimate of the great French historian Jules Michelet, another maudlin romantic who has been accused of national self-conceit: No historian has loved America so tenderly. To him that loved, much may be forgiven.[49]

CHAPTER **7**

From Marxism to Existentialism: Herberg

Woe to the man so possessed that he thinks he possesses God!
MARTIN BUBER, 1923

Berdyaev and Personalism: Herberg's Halfway Covenant

On the road to conservatism Dos Passos rediscovered Jefferson and the American Enlightenment; and Eastman came upon, by way of Hayek and Röpke, Adam Smith and the world of classical economics. Will Herberg ultimately discovered something both more conservative and more radical, less maudlin and less musty. He found, by way of Martin Buber, God.

Whether the discovery resulted from an unconscious "return" to Judaism or from an immediate existential "first encounter," Herberg was never quite sure. But during the early war years he visited what might be called his political Gethsemane. While Eastman was warning Americans about Stalin, and Dos Passos was singing praises to America's democratic spirit, Herberg was quietly experiencing a post-Marxist spiritual crisis. Confronted with the phenomenon of totalitarianism, he could not follow Dos Passos and Eastman back to the eighteenth-century world of rationalism and capitalism. Indeed there was no turning back, for the terrors of the twentieth century arose largely from the assumptions and illusions of the Enlightenment itself. Herberg soon realized that the logic of radical historicism must be reversed: the task of the philosopher was not to change the world but first of all to ponder it and understand it, perhaps even to mourn for it. Through the

269

tears of remembrance man may come to see that the innermost meaning of historical experience lies outside of history itself: "The events of the past thirty years have shown that it is sheer folly to look to history, in whatever form, for the solution of our problems. History cannot solve our problems; history is *itself* the problem."[1]

Few American writers repudiated Marxism with the intense introspection that characterized Herberg's thought in the forties. Hook tried to salvage the empirical elements of historical materialism, Dos Passos wrote superficially of "The Failure of Marxism," and Eastman dismissed socialism as a "utopian" dream ride into neverland. To Herberg such critiques were typically American, hence too provincial to penetrate to the heart of the problem. He wanted to elevate the issue from the pragmatic to the theoretical level, from science to philosophy. For the truth or falseness of Marxism was not simply a matter of its success or failure. The nonrealization of the socialist ideal does not necessarily impair the validity of that ideal, nor does its realization necessarily affirm it. Indeed, socialism may even be regarded as increasingly attainable, since, given the vast power of modern technology, its goals are increasingly accessible. Eastman, Dos Passos, and other American writers repudiated the dictatorial methods used to reach the socialist goals of freedom and equality, and thus their differences with communists remained mainly differences in tactics and programs. Herberg, on the other hand, began to wonder whether the goals themselves must be ultimately questioned, whether the ends as well as the means were desirable, whether man's struggle for total freedom and equality through political struggle led to man's subjection to total tyranny and hierarchy. The problem with utopia was not how to realize it but how to prevent its realization, how to resist those alienating, despiritualizing tendencies in modern society that made revolutionary socialism seem so morally desirable and thus politically inevitable. In this exercise America needed Dostoevski, not Dewey.

"Marxism was to me, and to others like me, a religion, an ethic, and a theology: a vast, all embracing doctrine of man and the

universe, a passionate faith endowing life with meaning, vindicat-
ing the aims of the movement, idealizing its activities, and guaranteeing its ultimate triumph."[2] Thus spoke Herberg shortly after
the war. But the spell had been broken years earlier, and the more
Herberg pondered the intellectual maladies of the age the more he
sensed that Marxism had absorbed the illusions of the Enlightenment: the rationality and moral improvement (if not perfectibility) of man, the worship of science and technology, and the belief
in history as the story of the progressive realization of man's freedom. He also sensed, and perhaps more acutely, that Marxian
socialism had likewise absorbed many elements of religious mil-
lenarianism, an argument he spelled out in "The Christian
Mythology of Socialism," published in the *Antioch Review* in
1943.

Earlier in the century several European scholars had seen parallels between socialism and religion in their respective doctrinal
convictions, organizational schisms and heresies, hagiographies and
cults, and other features suggesting a common psychological function hidden in each belief system. But Herberg, with his instinct
for asking ultimate questions, also perceived a similar "scheme of
human destiny." In both religion and socialism the drama of
human regeneration takes place in three acts: first, a primal state
of harmony, justice and happiness, the Edenic paradise of Christian myth and the "primitive communism" of Marxist doctrine;
second, the fallen state, in which man now finds himself estranged
and society divided, the condition of moral struggle in Christianity
and class struggle in Marxism; and third, the state of paradise
regained in which man, redeemed and transfigured, is both re-
stored to and elevated to his original primal innocence, and society, cleansed of all conflict, both returns to and advances to its
natural primal harmony.

At the heart of this great myth lies the riddle of the human
condition, both in the Christian context of "the spiritual alienation of man" and in the Marxist context of "his social self-aliena-
tion—the alienation of society." Christian theologians and socialist

theorists alike, observed Herberg, had difficulty accounting for "the Fall," and thus the whole drama of regeneration can only be explained through the doctrine of Christian paradox or through Hegel's dialectical logic of contradiction. Moreover, embedded in both organized Christianity and organized Marxism (i.e., Leninism) is a strong element of authoritarianism and elitism: both maintain that man overcomes his predicament only through work and struggle. Theologians claim that grace comes from above through the mediation of the Church; Leninists insist that revolutionary consciousness must be instilled from the outside through the mediation of the Party. Finally, Christianity and socialism both have cataclysmic and gradualistic elements. The Kingdom of Heaven may be ushered in by an apocalyptic catastrophe, or, as the modernists would have it, through a slow advance of mankind toward moral and spiritual perfection; similarly, socialism may be realized by a sudden proletarian revolution or, as the revisionists would have it, through a gradual accretion of social reforms.

These comparisons, and many others Herberg reflected upon, led to two conclusions: Christianity, both in its Hebraic and Greek aspects, had penetrated so deeply into the Western mind that it operates at the unconscious level and even those hostile to it cannot escape its influence; and mythological thinking arises out of any necessities that require the fervor of faith, the vital dynamism of great social movements as well as great religions.[3]

Did the discovery of a mythic strain in Marxism invalidate socialism? Not entirely. Herberg believed with Ignazio Silone that Christian Marxism could be "the seed of a new spirituality in which all that is best in socialist idealism will be absorbed and transfigured."[4] In this vision Kant would replace Lenin, for it was imperative to restore the Christian ethical tension between means and ends so that collectivism, elevated by communists to a "metaphysical" end in itself, will be recognized as the greatest danger facing the socialist world. Such recognition did not mean, as Eastman had concluded, that collectivism and democracy are incompatible. Herberg believed that some form of centralized economic control was the inevitable consequence of industrial development. How, then, would democratic collectivism be possible? Where was the answer to Eastman's quivering sense of freedom, Burnham's stark managerial predictions, and Dos Passos's scary bureaucratic visions? Herberg thought he had found the answer in a little book published in 1944, Nicholas Berdyaev's *Slavery and Freedom*.

Against society, the state, the nation, and every institution and ideology that made the whole greater than the part, Berdyaev's philosophy opposed all that degrades man, all that turns him from a person into a thing, a subject into an object; all those forces and ideas that represent not the moral nature of man but the "objectivization" of his spirit. Collectivist socialism is based on the supremacy of society and the state over the individual. But Berdyaev's idea of socialism, Herberg explained, affirms the absolute supremacy of the human person. Thus while man's economic activities may be socialized, his spiritual life cannot, for the latter realm represents both man's conscience and his consciousness, the sole creative force of his inner freedom. From Berdyaev Herberg developed his theory of socialist "personalism," the transcendent spiritual autonomy of the individual; and from Lewis Corey's *The Unfinished Task* he drew his theory of liberal "pluralism," the dispersion of political power among countervailing institutions. Herberg believed that both personalism and pluralism could be reconciled with liberalism and Marxism, since these two great secular ideologies had absorbed, even if unconsciously, the ethical philosophy of Judaism and Christianity. Indeed the religious reverence for personality is the moral essence of liberal individualism, German idealism, and Marxist socialism. It can be found in "Locke's denial that we are 'made for one another's uses as the inferior creatures are made for us'; Kant's precept of every human being as an end in himself; Marx's protest against the *Verdinglichung* [thingification] of men in bourgeois society."[5]

Herberg's essay on Berdyaev, "Personalism against Totalitarianism," was published as the first in a series of statements in a symposium that Dwight Macdonald ran in 1946 in his lively monthly, *Politics*. Conceived at a time when the bomb, the concentration camps, and the barbarities of Hitler and Stalin had shattered man's faith in himself, the symposium was an attempt to keep alive the spark of radical thought even though the flame of Marxism had burned itself out. In the continuing discussion on the "New Roads in Politics," Macdonald shared Herberg's reservations about Marxism. The idea of progress, Marxist or liberal, tends to justify the means by the end, the present by the future, wrote Macdonald in his seminal essay, "The Root Is Man." Moreover, in assuming that ethical values emanate from the historical process, Marxism precluded the possibility of an absolute moral standpoint. With Herberg, Macdonald concluded that value judgments are real and vital and belong to a realm of knowledge outside the reach of Dewey's scientific method and Marx's historical materialism.[6]

Although Macdonald and Herberg could assert the inviolability of man as the creator of value, Berdyaev's philosophy of personalism failed to satisfy all the questions troubling Herberg. As an anarchist, Macdonald saw no danger in making the individual the sole source of power and freedom, but Herberg began to sense that freedom itself cannot insure democracy. The development of the free, autonomous life does not necessarily implicate man in the responsibilities of civic life. In the Eastern orthodoxy of Berdyaev's philosophy Herberg soon discerned an "ecstatic spirituality" that would destroy the very basis of value by turning every self into a sovereign. Above all, Berdyaev's theology contained an eschatological theory of history envisioning a future state in which the rule of law gives way to the rule of love. To Herberg, Berdyaev's philosophy began more and more to resemble a variation of Russian messianism rather than a vision of Christian realism.[7]

Niebuhr and the Ironic Mode of History

In the writings of Reinhold Niebuhr Herberg found a less innocent and more heroic affirmation of post-Marxist philosophy. More than any other American thinker, Niebuhr related theology to politics by returning to the original problem of human nature, the doctrine of man's self-contradiction from which politics itself is born and takes divisive shape. From Niebuhr Herberg also gained an awareness of historical understanding from the perspective of neo-orthodoxy, a standpoint that denied the utopian illusions of Marx and the eschatological visions of Berdyaev. History could now be seen as paradoxical rather than progressive, ironical rather than logical (it could also be seen as dialectical, but without Hegel's redemptive telos).[8]

To Herberg, the Christian view of history illuminated many of the problems that bewildered Marxists and liberals. Studying the trade union movement, for example, he perceived what remained hidden from those who would explain the political by the economic: power had its own logic and bureaucracy had its roots deep in the very nature of organization. He also perceived what eluded Eastman, Dos Passos, and, to a certain extent, Burnham: justice and democracy, ideals that transcend history, become self-contradictory in the process of struggling toward their realization. Such knowledge was hardly academic to Herberg, who was now research and educational director of the New York Dress Makers Union of the ILGWU. He tried to bring theology to bear upon politics by explaining the ironies of labor history. Early unionism in America, he observed, had been a genuine workers' movement, an idealistic and reformist effort aiming toward the democratic self-liberation of the poor and exploited. To achieve these goals trade unions were forced to grow, expand, and develop into hierarchical structures in order to confront the might of industrial capitalism. Only through organizational strength could the workers achieve some measure of security and welfare, yet in realizing their economic well-being workers relinquished self-government to professional administrators, bargaining agents, and other "outside clerks." Through power, workers realized justice, and, through power, their freedom disappeared into the labyrinth of bureaucracy. This dual nature of power, moreover, may very well reflect the dual nature of man himself, whose idealism and self-interest are so completely fused that his egotism may serve as the instrument of justice while his benevolence may hide his drive for power. Thus institutions like labor unions, the creations of man, mirror the contradictions inherent in man. If organization is the disease of death, as Dos Passos cried, it is also the dynamic of political power and the logic of social life. The Niebuhrian sense of irony enabled Herberg to appreciate institutions as the source of freedom as well as tyranny, just as the human heart is the source of love as well as evil. It also enabled him to understand what escaped Dos Passos's rage against the New Deal: no historical movement, whether revolutionary or reformist, can avoid corruption. "The lust for power easily penetrates the most idealistic causes, for all causes, even the most idealistic, require power for their realization in history."[9]

Through Niebuhr's writings Herberg could also reintroduce the unmentionable concept of "sin." Eastman had criticized Marx for avoiding the question What is Man? But even Eastman was confident that man's irrational and aggressive behavior could be rationally explained without dredging up the stale idea of original sin. Herberg was convinced that one could no longer do without this concept when confronted with the ambivalent nature of man and the ambiguous nature of freedom. Like Niebuhr, Herberg saw man as tragically divided within himself. Man is neither wholly good nor wholly bad; he is both, and his character grows from the tension between the two forces at war within his soul. Thus through reason and moral will man may achieve dignity, but his egotism and self-centeredness render him incapable of escaping the stain of sin. Translated into politics, man's capacity to transcend selfishness and aspire to impartial justice makes social order possible, while man's basic egotism and aggressiveness make democratic pluralism necessary. This essentially Niebuhrian axiom Herberg projected back onto the Anglo-American concept of freedom in general and the political thought of the Founding Fathers in particular. The authors of the Constitution rejected both the Hobbesian view of man's utter depravity and the Rousseauistic view of man's natural goodness. One led to absolutism, the other to anarchism; one made morality inconceivable, the other rendered society unmanageable. The *Federalist* authors rightly founded government on the suspicion that neither the single leader nor the masses of men were good enough or wise enough to be entrusted with power, an attitude that derived from their "somber theological realism." Democracy, Herberg concluded,

is the institutionalization of permanent resistance to human sinfulness in politics, which, as we have seen, manifests itself primarily in the egotistical self-assertion of power. So thoroughly aware is democracy at its best of the inevitable moral dubiousness of all governments, that it embodies the principle of resistance to government in the very structure of government itself.[10]

Like Dos Passos, Herberg asked too much of the Founding Fathers. He returned to the eighteenth-century Enlightenment in order to find a political theology that perhaps could better be found in seventeenth-century New England Calvinism. Herberg's dilemma lay in his misreading intellectual history, in his attempt to identify personalism with pluralism while at the same time trying to validate both historically by invoking classical American liberalism. He was convinced that the "emphasis on the high dignity of man and his absolute worth as a person is the first principle of democracy; it is the principle of personalism."[11] The difficulty here is that the Founding Fathers built a government on the basis of pluralism precisely because they had so little faith in personalism. Herberg's concept of personalism made man the measure of politics, but Madisonian pluralism made institutions and the "machinery of government" the mediator of man. Herberg found in Berdyaev's philosophy the possibility of restoring individual conscience to political life, yet under the system of "checks and balances" devised by the *Federalist* writers there would be no role for the man of conscience in American politics. Ironically, in his attempt to go beyond Marxism Herberg actually returned to the epistemological premises of Marxist philosophy when he tried to combine Christian personalism with liberal pluralism. For both Marx and the *Federalist* authors were materialists; that is, they recognized no other reality than that which is measurable and corporeal, man's external actions and interests rather than his subjective beliefs and values. They were both convinced that there could be no appeal to purely ethical standards and disinterested ideals, since man's behavior will always be determined by personal interests. Denying the possibility of self-transcendence, Madison conceived a structure of government and Marx a philosophy of history in which there would be no need for moral man.

There is a note of Weberian tragedy in Herberg's dilemma. Passionately interested in ultimate ethical questions, he believed that politics and government must be elevated above interests and institutions so that man's inner life may be brought to bear upon his social life. His attempt to reconcile personalism and pluralism was, in short, nothing less than an attempt to reconcile religion and politics. Perhaps the tension between the two, between the normative "ought" and the empirical "is," can never be reconciled. Herberg was too steeped in pluralism to believe that politics could be ultimately purified, but he was too steeped in Judaism to relinquish what Weber called "the flame of pure intentions." Still the radical moralist in search of salvation, Herberg would never be comfortable with the full implications of conservative realism. "He who seeks the salvation of souls, his own as well as others," advised Weber, "should not seek it along the avenue of politics."[12]

"Either-Or"

In the late forties Herberg was invited to participate in a two-year conference conducted at Princeton University by the Program in American Civilization. Financed in part by the Rockefeller Foundation, the conference was devoted to the theme of "Socialism in American Life," the title used for the two-volume work that Princeton University Press later published. It was an ambitious conference that ranged over a broad number of subjects presented by socialist theoreticians, ex-Marxists, and academic scholars: Albert T. Mollegen and Stow Persons on the religious roots of socialism; E. Harris Harbinson and Harry W. Laidler on European socialism; David Bowers on the socialist theory of history; Paul Sweezy on Marxian economics; Wilbert E. Moore on the socio- logical aspects of socialism and George W. Hartman on its psycho- logical implications; Willard Thorp on American writers and Donald Drew Egbert on American art; Sidney Hook on the philo- sophical basis of American Marxism and Daniel Bell on the history of Marxian socialism in the United States; and Herberg on Ameri- can Marxist political theory. In his contribution Herberg stressed the flaws in the socialist attitudes toward power and the state, and he re-emphasized his commitment to a "neo-liberal socialism" grounded "theologically" in a libertarian respect for individual freedom and a personalistic reverence for man as the source of humanist values.[13]

Irving Howe, reviewing *Socialism in American Life* in 1952, called Herberg's essay "the major theoretical article" in the huge book, though he criticized Herberg for turning political moralist and peddling "maxims" as though democracy were a matter of moral preference rather than historical struggle, and he chided his conversion "from Lovestone to Jehova."* Yet in his thirty-eight- page review in the *New International*, Howe almost ignored other contributors as he returned again and again to Herberg's extraordi- nary essay. Clearly what troubled Howe was Herberg's theological reflections, a subject for which Trotskyists had little patience (and preparation) except the familiar annihilation by polemic. "This 'power drive,'" stated Howe in reference to Herberg's view of

* A few years earlier Howe had written, "The most pathetic evidence of the destruction of an entire revolutionary generation is the fate of the Lovestone group. This once proud Marxist tendency committed suicide *en masse* at the outbreak of the war, an act which has few precedents in the socialist movement. Of its three main figures, one, Lovestone, has become a 'think man' for a trade union bureaucracy; another, Wolfe, is now a Menshevik who defends Chiang Kai-shek's regime . . . and the third, Herberg, has been converted to orthodox Judaism. *Tempus fugit*, indeed!" Irving Howe, "Intellectuals' Flight from Politics," *New International*, XIII (Oct. 1947), 241.

human corruptibility, "is a category of political moralists, not of psychologists or anthropologists, who in fact have marshalled considerable evidence to show that in some societies (particularly among savages who have read neither Kierkegaard nor Niebuhr) it does not exist."[14]

Herberg's theological convictions also troubled Sidney Hook and Daniel Bell, two participants at the Princeton conference and two major figures in the American Committee for Cultural Freedom. The subject came up during a panel discussion on "The Ethics of Controversy," held at the New York Tamiment Institute under the auspices of the ACCF in 1952. Chaired by Hook, the panel featured Bell, Herberg, the journalist Henry Hazlitt, and the poet W. H. Auden. In his opening statement Herberg claimed that the struggle with communism was a "conflict of ultimates which no rational discourse can resolve." Although he realized that one cannot "simply translate the absolutes of religion into the relativities of politics," Herberg was convinced that a deep feeling for spiritual values better enabled one "to act resolutely and with conviction, yet without self-righteousness or fanaticism." Controversy with communists, on the other hand, was useless, since communists respect only power, not ideas, and least of all ethics. Thus "on the level of a basic religio-philosophical commitment, the choice is either-or." Hook and Bell could not understand Herberg's refusal to engage communists in debate, nor could they accept his argument that democracy rests on "religio-philosophical" truths about man's fallibility and that theology may be a possible bulwark against totalitarianism. They could not help but wonder whether Herberg's surprisingly militant anti-communism and his peculiar attitude toward McCarthy (discussed below) were somehow connected with his newly found spiritual passions. The following exchange captures some of the countercurrents within the ACCF.

Hook: . . . why can't I have a controversy . . . with a Communist or a Fascist? I am prepared to discuss with anybody when I come to the conclusion it is worth discussing. And I am not prepared to use his methods. I will argue with a Communist, and I will try to use the methods of logic. I will try to use evidence.

Herberg: You practically answer my question for me. If a person is ready to listen to you and agree in advance on certain intellectual and moral presuppositions that is—

Hook: He doesn't have to agree with me. All I want him to do is listen, give me a chance to talk, have his OK.

Herberg: You are so fond of talking, it is all right. Is there any point in that kind of controversy? A person may be ready to listen to your talk, because he wants time to take out his dagger and stab you in the back. That is not a far-fetched example. That is very applicable to Communists.

One of the reasons I mention that you cannot engage in controversy with Communists is because for Communists controversy, that is using words and talking about things, and so on, is not really a discussion of the content of what is talked about but merely an instrument of camouflage for a world-wide conspiracy of domination and enslavement.

Bell: We seem to be sort of bewitched by the poetic charm, the theological transcendence. I think the real problem is not so much should we not engage but there are people engaging us in controversy in a particular way, and what is happening is there is a breakdown in rational discourse in this country.

When a man comes along and says if there were no Communists in our government, why did we delay the H-bomb eighteen months, you are being engaged in controversy in a particular way. Somebody once said, if there are no Communists in government, why did we lose the Battle of Bull Run.

Herberg: That doesn't answer my question.

Bell: I am saying let's get away from some of these problems to something which is more tangible to the nature of controversy today. A certain kind of controversy is spreading in this country, a certain breakdown is creeping around, threatening a breakdown of discourse. It is to the practical interest of the people who talk about creeping socialism—

Hazlitt: It is not creeping.

Bell: I am trying to get this discussion off from creeping around. It seems to me the stake here is that willy-nilly we are being forced into certain kinds of controversy in terms of people who will only argue on either-or basis. It is very nice for you to say either-or is true theologically, but it is not true in terms of politics. Yet people today take an either-or. You are forced into these choices. That is what is happening today. That, it seems to me, is the problem of controversy.

Herberg: That is one problem. I think you are quite right. If you translate your fundamental absolutes into politics, you are going to get a destructive and suicidal politics, but it is very important to remember what is called—

Hook: What is the point? What are you trying to make? Why are we forced into a choice of either-or?[15]

The "either-or" proposition, the demand of the single alternative that had plagued writers in the thirties on the question of Joseph Stalin, had curiously returned to haunt them in the fifties on the question of Joseph McCarthy. McCarthyism raised again the issue of means and ends, and Bell and Hook could only wonder why those who had broken with the communists in the thirties because of their methods were now willing to tolerate McCarthy's methods. Herberg wanted to convert politics into moral confrontations, yet his definition of religion as an "either-or" total commitment seemed perilously close to the mentality of McCarthy's anticommunist crusade. Where, then, did Herberg stand on McCarthy?

Herberg answered this question sporadically in the course of his debates with Bell and Hook, but he developed his position later in articles in the *New Leader* and the *New Republic*. It is curious that he presented his views in these social democratic and liberal journals, for Herberg was one of the first American writers to interpret McCarthyism as a threat from the Left, as the demagogy of mass politics. The senator from Wisconsin was a classical "rabble-rouser," a crude, reckless master of the harangue and tirade, "a primitive plebeian, not a Pericles but a Cleon." He appealed directly to the people, flouted congressional channels and constitutional procedure, attacked wealth and the intellectual elite, and hence represented a modern version of Madison's nightmare— "direct democracy." Significantly, it was McCarthyism perhaps even more than communism that led Herberg to express, for the first time, "a feeling for a responsible neo-Burkean conservatism" in America.[16]

Peter Viereck was "so impressed by the original insights" of Herberg's *New Leader* article that he proposed to Sol Stein, executive director of the ACCF, that it be reprinted and circulated through the committee's mailing list. Viereck drew upon Herberg's analysis in his Town Hall debates with Senator Wayne Morse, and used it to develop his own controversial interpretation of McCarthyism as a form of neo-populism.[17] Other anti-communist intellectuals, however, wondered whether Herberg was attacking McCarthy or democracy. For Herberg insisted that McCarthy did not create the technique of "rabble-rousing" but merely exploited to the fullest a plebiscitarian tactic employed by many American politicians, even by former President Roosevelt, who used his "fireside chats" to circumvent Congress and the Court, and by President Eisenhower, who used the political "television show" to sustain his popularity with soothing grins and empty homilies. Some writers also wondered whether Herberg hated McCarthy less than his enemies. For Herberg refused to indulge in the " 'liberal' hysteria about hysteria." Particularly distasteful to him was the "delusive parallel" that Senator Ralph Flanders and journalist Marquis Childs had drawn between McCarthy and Hitler. True, McCarthy exploited anti-communism, but he was not anti-Semitic, Herberg pointed out, and if his financial support came from corporate wealth so did that of the Republican and Democratic parties. Moreover, unlike Mussolini, Hitler, and even Lenin, McCarthy had no ability to transform a mood into an organized totalitarian movement. "Joe McCarthy does not possess a demonic power because . . . there is nothing but emptiness at the heart of McCarthyism, no idea, no cause, no program, nothing." Indeed, McCarthy was to a large extent the "creature of his enemies," the liberal politicians, intellectuals, and journalists who, through their "compulsive" counterattacks, made him a political force by endowing him with the power of publicity. What

to do? Herberg's advice to the *New Republic* turned on its head
Edmund Wilson's counsel twenty years earlier: Take anti-
communism away from the anti-communists.[18]

Repelled by McCarthy, and disgusted with the anti-McCarthyites who did not take seriously enough the danger of communism
to the United States, if not *in* the United States, Herberg grew
weary of "ritualistic liberalism" in general. Reviewing Robert K.
Murray's *Red Scare: A Study in National Hysteria, 1919–1920,* he
chastised the liberal historian for using adjectives like "rabid,"
"frantic," and "hysterical" to characterize the anti-communist
activities of an earlier generation. The problem of loyalty and
security was too complex a matter to be left either to tolerant
liberals or intolerant patriots. And the loyalty oath, which was
being forced upon the academic community in the early fifties,
was not the proper means of preventing subversion and assuring
political allegiance. Anti-communism would remain sterile and
negative, Herberg was convinced, unless it arose from a deeply felt
moral commitment instead of a neurotic reflex or a nationalistic
impulse. Communism was a multi-dimensional phenomenon—
military, political, economic, and, above all, spiritual—and
America had only responded successfully to the first three challenges. Herberg was certain the cold war would be won or lost in
the fourth dimension as well, and to answer this challenge American society needed a new spiritual foundation, not old-time religion. To show America the way to this new authentic faith became Herberg's political mission.[19]

Beyond Nature and History: The Theology of Crisis

"Until nine or ten years ago, I was a thoroughgoing Marxist."
With that opening sentence, Herberg confessed his long journey
to Judaism in *Commentary* in 1947. His conversion to the orthodox Jewish faith was deeply existential, fusing the primacy of personal experience with the power of ontological reflection. It grew
out of the philosophical void left by the miscarriage of Marxism.

Perhaps it would be more accurate to say misconception, for to Herberg communism was not merely an "experiment" butchered by Stalin, an attitude that enabled one to plead poor judgment while escaping the torment of bad faith. On the contrary, the believer is what he believes, and since all ideologies are at the mercy of their consequences, one must accept responsibility for theory as well as practice, for the idea that deceives the thinker prior to the act. Hence Marxism, once Herberg's idée maîtresse, was now subjected to a critique in every branch of knowledge. Its redemptive philosophy of history, its dialectical epistemology, its fetishism of the forces of production, its amoral ethical relativism, and, above all, its naturalistic theory of man were ideas that Herberg repudiated as though he were asking God's forgiveness for his Promethean sin of intellectual pride. Neither human behavior nor human destiny could be understood, Herberg maintained, within the "two-dimensional plane of nature and history." The ultimate meaning of life must be found beyond life—in the "supernatural." From now on the image of Scriptural man would hover like a monad over everything Herberg wrote.[20]

In his Commentary article Herberg envisioned "a great theological reconstruction" arising from the works of Catholic scholars like Jacques Maritain and Protestants like Karl Barth and Emil Brunner. A few years earlier John Dewey and Sidney Hook had dismissed such efforts as a "new failure of nerve." To America's leading pragmatic philosophers, Herberg's call for a religious awakening represented an escape from the responsibilities of political life and the uncertainties of worldly experience. The current preoccupation with subjects like mind, self, consciousness and value signified a desperate search for a new metaphysical theory of existence that would restore the false consolations of spiritual peace. Above all, the "defeatist" retreat to religion meant an abandonment of the greatest cultural heritage of Western man—natural science and the empirical method. And science, Dewey and Hook insisted, is the foundation of truth, the instrument of democracy, and the agency of progress and social justice.[21]

Herberg answered these and other attacks on traditional religion in his first major work, *Judaism and Modern Man*. Published in 1951, the book conveyed Herberg's consuming quest for ethical salvation in a secularized world. But more than a one-man's philosophical pilgrimage, it was also something of a seminal study in modern American intellectual history. With the exception of Niebuhr's writings, *Judaism and Modern Man* offered the first extended analysis by an American writer of the relationship of religious existentialism and social philosophy. The work was highly praised by Jewish scholars, and Niebuhr himself believed that the book "may well become a milestone in the religious thought of America."[22]

Judaism and Modern Man is a powerful intellectual story of the "twice-born" soul. Seeking to awaken Americans to the reality of authentic existence, Herberg began his book with a grisly catalogue of the political terrors of the twentieth century. Classical philosophy, so arrogantly confident about man's self-sufficiency, had done nothing to prepare modern man for the horrors of human evil that brought the world to "the brink of the abyss." Confronted by the demonic forces of destruction all about him, man encounters for the first time the "meaninglessness, absurdity, and despair" of his predicament, the "homelessness" of his spirit and the agonizing "special solitude" of his self. He now realizes that "human existence is crisis . . . insecurity, peril, conflict, urgency, judgment, and decision." And the awareness of choice generates anxiety, for modern man is free to act but he does not know where to turn to find new truths and values on which he can ground his decisions. Without faith in a Supreme Being, he must choose from inside himself. He finds nothing there. Suddenly he is confounded, consumed by a vague but real "metaphysical dread."[23]

Traditionally man had looked to science for knowledge and power, but science itself is powerless when confronted with the human condition. It cannot tell us anything about our concrete, particular selves because it deals in abstractions and universals. It cannot illuminate the meaning and purpose of life because it has excluded metaphysical questions from its definition of reality. It cannot guide man to moral knowledge because it has devaluated the very concept of value. It cannot explain the subjective core of existence because it has reduced man to an object of nature, a tissue of matter, an organism, a mechanism, a "cell of society." In short, the discipline of science, like the doctrine of Marxism, denies the realm of "inwardness," translates knowledge into action and power, and thus turns man outward to seek in labor what has been lost in life. Even psychoanalysis, the latest development in social science, is incapable of penetrating beyond natural causation to what is within man's essence and being. It is the same illusion of technology offered as therapy, the draining of power away from man's moral will. The "peace of mind" psychoanalysis offers, Herberg observed, "is not the 'peace that passeth understanding'—which no practitioner can give—but the 'peace' that comes from the dulling of the conscience, the blunting of moral sensitivity and the shameless encouragement of an almost lascivious preoccupation with self." Science, then, is silent where it should be articulate, timid where it should be daring. The only way out of this naturalistic impasse is to make the ultimate decision—"the leap of faith," the ontological plunge that carries man beyond experience, science, and objective knowledge. Only from God, the transcendent source of life, can come the power of deliverance.[24]

Herberg realized that his affirmation of God left him open to the charge that he was in the grip of an anguished search for spiritual shelter, a "new failure of nerve," as Hook and Dewey put it. From Feuerbach to Freud, he pointed out, religious faith has been regarded as mere "wish-fulfillment" and therefore empirically untenable. But this charge has no basis in existential religion, which, Herberg responded, far from offering a comforting illusion, is a challenging imperative, an ethical demand that both shatters and reconstitutes man's very being. It involves "risk, venture, and decision"; it is a total commitment without total assurance, a faith that still leaves man struggling with choice and trembling with moral responsibility in a state of "holy uncertainty."[25]

Herberg's theology was openly eclectic. Combining the Judaic tradition of ethical inwardness with the existential ontology of Protestant neo-orthodoxy, it drew basically upon three sources: Reinhold Niebuhr, Sören Kierkegaard, and Martin Buber. From Niebuhr and classical Hebraism Herberg inherited a view of man as neither entirely spiritual nor entirely natural but a dynamic unity of both. Man is in nature and yet above it; he is subject to natural necessity and yet retains his freedom and self-determination; he is a finite creature who rebels in despair against his creatureliness. This effort at transcendence, religious in nature, is best expressed in Kierkegaard's definition of the "self" as "spirit." But man's encounter with God in the dialogue of the self with itself seemed to Herberg confining and privatized, isolating man from fellow man. More satisfying was Buber's triadic formulation of the primal reality of religious experience: the self, God, and one's neighbor. Authentic life is "meeting," and man achieves his essential being in real relationships with others as well as with God.[26]

Buber's model of the "dialogic life" and his "I-Thou" ethical motif gave Herberg a new theological foundation for his social philosophy and political commitment. Earlier, in Commentary, he had maintained that his Judaic religion was "not an escape from social responsibility, but a more secure spiritual groundwork for a mature and effective social radicalism." Although he had abandoned Marxist metaphysics, he was certain that the Judaic passion for social justice would make him "a better socialist" and even a "better Marxist, taking Marxism in terms of its best insights and ultimate ideals." He thus desired to "conserve" the "great contributions" of Marxism in the "fields of economic understanding, social thought, and political action." With Buber's philosophy Herberg could incorporate Marx's ideals while rejecting his illusions. For the Buberian affirmation of community repudiated both the atomistic individualism of capitalism and the totalitarian collectivism of communism. Capitalism cut man off from man while communism coerced him into a false community. In one case man is found in cold solitude, in the other he is left in frozen solidarity.

Neither capitalism nor communism acknowledged the genuine communion of man with man; hence neither offered real deliverance of men from their spiritual and social isolation. What Herberg envisioned, in short, was "socialism with a human face" (to use a slogan later coined by East European Marxist humanists), a community vitalized by the warmth of personal relations and humanized by mutual respect and affection, a moral community in which the ethic of total social responsibility "finds its source and power in the perfect love of God."[27]

A critical analysis of *Judaism and Modern Man* yields several difficulties which make the work more a personal statement than a philosophical treatise. First is the problem of subjective experience and objective truth. In his *Commentary* article, it will be recalled, Herberg confessed that Marxism had been to him "a religion, an ethic, and a theology: a vast, all-embracing doctrine of man and the universe, a passionate faith endowing life with meaning." One cannot help but wonder whether Judaism answered the same need. For unlike Eastman and Dos Passos, Herberg could not accept contemporary history as mere temporal experience or blind chaos. "Some overall affirmation about the totality of life and history is necessary if life is to receive any validation and history any meaning." The philosophy of history itself was not even a "theoretical question" to Herberg, but rather a matter of political survival and personal salvation—"quite literally a question of existence."[28] So impelled, Herberg saw behind the absurdity of events the drama of a great metaphysical schema, not the self-regenerating Hegelian dialectic of Marxism, but the intriguing interplay of God's will and man's efforts as revealed in the Bible. Scripture, therefore, may be used as "revelation . . . to disclose God's ways and purposes in the redemption of mankind and to open up to us the possibility of becoming part of that process by making redemptive history our own."[29] These are strange words coming from an author who stated in his foreword, "What I owe to Reinhold Niebuhr in the formation of my general theological outlook, every page of this book bears witness."[30] To Niebuhr, who associated teleological history with both a pagan Marxism and a proud Christianity, God reveals His "ways and purposes" but through a glass darkly, and to claim to make "redemptive history our own" is to risk identifying our will with that of God.[31] All this raises a delicate question: Did Herberg carry over from his radical past the psychology of Marxism, the need, that is, to endow history with purpose and destiny with, in theological language, a final *eschaton?* Even though the ultimate meaning of history now lay beyond history, the will to believe *in* history remained characteristic. From Hegelian Marxism to Hebraic eschatology the riddles of history and the anxieties of existence are overcome only when man can believe in the metaphysical certitudes and even the dialectical paradoxes that explain and justify history. From this perspective, Herberg's "leap of faith," while existentially authentic, risks mistaking therapy for truth.

Another conviction of Herberg's also rings more willed than true—that only religion will save mankind from political holocaust. No doubt the experience of totalitarianism opened Herberg to the urgency of faith, but his conviction that only a sense of the supernatural would enable man to preserve freedom could hardly be demonstrated historically. The Roman Catholic Church in Mussolini's Italy and the various Protestant churches in Hitler's Germany scarcely offered models of fervent resistance. Moreover, there was a theological determinism in Herberg's explanation of recent history which made him see totalitarianism as a kind of delayed political consequence of original sin. "Social institutions, too, necessarily reflect and tend to perpetuate oppression and injustice. But institutions are men writ large, and the wicked, tyrannical power-lusting man, at whose door the responsibility is to be laid, is—everyman. Whatever be the line of inquiry, the thread leads back to man. Man is the problem. . . . The horrors we glimpse are not merely the horrors of the hell without; they are also—and primarily—the horrors of the hell within, the chaos and the evil in the heart of man."[32] Such a line of inquiry can lead everywhere and nowhere. One may grant that all historical crises are basically moral and rooted in man's imperfect nature, but an eternal human condition does not explain why totalitarianism arose historically at a particular time and in a particular place. The source of tyranny and injustice may lie "within," but institutions determine whether man's capacity for evil is restrained or allowed free reign. Even man's inclination to sin is an eternal possibility rather than a natural necessity. (Niebuhr called it "inevitable but not necessary."[33]) Herberg seemed to want to implicate "everyman" in the crimes of Hitler and Stalin. Yet if it was necessary to have fascism and communism in order to dramatize man's precarious spiritual condition and to awaken him to God, the only conclusion to draw is that one must experience evil to overcome it. And this line of reasoning leads back not so much to theology as to theodicy—the question of God's justice. Indeed one is almost tempted to say that with Hitler and Stalin it is God, and not man, that is the problem.

Herberg's attempt to wrestle with the problem of God also reveals the limitations of existentialism as a religious proposition. He was willing, in the Hebraic tradition, to leave the ultimate nature of God a mystery while accepting His intentions as good and purposeful. As for God's existence, this was a phenomenological experience. Herberg was well aware of the various developments in social science that had stripped the world of supernatural significance, and he accepted Freudianism and modern psychology as the greatest challenge to existential religion. But Herberg could not completely answer the challenge. It was absurd to assume that the idea of God had its origins in the child's unconscious veneration of the father. A king, a teacher, indeed any authority figure may be so venerated and yet their reality is scarcely a figment of the disturbed imagination. What naturalists fail to see is "that the very tendency to project the father-image as God already presupposes an impulse in man toward the divine and cannot therefore be used to explain its origin." The depth psychologist C. G. Jung came close to perceiving this truth. Jung related religion to the "racial archetypes" and the "primordial images" of the soul, to the symbolic manifestations of the spirit that science could not challenge because they were "incommensurable." Yet Jungian analysis, Herberg realized, can be used to validate any religion, even "neo-pagan mysticism." Thus he was forced to the conclusion: "No, our religious affirmation neither needs nor can make use of such vindication. Psychology, both Freudian and Jungian, can throw a great deal of valuable light on various aspects of the religious 'problem.' But the fundamental affirmation of faith comes into being on a level of existential reality that not even the deepest of depth-psychology can reach."[34]

Herberg tried to restate the problem of God in existential terms, but he still could not escape the experiential relativism that he regarded as the curse of science and naturalism. On the basis of his own personal encounter with the miseries and tyrannies of the modern world, he was impelled to infer a universal spiritual force that transcended the world. Overcome with anguish by the thought that there may be no metaphysical purpose to events, his "leap of faith" enabled him to comprehend the nature of a truth beyond history on the basis of what he had experienced in history. Thus religion was reduced to the claims of authenticity, to what is emotionally real rather than what is true; and knowledge of God, as an epistemological proposition, still remained tenuous and relative, subject to the quality of personal experience. Unless "everyman" felt Herberg's *Angst*, God was unknowable, and He would remain so, curiously enough, to Eastman, Dos Passos, Burnham, and a whole generation of writers who responded dissimilarly to a similar historical experience. The theology of crisis could not resolve the crisis in theology.

When all is said, however, Herberg's theological writings were profoundly radical in the sense of "going to the root" and asking ultimate questions. As such, they shattered many of the assumptions of capitalism and socialism, neither of which had ever developed a satisfactory moral philosophy of obligation, a theory of personal community that would free man from the fetish of labor that binds him to his state of alienation. In this state man cannot see fellow man as a human person; instead he sees what Sartre called "the relationship of thing to thing."[35] Herberg's writings, like Sartre's in the mid-forties, reflected the same disenchantment with science, determinism, materialism, and the abstract reason of Hegel, and they expressed the same desperate affirmation of will, choice, freedom, and consciousness. Nevertheless, while Herberg could agree with Sartre that "man is condemned to be free," he could not accept the closing sentence in *L'Être et le Néant*. "To be man," Sartre had written, "means to try to be God." This "pure effort to become God, to become *ens causa sui*," Herberg regarded as the culmination of atheistic existentialism in "the most monstrous illusion of all—in man's deification of himself!" With Sartre a "proud stoicism" had been converted into an "idolatrous cult" that would lead to the "absolutization" of man— an argument Herberg then only touched upon but would return to twenty years later when he rejected completely existential ethics.[36] Yet while Herberg tried to reassert the dialectical tension in man's estrangement from and dependency upon God, he shared Sartre's hope in the potentiality of man as a free, self-determining, moral being. The entire edifice of Herberg's theology rested on the premise that man is basically *homo religioso*, a creature possessed with an inner drive to worship a supernatural power that transcends himself and from which he draws his strength. This premise would collapse when Herberg took a hard look at American society in the fifties and discovered that the promise of a genuine religious revival turned out to be a mockery and a farce. The theological existentialism Herberg offered Americans, the heroic religion which dramatized both the tragedy and grandeur of human existence, never took root in America. With his faith in religious man shakened, Herberg was to turn from humanism to historicism, from Martin Buber to Edmund Burke.

Historicism the Hard Way

At its deepest level, the conflict between Soviet-Communism and the free world is a religious conflict. It involves not merely a clash of na-

tional interest, economic system, and political purpose, though these
are certainly important. At bottom, it reflects a radical divergence in
the basic attitude to life. In their conception of man's nature and
position in the world, of his dignity and responsibility, of his relation
to his fellow men, to society, and to the Power that is beyond man
and society, Communism and the faith that underlies American
democracy confront each other in a conflict that admits of no compromise because it is a conflict of ultimates. Quite literally, it is a
struggle for the soul of modern man.[37]

The above statement comes from the opening passage of a paper
Herberg delivered to the National Conference on the Spiritual
Foundations of Our Democracy. Held in Washington in 1952, the
conference had been called in an effort to develop an anti-
communist "religious front" among the Protestant, Catholic, and
Jewish faiths. More than two hundred officials and representatives
attended the various sessions, and President Eisenhower spoke at a
luncheon meeting. Herberg found the conference encouraging,
but he was not entirely at ease with some of the shallow rhetorical
pieties that he had heard, and in Commentary he discussed the
problems of mobilizing religion for ideological purposes. The
Jewish-Christian faith, he wrote, offers both a deeper understanding of democracy and a powerful "spiritual dynamic with which to
meet communism on the ultimate level." Religion and democracy,
however, are distinct, and to make democracy the object of a
religious cult is to render a political instrument idolatrous. The
truly religious person can only have allegiance to a democracy that
"refuses to absolutize itself, as [he] refuses to absolutize any idea,
institution, or 'ism'—to a democracy, in short, that explicitly or
implicitly recognizes a majesty beyond itself." Herberg feared the
simple equation of Judaic-Christian faith and ethics with the values and traditions of Western culture, and Christian action with
the defense of democracy, because he feared the political uses of
religion in defense of the secular. "It is not easy," he warned, "to
grasp this paradox of the absolute and the relative, of faith and
politics, and many religious people tend to be impatient with such
subtleties."[38]

Herberg had good reason to express reservations about making religion serve the cause of democracy, even as a weapon against communism. When he wrote *Judaism and Modern Man* he believed America was on the verge of a religious revival. The postwar return to the synagogue and seminary, the rising student interest in Niebuhr, Tillich, Barth, and Buber, the introspective mood of existentialism, and the new respect accorded doctrinal thought, theology, and God-centered social philosophy were all healthy signs. But there were also disturbing countercurrents. In 1950 the *Partisan Review* published a symposium on "Religion and the Intellectuals." A revealing document in American intellectual and social history, it illustrates again the problem of consciousness on the one hand and society on the other, the mind of the intellectual and the mind of the masses.

"How can anyone who has swallowed the doctrines relating to penis-envy, or the withering away of the State, strain at the doctrine of Transubstantiation?" asked James Agee in the opening statement of the symposium. In that single question one may find a clue to Herberg's conversion. But it is significant that even the devout Catholic Agee wondered whether the intellectual could undergo an "amphibian" return to religion. Consciousness, knowledge knowing its ignorance, prevented the modern intellectual from giving himself over to a religious life that can be lived without being questioned. Consciousness, the tension between belief and knowledge, moved like a shadow of metaphysical gloom behind everything uttered in the symposium. Yet, at the same time, many writers realized that society may accept religion because the masses of men lacked the "strain" of consciousness that resides only in the mind of the individual artist or writer. And the religion of society is false because, as Robert Gorham Davis observed, modern, secular society cannot nurture the "symbolic and associative faculties" that enrich the spiritual imagination and thereby reanimate the meaning of ritual, myth, dogma, and mystery. Such faculties may be found in a Joyce or a Dostoevski, Rahv noted, but neither these nor any other modern novelists could reconcile faith and reason, nor could many contemporary writers re-experience the deeply personalized religious emotions of those great artists of the past who rebelled against God in order better to embrace Him. Not all the contributors to the symposium may have agreed with these agnostic sentiments, particularly Auden and Tate. But it is significant that almost all, with the exception of theologians Maritain and Tillich, regarded with aloof disdain the religious revival supposedly taking place in America, as though it were an ironic re-enactment of the "false consciousness" that Marx promised would disappear with industrial progress. There is a current revival, William Barrett conceded.

But it won't do for a religion. Religion itself is total or it is nothing, and I will begin to believe that a new leaven is working when I see the Catholic faithful walking barefooted through the streets of our cities on Good Friday, or climbing the steps of St. Patrick's Cathedral on their knees. Nineteenth-century materialism offered the theory that the religious sense of mankind would weaken and disappear as the material level of the masses rose. It is very easy to sneer at this as an over-simplification; as a real solution to the religious problem it is indeed a gross over-simplification; but as a sociological hypothesis it seems very apt, and certainly describes what has happened to the American masses, who, immersed in their gadgets, radios, television sets, automobiles, know nothing of the religious passion that once characterized the peasantries of Europe.[39]

Herberg had looked to the intellectual community to inspire and guide America's religious revival. But the *Partisan Review* symposium presaged the dilemma he faced: intellectuals, for the most part unable to believe in Biblical God, could not impart to society the authentic religion Herberg felt it needed, while society, too eager to believe, settled for a false religion. How and why this occurred was the subject of Herberg's second book, *Protestant, Catholic, Jew: An Essay on American Religious Sociology*.

The book was published in 1955. The date is significant, for it was exactly the time that Eisenhower's politics of moderation seemed to echo a new culture of conformity, a period when the country's best intellectuals, recoiling from the ideological conflicts of the past, were discovering that American society and history had been blessed by a remarkable degree of consensus and continuity. Herberg discovered something else—that American society was at once one of the most religious irreligious cultures that had ever existed. The paradox of the revival of the fifties was that it was characterized by a "mounting religiosity" together with a "pervasive secularism." All the evidence pointed to a real upsurge in religion: the dramatic rise in church membership; the vast sums of money spent on popular religious literature like the Bible, which everyone needs and no one reads; prayer at cabinet meetings and the public professions of faith by politicians and celebrities (God, said movie star Jane Russell, is a "livin' Doll"). But to Herberg all this only meant that America was experiencing a religion without faith, or perhaps more accurately, a faith in faith itself. President Eisenhower best expressed this attitude when he advised Americans: "Our government makes no sense unless it is founded in a deeply felt religious faith—and I don't care what it is."[40] The emphasis was added by Herberg, for a faith that could mean anything and everything meant nothing. A religion without intellectual conviction and theological content was hardly the religion that Herberg had in mind, where man would encounter absurdity, loneliness, doubt, decision, and the agony and beatitude of moral effort.

From Herberg's existentialist perspective, there were two great dangers in the shallow, polite religion that was running across America like Hawthorne's "Celestial Railroad." One was the problem of patriotism and religion. "Recognition of the Supreme Being," President Eisenhower declared in 1955 in his "Back to God" address to the American Legion, "is the first, the most basic, expression of Americanism. Without God, there could be no American form of government, nor an American way of life." To Herberg these commonplace utterances were as insidious as they were idolatrous. The identification of God and country could easily result in Niebuhr's nightmare—"a spiritual reinforcement of national self-righteousness and a spiritual authentication of national self-will." There was danger that the peculiarly American-ized religion was being embraced not because it was true but be-cause it was useful. Herberg quoted a Protestant minister: "The storehouse of dynamic power on which you may draw is faith. Not religion, not God, but Faith." And Herberg cited an advertise-ment: "There are times in your life when faith alone protects. We all reach these times in hours of crisis which dot life's span. Regu-lar church attendance helps you build your own personal reserve of faith." A religion that ignored the substance and structure of be-lief, and hailed instead the power and promise of belief, brought from Herberg the harsh outcry "What is this but picturing God as a great cosmic public utility, and religion and church-going as a way of charging one's storage battery of faith for use in emer-gencies."[41]

The quotes that Herberg cited are Menckenesque specimens that tell us a great deal about American society in the fifties. But in many respects Herberg's complaint echoed Kierkegaard's *The Attack upon Christendom*. Indeed, acquainted with the sociology of David Riesman, Herberg could readily validate Kierkegaard's prophetic insights about the institutionalization of religion that would accompany the rise of mass society—the disappearance of the inner-guided moral individual and the triumph of the "other-directed" man. Herberg believed with Kierkegaard that Christian-ity must begin with the individual alone, in a "dialogic" encounter with God; and he believed with Buber that Hebraic faith gives man the power to relate to others as he relates to God. Yet in America the "depersonalizing pressures" of contemporary life had made religion a social affair, a "way of life" and a means of "belonging" to and "identifying" with others, rather than a way of reorienting one's self to God and to fellow man. The cult of "positive think-ing," the promise of "peace of mind" brought home to Herberg the reason for Kierkegaard's "fear and trembling"—Christians cannot bear the burden of Christianity.[42]

Nor can Americans take too much theology. Indeed "Ameri-canism" and neo-orthodoxy were incompatible: on the one hand optimism, innocence, and progress, on the other pessimism, sin, and hubris. In this contest Niebuhr and Buber were no match for Billy Graham and Norman Vincent Peale, the "spiritual advisers" of the nation and the friends of presidents. Herberg was appalled to find Americans using religion to "identify the American cause with the cause of God" and to promote "prosperity, success, and advancement in business." Herberg's dilemma is fraught with irony; his own use of religion was part of the problem. Despite his fear of "absolutization," Herberg himself had maintained that America's struggle with communism was a "conflict of ultimates" because American democracy was grounded in Biblical truth; Eisenhower maintained that "recognition of a Supreme Being" was the moral foundation of American government. To Herberg, Eisenhower was expressing a dangerous "civic religion" that would sanctify "the American way of life."[43] Still, it was the religious "temptation" that led both the theologian and the statesman to see the cold war in absolute terms, and in this context Herberg's distinction between a democracy grounded in spiritual truths and an "Americanism" nourished by a shallow religiosity is a distinction without a difference.

It was without real distinction because Herberg was in no position to deny to others the personal, psychological, and even political uses of religion. In *Protestant, Catholic, Jew* he complained that religion in America had become "a spiritual anodyne designed to allay the pains and vexations of existence." But in *Judaism and Modern Man* existential religion was also offered as a mind cure for alienation; in fact, religion was a "power" that "offers us the unfailing resources of grace by which we may, if we will, be saved from the utter forlornness of a life cut off from God. It is this power that gives meaning and promise of fulfillment to life amidst its confusions, frustrations, and defeats and thus provides us with a transcendent security that nothing can shake."[44] All this merely indicates that existentialism could not resolve the epistemological anarchy of pragmatism; from James's "momentous live options" to Sartre's and Herberg's cult of "authenticity," the implications are the same: the power and will to believe gives man the right to believe in whatever he feels may be useful and good. Whatever Herberg thought about America's mindless religiosity, Eisenhower felt good about God.

In addition to the implicit theological dimension in *Protestant, Catholic, Jew*, there was also a more explicit sociological dimension, a thesis that Nathan Glazer praised as "the most satisfying explanation we have yet been given as to just what is happening to religion in America."[45] Since American religiosity was not founded on genuine faith, Herberg turned to extrareligious sources for an explanation; and, drawing upon the historical studies of Oscar Handlin and Marcus Hansen, he proposed that the prime movers behind the current revival were social pressures in general and immigrant and ethnic factors in particular. The recent upswing in religion resulted from the third generation of immigrants returning to the respective churches of the first generation, to the very religious culture the second generation rejected in its desire to become Americanized and to shed its foreign and alien ways. The third generation, that of the forties and fifties, took Americanization for granted but still needed to define the nature of its Americanness. Finding American society divided into many subcommunities, the third generation felt the need to create and join groups and associations as a means of "belonging," and the Church fulfilled this need. Thus in America's diffuse, mobile social structure, the religion of the fifties functioned as a means of providing "self-identification and social location."[46]

Although Herberg's analysis was stated in the cool language of social science, he was profoundly ambivalent about his own findings. On the last page of the book he expressed hope that some "deeper stirrings of faith" would still arise in America. Yet his own sociological interpretation, which occupied ten of the book's eleven chapters, was almost an admission that such "stirrings" were but the last ripples of religious consciousness in a culture swamped by the high tide of secularism and idolatry. American religion might continue to function as a stabilizing force in

James Burnham writing *The Struggle for the World*, Kent, Connecticut, 1946.

Will Herberg, 1947, then pondering ideological alternatives.

Reinhold Niebuhr, the ex-Marxist and leading Protestant theologian who had considerable influence both on Herberg's conservatism and Schlesinger's liberalism, 1946.

Harvard historian Arthur Schlesinger, Jr., steady opponent of communism and later a critic of William F. Buckley, Jr.'s style of anticommunism, 1947.

Max Eastman and Sidney Hook, professor of philosophy at New York University, at Freedom House rally to form Americans for Intellectual Freedom to oppose Stalinist-oriented Cultural and Scientific Conference for World Peace, then meeting at the Waldorf Astoria Hotel, March 26, 1949.

Novelist James T. Farrell, friend of Dos Passos and Eastman, speaking at the "International Day of Resistance to Dictatorship and War" anti-communist congress—a counter-meeting to the World Peace Conference—at the Sorbonne, Paris, April 30, 1949.

"Resistance Day" congress at the Sorbonne. (*From l. to r.*) Hook; Michael Josselson, later executive director of the International Congress for Cultural Freedom; Melvin J. Lasky, later editor of *Encounter*; and West German delegate Franz Borkenau, May 2, 1949.

Ex-communists James Burnham and Arthur Koestler in the rubble of postwar Berlin, attending the international meeting at which the International Congress for Cultural Freedom was formed, June 1950.

Eastman, then roving editor for *Reader's Digest*, speaking at conference of the American Committee for Cultural Freedom (successor to Americans for Intellectual Freedom), Waldorf Astoria, New York, March 29, 1952: (*l.* to *r.*) Elmer Rice, playwright, and Richard H. Rovere, *New Yorker* staff writer.

Ex-communist Granville Hicks broadcasting to the Russian people over CIA-sponsored Radio Liberation on the anniversary of Dostoevsky's death, February 9, 1956.

John Dos Passos in the mid-1960s when he wrote for *National Review*.

Will Herberg, contributing
editor of *National Review*
since 1961, c. 1970.

Max Eastman addressing the Asian office of the International Congress for Cultural Freedom, New Delhi, 1965.

John Dos Passos speaking at tenth anniversary banquet of *National Review*, 1965.

Daniel J. Boorstin, once member of communist "cell" while a Harvard student, now conservative historian of "consensus" view of American past, c. 1973.

James Burnham with William F. Buckley, Jr., editor of *National Review*, and Priscilla Buckley, managing editor, at a bi-monthly meeting at *Review* offices, New York City, 1966.

Buckley addressing Young Americans for Freedom, Manhattan Center, 1961.

America's social structure; even the immigrant, Herberg knew from the scholarship of Hansen, has turned out to be a conservative rather than a radical force, an empirical fact by no means unimportant to Herberg's growing conservative reflections. But without real theological content, without passion and conviction, religion could not serve society and at the same time serve God.

In 1960 *Christian Century* asked Herberg to contribute to its symposium on "How My Mind Has Changed." In an essay entitled "Historicism as Touchstone," Herberg admitted that he had indeed undergone a change of philosophy so great that he would now be unable to write *Judaism and Modern Man* in the same vein. Ten years ago, he recalled, "I was still living in the afterglow of the 'situation of *kairos*.'" In that time of "great expectations," history did not figure in his thought, and even the great philosophers of the past he cited merely as "a foil to my theologizing." But theological understanding alone, the realm of the "inward," proved inadequate to cope with the social and political problems of the day. Many Protestant existential theologians were trying to operate without "concepts involving enduring structures of value and meaning." Jacques Maritain, however, had all along sensed the dangerous pretentions of "situational ethics," as did Niebuhr, whose historical approach to theology seemed far more sound than Tillich's self-contained ontological system. Herberg could never quite forget Niebuhr's statement "The human person and man's society are by nature historical, and the ultimate truth about life must be mediated historically." He was now convinced that even theology could not provide metaphysical truths that transcended historical experience. Neither man nor society possesses a pure, rational essence; on the contrary, the nature of both can only be comprehended in their historical development. With this discovery Herberg arrived at historicism—the assertion that the fundamental distinction between theological and historical questions cannot be maintained. Politically this new perspective of historicism brought Herberg to Edmund Burke, who also understood that in times of crisis "the preservation of the historical stabilities and continuities against the incursion of the demonic becomes the primary concern and responsibility." Intellectually, the new perspective had both a humbling and a broadening effect on the future development of Herberg's thought:

If man is indeed an historical being, his thought too is historically elaborated, and one must take with the utmost seriousness the continuing conversation through the ages about the "highest things" that the history of philosophy reveals to us. Plato, Aristotle, Thomas Aquinas and Maimonides speak to us today just as contemporaneously as Heidegger, Sartre or the linguistic analysts, not because they utter eternal truths (though they may), but because they speak out of the historical reality that constitutes our own mind and culture. I have never been so convinced that the dialogue between philosophy and theology ought to be resumed and that the "classic" philosophers have something important to say to us in our theological concerns as I am today—precisely because of my new historicism.[47]

Ten years earlier Herberg had mournfully advised man not to look to history for answers, because history itself was the problem. Now the problems of historical reality themselves called for historical understanding, and any political solution to them called for action taken only within the historical context. This profound reorientation reflected Herberg's growing awareness of the inadequacies of abstract theology and existential ethics as well as his increasing disillusionment with America's religious revival. His path to conservatism was a long and arduous ordeal, and if it has taken us some distance to trace his intellectual footsteps, it is because his path took so many interesting turns: personalism, humanism, pluralism, Judaism, neo-orthodoxy, existentialism, and, finally, historicism. Herberg had no easy time getting to the other side, and it is a measure of his intellectual honesty that once he got there he would still be discontented with "what passes for conservatism in contemporary American politics."[48]

CHAPTER 8

Social Theory and the Cold War: Burnham

> Any estimate of Machiavellianism is made difficult by the presence of
> real thought intermingled with what is not thought—Machiavelli's
> political science being at the service of emotions and passions that
> have little or nothing to do with the science itself.
>
> ALBERTO MORAVIA, 1950

From Marx to Machiavelli

In 1947, when European existentialism was enjoying a sudden
vogue in the United States, *Partisan Review* asked James Burnham
to contribute an observation on the novels of Franz Kafka. "At the
literal level," wrote Burnham,

> it is as if Kafka pours on the body of the world a kind of acid, which
> dissolves all the connective tissue, leaving only the discrete elements
> of an organism. He then selects from among the elements according to
> an arbitrary will of his own, and re-unites these by ligaments spun out of
> his own spirit. The laws, therefore, of the world as we normally know
> it, do not, or need not hold. The relations of space, time, causality,
> identity, the divisions between dream and waking, reality and illusion,
> all the categories through which we stabilize—and thus also in part
> hide—the flux of experience are dissolved, or distorted. The ego's
> "reality" principle is suspended.[1]

Will Herberg had seen in *The Trial* a literary expression of
Buber's "triadic relation" of the self, God, and one's neighbor.
Burnham was concerned neither with man's spiritual isolation nor
with the metaphysics of "the door" of meaning; he found almost
intolerable Kafka's suspension of "reality" by an "arbitrary" act of

303

the aesthetic will. Burnham felt no epistemological tension between the visible and the transcendent, and in his conservative writings he would express certainty that metaphysical ideas are unknowable and unborn moral ideals therefore unrealizable. Herberg had come to view man as basically *homo religioso*, but Burnham came to view man as basically a political animal for whom the psychology of the soul was merely the disease of the imagination. Kafka's obsession with authority and hierarchy became Burnham's obsession, yet Burnham was sure one could find amid the seemingly indeterminate maze of layer upon layer of authority structures a rational explanation in the brute fact of power itself. What was ultimately at the top of government, or perhaps behind or beyond it, Kafka left hidden in darkness, an allegory fully appreciated by Jewish existentialists like Buber and Herberg. To Burnham *The Castle* was not "the world as we normally know it."

To the moral, theological, surreal world of Herberg Burnham would juxtapose the rational, logical world of Vilfredo Pareto and other twentieth-century elitist ideologues. Burnham's sudden interest in the theory of hierarchy and the phenomenon of elitism is itself psychologically curious. The political scientist Robert Dahl's hypothesis that "for individuals with a strong strain of frustrated idealism, it [elitist theory] has just the right touch of hard-boiled cynicism"[2] may explain the jaded radicalism of a C. Wright Mills. Whether it tells us anything about Burnham is doubtful. As a Trotskyist, Burnham had occasionally expressed great faith in the rational will of the masses. "Let The People Decide!" he had declared in the late thirties when defending the Ludlow Amendment.[3] Whether such sentiment represented a lapse of Leninism or a real dedication to participatory democracy is hard to say. The ultimate goals of communism had not inspired Burnham as much as Marx's analysis of the weaknesses of capitalism and the fallacies of liberalism. It is difficult to see in Burnham's mind "a strong strain of frustrated idealism" or to perceive in his career the psychology of the disappointed lover of freedom who turns sour on democracy. His shift to an elitist vision of political reality might better be interpreted as the logical and necessary progression of his political theory. In *The Managerial Revolution* he had argued that socialism was an impossible dream because of the dynamic tendency toward hierarchy and centralization in all industrial societies. Once Burnham questioned the possibility of socialism, it was necessary for him to carry the analysis further and question the possibility of democracy itself.

He took his first, hesitant step in this direction in an essay in *Whose Revolution?*, published in 1941. In this symposium, addressed to the future of American liberalism, Burnham maintained that democracy must rest upon institutional foundations, rather than moral precepts, and upon a delicately balanced conflict among such "social forces" as trade unions, business interests, farmer cooperatives, religious affiliations, and consumer organizations. The people represented by these forces may not hold democratic ideals higher than their own interests; nevertheless democracy may survive to the extent that such associations remain autonomous and independent of the state. The primary threat to this democratic equilibrium came from the "professional democrats" who were demanding America's intervention into a modern, total war that could only lead to further state regimentation and eventual totalitarianism. The essay ends with the somber advice that those who put war first in the name of preserving democracy are actually undermining democracy. Americans could defeat Hitler, it seemed, but they may also defeat themselves:

... if we put the question in the popular form, "Will democracy win?" there can be little doubt that the answer must be, No. Democracy can never win. Democracy always loses, because the forces of democracy, in winning, cease to be democratic. Those who want democracy, therefore, must be willing to lose.[4]

Appeasement? Isolationism? Pacifism? Revolutionary defeatism? It is difficult to know what to make of Burnham's position. He himself qualified every generalization and hedged every prediction about the "probable" survival of democracy with a negative reservation about that very probability. In some respects Burnham's sentiments echo Randolph Bourne's World War I dictum that "war is the health of the state." In others they anticipate John Kenneth Galbraith's post–World War II argument for the plural-istic necessity of countervailing institutions. But why, when faced with the prospect of an all-out war against Hitler and the Third Reich, did Burnham have so little faith in democracy itself? The answer would appear that revolutionary Trotskyism is not the best education for democratic citizenship. From Marx Burnham had inherited a distrust of liberal democracy as a pretense and a sham; and as an ex-Trotskyist he extended this distrust to democracy in all its forms, socialist as well as bourgeois. His earlier disenchant-ment with the working class led to a complete disillusionment with mass democracy, and his temperamental unwillingness to take seriously American ideals as moral imperatives resulted in a hardened cynicism toward liberalism and equality in general. Yet Burnham could hardly challenge these principles by following Dos Passos's path back to Jefferson and the Enlightenment, the very seedbed of democratic idealism. Nor could he join Eastman in celebrating Adam Smith or Herberg in rediscovering original sin: *The Managerial Revolution* had relegated capitalism to the ash heap of history, and Burnham's scientific naturalism had relegated Christianity to the museums of metaphysics and mythology. How, then, to move beyond Marxism and liberalism without returning to the historical assumptions of progress and freedom out of which these very ideologies had been conceived? This was Burnham's dilemma, and he found the answer in the writings of European social theorists who came to be known as the heirs of Machiavelli.

The Machiavellians was published in 1943. It would be Burn-ham's last major theoretical work before he became caught up in the polemical heat of the cold war, and it was the first thorough study by an American of the sociological writings of Gaetano Mosca, George S. Sorel, Roberto Michels, and Vilfredo Pareto. There are two curiosities about *The Machiavellians*. Previously American scholars had become interested in European elitist thought when they were trying to unravel the twisted intel-

lectual roots of fascism.[5] Yet Burnham chose to call his Machiavellians "defenders of freedom." The book appeared during the
midst of the greatest ideological war in modern history, when most
Americans fervently believed that the defeat of the fascist powers
would be a victory for democracy. Yet Burnham set out to prove
that democracy was a myth, an illusion, a fiction, and a lie.

The book's first several chapters are a brilliant tour de force.
Burnham opens with a passage from the 1932 Democratic Party
platform, and then, turning back six centuries, proceeds to contrast the "formal" and "real" meanings of Dante's *De Monarchia*
with Machiavelli's *The Prince*. Dante's treatise represented "politics as wish," pointless metaphysical distinctions and logical deductions drawn from a theology that had no relevance to the actual
world of space, time, and events. The "real" purpose of *De
Monarchia*, the immediate issues that brought the text into being,
was the protracted conflict between the forces of the papacy and
the forces of empire during the twelfth to fourteenth centuries.
Like the designers of the 1932 Democratic Party platform, however, Dante was reluctant to acknowledge the real power struggle
taking place before his eyes; he failed to demonstrate how his
abstract, idealistic goals for saving the Holy Roman Empire could
be reached, since "being unreal, they cannot be reached." Machiavelli, in contrast, took as his data phenomena that were truly
political; his method of inquiry was non-transcendental, confined
solely to the "field" of real power relationships among men.
Machiavelli was the first theoretician of praxis, the first political
philosopher to give man ideas that can be acted upon and translated into social practice.

It was this "science of power" that was carried forward into the
twentieth century by the neo-Machiavellians. Mosca, Michels,
Pareto, and Sorel followed Machiavelli in divorcing ethics from
knowledge, taking human nature as it is, rejecting all monistic and
metaphysical theories of history, and investigating political behavior in the "anti-formal" mode of refusing to accept at face value
what men say, think, or write. In their works Burnham found all

the intellectual ammunition he needed to wage his two-front war against socialism and democracy. One by one they come forward with their wisdom: Mosca, with his theory of the ruling class as an organized minority, his rejection of representative government as an empty fiction, and his empirical outline of the permanent stratification of society; Michels, with his "iron law of oligarchy," his thesis that direct democracy is impossible for "technical" and "mechanical" reasons, and his demonstration that ultimate sovereignty cannot be dispersed and that the masses psychologically depend upon autocratic leadership; Sorel, with his belief in the emotive and activating power of myth, his recognition of the necessity of violence to challenge institutions based on force, and his savage attack on the squalid fraud of nineteenth-century bourgeois parliaments; and, above all, Pareto, with his principle of the "circulation of elites," his view of politics as primarily the arena of non-logical conduct, and his theory of "residues" and "derivations"—roughly, the constant habits or impulses of human behavior and the rationalizations or ideologies used to justify them.

That there exists a sharp separation between the rulers and the ruled, that governments operate on force and fraud, and that all political groups and institutions degenerate into hierarchies and elites were theorems Burnham fully endorsed. But his conclusion was far from pessimistic. If democracy, conceived in Lincolnesque terms as popular sovereignty and government by the people, was theoretically impossible, liberty and freedom, as expressed in and through organized opposition, could still prevail. Mosca's principle of "juridical defense" demonstrated how the individual could be protected from arbitrary personal power, and both Mosca and Machiavelli demonstrated how liberty would emerge out of the continual clash of opposing factions, interest groups, and social forces. However, new threats to liberty were arising everywhere. The war, Burnham pointed out in the last chapter, was a "stage in a world social revolution." New power alignments will evolve even though the elitist structure of power itself remains intact. The military may now join the technicians and managers as a new "Bonapartist" ruling class based on plebliscitary democracy. This trend can be checked if various elites resist the total concentration of power in the state. However—and here is the crux—to do so elites may have to defy a democratic public which can never be induced to think logically and scientifically. How, then, can elites, whose scientific skepticism alienates them from the masses, preserve liberty and at the same time sustain their own deference and power?

A dilemma confronts any section of the elite that tries to act scientifically. The political life of the masses and the cohesion of society demand the acceptance of myths. A scientific attitude toward society does not permit the belief in the truth of the myths. But the leaders must profess, indeed foster, belief in the myths, or the fabric of society will crack and they will be overthrown. In short, the leaders, if they themselves are scientific, must lie.[6]

An argument for dishonesty honestly argued; Burnham was at least true to Machiavelli.

"On the whole I find [Burnham's theory] plausible," wrote the great Italian philosopher Benedetto Croce. *The Machiavellians* seemed to Croce a convincing defense of liberty and a lucid exposition of contemporary post-Marxist social thought. Beyond that, Croce offered several telling criticisms. First of all, Burnham confined his analysis solely to political forces and thus made liberty purely a political product that scarcely took account of man's deeper moral or religious impulses. Moreover, it would be impossible to deceive the masses but not ourselves, since one cannot convince others of beliefs one does not fully share, and there is the danger that elitists may become their own "dupes" and end by believing the myths they have perpetrated. And lastly, Burnham possessed a narrow version of myth. Like the Hegelians who believe that error is merely incomplete thought, Croce the neo-idealist maintained that myth is "not falsehood but imperfect truth," and the Italian philosopher called upon the "purer artists and finer minds" to recognize that myths like freedom are born, not made, and are true because they embody high ideals and hence are "beautiful."[7]

Crocean neo-idealism offered cold comfort to those "finer minds" in America which had to come to grips with *The Machiavellians*. Most American reviewers found the book blatantly wicked. To the Marxist Left, especially the Trotskyists, it was treasonous; to the liberals, especially the old-fashioned progressives, it was scandalous. But the response was something more than a sifting of the tough minds from the tender hearts. Even Reinhold Niebuhr, who could share some of Burnham's scorn of liberal cant, maintained in the *Nation* that the masses could better distinguish truth from "pretense" because they must suffer the consequences of actions taken by an elite. Others believed Burnham protested too much his own objectivity. Malcolm Cowley claimed in the *New Republic* that Burnham used the rhetoric of empiricism only to better disguise his own emotions; John Mac-Cormac, the New York *Times* reviewer, found Burnham's language "more apocalyptic than scientific."[8]

In American political theory *The Machiavellians* is doubtless a daring, pioneering work challenging the moral pieties of liberalism and the classless illusions of Marxism. Yet there is a perversity of brilliance in the work that makes one wonder whether intellectual history is being used or abused. One of the major embarrassments is its shifting criterion of truth. Approaching knowledge as an anti-formalist, Burnham denied the autonomy of political theory. He maintained that the "real" meaning of any political doctrine could only be understood against the background of time and place, and, above all, in light of the social forces that had produced it. Although he applied this criterion to Dante, he dropped it when he moved into the twentieth century and discussed the neo-Machiavellians. Here we learn nothing of the social and political context of their writings, for Burnham treated their theories almost as universal principles, as though he had discovered the timeless "iron laws" of political geometry. The conspicuous feature of modern elitist theory, however, is that it arose out of a particular political culture; indeed, it developed predominantly in Italy, a country where liberal democracy had not been fully developed, a culture wherein the moral cynicism of the intellectual class reflected the actual oligarchical power structure of the ruling class. Burnham believed he could extract theories peculiar to pre-fascist Italy and apply them to politics in general, even to America, where there had been no historical political traditions resembling the elitist patterns of the Old World. Had Burnham turned to the Founding Fathers he would have discovered a quite different assumption— not that their own oligarchy would be perpetuated, but that democracy would be inevitable unless curbed and deflected by the "machinery of government." The fears of the Founding Fathers were well founded. Since the age of Jackson the complaint of great American conservatives, from Henry Adams to Walter Lippmann, has not been the "circulation of elites" but their decline and leveling under the pressures of mass democracy. A decade earlier Burnham had tried to bring Marx to America, now he tried to import Machiavelli. Both were exercises in formalism confounded by "American exceptionalism."

The Machiavellians came to be regarded as the theoretical and moral foundation of Burnham's later attitudes toward the cold war. On the basis of his reading of Machiavelli, a leader or political elite could justify the unlimited use of force, violence, and even political lying in international affairs, not merely as traditional power politics, but on ethical grounds. Burnham was convinced that Machiavelli had not eliminated ethics from politics but had simply refuted Dante's otherworldly, transcendental ethical ideals because they were unattainable. He did this, Burnham maintained, "in order to bring politics and ethics more closely into line, and to locate both of them firmly in the real world of space and time and history, which is the only world about which we can know anything."[9] We rub our eyes at this. The "real world" is the domain of factual knowledge about which we can know nothing of moral knowledge. Ever since Hume philosophers have seriously questioned whether the slightest glimmer of ethical insight can be derived from a study of the objective world. Surely Burnham was aware of the dualism between science and ethics, and Herberg could have reminded him that knowledge apart from morality cannot determine choice. Most men want to feel there is a reasonable correspondence, a just measure of appropriateness, between what they think they know about the world and what they think "ought" to be done in the world. The Machiavellians failed to answer this need for ethical knowledge.

To a large extent the book also failed to answer the need for practical knowledge. It is difficult to see how neo-Machiavellian thought helped illuminate the meaning of many contemporary historical events and movements. In The Machiavellians there is no attempt to confront the dynamics of historical change or the novel phenomenon of totalitarianism in general or Stalinism in particular; nor is there any effort to analyze the reasons for the hegemony of elites or explain why elites must deteriorate (if Pareto's "circulation of elites" explains the Soviet purges, then Yezhov must be judged "superior" to Bukharin). Similarly, there is no effort to develop a theory of human nature or to explain the persistence of irrationality in politics; nor is there any convincing reason given why elites, and only elites, would think scientifically and rationally (the Founding Fathers, elitist themselves, did not trust government by elites because even the "best minds" were disposed to "self-delusion"; Mussolini, an admirer of Sorel and Pareto, was hardly a model of "logical conduct"; Stalin, an admirer of Stalinism, was perhaps too logical). Even more serious, The Machiavellians offers no penetrating causal interpretation of the struggle for power or any analytical perspective for anticipating the future course of history (it is far more difficult, Mosca observed, to foresee exactly what will happen than merely to foresee what is never going to happen). About all we can learn from The Machiavellians is that power struggles among men and nations will continue forever because man by nature is driven to struggle for power. Eastman and Herberg had at least tried to offer reasons for man's aggressive nature. Burnham did not explain it, he assumed it; and in doing so he offered a tautology instead of a theory.

Obviously Burnham was using Machiavellianism as shock therapy for liberals and socialists, the fuzzy-minded intellectuals whose moral sentiments blinded them to power realities. In the neo-Machiavellians he believed he had found a "scientific" body of knowledge that illuminated the flux of events, and he was certain that a proper understanding of Machiavelli would demonstrate why it was necessary to exclude moral considerations from political inquiry. Burnham's argument did not, as his critics charged, conceal value commitments that would justify a ruthless, militant response to the Soviet Union. What renders Burnham's work questionable is his simplistic interpretation of the meaning of Machiavelli. "We find," Burnham wrote, "that Machiavelli uses languages in a cognitive, scientific manner. That is, except where he is frankly urging his readers to action, he uses words not in order to express his emotions or attitudes, but in such a way that their meaning can be tested, can be understood in terms of the real world. We always know what he is talking about."[10] On the contrary, the author of *The Prince* and *The Discourses* used language in such ambiguous ways that Machiavellianism has far more than one meaning. Some scholars, seeing more satire than science, cannot even take the prose literally; others, especially political philosophers with ideological commitments, can easily make Machiavelli serve different political purposes. The Marxist Antonio Gramsci hails *The Prince* as a call for the dictatorship of progressive forces against an obsolete feudal aristocracy (Burnham also took this view); the conservative natural law philosopher Leo Strauss regards Machiavelli as an anti-Christian "teacher of evil"; the existentialist Merleau-Ponty sees him as a modern humanist operating in a universe hushed in moral silence; and the liberal historian Sir Isaiah Berlin maintains that Machiavelli realized the "irreconcilability of equally dogmatic faiths, and the practical improbability of complete victory of one over the other," and thus inadvertently opened the path to "empiricism, pluralism, toleration, compromise."[11]

The variety of these interpretations seriously question whether Burnham's politics rested on clear theoretical foundations. In his cold war phase, Burnham would pose as the "romantic Machiavellian" (Arthur Schlesinger, Jr.'s, description),[12] the proponent of heroic realpolitik who would bring all American power to bear on the liberation of Eastern Europe. Yet the cold war became anything but a cool, logical exercise in Machiavellian statecraft, which stresses the limited efficacy of force and aspires to the "pure" use of power, undefiled by motives of personal pride or political humiliation. Indeed, the cold war reintroduced on a grand scale the very emotional ingredient that Machiavelli tried to eliminate from politics—the language of moral passion.

Burnham's mind and temperament were unsuited to the advice that Machiavelli offered. Although the Renaissance philosopher wanted to use the "new" science of politics to control the imponderables of politics, he desired to sensitize the political leader to the discontinuities of historical experience and the ironies of political action. "Above all," Sheldon Wolin has written, Machiavelli's "political actor needed a temperament which could endure acting without assurance of certainty."[13] This anguished capacity to perform with "negative capability" (Keats's phrase), to confront the world of power and at the same time realize there are limits to man's knowledge of that world, scarcely described Burnham's mechanistic approach to cold war politics, where the movement of power would be predicted with geometric precision by a strategist who knew the "real world."

This curious discrepancy between Burnham's professed political theory and his actual political behavior, between Machiavelli's sense of skepticism and moderation and Burnham's absolute certainty about the course of history, raises a final question. If Machiavelli is not the theoretical foundation of Burnham's cold war convictions, what is? Were we to adopt Burnham's own anti-formalist method of inquiry and use the categories of Pareto, Burnham's neo-Machiavellianism would appear to be the "derivation" of his anti-Stalinist "residue." Burnham's new-found theories are less expressions of a "frustrated idealist" than those of a frustrated ex-Trotskyist, and his impassioned cold war convictions less those of a "scientist" than of someone whom Machiavelli himself might suspect as being concerned with the petty politics of *vendetta*. So much for the "real" meaning of *The Machiavellians*.

Stalin's Advocate or Adversary?

Trotskyism was the last great illusion of the Old Left. Even after his death in 1940, and long after his shibboleths had become stale and embarrassing, many of Trotsky's assumptions about the nature of Stalinism still lingered in the minds of several literary intellectuals, particularly those associated with the *Partisan Review*. In "Lenin's Heir," published in that journal in 1945, Burnham resurrected the intellectual legacy of Trotskyism for the last time, and then buried it in a grave of errors.

Cleverly provocative, Burnham's article was also brilliantly pernicious. He argued that Stalin, far from betraying the revolution, had actually fulfilled it. Trotsky and his followers could not see this because they had always dismissed Stalin as an uncultured mediocrity who triumphed more by stealth than by skill, an "apparatus man" who could not even write or speak with elegance or theoretical sophistication. Once the intellectual disabuses himself of this literary snobbery, Burnham contended, he may have to admit that Stalin is a "great man," and the source of his greatness lies not only in his role as military leader in the war but in a "creative political imagination" that has produced two profound changes in communist policy: first, "a multi-national Bolshevism" which now allows Russia to avoid the mistakes of the early Comintern and exploit the deeper currents of nationalism and national liberation; second, "a geopolitical vision" that enables him to orchestrate every isolated military move into a unified diplomatic offensive. Burnham dramatized this total movement in Platonic metaphors:

Starting from the magnetic core of the Eurasian heartland, the Soviet power, like the reality of the One of Neo-Platonism overflowing in the descending series of emanative progression, flows outward, west into Europe, south into the Near East, east into China, already lapping the shores of the Atlantic, the Yellow and China Seas, the Mediterranean, and the Persian Gulf. As the differentiated One, in its progression, descends through the stages of Mind, Soul and Matter, and then through its final return back to Itself; so does the Soviet power, emanating from the integrally totalitarian center, proceed outward by Absorption (the Baltics, Bessarabia, Bukovina, East Poland), Domination (Finland, the Balkans, Mongolia, North China, and tomorrow Germany), Orienting Influence (Italy, France, Turkey, Iran, central and south China . . .), until it is dissipated in MH ON, the outer material sphere, beyond the Eurasian boundaries, of momentary Appeasement and Infiltration (England, the United States).[14]

Only in his stress on nationalism can Stalin be said to have departed from Bolshevism, and even this revision merely indicates that revolutionary movements define themselves by deeds rather than by doctrine. Collectivization, the purges, the conspiratorial party dictatorship all followed logically from the conception of revolution originated in the founding of Bolshevism in 1903 and from the practice of revolutionary terror of 1918. Stalin, not Trotsky, is Lenin's rightful heir. Indeed, Trotsky was a "Platonic communist," stated Burnham as though he were reinvoking Eastman's Leninist critique of Menshevism. Trotsky was at his best in rhetoric and literature, not in the life of action. He did participate in the real "historical world of Becoming" in 1917, but history soon left him stranded, bewildered by the unexpected turn of events. Stalin, in contrast, "was the best Bolshevik just for the reason that he did not try to impose on history an a priori conception of the nature of revolution, but was ready to accept the revolution, with all its historical consequences, as it revealed itself to be in real life." These are "very unpleasant truths," Burnham concluded, "discovered by others at different turning points during the last generation, by some, like myself, rather late in the day."[15]

Burnham's article exploded like a tempest at Trotsky's wake. Former disciples immediately rushed to the defense of the "old man's" good name. Burnham regarded Trotsky's thesis "unpleasant," Lionel Abel insisted, because it was in fact false, and the pain arose from Burnham's effort to make it true.[16] Dwight Macdonald, who recalled that Burnham had also attributed features of greatness to Hitler in The Managerial Revolution, maintained that one could evaluate Burnham's "intellectual career as a restless quest for a Father, for authority, from Thomas Aquinas to Trotsky to Pareto to Hitler to Stalin." Macdonald further chastised Burnham for failing to take seriously the idealistic program of a Bolshevik leader, for directing his animus against a fallen revolutionist with whose values he agrees while admiring a "successful butcher" whose morality appals him, and for eliminating values entirely from historical inquiry by accepting what in fact happens rather than what one wants to happen. Macdonald protested the appearance of the article in Partisan Review, which brought an extended reply from editor William Phillips, who tried to take a middle ground while admitting that Burnham's critics had not addressed themselves to the central issue—Why have so many predictions and expectations of the Left opposition to Stalin been belied by history?[17] Macdonald had addressed himself to the motive of Burnham's article, and his speculations well illustrate why so many writers expressed frustration when trying to interpret it:

There are at least three mutually contradictory "readings" that may be made of "Lenin's Heir." It can be read as an anti-Stalinist article; it can be read as a lefthanded apology for Stalinism, designed to paralyze all opposition by suggesting that Stalin's world triumph is inevitable; or it can be read as an ironic, even quasi-anarchistic debunking of the whole concept of great men and power politics (for are they not presented as morally repugnant?). It can be read in all three ways because Burnham has all three attitudes at once: he wants to fight against Stalinism, he wants to submit to it, and he wants to complain about it. All three attitudes exist, but it is my opinion that the second is the one which subjectively motivated Burnham to write the article.[18]

Macdonald complained of the article's "ambiguity," and with good reason. "As Stalin expands in size before us," Burnham had written, "we can more readily grant his legitimate succession." What did he mean? The question troubled many intellectuals in Europe as well as in America, and one writer who came forward with an interpretation was the British novelist and political essayist George Orwell.

Orwell's essay, "Second Thoughts on James Burnham," is a classic in the literature of political criticism and historical and philosophical analysis. Orwell had been following closely Burnham's writings; he was familiar with *The Managerial Revolution* and *The Machiavellians*. Not until the publication of "Lenin's Heir," however, did he feel impelled to express profound disagreement with Burnham's entire approach to history, politics, and morality. Orwell was particularly incensed at the way Burnham had written off democratic England in *The Managerial Revolution*, and he chided Burnham for many of the book's unfulfilled predictions, particularly the victories of Germany and Japan. Examining "Lenin's Heir" along with *The Machiavellians*, Orwell now believed he possessed the key to Burnham's lofty indifference to democracy: he is intoxicated by a fascination with power. His eyes are always fixed upward, gazing at the apex of political authority. So transfixed, he tries to hypnotize the reader by building up a "picture of terrifying, irresistible power" in which Stalin becomes an epochal hero embodying the march of destiny. Moreover, this mental disease distorts Burnham's understanding of history. "Power-worship blurs political judgment because it leads, almost unavoidably, to the belief that present trends will continue." Not only does he predict the future simply by extending the present forward, Burnham sees history itself as one continual apocalypse. "Nations, governments, classes, and social systems are constantly described as expanding, contracting, decaying, dissolving, toppling, crashing, crumbling, crystallizing and, in general, behaving in an unstable and melodramatic way." It is this cataclysmic vision, together with his Machiavellian power fetish, that explains Burnham's new-found admiration of Stalin. Whether engrossed by Nazi Germany or Soviet Russia, by managerialism or bureaucratic collectivism, "in each case he was obeying the same instinct: the instinct to bow down before the conquerer of the moment, to accept the existing trend as irreversible."[19]

Although he provided a penetrating analysis of Burnham's philosophy of power and history, Orwell was completely wrong about Burnham's political position. So too were Macdonald, who suggested that Burnham's real attitude lay in the second "reading" —submission to Stalinism—and Abel, who called Burnham "Stalin's Advocate." Burnham fooled everyone by becoming, among the American intelligentsia, Stalin's greatest adversary. Years later he admitted in an interview that he had written the article as a "put-on," an effort to challenge intellectuals to think of Stalin as neither Trotsky's "mere cipher" nor as Roosevelt's "genial Uncle Joe."[20] Indeed, six months before the article appeared Burnham was secretly at work on a study of Bolshevik diplomatic goals for the Office of Strategic Services, a study which was to be analyzed in preparation for the Yalta conference. Parts of this study were incorporated into Burnham's next book, and when it appeared intellectuals would never again have to wonder whether they were reading Burnham correctly.

The Truman Doctrine

The Struggle for the World was published in 1947. A marvelous exercise in pamphleteering, it reads like Lenin's What Is to Be Done? and Tom Paine's Common Sense. The opening sentence expresses Burnham's usual apocalyptic belief in Armageddon: "The Third World War began in April, 1944." Burnham was referring to a mutiny of communist-led Greek sailors in Alexandria, a clear sign that the Soviet Union now intended to turn the anti-fascist resistance against the West. It was the opening round of a total war that "may begin at any moment, today, tomorrow; it may even have begun before these sentences are published." The inevitability of war, Burnham insisted, was the consequence of the "transcendent power" now concentrated in atomic weapons, a new technological development that makes possible for the first time in modern history the domination of the world by a single state. The struggle will be fought to the complete triumph of either the United States or the Soviet Union, the only two remaining power centers. Communism, emanating from Russia, will extend its ruthless drive to conquer the world; and America, though presently confused and vacillating, must resist this challenge by whatever means: blocking, through military and economic pressure, the Soviet consolidation of "Eurasia" (Greece, the Middle East, China, and India); undermining communist power in Eastern Europe, northern Iran, Afghanistan, Manchuria, northern Korea, and China; securing a monopoly of atomic weapons; and outlawing the Communist Party in the United States. Deeply influenced by Toynbee's *A Study of History*, Burnham believed that world conditions demanded the establishment of a new "universal empire." In this "time of troubles" a new alignment of power must be forged, which Burnham variously called "the American Empire," a "non-communist world federation," or a "world democratic order." It would be composed of continental nations not presently under Soviet domination—England and the British dominions and the Western Hemisphere countries—all accepting the realities of American power and hence its inevitable political hegemony.

The most revealing chapters of the book deal with Burnham's attitudes toward the meaning of communism. He defined communism as "a world-wide, conspiratorial movement for the conquest of a monopoly power in the era of capitalist decline." He drew on Lenin's writings to embellish the definition, and, with similar knowledge of Comintern history, he had no trouble demonstrating that Soviet policy was completely identified with the world communist movement. Communism, in short, was a monolith. Moreover, the logic and direction of communism could be grasped through the concepts of geopolitics. Thus Burnham worked out an actual spherical diagram of the world as it existed in August 1939, placing the Soviet Union at the center and drawing, around a dark inner circle, a series of concentric rings, each demarcating vividly the presence or influence of Soviet power. Lest the diagram imply a static image of the communist monolith, Burnham cleverly used the language of physical motion and force to depict it as a political dynamo. The Soviet Union is the "inner, magnetic core," the "defensive ring" from which, offensively, "pressure pushes" extend forever outward in a "thrust" of "direct power from the Heartland." The image was awesome, and it served to dramatize Burnham's argument that motion continues through a vacuum until it is resisted, that power must be answered with power.

Would America resist? Burnham was doubtful. Americans were too immature and their leaders too irresolute. Yet the West will inevitably have to face the awful decision somewhere sometime. And to carry out Burnham's policy will be, he admitted, "a long, difficult and perhaps most terrible process." "The most hopeful route out of the crisis will be hard and painful and, most probably, bloody." It will be a struggle "such that one or the other, or perhaps both, of the contestants must in the end be defeated." Nevertheless, Burnham could—by somehow mixing Toynbee with Machiavelli—conclude that the cold war is the challenge to which America must respond or accept its own decline and fall. Christian grace offers man another chance to repent and choose again; History, on the other hand, "offers each of its great challenges only once. After only one failure, or refusal, the offer is withdrawn. Babylon, Athens, Thebes, Alexandria, Madrid, Vienna sink back, and do not rise again."[21]

The Struggle for the World appeared at a turning point in modern American diplomatic history. It was published during the week in which President Truman announced his decision to come to the support of Greece and Turkey, to extend assistance to all

322 | The Middle of the Journey: 1940-1955

322 | The Middle of the Journey: 1940-1955

"free peoples" resisting external subjugation, and to mobilize American military power in an effort to halt communist expansion. Burnham's book was linked to what came to be known as the "Truman Doctrine." *Time* magazine treated the publication as a news event in its "International" section, and *Life* devoted thirteen pages to a condensation of the book's contents. *Christian Century*, which returned to the book again and again in its weekly editorials, stated gloomily, "It fits the 'stop Russia' policy of the Truman Doctrine so exactly that one can hardly read it without thinking, 'Here, whether they realize it or not, is what the senators and representatives who voted for the initial move under the new doctrine—the Greek-Turkish aid bill—were really approving as the foreign policy of the United States."[22]

The popular press had mixed feelings about the book. Reviewers could accept Burnham's analysis of the Soviet Union, but they shuddered at his grim solutions and bristled at his elitist criticism of the immaturity of the American people. As Burnham went on the radio to defend Truman's new policy, the intellectual community took a close look at the controversial book, now listed among the best sellers. The Christian internationalist Charles Clayton Morrison criticized Burnham for misinterpreting Toynbee and offering a diplomatic "blueprint for destruction." The isolationist Harry Elmer Barnes went further: "This is probably the most dangerous and 'un-American' book and, at the same time, in its grim way, the leading joke book of the year." Liberals like Henry Bamford Parkes and James Reston praised Burnham's analysis of America's floundering foreign policy but were taken aback by his melodramatic exaggerations and "melancholy" visions. Arthur Schlesinger, Jr., who preferred Burnham's anti-Stalinism to the "confusion and messy arguments of the appeasers," took issue with his concrete proposals and expressed relief that Burnham was not secretary of state. The anti-Soviet Marxist Left attacked Burnham for ignoring the economic implications of the cold war, and the Trotskyists in particular, who had more intimate knowledge of the unpredictable workings of his mind, could not resist pointing out a glaring inconsistency in his newest position: the same Burnham who had recently informed readers of *The Machiavellians* that all governments are controlled by ruling elites using the techniques of force and fraud, was now calling for the legal suppression of the Communist Party because it does not play by the "rules of the game."[23]

Burnham realized that the United States would have to rely solely on power pressure when confronting Russia diplomatically, and he knew that Truman's talk of the "free world" was, like Stalin's talk of "peoples' republics," hypocritical nonsense. Nevertheless, for all its vaunted "realism," *The Struggle for the World* failed to anticipate two historic events that occurred a year after its publication: Yugoslavia's break with the Soviet Union and Tito's courageous defiance of Stalin, and the Chinese communists' successful drive against Chiang Kai-shek's nationalist forces, culminating in a victory Stalin had neither foreseen nor tried to bring about. These events did not cause Burnham to revise his geopolitical schema. The distinction between Chinese and Soviet communism remained academic, for the "third world war" had begun long ago and there was still no basis for believing that international communist expansion would disappear merely because the communist monolith appeared to be disintegrating. Events in Europe in the late forties stiffened Burnham's attitude. The Berlin airlift was "a decision not to decide," a timid effort to avoid a Soviet confrontation instead of sending an armed convoy through the blockade, a "minute risk" that would have brought "enormous gain" by demonstrating to the world that the communists can be beaten at their own game.[24]

Burnham now began to re-examine the Truman policy that he once supported, and in *The Coming Defeat of Communism* (1950), he spelled out its defects: the lack of unified application and clear objectives; the defensive nature of America's response, which, by implication, conceded past victories to the communists;

and the failure of the Marshall Plan to unify Europe economically and to thwart communist strength in Italy and France. As the title suggested, however, Burnham was, for the first time, mildly optimistic. War may no longer be inevitable because of the nuclear balance of terror, and the communist "empire" shows signs of weakness. Now is the time to reject the Soviet offer of "co-existence" and to exploit the enemy's weaknesses by embarking upon an "offensive-subversive war" that will defeat communism through sustained propaganda, economic pressure on Western countries trading with Russia and her satellites, and material and moral support to resistance movements behind the Iron Curtain.

With *The Coming Defeat of Communism*, "Burnhamism" and "Burnhamite" became familiar terms in European intellectual circles as well as in America. The ex-Trotskyist, once known only remotely as the eccentric author of *The Managerial Revolution*, was now regarded as the chief American theoretician of a dangerously aggressive foreign policy. In Europe it was believed, among many socialists generally, and British Laborites in particular, that the split between the communist East and the democratic West must be accepted as a permanent reality, an unpleasant fact of political existence that should not be allowed to interfere with the reconstruction of Europe on the ideas and values of democratic socialism. What endangered this effort, R. H. S. Crossman informed American liberals, were the attitudes of embittered ex-communists like Burnham and Arthur Koestler, who accused Western intellectuals of "cowardice" for flinching from the consequences of taking the "strategic initiative."[25]

Among the European continental Left "Burnhamisme" also became a phrase of fear and revulsion, particularly in France, where Burnham's writings had been translated and widely discussed. In 1947 *The Managerial Revolution* was published as *L'ère des organisateurs*, with a long, critical, but respectful preface by the former socialist premier Léon Blum. A few years later Burnham's *Containment or Liberation?* was published in Paris with a dissenting introduction by the liberal social philosopher Raymond Aron. Most controversial of all were Burnham's dialogues with André Malraux, which first appeared in *Partisan Review* and then were published as a book, *The Case for De Gaulle.* Here Malraux and Burnham, who shared a post-communist admiration of elites, discussed the possibility of a European federation, the threat of Soviet communism, the nature of Gaullism, the prospect of a "third force" between the United States and Russia, and the overriding imperative of "decisiveness." Such discussions struck horror throughout the French intellectual Left; because of his association with Aron and Malraux, Burnham was identified with "reactionary" Gaullist nationalism in France and with "fascist" McCarthyism in the United States. The French communist Pierre Courtade, who had been in America in 1950 as *L'Humanité's* correspondent, equated Burnham's idea of a managerial elite with the racial-imperialist ideas of the Nazi Alfred Rosenberg. Courtade, who regarded Burnham as the intellectual architect of American hegemony, published a novel supposedly based on Burnham's career, *Jimmy,* later translated by the Leningrad review *Zvedva.* Unknowing Frenchmen could read of the anti-communist "police state" apparatus of Governor Thomas Dewey and Judge Harold Medina, who were suppressing the voices of progressive Americans, represented by the black communist Paul Robeson, while allowing anti-Semitism and racism to run rampant in a country succumbing to "*l'hystérie burnhamienne.*"[26]

"The great importance of your books, in my view," Malraux remarked to Burnham, "lies in the fact that they try to make this different reality apparent to us."[27] Malraux was referring to the phenomenon of bureaucracy outlined in *The Managerial Revolution,* the new "reality" that rendered obsolete Marx's theory of a declining bourgeoisie and a rising proletariat. Burnham seldom received such compliments from liberal or socialist intellectuals in the United States. As in Europe, the term "Burnhamism" no longer stood for the author of a minor classic in industrial sociology. By the early fifties it signified the quintessence of the conservative cold warrior, a new intellectual species that could not survive long with the American Left.

Burnham, the Congress for Cultural Freedom, and Arthur Schlesinger, Jr.

The non-communist Left in America was slow to realize the conservative direction in which Burnham was rapidly heading. Even after he clearly put forth his hard-line cold war policy in *The Struggle for the World*, he remained on good terms with *Partisan Review* and the American Committee for Cultural Freedom. This tenuous rapport could be maintained for several reasons. For one thing, until the McCarthy controversy and the presidential candidacy of Adlai Stevenson in 1952, the democratic Left assumed a cold war position that conceded ground to Burnham's indictment of ritualistic liberalism. At the Congress for Cultural Freedom meeting in Berlin in 1950, for example, Burnham delivered an attack on neutralism, pacifism, and the "pious litany of the Left" in general, and *Partisan Review* published the address even though editor Rahv felt that certain passages could be misinterpreted as advocating the use of atomic bombs.[28] Left intellectuals could also delight in Burnham's attack on the capitalist class for its suicidal blindness. "In relation to the struggle against communism," Burnham wrote, "the American businessman is too ignorant, too greedy, too reactionary, and, in a certain sense, too cowardly."[29] Moreover, Burnham was still held in esteem by many literary intellectuals. The *Partisan Review* editors could continue to count on him for discerning essays on aesthetic philosophy as well as strategic diplomacy, and ACCF officials would regard him as a valuable cultural asset, a writer who could explicate Malraux's mysticism and Machiavelli's realism. When *Encounter* started publishing in the early fifties, ACCF secretary Irving Kristol advised Stephen Spender to contact Burnham, "a first-rate essayist on cultural matters."[30]

Burnham had been one of the founders of the ACCF, which may also explain why the mésalliance took so long to surface. This organization—which awaits its historian[31]—was in some respects a revival of an older committee by that name started in the late thirties by John Dewey, Sidney Hook, and Norman Thomas. Its revival in 1951 was largely in response to the notorious "Cultural and Scientific Conference for World Peace" held at the Waldorf-Astoria in New York in 1949. The "Waldorf Conference" was clearly dominated by communists, fellow travelers, and Russian sympathizers. Dissident anti-Stalinist intellectuals attending, represented by Hook, Macdonald, A. J. Muste, Schlesinger, Herman J. Muller, George Counts, and Bertram D. Wolfe, protested the refusal of the program committee to allow Hook to read a paper before one of the panels (the paper, criticizing the notion of racial, national, and class "truth," had been previously accepted and then later rejected after Hook submitted an abstract). This group departed from the conference and reconvened at Macdonald's house, whereupon it decided to hold publicly its own countermeetings and adopt the name American Intellectuals for Freedom. The American opposition inspired a similar meeting at the Sorbonne among French anti-Stalinists, who also desired to protest the suppression of freedom in the Soviet Union while Parisian communists celebrated the "International Day of Resistance against War and Fascism." Shortly afterwards several American writers, including Burnham, went to Berlin for an international meeting at which the Congress for Cultural Freedom was formed. When they returned home, the ACCF was organized as a loose affiliation.[32]

As a founding member of the ACCF, Burnham first expressed dissent over the issue of McCarthyism. At an executive committee meeting in April 1952 Daniel Bell and Irving Kristol submitted a resolution—prompted in part by Eastman's statement to the press blasting McCarthy's critics—condemning both communism and "certain types of anti-communism." Burnham objected to the resolution, claiming it would provoke a split in the organization if it pertained only to McCarthy in particular rather than to the general "use of lies as political weapons" by all partisans. Action on the resolution was postponed, more out of weariness than wisdom.[33]

The following year Burnham himself brought on the very split he feared. In fall 1953 he wrote a preface to a book by Medford Evans, *The Secret Fight for the A-Bomb*. Evans, a former employee of the Atomic Energy Commission, accused American scientists of relaying secrets to Soviet agents and allowing assembled fissionable material to be stolen from nuclear plants in the United States. Some American scientists were prepared for the charge, which Evans had published earlier as an article in *The Freeman*. But when the book appeared with Burnham's preface, physicists in the ACCF, most notably Herman J. Muller, Robert Oppenheimer, and Harold Urey, were furious. Eugene Rabinovitch, editor of the prestigious *Bulletin of the Atomic Scientists*, demanded that Burnham be forced to resign from the ACCF's executive committee or else he and other physicists would dissociate themselves from the organization.[34]

Rabinovitch's ultimatum created a "great stench," as Sol Stein put it, within the inner circles of the ACCF. Stein, the executive director, quickly consulted other members. Nathan Glazer believed that it was wrong to attack Evans and Burnham for writing what Rabinovitch called "pathological and slanderous abracadabra." Evans had documented his case, Glazer told Stein, and he should be factually refuted and not just denounced. David Riesman, on the other hand, assured Stein of Rabinovitch's impeccable reputation among physicists, and Herman Muller suggested that Burnham might not be in full agreement with all Evans's charges and hence would be willing to write a disclaimer. Burnham was outraged by the suggestion, which to him smacked of censorship. The controversy continued for over a month, with the scientists lining up solidly behind Rabinovitch. Eventually it was decided not to expel Burnham, lest the ACCF lay itself open to the charge of, in Milton Konvitz's phrase, "doctrinal *Gleichschaltung*." While this controversy had been raging within the ACCF, moreover, Burnham had been asked to resign from the *Partisan Review's* advisory board because of his "neutralism" on McCarthy. In light of this sudden action it would be, Bell advised Hook, "fanning the flames for us now to step in and ask Burnham to go; it would only polarize the situation."[35]

Six months later, in July 1954, Burnham resigned from the ACCF on his own initiative. In his confidential statement to the executive director, he stressed that although he was never an ardent McCarthyite he was now certain that he was an "anti-anti-McCarthyite."

In my opinion those anti-communists who consider themselves to be anti-McCarthyites have fallen into a trap. They have failed so far to realize that they are, in political reality, in a united front with the Communists, in the broadest, most imposing united front that has ever been constructed in this country. As in all united fronts, only the Communists can benefit from it. Politics has an objective logic of its own. The united front doesn't have to be "formalized" in a signed pact. It is constituted by a certain relationship of political forces. And not all the good intentions or pained disavowals of all the liberals can alter the political reality.[36]

Burnham's "objective logic" surprised few who knew how his mind worked. Daniel Bell anticipated it; in response to the ACCF controversy, Bell had talked to several scientists at the Massachusetts Institute of Technology. "These people are not Russian dupes," he told Hook. "[Jerome] Wiesner is close to Schlesinger and A.D.A., but that is a far cry, of course, from being pro-Russian, unless one wants to apply Burnham's inverted Leninism of looking at the 'objective' consequences of their political positions."[37] Burnham went on to write his own version of scientific espionage in *The Web of Subversion*, published in 1954 by the John Day Company and reissued in 1961 as an "American Opinion" publication of the John Birch Society. Burnham chose to apply the method of "inverted Leninism" not only to scientists but to liberals in general. And in the instance of Arthur Schlesinger, Jr., he extended the doctrine of guilt by association to corruption by marriage. In "The Case against Adlai Stevenson" in the *American Mercury*, Burnham explained why the liberal historian was not to be trusted. "Schlesinger is married to the sister of John K. Fairbank, of Harvard, the O.S.S., the O.W.I., Amerasia, and the Institute of Pacific Relations. It would be a cruel thing to hold a man to blame for his brother-in-law. But Schlesinger has taken explicit political as well as personal responsibility for the *bona fides* of Fairbank—of whom it has been testified under oath that he was a member of the Communist Party, and who has been undeniably proved the active associate of Communists and pro-Communists."[38]

The bitterness between Burnham and Schlesinger had been building for some time. Each represented opposite tendencies within the ACCF. Schlesinger wanted the committee to speak out publicly against McCarthy, and he would withdraw from the organization for the exact opposite reasons that led Burnham to resign. Writing to the new chairman, James T. Farrell, in 1955, Schlesinger complained that the ACCF had lost sight of cultural freedom and had become obsessed with anti-communism long after the threat of internal communism had passed.[39] Burnham and Schlesinger also took diametrically opposing foreign policy views. During the 1952 presidential campaign Schlesinger, one of the leading intellectual spokesmen for the Democratic candidate, Adlai Stevenson, defended the party's containment policy against critics like Burnham. ACCF officials, well aware of the growing rift,[40] and upset by Burnham's attacks on Schlesinger in the *American Mercury*, tried to bring the two together in debates sponsored by the organization.[41] Schlesinger agreed to debate Burnham on several occasions, sometimes with Hans Morgenthau and Philip Mosely on the panel. When Burnham's *Containment or Liberation?* was published in 1953, he wrote a savage review in the *New Republic*. The book was "a careless and hasty job, filled with confusion, contradiction, ignorance and misrepresentation." Burnham is a man "in permanent apocalypse," Schlesinger scoffed, a catastrophic thinker whose tiresome prophecies of doom can only dazzle once.

"He is the Bix Beiderbecke of our political journalism, only he has hit that high note once or twice too often."[42]

Who Will Die for Containment?

In fall 1953 Max Eastman and others, perhaps with Schlesinger's review in mind, wrote to the *New Leader* complaining that Burnham's *Containment or Liberation?* was being sabotaged by bookstores and reviewers.[43] Actually Burnham's book, if coldly received in liberal circles, was widely discussed in the daily press and in the major periodicals. As with his other major works, *Containment or Liberation?* was timely, provocative, and deliberately unsettling. It appeared shortly after the campaign of 1952, when Stevenson and Schlesinger opposed the Eisenhower–John Foster Dulles policy of committing America to freeing peoples presently under Soviet domination. It appeared during the height of the Korean war and the McCarthy hysteria, when the public was most susceptible to criticisms of the failures of American foreign policy. For once Burnham was in touch with the masses.

Ironically, it was the elite, the only class Burnham had once believed capable of logical thinking and rational behavior, that was responsible for America's winless foreign policy, and supposedly the elitist "architect" of that policy was George Kennan. Burnham devoted several chapters to a close analysis of Kennan's famous "Mr. X" article in *Foreign Affairs* in 1947, and to his seminal treatise on realism versus idealism in international relations, *American Diplomacy, 1900–1950.* Burnham's critique was perceptive and, as it turned out, prescient. Looking back, it does appear that Kennan was unduly optimistic about the possibility that containment could effect real changes within the Kremlin (Kennan himself later conceded this). Exactly how containment would bring about a "gradual mellowing of Soviet power" was never convincingly explained. Burnham effectively challenged the liberals' assumption that communism was simply a "natural" response to a poor economic environment: there was no clear geographical correlation or historical pattern between communist strength and economic conditions. Communism was a "political apparatus," not a natural development, as Lenin's criticism of "spontaneity" proved again and again throughout the twentieth century.

Burnham was at his best exposing lucidly the fallacies of containment. Yet he himself became vague and problematic when he turned to liberation as the solution. He advocated recognizing governments in exile, recruiting and training national paramilitary armies in preparation for an invasion, and developing opposition movements behind the Iron Curtain. The key was resistance—the will to act decisively and struggle bravely. Greece and Finland had the will, and they remained free; Poland and Czechoslovakia did not, and they were swallowed up. The lesson? We can help the captive peoples restore the will to resist by demonstrating to Russia that America is ready to come to their support and is prepared for "whatever military action may be required" to assure the success of their struggle. Burnham never acknowledged that the success of Greece and Finland in remaining out of the Sovet orbit was due to Stalin's acquiescence to geopolitics as much as their own firmness. Nor did he, like Kennan, bother to explain how the Soviet ruling class could abandon a militant posture toward the West without giving up its own claim to power within the Russian bureaucracy. Why would the Soviet Union tolerate liberation? No ruling class relinquishes power to those who would destroy it. Both Marx and Machiavelli could agree to that truth. Was Burnham now a Wilsonian liberal speaking the language of "national self-determination" (used frequently in the book)? Or was he still an unconscious Trotskyist who continued to harbor illusions about the internal weaknesses of Stalinism and who saw his national liberation armies as the Fourth International redivivus? Whatever the answer, one thing seemed clear: Burnham was no longer the managerialist or the Machiavellian; he had no consistent theory of power to liberate the victims of total power.

Nor did Burnham offer a consistent theory of political knowledge with which to interpret historical events. This is no place to plunge into a historiographical discussion of the debate over the "origins" of the cold war. But it is obvious that at the heart of that debate is a fierce controversy over the *intent* of Soviet foreign policy. Was Stalin's policy aimed at Russia's national security or at world communist expansion? Burnham had no doubt it was the latter, but to prove Soviet designs for world conquest he had to abandon his recent neo-Machiavellianism and return once again to Marxism. Machiavellianism led to a geopolitical perspective that traced the cold war to imperial Russia's limited, strategic ambitions in Eastern Europe and the Balkans. This perspective, shared by conservative writers like Walter Lippmann and, to a certain extent, by conservative statesmen like Churchill and De Gaulle, Burnham was forced to reject in order to stress the ideological background of the cold war. He now attributed to ideas a power he had formerly denied them. The Burnham who had warned readers in *The Machiavellians* against accepting at face value the documents and statements of political leaders—the fallacy of "formalism"—was now citing Lenin's pre–World War I writings as the operational code of Soviet foreign policy and Marx's *Communist Manifesto* of 1848 as the mental blueprint of the Soviet *Weltanschauung*—"You have a world to win."

All this was highly dubious. Ideology does play an important role in communist thinking, yet it is exceedingly difficult to ascertain whether ideology determines the nature of action or action determines the meaning of ideology. Which text do we use? *What Is to Be Done?* (1902) revises *Capital* (1868), *State and Revolution* (1917) updates *Two Tactics of Social Democracy* (1905), and October 1917 breaks the whole organic unity of Marxist theory and practice, so that in *Left-Wing Communism* (1920) Lenin can flagrantly derevolutionize Leninism itself. Whatever may be the motivating force of Marxist theory in pre-Revolutionary situations, the irony is that Burnham attributed Soviet political successes to ideological determinism, while in reality Russia's political experience since 1917 has, as R. V. Daniels observes, "revolved around the most exaggerated voluntarism."[44]

A curious pattern of thought emerges in Burnham's attitudes toward the Soviet Union. In the late thirties he used the categories of Marxian and managerial analysis to explain the failure of the Bolshevik Revolution. A few years later, in "Lenin's Heir," he used neo-Machiavellianism to demonstrate that Stalin "fulfilled" the revolution only by betraying Marxist ideas for power politics. Then a decade later, when it became clear that the realpolitik perspective led to a conservative interpretation of the cold war as a traditional clash of nation states struggling for contiguous spheres of influence, he was compelled to reinvoke the power of ideology in order to dramatize the menace of communism. Burnham moved back and forth between Machiavelli and Marx, between the idea of power and the power of an idea, changing his epistemology each time he wanted to explain reality.

Burnham wanted to foretell as well as explain, and as a result *Containment or Liberation?* retained the same flaw that one sees in his earlier works—the instinct to predict the future by projecting the past. "If the communists succeed in consolidating what they have already conquered, then their complete world victory is certain. The threat does not come only from what the communists may do, but from what they have done. We do not have to bring in speculation about Soviet 'intentions.' The simple terrible fact is that if things go on as they now are, if for the time being they merely stabilize, then we have already lost." In Burnham's thoughts about diplomacy one cannot help but see a kind of residual Marxism, a tendency to think that any stable situation was inherently contradictory and contained the seeds of inevitable conflict. Thus the logic of containment led to two diametrically opposed alternatives. "At most, containment can be a temporary expedient, a transition. As the transition is completed, containment must move toward one or the other of the two major poles, toward appeasement or liberation." The United States cannot really contain Russia, Burnham insisted, for the "Soviet imperial state" is by definition "a totalitarian power which seeks world domination." Ultimately America will have to submit to communist expansion or "get rid of Soviet rule." The inexorability of the either-or alternative displays not only Burnham's weakness for melodrama but also the close correspondence of his views with the communist version of the cold war. Reading Burnham, we are in the same political universe as Lenin in 1917, a world of inevitable conflicts, apocalyptic confrontations, and ultimate moments of truth. Accepting communist rhetoric at face value, Burnham could continue to expound his mechanistic view of diplomacy as a chessboard of predictable power moves in a vacuum of non-resistance.[45]

The question of resistance brings us to the weakest link in the chain of Burnham's argument: the ethical link. Burnham's dilemma lay in formulating a theory of politics that could be realistic without being cynical, a political theory that made "power" its central concept and yet somehow allowed for the role of moral ideals in human affairs. He was unaware of the dilemma until the cold war, when it became apparent that Machiavellian geopolitics meant accepting the status quo. Hence the critique of containment had to be ethical as well as political. Burnham now spoke of the need for "honor" in American foreign policy, of being faithful to certain ideals without which liberation would be a mockery and a sham. "Spirit must direct matter toward a goal, and a firm resolution must sustain an unyielding effort through periods of failure, loss and sorrow." Burnham did not say what the source of this "spirit" would be, but his political message was clear enough: "It is perhaps the crucial defect of the policy of containment that it is incapable of meeting this moral and spiritual demand. Who will willingly suffer, sacrifice and die for containment? The very notion is ridiculous. The average man cannot even understand the policy of containment, much less become willing to die for it. Will the captives of the Kremlin risk death for a policy that starts by abandoning them to the usurpers of their freedom?"[46]

The question was poignantly posed, but one can find no answer to it in the entire body of Burnham's writings. Who, one might ask, will fight for Michels's "iron law of oligarchy"? Who will storm the barricades for the cause of bureaucracy? Who will die for Pareto? Perhaps it is here that the full implications of Benedetto Croce's criticism of The Machiavellians become relevant. Burnham, Croce wrote a decade earlier, dismissed freedom as an empty myth, and he remained blind to the meaning of truths that are born of pure spirit:

Myth is not falsehood but imperfect truth, one-sided, vague, dubious, mixed with feeling and disguised in images. We can constantly correct it by purifying it, and thus take occasion to fortify the truth and even to enrich it with elements previously neglected. To mythologize in cold blood is tasteless, dishonest and vain, for myths are born, not made, and they are born of what we call truths and treat as truths in our reasoning. Myths have been born from the idea of freedom, and none are more beautiful than those born from the truth of Christianity, which the vulgar may have taken grossly and materially, but in which purer spirits and finer minds could feel and recognize the deep truth and high ideals which they embodied.[47]

In 1943, when Hitler had all but conquered Western Europe, Burnham proceeded to prove that freedom was an illusion. In 1953, when Stalin had absorbed Eastern Europe, he suddeny discovered the value of freedom without explaining how it could be realized. Sorel-like, he now asked East Europeans to fight for an ideal he once believed theoretically impossible, and he asked the American people to risk their lives in order to rescue Europe from Soviet domination—the very people who had remained mute witnesses to the destruction of East European nationhood in 1939. Burnham could even define liberation as a "crusade," since the cold war must be understood as a confrontation between "two ways of life, two conceptions of the nature and destiny of man, which are in ultimate contradiction." The cause of liberation would be America's last chance to redeem herself and expiate the sins of the past. "If we do not ourselves honor our own words, who will honor them?"[48]

The conservative might forgive Burnham for offering his advice ten years too late, against Stalin rather than Hitler. But even conservatives cannot escape the fact that there was something theoretically incoherent in the very notion of liberation itself. Burnham's idea of liberation embraced two incompatible world views: the geopolitics of power and national interests on the one hand, and the "higher politics" of morality and national commitment on the other. The first stresses the need for international security and stability, the second the imperative of ethical demands as the test of national morality. The first is soberly conservative, preferring the known to the unknown, Machiavelli's world of power rather than Dante's world of ideals. The second is radically adventurous, fired by romantic notions of glory and honor. In *Containment or Liberation?* Burnham tries to accommodate both views, but ultimately the prudence of political realism yields to the pride of Wilsonian idealism, the mind surrenders to the will. The result of this theoretical schizophrenia was a confusion between what was possible and what was "honorable." As Machiavelli might have predicted, and as the East European uprisings of 1956 would demonstrate, the doctrine of liberation gravely implicated America in political tragedy.

PART THREE

The Dilemmas of American Conservatism 1955–1974

In 1955 two events quietly occurred that were totally separate in motivation and yet totally related by implication. Professor Louis Hartz published *The Liberal Tradition in America*, and William F. Buckley, Jr., brought out the first edition of the *National Review*. Buckley's journal would never quite be able to answer the thesis that Hartz had spelled out, a thesis that stymied the Left as well, and one that would have significant implications for the future of American social thought.

According to Hartz, liberalism has been the dominant American ideology, but American liberal theory itself has for two centuries nurtured deeply conservative instincts. The ubiquitous liberal creed, the Lockian fetish of property rights and individual natural rights, was both the conception and the consummation of the American political mind. The absence of a feudal order enabled Lockianism to pervade all social classes and all geographic sections, making liberalism a "natural phenomenon" in American history. American liberalism is also a "colossal . . . absolutism," an ideology that is accepted as given, an established custom that has gone unchallenged because there has been no perspective outside of Lockianism from which to view critically American Lockian orthodoxy. Ironically, if Hartz's argument is correct—and no historian has successfully challenged it*—then liberalism has pre-empted

---

* The most intelligent effort to refute Hartz succeeds only in pointing out the ideological inadequacy of American liberalism; its historical ubiquity remains unchallenged. See Kenneth McNaught, "American Progressives and the Great Society," *Journal of American History*, LIII (Dec. 1966), 504–20.

the role of conservatism as the bearer of the traditional values of the past. One finds in American liberalism what Edmund Burke found in English conservatism—the "untaught feelings" and "prejudices" that are "cherished" simply because they have endured as mindless habits and thoughtless instincts.

Buckley and the *National Review* would have an intellectual vanguard of ex-radical writers armed with postradical ideas: Eastman with his economic philosophy, Dos Passos with his historical imagination, Herberg with his theological conscience, and Burnham with his doctrine of realpolitik. Buckley could also draw upon a peripheral, fugitive tradition of cultural conservatism in America. But could he reconcile anti-communist conservatism with philosophical conservatism so as to challenge effectively the hegemony of liberal consensus in America? Or was Buckley posing as Burke but thinking like Locke? The New Left had no real answer to Hartz's thesis. Did the New Right?

CHAPTER 9

To the *National Review*

The Marriage of Incompatibles: Eastman and Buckley

Max Eastman was the first Old Left intellectual to form a friendly acquaintance with William F. Buckley, Jr.; he and Burnham were also among the first to become members of the editorial board of Buckley's new conservative journal. Eastman came to know Buckley in the early fifties when they were both working for the *American Mercury*, Eastman as a contributor, Buckley as an associate editor. Buckley, a bright young *enfant terrible* fresh out of Yale, often consulted with Eastman, for whom he had "deep respect" and "affection," seeking editorial suggestions and the proper translation of Lenin.[1]

While Buckley was planning the founding of what became the *National Review* he kept in touch with Eastman. In one six-page letter defending his new magazine, Buckley said that writing the prospectus was a matter of considerable tension, since "on the one hand I had to attract the investor, and on the other I had to be completely honest." Buckley's idea of honesty was as diplomatic as it was prophylactic. Certain passages in the prospectus having to do with "absolutes, natural law, etc.," had to be "diluted" for fear of offending prospective contributors. There could be "no mention of the fact that I intend, in an early issue, to read Dwight Eisenhower out of the conservative movement. . . . Dissimulation is involved only in the sense that we both know that there are people

343

who, while subscribing to the principles I outlined in the prospectus, simply haven't faced the fact that our principles are round and Eisenhower is square." Nothing would be said about "the Texas millionaires (though they are not terribly relevant) even though I intend to blast them too—as unproductive (vis-à-vis conservatism) nuisances." Apparently Buckley rejected Eastman's advice that his new magazine be "discreet" as well as "brave."[2]

Eastman and Buckley disagreed strongly about *Time* and *Reader's Digest*, Eastman regarding these mass publications as allies in the conservative cause, Buckley reminding him that some of their editors and writers had supported the New Deal. *Time* is no more a conservative than *Fortune* is a spokesman for Big Business, Buckley complained. "Look who ran *Fortune* during the thirties—men like Kenneth Galbraith, and Archibald MacLeish, and Dwight Macdonald, and C. D. Jackson." Intellectually, the Right is "virtually impoverished." With the exception of the *Freeman*, *Human Events*, and the *American Mercury*, Buckley explained, "we have no press."

In February 1955 Buckley asked Eastman to become a member of the board of directors of what he referred to then as the "National Weekly." Eastman accepted, and when the *National Review* began in November, Eastman appeared from time to time with leisurely articles on the Sacco-Vanzetti case, Mark Twain and socialism, and the failure of the welfare state in Norway. He confessed "I Acknowledge My Mistakes" in the *National Review*, yet he remained an unrepentant defender of Lenin's heroic role in history. Lenin was not power-hungry or Marxist-crazed, he explained in a personal letter to the anti-communist Harry Schwartz, writer for the New York *Times*: "To me his totally dominating characteristic was *tseleustremlynnoct*—practicality, driving toward the goal." Eastman remained an unrepentant agnostic as well. "I agree that communism as a body of ideas has 'filled the vacuum created by the breakdown of organized religion,' " he wrote to R. N. Carew-Hunt, the Oxford scholar and author of the widely read *The Theory and Practice of Communism* (which drew upon Eastman's earlier critiques of Marxist philosophy). Eastman disagreed with Carew-Hunt's advice that communism "can only be combatted by opposing to it a conception of life based upon wholly different principles." There are as many conceptions of life, Eastman replied, as there are life styles; and "another religion, or another organized and generally accepted body of ideas having a similar character," would only replace one false creed with another, as though one needed spiritual dictum to fight social doctrine.[3]

A few years before he joined the *National Review*, Eastman had written a review of Buckley's *God and Man at Yale* for the *American Mercury*. He later confessed that he admired Buckley and "found brilliant and good things in his youthful book," but in the review he objected strenuously to Buckley's suggestion that the Yale alumni take a strong hand in determining curriculum policy as a way of bringing religion and capitalism back into the classroom. "He wants to replace collectivist indoctrination with a counter-indoctrination," wrote Eastman, who amusingly wondered why Buckley was struggling so hard to give a helping hand to an omnipotent deity. "He doesn't call it by that name; he calls it 'value inculcation'; but it comes to the same thing. . . . I can't imagine anything that would botch up the business of education and research more completely than a march on New Haven by the Yale alumni."[4]

Several years later, in 1955, when Eastman published *Reflections on the Failure of Socialism*, he continued his war against indoctrination. Senator Barry Goldwater, Eastman observed, simply did not understand that "God's will" has little to do with the historical foundations of freedom; on the contrary, Anglo-Saxon political freedoms were won only after heroic struggle against kings and barons who invoked the doctrine of divine right. Eastman singled out Whittaker Chambers as "very profoundly wrong" in his conviction that the struggle between Soviet communism and the "free world" is the struggle of atheism against religion. Communists, too, Eastman maintained, believe in a deified philosophy of history, and "Communists believe in man not as an independent power, but as a constituent part of the superhumanly ordained movement of the universe." Anti-communism in America was becoming God-intoxicated, with Christianity the opiate of conservatism.

To Eastman the new conservatism in America seemed almost medieval in its resistance to natural science. In the National Review in 1958, when he defended the legacy of John Dewey, he complained that conservatives were blaming the great American philosopher for all their woes: socialism, permissiveness, "life-adjustment" therapy, and utilitarian morality. Not so. Dewey rejected socialism as alien to American society, developed an educational philosophy that made discipline part of the cognitive process, and, while subscribing to the experimental method of knowledge, made "an effort to build spirituality into science." Eastman's defense of Dewey, and his harsh reference to religion as "primitive mythology," brought a brisk reply from the conservative philosopher Russell Kirk, who accused Dewey and Eastman both of casting aside tradition, precedent, and history in favor of innovation and experiment. The philosophy of pragmatism, America's one original contribution to modern philosophy, would never find a home in the National Review.[5]

In the light of his intense animus against religion, it is surprising that Eastman stayed with the National Review as long as he did. It was almost a decade before he left the journal, National Review's "only single resignation," Buckley boasted years later.[6] In January 1964 Eastman spelled out his case against Christian theism in the National Review, denying contributing editor Frank Meyer's argument that freedom is based on the existence of an "objective moral order" and challenging Brent Bozell's pronouncement that Christians owe their identity and destiny to "the central fact of history—the entry of God onto the human stage." He questioned Buckley's assertion that atheists are less inclined than Christians to fight valiantly against communism because "a Christian views the experience of man on earth as transitory and so is less likely to attach highest value to earthly things." Meyer's idea of freedom, Eastman responded, is a reversion to "pre-liberal ecclesiastical authoritarianism," Bozell's dictum parochial and self-defeating, excluding, as it does, more than half the world's population. And Buckley's assertion is embarrassingly illogical. Since freedom on earth is an "earthly thing," the only inference to draw is that it is otherworldly Christians who will forsake it rather than fight for it. Eastman likened the convictions of Cromwell to those of Bukharin; both the Christian and the communist identified their ruthless actions with the will of history, divine or dialectic. These criticisms were lost upon Buckley, who knew nothing of Marxist philosophy and even less of Eastman's earlier works on the subject. (Curiously, Herberg, the only *National Review* writer who knew his Marxism as well as his theology, stayed out of the debate.) "There are too many things in the magazine—and they go too deep," Eastman wrote Buckley, "that directly attack or casually side-swipe my most earnest passions and convictions. It was an error in the first place to think that, because of political agreements, I could collaborate formally with a publication whose basic view of life and the universe I regard as primitive and superstitious."[7]

Several years later, reflecting on the Eastman affair, Buckley maintained that a conservative can associate with an agnostic and even an atheist, but not a "God-hater" who regards those who believe in or tolerate religion as "afflicted with short-circuited vision." Buckley had asked Eastman to do the impossible. "The agnostic," wrote Buckley,

can shrug his shoulders about the whole thing, caring not whether, in his time, the conflict between the pro-religious and anti-religious elements within conservatism will be resolved. There are so many other things to do than think about God. "Are you anything?" a lady flightily addressed at her dinner table a scholarly gentleman and firebrand conservative who has always managed to nudge aside questions or deflect conversational trends that seemed to be moving into hard confrontations involving religion. He smiled. "Well, I guess I'm not *nothing*," and the conversation went on pleasantly. Max Eastman was nothing; and he could no more resist the opportunity to incant his nonbelief than the holy priest can resist the opportunity to prose-lyte; and so the tension.[8]

Eastman, however, could "shrug his shoulders" neither at the God that failed nor at the God that failed to appear, and he was too honest to refute Hegelian Marxism only to embrace Christian theism. He knew what he knew and what he didn't know. As for the "nothing" epithet, perhaps it would be more accurate to say that those who know nothing doubt nothing.

Eastman was eighty-one years old in 1964 when he broke with the *National Review*. At an age when most men are content to give up the fight and watch the world continue on its foolish ways, Eastman remained intellectually alert and his mind was as politi-cally alive as ever. He was vigorous enough to continue to reflect upon his own complex private and public past, and in 1965 the second volume of his memoirs, *Love and Revolution: My Journey through an Epoch*, appeared. Unlike the first volume of his auto-biography, which appeared in 1948, and which he enjoyed doing, the second volume was a "sad business" to write. To read over the old journals he had edited and see "the immortal elegance" with which he once espoused radical causes, and to know now that he was "dead wrong," brought "tears to my eyes."[9]

The many favorable responses to his autobiography, however, may have eased the tears of remembrance. Most reviewers found the work an impressive feat of art and recollection. In the *Saturday Review* Joseph Slater summed up *Love and Revolution* as "a sort of factual *Bildungsroman* rich and dramatic enough to compensate him—and history—for the fiction that did not get written." The anonymous reviewers in *Time* and *Newsweek* were put off by Eastman's egotism and by his timid, gushy descriptions of his amorous adventures, yet impressed by his intellectual honesty and self-criticism, "a quasi-religious scrupulousness, as if he will be punished severely if he leaves out a single embarrassment." In a long, respectful review in the *New Republic*, Joseph Featherstone called *Marxism: Is It Science?* "still one of the keenest critical studies of Marxist philosophy ever written." But a crucial review, by George Lichtheim in the prestigious *New York Review of Books*, can only be described as disappointing. Lichtheim praised Eastman's memoirs as a "monument" to the "vanished glories" of the "age of innocence" that had inspired the Greenwich Village rebellion. The German social democrat expressed as well a European envy for a writer who had the freedom and the good sense to disengage himself from politics to pursue, in a healthy, open manner, private affairs and "erotic conquests." "He was of course," Lichtheim chided, turning to politics, "strictly an indoor Marxman —not required to shoot anyone or even to denounce people for failing to be wholehearted about the Revolution." As an intellectual Eastman was also a dilettante. "Mr. Eastman is an ex-radical, but not an ex-professional. He was an inspired amateur from the moment a girl friend explained Marx to him in three easy lessons. (There is no evidence, despite his professions to the contrary, and an enthusiastic endorsement from Edmund Wilson, that he ever went deeper into the subject.)" Lichtheim's haughty dismissal reveals that he himself never went deeper into the subject. It is a case of a reviewer not doing his homework. Although he was one of the foremost scholars of Marxism in the Western world, Lichtheim was abysmally ignorant of Eastman's earlier philosophical critique of Marxism and his debates with Hook and Trotsky. All the more the pity, since Eastman's early work anticipates, in embryonic fashion, the epistemological problems in Marxism raised over a quarter of a century later by important European philosophers like Louis Althusser and Jürgen Habermas.[10]

Eastman spent the last years of his life following, for health reasons, the sun in New York, Barbados, and Martha's Vineyard, where he and his friends continued their practice of nude swimming during the summer months. He also continued to write for *Reader's Digest*. "I might be, from the point of view of aesthetics, a demi-prostitute," he joked. He became increasingly interested in animal behavior, and he analyzed the research of Robert Ardrey for the *Reader's Digest*. Obviously he was convinced that in the anthropological implications of zoology lie the refutations of socialism. Man's origins, instincts, and perhaps even his social institutions derive in large part from the animal's sense of property, territory, status, and prerogative. Eastman had a score to settle with the Right as well. More interested than ever in the philosophical riddles of ethics, he wrote an essay for the *American Scholar* on "The Cardinal Virtues," and his very last book, *Seven Kinds of Goodness*, was a lucid and breezy discussion of Buddha, Confucius, Moses, Socrates, Plato, Mohammed, and Jesus. By showing that there was more than one way to virtue and goodness, Eastman implicitly challenged Buckley's conviction that moral standards derive their validity from a belief in God. Eastman's gay and adventurous life ended—he died in 1969—in the same spirit as his rebellious career had begun, as the impious moralist whose politics needed no invisible means of support.[11]

Dos Passos, Goldwater, and Edmund Wilson

"I am not a conservative," Dos Passos remarked in an interview in 1959. "The conservatives must first discover what they have to conserve." That same year he wrote a foreword to Buckley's *Up from Liberalism*. Here Dos Passos gave his own neo-Jeffersonian interpretation of conservatism: personal liberty, decentralized government, the dignity of work, the value of opportunity, and the menace of bureaucracy. Dos Passos's passions were not an exact replica of Buckley's causes: God, free enterprise, abortion as damnation, and the menace of liberalism. Dos Passos's libertarian and Buckley's authoritarian conservatism added one more ingredient to the mésalliance of the intellectual Right in America.[12]

Dos Passos was among the early contributors to the *National Review*, writing in one of the first issues his serialized "Reminiscences of a Middle-Class Radical." The *National Review* had its share of journalists, philosophers, political scientists, and economists, but Dos Passos was the first important American novelist to identify with the magazine. His allegiance was deeply appreciated. An editorial by Buckley on "The Crime of Dos Passos" took on liberal and radical literary critics who dismissed the elder Dos Passos for losing the verve and passion that had once inspired his youthful social protest. Jeffrey Hart, the *National Review's* learned Dartmouth literary critic and Bolingbroke scholar, hailed Dos Passos as an anguished humanist at war with social institutions, a literary genius of "individual sensibility—outraged, suffering, disgusted, and defeated." Eastman said that Dos Passos's "incorruptible intelligence" shone like "a halo around his head."[13]

By the sixties, after the publication of *Midcentury* and *The Best Times*, Dos Passos had become an enigma and an embarrassment to the literary critics on the Left. He seemed a man without a cause, a prophet without hope who no longer thundered against injustice but had grown "crotchety" about union racketeering. Granville Hicks complained that Dos Passos had succumbed to "petulance" and "peevishness." Even Daniel Aaron and Dan Wakefield, two sympathetic critics, preferred Dos Passos's earlier rage of radical innocence to his wounded wisdom of experience. Aaron cited Blake: "The Tygres of Wrath are wiser than the Horses of Instruction." Gore Vidal was critical and caustic: Dos Passos was the "sour and mean" exponent of "our lost Catonian virtue," an old and tired novelist who "has mistaken the decline of his own flesh and talent for the world's decline." Maxwell Geismar was even more severe—this crude Parringtonian of the Left advised readers that "we should close our eyes to what Dos Passos has written since *U.S.A.*" Yet if judgment about Dos Passos's real value as an artist lay buried in controversy over his politics, judgment about his real character and integrity emerged as clearly as ever. That "dangerous honesty" of which Mike Gold spoke in the thirties still could not be denied, even by these new critics. Josephine Herbst was one of many writers who realized that Dos Passos's honesty sustained a nobleness of vision that could not be corrupted by politics. "Though I don't share his latter-day views," she wrote from France in 1963, "I don't despise them; far from it, they have relevance for they hold an odd residue of what was his profound reverence for life."[14]

The aging hero of the Young Americans for Freedom, novelist laureate of Buckley and the new American Right, infuriated his sympathetic critics on the Left when he became an arch-supporter of Senator Barry Goldwater. In 1964 Dos Passos covered the San Francisco Republican national convention for the *National Review*. He had always found electoral politics and campaigns distasteful. Nevertheless, as a journalist he described the maneuverings at the convention, the buzzing excitement in the hotel lobbies, the civil rights protesters out on the streets, the Young Americans for Freedom in the Cow Palace with their "We Want Barry" placards, the attempt of liberal governors Rockefeller, Romney, and Scranton to stem the conservative tide, the piles of technological gadgets and twines of electric cables on the convention floor, and the TV commentators who "sift and arrange events as they occur." Behind the scenes Dos Passos saw a power struggle with the promise of a healthy generational and geographical revolt. On the one side was the eastern establishment, politicians and opinion makers who had dominated government and business since the Truman era; on the other the "marching mobs of the frustrated," oppressed entrepreneurs, victimized small farmers, hard-working folk, and brave young activists "who look to the American tradition as the source of victories for individual opportunity." Clearly Dos Passos saw the Republican convention as a war between Main Street and Wall Street (Norman Mailer described it as "the Wagnerian drama of the Wasp"), and Goldwater as the Bryan of the young Right:

The place to see Goldwater at his best was at the Masonic Temple addressing an audience of YAFs. He is a Mason and he dearly loves young people. He is entirely at home. His two sons introduce him. He explains why his stake is in the young people. He and his wife have raised a family. They've seen their children grow up. To a certain extent they have grown up with them. He speaks reminiscently of the old days when they all went fishing and hunting together, camping out, looking up out of their sleeping bags through the pine-branches at the stars and talking in whispers about God and man.[15]

Goldwater's nomination lifted Dos Passos's spirits—he even suggested getting out a "new edition" of the *Federalist*, as though the bright-minted certitudes of the Philadelphia convention of 1787 had been brought back to life in San Francisco's Cow Palace. As the campaign rolled on in the summer and early fall and he realized that Goldwater's chances of winning the election were dim, Dos Passos lectured *National Review* readers on the moral and political significance of Goldwater's nomination. Ideas and principles can survive defeat, he wrote, and Goldwater's capturing of the Republican Party means that America has, for the first time since the years of Bull Moose and Bob LaFollette, an effective and meaningful opposition politics. Goldwaterism represents the negation of liberalism; and his presidential race, even if unsuccessful, can dramatize enough dissent so that the 1964 campaign "may well prove to be the opening of a consistent application of minority opinion to the power structure in Washington." Dos Passos wanted the Republican Party to win power in order the better to liquidate it, but his older anti-statism had softened in the sixties. It would be unwise, he advised Goldwater Republicans, to advocate "restoring free enterprise." Recent experience shows that "semi-socialized, semi-capitalist nations" are far more productive than both "completely" socialized economies, which have proved a "failure," and "pure" capitalism, which cannot succeed because it simply does not exist in the contemporary world. Dos Passos still believed that power breeds corruption as inevitably as organization breeds bureaucracy, but he was now willing to accept the "mixed economy" as efficient, rational, and progressive. He had come a long way since 1947, when he had denounced the British Labor government for ignoring the lessons of classical economics, believing with Eastman that democratic socialism paved the road to serfdom—a view that Buckley and Goldwater still shared. He had made his peace with Keynes, if not with Weber.[16]

Although Dos Passos had modified his attitude toward capitalism, his attitude toward communism remained as adamant as ever, and it was this issue that estranged Dos Passos from his close friend and best literary critic of the Old Left, Edmund Wilson—an estrangement that resulted in one of the great private literary-political quarrels of the 1960s.

Dos Passos and Wilson had been close friends for many years. When Dos Passos first met "Bunny" Wilson in the twenties, "a sandyhaired young man with a handsome clear profile" who, upon being introduced, proceeded to do a somersault, he took a liking to the "elfish" youth. Once, when swimming together in the heavy surf off Red Bank, the novelist and the critic became engrossed in deep conversation. (Dos Passos remembers the topic as being Henry James, Wilson as being Whitehead and modern physics.) While the waves pounded on them, and Dos Passos was "coughing and sputtering and hard put to it to keep from drowning, Bunny kept unreeling one of his long involved sentences in a quiet conversational tone. Except when he was interrupted by a wave's breaking over his head, he didn't miss a single dependent clause." In the thirties Dos Passos sent Wilson fifty dollars to pay for a needed medical checkup, and after the war he organized a literary committee to defend Wilson, whose book *Memoirs of Hecate County* had been suppressed by the state of New York as "obscene." Wilson, in turn, had taken a keen interest in Dos Passos's work. With the publication of each of his novels after *Manhattan Transfer*, Dos Passos could always count on a letter from Wilson, whose comments were intended not so much to praise a friend as to perfect an artist. Wilson often likened Dos Passos's work to that of the great Russian and French novelists, yet he did not hesitate to point out to his companion the "naturalistic impediments" in his writing: the awkward effort to mix didacticism with determinism, the lifeless dialogues of clichés and platitudes, and the inability to penetrate the minds of his characters. When Dos Passos wrote history or memoir, moreover, Wilson became a stickler for accuracy, correcting the factual details, the spelling and grammar, even the misplaced accents on foreign words. Wilson loved literature as much as life, and he knew that friendship could be constant even in criticism.[17]

Wilson was aware of Dos Passos's drift to the Right after the war. "We always speak of you with a toast and a tear," he wrote to Dos Passos from England in the early sixties, "but I suppose since your citation from Goldwater, you are insensible to such humble tributes." Political differences between the two had thus far been confined to private correspondence. But in 1963 Wilson wrote *The Cold War and the Income Tax*, and the following year Dos Passos responded with a blistering attack in the *National Review*. Wilson had neglected to file income tax statements for nine years, and when the government discovered the author's oversight, it proceeded to harass him with threats of imprisonment, fines, and royalty liens until a settlement was finally made between his lawyers and tax officials. Dos Passos could appreciate Wilson's "Kafkaesque" discovery of the power of federal bureaucracy, but he protested Wilson's reluctance to question the tax structure itself. In response Wilson questioned the military purposes for which the government spent the citizens' taxes. Reflecting on his own career, Dos Passos expressed sympathy for the "anti-militarists" and admitted that the "uselessness of war has been basic in my political thinking all my life." The cold war was another matter, and Dos Passos proceeded to justify the actions of the armed services, the building of bomb shelters (which Wilson had ridiculed in his book), and the development of antiballistic missiles. Wilson answered Dos Passos's "offensive article" in a personal letter from Paris. His defense of "the Army and Navy and Air Force men who are conscientiously trying to do their duty by experiments with new methods of warfare," wrote Wilson, quoting Dos Passos's own words, "reminds me of 'the final solution to the Jewish question' "; and your sympathy with the anti-militarists recalls Oscar Wilde on "these Christs that died upon the barricades"—"God knows that I am with them in some things." Wilson, who had been traveling through Poland and Hungary,

informed Dos Passos that communism in Eastern Europe would
never be able to suppress permanently the people's desire for
political independence; and the eradication of the antiquated
feudal regimes, he noted, has had a "stimulating effect" on the
youth in those countries. Convinced, like De Gaulle, that "old
fashioned" nationalism would eventually absorb communism,
Wilson asked Dos Passos,

What danger do you imagine the Soviet Union is threatening us
with? Invasion and occupation of the United States? I don't see how,
at your age, you can continue to believe in these bugaboos and see
everything in terms of melodrama. It seems to me that you are just
as gullible as you ever were in the twenties. I get more and more
skeptical myself.[18]

Wilson and Dos Passos continued to exchange heated letters
during the sixties. The novelist sent the critic his articles on Goldwater and the San Francisco convention. How can you take seriously, Wilson replied, a politician who wants to escalate the cold
war and at the same time eliminate the income tax? Goldwater "is
surely one of the biggest asses in our asinine country." But Dos
Passos loved his "chosen country," despite Vietnam and the racial
crisis, and when shortly afterwards he gave a pious lecture in
Rome, praising American society, Wilson lashed back: "And what
do you mean by saying that 'the plain men and women who do the
work of the world and cope with the realities of life'—these
phrases are hollow clichés in a class with the Communist 'toiling
masses'—'respond almost automatically to these values'? What
values? Different societies have different values. Then, later on,
you talk about the 'firm belief that good is good and evil is evil'
and an indispensable 'conviction of right and wrong.' Well, what
is your conception of these moral abstractions?"[19]

During this period both Dos Passos and Wilson were writing
American history, the novelist steeped in the moral certitudes of
the Founding Fathers, the critic in the "patriotic gore" of the
Civil War. And as the one grew more righteous about contemporary America, the other grew more skeptical. Dos Passos's pro-

nouncements on current events gave Wilson "the creeps," he told his friend, and the novelist's articles in the *National Review* "sound to me like some of the messages from Mark Twain and Oscar Wilde that are supposed to be transmitted through mediums." Specifically, Wilson questioned Dos Passos's conviction that the anti–Vietnam war movement had been taken over by communists. He conveyed to Dos Passos his belief that the Kennedy assassination was, if at all a conspiracy, most likely the work of the right wing, and not of Russian or Cuban communists. Then, drawing upon his travels in Hungary, he stressed to Dos Passos that even though Washington "stupidly refused" to recognize the Kadar regime, people behind the Iron Curtain "yearn constantly toward the West and especially toward the United States, which they—disturbingly to me—idealize." Above all, Wilson wondered whether Dos Passos really had it in him to be a cold warrior. "I note that you are having nowadays some difficulty in reconciling your early resentment against our government for vilifying Germany with your later complete acceptance of its behaving in the same way about Russia."[20]

As a former anarchist and pacifist, Dos Passos underwent a political metamorphosis under the impact of the Soviet-American confrontation. The more he hated Russia, the more he loved America; and the more he accepted the inevitability of the cold war, the more he had to accept the inevitability of big government and big business. His philosophy continued to rail against power and technology, but his politics condoned the power and the glory of the Pentagon, the very war machine he rebelled against in his first two novels. Starting with Jefferson, he ended with Burnham. Inspired by the power of reason, he embraced the logic of power.

Dos Passos's dilemmas resulted from domestic events as well. The novelist who once demonstrated against the ethnic and political discrimination in the fatal Sacco-Vanzetti trial now witnessed young white and black pickets demonstrating against racial discrimination in education and employment, and he found the civil rights movement a "very depressing situation" that had fallen into the hands of "very sinister people," as he told a reporter in 1964. "Black racists are as undesirable as white racists," and before any progress could be made it was necessary for the "level-headed members of the Negro community" to regain control of the movement. The novelist who had once gone to Harlan County, Kentucky, to publicize rural poverty during the Depression now criticized President Lyndon Johnson's "war on poverty" as a "phony" diversion conceived by "a man who lives and thinks pure politics." And the novelist who had once lampooned "Meester Veelson" for sending the marines to Vera Cruz now praised President John Kennedy for setting up a blockade around Cuba. Although Dos Passos had voted for Richard Nixon in 1960, shortly after Kennedy assumed office Dos Passos stated during the Cuban missile crisis that "Kennedy might just turn out to be extremely good for us. . . . I'm absolutely cheering for him 100% right now." Dos Passos no longer applauded when Kennedy lifted the blockade, and he remained disappointed with the rest of Kennedy's foreign and domestic policies. The young president's appeal was not altogether denied all the same. A year after the tragic assassination Dos Passos referred to the late president as a "very attractive flower." Even conservatives may yearn for Camelot.[21]

The youth rebellion of the 1960s caught Dos Passos by surprise, as it did so many others. In 1959 he had dismissed the "Beat Generation" of the fifties, and generational conflict in general, as a "crashing bore." He found the young of the "silent" decade corrupted by professors whose permissive and relativist ideas gave students nothing to react against. In this intellectual void of nonresistance, students desired freedom and opportunity yet craved security. Dos Passos was not entirely pessimistic. "When new rebels come along," he speculated, "something exciting may be produced."[22]

The sudden uprising of the New Left, however, was not what he had in mind. "Spooks out of the past," he scoffed as he rattled off the lessons of his generation: the Popular Front, the Oxford Pledge, Munich, Yalta, and Potsdam. Dos Passos could not see that the New Left was protesting, in addition to the Vietnam war, the very abuses of power that he had raged against his entire life: bureaucracy, technology, centralized government, corporate capitalism, the "multiversity," all institutions that deny the autonomy and humanity of the individual. He seemed unaware that the Students for a Democratic Society had openly denounced authoritarian communist regimes in Eastern Europe. Dos Passos did not sense that his own advice also resembled a specter out of the past. He chastised the student radicals for adopting the tired clichés of Marxism, stating that a "Left that is really new might be worth having." Yet while he asked the young Left to think "new" thoughts, his own thoughts on communism were distinctly old, stale, and perhaps a little paranoiac. "As some spiders anesthetize their victims before devouring them, the Communists endeavor to anesthetize the thinking strata of the nations that stand in the way of world conquest." Everywhere he saw a monolithic conspiracy, as though Stalin's ghost had returned to betray American youth the way he had been betrayed on the battlefield of Spain. "It is no accident that when part of a graduating class walks out on a speech at some American college," he wrote in the *National Review*, "the event coincides with the disturbances of certain self-styled Buddhists in Saigon." In 1970, when Nixon ordered the invasion of Cambodia, and students throughout the country rose in massive protests which led to the tragic deaths of four youths at Kent State University, Dos Passos, once the author of the anti-war *Three Soldiers* and an admirer of the conscientious objector Randolph Bourne, defended the invasion as "the first rational military step taken in the war." Dos Passos's last political statements have a monomaniacal sadness.[23]

By the end of the sixties Dos Passos was receiving letters of warm praise from Buckley, Senator Harry Byrd, President Nixon, and Vice President Spiro Agnew. He did not live to see Nixon, the get-tough anti-communist, announce his "détente" with Russia and China, nor to witness the Watergate scandals in the name of "national security"—the communist world recognized and rendered respectable, the American Republic shamed by her own leaders—the brutal ironies of the temptations of power. Dos Passos died innocently, in September 1970, at the age of seventy-four, without having to suffer the full consequences of his own politics.[24]

Herberg and the 1960s Heroes: Martin Luther King, Erich Fromm, Jean-Paul Sartre

Will Herberg did not appear in the *National Review* until the early sixties. In the previous decade he had still been publishing in mainstream intellectual journals like the *New Republic*, *Commentary*, and *Christian Century*. But the perilous optimism in the liberals' rational approach to knowledge and social problems continued to drive him further to the Right. One of Herberg's first articles for the *National Review* was on Reinhold Niebuhr, the saintly hero of American liberals, perhaps liberalism's best critic of itself. Herberg was the conservative Niebuhrian, in contrast to Schlesinger's Niebuhr; and to Buckley Herberg would be the answer to conservative atheism, the theologian who would save modern man from skepticism, nihilism, fanaticism, and pride. In the *National Review* Herberg intelligently defended genuine religion founded on sound theological doctrine. There were others, however, who appropriated similar doctrines for different political purposes. Herberg always knew there was danger that religion could be Americanized, but he had not fully anticipated that existential theology could also be politicized. Religion in the sixties made every man his own theologian and enabled every youth to find his own way to Jesus. Religion had become "relevant," but was it religion?[25]

The liberal is "the Jacobin *sans* guillotine," wrote Herberg in the *National Review*. Tracing the historical relationship between liberalism and secularism, he showed how the whole tradition of Western liberalism, beginning with the French Revolution, represented an attempt to dethrone religion by making it a "private matter" and excluding affairs of the soul from public life. Drawing upon Burke and Tocqueville, he argued the necessity of religion as a "civilizing force" that enabled the body politic to survive as a moral entity, yet he confessed uneasiness with the instrumental use of religion by conservatives. Religion must be something more than an "idolatrous cult" that sanctifies the existing social order. Rather, genuine religion must offer a perspective above and beyond society, a standpoint that "subjects it to a radical, and what must sometimes seem a shattering, criticism." Thus the authentic man of faith must protest against any Western religion which is "robbed of its transcendence."[26]

Central to Herberg's case for religion as the basis of the "New Conservatism" was the doctrine of natural law. He was aware that natural law theory had been discarded by modern legal scholars like Oliver Wendell Holmes, Jr., and Roscoe Pound, yet Herberg delved into intellectual history in order to demonstrate that "the conviction that all man-made law stems from a source beyond man, from a 'higher law,' and derives its legitimacy from that source, is one of the oldest and most fundamental convictions of mankind." Not only fundamental but vital, Herberg explained, as he proceeded to describe the dilemmas German Protestant theologians had once faced when trying to confront Hitler, armed only with a "Barthian transcendentalism" that offered no criteria for articulating an opposition, no ethical guide to political action against the Nazi regime. After World War II natural law regained respectability in the writings of Jacques Maritain; and even the anti-Thomist Niebuhr, Herberg observed, spoke of the "enduring structures of meaning and value." Only liberals, mired in cultural relativism and legal positivism, continued to regard law as either the legitimization of public opinion, or, as Roscoe Pound put it, "merely organized force." Herberg called upon conservatives to help persuade liberals to see their false assumptions and thus enable them to return to the "vital center" of America's moral and political consensus. "What, now, is the upshot of this survey?" he concluded after taking the *National Review* reader through two centuries of intellectual history. "It is that some doctrine of higher law beyond the sheer will of the sovereign or the folkways of the community would seem to be necessary if the right is not to be reduced simply to the power of the stronger."[27]

The doctrine of natural law is as politically dangerous as it is philosophically ambiguous. No sooner had Herberg expounded his view than Dr. Martin Luther King, Jr., began to lead civil rights marches through Southern cities. A former divinity student steeped in Kierkegaard, Heidegger, and Sartre, a doctor of theology who had written his dissertation on Tillich, King translated religious existentialism into social action in the name of the "higher" morality of natural law. Horrified, Herberg reached for his texts. He denied King's theological presumption that "unjust laws" could be broken as a matter of Christian conscience. Citing St. Paul and Augustine, he maintained that civil disobedience is justified only when earthly rulers demand the ultimate allegiance and worship that belongs only to God—in a word, idolatry. A year later, when the Watts riots erupted in 1965, Herberg singled out King and his followers: "If you are looking for those ultimately responsible for the murder, arson, and looting in Los Angeles, look to them: they are the guilty ones, these apostles of 'non-violence.' " Herberg now asserted, drawing upon Niebuhr, that justice is second to order, on the grounds that without order there could be no justice and no society. Herberg's argument overstepped itself and came close to sliding into secular morality. Presumably religion would now afford no transcendent perspective. The existing social order, however unjust, must be preserved at all costs; and the religious conscience, however virtuous, must be subdued. An argument that may have satisfied *National Review* readers, it hardly had solid foundation in existential or scholastic theology. Thus King could also draw upon Niebuhr (who supported the civil rights movement) to maintain that passive resistance was necessary because no privileged groups give up their social position voluntarily. Moreover, from the very doctrine of natural law that Herberg had espoused as the conscience of civilization King drew the conclusion that social acts should be judged in light of transcendent moral laws. Like Augustine, King insisted that unjust laws are no laws at all; and, citing Aquinas, he declared that "an unjust law is a human law that is not rooted in eternal and natural law."[28]

In the seventies, when the civil rights movement had subsided, Herberg would take a more sympathetic view of the black Americans' struggle for racial justice.[29] But the race crisis posed a serious dilemma for Herberg's theology. He assumed, as did other conservatives, that civil disobedience would be destructive of law and order, not that it might bring secular law into closer congruence with justice and morality, two central ethical principles of "higher law" theory. Confronted with the civil rights movement, Herberg was willing to allow the "folkways of the community" to prevail, and thus, in his own previous words, to reduce "right . . . simply to the power of the stronger." So much for natural law in action.

In the early sixties an even greater challenge to Herberg's theology came from a most unexpected quarter—the Holy Vatican. Pope John XXIII's liberalization of the Roman Catholic Church, once the bastion of natural law doctrine, greatly disturbed Herberg. To *National Review* readers he confessed that he once admired the Catholic Church as the "most significant positive force of the West" because it alone resisted the pressures of secularization in the nineteenth century. Pope John's encyclicals, *Mater et Magistra* (1961) and *Pacem in Terris* (1963), seemed to indicate that the papacy too was succumbing to liberal cant. Herberg was upset politically by the encyclicals—which endorsed the rights of labor, criticized capitalist materialism, and called for peace, disarmament, and world community—and he complained of the Pope's "silence" on communist totalitarianism. Theologically, he protested the assertion by some Catholics that the encyclicals were teachings whose authority derived from papal infallibility, a doctrine that relates only to teachings on faith and morals, and not to social and political issues. Thus Herberg hailed *Politics and Catholic Freedom* by the young Catholic classicist Garry Wills, who challenged the notion that all Catholics must give the encyclicals "interior as well as exterior assent and obedience." While Herberg bemoaned the drift of Catholicism, the behavior of Protestant theologians was equally discouraging. Protestants now applauded the Supreme Court decision of the early sixties that had reaffirmed the separation of church and state by prohibiting religious worship in public schools. As the author of *Protestant, Catholic, Jew*, Herberg shared the fears of those who believed that religion was dissolving into culture, but he maintained that they failed to understand that a political order attains legitimacy only insofar as its citizens recognize a "higher majesty beyond themselves." Americans have regarded themselves as "subjects of the Governor of the universe," Herberg insisted by quoting Madison, and thus it followed that Americans needed religious symbols and ceremonials in public life.[30]

Herberg was desperately fighting a leftward religious current in the sixties. The theology of the previous decade had dramatized sin, corruption, and the imperfections of the human condition. Translated into politics, these themes dignified law, institutions, and social restraint. The sixties witnessed a thoroughgoing reorientation of religion. The new antinomianism could be seeen in the turning away from theology to sociology, from God-centered dialogues to human relations and "rapping"; in the revolt against institutional authority, particularly among young clergy in the Catholic Church like the Berrigan brothers; and in the "festival of fools" ethos that overcame the previous pall of theological gloom as Harvey Cox replaced Niebuhr as the high priest of the era. The radicalization of religion helped produce a new breed of "mystical mutants," college dropouts and drifters who became either the flower children of the counterculture or the direct confrontationists of the New Left. In the *National Review* Herberg addressed himself to the alienation of the young intelligentsia in general and to the hippie phenomenon in particular. Deracinated youth, Herberg explained, have taken up their "positions of conscience" on Vietnam and racism, but such stances are the expression, not the cause, of their alienation and dissent. The intelligentsia, unlike the workers, had not been integrated into society and therefore felt more acutely the moral chaos and psychic rootlessness of the modern social order. As free-floating *"frondeurs,"* young radicals use moral causes as "both the mask and the instrument of revolution in our society."[31]

If the New Left sought unjustified power, the sin of the hippies lay in seeking unrestrained pleasure. Herberg analyzed in detail the hippie phenomenon for readers of the *National Review*. He was not alone in his curiosity about a new counterculture that defied old political categories. The historian Arnold Toynbee took a walk through San Francisco's Haight-Ashbury neighborhood in 1965 and came away convinced that he had witnessed a religious revival. The sociologist Daniel P. Moynihan asked, "Who are these outrageous young people? I suggest to you that they are Christians arrived on the scene of Second Century Rome." Herberg also acknowledged a religious dimension in the hippie life style, maintaining that the flower children resembled the Adamites, an anarcho-nudist sect of the early Christian Church. But Herberg was less tolerant than Toynbee and less affectionate than Moynihan. The hippies' sense of "primal innocence" left them without knowledge of good and evil; their antinomian hostility to all authority and institutions was politically unrealistic; and, above all, their mystique of love, their sole ideology of ecstasy, was merely "an orgiastic feeling in which they wallow in self-indulgence." Nor did Herberg give hippies credit, as did a few theologians, for injecting metaphysical questions into American culture. The thinking of the "inner expatriates" was more primitive than profound, and even their rock music lacked the angry, creative ferocity that characterized the poetry of the older beatniks. The unsentimental Lenin would have no use for these gentle "Adamites," Herberg told his *National Review* readers, and neither would St. Augustine. Let us not be seduced by those who are in love with love.[32]

Herberg regarded the New Left and the counterculture as products of the growing disintegration of modern American society.

But their *Zeitgeist* was the result of perverted ideas as much as social pressures. In effect, the radicalism of the sixties sprang from the liberal ideologies of the fifties, the son's errant deeds the result of the father's erroneous doctrines. Herberg's indictment of the liberalism that made radicalism possible can be reduced to three alleged crimes against intellectual history.

First was Freudianism. Herberg had little patience with neo-Freudians like Erich Fromm and Karen Horney, and in "Freud, Religion, and Social Reality," first published in *Commentary* and later anthologized in Benjamin Nelson's *Freud in the 20th Century*, he attacked Fromm in particular for domesticating the ideas of the great Austrian psychologist in order to render them compatible with American liberalism. Herberg enumerated the distortions: Where Freud was dualistic, seeing man's nature in conflict with itself at the very structure of the psyche, Fromm is harmonistic, seeing man as unified, intact, morally complete. Where Freud assumed a kind of biological Manicheanism that dramatized the tragic antinomies of existence, Fromm tends to an "extreme Pelagianism" that glorifies human autonomy and perfectibility. Herberg was closer to Freud in reasserting the irrational and aggressive nature of man against Fromm's claim that man is essentially good and rational and desires nothing more than human "relatedness" and meaningful "productiveness" in a society freed from the market place. He was also close to Herbert Marcuse, the Hegelian apostle of the New Left, who demonstrated persuasively that the revisionists had "mutilated" Freud's instinct theory. But while Fromm tried to transform Freud's pessimistic view of human progress into a therapy of redemption, and while Marcuse tried to introduce the notion of "surplus repression" in order to prove that Freud's harsh theories had been conditioned by the obsolete specter of economic scarcity, Herberg saw Freud as a brave stoic who had destroyed all illusions about the possibility of overcoming alienation, an honest atheist who conceived man as God (or nature) had created him—a bundle of contradictions.[33]

A second liberal fallacy led to the radicalism of the sixties. This

was the "Death of God Theology." How is it possible, Herberg
asked in a series of lucid articles in the *National Review*, for
Christian thinkers to claim that God, once so alive and well, no
longer lives? To answer the question, Herberg explained the implications of phenomenology, a branch of epistemology that identi-
fies being with meaning and thereby reduces truth to the needs of
the knowing subject. In view of this subjective criterion of knowledge, Biblical God has indeed lost meaning and relevance for
modern man, and contemporary theologians have now fallen back
on the pietistic cult of Jesus and converted Him into an exemplary
image of the "religious superman." Herberg traced this development to three thinkers he admired: Dietrich Bonhoeffer, who believed that the world had "come of age" and man was on his own;
Friedrich Nietzsche, who first cried out not only that "God is
dead," as his followers insisted, but that man had "murdered"
God and thus must suffer the "darkening of the world"; and
Martin Heidegger, who claimed that the modern age was a "time
of the gods who have fled and the gods who are coming." Herberg
pointed out that contemporary theologians failed to grasp the profound despair of Nietzsche and Heidegger, whose radical indignation was directed less at God than at man. He maintained that
phenomenological analysis cannot prove that God does not exist
but only that He has been eclipsed. "An eclipse of the sun,"
Herberg quoted from Buber, "is something that occurs *between*
the sun and ourselves, not in the sun itself." Herberg reversed the
atheistic conclusions of phenomenology: God the divine object is
still alive and well; it is man the dull subject who is dead.[34]

The eclipse of God also spelled the erosion of ethics—the third
fallacy of liberalism. In the *National Review* Herberg became an
authoritative voice on moral philosophy, addressing himself to
such delicate issues as abortion and the doctrine of separation of
church and state. Convinced that social problems are at bottom
moral problems, he believed with equal force in the existence of
immutable principles of universal justice and morality. The plight
of contemporary ethical thought, however, distressed Herberg, and

he analyzed its dangerous drift in "The 'What' and 'How' of Ethics," published in 1971 in *Modern Age*, a learned theoretical journal of philosophical conservatism.

Turning back to classical Greek and Hebraic thought, Herberg sought to demonstrate that moral truth was not something created but rather "handed down" and "received," timeless principles rooted in traditional values and ancestral virtues. Another strain of moral philosophy, however, offered a radically different approach. The ethics of contemporary existentialism, Herberg explained, can be traced back to Augustine, Luther, and Kierkegaard, all of whom expounded a variation on the theme of authenticity: "Love, and do what you will." This theme culminates in the philosophy of Sartre, who advises modern man to "Do it in freedom, and do what you will," and to create personal codes rather than be guided by public standards. "I am in bad faith," Sartre announced, "if I choose to declare that values existed before me." Thus it was no longer important "what" one believed but "how" one acted on his beliefs. The style of personality replaced the substance of morality. Even Sartre's Kantian dictum—"When you choose, you choose not only for yourself but for all mankind"—fails to resolve the problem of what choices the individual ought to make, particularly when every self is regarded as sovereign. Simone de Beauvoir, Herberg observed, believed the Marquis de Sade was a "great moralist" because of his "headstrong sincerity." According to this reasoning, the cult of authenticity led to a ghastly conclusion: The "what" (hedonism, brutality, murder, etc.) is nothing because the "how" ("sincerity") is everything. The upshot is that Sartre's moral philosophy is a philosophy without moral demands. Although Sartre had rightly located morality in individual consciousness, he reduced consciousness to an encounter with "nothingness," and hence his existential ethic lacked a moral imperative.[35]

Herberg was himself too steeped in theological existentialism to return to scriptural dogma or classical philosophy. He realized that thoughtless obedience to unambiguous doctrinal truth left little room for individual freedom and human responsibility. Thus he advocated binding together the "what" and the "how" in creative tension. Recalling Kant, he stated that "the 'how' without the 'what' is empty; the 'what' without the 'how' is dead." Indeed, knowledge of the "what," that is, an awareness of the content of moral values, actually implied the "how," a commitment to truth, genuineness, authenticity, and sincerity. But the latter could not be possible without the former. Herberg would agree with André Gide: "To know how to free oneself is nothing; the arduous thing is to know what to do with one's freedom."[36] "What to do with one's freedom"—that is the crucial question that moral philosophy must be able to answer. Herberg was convinced the answer could be found only by recovering a sense of "standards," which in turn implied a respect for the authority of "tradition."[37]

Herberg had effectively analyzed the fallacies of liberalism and radicalism that lie in neo-Freudianism, the "Death of God Theology," and existential ethics. But where does one find the grounds for "standards" venerated by "tradition" in America? This is precisely the question that has troubled all American philosophers of conservatism. To Herberg especially the question posed many difficulties. Fifteen years earlier, in *Protestant, Catholic, Jew*, he had found in America no tradition worthy of the name, save the insidious cult of "the American way of life." Responding to the book, the Unitarian historian Sidney Mead and the Catholic sociologist Andrew Greeley criticized Herberg for treating America's "civil religion" too harshly. In an essay written in 1973 Herberg revised his views somewhat, agreeing that the power of religion in America had served a positive historical role in forging unity, consensus, and stability. Nevertheless, what could be evaluated culturally could not be accepted theologically. Because civil religion in America had become so assimilated with American culture, Americans confused allegiance to their country with ultimate and absolute allegiance to Christianity and Judaism. Like Burke, Herberg saw that religion was useful; but unlike Burke, he was not content to allow sentiment, prejudice, and "untaught feelings" to determine the foundation of morality as well as stability. Civil religion, therefore, is still merely a "way of life," a system of mores and manners that reflect *how* Americans live but not a body of beliefs that illuminate *what* they should live for, and why. Religion in America remains a custom of morality without a real conception of moral life.[38]

Cold War Dialectician: Burnham versus George Kennan, Walter Lippmann, and Hans Morgenthau

Herberg became the theological conscience of the *National Review*. James Burnham had been its geopolitical theoretician from the beginning. He became acquainted with Buckley personally in Washington, D.C. He was named associate editor of the *National Review* when it published its first issue in November 1955. Since 1955 he has been writing a regular column in the *National Review*, "The Third World War," later, in the 1960s, retitled "Protracted Conflict." For almost a quarter century the cold war would be Burnham's biweekly vigilance.

Burnham found little to cheer as he surveyed the diplomatic scene in his early columns. The Korean war had finally ended, but it was militarily terminated, not politically consummated—the bitter fruit of the "limited war" doctrine that constricted the Truman administration. Reviewing the former president's *Year of Decision*, Burnham pointed out to *National Review* readers exactly at what turning points the "man of decision" recoiled from choice: holding back General Patton from advancing into Czechoslovakia, permitting the Russians to enter Berlin first, allowing China to fall, and going "along with Moscow on Tito." To Burnham even Truman's diplomatic achievements must have seemed like Emerson's "law of compensation": America saved Greece and sacrificed China, recognized Palestine and relinquished Poland, liberated Germany and lost Berlin.[39]

The Eisenhower administration was an even greater disappointment to Burnham and the *National Review*. In the early fifties

Eisenhower's Secretary of State, John Foster Dulles, had adopted the spirit of Burnham's doctrine of liberation. By 1956 the Republican Party had yet to translate doctrine into action. During the presidential campaign of that year, the *National Review* debated whether to endorse Eisenhower's re-election. Burnham and John Chamberlain, arguing against William S. Schlamm and Frank S. Meyer, supported the choice of the Republican Party. Burnham insisted that a third-party alternative would weaken the conservative cause and probably bring over to their side "fascists," "anti-Semites," and "cranks" as well.[40]

No sooner had Eisenhower and Nixon won re-election than the doctrine of liberation was put to its severest test. In November 1956, while the administration refused to support France's and Britain's attempt to regain the Suez Canal after Nasser had nationalized it in the name of Egyptian anti-colonialism, Khrushchev ordered Russian troops to move into Budapest and crush the Hungarian uprising. The State Department watched the bloodbath helplessly. Burnham refrained from offering a diplomatic or military solution to the tense situation in Eastern Europe, and the *National Review* offered only moral gestures. Editor Buckley advocated issuing an "ultimatum" stating that the use of Soviet troops against "any of the East European peoples would constitute a *causus belli*. We believe that Moscow would have to back down from such an ultimatum." The use of the future "would" indicates that the *National Review* was hoping for the best while refusing to admit the worst had already happened. If the Soviets do not back down? The United States, Buckley insisted, should withdraw its ambassador to Moscow and refuse to compete with Russian athletes in the Olympic games! Burnham and the *National Review* later criticized the Eisenhower administration for its restraint during the Hungarian uprising, but Burnham himself remained restrained and silent for more than a month during the crisis. When he finally wrote on Hungary he addressed himself to the demands of the rebels: representative democracy, freedom of opposition parties, abolition of the secret police, workers' control of industry and peasants' voice in determining collectivization policy, diplomatic independence and neutrality, but not, Burnham honestly admitted, quoting a Budapest radio broadcast, the return of "landlords, big capitalists or mining tycoons."[41]

The Hungarian revolt apparently chastened Burnham, for he now realized that any hope for attaining the rebels' demands could be entertained only by abandoning the doctrine of liberation. He called for the withdrawal of both Soviet troops from Eastern Europe and NATO forces from Western Europe. Burnham believed his policy would be attractive to the Soviet Union, now presumably convinced that it had lost control of the situation in the East, and always ready to experiment with Lenin's tactic of one step backwards in the hope that later the opportunity would arise to take two steps forward. This policy for neutralizing Central and Eastern Europe, which Burnham referred to as "the Austrian solution," was strikingly similar to Walter Lippmann's proposal in 1947, and one that George Kennan would advocate in 1958 as the strategy of mutual "disengagement." Burnham's new turn, in short, was tainted with liberalism, which probably explains why he failed to sell the idea to fellow conservatives. In the *National Review* Meyer and Schlamm maintained that Burnham's policy, based upon the premise that atomic war is unthinkable, substituted a strategy of gradual surrender for the conservative strategy of "aggressive pressure." Burnham also failed to explain why disengagement would be acceptable to the Soviet Union. The Polish and Hungarian uprisings were, after all, responses to Khrushchev's Twentieth Party Congress speech denouncing Stalin, a dramatic speech that was not published in the USSR but gained widespread notoriety abroad and helped spark rising hopes in Eastern Europe for political independence and liberalization. Burnham expected the Soviet Union to relax its grip on Eastern Europe just when its grip was slipping, and he never seemed to consider that Hungary's demands consisted of those "Western" ideas for structural democratization that would challenge, and thereby threaten, the bureaucratic despotism of the Soviet state.

Burnham was honest enough to revise his policy of liberation in response to the Hungarian tragedy, but his new theory of disengagement ignored the logic of totalitarianism—a strange oversight by the author of *The Managerial Revolution* and *The Machiavellians.*[42]

Disgusted with the Eisenhower-Dulles posture of stalemate, Burnham responded favorably to the new administration of John Fitzgerald Kennedy. At first he was impressed by Kennedy's strategic sophistication, his emphasis on paramilitary operations, and his "brave and lofty" words about defending freedom in Laos. Burnham was also impressed by Kennedy's Secretary of Defense, Robert McNamara, who finally brought some rational direction and coordination to the various programs of the Pentagon. In April 1961 Burnham visited Washington and described the good will and youthful optimism in government circles. Only the resigned and cynical veteran administrators saw the new president "as a young David facing the Soviet Goliath—but with no God-granted guarantee of the outcome; a youthful Perseus flying toward the dragon without benefit of magic sword or shield; a boyish Atlas bent under the strangling load of the million-armed bureaucratic octopus." Burnham hoped that Kennedy would be able to break through the State Department's bureaucratic inertia and reverse the "lethargy and creeping retreat" in American foreign policy. Strategic reasons dictated that Laos not be the place to embark upon this decisive new turn. Instead Cuba, where the rising "anti-Castro revolt does seem to have Mr. Kennedy's backing," is the beachhead where America may redeem herself. "What is crucial," Burnham told *National Review* readers in April 1961, "is that we should *somewhere*, in *some* theatre or on *some* vital issue, make a stand of unconditional firmness: that we should strike a blow against the enemy." Ten days later Burnham's hopes were dashed with the Bay of Pigs fiasco. Kennedy lost his nerve, Burnham complained, when he refused to provide air support to the invaders. Burnham now referred to Cuba as Khrushchev once spoke of Berlin—"a bone in our throat."[43]

Kennedy's adroit firmness during the Cuban missile crisis scarcely impressed Burnham. Although Khrushchev removed the missile sites, nothing substantial had been accomplished. The Castro regime remained intact, and communism in South America was still a threat. In Burnham's eyes Kennedy's halfhearted actions in the Caribbean foreshadowed America's feeble policies in Vietnam. In the early sixties he toured Indochina and described to the *National Review* the disillusionment of Asians with America's timid response to Cuba. He recounted General Bill Donovan's "domino theory," which presumably explained through the verbal ingenuity of metaphor why America's capitulation in Laos convinced the communists that victory in Vietnam was possible. Burnham was certain that America possessed the power to win in Vietnam but lacked the will and courage. "What if," he asked *National Review* readers, "the incredible chemical and biological weapons now available to Americans were turned against the Viet Cong and the North Vietnamese? If really massive combined forces were assembled from the U.S., Philippines, Free China and Australia? If Chinese north-south communications were cut, as they can be without too much difficulty? If operations into the Chinese mainland were launched?" Would not such actions precipitate nuclear war between the two superpowers? "Poppycock," scoffed Burnham: Khrushchev will not sacrifice Moscow to save either Saigon or Havana. Here Burnham could certainly cite Russia's backing down in the missile crisis, but he lost all sense of geopolitics when he spoke of launching operations into the Chinese mainland, as General MacArthur could have reminded him from the Korean experience. Nevertheless, Burnham's respect for power politics remained as pronounced as ever. Kennedy liberals, so squeamish about world opinion and so scrupulous about their own political purity, are blaming President Ngo Dinh Diem for their failures in Vietnam. True, the Diem government is not democratic, Burnham admitted, "but what sort of political cretins can they be who think South Vietnam could be ruled like England or Switzerland?" On one issue Burnhamite conservatives and New

Left radicals were in agreement: The struggle is against communism, not about democracy. In the cold war the Machiavellians and the Marxists had found a consensus.[44]

More ominous than Kennedy's tender democratic sensibilities was his nuclear test ban treaty with Moscow. As the President steered the bill through the Senate in 1963, Burnham protested angrily in his column, drawing parallels between the treaty and the Munich Conference, citing A. L. Rowse's *All Souls and Appeasement* as evidence that an "aggressive totalitarian movement" cannot be curbed by negotiation, compromise, and conciliation. Kennedy, it might be noted, had earlier reached this conclusion in *Why England Slept*, a Harvard senior's thesis published in 1939—when Burnham was arguing with Trotsky why one should sit out the war against Hitler. Be that as it may, Burnham saw in Kennedy's effort to relax tensions between the U.S. and Russia, and to find "areas of agreement" on which to build a "détente," a repetition of "the Yalta strategy." Specifically, the test ban would prevent America from continuing critical research and development of long-range armament and antiballistic missile systems. Generally, it was based on a set of widely shared and highly questionable assumptions. Khrushchev might want the treaty to lift the burden of the arms race off the Soviet economy, but that is no argument in favor of America signing it, Burnham noted. The treaty might inhibit the spread of atomic weapons, but is it not in America's interest to see the French develop nuclear capability? Everyone assumed the treaty would be a victory for Moscow over Peking, but Russia's strategy of covert infiltration is no less dangerous than China's strategy of overt revolution. Indeed, why, Burnham asked, should not America "seek to *increase* the tension that causes conflict between the Communist powers, that divide Moscow from its satellites, that set the people of the Communist sphere against their despotic governments?" The test ban treaty, Burnham concluded, only makes it easier for Khrushchev and his *apparatchiks* to preserve their totalitarian regime.[45]

As with the early Kennedy administration, Burnham saw in the first years of the Johnson administration the possibility that America would take the initiative and produce a decisive cold war victory. Lyndon B. Johnson's saving grace was geographical—he did not come from the eastern establishment. Only a man from Texas had the guts to spurn liberal "isolationists" and escalate the Vietnam war through systematic aerial bombardment. Burnham delighted in describing what liberals despaired in discovering: "So far as foreign policy goes, Lyndon Johnson expresses the same temperament and policy as Barry Goldwater. The citizens who in 1964 voted for Goldwater are today, in general, the firmest supporters, outside of the professional military men, of Johnson's intervention in Asia." Equally encouraging was the performance of Defense Secretary Robert McNamara, whom Burnham described as "a perfect exemplar of the top level of the new managerial class." McNamara was attempting to integrate the industrial economy and the war machine through "program definition, cost-efficiency, systems analysis, centralized procurement, computerized inventory control, ultra-speed internal communications, etc." Burnham, the technological elitist, was deeply moved, and in the *National Review* he wrote an intelligent defense of McNamara against his military and business critics on the Right and his intellectual and student critics on the Left. Soon Burnham himself became a critic. All along he had doubted whether Johnson, a consummate politician, would be enlightened enough to rise above partisan, domestic issues and devote his energies primarily to foreign affairs. By 1967 it became clear that the Johnson administration would not ignore the anti-war pressures mounting across the country. Burnham now criticized McNamara for failing to step up the bombing by knocking out North Vietnam seaports and destroying its irrigation systems and food supplies through "biological or chemical means." The State Department, Burnham maintained, was faltering not so much out of fear of risking China's intervention as of jeopardizing "the policy of Soviet-American convergence that dominates, in the last analysis, the Administration's global thinking." Since neither McNamara nor Johnson offered an aggressive alternative to the

Vietnam stalemate, all that remained was the "catastrophic" policy of gradual pullout. In the end LBJ, like JFK, had feet of clay.[46]

Developments in Europe were no less distressing to Burnham. The spectacular economic boom in the postwar years pleased liberals who saw industrial development as the answer to revolution, but the "theory of belly communism," Burnham noted, was contradicted by the sustained party strength of the French communists and the increasing electoral strength of the Italian communists. Moreover, the "opening to the Left" advocated by the Italian socialists, and endorsed by some Christian Democrats and even tacitly by the Vatican, conjured up in Burnham's mind the ghost of the Popular Front. Worse still, in France Charles de Gaulle, a patriot and Catholic, and once the object of Burnham's and Malraux's praise, now seemed a Napoleonic anachronism, a visionary who was playing into the hands of the Soviet Union with his lofty dismissal of ideology and his stubborn faith in nineteenth-century nationalism. While the president entertained illusions of French power, he refused to take communism seriously, advised America to forget Castro and deal with Cuba, and broke with London, Washington, and the Common Market, all of which endangered NATO. Only on one matter could Burnham agree fully with De Gaulle: As presently prosecuted, the war in Vietnam will be lost by the United States.[47]

Events in Asia also distressed Burnham. The Sino-Soviet split that emerged in the early sixties seemed to confirm what De Gaulle had always suspected—beneath the ideology of communism lay the deeper emotions of nationalism and the deeper impulses of power. Burnham did not deny that the Soviet state comprised a fusion of Russian and communist elements, even though, as World War II demonstrated, each element shifted in relative weight from time to time. What he denied was the ultimate historical significance of the Moscow-Peking rivalry. For the rift between European and Asiatic Marxist Leninism created the impression that there now existed two distinct communist postures: Russia's "soft" line of peaceful coexistence, and China's "hard" line of permanent revolutionary struggle. And this impression led to the assumption that the United States should support the policy of coexistence to demonstrate that the democratic West also desired peace. Burnham challenged these assumptions one by one.

The nature of the Sino-Soviet dispute is "verbal only," Burnham maintained. Peaceful coexistence versus revolutionary struggle is merely a debate "over how best to bury us." Burnham pointed to Zanzibar, Angola, and Yemen as evidence that Russia as well as China supported communist revolutionary activity, and to Indonesia, where both Moscow and Peking supported Sukarno's "crush Malaysia" adventure. The split is not between China and the Soviet Union but between Chinese and Russian communists. Burnham acknowledged the ethinic, economic, and cultural differences between the two great powers. But the split is basically a factional quarrel, an organizational struggle for control and direction of the world communist movement. From a Leninist perspective, the split could be viewed as an "intra-revolutionary dispute" in many respects resembling the old rivalry between the Bolsheviks and the Social Revolutionaries; and the debate over the "hard" and "soft" lines echoed the disputes that marked the earlier Comintern shift from the Second to the Third period, from the strategy of consolidation based on the apparent stability of capitalism in the 1920s, to the strategy of revolutionary offensive that began on the eve of the Depression. "Khrushchev and Mao take their stand foursquare on Lenin," Burnham insisted, and thus "the objective and the method of the struggle are according to the Communist mode."

What to do? Although it may be necessary to side with the "weaker" Chinese, America must do everything possible to exacerbate the split. We should use the UN, Burnham advised, "to needle Khrushchev with what Maoists have said about him, and Mao with Khrushchevian insults." America can even stoop to conquer. "We should actively help—in this case our means would have to be black—to establish anti-Moscow Communist parties in every country—Maoist parties, and where feasible Castroite, Titoist, Trotskyite or what-not parties, the more, and the more irreconcilable, the better." And America can also, Burnham suggested, drawing a lesson from the thirties, set up "front organizations" of youth, labor, students, peace groups, and journalists. Communism can be beaten with communism, counseled the ex-Trotskyist who once knew what it meant to be beaten by Stalin.[48]

Burnham had no qualms in advising America to become aggressive and take the cold war offensive. For what the Hungarian uprising proved is that the Soviets could handle their "domestic matters" without fear of outside interference. This was the essence of "peaceful coexistence," a doctrine that pre-empted Western interference only. The communists, Burnham maintained, operate on the assumption of two zones: the "zone of peace," the land under communist rule, is off limits, and any effort to disturb the status quo is considered counterrevolutionary and right-wing, to be crushed by whatever means necessary. The "zone of war" is the territory still free from communist domination, and within this zone any attempt that seeks to change or overthrow a government is "progressive," to be supported by "all freedom loving peoples." The United States has been duped into regarding Cuba and North Vietnam as "zones of peace," and hence America naïvely announces to the world that its foreign policy does not aim to overthrow the governments of Castro and Ho Chi Minh. The Marxists, it seemed, also had their corollary to the Monroe Doctrine.[49]

Any judgment one makes of Burnham's theory of the two zones is bound to be a matter of political sentiment. The point, however, is to match "selective indignation" with objective selection. If the Soviets engaged in two-zone diplomacy, clearly the West originated it with the Allied intervention during the Russian Revolution and Civil War in 1918–1920; and if the Soviets perfected it, the United States nonetheless practiced it—witness, for example, the State Department's role in the overthrow of Mossadegh in Iran and the CIA's involvement in subverting the communist-supported Arbenz government in Guatemala. As for penetrating beyond the enemy's borders, the Soviets take the low ground with communist spy networks, and America takes the high ground with U-2 reconnaissance flights deep into Russia's heartland. Burnham could complain that the Soviets supported and exploited revolutionary uprisings in Greece, Angola, Cuba, and Zanzibar, but he could not prove that they had created them.* In giving the Soviets more credit than they deserved, Burnham's thoughts once again reflect the mirror image of the communist mentality. As an anticommunist cold warrior, Burnham retained his Marxist vision of totality, the tendency to see all political phenomena as interrelated and emanating from a single source. It is not surprising that both Burnham and the communists had difficulty acknowledging indigenous nationalist movements, whatever their political nature, working class or bourgeois. Burnham detected the long hand of Moscow in communist activities in Africa, and the communists saw the long hand of Washington in counterrevolutionary movements in South America. Neither the Left nor Right, it seemed, could successfully take action independent of Russia or the United States. Whatever the validity of this world view—the Indonesians who took it upon themselves to oust Sukarno apparently did not share it—two could play the game while each professed clean hands. On the question of democracy, Burnham himself succumbed to the two-zone distinction. He accused liberals of being

---

* As to the distinction between exploiting and creating a revolution, we should return to the outset of the cold war. In The Struggle for the World, Burnham dramatized the Greek revolt of 1944 as a Soviet-inspired maneuver and thus the actual beginning of the "Third World War." Regarding a mutiny in the Greek navy, which he presumed had been instigated by the Moscow-controlled Greek Communist Party, Burnham wrote, "We do not know the details of what happened in the mutiny; but the details, important as they may be for future scholars, are unnecessary. We know enough to discover the political meaning of what happened, and for this details are sometimes an obstacle" (p. 1). A recent thorough and scholarly study of this affair, wherein "details" inform rather than "obstruct," presents a quite different picture of the "political meaning" of a resistance movement that Stalin himself would later allow to be crushed. See John O. Latrides, Revolt in Athens: The Greek Communist "Second Round" 1944–1945 (Princeton, 1972).

political "cretins" for refusing to understand that representative government and liberty are impossible in South Vietnam because of the lack of a democratic heritage. The logic of this rationale applies to Russia and much of Eastern Europe as well. Surely the Russians, the old fellow travelers used to chide liberals (as do the new pilgrims to Peking), could not claim to have lost under communism what they never possessed under Czarism. Burnham's two-zone thinking enabled him to defend the anti-democratic coup of the Greek colonels in 1968, but not to defend the democratically elected Marxist government of Salvador Allende in Chile in 1972. Determined to see the Soviet Union liberated in the name of democracy, Burnham was willing to allow democracy to be liquidated in the name of the "free world." It was all a matter of "zones." (Orwell, Orwell, where art thou now?)[50]

But moral judgment, as desirable as it is dangerous in the study of international relations, will probably not yield understanding of the cold war. Far more essential is a plausible mode of analysis with which to interpret the meaning of historical events. In this respect, it was the liberals who did not share Burnham's vision of the cold war—not the radicals. Burnham reserved his greatest scorn for writers who assumed "the Kennan-de Gaulle-Morgenthau-Lippmann approach" and mistakenly interpreted the Sino-Soviet split and Khrushchev's "de-Stalinization" policy as evidence that communism had run its course. Kremlinologists of this school perceived communism in the traditional categories of national interest and security, substituting for ideological clashes historical counters that arose from concrete geographical settings. These same writers asked Americans to understand that the Soviet's security concerns were similar to those of pre-Revolutionary Russian governments and, by the same reasoning, that America's national interest and security were not at stake in Vietnam. Such theorists take geopolitics too seriously, complained Burnham, who once believed that *raison d'état* and realpolitik gave the only true perspective on the cold war. "De Gaulle's theory and practice of international politics are based on the following conceptions: 1) the primary counters of the game are nations with deeply ingrained traits that change very slowly, if at all; 2) as a corollary, 'ideologies' (communism, fascism, Liberalism, etc.) are secondary and superficial; 3) the rules of the game are Machiavellian: significant moves express changing relations of power and interest, not ideological or moralistic abstractions about 'justice,' 'freedom,' 'peace,' or what not." De Gaulle's error lay in following literally the advice Burnham put forth in The Machiavellians: Power is everything, ideology nothing.[51]

Burnham, like Pareto, had once attacked as fallacious the liberal assumption that people act as they do because of the beliefs they hold. Then with the impact of the cold war, as we have seen, he was compelled to attack liberals for failing to take beliefs and ideologies seriously. In the late fifties and the sixties, with the ideological shift to the doctrine of peaceful coexistence, and with the development of the Sino-Soviet split and de-Stalinization, Burnham turned the angle of his epistemological prism once again. He now called upon Kremlinologists to concentrate upon deeds rather than doctrine. "Suppose we ask the experts what this dispute is all about. Can you prove it? Yes, they will reply, and they will produce hundreds of Soviet statements proclaiming peaceful coexistence and hundreds of matching Chinese statements denouncing peaceful coexistence and calling for revolutionary struggle." All such statements are "notoriously unreliable," maintained Burnham. "Let's forget for a moment what they say. What do they do?" he asked as he proceeded to use Zanzibar, Yemen, and Indonesia as test cases.[52]

Burnham had little respect for American scholars of the Soviet Union. In the fifties he blasted the Russian institutes at Columbia and Harvard, the "mass production . . . factories" of which "99 per cent of their publications have not the slightest intellectual, scientific, or political interest." A rare exception in American scholarship was Gerhart Niemeyer's An Inquiry into Soviet Mentality. Niemeyer's book demonstrated that communist behavior is not "rational," because it aspires beyond "the limits of normality in action"; that an "East-West dialogue" could not take place because of the communist *Weltanschauung*; and that "peace . . . is not possible with an adversary who rejects the very right of other societies to exist." Such conclusions were like an ice bath of diplomatic realism from which "nearly all Americans draw blindly back," observed Burnham, who praised Niemeyer for single-handedly "inquiring into the categorical presuppositions of our knowledge of Communist behavior."[53]

With what "categorical presuppositions" did Burnham now propose to explain communist behavior? Burnham's own perspectives had shifted with each episode in his intellectual career—from managerialism to Machiavellianism to Marxist Leninism. In the sixties many of the most prestigious American writers were articulating the Machiavellian, geopolitical viewpoint that Burnham had advocated in the forties. From this perspective of political "realism," Kennan, Morgenthau, and Lippmann interpreted the Sino-Soviet split as a nationalistic rivalry, and de-Stalinization and peaceful coexistence as the triumph of experience over dogma. In response, Burnham now challenged the American scholars' view of the Sino-Soviet split from a Leninist perspective as essentially a conflict to decide the question that had always been the crux of the inner-communist struggle—Who shall be master of the international revolutionary movement? Similarly, the riddles of Soviet behavior—that the Russians, for example, can "simultaneously want and not want coexistence"—must be understood by simple Marxist logic. "What the Kennans, etc., say is true enough (this is what gives it plausibility), but true only in one historical dimension of a multi-dimensional reality. They fail, a Marxist would say, to comprehend dialectics: fail to realize that simultaneously in our age there is taking place an international competition of national states and empires (new and old), as in the past several centuries, *and also* an unprecedented revolutionary struggle that is world-wide and civilization-deep." When Lippmann and Morgenthau tell us that American interest and security are not at stake in Vietnam, their "premise is based on a superficial, too mechanical idea of the national interest." And when they view the Sino-Soviet split as real and permanent, they are likewise reasoning mechanically rather than dialectically. To separate the strategy of peaceful coexistence from that of revolutionary struggle is to confine oneself to a one-dimensional perspective, an a-historical perspective that fails to see the conflict as merely an extension of the "old legal-illegal dispute," reform versus revolution. Rather than a renunciation of communism, the split is a phase of revisionism that will itself be revised in a revolutionary direction. "A true dialectician would see it as once more exemplifying the law of the unity of opposites. On a higher plane, the Russian thesis of coexistence and the Chinese antithesis of militancy fuse into a synthesis of true revolutionary struggle."[54]

Not until the end of the sixties did Burnham and the *National Review* grudgingly admit a genuine rupture between China and Russia.[55] Meanwhile, in order to drive home the significance of the dialectical viewpoint, Burnham purported to convey in his columns the communist vision of reality through the "eyes of the Kremlin." Striving for authenticity, he organized his columns as secret diplomatic dispatches to the CPUSSR:

To: The Secretariat
From: Intelligence Section
Subject: Weekly Summary, International (excerpts)

The present (or Geneva) period is characterized dialectically
in the following manner: a) thesis—unprecedented freedom of
maneuver for the camp of socialism; b) antithesis—unprecedented inertness on the part of the enemy . . .[56]

Burnham was convinced that the best way to understand Soviet communists was to see them as they saw themselves through the mediation of the Marxist-Leninist mind. Perhaps a student of R. G. Collingwood would appreciate Burnham's effort to "think himself into" historical action in order to discern the thought of his antagonist. But one wonders, for example, whether Burnham's Marxist-Leninist perspective could explain many of the cold war's erratic events and surprising turns. What would Lenin say of the sporadic uprisings in Yemen and Zanzibar? And Stalin, who never lifted a finger to help Mao or Tito, what would he say of Khrushchev's attempt to rescue Castro by planting missile sites in Cuba? And how would Khrushchev, who denounced the "crimes of Stalin," react to the New Left's exoneration of Stalin's role in the cold war?

Burnham demanded that every Kremlinologist become a "true dialectician." He was convinced that the contradictions in Soviet diplomacy could be seen as more apparent than real only when writers overcame a mechanistic, linear view of historical development and appreciated the "unity" that lay behind "opposite" tendencies—the "higher plane" of historical understanding. From this privileged epistemological position, he criticized De Gaulle and Kennan for not understanding "the enemy's dual nature," Russia's "synthesis" of Soviet nationalism and communist internationalism, of peaceful coexistence and revolutionary struggle.[57] There is an embarrassing irony in this criticism of the dichotomy of national interests and ideology, for it is precisely the indictment Trotsky leveled at Burnham himself a quarter century earlier. Trotsky also had been convinced that Russia was characterized by what he called, in his debates with Burnham and Max Eastman, a "dual nature," and he too believed that the "contradiction" between the Soviet Union's revolutionary ideology and Stalin's counterrevolutionary nationalism would resolve itself on the battlefield in a new fusion of war and liberation. But when Trotsky asked Burnham to accept the principle behind the paradox and support the USSR while opposing Stalinism, and when he called upon his American followers to discard the "banalities" of "common sense" and discipline themselves in the "dialectical training of the mind," Burnham replied, "I stopped arguing about religion long ago." As a cold warrior, Burnham was now, twenty-five years later, asking Kennan, Lippmann, and Morgenthau to take up again the "religion" of dialectical reasoning and to see Russia through Trotsky's eyes, thereby grasping the negation of peaceful coexistence ("socialism in one country") by the higher synthesis of "permanent revolution." With this demand, the epistemology of the cold war had come full circle.

Although no single writer dominated right-wing foreign policy strategy in America, Burnham's influence was considerable. In 1944 Burnham conducted research and analysis for the OSS, and in the early years of the Nixon administration he was appointed to review the publications of the United States Information Agency. Burnham's diplomatic writings, which span the entire cold war, had perhaps the greatest impact during the Korean war, when the Democrats' containment policy came under severe partisan attack. Townsend Hoopes describes well the atmosphere that made Burnham's offensive alternatives so attractive:

> In early 1950, there appeared on the Washington scene a small book which gave focus and a certain measure of intellectual respectability to what had previously been, in the main, an inchoate collection of doubts and anxieties. Written by James Burnham, a professor of political science at Georgetown University, *The Coming Defeat of Communism* expounded the thesis that, in its mortal struggle against the "Communist octopus," the West must now "turn to the offensive" for "if we do not smash the communist power, we shall cease to exist as a nation and a people." From a competent analysis of weaknesses in the "overextended Soviet empire," Burnham moved to the prescription of detailed measures for exploiting these, thus bringing down what he perceived as a house of cards. The book struck profoundly sympathetic chords in important segments of the State Department, the Central Intelligence Agency, and among military planners at the Pentagon. And when the attack on South Korea came a few months later, dramatically reinforcing the argument of those who already saw inadequacy in a purely defensive American response, there proved to be decisive sentiment in the upper reaches of the national security bureaucracy for putting the liberation-rollback doctrine to its first practical test.[58]

To the conservative Right, Korea was the turning point in the cold war at which America failed to turn. The Truman liberals rejected the counsel of the Burnhamites in the State Department, the CIA, and the Pentagon. The coming defeat of communism would be a long time in coming.

CHAPTER **10**

The Postwar Intellectual Right

Conservatism: "The Forbidden Faith"

American history, the graveyard of European radicalism, has also been the cancer ward of American conservatism. The very label "conservative" became a taint, and as the stigma spread into the larger political domain, the wisdom of conservatism was reduced to a whisper.

In 1948 the New York *Times* questioned leading American statesmen about their ideological convictions. All those interviewed, including President Harry Truman, Governor Thomas Dewey, Henry Wallace, and even Senator Robert Taft, identified themselves as "liberals." The following year Peter Viereck observed that "conservative . . . is among the most unpopular words in the American vocabulary. To be praised as a conservative has become an insuperable handicap." The Burkean scholar Raymond English summed up the dilemma of American conservatism in three words: "The Forbidden Faith." Conservatism suffered defamation not only in politics but in culture as well. In 1950 the literary critic Lionel Trilling went so far as to deny conservatism even the status of an idea.

In the United States at this time liberalism is not only the dominant but even the sole intellectual tradition. For it is the plain fact that nowadays there are no conservative or reactionary ideas in general circulation. This does not mean, of course, that there is no impulse to

387

conservatism or to reaction. Such impulses are certainly very strong, perhaps even stronger than most of us know. But the conservative impulse and the reactionary impulse do not, with some isolated and some ecclesiastical exceptions, express themselves in ideas but only in action or in irritable mental gestures which seek to resemble ideas.[1]

It is curious that the term "conservative" did become anathema, for Americans as a people can scarcely be described by any other political category. Political definitions are always hazardous, alternating as they do from one criterion to another as one examines attitudes toward change, class sympathies, programs, convictions, and ideologies. Nevertheless, it would be difficult to describe Americans as liberals, if by that term we mean a deep commitment to the Bill of Rights and the ideals of the Declaration of Independence. Nor would it be anything but a utopian daydream to categorize Americans as radical, a nation of people presumably about to break the chains of history and to abolish class distinctions and capitalist property. Perhaps Tocqueville's description of the mentality that tied together the Jacksonian and the Whig still applies to the mentality that binds together the Democrat and the Republican. The American, Tocqueville wrote over a century ago, is a person who desires change as much as he resists it, who stands in awe of economic transformation and recoils in fear of political radicalization. This "venturous conservative" (Marvin Meyers's apt phrase) enjoys equality of condition but rejects equality of conviction. With bourgeois liberals he denounces authority in favor of opportunity, but with bourgeois conservatives he quietly denies his individuality in favor of conformity. How does one define such a creature? Perhaps Louis Hartz is correct in saying that the American political character suffers from something of an identity crisis. Carrying Tocqueville's analysis further, Hartz persuasively argued that the American is a "huge hybrid figure," a schizoid personality who has never been quite sure whether he was a worker or a capitalist, or whether he loved democracy more than he feared the mob. Of two things he was certain: first, property; second, more property. This was the possessive individualism of Locke minus the moral individualism of Jefferson, or what Richard Hofstadter called the "entrepreneurial radicalism" of Jacksonian democracy minus the peripheral social radicalism of William Leggett and the Jacksonian Left. Opportunity, expansion, enterprise—these were the watchwords of a Lockian philosophy that has come to dominate American political culture since the mid-nineteenth century. More a compulsion than a conception, Lockianism is the Herculean life of action, composed of both liberal restlessness and conservative sobriety. It is a political life more driven than defined, less analyzed than acted upon. Thus at the base of liberal democracy in America is the conservative confusion of the American democrat—"a Hercules with the brain of a Hamlet."[2]

These problems of definition will become more apparent than real once we distinguish the idea of "philosophical conservatism" as it developed in American history. But first it is necessary to explain why, despite the essentially conservative temperament of Americans, the idea of conservatism itself fell into disrepute in the immediate post–World War II period. The reasons for the obloquy go to the heart of the conservative dilemma in America: resistance to liberalism. In the thirties Roosevelt's New Deal did more than any other modern political movement to revive the ideology of liberalism. At the same time, and with an irony that frustrated both the Left and the Right, it made Americans more conservative than ever by integrating the mass of citizens into the security of the welfare state as the Republican Party's opposition to the New Deal, and its Midwestern opposition to Roosevelt's foreign policy after the outbreak of World War II, were repudiated again and again at the polls, climaxed by Truman's stunning upset of Thomas Dewey in 1948. In domestic politics and international affairs conservatism took on a negative connotation and became identified with the discredited economic individualism of Herbert Hoover and the diastrous diplomatic isolationism of Robert Taft. Until the appearance of Barry Goldwater in the sixties, conservatism was the kiss of political death in America.

In the early years of the Republic, conservatism had been a badge of honor. Indeed the Federalist era might be characterized as the "golden age" of American conservatism, the last period in history when the country enjoyed a brilliant fusion of power and intellect. Although gripped by dark thoughts, early American conservative thinkers were inspired by high hopes. Self-made demi-aristocrats, they were perhaps the first political philosophers in modern history who wrote a constitution to check the power of their own class. Thanks to the framers, American conservatism began on a genuinely lofty plane. James Madison, Alexander Hamilton, John Marshall, John Jay, James Wilson, and, above all, John Adams aspired to create a republic in which the values so precious to conservatives might flourish: harmony, stability, virtue, reverence, veneration, loyalty, self-discipline, and moderation. This was classical conservatism in its most authentic expression. Critical, reflective, deeply conscious of history and tradition, and endeavoring to elevate political society to the highest possible standards of excellence, this is the meaning of "philosophical conservatism." Dos Passos was right to return to the Founding Fathers in order to recover the forgotten truths of the past; and Eastman too could have found a healthy streak of skepticism in Madison, Herberg a deep sense of sin in Adams, and Burnham a keen grasp of power in Hamilton.

There was, however, an ironic flaw in the conservative thought of the Founding Fathers—or perhaps more accurately, a hidden liberal premise. Although they believed in the dignity of man, they created a government in which there would be no need for the man of dignity. With a touch of generational egotism, the framers were convinced that future America could not count on the reappearance of leaders of their caliber. Good government, not good men, would save the Republic. Thus the Founding Fathers devised a well-functioning "machinery of government" built upon a geometric equilibrium of "checks and balances" and division of powers. Here lies the paradox. At its best, conservatism is a philosophy of moral and aesthetic sensibility, yet the framers developed a Constitution based upon mechanical contrivance. How could the human principles they esteemed (e.g., "virtue") be realized when politics is taken out of the realm of conscience and reduced to a system of mechanisms? How could interest politics (e.g., "factions") be elevated to moral politics? In short, can personal values be derived from the functioning of impersonal institutions, and can a good mechanical whole be constructed out of defective human parts? Raising such questions is merely another way of saying that the Founding Fathers started with conservative concerns and arrived at liberal conclusions. Or to state it another way, they bypassed John Adams, who preferred the concept of virtue to the chaos of freedom. The *Federalist* and the Constitution represent the eclipse of political and moral authority and the legitimization of pluralism, individualism, and materialism, the very Lockian liberalism that would remain hanging like an albatross around the neck of the conservative intellect in America.

With the advent of Jacksonian democracy, classical American conservatism passed into oblivion. When the commercial-minded Whigs replaced the patrician-minded Federalists as the party of the Right, Lockian liberal capitalism absorbed the entire political spectrum. Moreover, the day of the intellectual elite in politics ended as power passed to the arriviste of banking and manufacturing. And by 1840 even the "conservative" Whigs, after unsuccessfully resisting universal suffrage, found that they too could stoop successfully to mass politics. Adopting "log cabin" candidates, the Whigs joined the Jacksonian Democrats and went whoring after the "common man." Whatever its achievements in formulating programs for economic development, American Whiggery became the philosophy of opportunity and banality. "Of all the parties that have existed in the United States," wrote the young conservative Henry Adams, "the famous Whig party was the most feeble in ideas." As liberalism became identified with the anti-intellectual vulgarities of Jacksonian politics, and conservatism became synonymous with the squalid growth of commercial capitalism, the American intellectual often found himself alienated from political life. The Transcendentalists could only conclude what John Adams had feared and Tocqueville had confirmed: political thought would be at the mercy of public opinion, and the demands of truth would be sacrificed to the "tyranny of the majority." In an age of mass politics and economic activity, conservatism no longer had claim to philosophical dignity. Inspired by power alone, it lost its power to inspire. "Conservatism," wrote Emerson, "makes no poetry, breathes no prayer, has no invention; it is all memory."[3]

"Memory" is indeed the appropriate word to describe the quality of conservative thought that lingered in the South. The antebellum South, as Hartz has shown, was the only region that seemed to escape the Lockian liberalism that had consensualized the American political mind. Against the Northern doctrines of democracy, liberty, and individualism, the South responded with an ideology that stressed the virtues of aristocracy and authority, the delusions of natural-rights liberalism, the permanency of class divisions, and the primacy of organic community. In reality, however, Southern conservatism was half rhetoric and half romance. For one thing, the Southern economy belied the neo-feudal pretensions of Southern writers like John C. Calhoun and George Fitzhugh. The supposed aristocratic virtues of the Southern planters rested as much on market profits and entrepreneurial enterprise as did the economy of the industrial North. The imperatives of economics killed the "feudal dream" of the South, forcing Southern "gentlemen" to live with the bourgeois values of the nation at large, even while attacking the "cupidity" of those capitalist values. Moreover, the South was just as ambivalent about liberalism. Although Calhoun brilliantly developed an organic, Burkean theory of society and tradition in order to repudiate the contractual rationalism of Locke and the natural rights doctrines of Jefferson, he was compelled to draw upon that Lockian-inspired, Jeffersonian document, The Declaration of Independence, as his only means of justifying state sovereignty and the revolutionary right of secession. The embarrassing disjunction of the Southern mind is best captured in Hartz's felicitous phrase "the reactionary Enlightenment." The phrase is packed with irony. Calhoun not only used the doctrine of the natural rights of man to resist the emancipation of man, he tried to oppose the heresies of liberalism by invoking the heritage of liberalism.[4]

Whither American conservatism? Stained by the sin of slavery and racism in the South, driven out of national life by the pursuit of property, and purged from political discourse by the pervasive language of Locke, genuine philosophical conservatism could find refuge only in the classical literature and philosophy of the nineteenth century. In the psycho-metaphysical allegories of Nathaniel Hawthorne and Herman Melville, in the anti-egalitarian social novels of James F. Cooper, and in the theological discourses of Horace Bushnell and Orestes Brownson, American conservatism survived, however obliquely, as a cultural force. Here one finds the most penetrating analysis of the two foundations of modern liberalism and radicalism: eighteenth-century French Enlightenment, and nineteenth-century German idealism. Over these two radiant philosophies fell "the power of darkness" (Harry Levin's phrase). Hawthorne and Melville especially exposed the impulses of egotism hidden in the soul of everyman. The great "sin of intellectual pride" was the refusal to acknowledge the reality of evil, the opacity of knowledge and experience, the ambiguities of human nature, and the illusions of progress and perfectibility. The radical quest for innocence was an attempt to deify man and naturalize God, both of which remained as "inscrutable" as Melville's white whale. For the conservative intellectual, wisdom begins where *Moby Dick* ends—in the recognition of the tragic limitations inherent in the human condition.

Such recognition scarcely characterized what passed for conservative thought in late nineteenth- and twentieth-century America. After the Civil War, industrialists and financiers engaged in what Clinton Rossiter has wryly termed "the great train robbery of American intellectual history." All that was best in the conservative tradition was misappropriated and made into an apologia for laissez-faire economics. Turning Hamilton on his head, American capitalists became the first Right in history to turn against the constructive power of the state. Turning Jefferson inside out, they used the Constitution to assert the inviolability of property rights over human rights. As the old order gave way to plutocracy, conservatism became identified with industrialism, Social Darwinism, the gospel of success, and the Algerism of self-help. The result was that nineteenth-century conservatism became almost indistinguishable from liberalism. Committed to capitalism, both conservatives and liberals dabbled in civic reform, debated the tariff, and shared a creed of cosmic optimism. Those who regarded themselves as conservatives in the nineteenth century represented a curious anomaly—the first Right in history to turn its face bravely toward the future. Only a handful of alienated American intellectuals, perhaps best epitomized by Henry Adams and Mark Twain, looked forward with fear and backward with hope, reaching deep into the past to find the sense of order and unity that Dos Passos yearned for in his later writings. In an age of exuberant optimism, it was the dissenting intellectuals who again displayed a solemn pessimism that was characteristically conservative.[5]

In the twentieth century, laissez-faire conservatism, the ideology of big business, was challenged by the liberal progressive movement, a political phenomenon that was itself ambiguous about the values of capitalism and individualism. Philosophical conservatism remained as isolated as ever from the mainstream of political life. George Santayana, America's greatest conservative philosopher, exiled himself from an American culture which, the aesthetician of beauty protested, stifled art and starved the spiritual imagination. America's greatest conservative poets, T. S. Eliot and Ezra Pound, also failed to find aesthetic and spiritual nourishment in America. Between the two world wars, philosophical and literary conservatism, the highest expression of conservatism as a body of transcendent principles, survived only in two countertendencies in American thought that came to be known as "New Humanism" and "Southern Agrarianism."

Led by Paul Elmer More and Irving Babbitt, the New Humanists were at war with both history and modernity, with the shallow "genteel" culture of polite and practical idealism of the late nineteenth century, and with the contemporary liberal culture of innovation and freedom, flux and chaos. (More, it will be recalled, likened Dos Passos's *Manhattan Transfer* to "an explosion in a cesspool.") The New Humanists stood for standards, tradition, form, decorum, duty, and the ethical imperative of the "inner check." They drew upon a syncretic intellectual heritage that embraced Buddhism as well as Platonism, and their ideals were harmony, restraint, repose, and the stillness of desire. The New Humanists defended the seventeenth-century Puritans against contemporary Freudian and Marxist critics who, like Eastman and the young Herberg in the twenties, saw religion as a mechanism of repression and thereby remained blind to the moral heroism exemplified in the Calvinist life of austerity. The New Humanists went even beyond Puritanism in their ontological beliefs. Against the culture of Protestantism, liberalism, and Marxism they substituted for the doctrine of work something approaching the doctrine of grace—the labor of the heart, self-regeneration. Their political philosophy had no basis in American values or traditions. Peter Viereck claims that Babbitt and More are "the legitimate heirs of our classic conservatives of the Federalist Papers," but the New Humanists went far beyond the Founding Fathers in their crusty political elitism. The framers gave us a government of mechanisms, not of men, whereas the New Humanists desired to see a timocracy, a government ruled by men of honor. America must substitute "the doctrine of the right man for the doctrine of the rights of man," advised Babbitt in 1924. Madison devised a Constitution to prevent exactly what Babbitt prescribed.[6]

During the early years of the Depression the Southern Agrarians emerged as the new force of critical conservatism in America. This literary intelligentsia included Donald Davidson, John Crowe Ransom, Allen Tate, Robert Penn Warren, and Stark Young. Originally called the "Nashville Fugitives," they were later joined by a group of distributists, among them the historians Herbert Agar and Frank Owsley. In 1930 the Agrarians issued a manifesto, *I'll Take My Stand*, and a few years later they published *Who Owns America?* and contributed to Seward Collins's *American Review*, the major philosophical forum of the right-wing cognoscenti in the thirties. Here the Agrarians attacked modern industry, technology, and science as the sources of the deracinated fragmentation of modern man. One of their enemies was the radical empiricist Max Eastman, who claimed in *The Literary Mind* that poetry would soon yield to science the task of interpreting experience. For the Agrarians as well as the New Humanists, literature and poetry constituted the real repository of value and meaning, the last refuge of intelligence in a scientific culture that can only answer "how" when man desperately asks "why." Like religion, poetry affords an intuitive feeling for the particular, the concrete, and the contingent, a reverence for the intangible and the immeasurable, and a humility before the mysteries of character.

Defenders of tradition in aesthetics, the Agrarians advocated a Burkean worship of continuity and the organic in politics. Regional self-determination and the supremacy of agricultural life was the South's answer to Northern capitalism. Less Calhoun's feudalistic fantasy, however, and more Jefferson's yeoman idyll inspired the contemporary Southern literati. Although they shared some of the political elitism of the New Humanists—and a few succumbed to racist utterances—their social and economic doctrines were profoundly radical. Influenced by the English distributists G. K. Chesterton and Hilaire Belloc, the American Agrarians demanded that the industrial economy be decentralized, that government purchase the property of corporate and absentee owners, insurance companies, and some large planters, and that land be redistributed to the landless. The way back to conservatism was through the soil, particularly the good earth that nourishes the concrete organic community, like that of the Old South. In offering such proposals, Southern writers, fired by nostalgic romance, may have revived what Richard Hofstadter called, in reference to nineteenth-century populism, "the agrarian myth"—the notion that the American farmer was a humble toiler more interested in the value of the land than in land values. But the Southern Agrarian at least took seriously both sides of the Jeffersonian heritage: All men have the right of property and—the forgotten ideal—the right to property.

Qualify the last statement by inserting the implied restriction, "for all white men," and one can understand why the distributists had little appeal to intellectuals outside the South. In fact, in the thirties New Humanism and Southern Agrarianism were attacked by the Left as expressions of native American "fascism." The charge is unfair; still, the conservatives did love community and morality more than democracy and liberty, and the *American Review* did support Mussolini and Franco while chastising the Soviet "experiment" so dear to liberals. Such heated issues cut off all possible dialogue between the literary Right and the Marxist Left in the thirties. Curiously, three decades later it was not the Old Left but the young student New Left, with its pastoral idyll of small self-sufficient communities pursuing happiness through the joys of soil labor and craftsmanship, that would raise again the questions of decentralization that had occupied the Agrarians. Technology's children would find in rock music and drugs what the older conservatives had claimed for poetry—imagination, mystery, and the inviolability of consciousness against the threat of science. The link between the Old Right and the New Left is not made to argue a generational continuity but only to suggest why they both failed, why they were defeated by the common enemy: liberalism.

In the years immediately following World War II the ideology of liberalism, "the vital center," as Arthur Schlesinger, Jr., put it, temporarily flourished while conservatism lay in limbo. Philosophical conservatism had been disgraced by its apparent support for the lost causes of the European Right, and economic conservatism, as we have seen, had been repudiated because of its opposition to the New Deal. After 1949 liberalism also found itself on the defensive. The unfulfilled promises of the welfare state and the persistence of business cycles and recessions cast doubt upon the liberal idea of a regulated economy. Even more seriously, the advent of the cold war dampened liberal hopes for a rapprochement with the Soviet Union, and the resurgence of Stalinist terrorism, dramatized in the Czechoslovakia coup of 1948 and later in the anti-Semitic "doctors' plot" of 1952, dispelled for good the liberals' image of the USSR "as a kind of enlarged Brook Farm community, complete with folk dancing in native costumes, joyous work in the fields and progressive kindergartens."[7] The words are Schlesinger's, one liberal who was willing to admit that liberalism had not prepared American intellectuals for Stalin. The apparent failure of the Left to meet the challenge of communist totalitarianism discredited liberalism and helped shape the mood of disillusionment from which the intellectual Right drew its appeal. With liberalism at bay, William F. Buckley emerged seemingly out of nowhere to forge an intellectual movement that came to be known as the "New American Conservatism." Buckley was the catalysis and synthesis of the intellectual Right in postwar America, the first editor to attempt to integrate the new anti-communist conservatism with the older traditions of philosophical conservatism discussed above. Combining Burnham and Burke, the *National Review* answered the fears of the present with the faiths of the past.

The postwar conservative revival, in part a product of anti-communist tensions, derived from a variety of sources. Most prominent in wider intellectual circles was Peter Viereck, the poet-historian of aristocratic sensibilities and democratic sympathies. Viereck's *Conservatism Revisited* (1949) attempted to define neo-conservatism as "the rediscovery of values" in the cultural context of classicism and humanism. It was also an effort to rehabilitate the historical role of Count Metternich, not as the dark reactionary and enemy of liberalism, but as the responsible statesman whose answer to revolution was the slow ripeness of wisdom that lay in gradualism and social reform—"*le socialiste conservateur.*" Viereck's thankless effort to synthesize philosophical conservatism with political liberalism, evidenced by his support of the New Deal and his enthusiastic backing of Adlai Stevenson, appeared to *National Review* intellectuals as a halfway covenant with the devil.[8]

Far more acceptable was Russell Kirk, the philosopher-hero of the *National Review. Kirk's The Conservative Mind* (1953) offered Americans an elegant explication of the philosophical and literary implications of "critical conservatism." Deeply influenced by Burke, and indebted to Babbitt and the New Humanists, Kirk elaborated six canons of conservative thought: (1) that society is ruled by "divine intent," and hence political problems are basically moral and religious problems; (2) that one must respect the "proliferating variety and mystery of traditional life"; (3) acknowledge that "civilized society" requires distinct class strata; (4) accept the inseparable connection between property and freedom; (5) believe in the politics of prescription, since only "tradition and sound prejudice provide checks upon man's anarchic impulses"; and (6) recognize that change and reform are not identical, since organic change conserves the past, while innovative reform devours it. Kirk is a Burkean with tears. His English idol could love his country because his country was lovely, and he could therefore defend the existing order as he wrote lyrically about the merry countryside; Kirk, in contrast, is a discontented intellectual in an industrial nation that is "ugly," "sterile," and "purgatorial." Passionately intent on restoration rather than conservation, he longs for the eighteenth-century world of John Randolph, a world that would not stand still even for Randolph or Fisher Ames. Although hailed by Goldwater and the Cadillac conservatives of modern suburbia, Kirk himself lived in an ancestral home in Mecosta, Michigan. For a long time he drove a 1930 Chevrolet, and he composed his thoughts on his "great-uncle Raymond's typewriter, an L. C. Smith, No. 1, circa 1907." In *Confessions of a Bohemian Tory,* Kirk described himself as possessing a "Gothic mind, medieval in its temper and structure. I did not love cold harmony and perfect regularity of organization; what I sought was variety, mystery, tradition, the venerable, the awful." Kirk's honest, independent philosophical stance illustrates how far Burkean conservatism was from the American conservatism of rugged individualism. Even Goldwater did not pay him the compliment of reading his works. Kirk's universe is the dark, shadowy world of Coleridge and Hawthorne, impenetrable to the disciples of Coolidge and Hoover.[9]

The postwar conservative revival saw a rich harvest of philosophical rumination. Recoiling from the experience of European totalitarianism, intellectuals in almost every discipline submitted the entire tradition of Western thought to intense scrutiny, as though one could find in intellectual history the precise moment when the mind of modern man had lost its soul. In *Metapolitics* Viereck had earlier argued that the descent into political hell began with German Romanticism. For the neo–Southern Agrarian Richard Weaver the primal fall occurred in the fourteenth century, when the nominalism of William of Occam replaced spirit for phenomena. Eric Voegelin traced it to Joachim of Flora, the twelfth-century Christian whose gnostic belief in the "redivinization of society" through the symbol of the Holy Trinity expressed the chiliastic hypostasization of history that would later manifest itself in the dialectic of Hegel and Marx. Other philosophers moved the analysis forward to the eighteenth century. The French Enlightenment was seen as the erosion of democracy's moral foundations (John Hallowell), the era when historical experience was rejected for an ideology "independently premeditated" through "rationalism" (Michael Oakeshott), a period when Machiavelli and Locke culminated in the empiricist separation of values from facts in the name of a political "science" no longer concerned with the ultimate ends of political life (Leo Strauss). Catholic conservatives like Anthony Harrigan, Frederick Wilhelmsen, and Ross J. S. Hoffman joined in the revolt against modern secularization, assimilating Aquinas and Burke in a philosophy that made the divinely ordered state as sacred as the nuclear family. Not all conservative intellectuals felt it was necessary to do God's work. A yawning gulf, for example, separated Viereck's respect for reason and Kirk's faith in religion.[10]

In the fifties conservatism enjoyed a vogue on college campuses, particularly at the University of Chicago, where Leo Strauss and Milton Friedman turned out budding political philosophers of ethics and, ironically, free market economists who had no need for ethics; and where, to add to the irony, the historian Daniel J. Boorstin claimed that the "genius" of Americans was their ability to live without political philosophy or economic theory. In the academic community at large there were no common theoretical premises even within common subjects. In no discipline were the differences greater than in economics, which encompassed the corporatist capitalism of Peter Drucker, the classical laissez-faire school of Friedman, and the anarcho-libertarianism of Murray Rothbard. Such dissenting tensions could be found in other fields as well. Philosophers William Ernest Hocking and Mortimer Adler differed over the validity of Thomistic metaphysics, literary critics Hugh Kenner and Eliseo Vivas over the ontological status of poetry, psychologists Ernest van den Haag and Richard LaPiere over the meaning of Freud, and sociologists Robert Nisbet and Talcott Parsons over the importance of structural functionalism. In the discipline of political science, Willmoore Kendall looked to the Madisonian mechanisms of government to resolve social conflicts, while Harry V. Jaffa maintained that government rises to greatness only with the appearance of great men like Lincoln, whose achievement could be understood not on the basis of the *Federalist* but on that of *The Nicomachean Ethics*. And in American history Samuel Eliot Morison tried to restore the life of the mind in the American past, while Boorstin wrote three volumes to prove that it did not exist.

Despite the lack of consensus, or perhaps because of it, conservative periodicals sprouted like lilies in the field during the fifties and early sixties. The *Southern Review* and *Kenyon Review* had earlier origins, but other scholarly publications, like *The Mod-*

ern Age and *The Intercollegiate Review*, emerged with the postwar conservative revival. The academic journals on the Right included *University Bookman*, *Orbis*, *The Political Science Reviewer*, and the Catholic quarterly *Thought*; and on the libertarian fringe were the *New Individualist Review*, *The Alternative*, *Reason*, and the *New Guard*. Kirk's sophisticated theoretical journal, *The Modern Age*, might be regarded as the cultural beacon of the Right, as *Partisan Review* had once been the lodestar of the Left. But the best known periodical was *National Review*, whose editor called upon many of the writers mentioned above when he compiled an anthology of contemporary conservative thought. Appropriately, his subtitle was *Did You Ever See a Dream Walking?* In William F. Buckley, Jr., the new American conservatism had found its dream merchant.[11]

Between God and Man: William F. Buckley, Jr.

"We have long needed a good conservative magazine," Dwight Macdonald wrote in response to the *National Review* in 1956. "This is not it." Macdonald's curt evaluation anticipated the scant and sarcastic attention the Left would pay the *National Review* for years to come. The *National Review's* editor could not so easily be dismissed. As a popular "celebrity intellectual," an eloquent debater who could reduce infallible arguments to fallacious premises, and a witty polemicist who knew the art of annihilation by aspersion, William F. Buckley, Jr., was the bane of the liberal and socialist Left in America.[12]

Buckley was born in 1925. In Sharon, Connecticut, his large family (three sisters and six brothers) lived on an appropriately large estate. From his father, a self-made millionaire, estimated to be worth more than $100 million in 1958, with "interests" in oil markets, he inherited both the ease of wealth and the enlightenment of "a rigid ideology based on free enterprise and the survival of the fittest." His mother, a devout Catholic, saw that young William received the best spiritual training, first by private tutors, then at St. Thomas More School and St. John's in England, before finishing secondary education at Millbrook School in New York. After serving two years in the army as a second lieutenant during the war, he attended Yale from 1946 to 1950, graduating with honors. The following year he wrote *God and Man at Yale*, one of the few documents in American intellectual history in which youth attacks age for its liberal permissiveness. Having made a reputation as a young fogier-than-thou conservative, Buckley became an editor of the illiberal *American Mercury*. In 1954, in collaboration with his brother-in-law, L. Brent Bozell, he published *McCarthy and His Enemies*, a book that inspired ecstasy on the Right and apoplexy on the Left. "It is written in an elegantly academic style," fumed Macdonald, "replete with nice discriminations and pedantic hair-splittings, giving the general effect of a brief by Cadwallader, Wickhersham & Taft on behalf of a pickpocket arrested in a subway men's room."[13]

While the Left fumed, Buckley flourished. He put up $10,000 of the $290,000 raised to start the *National Review*, making his initial pitch, as we saw in his letter to Eastman, as noncommitted and as broad as possible. The *National Review* eventually picked up advertising support from American oil companies, producers of farm machinery and industrial synthetics, the Conservative Book Club and the Henry Regnery publishing house, and tourist offices boasting of the beauties of Greece, Portugal, and South Africa. By the sixties the biweekly magazine increased its circulation to more than 100,000. The *National Review*'s political point of view was predictable, but its tone varied from flippancy to pomposity to occasional profundity, qualities that reflect the different temperaments of the editorial board as well as the editor's personality.*

* The editors were James Burnham, Willmoore Kendall, Suzanne LaFollette, Jonathan Mitchell, and William S. Schlamm; the associates and contributors, L. Brent Bozell, John Chamberlain, Frank Chodorov, John Abbot Clark, Forest David, Max Eastman, Medford Evans, Karl Hess, Russell Kirk, Eugene Lyons, Frank S. Meyer, Gerhart Niemeyer, E. Merrill Root, Morrie Ryskind, Freda Utley, and Richard Weaver; the foreign correspondent, Wilhelm Röpke.

No doubt Buckley's energetic and effervescent style did much to promote the conservative cause in postwar America. A rare mixture of cunning and charm, his style has yet to wear thin. Today, in addition to editing the *National Review*, Buckley writes a syndicated column, "On the Right," receives about six hundred letters a week, accepts numerous invitations to speak and debate, politicks and campaigns (in 1970 he ran for mayor of New York City), edits books that are reasonably learned (*American Conservative Thought in the Twentieth Century*), writes some that occasionally rise above polemic to perceive the fallacies of conventional wisdom (*Four Reforms*), and, as an evening activity, conducts his lively television show, *Firing Line*, where his composed aristocratic image comes through to millions of Americans: legs crossed and relaxed, pencil in hand, wavy head thrown back, voice simultaneously inhaling and expressing, tongue flicking in anticipation of a joke, lips pausing to savor a polysyllable, eyes twinkling devilishly —a performance in which the host never fails to get in the last word. Buckley came to be the public's favorite conservative intellectual.

Buckley never went through the introspective ordeal of a political conversion. Even as a youth he had no infantile infections of Marxist socialism or, more incurable still, chic liberalism. Buckley's conservatism seems to be living witness to the Catholic doctrine of the Immaculate Conception: a virgin birth unsoiled by the sins of the Left. Many other *National Review* writers, however, were haunted ideologues, ex-radicals with stained pasts. Aside from Eastman, Dos Passos, Herberg, and Burnham, the *National Review*'s lineup of editors and contributors included former members of the militant left (Frank Meyer and William Schlamm), crypto-communists and notorious socialists (Whittaker Chambers and J. B. Matthews), early supporters of the Soviet Union (William H. Chamberlin and Eugene Lyons), fellow travelers and Marxist theoreticians (Freda Utley and Eliseo Vivas), Trotsky sympathizers (Suzanne LaFollette and Morrie Ryskind), little-known radical partisans (Frank Chodorov and Ralph de Toledano), and well-known radical critics of native American progressivism (John Chamberlain and Henry L. Hazlitt). In the sixties the *National Review* could even claim a defector from the New Left, Phillip Abbott Luce, a young political science student who had made the pilgrimage to Castro's Cuba as an avid radical and returned home to find the Progressive Labor Party demanding that he go "underground" and accept the dictates of the Chinese Communist Party.[14]

The *National Review*, Buckley announced in his opening editorial, "stands athwart of history, yelling Stop, at a time when no one is inclined to do so, or to have much patience with those who so urge it." The *National Review*'s wail soon became a familiar "*trahison des clercs*" that made the intelligentsia the demiurge of history. "Ideas rule the world," the "ideologues" control the power, and thus conservatives must expose "the inroads relativism has made on the American soul." The enemy is everywhere. "Drop a little itching powder in Jimmy Wechsler's bath and before he has scratched himself for the third time, Arthur Schlesinger will have denounced you in a dozen books and speeches, Archibald MacLeish will have written ten heroic cantos about our age of terror, *Harper's* will have published them, and everyone in sight will have been nominated for a Freedom Award." To save the Republic, conservatives must rescue America from the corrupting and ubiquitous fallacies of liberalism. The early issues of *National Review* rose to the occasion. Frank Meyer attacked cultural relativism, Morrie Ryskind lampooned psychoanalysis, Senator William Knowland denounced disarmament and William Chamberlin diplomatic defeatism, Aloise Heath assailed "pink professors," and Buckley scolded Henry Ford, Jr. (whose foundation supported the Fund for the Republic). The *National Review*, advised Willmoore Kendall, "must keep a watchful eye on the day-to-day operations of the liberal propaganda machine."[15]

Anti-liberalism provided the *National Review*'s emotional fuel, but it was scarcely sufficient to forge a conservative consensus. The issue of religion, which led to Eastman's defection, likewise led to the expulsion of Ayn Rand and her followers. Buckley agreed with Chambers that the Randian philosophy of "Objectivism" was godless in its hedonistic cult of self-interest, anti-Christian in its worship of triumphant individualism, and dehumanizing in its cold denial of the promptings of the heart and the secrets of the soul. Buckley found equally suspect the neo-anarchism of Murray Rothbard. He was an intelligent economist who did much to revive laissez-faire ideas, but Rothbard's total distrust of the state amounted to a "demonology" rooted not in historical experience but in "his epistemological doctrine of 'extreme apriorism.'" Buckley accepted this judgment by Hazlitt, and the editor read the Rothbardian libertarians out of the "mainstream" of American conservatism, thereby polarizing the *National Review* and the *New Individualist Review*. Similarly, Buckley was willing to forsake L. Brent Bozell, the volatile cold warrior whose name disappeared from the *National Review*'s masthead in the early sixties, when Bozell's violent anti-abortion crusade turned out to be more Catholic than Christian. And the magazine suffered a far greater loss—if intellect is the criterion—in Garry Wills. A young Catholic trained in classics, Wills was chastened by the events of the late sixties, especially the repression of student anti-war protesters and the police harassment of black Americans. In *Nixon Agonistes* he repudiated conservative politics as a "mishmash" of alliances with no theoretical bond other than a common nervous impulse to defend the powerful against the powerless. To make matters worse, long before these individual desertions Buckley and the *National Review* ran into Robert Welch and the John Birch Society, the lumpenpatriots of the far Right. Buckley objected vigorously to Welch's conspiratorial view of history, in which one is allowed to infer subjective (and subversive) intent from objective results. The essence of Welch's cold war methodology, Buckley noted, is the gift-wrapped syllogism: "(A) We were all-powerful after World War II; (B) Russia is now as powerful as we are; therefore, (C) We willed the enemy's ascendancy." Nicely formulated. But one cannot reason someone out of what he had not reasoned into, as liberals earlier discovered when trying to combat McCarthyism, and thus the *National Review*'s only retort to the Birchite mentality was Russell Kirk's whimsical comment: "Eisenhower isn't a communist—he is a golfer." Thousands of rightwingers never forgave Buckley for "throwing mud" at Robert Welch, but the *National Review* resisted the temptation of *pas d'ennemi à droite*.[16]

Buckley's philosophy of conservatism represented a tenuous combination of Catholic theology and economic orthodoxy. His halfhearted attempt to assimilate papal doctrine with Ludwig von Mises ended in frustration. (Indeed conservatism, capitalism, and Christianity present, as we shall see in the conclusion, an impossible synthesis.) In theory Buckley subscribed to the Catholic vision of society as an organic unity, ordained by God and legitimatized by transcendent natural law. He tended to reject much of classical economic liberalism and the utilitarian ethics of laissez faire, the dynamic philosophy of change and the calculus of pleasure that undermines the moral restraints of custom, religion, family, and community. With the Catholic Church he could, therefore, blame the curse of secularization upon the original sin of liberalism. Yet Buckley wrote too much and read too little. In truth, he never absorbed Catholic social doctrine, the papal encyclicals of Pope Leo XIII that advocated social justice as the answer to nineteenth-century liberal capitalism and radical socialism. Thus when Pope John XXIII's *Mater et Magistra* (1961) called for aid to underdeveloped countries and criticized capitalists for ignoring the plight of the poor, the *National Review* dismissed the encyclical as theological nonsense. Defying the Vatican, Buckley continued to oppose social security, progressive taxation, federal subsidies to farmers, and government protection of labor—all threats by the omnipresent state. Ultimately Buckley reverted to the classical economic liberalism of nineteenth-century capitalism, asking that it do precisely what the Church realized it had undone —preserve moral community.[17]

Buckley's approach to the racial problem was also fraught with irony. For many years he dealt with the issue obliquely, deploring the erosion of state sovereignty at the hands of civil rights activists backed in part by the federal government. After the 1954 Supreme Court decision on school desegregation, Buckley became the George Fitzhugh of the master class, defending the right of a Southern minority to maintain its hegemony on the grounds that the "claims of civilization (and of culture, community, regime) superseded those of universal suffrage." Buckley, however, wisely shunned the logic of racism. The superior position of the white man was circumstantial, not natural. "There are no scientific grounds for assuming congenital Negro disabilities. The problem is not biological, but cultural and educational." Buckley conceded this much and nothing more. What the force of circumstance had created could not be immediately altered by forcing a change of conditions. Segregation is "a problem that should be solved not by the central government, but locally—in the states . . . and in the hearts of men." Buckley thus encouraged Southerners to resist and circumvent the Supreme Court's decision, and at the same time he rendered advice to black Americans that began to sound curiously like the counsel of Malcolm X. Buckley believed that black pride and solidarity could be revitalized only when plans for social reconstruction were conceived, financed, and directed by Negroes themselves.[18]

Yet Buckley evinced little sympathy for black aspirations, respectable or radical. While running for mayor of New York City, he indiscriminately linked together Adam Clayton Powell and Bayard Rustin, claiming that both the opportunist congressman and the conscientious writer who tried to steer the civil rights movement away from confrontation and toward electoral politics were equally responsible for the white backlash. Along with Herberg he attacked Martin Luther King's non-violent marches as destructive to social order, and at the time of Robert Kennedy's assassination, Buckley announced in the National Review, "Dr. King's discovery of the transcendent rights of the individual conscience is the kind of thing that killed Jim Crow all right. But it is also the kind of thing that killed Bobby Kennedy." The strange relationship that Buckley drew between these two tragic deaths left his critics gasping for an explanation. Is Buckley saying, Joseph Epstein asked, that the two courageous exponents of non-violent civil disobedience were victims of their own doctrine, killed by an "act of civil disobedience" by assassins responding to "individual conscience"?[19] Whatever the answer, it was a strange formulation by one who had earlier encouraged Southerners to flout the integrity of the Supreme Court, the ultimate law of the land. Conservatives no less than liberals have trouble reconciling the commands of law with the demands of conscience.

Toward the end of the sixties Buckley could no longer readily invoke local self-government as the answer to the racial problem. Ironically, the New Left pre-empted much of the issue with its programs of community action, and even the Black Panthers began to sound like reformed Buckleyites when they put down their guns and started espousing the gospel of ghetto self-help. The principle of localism for him came too close to home when blacks in Northern cities demanded local control of their own community schools. Other conservative causes were also overcome by the bizarre developments of the sixties. No longer could Buckley expound the blessings of religion when religion itself had been radicalized in social protest, and it was awkward to praise the virtues of capitalism while corporation executives were being prosecuted for anti-trust violations and huge insurance company conglomerates collapsing amid a rubble of fraudulent stock. In an age of radical scandal and conservative shame there seemed to be only one sacred cause left—anti-communism.

Buckley fully shared Goldwater's attitude that there could be no peace until the "prior defeat of world communism," and he found eloquent Goldwater's campaign slogan (composed by Harry Jaffa): "Extremism in the defense of liberty is no vice, moderation in the pursuit of justice is no virtue." Translated into action, Castro must be liquidated and Eastern Europe liberated, even at the risk of nuclear war. Good men are prepared to die for their beliefs, Buckley exhorted, for those who are willing to do so realize that their bereavement will not be greater because a hundred million countrymen have died with them. True, nationhood and community may temporarily perish, but only "pagans" will mourn such losses, for human life and human freedom are "more valuable than all the perdurable treasures of the earth." Buckley never expressed much faith in the masses, but for the sake of defeating communism he was willing to democratize the glories of nobility. "If it is right that a single man is prepared to die for a just cause, it is arguably right that an entire civilization be prepared to die for a just cause." Who decides? Those who know there is no alternative except a *guerre à mort* of one side or the other. "Better the chance of being dead," Buckley concluded, "than the certainty of being Red. And if we die? We die."[20]

Buckley seldom bothered to discuss the diplomatic and military complexities of the cold war. His hatred for communism amounted to a consuming religious obsession that transcended the mundane realities of world politics. Walter Karp, who described Buckley as "a kind of Anthony Comstock of the Cold War era," perceived well the spiritual psychology behind this monomania:

For Buckley, Communism is not merely a pernicious doctrine or a vile social system—the two meanings are not even distinguished in his essays. It is nothing less than an indivisible, absolute, moral evil. It is so evil that its evilness is beyond comment, so evil that it ought to be extirpated even at the risk of nuclear war, even, as Buckley will argue, at the *expense* of nuclear war. Note the point: Communism, for Buckley, is not evil because it endangers us, it endangers us because it is evil.[21]

George Kennan once remarked that Russian communists hate Americans not because of what we do but because of what we are. The same attitude would apply in reverse to Buckley. Indeed this distinction between being and doing suggests again the curious strain of radicalism in what passes for anti-communist conservatism in America. As a conservative Catholic, Buckley professed to recognize the permanent reality of evil in the universe. Yet, instead of siding with Burke in order to work for world stability, he aligned himself with Robespierre and Lenin in a utopian effort to eradicate evil from the face of the earth. In his search for absolutes in world affairs, Buckley would not rest until America achieved absolute security, absolute amity, and absolute harmony. And like Melville's Ahab, he would commit others to his obsessive quest to deliver mankind from the forces of darkness. A world without evil—is not this the radical "sin" of intellectual pride?

For Buckley, the pure evil of communism could not be possible without the primal curse of liberalism, the great temptation of modern man. Buckley touched upon this theme in *Up from Liberalism*, but it was left to Burnham to analyze the fallacies of a misbegotten doctrine and to provide the final autopsy.

The Suicide of the West: The Liberal Death Wish

Burnham's *Suicide of the West: An Essay on the Meaning and Destiny of Liberalism* was published in 1964, a triumphant year for conservatism that saw Goldwater make his bid for the presidency. It is a curious work, an exercise in philosophical and psychological speculation, loose in structure, and ranging over the whole course of world history since 1914. Several chapters derived from a series of lectures on "Liberalism as the Ideology of Western Suicide," delivered before the Christian Gauss Seminar in Criticism at Princeton University. Almost forty years earlier Burnham left his alma mater an ex-Catholic; now the ex-Marxist returned and "suffered the slings and arrows" of the Gauss seminar as he brooded eloquently over the fate of the West.[22]

Characteristically, the book opens with the drama of apocalypse. The West is shrinking because it is dying. Words will not do, not even the Spenglerian metaphors "decline," "ebb," "waning," and "withering." Instead, the reader is invited to examine an atlas of the world as it was in 1914, and to compare that map to one of 1964. The reader quickly senses all that has been lost because of the collapse of the monarchical dynasties of Europe and the spread of communism after World War I. The process that started at Sarajevo and St. Petersburg continues relentlessly. Today, Burnham wrote in the book's final pages, Western civilization, slowly decaying in Europe, has also lost its grip on the Third World:

The great harbor of Trincomalee, commanding the western flank of the Bay of Bengal, southeast Asia and the Strait of Malacca, ceases to be a Western strategic base. Gone too are the mighty ports of Dakar and Casablanca, looming over the Atlantic passage. Of the guardian bases of the north African littoral, southern flank of Europe, only Mers-el-Kebir remains, no longer of any importance and scheduled to be soon abandoned. Bombay, overlooking the Arabian Sea; Basra, watching the Persian Gulf and opening toward the northern plateau and the passes from the steppes; the staging areas of the Middle East and those of East Africa guarding the Indian Ocean—all abandoned; Hongkong, left as a pawn in the arms of communist China; Singapore, shedding its strategic utility for the West as it phases into an independent Malaya; the mighty NATO air base at Kamina in Katanga, air power axis of sub-Saharan Africa, abandoned; the half-billion-dollar system of American-built air bases in Africa's northwest salient into the Atlantic, hub of a great wheel holding within its compass all north and central Africa, the Near East, and Europe right out to the Urals, and linked at its western rim to the Americas: abandoned. Suez, the Canal and the Isthmus: the water passage from Europe to Asia and East Africa, the land bridge between Asia and Africa, abandoned.

The contraction of the West, Burnham maintained, cannot be explained by a lack of economic resources or of military strength. Neither can it be explained by a deficiency in the two factors that in the past have stymied the growth of civilizations and empires—population and land. Nor can it be accounted for by the material capacity of any power external to Western civilization. Therefore, Burnham concluded with syllogistic flourish, the West must be contracting because of internal reasons. It has lost "the will to survive," and this atrophy of nerve and resolution characterizes liberalism, the ideology of a dying political culture.

Burnham acknowledged that liberalism contained neither a common body of doctrine nor a single intellectual legacy. Nevertheless, he developed a "syndrome" of liberal attitudes and ideas by cleverly formulating thirty-nine propositions involving such matters as racial segregation, tolerance, welfare and humanitarianism, war, the United Nations, colonialism and imperialism, crime and juvenile delinquency, cultural relativism and ethical permissiveness, free education and academic freedom, and, inevitably, Joseph McCarthy. Drawing partly upon Michael Oakeshott's *Rationalism in Politics*, he then elaborated nineteen basic liberal beliefs, which can be reduced to five core convictions: (1) a view of man's changing, malleable, "plastic" nature, with no intrinsic limits to achieving the goals of peace, freedom, and justice; (2) a "rationalism" that is both skeptical and optimistic, a "faith in intelligence" (Hook's phrase) that enables man to subject all problems to critical inquiry on the assumption that the mind alone, "the power of reason," can determine the "worth of a thing, the truth of an opinion or the propriety of an action" (Oakeshott); (3) a conviction that the only obstacles to the good society are the external factors of ignorance and bad social institutions; (4) a vision of "historical optimism" in which the world is redeemed by human power from poverty and tyranny; (5) an anti-traditionalist perspective in which the habits and customs of the past are to be liquidated rather than venerated. These liberal fallacies are the fruits of ideological thinking, which Burnham defined as thought that is "independently premeditated" (Oakeshott), ideas that are born of pure reason and hence have little to do with the real world of space, time, and events. Whether of the Right or of the Left, the ideologist is enamored of ideas and convictions that remain untouched by logical analysis or empirical evidence. The liberal in particular, the most influential modern ideologue, breathes deductions and lives by abstractions. The world "unfiltered" by ideology is not his cup of tea.

"Do liberals really believe in liberalism?" Burnham asked. Their daily conduct seldom is in uniform accord with their beliefs: advocates of racial integration who send their own children to exclusive white schools; egalitarians who fear the vulgarization of popular culture; bureaucrats who complain of bureaucracy. Yet liberals not

414 | The Dilemmas of American Conservatism: 1955–1974

only believe in principles they have difficulty practicing, they also believe in ideas that have no logical meaning or cognitive status. The ideology of liberalism is "a matter of prejudice, sentiment or faith," what Pareto would call "derivations." Why then do liberals believe in it? The answer cannot be found in a doctrine's objective claim to truth, which, even if valid, is the least of the motives that drive man to believe in it. Instead, the liberal's desire to improve the world by his ideology actually stems from an unacknowledged residue of guilt, a feeling of bad conscience that he is more fortunate than others. The liberal is wracked by *mauvaise foi* because he cannot believe in Christianity, the one doctrine that "faces the reality of guilt, provides an adequate explanation for it, and offers a resolution of the anxiety to which it inevitably gives rise." Instead of understanding guilt as a state of sin that can only be overcome by faith, the liberal externalizes the problem by attaching his unanalyzed spiritual condition to the "unhappy" situation of others, thereby giving his inner state "some sort of objective, motivating structure." This is why liberals are less concerned with the validity or results of their ideas than with the good intentions behind them: "The real motivating problem, for the liberals, is not to cure poverty or injustice or what not in the objective world but to appease the guilt in their own breasts; and what that requires is some program, some solution, some activity, whether or not it is the correct program, solution and activity."

Attempting to purify the heart, the intellectual perverts the head. The West is dying, Burnham concluded, because of the good will of liberals, who are determined to believe they have no enemies on the Left, only on the Right. Liberals do not respond to communist aggression with the same hostility they display over fascist aggression, and the atrocities of the Left are dismissed as essential to liberation, while those of the Right are denounced as willful evil. Liberals engage in "selective indignation" because they share the same attitudes as communists hold on human nature, social justice, equality, and secularism. For much the same reason liberals believe Russia and the United States are moving closer toward a similar political culture. To the fellow travelers of the past, and to the theorists of convergence today, "communists seem not much more than liberals with guts." Such assumptions enable liberals to explain away "defeat as victory, abandonment as loyalty, timidity as courage, withdrawal as advance." Born in guilt, liberalism is the rationalization of failure, the strategy of Western suicide in the name of sanity and morality, self-extermination through expiation.

Suicide of the West became the gospel of conservative prophecy in the sixties. The many faithful *National Review* readers at last had a comprehensive explanation for the political defeat and cultural malaise of the age, and several thousand other Americans were enticed to become *National Review* subscribers by a bonus copy of Burnham's book. As Burnham might have expected, however, the New York literary circles dismissed the work as a simplistic diatribe that read like a coroner's report on modern liberalism. "*Suicide of the West*," wrote Charles Frankel, "is the pure Platonic Form of which Barry Goldwater is only the pale, stammering shadow." Irving Howe, seeing the work as a "Barnes & Noble handbook" with which campus conservatives would pepper their liberal professors, parodied it as a "rodomontade blending academic hauteur with fanatic shrillness," an "odd yoking of Ortega y Gasset and General Jack D. Ripper."[23]

Like most controversial books, *Suicide of the West* was more a clever argument than a convincing analysis. One of the major premises of the work was the equation of civilization with military and political boundaries. Burnham could argue that Western dominion had been cut to half of what it was in 1914 by tracing the recession of the lines of political sovereignty and physical force on his atlas. But while this contraction of power was taking place, Western culture was also expanding, and it was in those very Third World countries that Burnham listed that the hegemony of the West was being challenged by leaders who claimed for their own nations political rights the West once claimed to be universal. Although Burnham anticipated the criticism of identifying civilization with power, he scarcely acknowledged that westernization itself deprived the West of its claim to moral and political superiority. If this be the "suicidal" logic of liberalism, it is also the rational logic of modernization, a logic that both Marxists and capitalists share.

The notion that liberalism is responsible for the decline of the West can be traced to Nietzsche and Spengler, and it received impassioned expression in the humanist writings of Lewis Mumford and Archibald MacLeish during the World War II years. Burnham's argument, however, was political rather than moral, more concerned with the survival of Western power than with the preservation of Western culture. Indeed, he all but purged liberalism from the Western tradition. For Burnham, the crisis of modern Western culture begins with the October Revolution. The Bolsheviks "broke totally away" from the West, and the new Russian empire "became not merely altogether separate from Western civilization but directly hostile to it in all these senses, in the moral, philosophical and religious as well as the material, political and social dimensions." Such a reading of history might serve to expunge Marxism from Western culture and explain the Soviet state as an outgrowth of Slavic institutions and character. But while Burnham maintained that Bolshevism repudiated the West, he also claimed that the contraction of Western civilization was the result of a series of Soviet advances, a movement that drew its ideological strength from the attitudes that liberals and Marxists held in common. "Liberalism is infected with communism in the quite precise sense that communism and liberalism share most of their basic axioms and principles, and many of their values and sentiments." Here all sense of historical understanding breaks down under the weight of causal explanation. Apparently Burnham assumed that a cause must resemble its effect, for he doubtlessly presumed that liberalism and communism were similar and that the latter somehow issued from the former—if not in origin at least in expansion. But Burnham could not have it both ways. It was one thing to claim that Soviet diplomatic victories were due to the illusions of fellow travelers, in which case he could rightly indict a specific liberal mentality. It was quite another thing to claim, in order to discredit liberalism, that Marxism itself partook of the liberal tradition, in which case the Soviet Union could be seen not as the negation of the West but as its "higher" synthesis.

Whatever the line of reasoning, Burnham faced the same difficulty that Eastman encountered when the latter attributed the success of communist expansion to democratic socialists and their collectivist illusions: how to explain the resistance to communism in the democratic West and the receptivity to communism in the underdeveloped world? Indeed Burnham's dilemma was greater, for when he ticked off a list of Third World countries in order to dramatize their "abandonment" by the West, he implied that the West had a legitimate right to control those countries it had once possessed and had presumably "lost." Ostensibly writing about liberalism and "civilization," Burnham was actually thinking about imperialism and power. In Paretan vocabulary, this might be called Burnham's Marxist "residue." Since the beginning of the twentieth century Marxists could never distinguish liberalism from imperialism; and ex-Marxists, it would seem, retained an attitude carried over from the communist theory of "social fascism" to the anti-communist theory of McCarthyism: We must disgrace and defeat liberalism to save the West.

All of which suggests that Marxists and conservatives share a peculiar understanding of liberalism, as do political "realists" and neo-orthodox theologians. This misleading conception may explain why Burnham could not come to grips with the major antagonist of his book, Arthur Schlesinger, Jr., and his *The Vital Center*. The caricature of liberalism that emerges in *Suicide of the West* reads like a parody of intellectual history. One finds, first of all, the vulgar equation of liberalism and perfectionism in order to identify both with communism. "What communism does is to carry the liberal principles to their logical and practical extreme: the secularism; the rejection of tradition and custom; the stress on science; the confidence in the possibility of molding human beings; the determination to reform *all* established institutions; the goal of wiping out all social distinctions; the internationalism; the belief in the welfare state carried to its ultimate form in the totalitarian state." What would Trotsky say, who railed against the New Deal and dubbed liberalism the "banality" of "common sense"? "An optimistic theory of human nature and history," Burnham continued, "is integral to, logically inseparable from, the whole body of liberal doctrine." What would Jefferson say, who regarded "man as a destroyer," a predator of his own species, "the only animal which levied war against its kind"?[24] Intellectual history was at the mercy of politics. Drawing heavily upon Oakeshott, Burnham clearly mistook the tradition of democratic radicalism, which had its origins in French utopianism, for the tradition of Anglo-American liberalism, which derived from the skepticism of Locke and Hume. The latter heritage reflected "a philosophy of sobriety, born in fear, nourished in disenchantment, and prone to believe that the human condition was and was likely to remain one of pain and anxiety."[25]

In the thirties, it is true, many American Soviet sympathizers were seized by a fit of absent-mindedness as they wrote what David Caute has called a "postscript to the Enlightenment," abandoning Anglo-American skepticism and affirming the classical French utopian worship of reason, science, and progress.[26] But fellow-traveling liberalism represented a brief wayward episode in modern progressivism that Schlesinger himself repudiated in *The Vital Center*. Burnham acknowledged that Schlesinger's book was thick with references to Kierkegaard, Dostoevski, Nietzsche, Proust, and other contemporary anti-Enlightenment voices of the irrational, the contingent, the imponderable. But he dismissed Schlesinger's existential liberalism as "intellectually stylish," and as for Schlesinger's Niebuhrian denials of the liberating power of knowledge and morality, Burnham exclaimed, "But the denials are like Peter's." Under Burnham's diagnosis the American liberal was doubly diseased: if he is optimistic, he is suicidal; if pessimistic, insincere.

Burnham's most perceptive analysis was his treatment of liberal guilt. This was a forbidden subject in the early sixties, spoken only in whispers at the time he wrote the book. But by the end of the decade, as liberal professors gave in to escalating demands of New Left and Third World students, few could deny that the liberal's flexibility of spine was a measure of his fallibility of conscience. The campus confrontations of 1967–1969, far more than the show-downs with the Soviet Union, may have validated Burnham's interpretation of the liberal mind. Yet in his book he had no solution to the problem he had uncovered. He maintained that Christianity could appease guilt—only "if it is true"—and Burnham had long ago ceased believing in Christian doctrine. A man without faith could offer the liberal no means of redemption from his individual guilt. Indeed, it was Burnham who grew wistful and even utopian at the prospect of living with Schlesinger's existential liberalism. Liberal ideology, he protested, blinds the intellectual to the reality of his inner condition, the spiritual unease that is be-hind his restless activism, compelling him to engage in endless and unsatisfying tasks of secular reform. Hence Schlesinger in *The Vital Center:* "We are forced back on the reality of the struggle. The choice we face is not between progress with conflict and progress without conflict. The choice is between conflict and stag-nation. . . . Out of the effort, out of the struggle alone, can come the high courage and faith that will preserve freedom." Such an ethic, Burnham argued after quoting Schlesinger, accounts for the "liberal emphasis on continuous change, on methods rather than results, on striving and doing rather than sitting and enjoying." Longing for peace and repose, Burnham the Machiavellian realist became a Thoreauvian escapist. "Within the universe of liberalism there is no point at which the spirit can come to rest; nowhere and no moment for the soul to be able to say: in His Will is our peace." The author of *The Struggle for the World* once accused tender-minded liberals of shrinking from the realities of conflict

420 | The Dilemmas of American Conservatism: 1955–1974

and power. When liberalism became existentially tough, he complained that *The Vital Center* failed to show the way to Walden Pond.

Burnham's shifting perspectives reveal a shift in his perception of the function of the intellectual in modern society. Previously, in *The Managerial Revolution* and *The Machiavellians*, he saw the intelligentsia as driven by motives of status and power, technicians who would use their talents and ideas as a means of securing influence and control over the state. This description, while perhaps relevant to the Stalinists of the thirties (the "totalitarian liberals" who wanted, as Dwight Macdonald remarked, "to identify with power without feeling guilt"), hardly fitted the contemporary existential liberal, whose activist itch seemed to offer a kind of masochistic pleasure in struggle itself. Thus Burnham became the psychologist of the soul as he probed the motives of guilt that lay behind liberal ideology. From this perspective, liberalism could be seen as the opiate of the ineffectual class, the swan song of a dying cultural elite which, incapable of self-analysis, could neither recognize the enemy nor respond to the aggressor. Liberalism functioned to soothe the intellectual's conscience and distort his perception of reality. It enabled an economist like W. W. Rostow, for example, to see Soviet industrial growth as a source of stability instead of a threat, and others to mistake Soviet imperialism for national liberation. In its most grotesque moments, liberalism could even allow the intellectual to identify with the aggressor, whose revolutionary actions would solve the social problems that tormented the generous and anguished mind. "What liberalism can and does do, what it is marvelously and specifically equipped to do, is to comfort us in our afflictions; and then, by a wondrous alchemy, to transmute the dark defeats, withdrawals and catastrophes into their bright opposites: into gains, victories, advances."

The charge of liberal guilt was indeed damaging to liberalism, opening up a new dimension of false consciousness, a hidden ethical anxiety that belied the moral claims of liberal humanitarianism. One might reply that Burnham's own aggressive anti-communism reflected the guilt of an errant ex-Trotskyist trying to expiate his past. These more difficult questions of ultimate "motives" will be discussed in the final chapter. Here it might be asked how Burnham himself managed to solve the problem of guilt. By what process of self-knowledge did he escape the psychology of liberalism? In *Suicide of the West* he displayed some awareness of the problem of poverty. He told of his acquaintance with two black workers, "cheerful, pleasant fellows," whom he would regularly see at work in New York collecting piles of old paper boxes. Their IQ's "were almost out of sight," but they seemed happy, took "pride in their work," and managed to eke out a living from it. Mayor Robert Wagner, however, was demanding that the state raise the minimum wage to $1.50 an hour, a move that would deprive the two blacks of their jobs and throw their families on welfare. Liberals like Wagner could not see the consequences of their actions, nor could they understand that unpleasant scenes like Skid Row cannot be erased, for "Skid Row is the end of the line; and there must be an end of the line somewhere." Poverty, in a word, is fated, and one cannot hold oneself morally responsible for what cannot be changed. Nothing was more ridiculous and repugnant to Burnham than President Kennedy's declaration: "We have the ability, we have the means, and we have the capacity to eliminate hunger from the face of the earth." A decade before the young liberal president set out to conquer "new frontiers," Burnham had reached a totally different conclusion about hunger and misery. He eloquently recorded his poignant impressions in an essay written shortly after leaving India:

It is through the eyes, those windows of the soul, that the main thrust is carried. We, whose culture is Anglo-Saxon as well as European, have decided, for the sake of business and tranquility, not to look at many things. Our animals are murdered by professional executioners, in parts of town which we do not visit, and we receive into our ken only the unreproaching steak and chop. Our idiots and halt and senile, we lock up behind walls and grass and trees, where we seldom ever pass. We thrust birth and disease and death into the sterilizing pans of our hospitals. We consider beggars in the streets a crime against the law as well as nature. The poor, if they are always with us, are taught to be decent and respectable, to keep the floor clean and the curtains drawn. In the extremity of our squeamishness, we even begin to abolish poverty itself.

But India, with the pedantry of the traditional villain who compels the fair maiden to witness the torture of her lover, puts everything naked before us. This poverty, compared to which our lowest Neapolitan slum is a palace, is neither decent nor respectable, but stark, abject, disease- and dirt-ridden, absolutely and unyieldingly wretched. These are no quaint and human beggars: alcoholic Irishmen who you know will use the quarter for a shot of bad whiskey, or picturesque town characters adding a little spice to the night life, or, perhaps, a fellow who has had a bad break and may make a comeback with a bit of help to tide him over. These beggars are thoroughbreds, born and trained for the sport of saints. They arise out of the ground at the approach of a stranger, like the damned before Dante and Vergil in the wildest chasms of Hell. They are thinner than skeletons, with distorted strings of black hair, backward twisted feet, stumps for arms, with sprouts of cartilage or flesh growing out in a dozen directions like new shoots from the stump of a maple, blind eyes with dripping sockets, withered babies, pus-filled sores, and voices that whine like sawmills.[27]

When Burnham wrote these words in 1951, he could still say of America, "In the extremity of our squeamishness, we even begin to abolish poverty itself." In 1964 a walk through Harlem or the Bowery no longer brought such a response. Sadly, the cold war had hardened a sensitive, intelligent conscience. One of the finest minds of the Old Left, Burnham could only offer a younger generation two options: one must choose either the sins of liberal guilt or the sang-froid of a conservatism without compassion. Diplomatically, too, one must choose between a liberalism that is "the ideology of Western suicide," and a conservatism that held out the consolation of Buckley's cold war death instinct: "If we die? We die." On the one hand unconscious slow death, on the other martyrdom for the sake of *machismo*. Sometimes, observed Montaigne, it is a good choice not to choose at all.

CHAPTER 11

Conservative Paradoxes

"A Twice-Born Generation"

"The ex-communist," wrote Isaac Deutscher in 1950, "is the problem child of contemporary politics." Scholars and journalists have generally either sympathized with this "problem child" or admonished him. Those whose own careers were close to the Old Left—most notably Daniel Aaron, Daniel Bell, and Murray Kempton—treat the radical writers of the thirties as political prodigal sons, fellow travelers who lost their innocence abroad and returned home better Americans. Belated heretics of Marxism, Old Left intellectuals presumably forsook their faith in the end of "pre-history" and thereby regained their reason. "Ours, a 'twice-born' generation," observed Bell in *The End of Ideology*, "finds its wisdom in pessimism, evil, tragedy, and despair. So we are both old and young 'before our time.'" Similarly, Aaron asks readers of *Writers on the Left* to exercise forbearance, understanding, and compassion as they "think back on us"—a line from one of Cowley's poems. "We who precariously survive in the sixties," Aaron pleads in the book's final passage, "can regret their inadequacies and failures, their romanticism, their capacity for self-deception, their shrillness, their self-righteousess. It is less easy to scorn their efforts, however blundering and ineffective, to change the world." And of the ideals that once had inspired such efforts, Kempton confesses in *Part of Our Time*, "I miss them very much and I wish we had them back."[1]

Other writers—notably David Caute, Isaac Deutscher, and Matthew Josephson—are more disturbed by the extent to which the "shrillness" and "self-righteousness" continued into the post-war era. Open a copy of the *National Review*, and we find the renegades from radicalism as cold war avengers. Positions have changed, but the passions remain. In "The Ex-Communist's Conscience," Deutscher's perceptive review of *The God That Failed*, we are told that a common mentality unites the New Right with the Old Left. In an effort to extirpate the ideologies he himself formerly embraced, the ex-communist becomes an "inverted Stalinist."

He continues to see the world in white and black, but now the colors are differently distributed. As a Communist he saw no difference between fascists and social democrats. As an anti-Communist he sees no difference between nazism and communism. Once, he accepted the party's claim to infallibility; now he believes himself to be infallible. Having once been caught by the "greatest illusion," he is now obsessed by the greatest disillusionment of our time.

Self-expiation was a politically and intellectually barren stance to Deutscher, who believed the ex-communist could better overcome his "blind hatred of his former ideals" by taking a broader look at the dynamics of revolution. He thus drew a historical parallel between Stalinism and the anti-Soviet nations on the one hand and Napoleonic France and the Holy Alliance on the other. Jefferson, Deutscher reminded American ex-radicals, was "the stanchest friend of the French Revolution," while Goethe and Shelley rose above partisan hatreds and thus interpreted events more truthfully than their "fearful" contemporaries. The lesson for today's contemporaries? It is as difficult to reconcile oneself to Stalin as it was difficult for the nineteenth-century intelligentsia to reconcile itself to Napoleon, the "despot" of another "degenerated" revolution. Nevertheless, Jefferson, Goethe, and Shelley saw that the "message" of the French Revolution lived on to echo powerfully

throughout the nineteenth century, and hence they looked upon
the Holy Alliance and the anti-Jacobin cause as "vicious, ridiculous
anachronisms." In the year of Napoleon's defeat, Shelley wrote to
Wordsworth:

> In honoured poverty thy voice did weave
> Songs consecrate to truth and liberty—
> Deserting these, thou leavest me to grieve,
> Thus having been, that thou shouldst cease to be.

To which Deutscher added, "If our ex-Communist had any historical sense, he would ponder this lesson."[2]

Deutscher's position was similar to Floyd Dell's in his unsent
letter to Eastman. Both advised Old Left writers to follow the
spirit of Jefferson and Shelley, not Coleridge and Byron, and avoid
identifying themselves with any "established Cause." This was an
honest plea, yet Deutscher's historical parallel was as confusing as
it was unconvincing, sidestepping as it did a whole series of theoretical problems regarding modern Soviet totalitarianism.* One
need not applaud Eastman, Dos Passos, Herberg, and Burnham as
they formulated their new conservative beliefs and allied themselves with the enemies of the Left. The four American writers,
however, did raise certain issues which Marxists, with their
vaunted "historical sense," need to consider more carefully. Certain
problems haunt the mind of the ex-communist intellectual: Marxism, Leninism and Stalinism, human nature, power and bureaucracy, and the philosophy of history.

The Problem of Marxism. What is living and what is dead in
the philosophy of Karl Marx? Can an idea be defeated by an
event? Does history negate philosophy? Those questions occupied

---

* Deutscher's categories, so clear in light of nineteenth-century realities, become vague and fluid in mid-twentieth-century Europe. Was Stalin a modern
Napoleon trying to bring the Russian "Enlightenment" into Czechoslovakia?
Or was he another Alexander I with a Slavophilic resistance to Western
liberalism? Deutscher tended to follow his mentor Trotsky and regard Stalinism
as an expression of counterrevolutionary "Bonapartism" even while questioning
the analogy. Yet while the "message" of the French Revolution did survive the
personal dictatorship of Napoleon, the Soviet Union continues as a totalitarian
state long after the passing of Stalin. The "message" of Marx still languishes
behind the Iron Curtain.

the Old Left as it began to sense, beginning with Hitler's consolidation of power and the Moscow trials, a profound crisis in Marxism. Previously Marxism had appealed to the Left because it offered a dramatic philosophy of history, a crisis theory of economics, a novel methodology of class analysis, and a vision of totality that enabled one to see the well-knit interrelationships of all aspects of society. Moreover, functioning as a "science" as well as an ethic, Marxism presumably could foretell as well as inspire. With the unexpected events of the thirties, Marxism lost not only its heralded—and much misunderstood—power of prediction, it also lost its claim to retrospective explanation. As a result Burnham broke with Trotsky over the issue of the dialectic, Eastman performed his final autopsy on philosophic Marxism, Herberg awoke to the problem of evil, and Dos Passos bid farewell to Europe and steeped himself in Jefferson and Paine. What remained of Marx as a "scientist" lay in ruins in Stalin's labor camps and Hitler's concentration camps. What remained of Marx as a "moralist" or "humanist" another generation would discover, which only proves that Marxism still possesses the power of inspiration, if not the power of realization.

"A lot of Hegel got mixed up with Marx's notion of history. Max Eastman pointed this out. The dialectic was a way in which Marx made the course of history coincide with his unconscious desires."[3] Those are the words of Mario Savio, an organizer of the Berkeley Free Speech Movement and an early leader of the New Left of the 1960s. Savio's empirical skepticism could hardly provide the emotional foundation on which Left movements are built. Nor could any New Left student who had read Eastman dare carry his psychological analysis to its logical conclusion. For when the young radicals of the sixties discovered a "new" Marx, they too may have been making history "coincide" with desire. Once Marxism itself can be analyzed as an ideology, even radical self-consciousness may be seen as an objective illusion. There is no end to this mode of analysis when ideas are reduced to motives and thought treated as the rationalization of wish; no one is safe from the accusation of "false consciousness," least of all the accusers. The Old Left may have needed to believe in Marxism as a solution to the contradictions of capitalism, but the New Left needed to believe in it as an answer to the paradoxes of alienation.[4] Thus the young radicals of the sixties seized upon Marx's essentially Hegelian concepts of "estrangement," "alienation," and "reification" in order to turn a predicament of the human condition into a platform for social emancipation.[5] After the belated discovery of the *Economic-Philosophic Manuscripts* of 1844, the meaning of Marxism would never be quite the same. The crucial distinctions that Eastman drew between Marxism and German idealism would now be reintegrated by the logic of perfect contradiction as Hegel reappeared in America as though the owl of Minerva were rising with the counterculture.*

The Problem of Leninism and Stalinism. Was Stalin the legitimate heir of Lenin, as Burnham argued in 1945? Or, as Eastman insisted for many years, was Lenin the creative genius of the October Revolution, Stalin its butcher, and Trotsky its conscience? Such questions were debated in the late thirties when the Old Left was trying to determine what went wrong in Russia. Yet even after the war Burnham and Eastman never resolved their differences: the latter saw Lenin as the heroic "engineer of revolution," while the former regarded both Leninism and Stalinism as nothing more than the ideologies of the managerial state. In the light of the universal significance of the Russian Revolution as a basic postulate in communist ideology, the distinction between Leninism and Stalinism, or their alleged lineal descendancy, remains a crucial issue. Can a revolution begin with the early Eastman's anarcho-

---

* The moral and political idealism of an older radical social movement or school of thought is often rediscovered by a future generation as a source of inspiration. A study of the deradicalization of a Left intelligentsia, however, suggests that the skepticism of one generation can seldom be transmitted to another generation. Not even Eastman's rhapsodic, life-celebrating "affirmative skepticism" would be adequate for the young radicals of the sixties, who wanted "relevance" and not the lessons of experience from the authorities of failure. See John P. Diggins, *The American Left in the Twentieth Century* (New York, 1973), pp. 136–52.

democratic aspirations and avoid Burnham's bureaucratic conclusions? Must all revolutions be betrayed? When Soviet tanks moved into Prague after the Spring of Freedom in 1968, Czech resisters put up posters exclaiming, "WAKE UP LENIN!" Eastman would understand the posters, Burnham the tanks.

The Problem of Human Nature. Why do oppressive power relationships continue when there is no longer any need for exploitation? This question goes to the heart of the dilemma in post-Revolutionary Marxist social thought. One thing can be said for Stalin: in eradicating traditional forms of property and social classes he achieved a great intellectual victory—the elimination of the economic motive from historical explanation. What was now needed was a post-Marxist theory of human behavior to account for Soviet tyranny, and this the Left could not provide. Hence Eastman turned back to Mark Twain's parables on human pretense; Dos Passos, wondering in *The Big Money* why radicals behaved "like such shits," found an answer in the Enlightenment's ethos of moderation; Herberg, painfully aware of the perilous ambiguity of political man, embraced existentialism in order better to comprehend the paradoxes of the human "power-drive"; and Burnham, rejecting Trotsky's interpretation of Stalinism, absorbed the writings of the neo-Machiavellians to account for the inevitable role of force in human affairs.

The Problem of Power and Bureaucracy. The emergence of new sources of power and the spectacle of "bureaucratism" in Soviet Russia deeply troubled Old Left writers. Was the "withering away" of the state a desperate pipe dream? Marxists have generally argued that such phenomena as bureaucratic power resulted from social inequality and economic scarcity, a consequence of attempting to establish a workers' state in a backward country without the prerequisite of "primary capitalist accumulation." Eastman, Dos Passos, Herberg, and Burnham had no patience with such explanations, for all became convinced that even the presence of equality of wealth in a society does not necessarily guarantee an equal distribution of status and influence. Thus each chose a different solution to the problem of power: free enterprise (Eastman), Jeffersonian individualism (Dos Passos), religion and ethics (Herberg), or pluralistic institutions managed by competing elites (Burnham).

The Problem of the Philosophy of History. As a theory of historical interpretation and causation, Marxism had provided the Old Left with a seemingly coherent perspective upon events, a profoundly dramatic, crisis-ridden perspective that made human experience rich with historical meaning. Rejecting Marxism, ex-radicals had now to adopt new outlooks to interpret the swirling flux of events. Aside from Eastman, who seemed to be able to live comfortably without a systematic philosophy, the other three writers discussed here attempted to develop a sense of the past that would help bring power under control and thereby allow liberty to survive. Significantly, no consensus emerged from their efforts. Herberg originally believed that history itself was "the problem," and thus he sought moral truth in metaphysical knowledge, only later to incorporate philosophy into history as he replaced Buber with Burke and referred to himself as a "historicist." In contrast, Burnham never confused personal salvation with political truth, and thus when studying history he could reduce moral problems to power relationships. Dos Passos consummated his own lifelong search for identity in the study of the past, deliberately creating a vision of historical salvation in the eighteenth-century American Enlightenment, an optimistic, rationalistic milieu offensive to both Herberg's Burke and Burnham's Machiavelli. Each writer looked for a history that would guarantee liberty; whether they could develop a philosophy of history that would be distinctly conservative is another matter, one to which we shall return shortly.

Deradicalization and the Limits of "Psychohistory"

The writers we have been dealing with could readily cite the problems of power, liberty, and history in order to turn Shelley's lament back upon Deutscher and ask the faithful men of the Left to "ponder these lessons." But merely to cite these issues neither justifies nor fully explains why Eastman, Dos Passos, Herberg, and Burnham felt the need to move so far to the Right. In Europe numerous ex-radicals confronted the same theoretical issues: W. H. Auden, Stephen Spender, Victor Gollancz, and George Orwell in England; André Gide, Boris Souvarine, André Malraux, Jean-Paul Sartre, Albert Camus, Maurice Merleau-Ponty, and Victor Serge in France and Belgium; Nicola Chiaromonte, Ignazio Silone, and Bruno Rizzi in Italy; and Arthur Koestler, Anton Ciliga, and Milovan Djilas in Central Europe. Stalinism and the Nazi-Soviet pact produced an anti-Stalinist intelligentsia in Europe; in America similar events produced, as well, apologists for free enterprise, power politics, religion, and maudlin nationalism.

Can we therefore describe the path from far Left to far Right as a peculiarly American phenomenon? A look at the postwar role of the German émigrés in America, especially the Frankfurt scholars associated with the Institut für Sozialforschung and the New School's "University-in-Exile," suggests a negative answer. With the exception of Herbert Marcuse, and possibly Franz Neumann, most of the German refugee scholars, including the brilliant sociologists of "critical theory," Theodor Adorno and Max Horkheimer, moved to the Right in the postwar years and supported America in the cold war. Like much of the American Old Left, the Frankfurt intellectuals abandoned Marxist capitalist categories and interpreted totalitarianism as a mass movement that defied orthodox class analysis. They also grew skeptical of economic planning, treated social problems as psychological or moral issues, and often adopted the anti-ideological "realism" associated with Hans Morgenthau and, later, Henry Kissinger. From Hannah Arendt to Karl Wittfogel, the legacy of the German refugee intellectuals was decidedly conservative and anti-communist.[6]

One cannot then conclude that the transformation of the American Old Left was either peculiar or parochial. There were many veterans of the thirties (Edmund Wilson, Dwight Macdonald, Malcolm Cowley, and Granville Hicks, among the old lions; Irving Howe, C. Wright Mills, Michael Harrington, and Paul Goodman among the cubs) who experienced the same betrayals and disenchantments of the era and yet continued to sustain a radically critical stance toward American society and American culture. Thus there is something unique about those writers who made the complete conversion. Historical experience alone cannot account for this behavior. Bertrand Russell and Max Eastman, for example, would both repudiate Soviet communism for its dogmatism and despotism and in turn support their own democratic governments; but while Russell went on to become a fiery critic of America's post–World War II anti-communist interventions, Eastman became a cold war militant. The same pattern of agreement and divergence is true of Dos Passos and Orwell. Both writers went through almost exactly the same trial of faith on the battlefields of Spain, and each came away convinced more than ever that the language of politics must be rescued from the enemies of freedom. Yet while Orwell could become a severe critic of Kremlin "doublethink" and Burnhamite realpolitik as well, Dos Passos came to believe he could be anti-communist without being anti-military. The difference boiled down to a choice of weapons: the pen alone, or the pen and the Pentagon.

As one surveys the ideological careers of various American and European intellectuals, it seems clear that there could be more than one intelligent and moral response to a given historical experience. It also seems clear that it is by no means reason alone that compels the American intellectual to reject Marxism and embrace conservatism. The four paths we have studied are strewn with scraps of conflicting evidence that make a general theory of motivation impossible. By what inner thoughts did our writers make their way to the *National Review?* In the process of undergoing deradicalization, were their minds manifestly cerebral, emotional, rational, ethical, environmental, or psychological? Or did their thoughts and reconsiderations express, to borrow the vocabulary of social science, "cognitive dissonance" born of the "disconfirmation" of expectations? Granting the trauma of "when prophecy fails," since other radicals and liberals responded differently, we must ask a delicate question: Do our four writers suggest a conservative character type, a thinker who projects his own personality into politics and thereby perceives reality according to his inner needs? We arrive at the treacherous but inevitable subject of "psychohistory."

Herberg's and Dos Passos's odysseys cannot be fully explained without some mention of the psychological dimension of politics. In Herberg we have the dilemma of the ethical Jew, one whose conscience as an intellectual urges him to look to authority, but one whose conscience as a radical moralist urges him to resist authority. The same tension between authority and liberty inspired Dos Passos's rebellious nature, though in the novelist's case the tension rose from childhood and family experiences rather than religion. Nevertheless, both Herberg and Dos Passos seem to have been driven by a need to find meaning and identity, a need that found conservative expression when Herberg turned to ancient theology and Dos Passos to American history. *Judaism and Modern Man* was Herberg's deliverance from spiritual anguish, for here he found outside of himself support for his own existence, and in a doctrine that offered, curiously enough, both moral authority and ethical freedom. Similarly, *The Ground We Stand On* ended Telemachus's search for patriarchal roots in Dos Passos's *Rosinante to the Road Again*. The novelist now found in "the clean words . . . our fathers spoke" the convictions his own father failed to provide, and hence the political wisdom that enabled him to face the "quicksands of the scary present" and identify with the founders of the Republic. In Herberg and Dos Passos there may be some relation between conservatism and "personality needs." Perhaps.

With Eastman, however, we find no suggestion of Herberg's quest for moral authority and existential freedom; nor do we see, as in Dos Passos's career, the pattern of generational rebellion and subsequent filial reconciliation. Eastman had no need to return to the religion of his parents, whom he forever admired with the deepest respect and affection. His beloved mother was "heroic and saintly," and his father "kind, reasonable, patient, courageous, sweet-tempered, generous, truthful, just."[7] Indeed Eastman's alliance with free enterprise capitalism would probably have prompted his parents, both liberal Congregational ministers, to pray for his soul. As for Burnham, the tensions of family and religion are almost completely absent from his political career. Although raised a Catholic, he never experienced anything resembling a spiritual crisis, and his defection from the Workers Party was marked by deliberate rational argument, by reason, logic, evidence. Other ex-communists—Whittaker Chambers, Howard Fast, Louis Budenz—have confessed to a kind of psychospiritual catharsis and self-transformation when they broke with the Communist Party. Burnham's resignation displayed more eloquence than emotional intensity. Does the very coolness of Burnham's mind conceal "deeper" desires and motives? Orwell, it will be recalled, insisted that Burnham's theoretical reflections were nothing more than the politics of "power-worship." Yet Burnham opted for Trotsky in the thirties and Buckley in the fifties, hardly the choices of a writer who equated the inevitable with the desirable as he panted for history. More recently, a young New Left historian has accused Burnham of being a corporate capitalist all along without knowing it. The Managerial Revolution, James Gilbert has argued, was part of a "collectivist" design by writers who were trying to "carve out for themselves an indispensable role" in society, to "mark off a function which would be their own speciality and justification," and thereby to "insure" themselves and their colleagues (who would be teaching in "universities") of "their own longevity as social engineers."[8] There is only one thing wrong with this psychopolitical interpretation: while teaching political philosophy at New York University Burnham wrote The Managerial Revolution to prove, among other things, that society could be run without political philosophers.

It is unavoidable that we deal with the underlying motives of the thinkers we are discussing; it is deplorable when an intellectual historian becomes obsessed by them. At its worst, "psychohistory" reduces thought to a desire for power, status, ego gratification, economic security, or personal revenge. At its best, however, it traces the roots of adult thought to childhood determinants and early psychospiritual tensions, both of which suggest an unconscious desire for social identity and moral authority. A psychological examination of political attitudes may help explain individual behavior but it cannot illuminate the different patterns of behavior among a whole generation of writers. Clearly the anti-communist Left had much in common with the ex-communist Right. Both groups were anti-totalitarian and critical of Marxism, and both remained alienated from the mainstream of American political life. Why, then, did Eastman, Dos Passos, Herberg, and Burnham become militant neo-conservatives and why did not more veteran radicals follow their path?

Divisive Issues: Means and Ends, McCarthyism, Liberalism

The four converts to conservatism all assumed an attitude toward communism that was at once anxious and suspicious. Far from being a mere "projection," however, their common attitude grew out of real experience that was more immediate and carried more enduring personal significance to them than to many other veterans of the Old Left. Floyd Dell might tell Eastman that he refused to become a Russian "hater" after being a Russian "lover," but the Soviet Union had always been a Platonic affair to Dell, just as it had been a political abstraction to much of the liberal Left in America. Eastman, however, witnessed firsthand the Stalinization of the Communist Party of the USSR, had himself been branded a capitalist spy by the GPU, and had known, through his third wife Eliena Vassilyevna Krylenko, and through such émigrés as Boris Nicolaevsky, of the murderous brutalities of collectivization and the purges more than a quarter century before

The Gulag Archipelago shocked the conscience of the world.* The wound of personal experience had also remained painful to Dos Passos, who learned in Spain in 1937 what Eastman learned earlier in Russia, that it is necessary to protest Soviet oppression and terror whatever the consequences. The political education of Herberg and Burnham, though deriving from different experiences, led to the same conclusion. As a Lovestoneite, Herberg encountered continual harassment by the American Communist Party even though he had remained silent in the face of Stalinist atrocities. As a theoretician of the Workers Party, Burnham himself devised many of the tactical schemes to infiltrate and absorb rival opposition groups, and he was, in Max Shachtman's words, "deeply affected and very adversely affected" when Trotsky later maneuvered factions against him and raised false issues in their debate over the Russian question, "arguments which were absolutely unworthy of Trotsky."[9] Both Herberg and Burnham

* Addressing the annual convention of the American Federation of Labor in 1948, Eastman stated, "There are, according to the most conscientious estimates, fourteen million slaves in GULAG, the slave empire ruled by the Soviet State Police. That is more than the total population of New York State, including Manhattan. It is more than the total number of unenslaved industrial workers in the Soviet Union itself." Eastman, *Reflections on the Failure of Socialism* (New York, 1955), p. 119.

Had he lived to witness Alexander Solzhenitsyn's exile, Eastman would have readily empathized with the Russian's rage against Western literary intellectuals who refused for so long to face the truth about Stalin's Russia. In 1933 Eastman received the following advice from Theodore Dreiser:

I would answer your question about those Russian prisoners at once, except that I am so much interested in the present difficulties in Russia and in Russia's general fate, that I am not prepared, without very serious consideration, to throw a monkey-wrench such as this could prove to be, into their machinery.

It seems to me, whether badly managed or well managed, that it is at least a set-up which should be preserved and fought for. If that means serious and, in some cases, seemingly cruel sacrifices, it is, as we say, just too bad.

But, after all, if, by any process whatsoever, (this, or any other) Russia is seriously crippled or destroyed, what good would freeing those prisoners do? (Dreiser to Eastman, April 26, 1933, Eastman Papers.)

What good, indeed!

emerged from the thirties convinced that a communist party is by definition a conspiratorial instrument for obtaining power illegitimately and holding power absolutely. The Czech coup of 1948, so stunning and unexpected to fellow travelers and liberals, only demonstrated to Burnham and Herberg the result of the Leninist deification of the *apparat*, the party machine that had already liquidated relatives and friends of Eastman and Dos Passos.

Although Eastman, Dos Passos, Herberg, and Burnham may have reached this conclusion sooner than others, many radical writers became rapidly disenchanted with one-party "socialist" regimes as a result of the Stalinization of Eastern Europe after the war. What then was the crucial difference separating the ex-communist conservative from the anti-communist liberal and social democrat? On the eve of America's entry into the war, Eastman tried to develop a distinction in a debate with James T. Farrell. "The real difference between us and you, in my opinion, is this: In a period when certain means we had all agreed upon for emancipating the working class, and therewith all society, have proved to lead in the opposite direction, we have remained loyal to the aim, you to the means."[10] Eastman returned to this distinction at the end of the war in his exchange with Dwight Macdonald over communism in Greece, and it was implicit in his arguments over anti-communism with Dell in the fifties. At the beginning of the cold war Eastman's distinction had some plausibility. The basic issue was whether, as Macdonald and the Old Left had hoped, there existed the possibility of a mass alternative to both Stalinism and capitalism, or whether, as Eastman and the New Right believed, popular, democratic movements stood a better chance of success fighting within spheres of the British and American empires. The choice of strategy was indeed crucial, but looking back, the entire history of the subsequent cold war casts doubt on both propositions. As events in Eastern Europe would demonstrate, no democratic movement against Soviet totalitarianism had a chance of success; and as events in Asia and Latin America would demonstrate, no Marxist movement against British and American hegemony could succeed without a Leninist-modeled party dictatorship. The tragic fate of Jan Masaryk foreshadowed the equally tragic fate of Salvador Allende. Czechoslovakian democracy was "subverted" by the GPU, Chilean democracy "destabilized" by the CIA. In the early years of the cold war Eastman and Macdonald were susceptible to desperate illusions; neither was guilty of bad faith.

Yet if Macdonald's dream could not be realized, neither could Eastman's distinction be maintained. The ex-communist may have revised his "means" of "emancipating" society from oppression, and doubtless Eastman originally was urging the Left to see the imperative of democratic processes and the disaster of proletarian dictatorships. But as the cold war spread to the Third World, conservative anti-communism became an end in itself, to be realized by any means possible, even by the despots and juntas of the "free world" whom Dos Passos defended just before his death in 1970. Against Castro and Allende the CIA served the historical function of Lenin's "vanguard," the conspiratorial will of the revolution, or rather, the counterrevolution. The burden of demonstrating how undemocratic means can lead to democratic ends— the very challenge which John Dewey had put to Trotsky—must be assumed by the ex-communist conservative.

The conservative does not begrudge that burden; he relishes it. The cold war is the great moral drama of our time, and the choice of allies is the test of integrity. On what grounds, then, can the conservative defend an undemocratic regime which violates the principles of free government? One may do so, Buckley and Burnham have been arguing recently in the *National Review*, because it is far more likely that a national populace can rise against and topple a right-wing autocracy than a left-wing dictatorship. Recent events in Portugal and Greece, when compared to the total political and cultural suppression of Eastern Europe and China, suggest that the conservative argument has some historical validity. But the *National Review*'s position is about as persuasive as Trotsky's appeal to the American Left to support Stalin's Russia in order better to defeat Stalinism. Buckley and Burnham supported the Greek junta because it supposedly was the only element capable of resisting a communist takeover; they then maintained that the collapse of the junta proved that the Right was responsive to popular pressures and therefore preferable to the Left, even though the collapse risked what the Right set out to prevent—a communist seizure of power. The *National Review* thus must look to a radical Left to prove by the strength of its insurrectionary actions why a conservative Right cannot become a permanent dictatorship. For without such a Left as an opposition force, the lesson the *National Review* must ponder is this: If there is one historical experience rarer than a right-wing dictatorship achieving the genuine social progress necessary to defeat communism, it is a right-wing dictatorship transforming itself into a genuine democracy. And if the *National Review* supports a right-wing regime which has as its aim the suppression of the democratic Left, one can only conclude, by the magazine's own logic and by Eastman's distinction between being "loyal to the aim" rather than to the means, that the conservative is on the wrong side of the barricades.

The second issue which separated the anti-communist conservative from the anti-Stalinist liberal or socialist was McCarthyism. Nearly all of the writers who found their way to Buckley's *National Review* supported McCarthy's inquisition and efforts of congressional committees to purge former Russian sympathizers and Fifth Amendment witnesses. Subversion, espionage, atomic secrets, security risks, Whittaker Chambers's blood-curdling revelations—such issues caused Eastman, Dos Passos, Herberg, and Burnham to see McCarthy as one of the few political leaders willing to raise embarrassing questions about the sins of the Left. They may have been uncomfortable with McCarthy's "methods," but they felt strongly that the senator saw communism in its proper perspective, not as a popular mass movement but as an internal conspiracy of assassins. More than anything else it was the McCarthy controversy that split the ranks of the American Committee for Cultural Freedom, dividing the anti-communist conservative from the liberal intelligentsia. Here the difficulty arises. Conservatives identified with McCarthy, but did they not confuse a political campaign for a moral cause? What did McCarthyism have to do with the goals of anti-communism? Richard Rovere raised this telling question in a letter to Arthur Schlesinger, Jr., in 1952:

I am fairly well convinced that most of the committee members are willing to take a firm position on McCarthyism, but I also know that taking the position would result in a split of some sort. I can understand the reluctance of Hook and some of the other founding members to allow this to happen, but I think it would really be an excellent thing. People like Max Eastman don't give a damn about cultural freedom; Eastman, in fact, said just this in the opening remarks of his speech—I forget his exact words, but they were to the effect that there is really no question of cultural freedom, there is only the question of winning the war against Stalinism—and I think it would take very little effort to show that Eastman is really hostile to the basic purposes of the organization. His intellectual home is the *Freeman*. . . . That, it seems to me, is clearly the place for anyone who can call McCarthy a "clear-headed patriot of freedom."[11]

Rovere's complaint would scarcely move the conservative intellectual. The McCarthy controversy went deeper than the goal of cultural freedom or even political freedom. What was the issue? In a word, it was "conformity." That was the thesis propounded in *McCarthy and His Enemies*, which Buckley wrote with his brother-in-law, L. Brent Bozell. McCarthyism represented a "consensus," a widely shared conviction that communism posed a threat to American values and that therefore communists and communist sympathizers should be eliminated from public life and liberals should be exposed as "atheistic, soft-headed, [and] anti-anti-communist."[12] A strange argument. Only in America do conservative elites turn to the democratic masses for popular support against non-conforming liberals. Be that as it may, *McCarthy and His Enemies* flagrantly skirted the basic issue. The real question was not whether communism posed a threat to American values—clearly the position of the ACCF—but whether McCarthyism was a matter of posture rather than principle, a stance that enabled the politician to be against liberalism without necessarily being against *real* communism. The career of McCarthyism's finest creation, Richard Milhous Nixon, indicates strongly that the ACCF intellectuals were right, that anti-communism in America had become an expedient political issue rather than a deep moral commitment. The *National Review*, it should be noted, supported Nixon as Eisenhower's choice to stay on as vice president in the election of 1956, and that support was based on the single-minded conviction that Nixon was an authentic anti-communist and nothing else really mattered. As John Chamberlain explained the case, Nixon, while shifty on economic issues, possessed an "intellectual understanding of Marxism in both its theoretical and practical aspects," displayed "a clear perception of the nature of Communist dynamism in international affairs," and was, despite all the talk of "Tricky Dick," a "rather open young man with decent impulses."[18]

All this might suggest that conservatives need to choose their comrades a little more carefully. Buckley claimed that McCarthy's enemies were "soft" on communism, but it was McCarthy's friends who feared the Red presumably under the bed more than the Red who was actually in it. Buckley also maintained that since Americans were anti-communist McCarthyism represented the "consensus" of American values and attitudes. On the contrary, McCarthyism violated American values, since it had no commitment to any value. (Herberg discerned this ethical void.) Indeed, if one surveys the heritage of McCarthyism in the 1970s, one finds a disturbing consistency between the past tactic of McCarthyite slander and the present strategy of Moscow summit, between the old witch hunter and the new fellow traveler. In Nixon's heralded détente with Russia and China, one sees that a politician nurtured on McCarthyism can be anti-communist without being anti-totalitarian; in the Watergate affair, one sees that an administration founded on "law and order" can resort to illegal and quasi-totalitarian methods allegedly to protect the "free world" from totalitarianism; and in the recent Moscow negotiations, one sees why a chief of state who tried to silence the American press can stand idly by while Soviet authorities pull the cables on American journalists who are trying to report on Russian dissidents. It is the grimmest irony of the cold war that Nixon did more than any other modern statesman to bestow legitimacy on communist China and Russia. The irony is compounded when one considers that détente itself is an exercise in the very Machiavellian power politics that Burnham had once believed essential to the defeat of the communist world.*

Who, then, is "soft" on communism? President Gerald Ford tells students at Ohio State University that Red China deserves America's "respect" because of the regime's "discipline."[14] One recalls that it was the Stalinists who extolled the virtues of "discipline" in Russia while Eastman was renouncing the Soviet Union because of its denial of the cultural and political freedoms so precious to the democratic Left. Somehow it is easier to believe that Eastman was closer to American values in 1937 than it is to accept Buckley's argument that McCarthyism represented the American "consensus" in 1952.

The third issue dividing the intellectuals of the New Right from the veteran intellectuals of the Old Left is liberalism itself. In the introduction to this book some mention was made of the continuity of contempt for liberalism that runs through the careers of Eastman, Dos Passos, Herberg, and Burnham. Before their break with the Left these writers chastised liberalism for its inability to

---

* It is to Burnham's credit that he has resisted this obscenity. In August 1974 Burnham spoke out against the Nixon-Kissinger rapprochement with the Soviet Union, not to rekindle the dying flames of the cold war, but, more admirably, to protest the administration's silence on Soviet domestic repression. As Burnham noted, the Nixon-Kissinger policy conveyed the same moral atrophy that characterized the Wallace Progressive Party of 1948 (Burnham, "Détente (Deletions)," NR, XXVI [August 2, 1974], 857). Yet Burnham's own admiration for realpolitik appeared to preclude the very protest he tried to make. In "The Kissinger Style" (NR, XXVI [Feb. 15, 1974], 118), Burnham had described Kissinger as the real Machiavelli would have esteemed the statesman who is "secretive," unconcerned about "what-might-have-beens," and willing to accept the status quo. Earlier, a "Machiavellian" approach required for Burnham a stance as a confrontationist who settled for nothing less than total victory.

make a social revolution; after their break, they condemned liberalism for its inability to prevent one. Now liberalism was seen not
only as having no future but as having been contaminated by the
misdeeds of the past: the Popular Front, Stalin as "Uncle Joe," the
Moscow trials as "progressive," isolationism at the outbreak of
World War II, silence on the Katyn Forest massacre, the Wallace
"peace" campaign of 1948, Alger Hiss, the censure of McCarthy.
This indictment was as one-sided as it was short-sighted.[15] When
Eastman attacked Soviet Russia in Harper's in 1937, he made a
plea for freedom that was based essentially on the liberal ideas of
equality and justice; when Dewey criticized Trotsky the following
year, his argument clearly derived from a liberal faith in the intelligence of the masses and a liberal skepticism of proletarian dictatorship as a means to freedom; and, to bring our survey up to
date, when Burnham recently criticized the Nixon-Kissinger policy
of rapprochement, even the political "realist" protested the administration's indifference to civil liberties in the Soviet Union.
Liberalism, in short, is the only stance the intellectual can take to
oppose the totalitarianism of the Left or Right, and thus the
National Review writers find themselves in the awkward position
of advocating liberalism in the communist world while ridiculing it
in the liberal world.

Yet while the conservative intellectual may defend liberal values
against communist realities, he still holds the ideology of modern
liberalism responsible for the problems of contemporary society.
To Eastman, liberalism meant the tyranny of planning and the
eclipse of economic freedom; to Herberg, the perils of believing in
man's rationality and goodness and the pitfalls of relativism; to
Burnham, the politics of "guilt" and a blindness to power; to Dos
Passos, the abuses of power and an itch to change that ignores the
wisdom of history. When Buckley wrote Up from Liberalism in
1959, he lucidly articulated many of these fears (and added a few
of his own). Buckley and other intellectuals of the New Right also
attempted to repudiate liberalism by offering their own version of
a "conservative affirmation." How well did they succeed in devel-

oping systematic and internally consistent political philosophy? Did the "New American Conservatism" really negate liberalism?

Tarnished Principles: Capitalism, Legitimacy, Sovereignty, Morality

"Please don't forget to eliminate the word 'liberal' from the blurb," Eastman wrote his publisher in 1939. " 'Progressive,' 'radical,' 'advanced,' 'thinking people' any and everything but 'liberal,' " he insisted.[16] What to call oneself posed an awkward problem for the Old Left–New Right intellectuals. For a number of years after the war our four writers were reluctant to label themselves "conservative." One reason for this was that the term in America had become almost synonymous with capitalism, the scourge of the thirties generation. The intellectual, even the conservative intellectual, has always felt uneasy with the capitalist as ally. Burnham believed the business class was too "cowardly" and "selfish" to be relied upon in the cold war, and Eastman had to agree with Hook that businessmen had little concern for political freedom. Herberg found the conservative tradition in America to be "thoroughly permeated with the timidities, inhibitions, and illusions" of "bourgeois" materialism.[17] Even Dos Passos, despite his reconciliation with his capitalist father, chided Goldwater about his blind faith in free enterprise. The predicament of the four neo-conservatives was best expressed in a personal letter to Eastman from William S. Schlamm, himself an ex-communist:

The older I grow, the more certain I am that the error of my youth was intellectual rather than moral. Morally (and esthetically) my disgust with the satiated is angrier than ever. The trouble is that one cannot save capitalism without saving the capitalists—and, boy, does that make me mad![18]

Eastman felt he could separate the concept from the creature. When he agreed with Sidney Hook that capitalists could not be relied upon to "defend political freedom against a regime of terror," Eastman replied, "That is indeed true—nor the workers either. . . . But it is not 'capitalists' but a capitalist economy on which we base our hopes." To Hook the reply seemed like a mystical distinction, as dubious as socialists looking not to the activities of socialists themselves but to a disembodied essence called "socialism."[19] Far more than an ontological quibble was involved in this exchange. The larger issue, one that confronts every intellectual on the Right, is whether capitalism and conservatism are compatible.

Alexander Hamilton made a brilliant attempt to synthesize the two under the discipline of a mercantilist state. But it was an impossible fusion, as even Russell Kirk acknowledged. The Old Left–New Right intellectuals fared no better in modern corporate America. The "capitalist economy" on which Eastman based his hopes means growth, change, social dislocation, whereas conservative social theory aspires to order, continuity, social stability. In the eyes of the philosophical conservative, the bourgeoisie is the demiurge in the drama of modern disintegration. Henry Adams vividly saw what John Adams vaguely sensed: commercial capitalism directed the movement of history not toward greater unity but more freedom. Eastman, who eventually came to call himself a "libertarian conservative," was scarcely troubled by such knowledge, but Herberg, Dos Passos, and Burnham were less complacent about the disruptive role of the free market. Herberg in particular also understood another terrible secret: capitalism may not only be incompatible with conservatism but with Christianity as well. The aim of capitalism is to maximize satisfactions, while that of Judaism and Christianity is to minimize desires. In Protestant, Catholic, Jew Herberg recognized that capitalist mass society had made a mockery out of religion, stultifying the interior "I-Thou" dialogue, socializing conscience, demystifying spirit, and setting man off on a frantic pursuit after "happiness." The contradiction between religious and conservative values and the industrial society of modern capitalism is one of many dilemmas facing the National Review intelligentsia.

Another is the problem of legitimacy in democratic society.

Where does lawful authority reside in the modern state? In contemporary America no one really knows for sure. As John Schaar observes, we are all whistling in the dark:

Authority is a word on everyone's lips today. The young attack it and the old demand respect for it. Parents have lost it and policemen enforce it. Experts claim it and artists spurn it, while scholars seek it and lawyers cite it. Philosophers reconcile it with liberty and theologians demonstrate its compatibility with conscience. Bureaucrats pretend they have it and politicians wish they did. Everybody agrees that there is less of it than there used to be. It seems that the matter stands now as a certain Mr. Wildman thought it stood in 1648: "Authority hath been broken to pieces."[20]

Open an early copy of the National Review, and we find the answer. Authority, the neo-conservative insists, must lie in some source external to and independent of man; in, for example, the Constitution (Kendall), or history and immemorial custom (Kirk), or the laws of nature and economics (Eastman), or the majesty of transcendent higher law (Herberg). In theory the conservative idea of legitimacy is highly satisfying, for it appears to offer an aura of normative certitude. In practice, however, it proves an awkward proposition. Conservatives cite the authority of the Constitution and the Supreme Court as the "highest law of the land" in order to protect property against interference and confiscatory taxation. When civil rights leaders cite the "equal protection" clause of the Fourteenth Amendment, the Constitution suddenly loses its moral force. The National Review advises blacks not to look to the sanctity of the law. Segregation, Buckley declared in 1955, "is a problem that should be solved not by the central government, but locally—in the states . . . and in the hearts of men."[21] The foe of liberal democracy, Buckley is the friend of local democracy on racial matters. He is Stephen Douglas holding forth against Lincoln. And siding with popular sovereignty, Buckley returns law to precisely that status from which Lincoln tried to rescue it. The legitimacy of law is now located not above man but in man's sentiments and feelings. Reduced to this level,

law becomes "merely organized force" (Roscoe Pound) and ultimate authority is simply "the police power" (Douglas).

Herberg had also once asserted that "some doctrine of higher
law beyond the sheer will of the sovereign or the folkways of the
community would seem to be necessary if the right is not to be
reduced simply to the power of the stronger."[22] But even Herberg
followed Buckley in recoiling from their common doctrinal position when Martin Luther King organized his movement around
the concept of "higher law." Obviously the National Review was
no longer talking about legitimate authority when it turned to the
racist "folkways of the community" and the unenlightened "hearts
of men." Nor, for that matter, were radicals any longer respecting
the "higher law" of conscience when they turned to "black
power." Once the foundations of legitimacy rest solely upon rhetoric, theory can no longer elevate power into authority, and the
position of the stronger rests ultimately upon the power that
comes from the barrel of a gun.

The difficulties the National Review encountered in trying to
maintain a consistent practical stance reflect the theoretical difficulties of conservatism itself. The problem of legitimacy is at least
as old as Socrates, who formulated the original inconsistency when
he urged civil disobedience to fulfill spiritual law in The Apology,
and submission to folkways to preserve social peace in The Crito.
The problem that divided ancient philosophers also divides modern conservatives. Among National Review writers, Frank Meyer
maintained that freedom depends upon the individual being free
to choose freedom, while Kirk and Willmoore Kendall (who
sympathizes with those who put Socrates to death) insisted that
freedom is preserved by the "divine" sanction of custom and tradition.[23] The difference between Meyer on the one hand and Kirk
and Kendall on the other is as great as the difference between Dos
Passos and Herberg, between the historian who sides with Paine
and liberty and the historicist who sides with Burke and order.
The tension that arises over the problem of legitimacy is characteristic of the conservative intellectual, who may rightly see in the

equivocation a genuine recognition of the ultimate incommensurability of values and reality. In this respect the dilemmas of conservative legitimacy are themselves intellectually legitimate. The same cannot be said, however, when we turn to the problem of sovereignty.

If the disparate *National Review* intellectuals committed themselves to one unifying principle of sovereignty in the fifties, it was federalism. Reacting to the centralization of power under the Roosevelt and Truman administrations, conservative writers returned to the framers to make an eloquent case for a republic of separated powers. All major conservative political theorists—Willmoore Kendall, Harry Jaffa, Ernest van den Haag, Martin Diamond, Garry Wills, L. Brent Bozell. Frank S. Meyer—drew upon the resouces of their academic disciplines to demonstrate that the federal government could not be assigned social responsibilities it was theoretically incapable of exercising and fulfilling. And every major conservative intellectual associated with the *National Review* was certain that centralized government posed a threat to liberty and the Constitution. The watchword of the conservative was federalism, and the answer to executive supremacy was congressional sovereignty. As a text, we can turn to Burnham's *Congress and the American Tradition* (1959).

Here we find not the managerialist prophesying the inevitability of the bureaucratic state, but the Madisonian restating the case for checks and balances. Along with other conservative political scientists, Burnham reasserted the primacy of Congress over the executive, specifically in legislative initiative and purse control, emphatically in the authority to make treaties and to declare war. "By the intent of the Founding Fathers and the letter and tradition of the Constitution, the bulk of the sovereign war power was assigned to Congress." However clear the intent, in the actual operation of government the prosecution and conduct of war was, Burnham admitted, a function that came to be "fairly evenly divided" between the two branches. Burnham also devoted learned chapters to the investigatory power of Congress, including the House

Committee on Un-American Activities. With more dispassion than Buckley had displayed in *McCarthy and His Enemies*, Burnham defended congressional investigations against three major liberal criticisms: that such inquiries properly belong to the judicial branch; that they are actually political "witch hunts" or "fishing expeditions" serving no legislative purpose; and that they violate the constitutional rights and privacy of the citizen.[24] During the fifties the doctrine of congressional supremacy rose to epigrammatical brilliance in the writings of the *National Review* intelligentsia. The following decade the doctrine stood as a blushing intellectual embarrassment to the conservative principle of sovereignty.

First came Vietnam. It was no longer Truman fighting a limited war in Korea; it was now Johnson and Nixon systematically escalating aerial bombing without congressional approval. The *National Review*, however, did approve, and happily allowed the chief executive unlimited freedom of action, even the right to withhold military secrets from Congress and the nation. Echoing the earlier liberals' support of Truman, and forgetting their own previous support of the Bricker Amendment, conservative writers opposed a vote to reconsider the Tonkin Gulf resolution on the grounds that the president's war power would be constricted. Next came Watergate. It was now Nixon, not Truman, who invoked executive privilege and immunity; and witnesses subpoenaed to face congressional grilling were no longer "soft on communism" scientists or Fifth Amendment playwrights, but well-trimmed lawyers and advertising agents, *nouveaux riches* Republicans who came to Washington with California suntans and business administration degrees.[25]

For several months after the Watergate break-in was headlined in the press, the *National Review* tried to brush aside the affair, and the more the evidence led back to the White House the more defensive Buckley became. The President, the *National Review* insisted, could very well be blameless even though his aides may be guilty of "idiocy" (innocence by dissociation); he has the right to make secret tapes and order wiretaps (all power to the Oval Office); he cannot be held responsible for the burglarizing of Dr. Ellsberg's psychiatrist's office since he and his staff were "proceeding on the assumption" of national security ("War is the time of Caesars"—Dos Passos); he may take tax deductions on state papers as have other officials (permissiveness by precedent); and, what is more, the press is politically prosecuting a man it hates merely for exercising the enormous executive powers developed under the Roosevelt and Truman administrations (the heroic burden of original sin). As for the Watergate Committee, Senator Sam J. Ervin, formerly quoted in the *National Review* for presaging the "twilight of federalism," now appeared to Buckley to be the Polonius of the Bible Belt, piously "sputtering indignation" in defense of the Fourth Amendment. Reversing every argument he and Burnham had put forth a decade earlier, Buckley went before the Yale Forum and declared (in a nationally televised debate with Senator Lowell Weicker) that the Watergate investigation had not only proved unproductive, it was an improper function of Congress, violated the legal rights and personal privacy of witnesses, and damaged their reputations in the eyes of the community. This was liberal anti-McCarthyism, circa 1950, the cant Buckley once attributed to pink professors now adopted in behalf of patriotic "plumbers."[26]

Not all *National Review* conservatives suffered from amnesia during the Watergate hearings. The distinguished syndicated columnists George F. Will and James Kilpatrick vigorously disagreed with Buckley when he first tried to dismiss the break-in as normal campaign chicanery. They also knew enough British constitutional history to understand that Nixon's behavior, while perhaps not criminally indictable, was nevertheless grounds for impeachment by the dishonor brought to the office of the presidency. Eventually Buckley himself grew critical of Nixon, who refused to heed his advice to take a "leave of absence," and in March 1974 he supported his brother, Senator James Buckley, in calling for the president's resignation.

Conservatives, of course, were not the only intellectuals who became schizoid on the subject of sovereignty. Liberals, too, completely reversed their roles during Watergate, now gleefully supporting congressional inquisitions and asking the informer, so despicable in the McCarthy era, to open his memory and "let it all hang out." Yet we expect more from conservatives because conservatives pose as the beacons of moral light in a world eclipsed by liberal relativism. America, warns Buckley, "is in danger of losing her identity" because of her "failure to nourish any orthodoxy at all." Liberal philosophy, the conservative maintains, is really a way of getting by without a philosophy. "The danger comes when a distrust of doctrinaire social systems eases over into a dissolute disregard for principles. A disregard for enduring principles delivers a society, eviscerated, over to the ideologists."[27]

What then are these "enduring principles"? This question brings us to another paradox of American conservatism. Buckley is convinced of the profound truthfulness of conservative morality. Yet if conservatism is a moral philosophy, wherein lies its ethical foundation? It cannot be found in capitalism, for Eastman, Von Mises, and other laissez-faire theorists tell us that the free market systematizes desires and allows man to flee the pains of scarcity and seek the pleasures of consumption. It cannot be found in religion, for American religiosity, Herberg pointed out, functions merely as a "way of life" without spiritual content, a sanctification of habits and attitudes that are already established. It cannot be found in politics and public affairs, for this is the "real" world of power and action and not, to use Burnham's categories, the "formal" world of ideals and moral vision. Neither can it be found in the principle of legitimacy, which is located in "higher law" one year and popular folkways the next; nor in the concept of sovereignty, which resides in Congress during one administration and in the executive for the duration of another. "The conservative movement in America," Buckley confessed in a moment of humility, "has got to put its theoretical house in order."[28]

Conservatives have always been keen on morality. In contrast to liberals and Marxists, conservatives believe that social problems are basically moral in nature and that the social order must have a moral foundation. Such may be the "human condition," but there is a futher paradox between the conservative conception of life as tragedy and the conservative conception of ethical responsibility. Man is a "poor fallen creature," Russell Kirk declares; his destiny is to struggle and suffer, for he is "not made for happiness, and will not find happiness."[29] To state the problem in these terms is by no means to resolve it. Indeed there is no reason why Christian paradox can rescue political conservatism from its own paradoxes. Man's "fallen" state, the doctrine of inherited guilt, can just as easily deny both the premise of moral freedom and the goal of social harmony that are so precious to conservatives. Nor is it clear that the idea of sin and redemption has only one meaning. What conclusion does the American conservative draw from the example of Christ dying on the cross for our sins? Does he ask the capitalist to learn the meaning of tragedy by aspiring to the "imitation of noble actions"? If anything, the Christian moral doctrine of sacrifice is closer to liberal neo-orthodoxy than to conservative social philosophy. According to Niebuhr, it is man's tragic fate to strive after an "impossible victory" and suffer an "inevitable defeat." Conservatives, in contrast, advise man to shun the impossible and accept the inevitable. This is hardly a moral demand, for it is characteristic of all ethical philosophers that they do not think in terms of mere actuality.[30] Kirk and Herberg are right in one respect. Man may never overcome all problems and find "happiness." But it was Jefferson, not Niebuhr, who identified "happiness" with "virtue." And it was Babbitt, not Buckley, who identified genuine moral life with the "inner check." Niebuhr's noble, if masochistic, proposition makes cowards of us all, but it reminds us that we need to take moral philosophy a little more moralistically. Indeed, until suffering is raised from the level of material fate to that of spiritual tragedy, until man is liberated from the realm of economic necessity and becomes conscious of the realm of freedom in the act of moral choice, it is difficult to see how conservatives can build an ethical system around the tragic vision of life. "Conservatives," Buckley has written, "must learn to agonize more meticulously."[31] Would a small dose of "liberal guilt" help?

A Rootless Search for Roots

The four paths we have followed crossed frequently before converging on the *National Review*, and those who traveled their own routes to conservatism came to know and admire one another. Yet no common theoretical outlook developed to give the *National Review* a unified philosophical stance. Nor did our pathfinders make an attempt to analyze the differences among themselves. Thus we have four different conservative minds, each with particular concerns and distinct attitudes and values. Dos Passos, for example, was preoccupied with the fate of the individual in large-scale organizations, while Burnham's thoughts start from the premise of organizational necessity, Herberg's from the pain of existence, and Eastman's from the joy of experience. In the context of American intellectual history, we might say that Dos Passos stands with Jefferson and liberty, Burnham with Hamilton and power, Herberg with Edwards and sin, Eastman with Franklin and pleasure.

The differences that separate the four writers are also marked by inner contradictions within their own thoughts. Thus Eastman cites the "laws" of the market place and animal anthropology to validate competition and the inevitability of human aggression as natural phenomena. Yet he felt no discrepancy in advocating birth control to fight overpopulation, thereby using technology to interfere with the natural rhythms of procreation. Eastman's position was, of course, anathema to Buckley, who, while scolding radicals for being "apriori" and "doctrinaire," opposed birth control because contraceptive devices violated papal doctrine. Herberg, the most catholic of the ex-communists, hoped that some of these differences could be ironed out by bringing Niebuhr into the conservative dialogue. But his expected "Great American Debate" never took place, and the "New Conservatism" remained a mood in search of a master. "Herberg may be able to delude himself into thinking he can agree simultaneously with Kirk, Rossiter, and Niebuhr," wrote Morton Auerbach in 1958. "But Kirk is obviously uncomfortable about Rossiter; Rossiter and Viereck are lucid in their repudiation of Kirk; the Southern Agrarians and Drucker do not live in the same world; Kirk is suspicious of Drucker; Rossiter thinks he can take him or leave him; Drucker doesn't understand any of them; Niebuhr keeps the entire group at arm's length; and while they all quote Niebuhr profusely, each manages to repudiate his position in some obscure corner of a book."[32]

Ultimately what vitiates American conservatism is not so much a lack of unity as a lack of historical continuity. To be a conservative means to become aware of the historical dimension of knowledge, to nurture, revere, and defend those values and institutions that belong to the past. Knowledge of the American past, however, is precisely the paradox of American conservatism. The same problem of American "exceptionalism" that confronted the Old Left in the thirties confronted the New Right in the fifties. For the same country that failed to produce a revolutionary proletariat failed to produce a conservative aristocracy. The Right, no less than the Left, must come to terms with the bourgeois ethos of Lockian individualism that resounds throughout American history like a choral fugue on the theme of liberal "consensus." Indeed, the dilemma is greater for the neo-conservative, for even while attacking contemporary liberalism and radicalism he is forced to defend America in terms of its liberal tradition. "If he had read Jefferson, Madison and John Adams," Dos Passos said of Milovan Djilas, "he would definitely have something to offer."[33] In the cold war the American writer, even the conservative writer, rises to the defense of the liberal values of freedom and individualism, and the *National Review* intellectual finds himself in the position of advocating the preservation of a social order based upon principles that offend him.

How does one revive what has never lived? Once again, this is not a problem to the liberal, who basks in his belief in progress, or to the radical, who follows Marx's advice and draws his "poetry" from the future, not the past. The American conservative, however, must find his ideological roots in America's historical experience. As a body of principles, conservatism cannot be created *ex nihilo* and instilled into society; rather, it develops organically from the wisdom of the ages. When the *National Review* intellectual turns to the American past, however, he finds himself in the awkward role of the anti-liberal conservative trying to conserve liberalism. To avoid the embarrassment, Russell Kirk may take the reader of *The Conservative Mind* abroad in order to bring home Burke and Coleridge by way of Adams and Calhoun. But his effort is no more convincing than Staughton Lynd's, who asks readers of *Intellectual Origins of American Radicalism* to import Marx by way of Thoreau. Ironically, both the radical and the conservative suffer from the same frustrations of liberal society: one cannot make a revolution, the other cannot create a tradition. Hence Lynd looks to Europe for a sense of class conflict, Kirk for a sense of community. It is by no means a coincidence that the only important conservative historian who stays entirely within the American tradition turns out to be completely unblessed with a conservative philosophy of history. Here we are speaking not of Dos Passos, who is in the same predicament, but of Professor Daniel J. Boorstin, another ex-radical from the thirties. In his magisterial three-volume study of the American experience, Boorstin describes Americans as fleeing from the past, rejecting the authority of moral theory and the structure of organic society. Boorstin finds American history to be "doctrinally naked," for the "genius" of the American people lies in their having abolished philosophy in order to take up the life of action. Intended as a critique of radical historiography by a brilliant ex-Marxist, Boorstin's history is hardly a testimony to intellectual conservatism. He glorifies American "genius" but he also denies Americans one of the highest principles of philsophical conservatism—consciousness, the ability of mind to become aware of itself and to create value through conscious human choice.[34]

All these tensions culminate in what might be called, to use the quaint language of the Old Left, the "final contradiction," which is the *National Review* itself. Buckley's journal represents an attempt to integrate two incompatible themes in modern American intellectual history: anti-communist conservatism, which turns out to be more Lockian than Burkean; and genuine philosophical conservatism, which is too contemplative and intellectually demanding for Boorstin's Americans and too academic for Burnham's causes. The latter theme is more a sensibility than an ideology, concerned primarily with the virtues of the good, the true, and the beautiful, with the prudence born of metaphysical skepticism, and with what Peter Berger calls the "humanism of compassion."[35] Cold war conservatism, on the other hand, springs from the wounds of national (or personal) humiliation, builds upon power politics and the hubris of total victory, tries somehow to combine federalism and private enterprise with the warfare state, and ultimately depends upon the crimes of communism and the "suicidal" illusions of liberalism. The inspiring symbol of the philosophical conservative might be John Adams's Republic of Virtue or Henry Adams's Cathedral of Chartres; for the anti-communist conservative it is the Berlin Wall. One image engenders faith in the dream of moral community, the other engenders fear in the reality of "permanent revolution" (Trotsky's dream became Burnham's nightmare). Philosophical conservatism suggests the American mind; anti-communist conservatism, the American will. The editor of *National Review* has his work cut out for him if he strives to resolve these paradoxes. Perhaps Burnham and Herberg, the two veteran ex-Marxists, can think of a "higher synthesis." I wish them luck.

The editor himself, however, will need more than luck. He is quite prepared to risk destruction of the Cathedral to bring down the Wall by a sheer act of will power. "Better the chance of being dead," wrote Buckley, "than the certainty of being Red."[36]

Buckley's comrades should have no trouble recognizing the language of inevitability, the "certainty" of communist victory. Philosophical conservatives may have more difficulty discovering what will remain to be conserved.

ABBREVIATIONS FOR UNPUBLISHED SOURCES

ACCF   American Committee for Cultural Freedom Files, Tamiment Library, New York University

AN   Allan Nevins Papers, Butler Library, Columbia University

BC   Bennett Cerf Papers (Random House), Butler Library, Columbia University

FD   Floyd Dell Papers, Newberry Library, Chicago

HL   Hoover Library, Stanford, California

JDP   John Dos Passos Papers, Alderman Library, University of Virginia

MC   Malcolm Cowley Papers, Newberry Library, Chicago

ME   Max Eastman Papers, Lilly Library, Indiana University

MS   Max Shachtman Transcripts, Oral History Collections, Columbia University

PR   *Partisan Review* Files, Rutgers University Library

VFC   Victor F. Calverton Papers, New York Public Library

WWN   W. W. Norton Papers, Butler Library, Columbia University

TA   Trotsky Archives, Houghton Library, Harvard University

ABBREVIATIONS FOR PERIODICALS

AM   *American Mercury*

C   *Commentary*

CS   *Common Sense*

H   *Harper's*

MM   *Modern Monthly*

MQ	*Modern Quarterly*
N	*Nation*
NI	*New International*
NL	*New Leader*
NM	*New Masses*
NR	*National Review*
NeR	*New Republic*
NYT	*New York Times*
PR	*Partisan Review*
RA	*Revolutionary Age*
RD	*Reader's Digest*
TMQ	*The Marxist Quarterly*
WA	*Workers Age*

Reference Notes

Introduction

1. Cristiano Camporesi, *Il marxismo teorico negli USA, 1900–1945* (Milan, 1973).
2. Floyd Dell, *Homecoming: An Autobiography* (New York, 1933), p. 251.
3. Max Eastman to Trotsky, Feb. 24, 1933, Max Eastman Papers, Lilly Library, Indiana University (ME).
4. Eastman, *Reflections on the Failure of Socialism* (New York, 1955), pp. 112–27.
5. *The Fourteenth Chronicle: Letters and Diaries of John Dos Passos*, ed. Townsend Ludington (Boston, 1973), pp. 413–30.
6. Ibid., pp. 640, 643.
7. Edmund Wilson, *Night Thoughts* (New York, 1961), p. 196.
8. Will Herberg, "The Biblical Basis of American Democracy," *Thought*, XXX (Spring 1955), 37.
9. James Burnham and Max Shachtman, "Intellectuals in Retreat," *New International*, V (Jan. 1939), 3–22.
10. Max Shachtman Transcripts, Oral History Collections, Columbia University, pp. 345–46.

CHAPTER 1
Exorcising Hegel: Max Eastman

1. Mabel Dodge Luhan, *Intimate Memoirs*, Vol. III, *Movers and Shakers* (New York, 1936), pp. 358–59.
2. Max Eastman, *Enjoyment of Living* (New York, 1948), p. 537. Reed's poem "A Dedication to Max Eastman" is reprinted in Eastman's appendix, pp. 594–95.
3. Joseph Freeman, *An American Testament* (New York, 1936), p. 103; Daniel Aaron, *Writers on the Left: Episodes in American Literary Communism* (New York, 1961), p. 375. Freeman's later reflections on Eastman, dated December 1, 1958, are quoted in a

459

letter from Freeman to Daniel Aaron. I am grateful to Professor Aaron for allowing me to examine his extensive Freeman correspondence.

4. Eastman's collaboration with Trotsky, which occupies a good portion of his correspondence deposited in the Lilly Library, Indiana University, is a separate study in itself, and one that requires thorough knowledge of Russian and sensibility to the demands of literary art. In the estimate of critic F. W. Dupee, "Eastman's admirable translation has made *The History of the Russian Revolution* an English classic" (Leon Trotsky, *The Russian Revolution*, F. W. Dupee, ed. [Garden City, N.Y., 1959], p. viii). Eastman also translated Trotsky's *The Real Situation in Russia*, *The Revolution Betrayed*, and *The Young Lenin*.

5. Max Schuster to Victor Gollancz, May 13, 1936, Max Eastman Papers, Lilly Library, Indiana University (ME).

6. Eastman, *Love and Revolution: My Journey through an Epoch* (New York, 1964), p. 127.

7. *Liberator*, I (Nov. 1918), 17.

8. Theodore Draper, *The Roots of American Communism* (New York, 1957), pp. 49, 403–4.

9. Eastman, *Love and Revolution*, pp. 350–56, 446–47; *Since Lenin Died* (New York and London, 1925); *Leon Trotsky: The Portrait of a Youth* (New York, 1925), p. v; "Lenin's Testament," Dec. 25, 1922, "Supplement," Jan. 4, 1923, ME. Such scholars of diverse political views as Leonard Schapiro and Isaac Deutscher have praised Eastman's *Since Lenin Died* for its prescience. See Leonard Schapiro, *The Communist Party of the Soviet Union* (New York, 1960), pp. 280, 296, 306; Isaac Deutscher, *The Prophet Unarmed: Trotsky: 1921–1929*, Vol. II (New York: Vintage edn., 1965), pp. 201–2.

10. Eastman, "Political Liberty," in *Freedom in the Modern World*, Horace Kallen, ed. (New York, 1928); pp. 159–82.

11. Freeman, *An American Testament*, p. 50.

12. Aaron, *Writers on the Left*, pp. 49–55.

13. Eastman, *Marx and Lenin: The Science of Revolution* (New York, 1927), p. 183.

14. Eastman, *The Literary Mind: Its Place in an Age of Science* (New York, 1932), pp. 3–11, 161–94. Two valuable treatments of Eastman as an aesthetician are Charles I. Glicksberg, "Max Eastman: Literary Insurgent," *Sewanee Review*, XLIV (July–Sep. 1936), 323–37; and Murray Krieger, *The New Apologists for Poetry* (Bloomington, Ind.: Midland edn., 1963), pp. 191–201.

15. Eastman, "Three Visits with Einstein," in *Great Companions* (New York, 1959), p. 27.

16. See I. A. Richards's review of *The Literary Mind*, in *Criterion*, XII (Oct. 1932), 150–55; and Eastman's reply, ibid. (April 1933), 488–91. See also Allen Tate's "Understanding Modern Poetry," in

On the Limits of Poetry (New York, 1948), pp. 115–19. In a public lecture Eastman maintained that the failure of Seward Collins to reply to *The Literary Mind* was an admission of the intellectual "defeat" of the New Humanists. Collins, editor of the important conservative journal *American Review*, informed Eastman that not only was *The Literary Mind* flawed by "numerous weaknesses and absurdities" but that he intended to do a full-scale critique of all Eastman's books under the title "The Pseudo-Scientific Mind" (Collins to Eastman, n.d., 1933, ME). Edmund Wilson, who had explicated the symbolism of modern writers like Joyce and Proust in *Axel's Castle*, was highly critical of Eastman's treatment of such writers in *The Literary Mind*. At the end of the decade, however, he reappraised the work. "A glance into *The Literary Mind* today," he wrote in 1941, "reveals, rather surprisingly to one who was prejudiced against the book when it first appeared, that it was distinguished by a deeper comprehension of the real issues raised by contemporary literature than almost anything that had been written in the twenties. . . . Max Eastman was almost alone in his attempt to work out as an enlightened modern man the larger relations of art and science to one another, and of both to the society behind them." Wilson, "Max Eastman in 1941," *Classics and Commercials* (New York, 1950), pp. 57–69.

17. Eastman to Calverton, Sep. 24, 1934, Victor F. Calverton Papers, New York Public Library (VFC). After Eastman resigned from the *Modern Monthly*, Calverton apologized to him for having "muddled that sentence which caused you so much irritation and pain." Calverton to Eastman, Sep. 28, 1934, ibid.

18. Eastman, *Love and Revolution: My Journey through an Epoch* (New York, 1964), p. 606; Eastman to Trotsky, Aug. 9, 1933, and Aug. 14, 1933; Shachtman to Eastman, Oct. 8, 1933, ME.

19. Eastman, *Love and Revolution*, pp. 602–3. Eastman, like Trotsky, was smeared as one of the "Pontius Pilates" of the Soviet Union by the communist Left in America. Yet at this juncture Eastman and Trotsky were protesting the corruption of the dream of the October Revolution under the bureaucracy of Stalin, not Bolshevism itself. When the British publishers of *Artists in Uniform* advertised the book as an argument in favor of life in democratic England, Eastman protested vigorously (Eastman to Stanley Unwin, April 8, 1935, ME). Juan Andrade, editor of the journal *Comunismo*, requested permission to translate the book for Spanish and Latin American readers (Andrade to Eastman, May 29, 1934, ME). For a debate over *Artists in Uniform*, see the *Modern Monthly*, VIII (Aug. 1934), 445–48; (Oct. 1934), 569–73.

20. Eastman, *Love and Revolution*, p. 606; Chevalier is quoted in Aaron, p. 318. For Chevalier's background, see David Caute, *The Fellow-Travelers: A Postscript to the Enlightenment* (New York, 1973), pp. 335–38.

21. Eastman, *Love and Revolution*, p. 607.

22. Eastman to Albert Boni, July 1, 1926, ME; Eastman to Calverton, June 23, 1934; March 28, 1935; March 18, 1936, VFC.

23. Eastman, "John Reed and the Old *Masses*," *MM*, X (Oct. 1936), 19–22, 31; Eastman is quoted from a letter to Granville Hicks which prefaced the article.

24. Eastman to Calverton, July 11, 1936, VFC; Calverton to Eastman, Aug. 12, 1936, ME; Hook to Calverton, Aug. 26, 1936, VFC.

25. Mabel Dodge to Eastman, May 10, 1938; Eastman to Dodge, May (?), 1938; Oct. 25, 1938, ME. For an excellent analysis of the contradictory testimony of Louise Bryant, Angelica Balabanoff, Benjamin Gitlow, and Louis Frania, see Theodore Draper, "The Mystery of John Reed," in *The Roots of American Communism* (New York: Compass edn., 1957), pp. 284–93.

26. Eastman to Calverton, June 29, 1934; July 30, 1934, VFC.

27. Eastman, "Discrimination about Russia," *MM*, VIII (Sep. 1934), 479–85.

28. Eastman to Calverton, June 12, 1935, VFC. During this period Eastman had been receiving chapters in Russian of Trotsky's forthcoming book, *The Revolution Betrayed*, a source of much of his factual information about events inside Russia. Since the early thirties Eastman had also been keeping in touch with Boris Souvarine, the first secretary of the French Communist Party. Eastman helped Souvarine find an English publisher for his monumental work, *Staline, Aperçu Historique de Bolshevisme*, a source which was perhaps more valuable to Eastman than Trotsky's book for understanding the phenomenon of Stalinism. Boris Souvarine to Eastman, Sep. 16, 1933; Sep. 23, 1936; April 16, 1937; April 18, 1937, ME.

29. Eastman, "The End of Socialism in Russia," *Harper's*, CLXXIV (Feb. 1937), 302–14. See also Eastman's "Russia and the Socialist Ideal," ibid., CLXXVI (March 1938), 374–85.

30. Benjamin H. Kizer to Eastman, March 2, 1938; E. J. Coit to Eastman, March 16, 1938; J. B. Matthews to Eastman, March 17, 1938; John Dewey to Eastman, March 3, 1938; Little, Brown & Co. to Eastman, April 19, 1937; Eastman to E. F. Tompkins, April 24, 1937; Eastman to Kenneth C. Wilson, Nov. 25, 1936; Maxwell Perkins to Eastman, May 16, 1939, ME.

31. Trotsky, "Statement Regarding Max Eastman," to the New York *Times*, dated Feb. 23, 1937, Trotsky Archives, Houghton Library, Harvard University (TA). Eastman's letter to Shachtman and Burnham, a seven-page typed statement entitled "A Few Remarks" (dated Jan. 18, 1939), has written in pencil, "Not sent" ME.

32. Eastman, "Socialism Revalued: The State of Ethics and Its Overthrow," *Common Sense*, IX (Feb. 1940), 12–15.

33. Aaron, *Writers on the Left*, p. 315.
34. Eastman, *Enjoyment of Living* (New York, 1948), pp. 23, 236, 293; *Heroes I Have Known* (New York, 1942), pp. 104–42; *Great Companions: Critical Memoirs of Some Famous Friends* (New York, 1959), pp. 299–312.
35. Eastman, *Enjoyment of Poetry* (New York, 1913), pp. 3–19, 136–53.
36. Eastman, *Love and Revolution*, pp. 14–16; *Enjoyment of Living*, p. 355.
37. Gustav A. Wetter, *Dialectical Materialism: A Historical and Systematic Survey of Philosophy in the Soviet Union*, trans. Peter Heath (New York, 1958), pp. 128–29.
38. Georg Lukacs, *History and Class Consciousness: Studies in Marxist Dialectics* (1923), trans. Rodney Livingstone (Cambridge, 1970), p. 10, passim; Karl Korsch, *Marxism and Philosophy* (1923), trans. Fred Halliday (New York and London, 1970), pp. 44–45.
39. Eastman, *Marx and Lenin: The Science of Revolution* (New York, 1927), pp. 13–18, 31.
40. Ibid., pp. 11, 19–64, 112, passim.
41. Ibid., pp. 16–88, 97–105.
42. Ibid., p. 46.
43. Ibid., pp. 141, 149–63. In direct contrast to Eastman, Lukacs insisted that the Leninist distinction between the "subjective factor" of historical awareness (the Party) and its object (the masses) could be reconciled by the proletariat, whose revolutionary activity not only "reflects" the processes of history but "transforms" them. Lukacs, *History and Class Consciousness*, pp. 1–26, 46–82, passim. For a critical analysis of Lukacs, see Morris Watnick, "Relativism and Class Consciousness: Georg Lukacs," in *Revisionism: Essays on the History of Marxist Ideas*, ed. Leopold Labedz (New York, 1962), pp. 142–65; and George Lichtheim, *Georg Lukacs* (New York, 1970).
44. Eastman, *Marx and Lenin*, pp. 28, 106–17, 150–74, 186–88, 191.
45. Foster to Calverton, Sep. 8, 1925; Mike Gold to Calverton, May 4, 1925, VFC; Bertram D. Wolfe, "Eastman Revises Marx," *The Communist*, VI (Nov. 1927), 403–12.
46. The Mussey review is in the *Nation*, CXXVII (Aug. 15, 1928), 159–60; Smith review in the *International Journal of Ethics*, XXXVIII (July 1928), 480–82; Kallen to Eastman, April 7, 1927, ME.
47. Eastman, *Love and Revolution*, p. 461; J. M. Keynes to Eastman, Dec. 22, 1926, ME.
48. Leif Björk to Eastman, July 12, 1926, ME.
49. Charles Rappoport, "Les Sophismes Révisionistes," *L'Humanité*, Dec. 5, 1926.
50. Lukacs, "Eine Marxkritik im Dienste des Trotzkismus," *Die Internationale* (Mar. 1927), 189–90.

51. Sidney Hook, "Marxism, Metaphysics, and Modern Science," *MQ*, IV (May–Aug. 1928), 388–94; ibid., VII (Sep. 1933), 511–12; Eastman to Calverton, Aug. 9, 1933, VFC.
52. Hook, "Marxism, Metaphysics," 390–94.
53. Hook, "From Hegel to Marx," *MQ*, VI (Summer 1932), 33–43. Hook expressed indebtedness to the work of Korsch and Lukacs though he believed Korsch underestimated the difficulties in making the "formal aspects" of Marx's thought "practical," and Lukacs linked "Marx up—unfortunately much too closely—with the stream of German classical philosophy." Hook, *Towards the Understanding of Karl Marx: A Revolutionary Interpretation* (New York, 1933), p. xii.
54. Hook, "From Hegel to Marx," *MQ*, VI (Winter 1931), 46–62; ibid. (Summer 1932), 33–43; ibid. (Autumn 1932), 58–67. "The fluidity of thing and fact and the changing context of judgment represent the heart of the dialectic, and not the antiquated terms in which Hegel dressed up the idea. Mr. Eastman may be surprised to learn that the dialectic—modified to be sure—appears in the instrumentalist logic. In any moving, developing situation the relation between 'need' and 'fulfillment' has been taken by Professor Dewey to be an instance of 'intrinsic opposites' whose resolution appears as a factor in other concrete situations which grow out of the first. But an existential bipolarity is the condition precedent to genuine thinking." Hook, "Marxism, Metaphysics," 393.
55. Bertrand Russell also discerned epistemological similarities between Marxism and pragmatism and, like Eastman, remained skeptical of both philosophies. See Russell, "Dialectical Materialism," in *Theories of History*, ed. Patrick Gardiner (New York, 1959), pp. 285–95; and "Why I Am Not a Communist," in *The Meaning of Marxism*, pp. 83–85. But Russell, who had from the beginning criticized Bolshevism along with Marxism, had equally strong doubts about Eastman's praise of Lenin (Eastman to Calverton, June 6, 1937, VFC). On the relationship between American pragmatism and Marxism, see also Leszek Kolakowski, "Karl Marx and the Classical Definition of Truth," in *Toward a Marxist Humanism: Essays on the Left Today*, trans. Jane Zielonko Peel (New York, 1969), pp. 38–66; Jürgen Habermas, *Knowledge and Human Interests*, trans. Jeremy Shapiro (Boston, 1971).
56. Hook, *Understanding of Karl Marx*, pp. 92, 100, 109–10. "We are now in a position to understand what Marx really means when he speaks of the historical inevitability of communism. Communism is not something fated to be realized in the nature of things; but, *if society is to survive*, communism offers the only way out of the impasse created by the inability of capitalism, despite its superabundance of wealth, to provide a decent *social* existence for its own wage-earners. What Marx is really saying is: either this (communism) or nothing

(barbarism). That is why communists feel justified in claiming that their doctrine expresses both the subjective class interests of the proletariat and the objective interests of civilization. The objectivity of Marxism is derived from the truth of the disjunction; the subjectivity, from the fact that *this* is chosen rather than *nothing*. . . . It is only when one accepts the first terms of the disjunction—which is a psychological, and, if you please, an ethical act, that he has a right to the name [of Marxist]. The choice is intelligent only if it takes note of Marx's analysis; but once the choice is made, it itself becomes an historical factor in making the revolutionary ideal come true." Ibid., pp. 113–14.

57. Hook, "From Hegel to Marx," *MQ*, VI (Winter 1931), 62.

58. Eastman, *The Last Stand of Dialectical Materialism: A Study of Sidney Hook's Marxism* (pamphlet, Polemic Publishers, New York, 1934), pp. 7–18, passim; "Marxism: Science or Philosophy?" *New International*, II (Aug. 1935), 159–63. For a different interpretation of this crucial passage in the "Theses on Feuerbach," see Hook, "Marx and Feuerbach, *NI*, III (April 1936), 47–57.

59. Hook, "Marxism and Values," *Marxist Quarterly*, I (Jan.–March 1937), 38–45.

60. See the various attacks on Eastman in "Marxism and Social Change: A Symposium," *MQ*, V (Winter 1930–1931), 427–50.

61. Will Herberg, "Workers' Democracy or Dictatorship? On Hook's Revival of Kautsky's Theories," *Workers Age*, II (Dec. 15, 1934), 3, 8.

62. Shachtman to Eastman, Feb. 13, 1934; A. J. Muste to Eastman, Aug. 22, 1934, ME.

63. Trotsky to Hook, April 10, 1933; Trotsky to *The Militant*, July 1929; "Perspectives on American Marxism," Ms. to Calverton, Nov. 4, 1932, TA; Eastman to Robert LaFollette, June 7, 1933; Eastman to William C. Bullitt, June 13, 1933; Dreiser to Eastman, May 26, 1933; Eastman to Trotsky, July 9, 1929, and Feb. 24, 1933, ME. According to Burnham, Trotsky had asked him and other writers in the *New International* to respond to Eastman's critiques of Marxist philosophy (interview with Burnham, June 11, 1971). Burnham was willing to defend Marxism but not dialectical materialism, which he saw as "only a disguised form of monistic objective idealism" that falsely guaranteed the inevitability of socialism. See John West (James Burnham), "Max Eastman's Straw Man," *NI*, II (Dec. 1935), 220–25.

64. Eastman, *Love and Revolution*, p. 627. For Tresca's career, see John P. Diggins, *Mussolini and Fascism: The View from America* (Princeton, 1972), pp. 134–39.

65. Eastman to Calverton, March 4, 1937, VFC.

66. John Dewey, "Means and Ends," *NI*, IV (Aug. 1938), 232–33.

67. James Burnham, "Science and Style," reprinted in Leon Trotsky,

In Defense of Marxism (against the petty-bourgeois opposition)
(New York: Merit Publishers, 1965), pp. 196–97; Trotsky to Burnham, Jan. 7, 1940, TA.

68. Hook, "Dialectic and Nature," *Marxist Quarterly*, I (April–June 1937), 253–84; "Dialectic in Social and Historical Inquiry," *Journal of Philosophy*, XXXVI (July 6, 1939), 365–78. Eastman applauded Hook's reconsiderations and described "Dialectic and Nature" as a "brilliant study" (Eastman, "Trotsky's Use of 'Dialectic,'" Ms., n.d., ME). Observing Hook "quietly changing his mind" about dialectical philosophy, some wondered whether Eastman's writings had any influence on Hook's "most startling" shift of attitude (Margaret Johns to Eastman, Dec. 7, 1938; Alfred Bingham to Eastman, Nov. 4, 1938, ME). It is doubtful that Hook would allow himself to be influenced by a part-time philosopher like Eastman. Perhaps the one thinker who impressed Hook in the thirties was Karl Korsch, whose lectures he had attended in Berlin. Hook tried to get Korsch to participate in various American symposia on Marxism, paid for his subscription to *Modern Quarterly*, and sent him his articles on Hegel and Marx (Hook to Calverton, July 14, 1934). In the late thirties Korsch, now living in the United States, reconsidered his earlier synthesis of Marxism and German idealism and stressed the differences between Marx and Hegel (Korsch, "Leading Principles of Marxism," *Marxist Quarterly*, I [Oct.–Dec. 1937], 356–78). In *Karl Marx* (London, 1938), he sought to convert Marxism into a theory of revolutionary practice and to free historical materialism from the contemplative spell of Hegel—somewhat the same approach Eastman advocated a decade earlier. Unfortunately, even though Calverton urged Eastman to read Korsch's articles and books, Eastman felt there was nothing more to be learned from a German Marxist philosopher (Eastman to Calverton, Feb. 28, 1939, VFC).

69. Hook, *The Hero in History: A Study in Limitation and Possibility* (New York, 1943).

70. Wilson to Eastman, Oct. 5, 1938, ME; Wilson to Dos Passos, April 27, 1938, John Dos Passos Papers, Alderman Library, University of Virginia (JDP); Phillips to Wilson, Aug. 31, 1938, and Wilson to Dwight Macdonald, Sep. 10, 1943, *Partisan Review* Files, Rutgers University Library (PR); Edmund Wilson, *To the Finland Station: A Study in the Writing and Acting of History* (Garden City, N.Y.: Anchor edn., n.d.), pp. 179–98, 372–402. Wilson, however, was less certain than Eastman that Lenin could be appreciated apart from Marxism. Although Bolshevism may not have been the historical actualization of the dialectic, Lenin identified his doctrines with the logic of philosophy. This raises the question whether Lenin could have, psychologically as well as philosophically, succeeded in making a social revolution happen without the conviction that he embodied the will

of Marxism. Although Wilson then avoided the issue (but later returned to it indirectly in *Patriotic Gore* [New York: Galaxy edn., 1966], pp. xvi–xix), a case for the argument had been made earlier by Waldo Frank:

> There is, moreover, no contradiction between the philosophy of Marx and the methodology of Lenin. Mr. Eastman (like most enemies of philosophy) is so simplistic that he cannot conciliate the concept of historical necessity (Marxism) with the necessity, *within that necessity*, of human will to determine its methods of action, to choose, to fight and to create (Leninism). The dynamism of Lenin as an engineer lies precisely in his being nurtured by the *Weltanschauung* of Marx, his intuition of life as an organism *with an internal direction*. Mr. Eastman, it seems to me, is unable to understand Lenin because he rejects what is profound and true to Marx. There is no antithesis between a social engineer and a prophet [*Modern Quarterly*, V (Winter 1930–1931), 448].

To Eastman, however, whether or not Lenin was acting in the name of Marxism proved nothing about the epistemological claims of Marxian philosophy, which demands that theory and practice be organically related. Eastman was an "enemy of philosophy" only to the extent that those who regarded themselves as philosophers failed to answer their own questions. "It seems to me," he wrote to another one of his critics who challenged him on the same issue,

> that this philosophical position of Lenin's ignores the essential problem which it pretends to solve. The problem about determinism and free will is how to reconcile the assumption of the mind that everything is determined with its assumption that by knowing these determinations, it can itself determine the future. Neither Engels nor Lenin approaches this problem, and the reason is, I think, that they are not interested in philosophical problems as such, but merely in arriving at a practical, working attitude of mind. . . . In short, if you will think longer about it, I think you will see that you cannot possibly attribute to mind—and that means will, thought, and feeling—a dynamic effect upon the ordered movement of matter without assuming that, at least where mind arises, there is an indetermination in that movement [Eastman to Peter Berlinrut, Sep. 16, 1933, ME].

71. See Hook's severe review of *Reason and Revolution* in *New Republic*, CV (July 21, 1941), 90–91.

72. Interview with Herbert Marcuse, Sep. 14, 1972.

73. John P. Diggins, "Pragmatism and Ideology: Philosophy or Passion?" *American Political Science Review*, LXIV (Sep. 1970), 899–906.

74. Hook, "Metaphysics and Social Attitudes," *Social Frontier*, IV (Feb. 1938), 153–58; "Hegel Rehabilitated?" *Encounter*, XXIV (Jan. 1965), 53–58; Shlomo Avineri, "Hook's Hegel," ibid., XXIV (Nov. 1965), 63–66.

75. Eastman, "Marxism: Science or Philosophy?" *NI*, 163.

76. There is a striking similarity between Eastman's and Veblen's attitudes toward Marxism. Veblen also believed Marx was caught up in nineteenth-century metaphysical assumptions. His "sublimated materialism" betrays the spirit of Hegel in the language of Darwinism, while his theory of class struggle "proceeds on the grounds of the hedonistic calculus" that is "closer to Bentham than to Hegel." "Animism" was also a favorite description of Veblen's. See Veblen, "The Socialist Economics of Karl Marx and His Followers," *Quarterly Journal of Economics*, XX (Aug. 1906), 578–95.

77. John Dewey, *German Philosophy and Politics* (New York, 1915); Thorstein Veblen, *Imperial Germany and the Industrial Revolution* (New York, 1915). See also Morton White, *Social Thought in America: The Revolt against Formalism* (Boston: Beacon edn., 1957), pp. 147–60.

78. Max Horkheimer, *Critical Theory: Selected Essays*, trans. Matthew J. O'Connell and others (New York, 1972), pp. 132–87.

79. Preface to Eastman's poem "Lot's Wife," quoted in *Reflections on the Failure of Socialism* (New York: Universal Library edn., 1962), p. 57. Eastman always regretted never having fully developed his notion of science, his "unborn magnum opus." See *Love and Revolution*, pp. 127, 200–3.

80. In *Karl Marx: His Life and Environment* (New York: Galaxy edn., 1963), Sir Isaiah Berlin called Eastman's *Marxism: Is It Science?* "an essay of characteristic brilliance by this sharp and original critic and excellent writer, bitterly condemned as a heretic by orthodox Communists" (p. 287). R. N. Carew-Hunt, *The Theory and Practice of Communism* (Baltimore: Penguin edn., 1963), pp. 48–49, 52, 55, 144, 153, 240, 298; Carew-Hunt to Eastman, Jan. 20, 1954, ME. For a critique of Eastman and Raymond Postgate, see T. A. Jackson, *Dialectics: The Logic of Marxism and Its Critics* (London, 1936), pp. 481–560. For a more recent Marxist review of the issue, see Edward J. Primbs, "Contemporary American Criticism of Dialectical Materialism," *Science & Society*, XXIX (Spring 1965), 129–72.

81. Edmund Wilson, "Max Eastman in 1941," *Classics and Commercials*, pp. 68–69. This collection reprints the review originally appearing in the *New Republic*, Feb. 1941.

82. Eastman, "Russia and the Socialist Ideal," *Harper's*, CLXXIV (March 1938), 374–85.

83. Leon Trotsky, "The Soviet Union Today: The Workers' State and the Question of Thermidor and Bonapartism," *NI*, II (July 1935),

116–22; id., *The Revolution Betrayed: What Is the Soviet Union and Where Is It Going?* trans. Max Eastman (New York: Merit Publishers edn., 1965), pp. 86–114, 231, 273–89, passim.

84. Eastman, "Russia and the Socialist Ideal," *H*, 382.

85. Trotsky, *In Defense of Marxism*, pp. 6, 72.

86. Ibid., pp. 3–22; Deutscher, *The Prophet Outcast*, pp. 457–62.

87. See, for example, Staughton Lynd, "How the Cold War Began," *Commentary*, XXX (Nov. 1960), 379–89.

88. Trotsky, *In Defense of Marxism*, p. 53.

89. Ibid., pp. 50, 54, 83.

90. Trotsky, "The U.S.S.R. in War," *NI*, V (Nov. 1939), 327.

91. Eastman and Hook still believed in working class struggle, which is not to be confused with the "proletariat." The former is a reality that can be studied in historical and sociological terms; the latter is an idea rooted in Marx's dialectical scheme of thought, a concept which can neither be affirmed nor refuted empirically, and hence better described as "philosophical." See Ralf Dahrendorf, *Class and Class Conflict in Industrial Society* (Stanford, 1959), pp. 27–32.

92. Eastman, "Russia and the Socialist Ideal," *H*, 382.

CHAPTER 2
"Organization Is Death": John Dos Passos

1. Max Eastman, *Love and Revolution*, p. 131; Malcolm Cowley, "Dos Passos: The Learned Poggius," *Southern Review*, IX (Jan. 1973), 3–4.

2. John Dos Passos, *The Best Times* (New York: Signet edn., 1968), p. 20.

3. Dos Passos, *Chosen Country* (Boston, 1951), p. 26.

4. Dos Passos, "A Humble Protest," *Harvard Monthly*, LXII (June 1916), 119.

5. Quoted in Daniel Aaron, "The Riddle of John Dos Passos," *Harper's*, CCXXIV (March 1962), 55–60.

6. Dos Passos, "A Letter from the Front" (Aug. 27, 1917), *New York Review of Books*, XX (June 28, 1973), 24; Aaron, "Riddle," 57.

7. Dos Passos, *One Man's Initiation: 1917* (Ithaca, N.Y.: Cornell University Press edn., 1969), pp. 165–66.

8. Ibid., p. 165.

9. Dos Passos, *The Best Times*, p. 148.

10. More is quoted in Frederick J. Hoffmann, *The Twenties: American Writing in the Postwar Decade* (New York: Collier edn., 1962), p. 169; Edmund Wilson, *Shores of Light* (New York, 1952), p. 431.

11. Dos Passos, "The New Masses I'd Like," *New Masses*, I (June 1926), 20.

12. Dos Passos, "Making of a Writer," *NM*, IV (March 1929), 23.

13. Dos Passos, "Whither the American Writer," *MQ*, VI (Summer 1932), 11–12.

14. Ibid., 11–12; Malcolm Cowley, *Exile's Return: A Literary Odyssey of the 1920's* (New York: Compass Books edn., 1956), p. 223.

15. Dos Passos, "Whither the American Writer," 11–12; "Back to Red Hysteria," *New Republic*, XIII (July 2, 1930), 168–69; "Intellectuals in America," *NM*, VI (Aug. 1930), 8.

16. Dos Passos, "Wanted: An Ivy Lee for Liberals," *NM*, LXIII (August 13, 1930), 371–72; "Whither the American Writer," 12.

17. Dos Passos's interview quoted in Georges-Albert Astre, *Themes et Structures dans L'Oeuvre de John Dos Passos*, II (Paris: Lettres Modernes, 1958), pp. 300–1.

18. *NM*, X (Feb. 27, 1934), 8–10, 24; (March 6, 1934), 8–9; Aaron, *Writers on the Left*, p. 350; Granville Hicks, "The Politics of John Dos Passos," *Antioch Review*, X (March 1950), 93.

19. John Howard Lawson to Dos Passos, n.d., John Dos Passos Papers, Alderman Library, University of Virginia (JDP).

20. John Dewey to Dos Passos, June 12, 1937; Margaret De Silver to Dos Passos, n.d., JDP.

21. Dos Passos to Scott Fitzgerald (Oct. ? 1936), in Fitzgerald, *The Crack-Up*, Edmund Wilson, ed. (New York, 1956), p. 311.

22. Dos Passos to Robert Cantwell, Sep. 1934; Dos Passos to Edmund Wilson, March 23, 1934, in *The Fourteenth Chronicle: Letters and Diaries of John Dos Passos*, ed. Townsend Ludington (Boston, 1973), pp. 435–36, 441–42.

23. Ernest Hemingway to Dos Passos, Oct. 30, 1951, JDP.

24. Hemingway to Dos Passos, June 26, 1931; March 26, 1932; May 30, 1932; Oct. 14, 1932, JDP.

25. Hemingway to Dos Passos, March 26, 1932, JDP; Dos Passos, "The Villages Are the Heart of Spain," *Esquire*, IX (Feb. 1938), 32–33, 151–53. See also Dos Passos's earlier "Young Spain," *Seven Arts*, II (August 1917), 473–78. According to Hemingway, Dos Passos was also an enormously popular writer among the Spaniards. Hemingway to Dos Passos, Jan. 26, 1932, JDP.

26. Carlos Baker, *Ernest Hemingway: A Life Story* (New York, 1969), p. 305; Dos Passos to Dwight Macdonald, n.d., Partisan Review Files, Rutgers University Library (PR).

27. Dos Passos, "A Farewell to Europe," *Common Sense*, VI (July 1937), 9–11.

28. Hemingway to Dos Passos, 1938 (n.d.), JDP; Baker, *Life Story*, p. 306.

29. Dos Passos to Malcolm Cowley, Nov. 25 (n.y.), Malcolm Cowley Papers, Newberry Library, Chicago (MC).

30. *NM*, XXXII (July 4, 1939), 21; *NeR*, XCIX (June 14, 1939), 163. For Dos Passos's reply to Cowley, see *NeR* (July 19, 1939), 308–

9, and Dos Passos to Dwight Macdonald, n.d., to William Phillips, n.d., and to Philip Rahv, n.d., PR; John Howard Lawson to Dos Passos, May 3, 1939, JDP. For Farrell's sympathetic review, see American Mercury, XVII (Aug. 1939), 489–94.

31. Dos Passos, "The Communist Party and the War Spirit," Common Sense, VI (Dec. 1937), 11–14; "The Situation in American Writing," Partisan Review, VI (Summer 1939), 27; "To a Liberal in Office," Nation, CLIII (Sep. 6, 1941), 195–97; Claude Bowers to Dos Passos, May 1, 1939; Edmund Wilson to Dos Passos, April 13, 1958, JDP.

32. For the psychological interpretation I have drawn upon two important articles: Blanch Gelfant, "The Search for Identity in the Novels of John Dos Passos," PMLA, LXXVI (March 1961), 133–49; and Martin Kallich, "John Dos Passos: Liberty and the Father Image," Antioch Review, X (Spring 1950), 100–5.

33. Gelfant, "The Search," 138.

34. Dos Passos, responding to questionnaire, "The Situation in American Writing," PR, 27.

35. David Sanders, "The Anarchism of John Dos Passos," South Atlantic Quarterly, LX (Winter 1961), 44–55.

36. Had there been an American Marxist critic with the mind of a Georg Lukacs, he might have seen that U.S.A. lacked an "organic" conception of reality enabling its author to grasp the "objective" and "essential driving forces of history." See Lukacs, The Historical Novel, trans. Hannah and Stanley Mitchell (Boston: Beacon edn., 1963), p. 206.

37. Dos Passos, "A Statement of Belief," Bookman, LXVIII (Sept. 1928), 26; Introduction, Three Soldiers (New York, 1932), p. viii; Dos Passos to Simon & Schuster, 1932 (n.d.), Max Eastman Papers, Lilly Library, Indiana University (ME). "Whither the American Writer," 11–12.

38. Robert Gorham Davis, John Dos Passos (Minneapolis, 1962), pp. 28–30.

39. Dos Passos, "Contemporary Chronicles," Ms. (n.d.), JDP.

40. Ibid., pp. 4–5.

41. Benedetto Croce, "History and Chronicle," in The Philosophy of History in Our Time, ed. Hans Meyerhoff (Garden City, N.Y., 1959), pp. 44–57.

42. Jean-Paul Sartre, Literary and Philosophical Essays (New York: Collier edn., 1962), pp. 94–103.

43. Charles Beard, "Written History as an Act of Faith," in Philosophy of History, pp. 140–51. In this famous address, delivered before the American Historical Association in 1932, Beard maintained that one could write history from the point of view of progress or cycles but not chaos, since the latter category admits no order to events and hence

472 | Reference Notes

no principle of understanding. The address was delivered while Dos Passos was in the midst of completing *U.S.A.*

44. Dos Passos, "Satire as a Way of Seeing," in *Occasions and Protests* (Chicago, 1964), p. 30.

45. Charles Horton Cooley, *Social Organization* (New York, 1909).

46. Émile Durkheim, *Suicide: A Study in Sociology*, trans. J. A. Spaulding and George Simpson (New York: Free Press, 1951). "Human passions," Durkheim observed, "stop only before a moral power they respect." *The Division of Labor in Society*, trans. George Simpson (New York: Free Press, 1964), p. 3.

47. Dos Passos to author, April 3, 1966. Dos Passos was referring to the author's article "Dos Passos and Veblen's Villains," *Antioch Review*, XXIII (Winter 1963–1964), 485–500.

48. Dos Passos, "The Technocrats of Missouri," Ms. (n.d.), 5950 AE, Box 23, JDP. In September 1934 Dos Passos wrote to Edmund Wilson, "Since I've been in bed I've been reading a good deal of Veblen. He takes a good deal of reading. I admire his delicate surgeon's analysis more and more. In spite of the fact that everything he deals with is abstracted for classroom use, I shouldn't wonder if he were the only American economist whose work had any lasting value. His work is a sort of anthropological footnote to Marx. If you haven't read him recently you should read him—The Vested Interests or the Nature of Peace or Business Enterprise—(I think The Leisure Class is more or less of a side issue, though it will always be considered the type Veblen satire). Imperial Germany makes an excellent prelude to Hitler Over Europe. . . . There certainly seems to me to be more ammunition in his analysis than in any other for us, because he seems to have been the only man of genius who put his mind critically to work on American capitalism—Stuart Chase and Howard Scott got their analysis directly from him. And certainly he's of an entirely different stature than the purely literary critics, like Van Wyck Brooks and Randolph Bourne, who have the same beforethewar limitations. Its amazing how fresh his clinical picture remains." Dos Passos to Wilson, Sep. 24, 1934, in *The Fourteenth Chronicle*, pp. 443–44.

49. Dos Passos, "The World We Live In," *NeR*, LXXIX (May 16, 1934), 25.

50. David Sanders, "Interview with Dos Passos," *Paris Review*, XII (Spring 1969), 157–58.

51. Dos Passos, Introduction to William F. Buckley, Jr.'s. *Up from Liberalism* (New York, 1959), p. viii.

52. Dos Passos, "A Humble Protest," *Harvard Monthly*, 117–20.

53. Karl Marx, "Economic and Philosophic Manuscripts" (1844), in *Writings of the Young Marx on Philosophy and Society*, eds. Lloyd D. Easton and Kurt Guddat (Garden City, N.Y., 1967), p. 310.

54. When *The Big Money* was published in 1936, the foster daugh-

ter of Taylor protested to Dos Passos the portrait of her father in the novel: "Fred Taylor was genuinely interested in the welfare of the workingman. The misapplication of his system of management to exploit labor deeply depressed him and was a fundamental cause of his early retirement. A passion for fair play and social justice was the central force of his work and life—a fact which you have singularly missed in your biographical sketch." K. P. A. Taylor to Dos Passos, Oct. 28, 1936, JDP.

55. Dos Passos, "A Humble Protest," 119.

56. Mike Gold criticized Dos Passos's position that it was not just the profit system but industrialism itself that "enslaves mankind." "The Education of John Dos Passos," *English Journal*, XXII (Feb. 1933), 87–93.

57. Dos Passos, *Rosinante to the Road Again* (New York, 1922), p. 93.

58. Dos Passos, *Occasions and Protests*, p. 278.

59. Max Weber, *The Protestant Ethic and the Spirit of Capitalism* (New York: Scribner's, new edn., 1958), p. 181.

CHAPTER 3
The Quest for Transcendence: Will Herberg

1. John Dos Passos, "The New Masses I'd Like," *New Masses*, I (June 1926), 20.

2. Will Herberg to author, Feb. 19, 1973; Interview, Sep. 29, 1974.

3. Sidney Hook to author, Sep. 12, 1973; Hook, "The Ethics of Controversy" (Forum sponsored by the American Committee for Cultural Freedom, April 8, 1952), Ms. typescript, Tamiment Library, New York University; Interview with Wolfe, Sep. 1, 1971; Irving Howe, "Critics of American Socialism," *New International*, XVIII (May–June 1952), 122.

4. In his Marxist years, Herberg was much impressed by V. F. Calverton's anthropological approach to religion as a "cultural compulsive." See his review of Calverton's *The Passing of the Gods*, in *Workers Age*, II (Nov. 15, 1934), 7.

5. Herberg, "Sigmund Freud," *WA*, VIII (Oct. 7, 1939), 4.

6. Herberg, "Darwinism and Marxism," *WA*, I (May 7, 1932), 3–4.

7. Herberg, "Communism and Science," *Revolutionary Age*, II (June 13, 1931), 4.

8. Herberg, "How Einstein Made the First Page," *RA*, II (Dec. 13, 1930), 3.

9. Herberg, "Einstein and Marx," *RA*, II (Dec. 20, 1930), 3.

10. Arthur Koestler, *Arrow in the Blue* (New York, 1952), pp. 293–94.

11. Daniel Aaron, *Writers on the Left*, p. 158.

12. Herberg, "Science and Determinism," *RA*, II (April 4, 1931), 3.

13. Herberg, "Theory of Relativity and Dialectical Materialism," *RA*, II (Dec. 27, 1930), 3.

14. Ibid., p. 3.

15. For an excellent discussion of the reluctant and belated reception of quantum physics and relativity theory in Russia, see Gustav A. Wetter, *Dialectical Materialism: A Historical and Systematic Survey of Philosophy in the Soviet Union* (New York, 1958), pp. 405–32.

16. Mike Gold, "Thornton Wilder: Prophet of the Genteel Christ," *New Republic*, LXIV (Oct. 27, 1930), 267.

17. Wilson's article on the "Literary Class War" contains two parts: an account of the Gold-Wilder controversy, and his own exposition on revolutionary literature. Significantly, the second part, which was the subject of Herberg's discerning criticism, was deleted when Wilson anthologized the essay in *The Shores of Light*. In this section Wilson discussed Joyce and Dostoevski as critics of the "sickness of bourgeois society" and then offered the curious advice that the mechanics of art and of science are potentially compatible:

> And the literary devices of the neo-Symbolists may well turn out to be among the technological improvements made under capitalism which communism will be glad to take over. "The last word of capitalism, the Taylor plan," wrote Lenin, "combined the regained cruelty of bourgeois exploitation with a certain number of scientific gains which are extremely valuable for the analysis of the mechanical movements necessary in working. . . . The Soviet Republic should take over every technical advance which is scientific in character and offers some adavntage." It should be possible to convince Marxist critics of the importance of a work like "Ulysses" by telling them that it is a great piece of engineering—as it is. Henry Ford bought the Johannson gauges because they were true to the millionth of an inch, and the Soviets would be glad to have them. The Joyces and the Eliots and the Cummingses possess the Johannson gauges of consciousness. One of the principal achievements of these writers, furthermore, has been the invention of a literary shorthand which syncopates the syntax of the old literary language, and this shorthand is likely, I should say, to play its role in the creation of the language of the future.

Edmund Wilson, "The Literary Class War," *NeR*, LXX (March 4, 1932), 319–23.

18. Herberg, "About the 'Literary Class War,'" *WA*, I (May 14, 1932), 4.

19. Herberg, "Marxism and Modern Political Thought" (New York: New Workers School, 1936), a typescript of a course outline for

a class Herberg taught at the school (New York Public Library); "The Liberation of American Literature," WA, II (Oct. 15, 1932), 4.

20. Herberg, "The Civil War in New Perspective," Modern Quarterly, VI (Summer 1932), 54–61. For the Herberg-Hacker exchange, see MQ, VII (Jan. 1934), 764–67; and Herberg to Calverton, Aug. 6, 1932, Victor F. Calverton Papers, New York Public Library (VFC).

21. Herberg, "Marxism and the 'Negro Question': Roots of Negro Subjection," RA, II (July 11, 1931), 4.

22. Theodore Draper, The Rediscovery of Black Nationalism (New York, 1970), pp. 63–67; American Communism and Soviet Russia (New York, 1960), pp. 315–56.

23. Herberg, "Are the U.S. Negroes a Nation?" RA, II (Feb. 14, 1931), 3; "Communists and Abolitionists," WA, I (April 9, 1932), 3.

24. Herberg, "Jews in Russia—Negroes in USA: A Lesson from the Soviet Union," RA, II (Aug. 1, 1931), 3; "The Negro and Communism: Worker Rule and Race Prejudice," WA, II (May 15, 1933), 5.

25. Engels to Marx, April 20, 1870, quoted in Shlomo Avineri, "Feuer on Marx and the Intellectuals," Survey, No. 62 (Jan. 1967), 154.

26. Herberg, "Lenin and Youth," Workers Monthly, V (Feb. 1926), 166–71; "Military Training at the Leagues' Schools," Daily Worker, Aug. 6, 1928.

27. Draper, American Communism, pp. 377–441. The author is indebted to Draper's excellent historical account of the Lovestone-CP split.

28. Ibid., pp. 422–23.

29. Herberg, "The Tenth Plenum ECCI," RA, I (Nov. 1, 1929), 15; (Nov. 15, 1929), 17; (Dec. 1, 1929), 15; (Dec. 15, 1929), 12; (Jan. 1, 1930), 11; Herberg to Calverton, April 5, 1933; Calverton to Herberg, Oct. 6, 1932, VFC.

30. Herberg, "The Viewpoint of the International Communist Opposition," Modern Monthly, VII (June 1933), 283–88. Although Modern Quarterly became Modern Monthly in 1933–1938, it was often informally referred to as Modern Quarterly. See also his "Have Communists a Right to Think?" RA, I (Feb. 1, 1930), 10; "The Real Meaning of the 'New Turn,'" RA, I (March 1, 1930), 6; (March 15, 1930), 6–7; "Exceptionalism and Leninist Strategy," RA, I (Dec. 15, 1929), 6.

31. Herberg, "Viewpoint of Opposition," 284–85.

32. Ibid., 285–86; "The Tenth Plenum, ECCI," RA, I (Dec. 15, 1929), 12. See also the editorials "The Results of the German Elections," WA, I (March 26, 1932), 4; "The Collapse of Illusions," WA, I (June 11, 1932), 4.

33. Herberg, "Viewpoint of Opposition," 287–88; "Trotskyism and the Communist Opposition," RA, I (Sep. 1, 1930), 8; "Whither

Trotskyism?" *RA*, I (April 21, 1930), 6. See also Herberg's response to Trotsky's "Perspectives on American Marxism," in Herberg to Calverton, Jan. 5, 1932, VFC.

34. Herberg, "Fascism and Democracy in Hitler's Germany: Trotsky as a Champion of Reformism," *WA*, II (Sep. 15, 1933), 3; "From 'Real Communism' to 'Real Democracy': Leon Trotsky Completes the Circle!" *WA*, II (Jan. 1, 1934), 3.

35. Herberg, review of *Modern Monthly*, in *WA*, II (July 1, 1933), 8; (Dec. 1, 1933), 8.

36. Hook, "On Workers' Democracy," *MM*, VIII (Oct. 1934), 529–44; Herberg, "Workers' Democracy or Dictatorship?" *WA*, III (Dec. 15, 1934), 3, 8; "Parties Under Workers' Rule," *WA*, IV (May 4, 1935), 5.

37. Hook, "Manners and Morals of Apache-Radicalism," *MQ*, IX (June 1935), 215–21; Will Herberg, "Professor Hook Loses His Temper," *WA*, IV (July 6, 1935), 3; "As to Multi-Party Dictatorship," *WA*, IV (May 11, 1935), 3.

38. Dos Passos, "Whither the American Writer," *MQ*, 11–12.

39. Herberg, "The Crisis of the Revolution," *RA*, II (Mar. 14, 1931), 3.

40. Herberg, "Unemployment and Labor," *RA*, II (Feb. 21, 1931), 3; "The NRA and American Labor," *MM*, VII (Oct. 1933), 519–24; "What Is the New Deal Labor Policy?" *WA*, VI (July 3, 1937), 3,8; "Roosevelt and the Liberty League," *WA*, V (Feb. 22, 1936), 4, 6; "The Communist Party and the 'Roosevelt Question,'" *WA*, V (June 13, 1936), 3.

41. Herberg, "The New Wages and Hours Bill," *WA*, VI (June 19, 1933), 3; "Is America Heading for Fascism?" *WA*, II (Aug. 1, 1933), 1, 4–5; "The Communist Party and the 'Roosevelt Question,'" 3.

42. Herberg, "Estimating Austria's Revolution," *WA*, III (Aug. 1, 1934), 7; "The Rise and Fall of Dual Unionism," *WA*, IV (Sep. 21, 1935), 3, 5.

43. Herberg, "Who Are the Fascists in America?" *WA*, V (Jan. 4, 1936), 1, 3; "War, Fascism, and the Middle Classes," *WA*, V (Feb. 1, 1936), 1; "The People's Front Policy versus the Teachings of Marx and Lenin," *WA*, V (Aug. 29, 1936), 2; "Inconsistency or Principle or Revolutionary Marxism?" *WA*, VI (April 10, 1937), 3.

44. Herberg, "The Bankruptcy of the People's Front," *WA*, V (April 25, 1936), 6; "The Civil War in Spain," *WA*, V (Aug. 15, 1936), 3–4; "Revolution and the People's Front," *WA*, V (April 18, 1936), 4, 6; "The POUM and the Spanish Revolution," *WA*, VI (April 17, 1937), 5–6.

45. For Dos Passos's views on revolutionary Spain after the Bolshevik Revolution, see *Rosinante to the Road Again*; see also Gerald

Meaker's excellent new study of Spain's response to Bolshevism, *The Revolutionary Left in Spain, 1917–1924* (Stanford, 1974). In fairness, it should be noted that Herberg had doubts whether there were "any truly revolutionary socialist forces in Spain today . . . any tendency that really champions the tested principles of Marxism so brilliantly applied by Lenin in the course of the Russian revolution" ("Civil War in Spain," 4). But it is unclear whether he believed that Spain was not ripe for revolution, in which case all the lessons of 1917 were irrelevant; or whether Spain only needed a Lenin and a Bolshevik-inspired organization, in which case the revolution was not inherent in Spain's economic development, a situation that makes the "tested principles" of Marxism more twisted than tried.

46. Herberg, "17 Years of Socialist Construction," *WA*, III (Nov. 1, 1934), 1–2.

47. Herberg, "The 'Russian Question' and the Moscow Trials," *WA*, VI (April 24, 1937), 3, 5. See also Jay Lovestone, "The Moscow Trials in Historical Perspective," *WA*, VI (Feb. 6, 1937), 3.

48. Herberg, "The Case of Leon Trotsky," *WA*, VI (Dec. 18, 1937), 3.

49. Herberg, "Events of 1917 Show War Brings Dictatorship," *WA*, VIII (May 17, 1939), 4; "The ALP and the War Issue," *WA*, VIII (Nov. 4, 1939), 1, 3; "An Analysis That Misses," *WA*, IX (Dec. 7, 1940), 4; "Confusion without End," *WA*, IX (Dec. 21, 1940), 4.

50. Herberg, "The Basic Dilemma of Socialism," *WA*, IX (June 8, 1940), 4; (June 15, 1940), 4; (June 22, 1940), 4.

CHAPTER 4
The Cerebral Communist: James Burnham

1. Max Shachtman Transcripts, Oral History Collections, Columbia University, pp. 335–39.

2. Matthew Josephson, *Infidel in the Temple: A Memoir of the Nineteen-Thirties* (New York, 1967), p. 108; interview with Bertram D. Wolfe, Sep. 11, 1971.

3. Interview with James Burnham, June 11, 1971; Burnham and Philip Wheelwright, *Introduction to Philosophical Analysis* (New York, 1932), pp. 3–25, 33, 37. Langer's praise, from the *Journal of Philosophy*, is quoted in "James Burnham," *Current Biography* (New York, 1941), p. 122.

4. Burnham, "On Defining Poetry," *Symposium*, I (April 1930), 221–30; "Progress and Tradition," ibid. (July 1930), 349–60; "Trying to Say," ibid., II (Jan. 1931), 51–59.

5. Burnham, Review of Trotsky's *History of the Russian Revolution*, in *Symposium*, III (July 1932), 370–80.

6. Burnham, "Marxism and Esthetics," *Symposium*, IV (Jan. 1933), 3–30.

7. Burnham and Wheelwright, "Comment: Thirteen Propositions," *Symposium*, IV (April 1933), 127–34.

8. T. S. Eliot, "A Commentary," *Criterion*, XII (July 1933), 642–47; Paul Salter, "Fascist Philosophers," *New Masses*, VII (July 1933), 13–14.

9. Burnham, "Comment," *Symposium*, IV (Oct. 1933), 403–13.

10. Ibid., p. 413; Interview with Burnham, June 11, 1971.

11. Burnham, "Comment," *Symposium*, IV (July 1933), 259–79.

12. Ibid., 279.

13. Burnham to Comrade Breier, n.d., Victor F. Calverton Papers, New York Public Library (VFC). In *Labor Action* and *New International* Burnham wrote under the pseudonym "John West," a satirical name used to associate the author and his revolutionary Marxism with a new Western renaissance. Interview with Burnham, June 11, 1971.

14. John West, "Roosevelt and the New Congress," *NI*, II (Jan. 1935), 1–3; "Roosevelt Faces the Future," *NI*, IV (Feb. 1938), 43–45.

15. West, "The Roosevelt 'Security' Program," *NI*, II (March 1935), 40–43; "The Wagner Bill and the Working Class," *NI*, II (Oct. 1935), 184–89.

16. West, "The Bands Are Playing," *NI*, II (July 1935), 113–16; Burnham, *The People's Front: The New Betrayal* (New York, 1937), pamphlet.

17. Interview with Burnham, June 11, 1971.

18. West, "Max Eastman's Straw Man," *NI*, II (Dec. 1935), 220–25.

19. Max Eastman, "Russia and the Socialist Ideal," *Harper's*, CLXXVI (March 1938), 374–85.

20. Ibid., 378–85.

21. Burnham, "Max Eastman as Scientist," *NI*, IV (June 1938), 177–80.

22. See Robert C. Tucker, *Philosophy and Myth in Karl Marx* (Cambridge, 1961); Peter Clecak, *Radical Paradoxes: Dilemmas of the American Left, 1945–1970* (New York, 1973); Allen W. Wood, "The Marxian Critique of Justice," *Philosophy and Public Affairs*, I (Spring 1972); and John P. Diggins, "Thoreau, Marx, and the 'Riddle' of Alienation," *Social Research*, XXXIX (Winter 1972), 571–98.

23. Eastman, "Russia and the Socialist Ideal," 379–85; Burnham, "Max Eastman as Scientist," 177–80. See also the exchange: Eastman, "Burnham Dodges My Views," *NI*, IV (Aug. 1938), 244–46; Burnham, "A Little Wool Pulling," ibid., 246–47.

24. Burnham and Max Shachtman, "Intellectuals in Retreat," *NI*, V (Jan. 1939), 3–22.

25. Irving Howe, *Steady Work: Essays in the Politics of Democratic*

Radicalism, 1953–1966 (New York: Harvest edn., 1966), p. 117; F. W. Dupee, Editor's Note, in Leon Trotsky, *The Russian Revolution*, trans. Max Eastman (Garden City, N.Y., 1959), p. vii; Dwight Macdonald, *The Memoirs of a Revolutionist* (New York, 1959), p. 15; EdmundWilson, *To the Finland Station* (New York: Anchor edn., n.d.), pp. 431–32.

26. M. S. Venkataramani, "Leon Trotsky and American Politics," *International Review of Social History*, IX, Pt. I (1964), 1–46; Macdonald, *Memoirs*, pp. 14–15.

27. Venkataramani, 27–32.

28. Leon Trotsky, *The Revolution Betrayed: What Is the Soviet Union and Where Is It Going?*, trans. Max Eastman (New York: Merit Publishers edn., 1965), pp. 86–114, 231, 273–89; "The Soviet Union Today," *NI*, II (July 1935), 118.

29. Isaac Deutscher, *The Prophet Outcast: Trotsky, 1929–1940*, Vol. III (New York: Vintage edn., 1965), pp. 313–18. Deutscher's criticisms of Trotsky's use of the Thermidor analogy are learned and perceptive, but his characterization of *The Revolution Betrayed* as Trotsky's "classical indictment of bureaucracy" (p. 302) remains a description in search of an explanation. From what sources did the phenomenon of Soviet bureaucracy arise? Deutscher never questioned Trotsky's interpretation, which held that it arose out of the "social contradictions between the city and the village; between the proletariat and the peasantry (these two kinds of contradictions are not identical); between the national republics and districts; between the differing groups of peasantry; between the different groups of consumers; and, finally, between the Soviet state as a whole and its capitalist environment." (Trotsky, "The Soviet Union Today: The Workers' State and the Question of Thermidor and Bonarpartism," *NI*, II [July 1935], 118.) This interpretation had the virtue of being dialectical and the defect of being universal. The "social contradictions" that Trotsky enumerated could apply as well to pre-1917 Russia when private property and class differences prevailed. (Even Tsar Nicholas and his feudal adherents felt threatened by the "capitalist environment" of the West.) Trotsky never explored the hypothesis that bureaucratic despotism was the product of total collectivization, an idea that began to occupy Burnham. The greatest critic of Stalinism was reluctant to confront the full logic of totalitarianism.

30. Dwight Macdonald, "Once More: Kronstadt," *NI*, IV (July 1938), 211–14; Trotsky, "Hue and Cry over Kronstadt," *NI*, IV (April 1938), 103–06.

31. "Violence, For and Against: A Symposium on Marx, Stalin and Trotsky," *Common Sense*, VII (Jan. 1938), 19–23.

32. Ibid., 19–20, 22–23; Trotsky, "Their Morals and Ours," *NI*, IV (June 1938), 163–73; John Dewey, "Means and Ends," *NI*, IV (Aug. 1938), 232–33.

33. Burnham and Shachtman, "Intellectuals in Retreat," 6.

34. Deutscher, *Prophet Outcast*, pp. 457–62.

35. Trotsky, *In Defense of Marxism* (*against the petty-bourgeois opposition*) (New York: Merit Publishers, 1965), p. 28.

36. Trotsky, "The USSR in War," *NI*, V (Nov. 1939), 325–32.

37. Burnham, "The Politics of Desperation," *NI*, VI (April 1940), 75.

38. Eastman to Burnham and Shachtman, Jan. 18, 1939, Max Eastman Papers, Lilly Library, Indiana University (ME).

39. Burnham, "Science and Style," reprinted in Trotsky, *In Defense of Marxism*, pp. 187–206.

40. Interview with Burnham, June 11, 1971.

41. Burnham, *The Managerial Revolution: What Is Happening in the World* (New York, 1941), pp. 71–95, passim.

42. Ibid., pp. 167–68, passim.

43. Ibid., p. 170.

44. New York *Times*, May 1, 5, 15, 1941; Burnham, "Coming Rulers of the U.S.," *Fortune*, XXIV (Nov. 1941), 100–01, 119–24; "The Theory of the Managerial Revolution," *Partisan Review*, VIII (May–June, 1941), 181–97; "Man and Managers," *Time*, XXXVII (May 19, 1941), 98–101; Peter Drucker, "The Rulers of Tomorrow," *Saturday Review of Literature*, XXIV (May 10, 1941), 9.

45. Lewis Corey, "A New Theory of Revolution," *Nation*, CLII (April 26, 1941), 505–06; Paul M. Sweezy, "The Illusion of the Managerial Revolution," *Science and Society*, VI (Winter 1942), 1–23; C. Wright Mills (with Hans H. Gerth), "A Marx for the Managers," *Ethics*, LII (Jan. 1942), 200–15. For an important critique of Burnham from the liberal perspective, see David Spitz, *Patterns of Anti-Democratic Thought* (New York: Macmillan edn., 1965), pp. 48–87.

46. Sweezy, "Illusion of Managerial Revolution," 6–23; Mills, "A Marx for the Managers," 203–15; Dwight Macdonald, "The Burnhamian Revolution," *PR*, IX (Jan.–Feb., 1942), 76–84.

47. Ralf Dahrendorf, *Society and Democracy in Germany* (New York, 1967); David Schoenbaum, *Hitler's Social Revolution: Class and Status in Nazi Germany, 1933–1939* (New York, 1966); Kendall E. Bailes, "The Politics of Technology: Stalin and Technocratic Thinking among Soviet Engineers," *American Historical Review*, LXXIX (April 1974), 445–69; see also *Power in Postwar America*, ed. Richard Gillam (Boston, 1971).

48. Of Burnham's theory of managerial revolution, Nomad wrote, "First hinted at by Michael Bakunin, later developed by the Polish revolutionist Waclaw Machajski, subsequently presented to the American public by this writer in his *Rebels and Renegades* (1932) and *Apostles of Revolution* (1939), it became the subject of a best-selling book by an author who gave no credit to his predecessors. He

was a teacher of ethics." Nomad, *Aspects of Revolt* (New York, 1951), p. 15.

49. Marshall Shatz, "Jan Waclaw Machajski: The 'Conspiracy' of the Intellectuals," *Survey*, No. 62 (Jan. 1967), 45–57; Anthony D'Agostino, "Intelligentsia Socialism and the 'Workers' Revolution': The View of J. W. Machajski," *International Review of Social History*, XIV, Part I (1969), 54–89.

50. Had Weber lived to witness the outbreak of World War II, one wonders how he would have responded to the following complaint by Burnham:

> Nowhere is the importance of bourgeois ideologies more apparent than among the youth, and the coming world, after all, will be the youth's world. The abject failure of voluntary military enlistment in Britain and this country tells its own story to all who wish to listen. It is underlined in reverse by the hundreds of distinguished adult voices which during 1940 began reproaching the American youth for "indifference," "unwillingness to sacrifice," "lack of ideals." How right these reproaches are! And how little effect they have had!
>
> In truth, the bourgeoisie itself has in large measure lost confidence in its own ideologies. The words begin to have a hollow sound in the most sympathetic capitalist ears. This, too, is unmistakably revealed in the policy and attitudes of England's rulers during the past years. What was Munich and the whole policy of appeasement but a recognition of bourgeois impotence?

Burnham, *Managerial Revolution*, p. 36.

51. Burnham, *Managerial Revolution*, p. 285. Burnham informed me, in an interview (June 11, 1971), of Rizzi's attempt to collaborate with him after the war. See also James M. Fenwick, "The Mysterious Bruno R.," *NI*, XIV (Sep. 1948), 215–18; Daniel Bell, "The Strange Tale of Bruno R.," *New Leader*, XLII (Sep. 28, 1959), 19. More than a quarter century later the debate continues; see the exchange between Rizzi and Mario de Ciampis in *La Parola del Popolo* (Chicago), XVIII (Oct.–Nov. 1968), 23–24; (Dec. 1968–Jan. 1969), 45–46; (Feb.–Mar. 1969), 17–18.

52.
The substitution of relations of authority for those of production in defining class is but a radical interpretation of some of the theories discussed in the preceding chapter. Djilas, Schumpeter, Renner, Geiger, and, above all, Burnham in his theory of managerial power, have paved the way for this step. But Burnham makes a curious mistake which is worth examining in some detail. There is an interesting nuance peculiar to his approach which rapidly turns into a consequential fallacy and renders his theory empirically non-

sensical and analytically useless. Burnham tries to supersede Marx's theory by replacing the narrow legal concept of property by a wider sociological concept. Quite rightly he defines property relations (the particular) by authority relations (the general). But with a theoretical inaccuracy which is characteristic of his work he now reverses this definition and declares authority relations (the general) to be property relations (the particular). The managers have property ownership because they have factual control. At best, this reversal results in a nonsensical extension of the concept of property to all forms of authority, in which case the head of the state would have property in "his" state. At worst, however, and this is Burnham's case, the logical somersault is followed by an empircal *salto mortale* consisting in the assertion that authority can exist only where there is property, or, as Burnham says himself, that "the instruments of production are the seat of social domination." Marx and Burnham meet in the premise that economic power is *eo ipso* political power, because there is no power except that based on ownership in the means of production. But both of them are wrong, and their error makes it necessary to pose the problem of the relations between economic and social power anew.

Ralf Dahrendorf, *Class and Class Conflict in Industrial Society* (Stanford, 1959), p. 141.

CHAPTER 5
Capitalism and Freedom: Eastman

1. Eastman, *Love and Revolution*, pp. 631–32.
2. On American opinion of Russia during the war, see Melvin Small, "How We Learned to Love the Russians: American Media and the Soviet Union during World War II," *The Historian*, XXXVI (May 1974), 455–78. See also the sardonic but perceptive comments of Irving Howe and Lewis Coser, *The American Communist Party: A Critical History* (New York: Praeger edn., 1962), pp. 431–36. Max Eastman tried to stem the tide of Russophilia in mass periodicals; see his "We Must Face the Facts about Russia," *Reader's Digest*, XLIII (July 1947), 1–14.
3. Eastman, "Stalin's American Power," *RD*, XXXIX (Dec. 1941), 39–48.
4. Eastman to Edmund Wilson, Feb. 17, 1941, Max Eastman Papers, Lilly Library, Indiana University (ME).
5. Eastman to Arthur Hays Sulzberger, April 25, 1942; May 19, 1942, ME.
6. J. K. Zawodny, *Death in the Forest* (Notre Dame, Ind., 1962), pp. 29–45.
7. Boris Nicolaevsky to Eastman, June 19, 1943, ME.

8. Wladyslaw M. Besterman to Eastman, July 3, 1943; J. Ciecha-nowski to Eastman, July 12, 1943, ME.

9. Charles Burlington to Eastman, Feb. 3, 1942; Eastman to Bur-lington, Feb. (n.d.), 1942; RD to "Dear Reader," Feb. 17, 1942, ME.

10. Eastman, "Stalin's American Power," 42.

11. Eastman to Acklom, April 1939 [?]; Gitlow to Eastman, April 6, 1939, ME.

12. Howe and Coser, American Communist Party, pp. 424–28; Joseph Starobin, American Communism in Crisis, 1943–1957 (Cambridge, 1972), pp. 54–55.

13. New York Times editorial, July 8, 1943, p. 18; also quoted in Eastman to New York Times, July 20, 1943, ME.

14. Ibid.

15. Eastman to Warder Norton, Jan. 15, 1941, W. W. Norton Papers, Butler Library, Columbia University (WWN).

16. Mebane to Eastman, Oct. 27, 1944, ME.

17. Eastman to James (NYT), May 28, 1945; Eastman to Jimmy Vincent Sheean, March 26, 1941; Eastman to Edward Weeks, Nov. 7, 1945; Eastman to Bennett Cerf, April 12, 1944; Eastman to Leon Henderson, Oct. 29, 1945, ME.

18. Francis Biddle to Eastman, Sep. 27, 1943; Barbara Stanwyck to Eastman, June 28, 1953, ME.

19. Erwin to Eastman, Nov. 29, 1941, ME.

20. Dwight Macdonald, "Eastmania," Politics, II (Feb. 1945), 58–60.

21. Lewis Mumford to Eastman, May 12, 1941; Clarence Streit to Eastman, May 11, 1941, ME.

22. "Max Eastman's New Faith" (Editorial), New International, VII (June 1941), 101; Dwight Macdonald, "Kulturbolschewismus Is Here," Partisan Review, VIII (Nov.–Dec. 1941), 442–51.

23. Eastman and James T. Farrell, "As to Values and Facts: An Exchange," PR, IX (May–June 1941), 204.

24. Most of the response to the Town Hall debate is in the folder "1946 Correspondence," ME. Eastman had brought to the debate typed-out passages from Laski's Reflections on the Revolution of Our Time, in which the British socialist "most eloquently describes the horrors of life under the Soviet communist regime," in Eastman's words. During the course of the debate, when Eastman commented on the "crimes" of the Russian communists, Laski replied, "It's no part of my case that Russia hasn't committed crimes and been guilty of grave blunders and committed inconceivable follies; so has the United States, and so has Great Britain." In response, Eastman read from Laski's book to see whether the crimes committed in the Soviet Union had been committed in the United States or England. After enumerating the various restrictions on freedom in Russia, Eastman was interrupted by the moderator, who turned to Laski and asked,

"Do you care to comment?" Laski, spreading his hands in a futile gesture, answered, "No." Unfortunately, Laski apparently never thought of bringing with him old copies of Eastman's *Liberator.* Eastman, *Reflections on the Failure of Socialism* (New York: Universal Library edn., 1962), pp. 61–62.

25. Eastman to Arthur G. Hayes, April 21, 1947, ME.
26. Boardman and Sally Robinson to Eastman, April 13, 1948; Upton Sinclair to Eastman, April 19, 1948; Harold Lord Varney to Eastman, Nov. 26, 1948; Ida Rauh to Eastman, Aug. 4, 1948; Floyd Dell to Eastman, April 16, 1948, ME.
27. Dell to Eastman, "Antescript," (n.d.); Dell, "Review of Max Eastman's *Enjoyment of Living,*" (n.d.), Floyd Dell Papers, Newberry Library, Chicago (FD); Letter to Eastman, Jan. 17, 1950; Letter to Eastman, Oct. 3, 1950, ME.
28. Jessica Smith to Eastman, June 1, 1948; Corliss Lamont to Eastman, June 4, 1948; Eastman to Lamont, June 8, 1948; Eastman to De Witt Wallace, n.d., 1948; Wallace to Eastman, July 20, 1948; George Papandreou to Eastman, Dec. 28, 1949; April 7, 1950; Laird Archer to Eastman, Sep. 5, 1949; Clare Boothe Luce to Eastman, May 22, 1946; May 27, 1946; "Ed" (Dept. of State) to Eastman, Sep. 21, 1950, ME.
29. Maxwell Perkins to Eastman, July 3, 1946; Oswald G. Villard to Eastman, July 9, 1946; Irving Fisher to Eastman, June 26, 1946; Herman Finer to Eastman, Sep. 20, 1946; Eastman to Carl Sandburg, Jan. 30, 1946; Sandburg to Eastman, March 5, 1946; Eastman to Joseph Freeman, n.d.; Eastman to K. C. G., April 18, 1947; Eastman to Glenway Wescott, Feb. 9, 1947; Eastman to Louis Untermeyer, July 24, 1950; Katharine Garrison Chapin to Eastman, Feb. 24, 1950; Robert Hillyer to Eastman, March 18, 1950, ME.
30. Eastman to Sol Levitas, April 11, 1948; Oct. 26, 1948, ME.
31. James T. Farrell to PR, Jan. 31, 1950; Farrell to Eastman, Jan. 31, 1950, ME.
32. ACCF, Executive Committee Minutes, April 16, 1952, American Committee for Cultural Freedom Files, Tamiment Library, New York University (ACCF).
33. George S. Counts to Eastman, Oct. 16, 1951; Eastman to Counts, Oct. 20, 1951; "Examination of Max Eastman at Martha's Vineyard, Mass., Confidential, regarding Charles Chaplin as Suspected Former Member of Communist Party," stenographic typescript, Oct. 22, 1952, ME.
34. General Albert C. Wedemeyer to Eastman, July 24, 1952; Eastman to Wedemeyer, June 5, 1952, ME.
35. Ben Gitlow to Eastman, March 26, 1948; June 10, 1948, ME.
36. Eastman to Viereck, Sep. 28, 1951, ME.
37. Eastman to Dell, Dec. 16, 1954, ME; Eastman to Dell, March 6, 1954, FD.

38. Eastman to Viereck, Sep. 28, 1951, ME.

39. Dell to Eastman, March 10, 1954. Dell's wife, B. Marie, cautioned him against sending the letter out of fear that Eastman would show it to the editor of *The Freeman*, Florence Norton. Miss Norton had previously published without permission a poem of Dell's that Eastman had showed her, and B. Marie feared she might do the same with the letter and ask Eastman to reply to it in a denunciatory manner, publicity which would unleash, Dell quipped, "the McCarthy smear-artists and hatchet-men." See "PS," Dell to Eastman, March 11, 1954, FD. Eastman apologized to Dell for Miss Norton publishing his poem without consulting Eastman or obtaining Dell's permission, Eastman to Dell, Nov. 23, 1954, FD.

40. Dell to Eastman, March 10, 1954, FD.

41. Dell to Eastman, "Thanksgiving Day," 1954, (p. 9), FD.

42. Ibid., 8–9.

43. T. W. Phillips to Eastman, March 27, 1955; Merwin K. Hart to Eastman, April 4, 1955; David Lawrence to Eastman, April 7, 1955; Ray Moley to Eastman, April 12, 1955; Vermont Royster to Eastman, March 30, 1955; John Chamberlain to Eastman, March 29, 1955; William Henry Chamberlin to Eastman, Feb. 28, 1955; Morrie Ryskind to Eastman, March 27, 1955; William S. Schlamm to Eastman, March 17, 1955; Milorad M. Drachkovitch to Eastman, Nov. 9, 1955; Vladimir Petrov to Eastman, April 7, 1955; Franklin Burdette to Eastman, Sep. 21, 1955, ME. Among those invited to Eastman's party were: Louis Bromfield, James Burnham, Francis Brown, William Buckley, John Chamberlain, Robert Considine, Igor Cassini, Frank Chodorov, Charles Duell, Hamilton Fish, John T. Flynn, Frank Hanighen, Gilbert Highet, Herbert Hoover, H. L. Hunt, David Lawrence, Fulton Lewis, Henry Luce, Eugene Lyons, Tex McCrary, Frank McNamara, Dwight Macdonald, Felix Morley, Raymond Moley, J. B. Matthews, Douglas MacArthur, Florence Norton, Westbrook Pegler, Orville Prescott, W. G. Rogers, Archibald Roosevelt, Ogden Reid, Charles Scribner, Herbert Swope, George Sokolsky, Robert Theobald, Gene Tunney, Irita Van Doren, Ludwig von Mises, and De Witt Wallace. "Eastman Party," April 27, 1955, ME.

44. Eastman, *Reflections on the Failure of Socialism* (New York: Universal Library edn., 1962), pp. 24, 56, 83, 101, passim.

45. Wilhelm Röpke to Eastman, April 21, 1952; F. A. Hayek to Eastman, May 24, 1948, ME.

46. Eastman, *Reflections*, pp. ii–iv, 51, 65–66, 100–111, passim.

47. My views on this issue are expressed in "Thoreau, Marx, and the 'Riddle' of Alienation," *Social Research*, XXXIX (Winter 1972), 571–98.

48. Van Wyck Brooks to Eastman, May 8, 1955, ME; Dell to Eastman, "Thanksgiving Day," 1954, FD.

49. Dell to Eastman, "Thanksgiving Day."

50. Eastman, *Reflections*, p. 108.

51. Long before the rise of the "free market" various political freedoms had evolved from the tradition of religious dissent and the struggle of the aristocracy and nobility against monarchical efforts to violate "ancient liberties." See Guido de Ruggiero, *The History of European Liberalism*, trans. R. G. Collingwood (Boston: Beacon edn., 1959).

52. Eastman to Saul Friedlander, Nov. 11, 1949; Eastman to R. N. Carew-Hunt, April 16, 1950, ME.

53. The debate between Hook and Eastman, carried in the *New Leader* on January 27 and February 3, 10, 1945, is reprinted in Hook's *Political Power and Personal Freedom: Critical Studies in Democracy, Communism, and Civil Rights* (New York: Collier edn., 1962), pp. 397–437.

54. Eastman, *Reflections*, pp. 37, 104.

55. Marx is quoted in Robert Tucker, *Philosophy and Myth in Karl Marx* (London: Cambridge University Press, 1961), p. 222. On Marx's scorn for liberalism, see also Allen W. Wood, "The Marxian Critique of Justice," *Philosophy and Public Affairs*, I, No. 3 (Spring 1972), 244–82.

56. For an informative critique of the role of autonomous economic laws in both Marxist and capitalist schools of thought, see Herbert Luthy, "L'Histoire du Monde: une déviation?" *Preuves*, X (May 1958), 68–78.

CHAPTER 6
Visions of Order: Dos Passos

1. John Dos Passos, *State of the Nation* (Boston, 1943), p. 5.

2. Dos Passos, *Tour of Duty* (Boston, 1946).

3. Dos Passos, "Americans Are Losing the Victory in Europe," *Life*, XX (Jan. 7, 1946), 22–25; "Report on the Occupation," ibid., XX (March 11, 1946), 104–15; "Vienna: Broken City," ibid., XX (March 4, 1946), 92–104.

4. Dos Passos, "The Failure of Marxism," *Life*, XXIV (Jan. 19, 1948), 96–108.

5. Ibid., 96.

6. Dos Passos, *The Grand Design* (New York, 1949), pp. 141–42.

7. Ibid., p. 418.

8. Granville Hicks, "The Politics of John Dos Passos," *Antioch Review*, X (March 1950), 85–98; Wilson's criticisms are cited in Hicks's article.

9. Dos Passos first investigated as a reporter some of the social material he used in the novel. See his two articles, "Revolution on the Farm," *Life*, XXV (Aug. 23, 1948), 95–104; "Where Do We Go from Here," ibid., XXII (Jan. 27, 1947), 95–104. Curiously, how-

ever, the articles express a mild optimism about America that contrasts with the pessimism and bitterness in *The Grand Design.*

10. *Washington Post,* July 16, 1959.

11. Malcolm Cowley, *A Second Flowering: Works and Days of a Lost Generation* (New York, 1974), p. 87; Dos Passos, "The Situation in American Writing," *Partisan Review,* VI (Summer 1939), 27; Dos Passos to Eastman, April 12, 1944, Max Eastman Papers, Lilly Library, Indiana University (ME); Henry Luce to Dos Passos, Jan. 4, 1946; James T. Farrell to Dos Passos, April 26, 1958, John Dos Passos Papers, Lilly Library, University of Virginia (JDP).

12. Dos Passos to New York *Times* (Book Review Section), March 15, 1945; Lewis Galantière to Dos Passos, December 15 (n.y.), JDP; Arnold Beichman to Dos Passos, May 27, 1956, American Committee for Cultural Freedom Files, Tamiment Library, New York University (ACCF).

13. Dos Passos, "Mr. Chambers's Descent into Hell," *Saturday Review,* XXXV (May 24, 1952), 11; Dos Passos to Glenway Wescott, Dec. 27, 1946, ME.

14. William Phillips to Whittaker Chambers, Dec. 16, 1948, *Partisan Review* Files, Rutgers University Library (PR).

15. Archibald MacLeish to Dos Passos, n.d.; Edmund Wilson to Dos Passos, April 13, 1958, JDP.

16. Dos Passos's interview is quoted in Hicks, "The Politics of John Dos Passos," 95; James T. Farrell to Dos Passos, Dec. 20, 1957, JDP.

17. Edward Grant Taylor to Robert Kennedy, March 22, 1958; Taylor to Dos Passos, April 1, 1958; Adolph Fram to Robert Kennedy, April 7, 1958; Fram to Dos Passos, Aug. 21, 1958, JDP; John Dos Passos, "Anonymously Yours," *Occasions and Protests* (Chicago, 1964), pp. 246–74.

18. Abbott Washburn to Dos Passos, March 14, 1959, JDP.

19. Dos Passos, "Thank You, Mr. Hitler," *Common Sense,* I (April 27, 1933), 13.

20. Dos Passos, "A Case of Conscience," *CS,* IV (May 1935), 16–19.

21. Dos Passos, "A Farewell to Europe," *CS,* VI (July 1937), 10–11.

22. Quoted from Dos Passos's reply to the symposium "The Situation in American Writing," *PR,* VI (Summer 1939), 27.

23. Dos Passos, *The Ground We Stand On* (London: Routledge & Sons, 1942), p. 3. (The American edition was published in 1941.)

24. Dos Passos apparently felt no epistemological embarrassment in the admission that he was both discovering history and creating it:

A set of ideas, a point of view, a frame of reference is in space only an intersection, the state of affairs at some given moment in

the consciousness of one man or many men, but in time it has
evolving form, virtually organic extension. In time ideas can be
thought of as sprouting, growing, maturing, bringing forth seed and
dying like plants. To make sense of the tangled jungle of men's
thoughts and impulses that makes up the history of a culture we
have continually to invent sequences which we can follow like foot-
paths through the thickets of what was.

Dos Passos, "The Use of the Past," in *Ground We Stand On*, p. 16.

25. *The Federalist*, No. 10.

26. Edmund Wilson, *The Shores of Light* (New York, 1952),
p. 431.

27. Wilson to Dos Passos, July 16, 1939, JDP.

28. Dos Passos, *Ground We Stand On*, pp. 381–401; *The Shackles
of Power: Three Jeffersonian Decades* (Garden City, N.Y., 1966),
p. 283.

29. Dos Passos quoted by Wilson in his letter to Dos Passos, July
16, 1939, JDP.

30. Dos Passos, *Ground We Stand On*, pp. 187–205; *Occasions
and Protests* (Chicago, 1964), pp. 52–36.

31. Dos Passos, *Ground We Stand On*, p. 4.

32. Ibid., pp. 23–183; Alan Simpson, "How Democratic Was Roger
Williams?" *William and Mary Quarterly*, XIII (Jan. 1956), 55–67.

33. Dos Passos, *The Living Thoughts of Tom Paine* (New York:
Premier edn., 1963), p. 47.

34. The full thrust of Professor Kenyon's argument deserves quoting:

> When he wrote *Common Sense*, he was like Marx writing the
> *Communist Manifesto*. Like Marx, he knew the existing system with
> all its evils; but of the system that was to come after the Revolution
> he knew only that it was to be good. Unlike Marx, Paine had an op-
> portunity to see the new world in operation, but his political thought
> was not much altered by the sight. One of the remarkable things
> about *The Rights of Man*, written almost fifteen years after *Com-
> mon Sense*, is that, except for historical narrative and some borrow-
> ing from Madison's attack on Montesquieu, it could just as easily
> have been written in 1776. If Paine learned anything about politics
> during the intervening years, the book contains no evidence of it.

Paine was a compulsive revolutionary, Kenyon continues:

> He belonged on the advancing front of that movement. His
> legendary declaration, whether literally accurate or not, is entirely
> characteristic: "Where liberty is not, there is my country." Had
> the French Revolution been the beginning of a general European
> overthrow of monarchy, Paine would almost certainly have advanced

from country to country as each one rose against its own particular tyrant. He would have written a world series of Crisis papers and died an international hero, happy and universally honored.

Cecilia Kenyon, "Where Paine Went Wrong," *American Political Science Review*, XLV (Dec. 1951), 1086–99. On the New Left and Paine, see Staughton Lynd, *Intellectual Origins of American Radicalism* (New York, 1968). For Dos Passos's response to the student radicals of the sixties, see his "The New Left: A Spook Out of the Past," *National Review*, XVIII (Oct. 1966), 1037–39.

35. Dos Passos, "A Note on Fitzgerald," in *The Crack-Up*, ed. Edmund Wilson (New York, 1956), pp. 69, 338–43.

36. See Winthrop D. Jordon, *White over Black: American Attitudes toward the Negro: 1550–1812* (Chapel Hill, N.C., 1968).

37. Perhaps it is worth noting that George Orwell, who went through somewhat the same political experience as Dos Passos in the Spanish Civil War, arrived at similar conclusions on the relationship of language to freedom. Like Dos Passos, Orwell protested the abuse of words, and he also believed that thought and language were so closely related that any tolerance for ambiguity threatened the existence of freedom, which depended upon clarity and honesty of expression. "Doublethink," Orwell wrote, "means the power of holding two contradictory beliefs in one's mind simultaneously and accepting both of them. . . . The process has to be conscious for it would not be carried out with sufficient precision; but it also has to be conscious, or it would bring with it a feeling of falsity and hence of guilt." Orwell, *1984* (New York, 1949), p. 215.

38. Blanch Gelfant, "The Search for Identity in the Novels of John Dos Passos," *PMLA*, LXXVI (March 1961), 133–49.

39. Wilson to Dos Passos, Sep. 5, 1950, JDP. (The source Wilson referred to was Roy Othley's *Black Odyssey*.)

40. Dos Passos, *Shackles of Power*, pp. 152–54.

41. "Government they considered the noblest preoccupation of man," wrote Dos Passos of the Founders. "The aim of government was the happiness of the governed. Happiness to the eighteenth-century Americans meant something more than an improved standard of living. It meant dignity, independence, self-government. It meant opportunity for the young, a serene old age and fearlessness in the face of death." (Foreword, *Prospects of a Golden Age* [Englewood Cliffs, N.J., 1959], p. vii.)

The idea of happiness had been a sacred principle to Dos Passos even in his early radical years. (See, for example, his "American and the Pursuit of Happiness," *Nation*, CXI [Dec. 29, 1920], 777–78.) Since the concept is so central to Dos Passos's political philosophy, the intellectual historian is forced to ask what the concept meant to the Founding Fathers. In truth, they themselves were not exactly sure, and the speculations they ventured clearly led to conclusions that would undermine Dos Passos's faith in the Enlightenment. John Adams believed happiness consisted in a good dinner and a good woman—in that order. Franklin believed it could only be understood negatively, as that which attracts man in his anxiety or "uneasiness" to flee the reality of pain, which was necessary in the nature of things. Madison identified happiness with the "unequal" acquisition of property, which made it an endless "pursuit" after an elusive possession. And Jefferson defined happiness as the pleasure of virtuous conduct motivated by social "utility," which implied, as John Schaar noted, that the meaning of happiness is taken from the individual's private conscience and aesthetic and ethical awareness and made into a public ethic of expediency and conformity. Dos Passos believed that by going back to the Age of Reason he could reassure Americans living in the Age of Anxiety that happiness was a natural right and a self-evident truth. But his piety toward his subject rendered him more complacent than even Franklin, who probably would have agreed with Archbishop Whately that happiness is no laughing matter. In the end Dos Passos could only guarantee American citizens what Howard Mumford Jones described as the ironic guarantee of Jefferson's idea of happiness: "the privilege of pursuing a phantom and embracing a delusion." (See Benjamin Franklin, A Dissertation on Liberty & Necessity, Pleasure & Pain [New York: Facsimile Text Society edn., 1930]; John Schaar, ". . . And the Pursuit of Happiness," The Virginia Quarterly Review, XLVI [Winter 1970], 1–26; Howard Mumford Jones, The Pursuit of Happiness [Ithaca, N.Y., 1966], p. 17.)

42. Dos Passos, Ground We Stand On, p. 3.
43. Dos Passos, Occasions and Protests, p. 11.
44. Leo Strauss, Natural Right and History (Chicago, 1953), p. 251.
45. Dos Passos, The Men Who Made the Nation (Garden City, N.Y., 1957), p. 56.
46. R. G. Collingwood, An Essay on Metaphysics (London, 1940), p. 75.
47. Maurice Merleau-Ponty, Signs, trans. Richard C. McCleary (Evanston, Ill., 1964), p. 223 ff.
48. Nicola Chiaromonte, The Paradox of History (London, 1971), p. 55.
49. The historian Nevins, with whom Dos Passos collaborated on a Gettysburg Centennial publication, wrote to the novelist, "Do give us as long an essay as you can, and indulge in as much philosophy as you can. You say that your reflections do not run to length. I think that when you get down to the full task of writing you may find that they do. The longer your paper, the better, and the more you indulge your unique gift for historical narrative, the better. I sometimes wonder whether you should not have undertaken to give first place to history rather than to fiction, but I am well content with your splendid books

in both fields." Nevins to Dos Passos, Dec. 4, 1963, JDP. See also Dos Passos to Nevins, Dec. 12, 1960; Jan. 1, 1961, Allan Nevins Papers, Butler Library, Columbia University, in which the novelist asked for help in finding unpublished personal narratives "from the doughboy level" to prepare his book on Wilson and World War I. He also consulted with Samuel Eliot Morison on colonial history; Morison to Dos Passos, Dec. 18, 1964, JDP. In 1942 John Peale Bishop, then Coordinator of Inter-American Affairs of the Executive Office of the President, asked Dos Passos to participate in a radio program in which the novelist's *The Ground We Stand On* would be discussed together with Carl Becker's *The Heavenly City of the Eighteenth-Century Philosophers.* Bishop to Dos Passos, Jan. 14, 1942, JDP. One wonders if this discussion took place. It is hard to imagine two books which approach the American Enlightenment so differently; it is even harder to imagine how Dos Passos would have responded to the ironic, philosophical skepticism that runs through Becker's book like acid dissolving ideas into illusions. For a critical assessment of Dos Passos as a historian by a brilliant literary scholar, see Irving Howe, "The Perils of Americana," *New Republic,* CXXX (Jan. 25, 1954), 16–17.

CHAPTER 7
From Marxism to Existentialism: Herberg

1. Will Herberg, *Judaism and Modern Man* (New York, 1951), pp. 27–28.
2. Herberg, "From Marxism to Judaism," *Commentary,* III (Jan. 1947), 25.
3. Herberg, "The Christian Mythology of Socialism," *Antioch Review,* III (Spring 1943), 125–32.
4. Herberg, "The Crisis of Socialism," *Jewish Frontier,* XII (Sep. 1945), 22–31.
5. Herberg, "Personalism against Totalitarianism," *Politics,* II (Dec. 1945), 369–74. See also Herberg's "Crucial Question," *Commonweal,* XLIII (Feb. 22, 1946), 473–76.
6. Dwight Macdonald, "The Root Is Man," *Politics,* III (July 1946), 194–214.
7. Herberg, ed., *Four Existentialist Theologians: A Reader from the Works of Jacques Maritain, Nicolas Berdyaev, Martin Buber, and Paul Tillich* (Garden City, N.Y., 1958), p. 16.
8. Interview with Herberg, July 24, 1969.
9. Herberg, "Bureaucracy and Democracy in the Labor Unions," *Antioch Review,* III (Fall 1943), 405–17; "The Ethics of Power," *Jewish Frontier,* XII (March 1945), 19–21.
10. Herberg, "Democracy and the Nature of Man," *Christianity and Society,* XI (Fall 1946), 18.

11. Ibid., 13–14.

12. Max Weber, "Politics as a Vocation," in *From Max Weber: Essays on Sociology*, eds. H. H. Gerth and C. Wright Mills (New York: Galaxy edn., 1958), p. 126.

13. Herberg, "American Marxist Political Theory," in *Socialism in American Life*, Vol. I, eds. Donald Drew Egbert and Stow Persons (Princeton, 1952), pp. 489–522.

14. Irving Howe, "An Answer to Critics of American Socialism," *New International*, XVIII (May–June 1952), 115–52.

15. "The Ethics of Controversy," Typescript, American Committee for Cultural Freedom Files, Tamiment Library, New York University (ACCF), 22–25, 29–31.

16. Herberg, "Government by Rabble-Rousing," *New Leader*, XXXVII (Jan. 18, 1954), 13–16.

17. Peter Viereck to Sol Stein, April 8, 1954; June 5, 1954, ACCF. For Viereck's interpretation of McCarthyism, see his "The Revolt against the Elite," in *The Radical Right*, ed. Daniel Bell (Garden City, N.Y.: Anchor edn., 1964), pp. 161–83.

18. Herberg, "Government by Rabble-Rousing," 14–16; "McCarthy and Hitler: A Delusive Parallel," *New Republic*, CXXXI (Aug. 23, 1954), 13–15.

19. Herberg, "Loyalty and Security in Historical Perspective," *NeR*, CXXXII (April 11, 1955), 20–22.

20. Herberg, "From Marxism to Judaism," 25–32.

21. John Dewey, "Anti-Naturalism in Extremis," in *Naturalism and the Human Spirit*, ed. Yervant H. Krikorian (New York, 1944), pp. 1–16; Sidney Hook, "Naturalism and Democracy," ibid., pp. 40–64.

22. Reinhold Niebuhr, review in the New York *Herald Tribune*, December 16, 1951.

23. Herberg, *Judaism and Modern Man: An Interpretation of Jewish Religion* (New York: Atheneum edn., 1970), pp. 3–41.

24. Ibid., pp. 25–29.

25. Ibid., pp. 37–40.

26. Ibid., pp. 47–129. See also Herberg's "Buber: Philosopher of the Dialogic Life," *NeR*, CXXXIV (Jan. 16, 1956), 26–28; "Three Dialogues of Man," ibid., CXXXII (May 16, 1955), 28–31.

27. Herberg, "From Marxism to Judaism," 27; *Judaism and Modern Man*, p. 134.

28. Herberg, *Judaism and Modern Man*, pp. 197–98.

29. Ibid., p. 248.

30. Ibid., p. vii.

31. Niebuhr, *The Irony of American History* (New York, 1952). See also Robert E. Fitch, "Reinhold Niebuhr's Philosophy of History," in *Reinhold Niebuhr: His Religious, Social, and Political Thought,*

eds. Charles W. Kegley and Robert W. Bretall (New York, 1961), pp. 292–310.

32. Herberg, *Judaism and Modern Man*, p. 6.

33. William John Wolf, "Reinhold Niebuhr's Doctrine of Man," in *Reinhold Niebuhr*, p. 239.

34. Herberg, *Judaism and Modern Man*, pp. 80–82.

35. Jean-Paul Sartre, *Being and Nothingness: An Essay in Phenomenological Ontology*, trans. Hazel Barnes (New York, 1956), p. 626; *Les Tempes Modernes* (June 1946), 15–16.

36. Herberg, *Judaism and Modern Man*, pp. 31, 187. For Herberg's later critique of Sartre, Buber, and existentialist morality in general, see "The 'What' and the 'How' of Ethics," *Modern Age*, XV (Fall 1971), 350–57.

37. Herberg, "The Biblical Basis of American Democracy," *Thought*, XXX (Spring 1955), 37.

38. Herberg, "Communism, Democracy, and the Churches," *Commentary*, XIX (April 1955), 386–93.

39. *Religion and the Intellectuals* (New York, 1950), pp. 8–15, 49–53, 106–11; Barrett is quoted on pp. 36–37. (The symposium was published as a *Partisan Review* pamphlet, series Number 3.)

40. Herberg, *Protestant, Catholic, Jew: An Essay on American Religious Sociology* (Garden City, N.Y.: Anchor rev. edn., 1960), pp. 1–4, 84.

41. Ibid., pp. 258, 263, 278, passim; Herberg, "Religion and Culture in Present-Day America," in Thomas T. McAvoy, ed., *Roman Catholicism and the American Way of Life* (Notre Dame, Ind., 1960), pp. 4–19.

42. Herberg, "Riesman's Lonely Man," *Commonweal*, LX (May 3, 1954), 538–40.

43. Herberg, *Protestant, Catholic, Jew*, pp. 263–66.

44. Ibid., p. 267; *Judaism and Modern Man*, p. 83.

45. Nathan Glazer, "Religion without Faith," *NeR*, CXXXIII (Nov. 14, 1955), 18–20.

46. Herberg, *Protestant, Catholic, Jew*, pp. 254–72, passim.

47. Herberg, "Historicism as Touchstone," *Christian Century*, LXXVII (March 16, 1960), 311–13.

48. Ibid., 312.

CHAPTER 8
Social Theory and the Cold War: Burnham

1. James Burnham, "Observation on Kafka," *Partisan Review*, XIV (Jan.–Feb. 1947), 190.

2. Dahl is quoted in D. A. Rustow, "The Study of Elites," *World Politics*, XVIII (July 1966), 690–717.

3. Burnham, *Let the People Vote on War!* (New York: Pioneer Publishers, pamphlet, 1937), p. 12.

4. Burnham, "Is Democracy Possible?" in *Whose Revolution? A Study of the Future Course of Liberalism in the United States,* ed. Irving DeWitt Talmadge (New York, 1941), pp. 187–217.

5. John P. Diggins, *Mussolini and Fascism: The View from America* (Princeton, 1972).

6. Burnham, *The Machiavellians: Defenders of Freedom* (Chicago: Gateway edn., 1963), p. 304.

7. Benedetto Croce, "Political Truths and Popular Myths," in *My Philosophy: Essays on the Moral and Political Problems of Our Time* (New York, 1962), pp. 91–95.

8. R. Fahen, "Machiavelli and Modern Thought: A Critique of James Burnham's Book," *New International,* IX (Dec. 1943), 334–37; for Parts II and III, see ibid., X (Jan. 1944), 24–28; (Feb. 1944), 50–54; Reinhold Niebuhr, "Study in Cynicism," *Nation,* CLVI (May 1, 1943), 636–38; Malcolm Cowley, "The Newest Machiavellian," *New Republic,* CVIII (May 17, 1943); John MacCormac, New York Times, May 2, 1943. For a favorable review, see Giuseppe Prezzolini, *Journal of Philosophy,* XL (June 24, 1943), 356–61; but see also Monroe C. Beardsley, "Mr. Burnham on the 'Elite,'" ibid., pp. 435–41.

9. Burnham, *The Machiavellians,* p. 44.

10. Ibid., p. 46.

11. Antonio Gramsci, *The Modern Prince and Other Essays* (New York: International Publishers edn., 1961); Maurice Merleau-Ponty, "A Note on Machiavelli," in *Signs,* II, 211–23; Leo Strauss, *Thoughts on Machiavelli* (Glencoe, Ill., 1958); Isaiah Berlin, "The Question of Machiavelli," *New York Review of Books,* XVII (Nov. 4, 1971), 20–32.

12. Arthur Schlesinger, Jr., Review of Burnham's *The Struggle for the World, Nation,* CLXIV (Apr. 5, 1947), 398–99.

13. Sheldon Wolin, *Politics and Vision: Continuity and Innovation in Western Political Thought* (Boston, 1960), p. 217.

14. Burnham, "Lenin's Heir," *PR,* XII (Winter 1945), 66–67.

15. Ibid., 61–72.

16. Lionel Abel, "Stalin's Advocate," *Politics,* II (May 1945), 146–48.

17. William Phillips, "The Lion and the Foxes," *PR,* XII (Spring 1945), 190–98.

18. Dwight Macdonald, "Beat Me Daddy," *PR,* XII (Spring 1945), 181–87. For Burnham's reply, see "The Politics of the Nursery Set," ibid., 188–90.

19. George Orwell, "Second Thoughts on James Burnham" (1946), in *The Orwell Reader: Fiction, Essays, and Reportage by George Orwell* (New York, 1956), pp. 335–54.

20. Interview with Burnham, June 11, 1971. Twenty years later Burnham also revealed in writing that "Part I of *The Struggle for the World* was originally part of a secret study prepared for the Office of Strategic Services in the spring of 1944 and distributed at that time to the relevant Washington desks." Burnham, *The War We Are In: The Last Decade and the Next* (New Rochelle, N.Y., 1967), p. 10.

21. Burnham, *The Struggle for the World* (New York, 1947), p. 248, passim.

22. "For That or Nothing," *Time*, XLIX (Mar. 24, 1947), 26–27; Burnham, "Struggle for The World," *Life*, XXII (Mar. 31, 1947), 59–68, 73–80. Letters to *Life* ran "about two to one against Burnham," which led the magazine to devote an entire editorial explaining its differences with his position; *Life*, XXII (Apr. 21, 1947), 38. "Blueprint for Empire," *Christian Century*, LXIV (May 21, 1947), 646–48. See also "The Truman-Burnham Parallel," ibid. (June 4, 1947), 702–03.

23. "Blueprint for Destruction," *Christian Century*, LXIV (May 28, 1947), 678–79; Harry Elmer Barnes, Review, *Annals*, American Academy of Political and Social Science, CCLII (July 1947), 106; Henry Bamford Parkes, Review, New York *Herald Tribune Weekly Book Review*, April 20, 1947, 6; James Reston, New York *Times*, March 16, 1947, 1; Arthur Schlesinger, Jr., *Nation*, CLIV (April 5, 1947), 398–99; Jack Weber, "James Burnham, A Modern Cato: Portrait of an Irresponsible," *New International*, XIII (Oct. 1947), 234–41.

24. Burnham, "Our Spineless Foreign Policy," *American Mercury*, LXX (Jan. 1950), 3–13.

25. R. H. S. Crossman, "Reflections on the Cold War," *NeR*, CXXIV (April 7, 1951), 10–12.

26. Burnham, *L'ère des organisateurs*, Preface by Léon Blum (Paris, 1947), pp. ix–xxi; Burnham, *Contenir ou Libérer*, Postface by Raymond Aron (Paris, 1953); Burnham and André Malraux, "The Double Crisis," *PR*, XV (April 1948), 407–38; id., *The Case for De Gaulle* (New York, 1948); Pierre Courtade, "James Burnham, le Nouveau Rosenberg de l'impérialisme Américain," *La Nouvelle Critique*, No. 18 (July–Aug. 1950), 14–28; id., *Jimmy* (Paris: Les Éditeurs Français Réunis, 1951). For a discussion of Courtade's Stalinist career, see David Caute's excellent study, *Communism and the French Intellectuals* (London, 1964), pp. 166–68, 177–78, 181–82, 224–25, 232.

27. Burnham and Malraux, "The Double Crisis," 414.

28. Philip Rahv to Burnham, Sep. 29, 1950; Burnham to Rahv, Oct. 4, 1950, PR Files, Rutgers University Library (PR); Burnham, "The Rhetoric of Peace," *PR*, XVII (Nov.–Dec. 1950), 860–71.

29. Burnham, "The Suicidal Mania of American Business," *PR*, XVII (Jan. 1950), 47–63.

30. Irving Kristol to Stephen Spender, April 24, 1953, American Committee for Cultural Freedom Files, Tamiment Library, New York University (ACCF).

31. Christopher Lasch, "The Cultural Cold War: A Short History of the Congress for Cultural Freedom," in *The Agony of the American Left* (New York: Vintage edn., 1969), pp. 63–114. "Thanks to the revelations of the CIA's secret subsidies," writes Lasch, "it is no longer a very novel or startling proposition to say that American officials have committed themselves to fighting fire with fire, and that this strategy is self-defeating because the means corrupt the end" (p. 110). Much as I sympathize with Lasch's position, his attitude toward the cold war is simple and one-sided. The late Max Shachtman used to say that one cannot "fight fire with gasoline," but even he realized that those who sympathize with communist dictatorships are in no position to tell the right wing which weapons to choose. Lasch himself is not really interested in the communist question; his main outcry is against the corruption of liberalism during the cold war. Yet does it follow that the Congress for Cultural Freedom was compromised because it received money from the CIA? The ACCF could, knowingly or unwittingly, serve the interests of the CIA providing the latter served the interests of the ACCF—financing the publication of Russian dissent literature, for example. It is not that the means corrupted the end but that the end of cultural freedom was itself lost sight of by conservative anti-communists like Burnham, John Chamberlain, Elliot Cohen, and Irving Kristol. This led to the resignation of a number of liberals, among them Arthur Schlesinger, Jr., Richard Rovere, David Riesman, John Kenneth Galbraith, and Diana Trilling. Lasch argues that the ACCF "took shape in a period of the cold war when official anti-communism had not clearly distinguished itself, rhetorically, from the anti-communism of the Right" (p. 81). An examination of the files of the ACCF indicates otherwise: the distinction was uppermost among liberals and socialists; that was what the internal debate over McCarthyism was all about. Lasch's account also lacks perspective, blurring the difference between the anti-Stalinism of the Korean war period and the anti-communism of the Vietnam war era. In this connection the British writer David Caute has, I feel, put the controversy over the CIA and ACCF in proper context. Comparing the causes of the fellow travelers of the thirties to those of the ACCF intellectuals of the sixties, Caute asks, "Did that Anglo-American tribe whose reputations floundered in 1966–67 really serve a better one? The answer seems to depend on which aspect of political life one considers: Soviet labour camps and purges suggest a 'yes'; the Vietnam war with its accompanying atrocities suggests a 'no.'" Caute, *The Fellow-Travelers* (New York, 1973), p. 300.

32. Sidney Hook to author, June 14, 1972; Dwight Macdonald, "The Waldorf Conference," *Politics*, VI (Winter 1949), 32a–32d (Appendix).

33. ACCF Executive Committee Minutes, April 16, 1952, ACCF.

34. Eugene Rabinovitch to Sol Stein, Nov. 17, 1953, ACCF.

35. Sol Stein to Peter Viereck, Dec. 3, 1953; Nathan Glazer to Stein, Dec. 10, 1953; David Riesman to Stein, Dec. 15, 1953; H. J. Muller to Stein, Nov. 28, 1953; Burnham to Stein, Dec. 5, 1953; Milton R. Konvitz to Stein, Dec. 9, 1953; Daniel Bell to Hook, Nov. 23, 1953, ACCF. For Burnham's resignation from the *Partisan Review*, see *PR*, XX (Nov.–Dec. 1953), 716–17.

36. "Confidential: Extract from a Letter from James Burnham to Christopher Emmet, July 17, 1954," ACCF. At the Paris meeting of the Congress for Cultural Freedom in 1955, Hook was quizzed about Burnham's resignation; see "Congrès pour la Liberté de la Culture, Réunion du Comité Executive," Jan. 24 and 25, 1955, ACCF.

37. Bell to Hook, Nov. 23, 1950, ACCF.

38. Burnham, "The Case against Adlai Stevenson," *AM*, LXXX (Oct. 1952), 11–19.

39. Schlesinger to James T. Farrell, March 14, 1955, ACCF.

40. Sol Stein to Robert Gorham Davis, April 28, 1954, ACCF.

41. Kristol to Schlesinger, Jan. 4, 1952, ACCF.

42. Schlesinger, "Middle-Aged Man with a Horn," *NeR*, CXXVIII (Mar. 16, 1953), 16–17.

43. *NL*, XXXVI (April 13, 1933), 28.

44. R. V. Daniels, "Fate and Will in the Marxian Philosophy of History," *Journal of the History of Ideas*, XXI (Oct.–Dec. 1960), 538–52. See also the same author's "What the Russians Mean," *Commentary*, XXXIV (Oct. 1962), 314–23; Bernard P. Kiernan, "Ideology and Foreign Policy: A Reconsideration," *Virginia Quarterly Review*, L (Winter 1974), 22–38; and Bertram D. Wolfe, "Communist Ideology and Soviet Foreign Policy," *Foreign Affairs*, XLI (Oct. 1962), 152–70. On the conceptual problems in trying to distinguish "practical" from "doctrinaire" behavior in politics and diplomacy, see John P. Diggins, "Pragmatism and Ideology: Philosophy or Passion?" *American Political Science Review*, LXIV (Sep. 1970), 899–906.

45. Burnham, *Containment or Liberation? An Inquiry into the Aims of United States Foreign Policy* (New York, 1953), pp. 217–18, 251.

46. Ibid., pp. 41, 211.

47. Croce, *My Philosophy*, pp. 94–95.

48. Burnham, *Containment or Liberation?*, p. 213.

CHAPTER 9
To the *National Review*

1. Max Eastman to William F. Buckley, Jr., Jan. 14, 1952; Buckley to Eastman, Jan. 20, 1955, Max Eastman Papers, Lilly Library, Indiana University (ME).

2. Buckley to Eastman, Aug. 3 (?), 1954, ME.

3. Buckley to Eastman, Feb. 28, 1955; Morrie Ryskind to Eastman, March 27, 1955; Eastman to Schwartz, Aug. 11, 1963; Eastman to Carew-Hunt, April 16, 1950, ME; Eastman, "I Acknowledge My Mistakes," *National Review*, I (Feb. 22, 1956), 11–14.

4. For Eastman's review of the Buckley book, see "Buckley versus Yale," *American Mercury*, LXXIII (Dec. 1951), 22–26. Four years later a bitter dispute arose between Sidney Hook and Eastman on the one side and Professor Robert MacIver on the other. In *Academic Freedom Today*, MacIver listed Eastman among Buckley's staunch supporters on intellectual regimentation. "The type of alumni control advocated by Mr. Eastman and Mr. Buckley," wrote MacIver, "would put indoctrination first, with enlightenment a poor second." Hook, who quoted this passage to Eastman, vigorously protested the distortion in his review of the MacIver book in the New York *Times*, and he suggested that Eastman write an "open public letter" to set the record straight. But the differences between Hook and Eastman remained: "And for heaven's sake, Max, please leave free enterprise out of it! The issue concerns much more than free enterprise or the T.V.A." Hook to Eastman, Oct. 16, 1955; Eastman to Frances Brown, Nov. 27, 1955; Brown to Eastman, Nov. 21, 1955, ME.

5. Eastman, *Reflections on the Failure of Socialism*, pp. 80, 84; "The Reaction against John Dewey," NR, VI (June 21, 1958), 9–11; Russell Kirk, "John Dewey Pragmatically Tested," ibid., 11–12, 23.

6. Buckley, ed., *American Conservative Thought in the Twentieth Century* (Indianapolis and New York, 1970), p. xxxii.

7. Eastman, "Am I Conservative?" NR, XVI (Jan. 28, 1964), 57–58; Buckley, *Conservative Thought*, p. xxix.

8. Buckley, *Conservative Thought*, p. xxxi.

9. Eastman, "Autobiographical Blues," *Saturday Review*, XLIV (April 22, 1961), 6.

10. Joseph Slater, "On Coming Home to Poetry," *Saturday Review*, XLVIII (Feb. 6, 1965), 30. "Cheerful Radical," *Time*, LXXXV (Jan. 8, 1965), 67; "Traveling Man," *Newsweek*, LXV (Jan. 4, 1965), 62; Joseph L. Featherstone, "An Exile from Socialism," *New Republic*, CLII (Jan. 16, 1965), 19–21; George Lichtheim, "The Romance of Max Eastman," in *Collected Essays: George Lichtheim* (New York, 1973), pp. 163–71. For the epistemological dilemmas in Marxism that Eastman had touched upon, see Louis Althusser, *For Marx* (New York, 1969), and Jürgen Habermas, *Knowledge and Human Interests* (Boston, 1971).

11. Eastman's remark on being a "demiprostitute" is quoted in *Time*, LXXXV (Jan. 8, 1965), 67; Eastman, "What Can We Learn from Animal Behavior?" *Reader's Digest*, LXXXI (Nov. 1962), 211–16; *Seven Kinds of Goodness* (New York, 1967).

12. Richard Whalen, "Conversation with Dos Passos," *New Leader*, XLII (Feb. 23, 1959), 20–21; John Dos Passos, Foreword to Buckley's *Up from Liberalism* (New York, 1959), pp. vii–xi.

13. Dos Passos, "Reminiscences of a Middle-Class Radical," *NR*, I (Jan. 18, 1956), 9–11; (Feb. 15, 1956), 9–12; Eastman, et. al., *John Dos Passos: An Appreciation* (New York, 1954), Pamphlet; "The Crime of John Dos Passos" (Editorial), *NR*, XVII (Jan. 26, 1965), 51–52; Jeffrey Hart, "John Dos Passos," *NR*, XIX (Jan. 24, 1967), 93–97.

14. Granville Hicks, "Of Radicals and Racketeers," *Saturday Review*, XLIV (Feb. 25, 1961), 25–26; Daniel Aaron, "The Riddle of John Dos Passos," *Harper's*, p. 60; Dan Wakefield, "Which Side Are You On," *Esquire*, LIX, (April 1963), 112–18; "Return to Paradise," *Atlantic*, CCXIX (Feb. 1967), 102–10; Gore Vidal, *Rocking the Boat* (New York, 1963), pp. 181–90; Maxwell Geismar, Introduction to *The Big Money* (New York: Washington Square Press, 1961), pp. xiii. Herbst is quoted in Wakefield, "Which Side Are You On," 118.

15. Dos Passos, "The Battle for San Francisco," *NR*, XVI (July 28, 1964), 640, 652.

16. Dos Passos, "What Chances of Maintaining a Conservative Opposition?" *NR*, XVI (Oct. 20, 1964), 907–08.

17. Dos Passos, *The Best Times*, pp. 156–57; Wilson to Dos Passos, Nov. 26, 1966; H. L. Mencken to Dos Passos, Jan. 27, 1947; Thomas Mann to Dos Passos, Jan. 24, 1947; Wilson to Dos Passos, Nov. 27, 1951, and Nov. 26, 1966, John Dos Passos Papers, Lilly Library, University of Virginia (JDP).

18. Wilson to Dos Passos, May 2, 1963; Jan. 18, 1964; and Feb. 1, 1964, JDP; Dos Passos, "Please Mr. Rip Van Winkle, Wake Up Some More," *NR*, XVI (Jan. 28, 1964), 71–74.

19. Wilson to Dos Passos, Jan. 18, 1964, and March 18, 1964, JDP.

20. Wilson to Dos Passos, Nov. 26, 1966; March 18, 1964; and May 18, 1964, JDP.

21. Dos Passos, interviewed in the San Jose Mercury, May 15, 1964.

22. Whalen, "Conversation with Dos Passos," 20–21.

23. Dos Passos, "The New Left: A Spook out of the Past," *NR*, XVIII (Oct. 18, 1966), 1037–39; *Fourteenth Chronicle*, p. 640.

24. Buckley to Dos Passos, July 22, 1970; Senator Harry F. Byrd to Dos Passos, June 18, 1970; Richard M. Nixon to Dos Passos, May 10, 1968; Spiro T. Agnew to Dos Passos, March 31, 1970, JDP.

25. Will Herberg, "Reinhold Niebuhr," *NR*, XI (Dec. 2, 1961), 379.

26. Herberg, "Conservatives and Religion: A Dilemma," *NR*, XI (Oct. 7, 1961), 230, 232; "Conservativism, Liberalism, and Religion," *NR*, XVII (Nov. 30, 1965), 1087–88.

27. Herberg, "Conservatives, Liberals, and the Natural Law," *NR*, XII (June 5, 1962), 407, 422; Part II (June 19, 1962), 438, 458.

28. Herberg, "A Religious Right to Violate the Law?" *NR*, XVI (July 14, 1964), 579–80; "Civil Rights and Violence," *NR*, XVII (Sep. 7, 1965), 769–70; Martin Luther King, "The Negro Is Your Brother," *Atlantic*, CCXII (Aug. 1963), 78–88. See also John W. Rathburn, "Martin Luther King: The Theology of Social Action," *American Quarterly*, XX (Spring 1968), 38–53.

29. Herberg, "America's 'Negro Problem' in Historical Perspective," *Intercollegiate Review*, VII (Summer 1971), 207–14.

30. Herberg, "The New Encyclical: A Question of Perspective," *NR*, XIV (May 7, 1963), 364–65; "The Limits of Papal Authority," *NR*, XVI (Aug. 25, 1964), 730–33; "Religion and Public Life," *NR*, XV (July 30, 1963), 61; "Pure Religion and the Secularized Society," *NR*, XV (Oct. 10, 1963), 188.

31. Herberg, "Alienation, 'Dissent,' and the Intellectual," *NR*, XX (July 30, 1968), 738–39.

32. Herberg, "Who Are the Hippies?" *NR*, XIX (Aug. 8, 1967), 844–46, 872; Daniel P. Moynihan, "Nirvana Now," *American Scholar*, XXXVI (Autumn 1967), 539–48.

33. Herberg, "Freud, the Revisionists, and Social Reality," in *Freud and the 20th Century*, ed. Benjamin Nelson (New York, 1957), pp. 143–63; Herbert Marcuse, *Eros and Civilization: A Philosophical Inquiry into Freud* (New York: Vintage edn., 1961), pp. 217–51. For an equally discerning critique of Fromm, see John Schaar, *Escape from Authority: The Perspectives of Erich Fromm* (New York, 1961).

34. Herberg, "The 'Death of God' Theology," *NR*, XVIII (Aug. 9–Sep. 6, 1966), 771, 779, 839–40, 884–85.

35. Herberg, "The 'What' and the 'How' of Ethics," *Modern Age*, XV (Fall 1971), 350–57.

36. André Gide, *L'immoraliste* (Paris, 1902), p. 13.

37. Herberg, "The 'What' and the 'How' of Ethics," 356–57.

38. Herberg, "America's Civil Religion: What It Is and Whence It Comes," *Modern Age*, XVII (Summer 1973), 226–33.

39. James Burnham, "The President and the Professor," *NR*, I (Nov. 26, 1955), 27–28.

40. Burnham, "Should Conservatives Vote for Eisenhower?" *NR*, II (Oct. 20, 1956), 12; John Chamberlain, "What's Wrong with Nixon?" *NR*, I (April 25, 1956), 13–14.

41. "Platonic Sorrows," Editorial, *NR*, II (Dec. 22, 1956), 4–5; Burnham, *The War We Are In: The Last Decade and the Next* (New Rochelle, N.Y., 1967), pp. 114–16.

42. Burnham, "Sighting the Target," *NR*, II (Dec. 29, 1956), 12. For Meyer's criticisms of Burnham, see his *NR* columns in *The Conservative Mainstream* (New Rochelle, N.Y., 1969), pp. 319–27. When Burnham collected his *NR* articles for his anthology *The War We*

Are In, published a decade after the Hungarian tragedy, he apparently forgot how cautious and restrained he was during that crisis:

. . . in writing about foreign affairs the temptation is almost ir-resistible, now and then, to consider how things might have been if a policy different from the actually prevailing policy had been followed. This temptation is especially sharp when the episode is critically important and when the actual policy can be shown to be sure to lead to undesirable results. Occasionally, in my running notebook on the Third World War, I succumb to this temptation and ruminate for a few paragraphs on what might have been if the American leadership had backed the Hungarian Freedom Fighters, supported instead of smashed the Anglo-French Suez expedition, acted on a program of liberation instead of co-existence, ordered air support at the Bay of Pigs, allied itself with Tshombe instead of fighting him, torn down the first props of the Berlin Wall instead of enduring them, pulled Yugoslavia into the Western camp instead of coddling Tito. [p. 108.]

43. Burnham, War We Are In, pp. 126–31.

44. Burnham, "Toujours, La Sale Guerre," NR, XIV (Jan. 29, 1963), 60; "Who Gives a Whoop?" NR, XIV (April 7, 1963), 279; "What Chance in Vietnam?" NR, XV (Oct. 8, 1963), 305.

45. Burnham, "False Analysis," NR, XV (Sep. 10, 1963), 181; "The Yalta Strategy," NR, XV (Sep. 24, 1963), 237; "Question Begging," NR, XV (Aug. 27, 1963), 148.

46. Burnham, War We Are In, pp. 104–06; "Why Do They Hate Robert Strange McNamara?" NR, XVIII (Nov. 15, 1966), 1152–62; "Does Johnson Have a Foreign Policy?" NR, XVI (March 10, 1964), 190; "McNamara's Non-War," NR, XIX (Sep. 19, 1967), 1012–14.

47. Burnham, "Food and Revolution," NR, XIV (June 18, 1963), 490; "Opening to the Left," NR, XIV (May 21, 1963), 400; "How De Gaulle Sees Things," NR, XVI (Oct. 6, 1964), 863; "De Gaulle, the Seducer," NR, XIV (March 26, 1963), 232.

48. Burnham, "Nikita Khrushchev: Maoist," NR, XVI (July 28, 1964), 644; "Kennedy, Khrushchev, and Mao," NR, XV (July 16, 1963), 17; War We Are In, pp. 53–61; "Bear-Baiting," NR, XVI (Aug. 25, 1964), 318.

49. Burnham, War We Are In, pp. 15–23.

50. Burnham, "Report of the Greek Referendum," NR, XX (Oct. 22, 1968), 1062–64; "Torture and the Colonels," NR, XX (Dec. 31, 1968), 1313.

51. Burnham, War We Are In, pp. 61–63, 195–97.

52. Ibid., pp. 56–58.

53. Burnham, "Their World and Ours," NR, II (Nov. 3, 1956), 19–20.

54. Ibid., 19; War We Are In, pp. 56–63, 99.

55. In 1960 Burnham edited and introduced a symposium, sponsored by the American-Asia Educational Exchange and published by the *National Review*, on the conservative response to the Sino-Soviet split. Here one may find well-reasoned, though subsequently disproved, arguments, particularly those by Stefan T. Possony and Karl Wittfogel, explaining why the split was more apparent than real and why China would be forced to remain subordinate to the Soviet Union. See Burnham, *Bear and Dragon: What Is the Relation between Moscow and Peking?* (New York, 1960).

56. Burnham, *War We Are In*, pp. 29–33.

57. Ibid., pp. 27–29.

58. Townsend Hoopes, *The Devil and John Foster Dulles* (Boston, 1973), p. 118.

CHAPTER 10
The Postwar Intellectual Right

1. Viereck is quoted in Raymond English, "Conservatism: The Forbidden Faith," *The American Scholar*, XXI (Autumn, 1952), 393–412; Lionel Trilling, *The Liberal Imagination* (New York: Anchor edn., 1957), p. vii.

2. Alexis de Tocqueville, *Democracy in America*, Vol. II (New York, 1945), pp. 144–47, 215–21, passim; Louis Hartz, *The Liberal Tradition in America* (New York, 1955), pp. 114–42; Marvin Meyers, *The Jacksonian Persuasion: Politics and Belief* (New York: Vintage edn., 1960), pp. 33–56.

3. Henry Adams, *Life of Albert Gallatin* (Philadelphia, 1879), p. 635; Ralph Waldo Emerson, "The Conservative," in *The Portable Emerson*, ed. Mark Van Doren (New York, 1946), p. 91.

4. Hartz, *Liberal Tradition*, pp. 145–200; William R. Taylor, *Cavalier and Yankee* (New York, 1961).

5. Clinton Rossiter, *Conservatism in America: The Thankless Persuasion* (New York: Vintage edn., 1962), pp. 128–62.

6. Peter Viereck, *Conservatism: From John Adams to Churchill* (Princeton, 1956), p. 104; Irving Babbitt, *Democracy and Leadership* (Boston, 1924), p. 246.

7. Arthur Schlesinger, Jr., *The Vital Center: The Politics of Freedom* (Boston: Sentry edn., 1962), p. 37.

8. Viereck, *Conservatism Revisited* (New York: Free Press edn., 1962). For a valuable intellectual and institutional study of the history of American conservatism, see Allen Guttmann, *The Conservative Tradition in America* (New York, 1967); also useful is Ronald Lora's *Conservative Minds in America* (Chicago, 1971). Viereck's book is lively and stimulating, but it is more an indictment of the politics of the forties and fifties than a sustained inquiry into American conservatism.

9. Russell Kirk, *The Conservative Mind* (Chicago: Gateway edn., 1960), pp. 7–8; Rossiter, *Conservatism in America*, pp. 220–21; Guttmann, *Conservative Tradition*, pp. 158–80; Lora, *Conservative Minds*, pp. 179–80.

10. Viereck, *Metapolitics: From the Romantics to Hitler* (New York, 1941); William F. Buckley, Jr., ed., *American Conservative Thought in the Twentieth Century* (Indianapolis and New York, 1970).

11. Buckley, *American Conservative Thought*, pp. xv–xl.

12. Dwight Macdonald, *The Memoirs of a Revolutionist: Essays in Political Criticism* (New York, 1957), p. 333. The phrase "celebrity intellectual" is Joseph Epstein's, in "The Politics of William Buckley: Conservative Ideologue as Liberal Celebrity," *Dissent*, XIV (Fall 1972), 602–16.

13. Macdonald, *Memoirs*, p. 326; Lora, *Conservative Minds*, pp. 195–96.

14. Phillip Abbott Luce, *The New Left* (New York, 1966).

15. "Publisher's Statement," *NR*, I (Nov. 19, 1955), 5; Willmoore Kendall, "The Liberal Line," ibid., 8.

16. Buckley, *American Conservative Thought*, pp. xv–xl; Garry Wills, *Nixon Agonistes: The Crisis of the Self-Made Man* (Boston, 1969), pp. 553–57.

17. *New York Times*, August 14, 1961; Buckley, "America's Bull," *NR*, XII (March 27, 1962), 92.

18. Buckley, "Segregation and Democracy," *NR*, I (Jan. 25, 1965), 5; Lora, *Conservative Minds*, pp. 206–08; Epstein, "Politics of Buckley," 610.

19. Epstein, 610–11.

20. Buckley, *American Conservative Thought*, p. 214; *The Jeweler's Eye* (New York, 1968), p. 126; Lora, *Conservative Minds*, pp. 210–11.

21. Walter Karp, Review of Buckley's *The Jeweler's Eye*, *Book World*, II (June 30, 1968), 14.

22. James Burnham, *Suicide of the West: An Essay on the Meaning and Destiny of Liberalism* (New York, 1964), p. 9. Unless otherwise indicated, all subsequent Burnham quotes are from this work.

23. Charles Frankel, "A Conservative Autopsy," *New Leader*, XLVII (July 20, 1964), 5–9; Irving Howe, "Bourbon on the Rocks," in *Steady Work: Essays in the Politics of Democratic Radicalism, 1953–1966* (New York, 1966), pp. 253–57.

24. Quoted in Daniel J. Boorstin, *The Lost World of Thomas Jefferson* (Boston, 1960), p. 174.

25. Sheldon Wolin, *Politics and Vision: Continuity and Innovation in Western Political Thought* (Boston, 1960), pp. 293–94.

26. David Caute, *The Fellow-Travelers: A Postscript to the Enlightenment* (New York, 1973), pp. 250–66.

27. James Burnham, "Parakeets and Parchesi" (1951), in *The New Partisan Reader, 1945–1953* (New York, 1953), pp. 469–70.

CHAPTER 11
Conservative Paradoxes

1. Isaac Deutscher, *Russia in Transition and Other Essays* (New York, 1957), p. 203; Daniel Bell, *The End of Ideology: On the Exhaustion of Political Ideas in the Fifties* (New York: rev. Free Press edn., 1965), p. 300; Daniel Aaron, *Writers on the Left*, p. 396; Murray Kempton, *Part of Our Time: Some Monuments and Ruins of the Thirties* (New York, 1955), p. 334.

2. Deutscher, *Russia*, pp. 203–16.

3. Quoted in Lewis S. Feuer, *The Conflict of Generation: The Character and Significance of Student Movements* (New York, 1969), p. 503.

4. For a criticism of the Marxist explanation of alienation, see John P. Diggins, "Thoreau, Marx, and the 'Riddle' of Alienation," *Social Research*, XXIX (Winter 1972), 571–98.

5. New Left philosophers in the sixties were engaged in a determined effort to refute Eastman and Hook and restore the dialectic to nature and reunite Marx and Hegel. See, for example, Michael Kosok, "The Dialectic of Nature: A Unified Field Theory of the Sciences," *Telos*, No. 6 (Fall 1970), 47–103. On the influence of Marcuse on the New Left, see *Critical Interruptions: New Left Perspectives on Herbert Marcuse*, ed. Paul Breines (New York, 1970). For Marcuse's view of the hippies and counterculture as possessing the new revolutionary "sensibility of praxis," see his *An Essay on Liberation* (Boston, 1968). For a criticism of this view, see John P. Diggins, *The American Left in the Twentieth Century* (New York, 1973), pp. 188–95, and Peter Clecak, *Radical Paradoxes: Dilemmas of the American Left, 1945–1970* (New York, 1973), pp. 175–229.

6. Joachim Radkau, *Die deutsche Emigration den USA: Ihr Einfluss auf die amerikanische Europapolitik, 1933–1945* (Düsseldorf: Berelsmann Universitatsverlag, 1971). I am grateful to Professor Martin Jay, author of *The Dialectical Imagination: A History of the Frankfurt School and the Institute of Social Research, 1923–1950* (Boston, 1973), for drawing my attention to Radkau's work. See also the special issue, "The Legacy of the German Refugee Intellectuals," *Salmagundi*, No. 10–11 (Fall 1969–Winter 1970).

7. Max Eastman, *Enjoyment of Living*, pp. 15–26.

8. James Gilbert, *Designing the Industrial State: The Intellectual Pursuit of Collectivism in America, 1880–1940* (Chicago, 1972).

9. Max Shachtman Transcripts, Oral History Collections, Columbia University, p. 341.

10. Eastman, "As to Values and Facts," *Partisan Review*, IX (May–June 1941), 204.

11. Richard Rovere to Arthur Schlesinger, Jr., March 30, 1952, copy from Schlesinger Papers.

12. William F. Buckley, Jr., and L. Brent Bozell, *McCarthy and His Enemies* (Chicago, 1954), p. 333.

13. John Chamberlain, "What's Wrong with Nixon?" *NR*, I (April 25, 1956), 13–14.

14. New York *Times*, August 3, 1974.

15. The notion, perpetrated by ex-radicals like Eugene Lyons, that liberal thinking in the thirties had been dominated by communists has been effectively challenged by Frank Warren in *Liberals and Communism: The "Red Decade" Revisited* (Bloomington and London, 1966).

16. Eastman to Warder Norton, Dec. 15, 1939, W. W. Norton Papers, Butler Library, Columbia University (WWN).

17. Will Herberg, "Conservative Worthy," *Commentary*, XVIII (July 1954), 88.

18. William S. Schlamm to Eastman, March 17, 1955, Max Eastman Papers, Lilly Library, Indiana University (ME).

19. Sidney Hook, *Political Power and Personal Freedom*, pp. 413, 426.

20. John H. Schaar, "Legitimacy in the Modern State," in *Power and Community: Dissenting Essays in Political Science*, eds. Philip Green and Sanford Levinson (New York: Vintage edn., 1970), p. 276.

21. Buckley, "Segregation and Democracy," *NR*, I (Jan. 25, 1956), 5.

22. Herberg, "Conservatives, Liberals, and Natural Law," 458.

23. Frank Meyer, *In Defense of Freedom: A Conservative Credo* (Chicago, 1962).

24. James Burnham, *Congress and the American Tradition* (Chicago, 1959), pp. 184, 241, passim.

25. Buckley, "The Bombing and Morality," *NR*, XXV (Jan. 16, 1973), 74–75; Burnham, "Open House," *NR*, XXIV (Feb. 4, 1972), 90.

26. "It does not seem probable," Buckley wrote in September 1972, "that anything much will come out in the trial, if any, of those who were picked up, or that anyone of public importance will be incriminated." Six months later: "A great deal of nonsense continues to be written about the Nixon aides implicated in the scandal. In fact, these men are not immoral or evil; Ronald Reagan was perfectly right when he remarked that they are not criminals at heart. They regard themselves as engaged in something more than a routine political contest, and came to regard their liberal and radical opponents not merely as rivals but as a threat to the nation. Not the least tragic aspect of this affair is that the conviction had some objective justification."

NR, XXIV (Sep. 29, 1972), 1054; NR, XV (Nov. 10, 1972), 1231–32; NR, XV (May 25, 1973), 565.

27. Buckley, *Up from Liberalism*, p. xiii.

28. Ibid., p. 161.

29. Kirk quoted in Ronald Lora, *Conservative Minds in America*, p. 221.

30. Ernst Cassirer, *An Essay on Man* (New Haven, 1944), pp. 60–61.

31. Buckley, *Up from Liberalism*, p. 160.

32. M. Morton Auerbach, *The Conservative Illusion* (New York, 1959), p. 237.

33. Richard Whalen, "Conversation with Dos Passos," *New Leader*, XLII (Feb. 23, 1959), 20–21.

34. John P. Diggins, "Consciousness and Ideology in American History: The Burden of Daniel J. Boorstin," *American Historical Review*, LXXVI (Feb. 1971), 99–118; "The Perils of Naturalism: Some Reflections on Daniel J. Boorstin's Approach to American History," *American Quarterly*, XXIII (May 1971), 153–80.

35. For the "humanist" position, see Peter Berger, "Two Paradoxes," *NR*, XXIV (May 12, 1972), 507–11. See also "The Achievement of Leo Strauss," Eulogies by Walter Bern, Werner J. Dannhauser, Harry Jaffa, and Herbert Storing, *NR*, XXV (Dec. 7, 1973), 1347–57.

36. Buckley, *The Jeweler's Eye*, p. 126.

Index

518 | Index

About the Author

A native of California and 1957 graduate of the University of California at Berkeley, John Patrick Diggins conceived of this book during the New Left confrontations at San Francisco State College, where he taught history on a campus in a three-year state of siege. Convinced that the experience of history is a guide to the present, he began to wonder whether today's leftists might be tomorrow's rightists, as some of the Old Left had become in their own day. This book is the result.

After receiving his PhD from the University of Southern California, he taught at San Francisco from 1966 to 1969; and he has been professor of history at the University of California at Irvine since 1969. His first book, *Mussolini and Fascism: The View from America*, was a nominee for the 1972 National Book Award in history, and it won the John H. Dunning Award of the American Historical Association. He is also the author of *The American Left in the Twentieth Century* and has been widely published in scholarly journals. In 1975 he received a Guggenheim Fellowship for a study on Thorstein Veblen and modern social theory.

Diggins lives in Laguna Beach with his wife, Jacy, and their children, Sean, ten, and Nicole, eight.